COMMUNICATION ENGINEERING

Communication Engineering

W. L. EVERITT, Ph.D.

Dean, College of Engineering
University of Illinois

G. E. ANNER, M.S. in Eng.

Associate Professor of Electrical Engineering
University of Illinois

THIRD EDITION

McGRAW-HILL BOOK COMPANY, INC.

New York   Toronto   London

1956

COMMUNICATION ENGINEERING

Library of Congress Catalog Card Number 55-12099

VI

19778

THE MAPLE PRESS COMPANY, YORK, PA.

PREFACE

In revising any book in a rapidly developing field it is possible to think of many items to add but difficult to decide on what to delete. This is particularly true when the field covered in a previous volume has expanded explosively.

When the first edition of this work was planned, it did not seem presumptuous to attempt to include in one volume the major fundamental concepts in the field of communication engineering. Since the publication of the second edition there have been many important developments and many excellent books and sets of books written on subdivisions of electrical communication. Such subdivisions include physical electronics, vacuum-tube circuits, antennas and propagation, electroacoustics, servomechanisms, information theory, pulse-generation and wave-forming circuits, computer systems, and many many more topics of importance in the processing of information.

In the third edition it has been decided to concentrate on the area which must precede the study of all other divisions of communication, namely, the fundamentals of linear-network analysis and synthesis, including the use of unilateral elements. This decision is influenced by the fact that the wide acceptance of the first two editions was based particularly on their emphasis in that area. However, in order to demonstrate the design requirements which are imposed on the linear portions of communication-system networks, both an analysis of various types of modulation and the transformation of transients from the time to the frequency domain are developed.

Naturally, although we can no longer hope to cover a major portion of the field of "Communication Engineering," we are retaining that well-known title.

The senior author wishes to thank the junior author for his major part in the revision, for it would never have been completed without his doing so much of the work.

The authors are indebted to their colleagues Profs. J. E. Williams and M. H. Crothers for their helpful comments on the sections on audio transformers and to Prof. W. J. Fry for information on piezoelectric crystals.

We also thank Berenice B. Anner, who did all the typing.

W. L. EVERITT.
G. E. ANNER.

v

CONTENTS

LIST OF PRINCIPAL SYMBOLS

A Voltage amplification; gain

A Real part of image transfer constant

B Magnetic flux density

B Susceptance

B Imaginary part of image transfer constant

b Normalized susceptance

BW Bandwidth

C Capacitance

C Channel capacity, bits per second

C Determinant cofactor

c Velocity of sound in air

D Determinant

d Diameter

$Dr(\ )$ Driving function

$D_t(x)$ Time derivative of x

E Voltage

E_g Generator voltage; grid voltage

E_{oc} Open-circuit voltage

E_R Receiving-end voltage

E_S Sending-end voltage

e Instantaneous voltage

e Naperian base $(= 2.718+)$

ε Electric field intensity

F An attenuation factor $(= e^{2\alpha})$

F Mechanical force

F_1 Over-all lower half-power frequency

F_2 Over-all upper half-power frequency

f Instantaneous mechanical force

f Frequency

f_1 Lower half-power frequency

f_2 Upper half-power frequency

f_c Cutoff frequency

f_h Highest frequency of importance

f_o Design-center frequency; null frequency

f_r Resonant frequency

f_∞ Frequency of infinite attenuation

Δf Frequency deviation

$f(t)$ Function of time

G Conductance

g Normalized conductance

g_m Mutual conductance

$g(f)$ Fourier mate of $f(t)$

H Scale factor

H Total information, bits

I Current

$\text{Im}\ \{x\}$ Imaginary part of x

i Instantaneous current

$J_n(x)$ nth-order Bessel function of the first kind

j $\sqrt{-1}$

k Design parameter

k Reflection factor

k Coupling coefficient

k Spring stiffness

L Inductance

L_{12}, L_m Mutual inductance

l Length

$\ln x$ Naperian logarithm of x

$\mathcal{L}$ Standing wave loss function $(= P_{\text{lost}}/\alpha l P_{\text{out}})$

M Mutual inductance

M Determinant minor

m Mass

m Design parameter

m_a Amplitude-modulation factor

m_f Frequency-modulation index

m_p Phase-modulation index

N Noise power

N	Number of turns	Y_{mm}	Self-admittance of node m
n	Number (of pulses, sidebands, etc.)	Y_{mn}	Nodal mutual admittance between nodes m and n
n	Design parameter	y	Distance from transmission-line receiving end
n	Impedance transformation ratio ($= R_{I1}/R_{I2}$)	y	Normalized admittance
P	Average power	y	Normalized frequency ($= f/f_2$)
p	Complex frequency ($= \delta + j\omega$)	y_{mm}	Driving-point admittance of the mth mesh
p	Number of meshes, nodes, or poles	y_{nm}	Mesh transfer admittance between meshes m and n
p	Instantaneous pressure difference	y'_{mm}	Nodal driving-point admittance between node m and reference node
p_o	A zero		
p_x	A pole	y'_{nm}	Nodal transfer admittance between nodes m and n
Q	Quality factor; figure of merit		
q	Instantaneous electric charge	Z	Impedance ($= R + jX$)
R	Resistance	Z_g	Generator impedance
R	Nominal filter impedance	Z_{I1}, Z_{I2}	Image impedances
R_o	Characteristic resistance	Z_{in}	Input impedance
$R(\ )$	Network response	Z_{it}	Iterative impedance
Re $\{x\}$	Real part of x	Z_o	Characteristic impedance
r	Normalized resistance	Z_{oc}	Input impedance of open-circuited network
r	Radius		
r_p	Vacuum-tube plate resistance	Z_{o1}	Input impedance at end 1, end 2 open-circuited
S	Signal power		
S	Standing wave ratio	Z_{o2}	Input impedance at end 2, end 1 open-circuited
S	Electrical elastance ($= 1/C$)		
S	Cross-sectional area	Z_R	Receiving-end (terminating) impedance
s	Spacing between parallel wires		
s	Stub length	Z_{sc}	Input impedance of short-circuited network
T	Signal duration; period		
T	Network transfer function	Z_{s1}	Input impedance at end 1, end 2 short-circuited
t	Time		
U	Real part of network immittance	Z_{s2}	Input impedance at end 2, end 1 short-circuited
$U(t)$	Unit step function	Z_t	Transfer impedance
V	Imaginary part of network immittance	Z_{mm}	Self-impedance of mesh m
		Z_{mn}	Mutual impedance between meshes m and n
v	Instantaneous velocity		
v_g	Group velocity	z	Number of zeros
v_p	Phase velocity	z	Normalized impedance
VA	Volt-amperes	z_{mm}	Driving-point impedance of mth mesh
W	Energy		
$W(\ )$	Immittance; network function	z_{nm}	Mesh transfer impedance between meshes m and n
X	Reactance		
x	Normalized reactance	z'_{mm}	Nodal driving-point impedance between node m and reference node
x	Mechanical displacement		
x	Distance from transmission-line sending end		
x	Normalized frequency variable	z'_{nm}	Nodal transfer impedance between nodes m and n
Y	Admittance ($= G + jB$)		

α Attenuation constant

β Phase-shift constant

β Feedback ratio

γ Complex propagation constant
$(= \alpha + j\beta)$

γ Per cent overshoot

δ Fractional deviation from
resonance $[= (f - f_r)/f_r]$

δ Real part of complex frequency
$p = \delta + j\omega$

δ Loss factor $(= QP_{\text{lost}}/P_{\text{in}})$

ϵ Permittivity

Θ Image transfer constant
$(= A + jB)$

θ An angle

η Efficiency

κ Relative dielectric constant

λ Wavelength

μ Amplification factor

μ Permeability

Φ Magnetic flux

ϕ An angle

φ Angle of reflection coefficient
$\rho = |\rho|\underline{/\varphi}$

ρ Angular modulating frequency
$[= 2\pi(\text{modulating fre-}$
$\text{quency})]$

ρ Reflection coefficient
$(= |\rho|\underline{/\varphi})$

ρ Density of air

σ Conductivity

τ Time

τ_g Group delay

τ_p Phase delay

τ_r Rise time, 10 to 90 per cent

ω Angular frequency $(= 2\pi f)$

CHAPTER 1

FUNDAMENTAL PRINCIPLES
OF COMMUNICATION NETWORKS

1-1. The Technical Problem of the Engineer. The fundamental problem of engineering is the utilization of the forces and materials of nature for the benefit of mankind. The problem of science is to understand nature, to answer such a question as: "If a certain combination of elements and conditions exists, what will happen?" Engineers are interested in an inverse type of question, viz.: "If one desires a certain result, what combination should be assembled to produce it with a reasonable degree of approximation and at a cost which can be afforded?"

The problems of science are therefore fundamentally those of analysis, while the problems of engineering are those of synthesis.

It should be pointed out that, in the development of tools for modern physical research, a great deal of excellent synthesis and design is necessary. This indicates that the distinction between the scientist and engineer is becoming more and more nebulous. However, one might claim that in designing a modern accelerator the physicist is demonstrating his ability to perform an engineering function. Most methods of synthesis require a thorough knowledge of and experience in analysis. Therefore engineering training in any area must place great emphasis on analysis.

A common method of synthesis involves making a sequence of intuitive guesses, testing the results of each guess by analytical methods, noting the degree by which the result differs from the desired one, making a new guess, and so approaching the answer by successive approximations. Experience in analysis and a feeling for the physical situation are invaluable aids in such a method. However, it is the aim of engineering to develop straightforward methods of synthesis which can either eliminate or greatly speed up the guessing and checking process.

Exemplifying the difference between analysis and synthesis is the *illustration* by contrasts between the differential and integral calculus. Straightforward methods exist for the calculation of the derivatives of a function, but basic integrals were obtained by guessing the answer and checking by taking the derivatives. The results may be tabulated so that each user of integrals need not repeat the process, and rules for combinations may be set up, but most new situations require a repetition of the use of intuition and checking.

The complex problems of engineering may be divided in many ways. One basis of division might be as follows: (1) the processing of materials; (2) the processing of energy; (3) the processing of information. Any actual problem will involve all three, but the communication engineer is interested primarily in the collection, transportation, and delivery of information. He must, of course, use materials and energy as means for this processing. In contrast, a power engineer will be interested primarily in the transformation of energy originally in chemical, atomic, or other form into an electrical form, its transportation with a minimum loss, and its reconversion on the customer's premises into some useful form such as light or mechanical motion. In this extensive process he also will have to solve certain problems of information processing in order to control his system, but this is auxiliary to his main purpose. It is obvious that both the communication and the power engineer must use a wide variety of materials, properly fabricated for the purpose.

The engineer may also be considered as interested in the problem of extending and supplementing the inherent capabilities of man. The processing of materials is of importance in meeting man's needs by modifying his environment and food supply and also in supplying the physical building blocks for his other wants. The processing of energy is of importance in supplementing man's muscles. The processing of information has as its function the supplementing of man's brain power and nervous system. For example, modern communication methods extend the sense of hearing by the telephone, radio, and public-address systems, the sense of sight by television, radar, electron microscopes, and radio astronomy, the sense of touch by many electronic sensing devices, and even the senses of smell and taste. Furthermore the development of modern computers has made it possible to process mathematical information much more rapidly than can the brain, and even to reach decisions based upon comparisons between two or more sets of data resulting from the processing. Debates have raged over whether such systems are truly "brains," but there can be no question that they can remove much of the repetitive drudgery formerly required of man's brains. Furthermore, because of their speed, they open up new possibilities of attacking problems by computational methods which previously were rejected because they required an excessive number of man-hours and were very susceptible to human error.

In a "jet air age" involving movements above the speed of sound, many decisions must be made in the control of airplanes within times so short that it is not possible to assemble, present, and assess the information on which action must be based using only primitive instrumentation and man's senses alone. Electronic communication systems provide the solution.

1-2. The Nature of Communication Systems. Information arises from two general sources: (1) ideas in the brain of a man; (2) changes in a physical environment. In all cases information represents some *change* from a previous state. A flow of information arises from a source in which changes are more or less continuous. The more rapid the changes, the greater can be the amount of information generated per unit time.

Information is useful only if it can be delivered to a receiver which can interpret it and make use of it. Corresponding to the two sources, there will be two types of receivers (sometimes called "sinks"): (1) the brain of a man; (2) a physical device which can respond to the signal or some transformed version of it.

Either type of source may be connected to either type of sink. When either terminal involves a man, the characteristics of the individual are of importance. The engineer will find a study of the results of experimental psychology invaluable. Designs of equipment should take into account statistical studies of the average reactions of individuals to physical stimuli, and in some cases the reaction characteristics of particular individuals.

In most situations the information originally generated is not in a form which can be readily transported to the receiver. It must go through a transformation, or coding, process, often in more than one step. For example, an idea may occur in a man's brain. This idea is translated into words within the brain. The brain, through long experience and practice, is able to send nerve impulses to the muscles of the throat and face to modify the character of the sound whose energy is obtained by blowing air past the vocal cords. Thus speech is produced. If the listener (receiver) is nearby, these speech sounds are now ready to be transmitted by acoustic waves through the transmission medium of the air to the ear of that listener. There these sounds must produce nerve impulses, which in turn can be interpreted by the brain.

If, on the other hand, the listener is at a distant point and an electrical transmission system is to be used, then there must be a transformation introduced which will use the acoustical energy emitted by the mouth to either control or generate electrical energy whose variation is a reasonable facsimile of the flow of acoustical energy. Such electrical signals may then be transported over an electrical communication system. In the above sentence the word "generate" is used in the sense of an electrical generator where the energy in a portion of the acoustical wave is transformed into electrical energy, while the word "control" implies a switching action where one source of energy turns on and off the flow of energy in a second system (as with a steam valve).   A carbon-grain transmitter and a vacuum tube are examples of such electrical control devices.

On the other hand, a particular electrical system (for example, long transoceanic cables without intermediate amplifiers) may not be able to transmit electrical variations which occur as rapidly as those involved in the pressure variations of speech.   This does not mean that transmission of information by electrical means is impossible.   Suppose that the individual whose brain represents the source translates his ideas into oral language words and then makes a second transformation, either in his mind or on paper, into written words.   The letters in these words can in turn be translated into the Morse-code dots and dashes.   All this can go on in the source brain, which can then send nerve impulses to its associated hand to manipulate a telegraph key.   Devices which make transformations in the form of information, which modify it so that it may be handled by the information-transportation system, may be called "coders."   A particular class of coders are called "modulators."

A class of devices also of importance are called "transducers."   The American Standard definition is:

A transducer is a device capable of being actuated by waves from one or more transmission systems or media and of supplying related waves to one or more other transmission systems or media.   Note: The waves in the input and output may be of the same or different types (e.g. electric, acoustic or mechanical). [ASA C42 65.06.450 (1953).]

Transducers can be either "passive" or "active."   The American Standard definitions are in turn:

A passive transducer is a transducer whose output waves are independent of any sources of power which are controlled by the actuating waves.   [ASA C42 65.06.456 (1953).]

An active transducer is a transducer whose output waves are dependent upon sources of power, apart from that supplied by any of the actuating waves, which power is controlled by one or more of these waves.   [ASA C42 65.06.458 (1953).]

An important group of transducers are those which transform one form of energy into another.   For example, an electromechanical transducer is defined as:

An electromechanical transducer is a transducer for receiving waves from an electrical system and delivering waves to a mechanical system or vice versa. [ASA C42 65.06.469 (1953).]

Examples of electromechanical transducers are microphones and loudspeakers, which are discussed in Chap. 16.

The simplest type of communication system, then, will contain the following five elements:

1. A source of information.

2. A coder, or transducer, for transforming the information into a form suitable for transportation over a transmission system.

3. A transmission system.

4. A decoder, or transducer, for transforming the signal into a form suitable for interpretation by the receiver.

5. A receiver of information.

Very frequently the transmission system must be used for several signals simultaneously, each arising from a separate source and each being addressed to individual receivers. Radio is an example where all the world is on a "party line." This common use can be accomplished by proper design of the coder. Each coder must modify the signals from its associated source so that there is a distinctive difference between the several coded signals, but the coding must not destroy the identity of the information. This process is called "modulation" and will be described later in the chapter. When modulation is involved in the coding process, the decoder must also be modified to perform two additional functions: (1) filtering out, i.e., selecting the desired signal for its addressee and rejecting all other signals; (2) transforming the signal back into a form in which it can be handled by the normal decoding process. This is called "demodulation."

A complete system from information source to information receiver is called an information, or communication, channel, whether a portion of the system is common to other channels or not.

It should be evident that, like all systems, error may creep in, i.e., the information may be distorted in the process of transportation. Common gossip is a good example of what may happen in the processing of information. Error arises from two major causes:

1. Distortion of the information may occur as it passes through successive links. This will be discussed later in the chapter.

2. Extraneous signals or noise may be introduced which will be interpreted by the receiver as part of the signal originating at the source. This noise may intrude at all links in the channel. Examples of noise source are static in radio, inductive interference from power and other telephone lines in telephony, and the random motion of electrons in resistors, vacuum tubes, and transistors in cases where high amplification is required. The block diagram of a communication system is shown in Fig. 1-1.

In order to be prepared to analyze and synthesize systems and to reduce disturbances which result in error, it is necessary to consider in more detail the characteristics of the signals which may be originated by

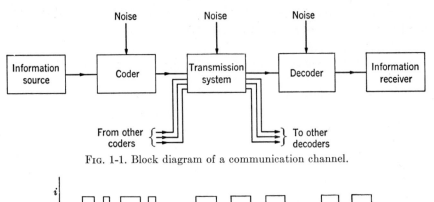

FIG. 1-1. Block diagram of a communication channel.

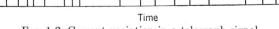

Time

FIG. 1-2. Current variation in a telegraph signal.

the sources or coding system and how these complex signals may be
analyzed into elementary forms so that the requirements for components
of the system may be specified.

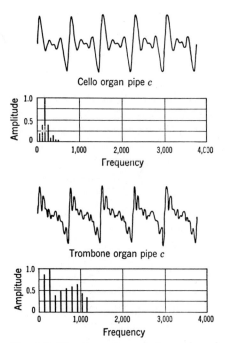

FIG. 1-3. Waveform of musical sounds and
their frequency spectra.

One of the simplest electrical communication signals is that originating from the dots and dashes of a telegraph key which applies a d-c voltage on an "all-or-none" basis, as illustrated in Fig. 1-2.

In music and speech the variation of pressure in a sound wave is complex. The nature of the fluctuation varies with every individual or instrument and with every word or note which is produced. Figure 1-3 shows the waveform of some sounds produced by musical instruments, while Fig. 1-4 shows the waveform of a particular spoken word.

In television events occur much more rapidly. It is necessary not only to transmit information on details of a picture at a rate of about 7,500,000 dots per second

(30 pictures per second each with a grain structure of about 250,000 dots)
but also to synchronize information to keep the scanning system at the

transmitter and receiver in step with each other.   Figure 1-5 shows the waveform of a typical black-and-white television signal.

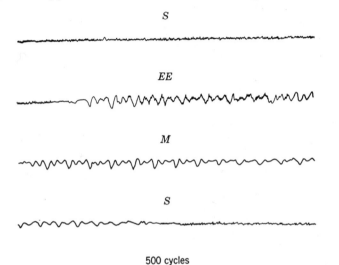

500 cycles

Fig. 1-4. Waveform of the word "seems."

Radar and computer systems deal with pulses somewhat similar to telegraph signals except that they are very much shorter, ranging from a fraction of a microsecond to a few microseconds in duration.   All show a fundamental characteristic of rapid change at the transmitting end and of unpredictability at the receiver.   To the extent that the signal can be predicted at the receiving end, the amount of information is reduced, as, for example, when a musical note repeats its waveform for a long period.

In order that the electrical system may be designed to handle time-varying signals, such as those of Figs. 1-3 to 1-5, more detailed knowledge of their nature is required.   In this regard, it will be shown that time-varying signals, no matter how complicated,

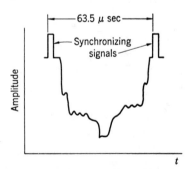

Fig. 1-5. Waveform of one line of a television signal.

may be analyzed in terms of a *frequency spectrum*, i.e., in terms of frequency components, with specified relative amplitudes.   The means for determining these frequency spectra are covered in detail in Chap. 2. For the moment, certain general ideas will be considered.

1-3. Analysis of Complex Waveforms. A current which varies with time can usually be analyzed into simpler elements. A method of analysis which can be applied to many problems is to reconstruct from the simplest elements a structure or form similar to that of the one being analyzed.

In Fig. 1-6a is shown a curve of the current flowing in a "carbon-grain" telephone transmitter when a pure tone, i.e., a sine wave of sound, is impressed upon its diaphragm.

The wave of Fig. 1-6a could be constructed by adding together the two components shown in Fig. 1-6b. It will be shown in Chap. 3 that each of the two components of Fig. 1-6b will divide in any *linear* network as though the other were not present. In a nonlinear impedance the components will react on each other in the manner described later.

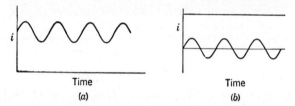

Fig. 1-6. Analysis of a pulsating current into components.

As an example of how the two components may be separated electrically, consider the effect of sending the current of Fig. 1-6b through a transformer. The voltage in the secondary depends upon the *variation* in flux and not on the amount. Only the alternating component will be effective in producing voltage in the secondary, and if a load were connected, the current would be a reproduction of the alternating components, but the d-c portion would be lost.

An application of a-c principles can be used to determine the transmission of the current of Fig. 1-6b in any electrical system. Whether a current actually reverses or not is immaterial; if it varies with time, it has alternating components. In fact, direct current can properly be considered as an alternating current of zero frequency. *The study of electrical communication is therefore based on a study of a-c circuits.*

1-4. Response of Network Elements to Sinusoidal and Nonsinusoidal Voltages. The sine wave is considered the fundamental, or simplest, waveform for reasons which will be explained later in the chapter. If a voltage with a complex waveform is impressed on a pure resistance, the current which flows will have the same wave shape as the voltage, because, by Ohm's law, the current is proportional to the *magnitude* of the voltage at every instant. Figure 1-7 shows an oscillogram of voltage across a resistance and current through it.

On the other hand, if the complex voltage wave is impressed on a pure capacitance, the current is proportional, at any instant, not to the magnitude of the voltage but to the rate at which it is changing.   This is

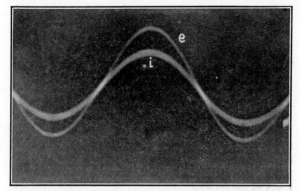

FIG. 1-7. Oscillogram of current and voltage in a resistance.

expressed by the equation

$$i = C\frac{de}{dt} \tag{1-1}$$

The waveform of current will therefore be quite different from that of the applied voltage, unless the latter is a pure sine wave.   If it is a sine wave, i.e., if

$$e = \hat{E} \sin \omega t \tag{1-2}$$

then from Eq. (1-1)

$$i = \omega C\hat{E} \cos \omega t \tag{1-3}$$

and the two waves will be similar to those shown in the oscillogram of Fig. 1-8a.   In this book an arc over a symbol (for example, $\hat{E}$ or $\hat{I}$) represents the peak, or maximum, value of the quantity.

The only difference between a sine and a cosine wave is a time displacement of one-quarter of a cycle.   There is no difference in shape, and so both are grouped under the general heading of "sine waves."

Similarly, if a complex wave of voltage is applied to a pure inductance, the current which flows will be such that, at every instant,

$$e = L\frac{di}{dt} \tag{1-4}$$

Equation (1-4) shows that the waveforms of the current and voltage will not, in general, be similar.   An exception occurs when the applied voltage is a sine wave of the form given by Eq. (1-2).   In this case

$$i = \frac{1}{L} \int \hat{E} \sin \omega t \, dt$$

$$i = -\frac{\hat{E}}{\omega L} \cos \omega t \tag{1-5}$$

An oscillogram of current and voltage for this case is shown in Fig. 1-8b.

Oscillograms of nonsinusoidal voltages and their resulting currents are shown in Figs. 1-9 and 1-10. In Fig. 1-9 the voltage is applied across a resistance, in Fig. 1-10a across a capacitor, and in Fig. 1-10b across an inductor. The waveforms of current and voltage are alike only in the case where the impedance is a pure resistance. It can be seen that in Fig. 1-10a the current is proportional to the rate of change

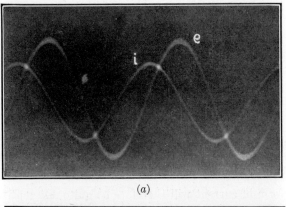

(a)

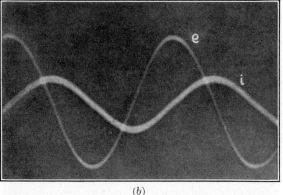

(b)

Fig. 1-8. Voltage and current in reactive elements.   (a) Capacitor.   (b) Inductor.

of voltage, while in Fig. 1-10b the voltage is proportional to the rate of change of current.

It is desirable to adopt the convention that when an alternating current of frequency f is referred to, it shall indicate that the current passes through f cycles/sec with a definite waveform. If any arbitrary waveform is taken as standard, other waveforms can be built up from this initial waveform. For example, suppose the arbitrary standard waveform selected were to be the triangular-shaped wave of Fig. 1-11a. The wave shape of Fig. 1-11b, which has the same period as that of Fig.1-11a,

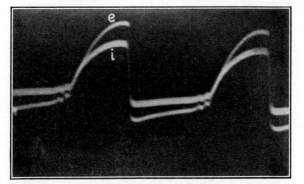

Fig. 1-9. An example of current and voltage waves when a nonsinusoidal voltage is impressed on a pure resistance.

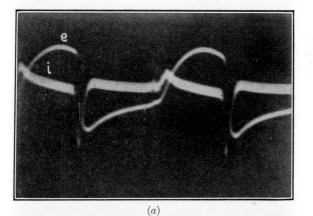

(a)

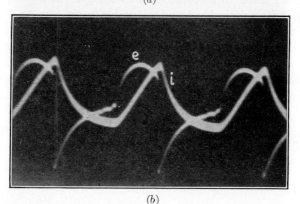

(b)

Fig. 1-10. Voltage and current in reactive elements when a nonsinusoidal voltage is impressed. (a) Capacitor. (b) Inductor.

could be approximated to any required degree by adding waves of the shape of Fig. 1-11a, these waves having frequencies which are integral multiples of the fundamental frequency.   This is apparent from the fact that a single triangular wave may be made to pass through any point in the first cycle of the wave of Fig. 1-11b and to pass through a similar point in each succeeding cycle.   *Two* triangular waves could be selected whose sum would pass through any two points in the wave of Fig.1-11b, and if the frequency of one were an integral multiple of the other, it would pass through corresponding points in all the later cycles.   Similarly,

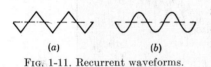

(a)   (b)

Fig. 1-11. Recurrent waveforms.

three waves could be selected whose sum would pass through any three points.   If enough different triangular waves were selected, each with a frequency which was an integral multiple of the first, their sum could be made to pass through any desired number of points in the first cycle and corresponding points in each succeeding cycle.   The sum of an *infinite* number of triangular waves could be made to coincide exactly with *all* the points on the curve of Fig. 1-11b or any other recurrent wave.

Hence, after the primary waveform has been selected, other waveforms can be analyzed in terms of a number of components of different frequency, but each with the shape of the primary wave form.   *For this reason when speaking of a single frequency, one must know what has been adopted as the fundamental waveform.*

If the triangular waveform were to be adopted as fundamental, a difficulty would immediately arise. If a voltage of this form were applied to a capacitor, the current would have a different waveform. Hence, if a single-frequency voltage were applied to the capacitor, the current would have to be considered as being made up of a number of frequencies.   It is desirable to adopt such a waveform that, if a single-frequency voltage is applied to a resistance, inductance, or capacitance, the current will also be considered as having a single frequency, i.e., as having the same waveform.   It has been shown that this occurs *only in the case of the sine wave*, for it is the only recurrent curve whose derivative (rate of change) and integral are of the same form as itself.   For that reason the sine wave has been adopted universally as the fundamental waveform, and it is understood in all electrical literature that, when a single frequency f is referred to, *it means a sine wave with f cycles/sec.* (It is common practice to shorten the dimensionally correct "cycles per second" to "cycles," and this will be done in the balance of this book.) The amplitude (maximum value) of a particular wave might vary with time. A sine wave has constant amplitude; hence, if the amplitude changes with. time, the wave must be specified in terms of more than one frequency.

Therefore, there is, strictly speaking, no possibility of setting up a true single-frequency current, for the current must have started some time, and hence a variation with time has occurred.   In spite of this it will be shown that analyses in terms of single frequencies give important information on actual networks.

1-5. Analysis of Transient Waveforms.   When complex waves, which repeat themselves over and over, are analyzed by the Fourier method, described in Chap. 2, the components obtained are integral multiples, or harmonics, of the frequency at which the wave recurs.   Rather than repetitive waves which continue for an appreciable time, communication systems are called upon to transmit transients, or waves which differ from the preceding and succeeding portions.   It is possible to analyze the results of such irregularities if the response to sinusoidal waves at all frequencies is known.

1-6. The Fourier Integral and Its Significance to Communication.   If a wave repeats itself 10 times a second, it can be analyzed into components of 10, 20, 30, 40, 50, . . . cycles.   If it occurs only once a second, then the wave will have harmonics which are integral multiples of unity, that is, 1, 2, 3, . . . 641, 642, 643, . . . cycles.   The amplitude of the individual harmonics will be decreased, but the frequency interval between harmonics will also be decreased.   If the time between successive impulses is still further increased, the individual components will be still closer together in frequency and smaller in amplitude. Finally, if an impulse occurs only once, the separation between individual components becomes infinitesimal and it is possible to plot a *continuous* curve of relative amplitude vs. frequency.   This is accomplished by means of a Fourier integral, which is a development of the Fourier series into the case where the fundamental frequency is zero.

The use of the Fourier integral in a formal analytical solution of transients can be applied only for relatively simple impressed impulses because of the difficulty of obtaining the necessary definite integrals. The other method of attack on transients, viz., the use of differential equations, is equally impotent for complicated impressed voltages.   *However, the existence of the Fourier integral does give the knowledge that any transient impressed voltage or current can be expressed as a continuous band of frequencies, and the response, or resultant, current or voltage at any part of the network can also be expressed as a continuous band of frequencies, the ratio of any frequency component in the impressed wave to the corresponding frequency component in the response wave being determined by the steady-state characteristic of the network at that frequency.*   This is probably the most important single idea in communication engineering, as the whole method of attack on communication networks is based upon it.   It will be developed in greater detail in the next chapter.

Owing to the continual change in waveform of the signal in communication systems, it is not possible to determine *analytically* the distribution or relative magnitude of the frequency components used in any transmission such as speech, music, telegraph code, television, etc. However, the distribution can be ascertained *statistically*. Statistics are in general resorted to where it is impossible to make definite predictions of an individual event, but these statistics make it possible to predict the distribution of a group of events. For example, it is not possible to predict accurately the exact date of the death of an individual (even if he has committed murder), but the financial stability of insurance companies is dependent on their ability to determine the distribution of deaths in a large group of individuals.

The statistical determination of the frequency distribution in impulses with the transient character of speech can be determined somewhat as follows: A telephone transmission system which will transmit only a

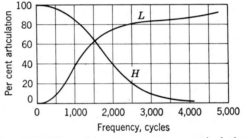

Fig. 1-12. Effect of frequency range on articulation.

limited but controllable band of frequencies is set up, and random unrelated speech sounds are sent over it. At the receiving end an observer records the sound which he hears. By comparison of the records at each end the percentage of words understood can be determined as a function of the band of frequencies transmitted. In order to be significant, thousands of observations should be made, for, in common with other statistics, the results are only significant when obtained from a large number of observations. Figure 1-12 shows two curves obtained by Crandall and MacKenzie, indicating the percentage of certain word syllables which were understood in two cases, as follows: curve *L* shows the percentage of sounds understood when all frequencies below the frequency indicated were transmitted and those above were eliminated, while curve *H* shows the percentage of sounds understood when only frequencies above the frequency indicated were transmitted. Curves of this character may be used to determine the width of the frequency band which should be transmitted for an acceptable understanding of telephonic speech. These would indicate that a transmission of 400 to 3,000 cycles might be acceptable for some purposes where only intelligibility is required.

In many cases it is desirable not only to have the words of the speaker understood but also to reproduce speech or music with naturalness. This is the case in broadcast transmission and phonograph reproduction. In this case, an artistic judgment must enter into the statistical determinations, and it has generally been agreed that a frequency range of 30 or 50 cycles to 15,000 cycles is desirable for so-called "high-fidelity" reproduction. Certain sounds, such as those of rattling keys and of percussion instruments, require the transmission of frequencies up to 15,000 cycles. In general, it is necessary to increase the cost of equipment as the bandwidth is expanded, and so engineering judgment must be introduced in any case to determine the actual requirements which should be met in the design of a unit, balancing increased cost against increased performance.

From this analysis one arrives at the following paradox: Because communication is carried on *exclusively* by *transients*, much of the analysis of the performance of communication apparatus is made in terms of the response of such apparatus to *steady-state* alternating currents, this response being determined over the range of frequencies found statistically to be of importance for the type of signal to be transmitted.

Where transmission of pulses is important, as in television and radio, the analysis of responses to sudden changes is significant and transient conditions may be examined directly. It will be shown in Chap. 2 that steady-state and transient response are directly related.

1-7. Response of the Ear. The ear is an important part of the decoding network in communication by speech or music and, in fact, plays an important part in determining curves such as Fig. 1-12. It is not equally responsive at all frequencies. Fletcher and Munson have given a set of curves of equal loudness as shown in Fig. 1-13. No sensation is produced by amplitudes lower than the zero level, which is called the *threshold of audibility*. The ordinate scale is given in decibels or logarithm of the ratio of the power to some reference power, the use of which will be explained in Chap. 6. The zero level corresponds to a sound power level of 10^{-16} watt/sq cm, which under normal conditions of temperature and pressure of the air is an alternating sound pressure with an effective value of 2.04×10^{-4} dyne/sq cm.

In the transmission of speech or music, if a component in the original sound falls below the threshold of audibility, owing to lack of energy or being outside the frequency range, then there is no advantage in transmitting it electrically. Hence, no matter what the waveform, it is generally considered necessary to transmit frequencies only within a limited range, although the wave may have components outside that range.

This applies to other signals as well, so that, for any given application, the circuit may be designed to handle a limited band of frequencies. The actual band required is determined by the nature of the signal as it emerges from the coder and the requirements of the receiver (or in some cases the decoder) for a signal which can be recognized within the required amount of allowable error.

1-8. Nature of Distortion.   As mentioned before, a communication network should deliver at the receiving end a waveform which is as nearly like the original supplied as is technically and economically feasible. Since control elements such as vacuum tubes and transistors may be used, the output may be greater in magnitude than the input, in which case

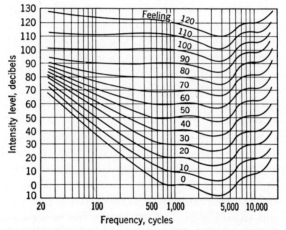

Fig. 1-13. Loudness-level contours.   (*Bell Telephone Laboratories.*)

the network is said to introduce a "gain," or it may be less, in which case the network introduces a "loss."

Since networks can produce either a gain or a loss, such gain or loss is not considered to be an important change in the original signal.   However, a change in *waveform* modifies the character of the signal, losing some of the original information, and is called "distortion."

Based on the idea that a complex transient can be analyzed into a band of sinusoidal waves, there are three types of distortion which occur in transmission.   These are defined precisely in Chap. 6 but for the moment may be described as follows:

Frequency distortion is that form of distortion in which the relative magnitudes of the different frequency components of the transmitted wave are altered.

Delay distortion is that form of distortion in which the time of transmission (or delay) of the different frequency components is not constant.

Nonlinear distortion is that form of distortion in which the output is not directly proportional to the input. The important result of this is that new frequency components, not present in the original input wave, are present in the output wave.

Frequency and delay distortion are usually due to the linear elements of inductance and capacitance, because their impedance varies with frequency. Delay distortion is not generally perceptible to the ear, if the unequal delay is kept to low limits, and therefore is of interest, in telephony, only on long transmission lines. It is of particular importance in telegraphy, where physical instruments interpret the signal, and in television.

If a pure sine wave of voltage is applied to a nonlinear impedance, the current will not be a sine wave. Such a wave can be analyzed into two or more sine waves, and thus there are introduced in the output new frequencies not present in the input. If a single sine wave is impressed, these new frequencies will be harmonics or integral multiples of the original frequency. If the impressed wave has more than one frequency component, the output will also have additional terms equal to the sums and differences of the input component frequencies and their integral multiples.

It is usually desirable in a network to make each unit as distortionless as possible. However, it is often possible to correct for *frequency* and *delay distortion* by additional meshes or elements which provide a counteracting distortion. For instance, in a cable the higher frequencies travel faster and are attenuated more than the lower ones. An equalizing network at the end should attenuate the lower frequencies and delay the higher ones. Such equalizing networks are considered in Chap. 14.

Nonlinear distortion cannot generally be compensated for in this manner. Once produced, the new frequencies can be eliminated only if they fall outside the band of those which are desired or if there is a total absence of delay distortion, when another nonlinear impedance with a reverse curvature may be used. All frequencies which do fall outside the band necessary for communication can be disposed of by networks, called "filters." These networks transmit effectively certain bands of frequencies and greatly attenuate other bands and are the subject of Chap. 7. As a rule nonlinear distortion must be prevented rather than corrected after its occurrence.

1-9. Frequency Translation, or Modulation. Nonlinear distortion, however, has extremely important uses for coding. A fundamental principle of communication is that a complex wave, represented by a band of frequencies, can be translated to any other band of at least equal width, if it is so desired, and later retranslated into its original form. This may be desirable because of a greater effectiveness of the transmitting medium at the new band or in order to convey several messages in the same medium. This translation can be accomplished by using nonlinear impedances and employing the fact that the current flowing in such an impedance contains new frequencies, equal to the sums and differences of those supplied in the input voltage.

Such a translation occurs in all radio and carrier telephone transmission. It is not feasible to build a radio antenna which will effectively radiate audio frequencies. The length of an antenna must be of the *order* of one-quarter the wavelength to be emitted. Such a length for 800 cycles would be 60 miles. Furthermore an antenna of this length could not radiate effectively frequencies of the order of one-half or twice its natural wavelength and so could not transmit the minimum band of 400 to 3,000 cycles needed for intelligible speech. It is necessary, therefore, to transmit a band of the same width at higher frequencies; e.g., it would be possible to use for intelligible speech 1,000,250 to 1,002,750 cycles

This translation, or modulation, may be compared to an automatic coding and decoding apparatus. Suppose all the words in an abridged dictionary were represented by Nos. 1 to 10,000. It would be possible to talk in terms of numbers, and in time the numbers would be as familiar to us as the words now used.

2,978-1-1,643-6,435-7,695-9,523-6,872-3,169 might be a sentence which meant "Having a fine time, wish you were here." Now suppose an individual suddenly inherits a typewriter which can write only numbers between 120,000 and 160,000 and he wishes to send a message home. The intelligence could be conveyed as well by a band from 120,000 to 130,000 as by the 1 to 10,000 band of numbers. He would agree, previously, with the individual to whom the message is to be sent to subtract 120,000 from the numbers received. The message would then be 122,-978-120,001-121,643-126,435-127,695-129,523-126,872-123,169.

Suppose at the same time he also wished to send a message to another member of the family, such as "Wire another hundred dollars." He might agree with this member that his messages were to be received in the band 150,000 to 160,000. The decoding would be accomplished by subtracting 150,000 from numbers in this group. Before coding this might read 7,843-819-3,245-1,298, and after coding it would become 157,843-150,819-153,245-151,298.

It would be possible to mix this message right in with the other, and yet there would be no confusion; e.g., the two messages together might be 122,978-120,001-157,843-121,643-150,819-126,435-127,695-153,245-129,-523-126,872-151,298-123,169.

Each person at the receiving end would know the band within which his message was to be received and would select numbers only in that band before applying the decoding process.

In the same way, several messages, originally in the same frequency band but in different channels, (see Fig. 1-1), can be coded, i.e., translated to new bands by nonlinear impedances, and then be introduced to and travel simultaneously in the same medium (either free space or a transmission line), be separated at the receiving end by appropriate filter networks, be transposed or decoded by nonlinear impedances to their original frequency band, and be delivered to the proper receiving point in substantially the same form as the original.

The principle of modulation is so important that it will be developed at somewhat greater length here, in order to understand its implications in the design of the networks covered in this book. However, the reader should refer to another text for detailed discussion of actual modulators and demodulators. One in general starts with some a-c phenomenon such as voltage, current, or electromagnetic field strength, generically referred to as waves.

Modulation of a wave is the process by which a characteristic of a so-called "carrier wave" of a higher frequency than any component of the signal is varied in accordance with the time variation of the signal. A general alternating wave may be represented by the equation

$$e = A \sin (\omega t + \phi) \tag{1-6}$$

Three groups of modulation methods are recognized:
1. Amplitude modulation, where A is varied by the signal.
2. Angle modulation, where ϕ is varied by the signal.
3. Pulse modulation, where the signal is turned on or off in pulses, and where the pulses themselves are modulated in amplitude or time of occurrence in accordance with the instantaneous values of the signal.

1-10. Amplitude Modulation.[1] In an amplitude-modulated wave the amplitude is varied about its mean value in proportion to the signal. Let the original signal (such as the sound pressure on the microphone) be represented by the function $f(t)$. Then the amplitude factor A of Eq. (1-6) is modified by $f(t)$ to give the amplitude-modulated wave

$$e = A[1 + bf(t)] \sin (\omega t + \phi) \tag{1-7}$$

where b is a factor determined by the design and operation of the modulating system and has dimensions such that $bf(t)$ is a pure numeric. b is usually a constant, but in some cases it is made a function of the signal frequency component. For example, if b is made to change with frequency in the proper manner, compensation may be secured for defects in the frequency characteristic of some other part of the system.

[1] W. L. Everitt, Frequency Modulation, *Trans. AIEE*, vol. 59, p. 613, November, 1940.

The amplitude variation cannot carry the amplitude below zero. Therefore the factor b should be so chosen by the operator that $1 + bf(t)$ never becomes negative. Hence $bf(t)$ should not exceed an absolute value of unity. This absolute value of the maximum of $bf(t)$ is called the *amplitude-modulation factor* and is given the notation m_a.

If the signal $f(t)$ is sinusoidal with a frequency $\rho/2\pi$, Eq. (1-7) becomes

$$e = A(1 + m_a \sin \rho t) \sin \omega t \qquad (1-8)$$

The curve of Eq. (1-8) is illustrated in Fig. 1-14 for $m_a = 0.5$ and $\omega/\rho = 10$. It will be noted that the wave crosses the axis at regular time intervals of $2\pi/\omega$ sec for both the modulated and the unmodulated waves.

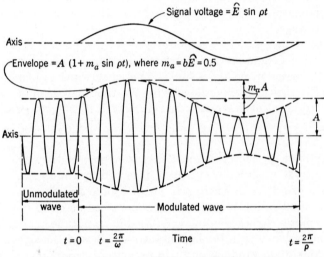

Fig. 1-14. An amplitude-modulated wave.

In alternating phenomena a single frequency is represented by the projection of a phasor of constant length rotating with the constant angular velocity $\omega = 2\pi f$. The wave of Eq. (1-7) could also be represented by a phasor rotating with a constant angular velocity ω, but the length of the phasor would be changing at a low frequency rate as given by the equation

$$\text{Length of phasor} = A[1 + bf(t)] \qquad (1-9)$$

The term $A[1 + bf(t)]$ is called the envelope of the wave. In Eq. (1-8) the envelope would be $A(1 + m_a \sin \rho t)$ as is illustrated in Fig. 1-14.

In drawing phasors which represent alternating phenomena it is common practice to consider that the observer is traveling on a platform which is also rotating about the same center with a velocity ω. The original phasor would then appear to be stationary and could be rep-

resented by a single drawing. However, if either the magnitude or the
phase of the phasor is changing with time, a series of successive drawings
is necessary to illustrate what is
happening.

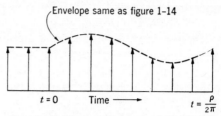

These successive drawings of
stationary phasors for the wave of
Fig. 1-14 are shown in Fig. 1-15
for time intervals of one-eighth
the period of the l-f wave producing the modulation.

FIG. 1-15. Phasor diagrams of the amplitude-modulated wave of Fig. 1-14 for successive instants.

At the receiver the demodulator
must produce a response which is
proportional to the envelope of the modulated wave (except for the constant component).

1-11. Interference of Two Amplitude-modulated Waves. If a second
amplitude-modulated wave of the same carrier frequency and phase is
added to the wave of Fig. 1-14, the resultant wave will have an envelope
which is the sum of the envelopes of the two waves, for the phasors will
be adding in phase. The interfering effect will be noticeable if the
undesired signal is as much as 1 per cent of the desired signal. Hence
it is desirable to make the value of m_a as large as possible, since the operator of a given communication system cannot control the modulation of
the desired wave by the undesired signal.

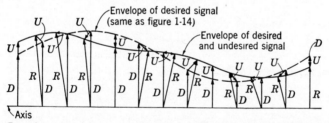

FIG. 1-16. Interference with an amplitude-modulated wave of a carrier of slightly
different frequency. (D is the desired, U the undesired, and R the resultant wave.)

If the frequency of the interfering wave is slightly different from the
desired wave (the difference being too small to eliminate it by selective
circuits), then the interfering wave will produce a variation in the envelope, which variation has an amplitude equal to the magnitude of the
interfering wave (even if it is unmodulated). This additional variation
will occur at a frequency which is equal to the difference between the
carrier frequencies of the desired and undesired signals, and will produce
an interfering modulation which is further superimposed on the resultant envelope. This is illustrated by the phasor diagrams in Fig. 1-16,
where the undesired signal has a frequency which exceeds the frequency

of the desired signal by $1.5\rho/2\pi$. It is seen that the resultant envelope is modified by an additional component equal to the magnitude of the undesired wave and so introduces interference proportional to the magnitude of the interfering wave.

Again it is apparent that the amplitude of the envelope of the desired signal should be kept as large as possible in order that the interference may be minimized. If Eq. (1-7) represents current or voltage, the amplitude of the envelope may be increased by increasing either the power or the amount of modulation (m_a).

1-12. Angle Modulation. In angle modulation (of which frequency modulation is a subdivision) the angle ϕ of Eq. (1-6) is given by a function of time which is related, but not, in all cases, directly proportional, to the signal function $f(t)$. The two principal subdivisions of angle modulation which have been extensively studied are phase modulation and frequency modulation.

1-13. Phase Modulation. In this type of modulation the phase angle ϕ is made to vary in accordance with the signal. That is,

$$\phi = b_1 f(t) \tag{1-10}$$

where b_1 is a *constant* determined by the design and operation of the modulating system. When Eq. (1-10) is inserted in Eq. (1-6), the wave becomes

$$e = A \sin [\omega t + b_1 f(t)] \tag{1-11}$$

The maximum value of $b_1 f(t)$ is called the *phase-modulation index* m_p. It is the maximum number of radians by which the phase of the carrier is altered during modulation. If the signal is sinusoidal with a frequency $\rho/2\pi$, Eq. (1-11) becomes

$$e = A \sin (\omega t + m_p \sin \rho t) \tag{1-12}$$

1-14. Frequency Modulation. In this type of modulation the *instantaneous frequency* is varied about the average value $\omega/2\pi$ in proportion to the instantaneous value of the signal. By definition, the use of the word 'frequency" is extended to the general equation (1-6) by the relation

$$2\pi f_{\text{inst}} = \omega + \frac{d\phi}{dt} \tag{1-13}$$

Since ω is a constant (2π times the carrier frequency), the signal must modify $d\phi/dt$ so that the instantaneous frequency is given by the relation

$$f_{\text{inst}} = \frac{\omega}{2\pi} + b_2 f(t) \tag{1-14}$$

where b_2 is a design and operating constant. The maximum value of $b_2 f(t)$ is the maximum deviation in instantaneous frequency of the modulated wave from the unmodulated one and is called the *frequency deviation*, Δf. If $f(t)$ is a sine wave of frequency $\rho/2\pi$ then

$$b_2 f(t) = \Delta f \sin \rho t \qquad (1\text{-}15)$$

If Eqs. (1-13) to (1-15) are combined,

$$2\pi f_{\text{inst}} = \omega + 2\pi \, \Delta f \sin \rho t = \omega + \frac{d\phi}{dt}$$

which gives

$$\phi = \int 2\pi \, \Delta f \sin \rho t \, dt = -\frac{\Delta f}{f_\rho} \cos \rho t \qquad (1\text{-}16)$$

where f_ρ is the frequency of the modulating signal. Equation (1-16) may be written

$$\phi = -m_f \cos \rho t \qquad (1\text{-}16a)$$

where m_f is called the *frequency-modulation index*. If this phase angle is inserted in Eq. (1-6), the result will be

$$e = A \sin (\omega t - m_f \cos \rho t) \qquad (1\text{-}17)$$

Equations (1-17) and (1-12), applying to a modulating signal of a single frequency, do not differ appreciably (except for a 90° shift in the modulation phase). In Eq. (1-17) the maximum shift in phase (corresponding to the phase modulation factor m_p) will be

$$m_f = \frac{\Delta f}{f_\rho} \qquad (1\text{-}18)$$

m_p in phase modulation and Δf in frequency modulation are arbitrary design factors. Unlike amplitude modulation they are not restricted to a maximum value of unity, for m_p may be hundreds of radians or Δf thousands of cycles if desired. The limitations on m_p and Δf will be determined by the allowable frequency spectrum and will be discussed later.

The distinction between phase and frequency modulation is as follows: if the frequency, but not the amplitude, of the modulating signal changes, m_p *is constant in phase modulation* and Δf *is constant in frequency modulation*.

It follows from Eq. (1-18) that in frequency modulation the phase deviation is inversely proportional to the modulating frequency. On the other hand, in phase modulation the frequency deviation is directly proportional to the modulating frequency.

Figure 1-17 is an illustration of angle modulation as represented by Eq. (1-12) for the case where $m_p = 0.5$ and $\omega/\rho = 12$. On a casual examination this would appear to be a single frequency wave. However, the intervals at which it crosses the axis vary throughout the audio cycle. In order to show this the first, fourth, seventh, tenth, and thirteenth cycles are expanded and shown in Fig. 1-18. It is seen that the varying shift in phase also produces a change in frequency which varies throughout the low-frequency (lf) cycle.

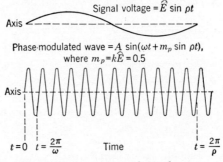

Signal voltage = $\hat{E}$ sin ρt

Axis

Phase-modulated wave = A sin($\omega t + m_p$ sin ρt), where $m_p = k\hat{E} = 0.5$

Axis

$t = 0$ $t = \dfrac{2\pi}{\omega}$ Time $t = \dfrac{2\pi}{\rho}$

Fig. 1-17. An angle-modulated wave.

The successive phasor diagrams for the angle-modulated wave of Fig. 1-17 (corresponding to the diagrams of Fig. 1-15 for an amplitude-modulated wave) are shown in Fig. 1-19. The signal wave is included for identification of the various instants.

The difference between phase and frequency modulation may be illustrated by the way the motion of the resultant phasor would appear to

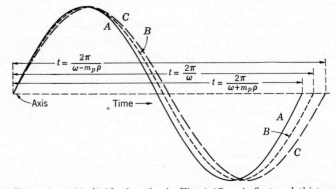

$t = \dfrac{2\pi}{\omega - m_p\rho}$

$t = \dfrac{2\pi}{\omega}$

$t = \dfrac{2\pi}{\omega + m_p\rho}$

Axis   Time →

Fig. 1-18. Expansion of individual cycles in Fig. 1-17. *A*, first and thirteenth cycles of Fig. 1-17. *B*, fourth and tenth cycles of Fig. 1-17. *C*, seventh cycle of Fig. 1-17.

an observer riding with the carrier phasor. In phase modulation two audio signals of equal amplitude, but of different frequencies, would produce equal angular *amplitudes* in the apparent swing of the resultant phasor. In frequency modulation two audio signals of equal amplitude would produce equal maximum angular *velocities* in the apparent swing of the resultant phasor. In this latter case (frequency modulation) the maximum angle of swing would be inversely proportional to the audio frequency [as is indicated by Eq. (1-18)]. This is illustrated by Fig. 1-20, where the phasors for both frequency and phase modulation are drawn for two signals with an audio-frequency (af) ratio of $2:1$. Note that in phase modulation the maximum angle ϕ_m is the same for both signals,

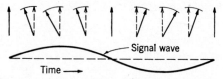

Time →

FIG. 1-19. Phasor diagrams of the angle-modulated wave of Fig. 1-17 for successive instants. Solid-line phasors are phasors of the modulated wave. Dashed-line phasors are phasors of the unmodulated wave.

while for frequency modulation the maximum angle ϕ_m for signal A (the lower frequency) is twice that for signal B. Since the angular *velocity* is proportional to the instantaneous value of the signal in frequency modulation, the phasor reaches its maximum angle of deviation when the signal is zero, while in phase modulation it reaches its maximum angle of deviation when the signal is a maximum.

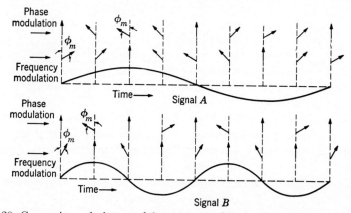

FIG. 1-20. Comparison of phase and frequency modulation by means of phasor diagrams. *Note.* ϕ_m is the same for both signals for phase modulation. ϕ_m is inversely proportional to signal frequency for frequency modulation. Maximum velocities of the phasors are the same for both signals for frequency modulation.

In radio transmission by angle modulation means are provided at the decoder so that the detected signal is proportional to the angle modulation (of the particular type selected) and at the same time this detected signal is made unresponsive to amplitude variations.

1-15. Interference of Two Angle-modulated Waves. When two angle-modulated waves of the same carrier frequency are added together, the total angle modulation is not the sum of the two individual modulations.

This can be illustrated by Fig. 1-21, where an angle-modulated wave B is represented by a phasor whose angle is changing with time. This is added to a larger phasor A which for the moment will be assumed to be unmodulated. The resultant phasor R will be the sum of the two phasors.

It is apparent that, if B is less than A, then no matter what the total angular variation of B may be (even if it is hundreds of radians) the total angular difference between R and A cannot exceed arctan (B/A). For instance, if $B/A = 0.5$, the maximum value of m_p for the phasor R when A is unmodulated is $m_p = 0.46$. If $B/A = 0.5$ and A in turn has its angle modulated, then the difference between the angle of A and that of R cannot exceed 0.46 radian at any instant. If the modulation factor m_p of A is made large in comparison with 0.46, the interference of B

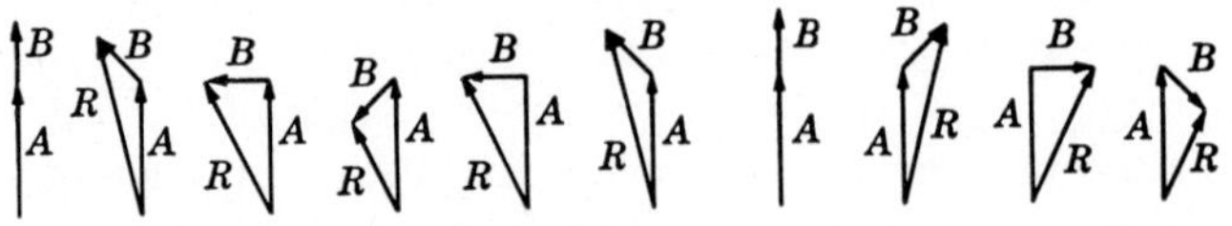

FIG. 1-21. Phasor diagrams showing interference in angular modulation. A, the desired signal phasor (unmodulated). B, the interfering signal phasor (same carrier frequency). R, the phasor of the total wave $(A + B)$.

becomes negligible, in spite of the fact that the magnitude of B is by no means negligible in comparison with A.

This analysis justifies the experimental results which show that when two frequency-modulated signals are picked up by a receiver, there is no appreciable interference between the two signals if the stronger exceeds the weaker by a ratio of $2:1$ or more.

It will be seen that the greater the value of m_p used for the desired signal the greater is the discrimination against the undesired signal, but this discrimination is not affected by the value of m_p used in the undesired signal.

The discrimination against interference obtained by angle modulation applies to all types of interference. In particular, static may be represented as a phasor of varying phase and magnitude. The selective circuits of the receiver admit only those components within the band to which it is receptive. If the amplitude of the admitted noise does not exceed half the amplitude of the desired wave, a very small amount of noise will be introduced into the output. The greater the average phase deviation in comparison with the angle 0.46 (approximately 0.5), the greater will be the discrimination against the noise. It should also be observed that components of the noise phasor which differ in frequency from the carrier by superaudible frequencies will produce superimposed angular velocities above audibility and so do not contribute to the noise, as long as the noise is small compared with the signal.

In radio operation it will be found that, if a portable receiver is driven in an automobile away from a frequency-modulated transmitting station, no appreciable noise will be experienced until the desired field strength drops to twice the noise field strength (taking into account only those components of noise accepted by the selective circuits of the receiver). The noise then rises rapidly, so that a sharp threshold is experienced.

Within the distance limited by the threshold, the signal-to-noise (S/N) ratio can be improved by either increasing the power or increasing the modulation factor (either phase or frequency).   Since power is proportional to the square of voltage or current in a given system, doubling the frequency deviation in frequency modulation has the same effect on the S/N ratio as increasing the transmitted power four times.   In general an increase in the maximum frequency deviation by a ratio n would be equivalent in its effect on the S/N ratio to an increase in power by the ratio n^2.

The major objection to the use of a large frequency deviation is that it would limit the number of stations which can serve a given area if a fixed total bandwidth is allowed for the service.

A compromise must be adopted and a standard set so that the receivers may work with the transmitters.   This is a function of government regulation.   In order to study the problem of the required allotment, a spectrum analysis must be made of the different classes of modulation.

1-16. Spectrum Analysis of Amplitude Modulation.   The wave of Eq. (1-8) may be expanded by the use of simple trigonometric identities. This equation becomes

$$e = A \sin \omega t + \frac{m_a A}{2} \cos (\omega - \rho)t - \frac{m_a A}{2} \cos (\omega + \rho)t \qquad (1\text{-}19)$$

Equation (1-19) shows that the wave which is amplitude-modulated by a single frequency may be analyzed into three component frequencies with the following designations:

$A \sin \omega t$	the carrier
$\dfrac{m_a A}{2} \cos (\omega - \rho)t$	the lower side frequency
$\dfrac{m_a A}{2} \cos (\omega + \rho)t$	the upper side frequency

The three components may be represented by three phasors rotating at different angular velocities.   Again if the observer were rotating with the carrier phasor, this phasor would appear to be stationary.   The upper-side-frequency phasor would appear to be rotating *counterclockwise* at a velocity ρ, and the lower side frequency would appear to be rotating *clockwise* at the same velocity ρ.

The three phasors corresponding to the wave of Fig. 1-14 are shown in Fig. 1-22. It will be observed that the upper- and lower-sideband phasors add together to form a phasor M called the modulation phasor,

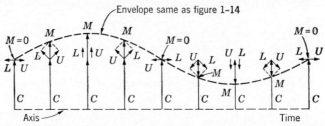

Fig. 1-22. Phasor diagram of the carrier and side frequencies in an amplitude-modulated wave. C, carrier phasor (constant length). U, upper-side-frequency phasor. L, lower-side-frequency phasor. M, modulation phasor (sum of U and L). Phasor of the complete wave is $C + M$.

which is always in phase with the carrier phasor but which varies in magnitude.

The three component frequencies of Eq. (1-19) are represented graphically in Fig. 1-23.

If the original signal were a complex wave instead of a single frequency, a spectrum analysis would show it to be represented by a band of frequencies. The lower and upper side frequencies would expand into two bands of frequencies each as wide as the band of the original signal. For instance, if the signal were restricted to a band of 0 to 5,000 cycles, the two sidebands would extend from 5,000 cycles below to 5,000 cycles above the carrier frequency. Since the quality of a signal depends upon the width of the band which may be transmitted, an improvement in the quality of transmission would require an extension of the frequency spectrum occupied by the radio wave. However, the narrower the frequency band which is used, the greater will be the number of stations which can be accommodated. In practice a compromise must be made. Standard broadcasting stations are assigned carrier frequencies in the range of 535 to 1,605 kc on a world-wide basis, these assignments being separated at intervals of 10 kc. In order to prevent interference, selective circuits are required in the receiver which are so sharp in most commercial models that sideband components more than 3,000 cycles away from the carrier are greatly attenuated. Hence the quality which is permissible in practical operation is limited by the major problem of interference.

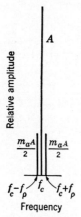

Fig. 1-23. Spectrum analysis of an amplitude-modulated wave. f_c, carrier frequency. f_p, signal frequency. $m_a = 0.5$.

1-17. Spectrum Analysis of Angle Modulation.   The angle-modulated wave of Eq. (1-12) may be expanded by the use of the identities

$$\sin (m_p \sin x) = 2[J_1(m_p) \sin x + J_3(m_p) \sin 3x + J_5(m_p) \sin 5x + \cdots]$$
$$(1\text{-}20a)$$
$$\cos (m_p \sin x) = J_0(m_p) + 2[J_2(m_p) \cos 2x$$
$$+ J_4(m_p) \cos 4x + J_6(m_p) \cos 6x + \cdots] \quad (1\text{-}20b)$$

where $J_n(m_p)$ is the nth-order Bessel function of the first kind.   Equation (1-12) may be written

$$e = A[\sin \omega t \cos (m_p \sin \rho t) + \cos \omega t \sin (m_p \sin \rho t)] \quad (1\text{-}21)$$

If Eqs. (1-20a) and (1-20b) are inserted in Eq. (1-21), the following result will be obtained:

$$e = A\{J_0(m_p) \sin \omega t + J_1(m_p)[\sin (\omega + \rho)t - \sin (\omega - \rho)t]$$
$$+ J_2(m_p)[\sin (\omega + 2\rho)t + \sin (\omega - 2\rho)t] + J_3(m_p)[\sin (\omega + 3\rho)t$$
$$- \sin (\omega - 3\rho)t] + J_4(m_p)[\sin (\omega + 4\rho)t + \sin (\omega - 4\rho)t] + \cdots$$
$$+ J_n(m_p)[\sin (\omega + n\rho)t + (-1)^n \sin (\omega - n\rho)t] + \cdots\} \quad (1\text{-}22)$$

This indicates that there are an infinite number of side frequencies for a single-frequency signal.   However, this is not as bad as might at first appear because, for any given value of m_p, there will be a value of n above which the coefficients $J_n(m_p)$ fall off rapidly and become negligible.   This is shown in Fig. 1-24. For example, if m_p is ½ radian or less, only the first pair of side frequencies is important.   On the other hand, if m_p is equal to 20 radians, side frequencies out to the twenty-fourth pair would be appreciable.   For large values of n this rapid falling off of $J_n(m_p)$ occurs just beyond $n = m_p$.   Observe also that the value of the carrier component is always reduced when modulation occurs since $J_0(m_p)$ is less than 1 for all values of m_p different from 0.   This is in contrast with amplitude modulation, where the value of the carrier is not affected by modulation.

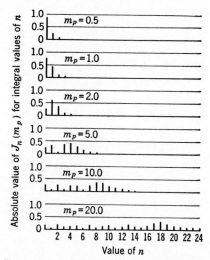

FIG. 1-24. Values of the Bessel function of the first kind for integral orders.

Figure 1-17 was drawn for a phase-modulation factor of 0.5, and so the first pair of sidebands are the only ones of importance.   If all other sidebands are neglected, the phasor diagrams including the side bands for different instants of Fig. 1-17 can be shown as in Fig. 1-25. The signal wave is shown for identification. The carrier and resultant phasors are the same as those shown in Fig. 1-19. The modulation phasor, which is the sum of the two sideband phasors, is always 90° out of phase with the carrier and varies in magnitude in the same way that the modulation phasor varies in amplitude modulation. The neglect of higher-order side frequencies is the same as an assumption that there is a negligible difference between the arc and a tangent line of the same length when the angle is small.

When the modulation phasor is added to the carrier phasor it causes the resultant phasor alternately to advance beyond and retard behind the carrier phasor. The maximum advance and retardation is approximately $\frac{1}{2}$ radian. The length of the resultant phasor is substantially

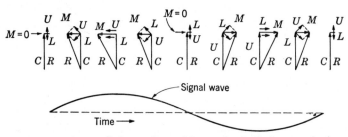

Fig. 1-25. Phasor diagrams of the carrier and first pair of side frequencies in an angle-modulated wave for low values of modulation index. C, carrier phasor. U, upper-side-frequency phasor. L, lower-side-frequency phasor. M, modulation phasor $(U + L)$. R, resultant phasor $(C + M)$.

constant. If the additional sidebands were included, the length of R would be exactly constant.

If the phase-modulation index exceeds $\frac{1}{2}$ radian, additional sidebands must be included because the arc and chord are no longer substantially the same. The addition of the phasors corresponding to these sidebands is illustrated in Fig. 1-26 for $m_p = 1$ and for one quarter of an audio cycle, the other three quarters being similar. It will be noticed that each pair of sidebands has associated with it a modulation phasor which maintains a constant phase with respect to carrier (assuming that phase reversals are taken care of by negative signs).

If the modulated wave represents a quantity whose square is proportional to power in a given system, the *average* power in an angle-modulated wave is not changed by the modulation, as the root-mean-square (rms) value of the wave is not modified if the amplitude remains constant. Therefore the sum of the squares of the carrier and all the sideband components remains constant for all values of m_p. The sideband power is obtained by a reduction in carrier power.   This is also proved by a well-known relation

$$J_0{}^2(m_p) + 2 \sum_{n=1}^{n=\infty} J_n{}^2(m_p) = 1 \tag{1-23}$$

for all values of m_p.   The number of terms which are of importance in the infinite series can be evaluated by setting

$$J_0{}^2(m_p) + 2 \sum_{n=1}^{n=s} J_n{}^2(m_p) \geq \lambda$$

Then if λ is taken as some value less than unity, the sum can terminate with a finite value of n equal to s.   If λ is equal to 0.999, then 99.9 per

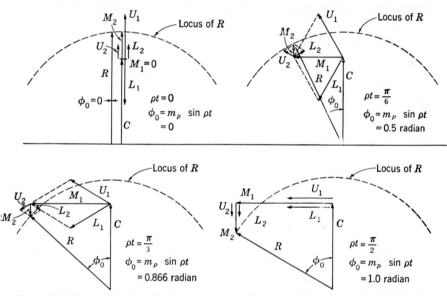

FIG. 1-26. Phasor diagram of a carrier and two pairs of side frequencies in an angle-modulated wave where $m_p = 1$. U_1, first upper-sideband phasor. L_1, first lower-sideband phasor. M_1, first modulation phasor $(U_1 + L_1)$. U_2, second upper-sideband phasor. L_2, second lower-sideband phasor. M_2, second modulation phasor $(U_2 + L_2)$. C, carrier phasor. R, resultant phasor.

cent of the energy in the wave would be due to sideband components corresponding to values of n equal to or less than s.

For example, if $m_p = 4$ and six components are taken in each sideband,

$$J_0{}^2(m_p) + 2 \sum_{n=1}^{n=6} J_n{}^2(m_p) = 0.157688 + 2(0.004356 + 0.132569$$

$$+ 0.185072 + 0.079017 + 0.017450 + 0.002411) = 0.999438$$

and all the components corresponding to $n > 6$ would contain only 0.0562 per cent of the energy.

The constancy of power output is in marked contrast to amplitude modulation where the carrier power remains constant and the sideband power is added. For this reason certain problems in design are simplified in a phase- or frequency-modulated transmitter.

1-18. Comparison of the Spectra of Phase and Frequency Modulation. In phase modulation the value of m_p is made directly proportional to the maximum amplitude of the signal. If two different signal frequencies have equal amplitudes, and modulate the signal in succession, the same number of sideband components would be necessary for each case and these components would have the same relative magnitude. It has been shown that to obtain the advantage of angle modulation in the reduction of interference requires the use of large values of m_p for the desired signal. If the value of m_p for a special case is taken equal to 20, then by Fig. 1-24 it is apparent that approximately 24 sideband components would be desirable for the upper sideband and a similar number for the lower sideband. Therefore if an audio signal of high quality containing components up to 15,000 cycles were to be transmitted, a bandwidth of approximately $2 \times 24 \times 15,000$, or 720,000, cycles would be required. This is obviously impracticable. For this reason phase modulation (as distinguished from frequency modulation) is seldom used for radio transmission.

In frequency modulation the value of Δf is made directly proportional to the maximum amplitude of the signal. If two different audio signals have equal amplitudes and modulate the signal in succession with equal values of Δf, by Eq. (1-18) the values of m_f for the two cases will be inversely proportional to the af. Thus if m_f is equal to 4 for 15,000 cycles, it would be equal to 40 for 1,500 cycles and equal to 400 for 150 cycles. A study of Fig. 1-24 shows that the number of components of appreciable magnitude in each sideband is slightly in excess of m_f. Therefore as the modulating frequency is reduced, the number of components necessary increases, and the modulated wave occupies almost a constant bandwidth in the spectrum. As an example, consider a case where the maximum frequency deviation is assumed to be 60,000 cycles. Then if a high-quality signal is to be transmitted, frequency components in this signal up to 15,000 cycles might be desired. If the wave were frequency-modulated with a 60,000-cycle deviation ($\Delta f = 60,000$), at 15,000 cycles m_f would equal

$$\frac{60,000}{15,000} = 4 \text{ radians}$$

For this case Fig. 1-24 shows that approximately six components in each sideband separated at intervals of 15,000 cycles are desirable, and the corresponding bandwidth would be 2 × 6 × 15,000, or 180,000, cycles. On the other hand, if the wave were to be frequency-modulated with a 60,000-cycle deviation by a 3,000-cycle wave, $m_f = 60,000/3,000 = 20$ and approximately 24 components in each sideband separated at intervals of 3,000 cycles would be desirable. The bandwidth for this signal would be 2 × 24 × 3,000 = 144,000 cycles, which is somewhat less than that needed for $m_f = 4$ at 15,000 cycles. Table 1-1 is constructed for a maximum deviation of 60,000 cycles, and a constant amplitude is assumed for the audio signal.

TABLE 1-1

Signal frequency	m_f for 60,000-cycle deviation	Approximate number of sideband components required	Approximate bandwidth, kc
30	2,000	4,030	120.06
60	1,000	2,020	120.20
600	100	208	124.8
2,500	24	46	140
3,000	20	24	144
5,000	12	30	150
10,000	6	16	160
15,000	4	12	180

The spectrum analysis for a deviation of 60 kc and modulating frequencies of 2,500, 5,000, 10,000, and 15,000 cycles is shown in Fig. 1-27, and it is apparent that the signal is contained within a bandwidth of approximately 200 kc in all cases.

As a practical matter, in typical audio signals the major portion of the energy is concentrated in the region below 2,000 cycles, the amplitudes of the higher frequencies falling off rapidly. Since Δf is proportional to signal amplitude, the very nature of typical signals is such that the required bandwidth is practically constant. For this reason it is found practicable to use a *maximum* deviation of 75,000 cycles for a total spectrum bandwidth of 200 kc.

The spectrum analyses for a modulating frequency of 15,000 cycles and deviation frequencies of 30, 15, 7.5, and 3.0 kc are shown in Fig. 1-28.

It is apparent from Figs. 1-27 and 1-28 that, when the frequency deviation is large compared with the signal frequency, the bandwidth required is approximately twice the frequency deviation, while, when the signal frequency is large compared with the deviation frequency, the bandwidth is twice the signal frequency. The latter case coincides with the situation in amplitude modulation. In other words, the bandwidth required is approximately twice the larger of the two frequencies (signal or deviation). If the signal and deviation frequencies are approximately equal,

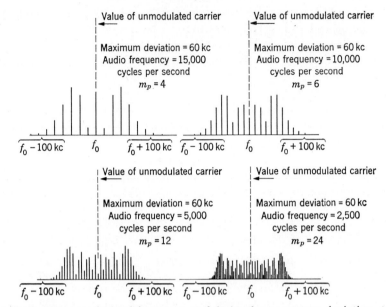

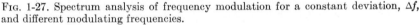

FIG. 1-27. Spectrum analysis of frequency modulation for a constant deviation, Δf, and different modulating frequencies.

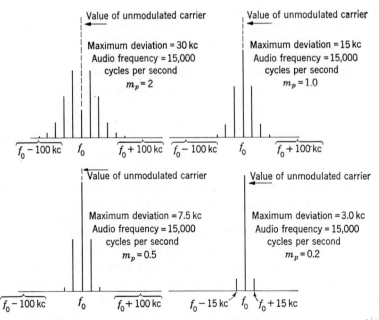

FIG. 1-28. Spectrum analysis of frequency modulation for constant modulating frequency and variable-frequency deviation. (Signal is for phase modulation.)

the bandwidth required is approximately four times that of the larger frequency (see Fig. 1-28 for $m_p = 0.5$, 1, and 2).

The spectra of Figs. 1-27 and 1-28 may be used for any other combinations of signal and deviation frequencies which have the same deviation ratio m_f by modifying the scale of abscissa so that the interval between adjacent components is equal to the af.

The reader must be cautioned that, if a signal contains two or more signal frequencies, the resultant spectra cannot be obtained by adding the spectra resulting from each signal frequency alone (as can be done in amplitude modulation).   However, the total spectra will remain approximately within the limits set by the maximum frequency deviation when the latter is large.

Although the discrimination against noise is proportional to m_f, it is impracticable to use large values of m_f at all signal frequencies because of the bandwidth involved.   However, noise and interference are the composite result of a larger number of noise components.   If frequency modulation is employed, the maximum value of m_f is obtained for each signal component in the signal which will at the same time keep the sideband components within the limits in the spectrum assigned to the transmission.   Therefore frequency modulation is the type of angle modulation which reduces the composite noise effect to the greatest practicable extent.

1-19. Simultaneous Modulation.   An amplitude-modulated wave and an angle-modulated wave can be transmitted in the same frequency band, provided the upper and lower sidebands of both are transmitted. Methods are available for the detection of amplitude modulation without responding to angle modulation, and, vice versa, methods are available for the detection of angle modulation without responding to amplitude variations.   However, in case two signals are transmitted simultaneously by amplitude and angle modulation, the requirements on the transmission system will be very stringent.   If one sideband is delayed a different amount from the other, then an angle-modulated wave will have amplitude variations proportional to its signal and an amplitude-modulated wave will have angle variations proportional to its signal.   The same result will occur if paired components in the two sidebands corresponding to a given component in the signal are not transmitted with the same gain or loss.   Under these conditions there would be interference (usually termed cross talk) between the two signals.

For simultaneous modulation, instead of using pure angle modulation for one of the signals, it could be transmitted by using only the first-order sidebands, even though the amplitude of the modulation phasor exceeds 50 per cent of the carrier.   This would keep the bandwidth of both signals identical.   This type of modulation is called "quadrature" modulation.   Amplitude modulation might, in contrast, be termed "inphase," or "direct," modulation.   Simultaneous direct and quadrature modulations are used to transmit two of the three video signals required in color television.

1-20. Single-sideband Transmission.   It is possible to filter out one of the sidebands of a modulated wave, transmitting information in a bandwidth equal only to that of the signal without further complication in coding.   In practice amplitude modulation is used to produce the original signal, and one sideband is then discarded.   With one sideband eliminated, both the phase and the amplitude of the resultant wave will vary in accordance with the signal, and so only one signal can be transmitted in a given band.   Since none of the signal information is contained in the carrier, it may be eliminated at the sending end.   However, the frequency of the carrier serves as decoding information, since the difference between its frequency and that of each component in the sideband identifies in turn the frequency of each component in the final signal in terms of the corresponding component in the original.

The carrier may be reintroduced at the receiving end by a local source, as long as the required frequency is known.   This is simple in the case of single-sideband transmission, because the reintroduced frequency need only be quite close to the original.   However, in case two sidebands are used, not only must the carrier frequency itself be exact, but the phase must be constant and correct if the identity of the angle or amplitude modulation is to be retained.   Therefore in simultaneous modulation it is absolutely essential that the carrier be transmitted and its phase relation to the two sets of double sidebands carefully preserved.

1-21. Interspersed or Comb Signal Separation.   When quasi-recurrent signals such as those resulting from the repeating lines of television are analyzed by the methods of Fourier, it will be found that the spectrum will show peaks of power at integral multiples of the recurrent frequency (in the case of television these would be at multiples of $30 \times 525 = 15,750$ cycles).   It is possible to introduce other signals, which have a similar characteristic and the same peak frequency separation, into the same frequency band, without appreciable interference.   This can be done for example for one additional signal by displacing it by one-half the frequency difference between peaks.   This method is used in the compatible color-television system adopted by the FCC, the second interspersed signal carrying both direct and quadrature modulation.   The original and interspersed signals thus transmit the three portions of the video information necessary to identify a color reproduction in a frequency band originally used only for black-and-white pictures.   As has been indicated, such a signal will place stringent limitations on delay and amplitude distortion in the transmission system or there will be interference between the three color components.

1-22. Pulse Modulation.   Both amplitude and angle modulation permit the separation of signals by means of frequency-selective networks or filters described in later chapters.   Systems making use of this method of coding and decoding for transmission of signals through a common transmission medium or network are generally called "frequency-division systems."

The use of pulse modulation introduces the possibility of another method of identifying signals of a particular channel on a "time-division" basis.   Pulse modulation is based on the concept of "sampling" a signal in accordance with the following theorem:

A signal of duration T whose highest frequency of importance is f_h can be completely specified by $2Tf_h$ [or $2T(BW)$, where BW is the bandwidth of the low-pass (LP) network necessary to transmit the signal] samples taken at equal time intervals of $1/2f_h$ sec.

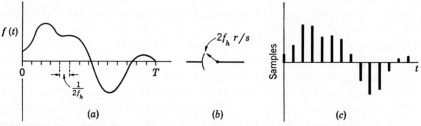

Fig. 1-29. The idea of sampling.   (a) A signal $f(t)$ of duration T.   (b) A simple rotating mechanical sampling switch.   (c) The amplitude samples corresponding to a.

The idea of sampling is shown in Fig. 1-29.   The theorem may be proved as follows: The signal $f(t)$ may be expanded into a Fourier series involving harmonics of $1/T^*$, that is,

$$f(t) = B_0 + \sum_{k=1}^{n} B_k \cos \frac{2\pi k}{T} t + \sum_{k=1}^{n} A_k \sin \frac{2\pi k}{T} t \qquad (1\text{-}24)$$

(Actually, when a Fourier series is used, the signal would repeat itself over and over again for values of time greater than T but all the information involved can be extracted in time T.)

By the specifications, f_h is the highest frequency of significance; hence n, the order of the highest harmonic in Eq. (1-24), will be

$$n = \frac{f_h}{1/T} = f_h T$$

There are, therefore, $2f_h T + 1$ terms in Eq. (1-24) whose amplitudes may be evaluated by setting up $2f_h T + 1$ simultaneous equations of the

* Fourier series are described in detail in Chap. 2.   It is suggested that the student return to this section after completing Chap. 2.

form of Eq. (1-24) at values of t corresponding to each of the samples. For typical values of f_h, $2f_hT + 1$ is essentially equal to $2f_hT$. Therefore, the samples contain all of the information necessary to specify $f(t)$.

Since the signal presumably has components extending from zero to f_h, the highest significant frequency, it is often convenient to replace f_h by BW, which is the bandwidth of both the signal itself and the network necessary to transmit it.

For a *continuous* signal (rather than one of duration T), the theorem may be restated as follows:

A continuous signal, whose highest frequency of importance is BW, can be completely specified by samples taken at a rate of 2BW per second.

It follows that, if the proper number of signal samples are taken and their magnitudes are identified with some characteristic (such as amplitude or position in time) of successive short pulses of a high-frequency (hf) wave, these pulses may be considered to represent a coded form of the signal. However, these pulses need not occupy *all* the time of transmission, and so the coded pulses of two or more signal channels may be interspersed in time, provided that at both the transmitter and the receiver there is a synchronous method of identifying the particular pulses of a given channel with the terminal equipment of that channel. Such a method of coding is termed "time-multiplexing."

In addition to the advantages of multiplexing by time division, various forms of pulse modulation show advantages in improving the signal to noise ratio. As in the case of frequency modulation this improvement in reducing noise is obtained at the expense of wider-frequency-band requirements in the transmission system.

It is also possible to use combinations of pulse and amplitude or angle modulation.

1-23. Hartley-Shannon Law. It has been shown that the amount of information in a signal of duration T and maximum frequency BW can be represented by $2T(BW)$ pulses, each of amplitude determined by the signal strength at the instants the samples are taken. At the receiving end, the amplitude of a signal never has an absolutely distinct value but has been, as it were, "smudged" by the introduction of noise from random disturbances encountered en route. Hence the value of a signal of power S is known only within a degree of error determined by the noise power N.

It is desirable to define the amount of information in a signal. In legal interrogation, there is always a desire to obtain simple "yes" and "no" answers to all questions. As a matter of fact, if there is a definite answer to a complicated question, it can always be secured if enough questions are properly phrased which do have an answer either yes or no.[1]

[1] See Matthew 5: 37.

This is particularly easy if the answer is quantitative. For example, if one asks an individual to think of any digit from 0 to 63, then not more than six questions with yes and no answers need be asked to determine the value of the digit. Suppose the number chosen is 43. Then the following questions, which are based on dividing possible numbers successively into two equal groups, will apply, together with the answers and conclusions indicated:

Question	Answer	Conclusion
1. Is $0 \leq x \leq 31$ true?	No	$32 \leq x \leq 63$
2. Is $32 \leq x \leq 47$ true?	Yes	$32 \leq x \leq 47$
3. Is $32 \leq x \leq 39$ true?	No	$40 \leq x \leq 47$
4. Is $40 \leq x \leq 43$ true?	Yes	$40 \leq x \leq 43$
5. Is x either 40 or 41?	No	x is either 42 or 43
6. Does $x = 42$?	No	$x = 43$

All the possible 64 values between and including 0 and 63 can be specified by no more than $\log_2 64 = 6$ answers to a corresponding number of questions which can be answered yes or no. By definition the possible choices among 64 possible values are defined as 6 *bits* of information corresponding to the 6 possible questions which can be answered yes or no. The term "bit" stands for "binary digit." The number of bits represents the maximum number of places in a binary number system which are required to designate the number of choices of values available. The binary number system is of much interest in communication work because it represents a simpler method of performing arithmetic operation and storage of information. However, since this book will deal largely with the analysis of the response of networks to continuous rather than quantized signals, this number system will not be developed further here.

Return now to a consideration of the information in a series of pulses describing a signal, each pulse having a voltage or current amplitude proportional to $\sqrt{S + N}$ and an uncertainty in value proportional to $\sqrt{N}$. Then the number of possible recognizable values of signal in the presence of noise is

$$n = \log_2 \sqrt{\frac{S + N}{N}} = \frac{1}{2} \log_2 \left(1 + \frac{S}{N}\right) \qquad (1\text{-}25)$$

Since the information in the original signal can be represented by $2T(BW)$ pulses, the total information H in the signal will be

$$H = T(BW) \log_2 \left(1 + \frac{S}{N}\right) \qquad \text{bits} \qquad (1\text{-}26)$$

The rate of transmission of information, or the capacity, of the channel in bits per second will be

$$C = \frac{H}{T} = BW \log_2 \left(1 + \frac{S}{N}\right) \qquad \text{bits/sec} \qquad (1\text{-}27)$$

Equation (1-27) is known as the Hartley-Shannon law.   Hartley provided the concept of the effect of bandwidth, and Shannon added the important effect of S/N ratio.

This law shows that an increase in information rate can be obtained by increasing either the bandwidth or the signal power or, alternatively, by keeping down the noise power.   However, it should be recognized that every communication system does not achieve the full capabilities inherent in the bandwidth and power used.   The design of the coding and decoding systems has much to do with the degree to which the limit of the channel capacity is approached.   Frequency modulation is just one method of obtaining improved S/N ratio by using wider bandwidths. Certain forms of pulse modulation obtain similar results at the cost of channel bandwidth required and increased complexity of coding and decoding.   Increased complexity in coding may also introduce appreciable time delay in order to perform the coding.

The fact that information capacity depends upon S/N ratio was not at first recognized.   However, consider the possibilities of a noiseless system.   In such a noiseless system one could identify the voltage of a single pulse with as many fine gradations as desired.   Then as many different messages could be sent with a single pulse as there were identifiable values of voltage, presumably an infinite number in this case. Hence one pulse could transmit any message.   One might list all possible messages ahead of time (theoretically possible but practically not achievable) and associate each message with a possible magnitude of a pulse.   The fact that voltage can in general be measured with only a finite accuracy indicates that this uncertainty in measurement is due to some random characteristic synonomous with noise in the general sense. This limits the amount of information which can be obtained with one reading.   In practice it is often easier to use n pulses whose presence or absence indicates yes or no answers than it is to produce the equivalent 2^n corresponding recognizable values of magnitude in a single pulse.

The ultimate range of any communication system is reached when the signal has dropped to a value where the S/N power ratio can no longer be tolerated.   This may be a relatively high value when the signal is to be used for entertainment, for example, in broadcasting, because it is easy to turn off the set and seek enjoyment in other pursuits.   A much lower value will be tolerated if the communication is vital, for example, in military applications.   However, even in the latter case, when the

S/N ratio becomes too low, the signal cannot be interpreted by the receiver and the communication becomes useless.

It is important to observe that once the S/N ratio falls below tolerable limits the signal cannot be restored by amplifiers, because they will amplify the noise along with the signal. The most carefully designed amplifier will introduce a certain minimum noise, due to the random motion of the electrons both in the input circuit and in the vacuum tubes or transistors themselves. Therefore signals, even though originally fairly noise-free and transmitted over circuits introducing very little noise, must not be allowed to fall to too low an intensity or they may not be recoverable by amplification. For this reason, in long-wire transmission systems it is necessary to introduce amplifiers at intervals, rather than attempting to add all the amplification at the ends. As an example consider the case of submarine cables which have a high loss when used over the band of frequencies necessary for telephone communication. Transatlantic telephony was not feasible over such cables until a method was developed which permitted the introduction of amplifiers at frequent intervals within the cable itself in spite of the fact that these amplifiers must be immersed deep on the ocean floor.

Figure 1-30 shows an illustration of the energy levels plotted on a logarithmic scale at different points along a telephone communication system. This illustration is purposely made somewhat noisier than would be good practice.

It should be observed that noise is originally introduced at the sending end because of sounds in the room of the talker and inadequacies of the microphone in the subscriber's set. The room noise is amplified by the sending microphone along with the signal. It is assumed that a negligible amount of noise is introduced by the local-line central office and first section of long line. However, the loss which has occurred in the first long-line section illustrated is so great that considerable gain is needed in the first repeater, and hence the inherent noise of the amplifier circuits is appreciable in comparison with the weak signal. The combination of signal and noise emerges from the repeater with a poorer S/N ratio than on entering. The second long line is assumed to be an open-wire line running parallel to a power line, and, in spite of the best precautions, some noise is introduced by induction. It is assumed that further noise introduced is not great until the S/N combination reaches the subscriber's set of the listener. There additional disturbing noise is introduced, largely due to local room noise, which enters in two ways. One way is through the ears of the listener (termed acoustic leakage), and the other is through the local microphone, which amplifies it, on through, but attenuated by, the subscriber set and back into the electrical circuit of the receiver. This latter source is called "side tone." There-

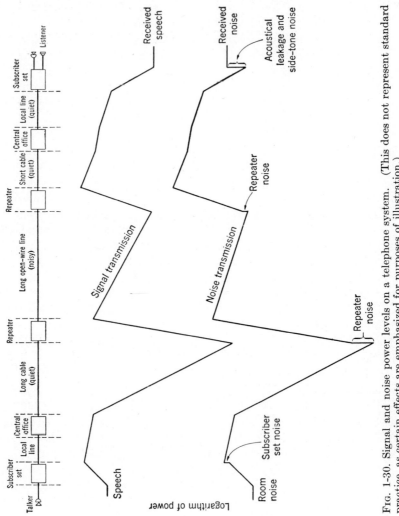

Fig. 1-30. Signal and noise power levels on a telephone system. (This does not represent standard practice, as certain effects are emphasized for purposes of illustration.)

fore the signal arrives with a S/N ratio inherently lower than when it started.

The fact that as much information cannot be passed over a noisy system in a given time as over a quiet system is illustrated qualitatively by the fact that frequent repetitions are required over a noisy telephone system.

It is the function of any communication-system design, be it telephone, radio, television, radar, computing system, or what have you, to ensure that (1) the S/N ratio will not fall below the allowable limit; (2) the signal itself is of sufficient amplitude to be interpreted or decoded by the ultimate user of the information, whether man or machine, or a combination of the two.

1-24. Summary.   In the design of electrical communication systems complex signals representing functions of time must be coded into electrical signals.   These signals may then be transmitted directly through networks to the point of delivery, or they may be further coded by frequency translation or other means before being introduced in the communication system.

In general a major feature in the design of communication systems involves the synthesis of a-c networks which can transmit desired signals represented by finite bandwidths without appreciable distortion and can reject signals or portions of signals in frequency ranges not desired. In this synthesis use will be made of passive elements having properties of resistance, inductance, and capacitance and of active elements such as vacuum tubes and transistors.   The balance of this book will be devoted to the analysis and synthesis of the linear networks.

Of comparable importance in the development of the communication engineer are the subjects of:

1. Ion and electron dynamics of importance in vacuum tubes.

2. Solid-state physics important to transistors.

3. Electromagnetic field theory and the application of boundary conditions set by antennas and wave guides to Maxwell's equations.

4. Application of nonlinearity to achieve devices for modulation and demodulation and power amplification of modulated waves.

5. Statistical information theory.

6. Electronic-system design.

Obviously these can no longer be compressed, even in their essence, within one volume.

CHAPTER 2

METHODS OF
NETWORK-BEHAVIOR ANALYSIS

Two basic concepts are encountered in the study of communication circuits: *analysis*, in which the network is given and its behavior is to be calculated, and *synthesis*, in which a network is to be designed to give a specified behavior. Fundamental to both these concepts is the idea of network behavior. This chapter will discuss several means by which this can be specified and calculated and the ways in which these means are related.

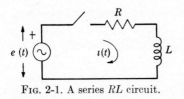

FIG. 2-1. A series RL circuit.

2-1. Transient-state and Steady-state Response. Consider the simple circuit of Fig. 2-1, where $e(t)$ is a cosine voltage suddenly applied at $t = 0$ such that

$$e(t) = 0 \qquad t < 0$$
$$e(t) = \hat{E} \cos \omega t \qquad t > 0$$

It is required to find the current i as a function of time. Thus, in this case, the network behavior relates $i(t)$ to $e(t)$. (Alternatively the voltage across R or L may have been required.) One basic method of finding the current consists in writing an equation relating $i(t)$ and its derivative (and its integral, if necessary) to the driving function $e(t)$ and the circuit parameters; hence, by Kirchhoff's voltage law

$$L \frac{di}{dt} + Ri = \hat{E} \cos \omega t \qquad t > 0 \qquad (2\text{-}1)$$

It is well known from the study of differential equations that the complete solution of Eq. (2-1) consists of two parts: (1) the complementary function which is independent of $\hat{E} \cos \omega t$ and is the solution to the homogeneous equation obtained by setting the driving function equal to zero in Eq. (2-1); (2) the particular integral which is dependent upon the form of the driving function and is a solution of Eq. (2-1). It will be shown later that these two parts of the complete solution have special physical significance.

44

As stated above, the homogeneous equation corresponding to Eq. (2-1) is

$$L \frac{di}{dt} + Ri = 0 \tag{2-1a}$$

One way by which this may be solved is to separate the variables and integrate.

$$\int \frac{di}{i} = - \int \frac{R}{L} dt$$

$$\ln i = - \frac{R}{L} t + \ln K$$

where K = constant

$\quad$ ln = napierian, or natural, logarithm

Rearranging and taking antilogarithms,

$$i = Ke^{-Rt/L} \qquad \text{complementary function} \tag{2-2}$$

The particular integral of Eq. (2-1) may be found by a straightforward method when the driving function is a cosinusoid, because in this case the derivative and integral are also cosinusoids. One can assume that the particular integral will have the form $i = |\hat{I}| \cos (\omega t + \phi)$, where $|\hat{I}|$ and ϕ are constants whose values must be determined. As a matter of convenience i may be written in another form by means of Euler's identity.

$$|\hat{I}| e^{j(\omega t + \phi)} = |\hat{I}| \cos (\omega t + \phi) + j|\hat{I}| \sin (\omega t + \phi)$$

or
$$i = |\hat{I}| \cos (\omega t + \phi) = \text{Re} \{|\hat{I}| e^{j(\omega t + \phi)}\} \tag{2-3}$$

where Re stands for "real part of."

Then substituting Eq. (2-3) into Eq. (2-1),

$$L \, \text{Re} \{j\omega|\hat{I}| e^{j\phi} e^{j\omega t}\} + R \, \text{Re} \{|\hat{I}| e^{j\phi} e^{j\omega t}\} = \text{Re} \{\hat{E} e^{j\omega t}\} \tag{2-4}$$

Since Re $\{ \quad \}$ and $e^{j\omega t}$ are common to all the terms, Eq. (2-4) may be rewritten Re $e^{j\omega t}\{|\hat{I}| e^{j\phi}(R + j\omega L) = \hat{E}\}$. Therefore

$$\text{Re } e^{j\omega t} \left\{ |\hat{I}| e^{j\phi} = \frac{\hat{E}}{R + j\omega L} = \frac{\hat{E}}{\sqrt{R^2 + (\omega L)^2}} e^{-j \arctan \omega L/R} \right\} \tag{2-5}$$

whence
$$|\hat{I}| = \frac{\hat{E}}{\sqrt{R^2 + (\omega L)^2}} \qquad \phi = -\arctan \frac{\omega L}{R} \tag{2-5a}$$

Then the particular integral of Eq. (2-1) is

$$i = \text{Re} \{|\hat{I}| e^{j(\omega t + \phi)}\}$$
$$= |\hat{I}| \cos (\omega t + \phi) \qquad \text{particular integral} \tag{2-6}$$

The complete solution of Eq. (2-1) is obtained by adding Eqs. (2-2) and (2-6).

$$i = Ke^{-Rt/L} + \frac{\hat{E}}{\sqrt{R^2 + (\omega L)^2}} \cos (\omega t + \phi) \tag{2-7}$$

The constant K is obtained from the initial conditions which prevail at $t = 0$. Since current cannot change discontinuously through the inductance, $i = 0$ at $t = 0$. Then, substituting in Eq. (2-7),

$$K = - \frac{\hat{E}}{\sqrt{R^2 + (\omega L)^2}} \cos \phi$$

From Fig. 2-2, $\cos \phi = R/\sqrt{R^2 + (\omega L)^2}$; so the complete solution is

$$i = - \frac{\hat{E} R}{R^2 + (\omega L)^2} e^{-Rt/L} + \frac{\hat{E}}{\sqrt{R^2 + (\omega L)^2}} \cos (\omega t + \phi) \qquad (2\text{-}8)$$

The first term in Eq. (2-8) is the *transient-state* part of the solution and is important only for finite values of time near $t = 0$. The second term is the *steady-state* part of the solution. In most circuits the parameters have values such that the transient-state term reduces to a negligible value in a fraction of a second and only the steady-state term prevails at large values of time. Thus the steady-state term describes the behavior of the circuit in response to the driving function after all transient terms have been reduced to negligible values.

2-2. Steady-state Response. A number of observations may be made concerning the method of obtaining the steady-state response or particular integral for a sinusoidal driving function as given in the last section. These serve as the basis for the usual j-operator, or complex-number, method of solving a-c circuit problems:

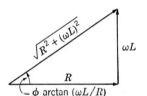

FIG. 2-2. Phasor diagram for evaluating $\cos \phi$.

1. Once the solution has been gone through step by step to lay the basis for the method, it is the usual practice to omit the Re { } and $e^{j\omega t}$ in Eq. (2-4).

2. The time derivative $d(\ )/dt$ is replaced by the multiplying operator $j\omega$, and the time integral $\int (\ ) \, dt$ is replaced by the multiplying operator $1/j\omega$. (The last statement was not demonstrated in the last section but may be proved by the student.)

3. In Eq. (2-5) the term $R + j\omega L$ may be identified with the usual complex impedance

$$Z = R + j\omega L \qquad (2\text{-}9a)$$

having a *magnitude*

$$|Z| = \sqrt{R^2 + (\omega L)^2} \qquad (2\text{-}9b)$$

and *angle*

$$\phi = \arctan \frac{\omega L}{R} \qquad (2\text{-}9c)$$

4. It is the usual practice in a-c-circuit theory to use the rms value of $|I|$ rather than $|\hat{I}|$, thus,

$$|\hat{I}| = \sqrt{2} \, |I| \qquad (2\text{-}10a)$$

and the "complex current" is represented by

$$I = |I|e^{j\phi} = |I|\underline{/\phi} \tag{2-10b}$$

A knowledge of the steady-state characteristic of a network as a function of frequency can be very useful. This may be obtained by calculating the response to a sinusoidal driving function of constant amplitude at many different frequencies and plotting the resulting data vs. frequency. Since the response will generally be a complex quantity, three quantities will be involved. By way of illustration, I for the circuit of Fig. 2-1 is plotted isometrically as a three-dimensional single-valued locus in Fig. 2-3a, the circuit-parameter values being $R = 10$ ohms, $L = 1.59$ mh, $E = 5$ volts. In the figure, the coordinates are the real and imaginary parts of I, and frequency.

It is fairly apparent that some simplified means of presenting these data are desirable, because the three-dimensional locus is difficult to draw on a two-dimensional plane, and even more difficult to interpret. Three such means are in common use.

The first consists in plotting the projection of the three-dimensional curve on the (Re $\{I\}$)-(Im $\{I\}$) plane. Since this projection results from collapsing the frequency scale, the frequency axis is lost. This difficulty is overcome in some instances by identifying points on the projection with their corresponding frequencies as in Fig. 2-3b. In other instances where the shape of the curve is of prime importance an arrow indicating the direction of increasing frequency may be used.

Another method consists in resolving the locus of Fig. 2-3a into its polar coordinates $|I|$ and ϕ,

$$\begin{aligned} I &= |I|e^{j\phi} = |I| \cos \phi + j|I| \sin \phi \\ &= \text{Re } \{I\} + j \text{ Im } \{I\} \end{aligned}$$

and of plotting these against frequency as in Fig. 2-3c.

A third method utilizes two projections of the three-dimensional locus: Re $\{I\}$ on the (Im $\{I\}$)(f) plane, and Im $\{I\}$ on the Re $\{I\}$)(f) plane. This presentation is shown in Fig. 2-3d.

In many applications the frequencies at which the behavior is of interest encompass such a large range that compression of the frequency scale is desirable. The psychological behavior of the human ear serves as a logical basis for this compression. The ear identifies equal frequency *ratios* as equal musical *intervals*. For example, if the two frequencies 128 and 64 cycles are heard simultaneously or in sequence, they seem to be separated by the same interval as if the two frequencies 1,024 and 512 cycles are sounded under similar conditions, even though the difference between them is 64 cycles in the first case and 512 cycles in the second. The key to this situation is that in both cases the frequency *ratio* is 2:1, and the corresponding interval is known as an "octave." Thus the ear's response to frequency is logarithmic; so logarithmic scales may be used to compress the frequency axis. An *octave* scale, based on powers of 2, may be used, in which case the frequencies 100, 200, 400,

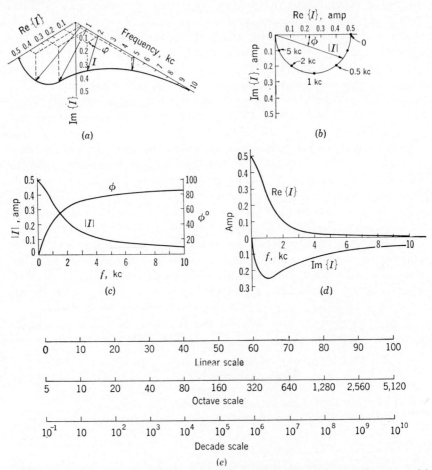

FIG. 2-3. Alternative methods of plotting the steady-state current of Fig. 2-1. (a) Isometric plot of three-dimensional current locus. (b) Projection of locus onto the (Re{I})(Im{I}) plane. (c) The polar coordinates of *b* plotted against frequency. (d) Projections of the three-dimensional locus on the (Re{I})(f) and (Im{I})(f) planes. (e) Comparison of linear and logarithmic scales.

800, . . . cycles would lie at equal intervals along the frequency axis. Because of the availability of semilogarithmic paper, however, it is the usual practice to use a *decade* scale, which is based on powers of 10. In this case the frequencies 10, 100, 1,000, 10,000, . . . cycles would lie at equal intervals along the frequency axis. It will also be found that the use of a logarithmic scale often simplifies the presentation of data. For example, in Chap. 4 a response curve is made symmetrical, and in Chap. 14 a curve is made linear over a wide frequency range by the use of logarithmic scales. The several scales are shown in Fig. 2-3e.

While the current has been chosen for graphical representation in Fig. 2-3, the student should realize that this need not be the case. For example, the impedance or the voltage across the inductance L in Fig. 2-1 could be chosen as the network characteristic, depending upon the requirements of the particular problem in hand.

2-3. Transient Response to Applied Step Function. In solving for the current of Fig. 2-1 it was seen that the constant factor K in the transient-state part of Eq. (2-7) is a function of the initial conditions existing in the circuit at the instant $t = 0$ and of ω of the cosine driving function. In the interests of providing a uniform basis for comparing different circuits, it is convenient to establish a standard condition for the transient response. A convenient standard is for the circuit to be initially at rest, i.e., no initial currents flowing and all capacitors uncharged.

A commonly used test signal for evaluating the transient response is the "step function," which, on a voltage basis, is equivalent to a battery of terminal voltage E applied at $t = 0$.

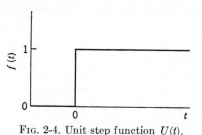

FIG. 2-4. Unit step function $U(t)$.

A unit step function (a step function of unit amplitude) is shown in Fig. 2-4. Mathematically, this function is described by

$$f(t) = 0 \qquad t < 0$$
$$f(t) = 1 \qquad t > 0 \tag{2-11}$$

and is usually symbolized by either $U(t)$ or $S_{-1}(t)$. It should be observed that multiplying a function $f_1(t)$ by $U(t)$ gives a new function $U(t)f_1(t)$ which equals $f_1(t)$ for $t > 0$ and which is identically zero for $t < 0$. Consider, then, the transient response of the circuit of Fig. 2-1 to a step function of voltage $EU(t)$. By Kirchhoff's voltage law

$$L\frac{di}{dt} + Ri = EU(t) \tag{2-12}$$

As before, the complementary function is Eq. (2-2), but the particular integral is

$$i = \frac{E}{R} \tag{2-13}$$

The student may verify this by substitution in Eq. (2-12). K may be shown to be $-E/R$; so the transient response to $EU(t)$ is

$$i = \frac{E}{R} (1 - e^{-Rt/L}) \qquad (2\text{-}14)$$

There are many reasons for choosing the step function as the basis for calculating transient response. For example, it may be shown that any nonrecurrent driving function may be analyzed as an integration of infinitesimal step functions properly weighted in amplitude and time. This is analogous to the method of the Fourier integral, whereby a non-recurrent driving function is analyzed into an integration of infinitesimal sinusoids properly weighted in amplitude and phase. Another reason for choosing the step function as a basic driving function is that the transient response, so calculated, is related to the steady-state response. This relationship is developed later in the chapter.

2-4. Time and Frequency Domains. In an earlier section a very basic problem of circuit analysis was considered when a time-varying current was calculated as the response of a network to a time-varying applied voltage. The current was found by solving the network differential equation. This method presents certain difficulties, particularly in a multimesh network where the solution of the simultaneous network equations results in differential equations of high order and hence algebraic equations of high degree. In such cases another method of solution which is based on the network's steady-state response can greatly simplify the work. In this method the network is conceived as an *operator* which is a function of frequency, $W(f)$. If, then, the time-varying driving function, $Dr(t)$, can be transformed into a corresponding function of frequency, $Dr(f)$, $Dr(f)$ can be operated upon by $W(f)$ to give the response $R(f) = W(f)Dr(f)$. A second transformation is then required to find the response as a function of time, $R(t)$. This alternate method, then, involves the transformation of the driving function from the time domain to the frequency domain, multiplication by $W(f)$, and transformation of the resulting response from the frequency to the time domain.

One fundamental limitation on this method is that the network must be *linear*, i.e., the magnitude of the response must be directly proportional to the magnitude of the driving force. If this linear relation does not hold, *modulation* will result and a given frequency component in $R(f)$ will not be a function solely of the corresponding component in $Dr(f)$.

Before the direct and inverse transformations between the time and frequency domains are considered, a few statements concerning $W(f)$ are in order. $W(f)$ is simply the steady-state network response that has been discussed earlier. It may give the relationship between voltage and current at a single pair of terminals, or it may relate voltage or current at one pair of terminals to voltage at another pair or current in another mesh of the network. Therefore this function may have the dimensions of impedance or admittance when it relates voltage and current, or it may be dimensionless when it relates voltage to voltage or current to current. Bode[1] has suggested that a suitable name for $W(f)$ may be "adpedance" or "immittance," the latter being in more common use.

The network function will always be a continuous function of frequency. If the driving force is recurrent, both it and the response will have components at only integral multiples of the fundamental frequency. As a consequence, if the phenomenon occurs less and less often, the number of components in a given frequency interval becomes greater and greater. In the limit when the phenomenon occurs only once, the frequency spectra become continuous. This concept will be developed in more detail later.

2-5. Fourier Series. The required transformation of the driving function from the time to the frequency domain may be accomplished by a "Fourier-series analysis" if $Dr(t)$ is repetitive or recurrent. By this means $Dr(t)$ may be analyzed into a number of sinusoidal components whose sum is known as a "Fourier series," which is identical to $Dr(t)$. As explained in Chap. 1, the frequencies of these component waves will be integral multiples of the number of times per second the nonsinusoidal wave recurs. Such integral multiples are termed "harmonics." In the interests of generality the Fourier series will be considered for a general time-varying function $f(\theta)$, θ being ωt, which has a period of $\theta = 2\pi$.[2]

If all the harmonic terms started at the same instant, there would necessarily be symmetry between successive half cycles, of the type of either Fig. 2-5a due to odd harmonics or Fig. 2-5b due to even harmonics. In order that the second half of the cycle may be controlled as well as the first, it is necessary to control both the *magnitude* and the *phase* of the harmonic terms. A harmonic of any frequency can be controlled in both phase and magnitude by adding two components in quadrature with each other, of the form $A_n \sin n\theta + B_n \cos n\theta$.

If the average value of the wave over a complete cycle were not zero, there would also be a d-c component to be added.

The general equation or Fourier series for any recurrent wave is,

[1] H. W. Bode, "Network Analysis and Feedback Amplifier Design," D. Van Nostrand Company, Inc., New York, 1945.

[2] The mathematician places additional restrictions on $f(\theta)$ for it to be expandable into a Fourier series. These restrictions are known as the Dirichlet conditions. See, for example, E. A. Guillemin, "The Mathematics of Circuit Analysis," p. 463, John Wiley & Sons, Inc., New York, 1949. It is fortunate for the engineer that most recurrent functions encountered in the physical world satisfy these restrictions, which will, therefore, not be considered here.

therefore,

$$f(\theta) = A_1 \sin \theta + A_2 \sin 2\theta + A_3 \sin 3\theta + \cdots + B_0 + B_1 \cos \theta$$
$$+ B_2 \cos 2\theta + B_3 \cos 3\theta + \cdots \quad (2\text{-}15)$$

$$= \sum_{n=0}^{\infty} (A_n \sin n\theta + B_n \cos n\theta) \quad (2\text{-}15a)$$

where, of course, the A's and B's must be determined for the particular $f(\theta)$. This may be done in the following manner:

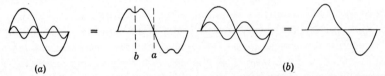

(a) (b)

Fig. 2-5. Symmetry. (a) Symmetry produced between positive and negative halves of the cycle by odd harmonics. *Note.* The wave displays even symmetry about b and odd symmetry about a. (b) Symmetry produced between positive and negative halves of cycle by even harmonics whose value is zero when the fundamental is zero.

Multiplying Eq. (2-15a) by $\cos k\theta \, d\theta$ (k being an integer) and integrating over any complete period from θ_1 to $\theta_1 + 2\pi$,

$$\int_{\theta_1}^{\theta_1+2\pi} f(\theta) \cos k\theta \, d\theta = \sum_{n=0}^{\infty} \int_{\theta_1}^{\theta_1+2\pi} (A_n \sin n\theta \cos k\theta + B_n \cos n\theta \cos k\theta) \, d\theta$$

$$= \sum_{n=0}^{\infty} \int_{\theta_1}^{\theta_1+2\pi} \left\{ \frac{A_n}{2} [\sin (n + k)\theta + \sin (n - k)\theta] \right.$$
$$\left. + \frac{B_n}{2} [\cos (n + k)\theta + \cos (n - k)\theta] \right\} d\theta \quad (2\text{-}16)$$

There appear to be a large number of terms to evaluate on the right-hand side of Eq. (2-16). However, it can be shown readily that the infinite summation reduces to a simple expression. The integral of a sine or cosine term over a complete cycle or integral number of cycles is zero since for one half of the cycle the term is positive, while during the other half it is negative. Therefore, terms where $k \neq n$, on the right-hand side of Eq. (2-16), are equal to zero.

On the other hand, terms where $k = n$ and $n \neq 0$ reduce to

$$\int_{\theta_1}^{\theta_1+2\pi} f(\theta) \cos n\theta \, d\theta = \int_{\theta_1}^{\theta_1+2\pi} \left[\frac{A_n}{2} \sin 2n\theta + \frac{B_n}{2} (\cos 2n\theta + 1) \right] d\theta \quad (2\text{-}16a)$$

Again the two trigonometric terms reduce to zero, and one has

$$B_n = \frac{1}{\pi} \int_{\theta_1}^{\theta_1+2\pi} f(\theta) \cos n\theta \, d\theta \qquad n \neq 0 \quad (2\text{-}16b)$$

If $k = n = 0$, Eq. (2-16a) yields

$$B_0 = \frac{1}{2\pi} \int_{\theta_1}^{\theta_1+2\pi} f(\theta) \, d\theta \qquad (2\text{-}16c)$$

By multiplying Eq. (2-15a) by $\sin k\theta \, d\theta$ and integrating from θ_1 to $\theta_1 + 2\pi$, the student may show in a similar manner that

$$A_n = \frac{1}{\pi} \int_{\theta_1}^{\theta_1+2\pi} f(\theta) \sin n\theta \, d\theta \qquad (2\text{-}16d)$$

If an equation can be written for $f(\theta)$, then Eqs. (2-16b) to (2-16d) can be evaluated analytically, but in many cases $f(\theta)$ can be expressed conveniently only in a graphical form. In this case the integrals in Eqs. (2-16b) to (2-16d) must be obtained by a point-to-point method such as the trapezoidal rule or Simpson's rule. A Fourier analysis can, of course, be applied to any recurrent wave, and $f(\theta)$ in these equations may represent any physical or mathematical quantity which is a function of θ.

2-6. Odd and Even Symmetry. In Eqs. (2-16b) to (2-16d) θ_1, the lower limit of integration, may be any angle whatever, the only requirement being that the integrations shall take place over a *complete* cycle.

Since $f(\theta)$ is recurrent, repeating itself at intervals of 2π for all values of θ, the angle $\theta = 0$ may also be chosen arbitrarily. Both θ_1 and $\theta = 0$ are usually selected according to the function involved so as to simplify the integrations. For example, if $\theta = 0$ can be chosen such that

$$f(-\theta) = -f(\theta) \qquad (2\text{-}17)$$

the function displays "odd," or "skew," symmetry. This would be the case in Fig. 2-5b if a were chosen to be $\theta = 0$. Under this condition the student may show that

$$A_n = \frac{2}{\pi} \int_0^{\pi} f(\theta) \sin n\theta \, d\theta$$
$$B_n = B_0 = 0 \qquad (2\text{-}17a)$$

Also, if $\theta = 0$ can be chosen such that

$$f(-\theta) = f(\theta) \qquad (2\text{-}18)$$

the function displays "mirror," or "even," symmetry and

$$B_n = \frac{2}{\pi} \int_0^{\pi} f(\theta) \cos n\theta \, d\theta$$
$$B_0 = \frac{1}{\pi} \int_0^{\pi} f(\theta) \, d\theta \qquad (2\text{-}18a)$$
$$A_n = 0$$

This would be the case if the angle b were chosen as $\theta = 0$ in Fig. 2-5b.

2-7. Calculation of Circuit Response by Fourier Series. If the function of interest is a recurrent function of time with a period $T = 1/f_1$ and if $2\pi f_1$ is designated by ω_1, then the set of equations becomes

$$f(t) = B_0 + \sum_{n=1}^{\infty} (A_n \sin n\omega_1 t + B_n \cos n\omega_1 t) \qquad (2\text{-}19)$$

where
$$B_0 = \frac{1}{T} \int_{t_1}^{t_1+T} f(t)\, dt \qquad (2\text{-}20)$$

$$B_n = \frac{2}{T} \int_{t_1}^{t_1+T} f(t) \cos n\omega_1 t\, dt \qquad n \neq 0 \qquad (2\text{-}21)$$

$$A_n = \frac{2}{T} \int_{t_1}^{t_1+T} f(t) \sin n\omega_1 t\, dt \qquad (2\text{-}22)$$

where again t_1 may be selected for convenience.

It would be simpler if Eqs. (2-19) to (2-22) could be included in a single equation. However, if Eqs. (2-20) to (2-22) are inserted directly in Eq. (2-19), there may be confusion, because the integration with respect to t must not affect the sin $n\omega_1 t$ and cos $n\omega_1 t$ of Eq. (2-19). One way to avoid this confusion would be to use a different variable such as τ in Eqs. (2-20) to (2-22), since, after integration, when the limits are applied, this variable disappears. Equations (2-19) to (2-22) could then be written in one equation as follows:

$$f(t) = \frac{1}{T} \int_{t_1}^{t_1+T} f(\tau)\, d\tau + \frac{2}{T} \sum_{n=1}^{\infty} \int_{t_1}^{t_1+T} f(\tau)(\sin n\omega_1 \tau \sin n\omega_1 t$$
$$+ \cos n\omega_1 \tau \cos n\omega_1 t)\, d\tau \qquad (2\text{-}23)$$

The integrations with respect to (τ) in Eq. (2-23) would then produce the coefficients A_n and B_n for all values of n, and there should be no confusion between the time variable τ, which must be integrated to determine the magnitude of each component in the frequency spectrum, and the time variable t associated with each individual frequency component in the summation.

Equation (2-23) can also be written as follows:

$$f(t) = \frac{1}{T} \int_{t_1}^{t_1+T} f(\tau)\, d\tau + \frac{2}{T} \sum_{n=1}^{\infty} \int_{t_1}^{t_1+T} f(\tau) \cos n\omega_1(t - \tau)\, d\tau \qquad (2\text{-}24)$$

But
$$\cos n\omega_1(t - \tau) = \frac{e^{jn\omega_1(t-\tau)} + e^{-jn\omega_1(t-\tau)}}{2}$$

Therefore
$$f(t) = \frac{1}{T} \sum_{n=-\infty}^{+\infty} \int_{t_1}^{t_1+T} f(\tau) e^{jn\omega_1(t-\tau)}\, d\tau \qquad (2\text{-}24a)$$

where the first, or d-c, term in Eq. (2-19) is now taken care of by the case $n = 0$.

In Eqs. (2-23) and (2-24) it will be observed that the integration for each value of n determines the magnitude of the corresponding component in the frequency spectrum and the summation of all these components gives the original function of time $f(t)$. The *integration* is therefore a process of *analysis* and the *summation* a process of *synthesis*. Going through both processes without any modifying action in between would correspond to taking a machine down into its component parts and then reassembling them back into the same machine. This may be instructive but is probably not very useful. On the other hand, if the parts are modified after they are taken apart, they may be reassembled into a new machine. Similarly if the frequency components of a driving force which is a function of time are determined and then subjected to modification by a network, the corresponding response when they are reassembled will be a new function of time. Consider the case where the driving force is a current $i(t)$, a recurrent function of time. Then this current may be broken down into a frequency spectrum by Eqs. (2-20) to (2-22). Suppose a voltage response is to be calculated. Then *each* component of voltage can be determined in both magnitude and phase if the impedance of the network, which relates the driving force and response, is known. If each of these components is computed and expressed as a corresponding function of time and the total summed up, then an expression for the *voltage response* as a function of time will be obtained.

Let the network impedance at a frequency nf_1 be given by the relation

$$Z_n = R_n + jX_n \tag{2-25}$$

Let the component of current at this frequency be given by the expression

$$i_n = A_n \sin n\omega_1 t + B_n \cos n\omega_1 t \tag{2-26}$$

and this current is flowing in the impedance Z_n. The resistance will produce a voltage in phase with the current, and the reactance will produce a voltage leading the corresponding current by 90° if X_n is positive. Therefore the corresponding component of voltage across the impedance will be

$$
\begin{aligned}
e_n &= R_n(A_n \sin n\omega_1 t + B_n \cos n\omega_1 t) \\
&\quad + X_n\left[A_n \sin\left(n\omega_1 t + \frac{\pi}{2}\right) + B_n \cos\left(n\omega_1 t + \frac{\pi}{2}\right)\right] \\
&= R_n(A_n \sin n\omega_1 t + B_n \cos n\omega_1 t) + X_n(A_n \cos n\omega_1 t - B_n \sin n\omega_1 t) \\
&= (R_n A_n - X_n B_n) \sin n\omega_1 t + (R_n B_n + X_n A_n) \cos n\omega_1 t \tag{2-27}
\end{aligned}
$$

Equation (2-23) may be modified, therefore, to give the relation between a current $i(t)$ and a voltage $e(t)$ related by an impedance which is a function of frequency as follows:

$$e(t) = \frac{R_0}{T} \int_{t_1}^{t_1+T} i(\tau)\, d\tau + \frac{2}{T} \sum_{n=1}^{\infty} \int_{t_1}^{t_1+T} i(\tau)[(R_n \sin n\omega_1\tau$$

$$- X_n \cos n\omega_1\tau) \sin n\omega_1 t + (R_n \cos n\omega_1\tau + X_n \sin n\omega_1\tau) \cos n\omega_1 t]\, d\tau \quad (2\text{-}28)$$

where, by Eq. (2-25), R_0 is the d-c resistance.

To generalize Eq. (2-28), let the driving force be represented by a function $Dr(t)$ and the response by $R(t)$. Further let them be related at a frequency nf by a network function (or immittance)

$$W_n = U_n + jV_n \qquad (2\text{-}29)$$

where U_n produces a response component in phase with the corresponding driving-force component and V_n a response component which leads the driving-force component by 90°. Then Eq. (2-28) becomes

$$R(t) = \frac{U_0}{T} \int_{t_1}^{t_1+T} Dr(\tau)\, d\tau + \frac{2}{T} \sum_{n=1}^{\infty} \int_{t_1}^{t_1+T} Dr(\tau)[(U_n \sin n\omega_1\tau$$

$$- V_n \cos n\omega_1\tau) \sin n\omega_1 t + (U_n \cos n\omega_1\tau + V_n \sin n\omega_1\tau) \cos n\omega_1 t]\, d\tau \quad (2\text{-}30)$$

W_n may be an impedance, an admittance, or dimensionless, depending upon what driving force is related to what response.

It has been pointed out that, in network analysis, it is convenient to replace sine and cosine functions by exponential functions. Then if the network is described by a complex function such as Eq. (2-29), the response at a given frequency can be obtained by straightforward multiplication. Thus if the component of a driving force at a frequency nf_1 is

$$Dr_n = A_n \sin n\omega_1 t + B_n \cos n\omega_1 t \qquad (2\text{-}31)$$

and since
$$e^{jn\omega_1 t} = \cos n\omega_1 t + j \sin n\omega_1 t$$

this can also be written

$$Dr_n = \mathrm{Re}\,\{(B_n - jA_n)e^{jn\omega_1 t}\} \qquad (2\text{-}32)$$

where, as before, the symbol Re means "real part of." Then if the network function is given by Eq. (2-29), the corresponding component of the response will be

$$\begin{aligned}
R_n &= \mathrm{Re}\,\{(U_n + jV_n)(B_n - jA_n)e^{jn\omega_1 t}\} \\
&= \mathrm{Re}\,\{[U_nB_n + V_nA_n + j(V_nB_n - U_nA_n)]e^{jn\omega_1 t}\} \\
&= (U_nA_n - V_nB_n) \sin n\omega_1 t + (U_nB_n + V_nA_n) \cos n\omega_1 t \quad (2\text{-}33)
\end{aligned}$$

Equation (2-33) may be compared with Eq. (2-27).

An alternate procedure is to consider the use of both positive and negative frequencies. In all network functions it will be found that the real part, U, involves only even powers of ω_1 and the imaginary part, V, will have odd powers of ω_1 in the numerator and even powers in the denominator. Therefore if positive and negative values of n are considered,

$$U_n = U_{-n}$$
$$V_n = -V_{-n}$$

Equation (2-31) may be rewritten in exponentials,

$$Dr_n = A_n \frac{e^{jn\omega_1 t} - e^{-jn\omega_1 t}}{2j} + B_n \frac{e^{jn\omega_1 t} + e^{-jn\omega_1 t}}{2}$$

If values of $e^{jn\omega_1 t}$ are multiplied by $U_n + jV_n = W_n$ and values of $e^{-jn\omega_1 t}$ are multiplied by $U_n - jV_n = W_{-n}$, then the following will be obtained,

$$\frac{U_n A_n e^{jn\omega_1 t}}{2j} + \frac{V_n A_n e^{jn\omega_1 t}}{2} - \frac{U_n A_n e^{-jn\omega_1 t}}{2j} + \frac{V_n A_n e^{-jn\omega_1 t}}{2}$$
$$+ \frac{U_n B_n e^{jn\omega_1 t}}{2} - \frac{V_n B_n e^{jn\omega_1 t}}{2j} + \frac{U_n B_n e^{-jn\omega_1 t}}{2} + \frac{V_n B_n e^{-jn\omega_1 t}}{2j}$$
$$= (U_n A_n - V_n B_n) \sin n\omega_1 t + (U_n B_n + V_n A_n) \cos n\omega_1 t \quad (2\text{-}34)$$

which is the same expression as Eq. (2-33).

Equation (2-34) avoids the cumbersome part of writing Re { } because any imaginary terms which may appear on the left side of Eq. (2-34) cancel out.

Hence it is apparent that Eq. (2-30) can be simplified in a manner similar to Eq. (2-24a) to

$$R(t) = \frac{1}{T} \sum_{n=-\infty}^{+\infty} \int_{t_1}^{t_1+T} W_n Dr(\tau) e^{jn\omega_1(t-\tau)} \, d\tau \quad (2\text{-}35)$$

Alternatively, Eq. (2-35) may be written in three equations as follows:

$$Dr_n = \frac{1}{T} \int_{t_1}^{t_1+T} Dr(t) e^{-jn\omega_1 t} \, dt \quad (2\text{-}36a)$$
$$R_n = W_n Dr_n \quad (2\text{-}36b)$$
$$R(t) = \sum_{n=-\infty}^{+\infty} R_n e^{jn\omega_1 t} \quad (2\text{-}36c)$$

It is not necessary to use (τ) instead of (t) in Eq. (2-36a) because there can be no confusion if the integration is performed first. Equation (2-36a) represents the analysis of the driving force as a function of time into its frequency spectrum. Equation (2-36b) represents the operation of the network in determining the frequency spectrum of the response for a giving driving force. Equation (2-36c) represents the synthesis of the frequency spectrum into the time function for the response.

2-8. The Fourier Integral. If the rate of recurrence of the repetitive driving function is made smaller and smaller while its shape is kept the same, the function will approach the condition where transient effects die out between successive events. In the limit the event may occur only once, and solutions for transients may be obtained. The summation of the Fourier series then becomes an integral and is called the Fourier integral. The transition from the series to the integral will now be considered.

For convenience let t_1 at the lower limit in Eq. (2-35) be $-T/2$, and let f be any frequency component in the spectrum. Then the fundamental frequency will be

$$f_1 = \frac{1}{T} \quad \text{and} \quad n = \frac{f}{f_1}$$

$$n\omega_1 = \omega \tag{2-37}$$

Assume that the event occurs only between the time $-T_0/2$ and $+T_0/2$ so that, at all other times between $-T/2$ and $+T/2$, $Dr(t) = 0$. Then Eq. (2-36a) would give the component at any value of ω which is a multiple of ω_1 as follows:

$$Dr(\omega) = \frac{1}{T} \int_{-T_0/2}^{T_0/2} Dr(t)e^{-j\omega t}\,dt \tag{2-38}$$

By way of a specific example, consider the repetitive square pulse of duration $T_1 = 1$ μsec, of period T, and of amplitude E as shown in Fig. 2-6. Then

$$Dr(t) = E \qquad \frac{-T_1}{2} < t < \frac{T_1}{2}$$

$$Dr(t) = 0 \begin{cases} -\dfrac{T}{2} < t < -\dfrac{T_1}{2} \\ \dfrac{T_1}{2} < t < \dfrac{T}{2} \end{cases}$$

By Eq. (2-38)

$$Dr(\omega) = \frac{1}{T} \int_{-T_1/2}^{T_1/2} Ee^{-j\omega t}\,dt$$

$$= \frac{E}{T} \left[\frac{e^{-j\omega t}}{-j\omega} \right]_{-T_1/2}^{T_1/2} = \frac{2E}{\omega T} \frac{e^{j\omega T_1/2} - e^{-j\omega T_1/2}}{2j}$$

Multiplying numerator and denominator by $T_1/2$,

$$Dr(\omega) = \frac{T_1 E}{T} \frac{\sin (\omega T_1/2)}{\omega T_1/2} \tag{2-38a}$$

Equation (2-38a) gives the *envelope* of the square-pulse-driving-force spectrum, but its magnitude has significance at only those frequencies which are integral multiples of the fundamental repetition rate, $1/T$. This is illustrated in Fig. 2-6, where the spectra are shown for three different values of T, T_1 being held constant. If the pulse occurs 500,000 times a second ($T = 2$ μsec), the spectrum contains components at 500, 1,500 kc and all other odd integral multiples of 500 kc as shown in Fig. 2-6a. If the pulse occurs 50,000 times per second ($T = 20$ μsec), the spectrum contains components at integral multiples of 50 kc as shown in Fig. 2-6b. In the second case there are 10 times as many frequencies present in the spectrum. The *envelopes* have the same shape, but in the second

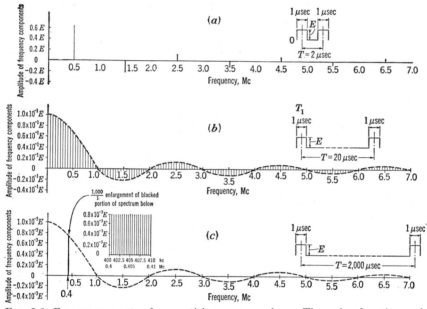

FIG. 2-6. Frequency spectra for repetitive square pulses. The pulse duration and repetition period are shown for each case. An enlarged portion of the spectrum for c is shown in the inset.

case the magnitude is $\frac{1}{10}$ the magnitude of the first. Since the power is proportional to the square of the amplitude of either voltage or current, the *total* power in the second case is 10 per cent of that of the first (10 times as many components with relative power per component of $1/10^2$).

Still a third case is shown in Fig. 2-6c, where $T = 2,000$ μsec. The envelope still has the same shape, but, in comparison with the first case, there are 1,000 times as many components, and the envelope amplitude is reduced by 1,000 and the total power to 0.1 per cent. In the limit as $T \rightarrow \infty$, when the driving function becomes a single pulse, the spectrum becomes *continuous*, all frequencies being present, each being of infinitesimal amplitude.[1] This will now be shown.

---

[1] Note that there is a finite amount of energy in the pulse, but since, in order to compute power, one must divide this finite energy by infinite time, the total *power* of all these components is actually zero.

As the interval between recurrences becomes larger and larger, $1/T$ becomes very small and so it would be preferable to write the fundamental frequency (which is also the frequency interval between successive components in the spectrum) as $f_1 = \Delta f = 1/T$. Then Eq. (2-35) would become

$$R(t) = \frac{1}{2\pi} \sum_{n=-\infty}^{+\infty} \Delta\omega \int_{-T/2}^{T/2} W_{n\omega_1} Dr(\tau) e^{jn\omega_1(t-\tau)} \, d\tau \qquad (2\text{-}39)$$

But, in the limit as $T \to \infty$, Δf approaches df, and the summation becomes an integration. Therefore, for an event which is not recurrent

$$R(t) = \int_{-\infty}^{\infty} df \int_{-\infty}^{\infty} W(f) Dr(\tau) e^{j\omega(t-\tau)} \, d\tau \qquad (2\text{-}40)$$

where the network function is now expressed as $W(f)$ since $n\omega_1$ has been replaced by ω and the spectrum is now continuous.

Equation (2-40) can also be written as three equations which are analogous to Eqs. (2-36a) to (2-36c).

$$Dr(f) = \int_{-\infty}^{\infty} Dr(t) e^{-j2\pi ft} \, dt \qquad (2\text{-}41a)$$

$$R(f) = W(f) Dr(f) \qquad (2\text{-}41b)$$

$$R(t) = \int_{-\infty}^{\infty} R(f) e^{j2\pi ft} \, df \qquad (2\text{-}41c)$$

Equation (2-41a) analyzes the driving function of time into a *continuous* frequency spectrum. Equation (2-41b) determines the corresponding spectrum of the response resulting from the operation of the network. Equation (2-41c) synthesizes the response spectrum into a function of time.

It should be observed that, while the spectrum is now continuous, the amplitude of each component has become infinitesimal. However, the sum of all these infinitesimals gives a finite response. This is not surprising, for, in all integrals which have a value, this value is obtained by summing up an infinite number of infinitesimals.

In Eq. (2-41a) the limits of integration are over all time. If the driving function has a value over only a limited interval, then the integration will have finite limits. This would also apply to Eq. (2-40).

It is frequently desirable to investigate the frequency spectrum of particular driving functions to determine their character. Of particular interest is the case of a d-c pulse. Suppose the driving function is a voltage described by the equations.

$$\begin{aligned} e(t) &= 0 & t &< 0 \\ e(t) &= E & 0 &< t < T_1 \\ e(t) &= 0 & t &> T_1 \end{aligned} \qquad (2\text{-}42)$$

Then by analysis by Eq. (2-41a)

$$e(f) = \int_0^{T_1} E e^{-j\omega t}\, dt$$

$$= -\left[\frac{E}{j\omega} e^{-j\omega t}\right]_0^{T_1} = -\frac{E}{j\omega}\left(e^{-j\omega T_1} - 1\right) \tag{2-43}$$

$$e(f) = E\left(\frac{\sin \omega T_1}{\omega} - j\,\frac{1 - \cos \omega T_1}{\omega}\right) \tag{2-44}$$

In this analysis the real part represents the envelope of the spectrum of the cosine terms and the negative of the imaginary part gives the spectrum of the sine terms. As a general situation the spectrum must be represented by two functions, which may be either the functions of the sine and cosine terms or the functions of amplitude and phase.

As in the case of the Fourier series, the analysis may sometimes be reduced to a single function if a proper choice of time axis can be selected to give symmetry. For example, suppose the time was selected so that the d-c pulse started at time $t = -T_1/2$ and ended at time $T_1/2$. (The pulse then becomes the limiting case as $T \to \infty$ of Fig. 2-6.) Then there will be only cosine terms. Equation (2-41a) would then give

$$e(f) = \int_{-T_1/2}^{T_1/2} E e^{-j\omega t}\, dt$$

$$= \frac{E}{j\omega}\left(-e^{-j\omega T_1/2} + e^{j\omega T_1/2}\right)$$

$$e(f) = \frac{2E}{\omega}\sin\frac{\omega T_1}{2} = E T_1 \frac{\sin(\omega T_1/2)}{\omega T_1/2} \tag{2-45}$$

Since $e(f)$ is real, there will be only cosine terms with relative amplitude given by Eq. (2-45). The general form of this spectrum for positive values of frequency is identical to the spectrum envelope in Fig. 2-6a to c. Since the $\sin u/u$ factor is an even function of u, the spectrum for negative values of frequency is the mirror image of that for positive frequencies.

Equations (2-41a) to (2-41c) are of far-reaching significance, for they show that *the transient characteristic of a network is uniquely determined by the steady-state network characteristics.* This follows at once from Eqs. (2-41). If $Dr(t)$ is known, then since $Dr(f)$ is unique, $R(f)$ and hence $R(t)$ will be determined uniquely by $W(f)$ operating on $Dr(f)$. For emphasis the statement in Chap. 1 will be reiterated: *It is because of the transformation possible by the Fourier integral that so much of the analysis and synthesis of communication circuits can be carried out on a steady-state, sinusoidal basis, even though communication signals themselves are inherently transient in character.*

Some typical applications of the Fourier integral to the calculation of the response of some so-called *ideal* networks will now be considered to illustrate the method. One important result of these calculations shows that these particular circuits are actually not physically realizable. Other results may be carried over to practicable circuits as convenient intuitive conclusions.

2-9. Transient Response of an Ideal Low-pass (LP) Filter to a Step Function. Consider the response to a step driving function shown in Fig. 2-4. It might be expected that the analysis of this step function could be determined by making $T_1 \to \infty$ in Eq. (2-43). However, other methods are preferred because there is difficulty in interpreting the meaning of sinusoidal functions at the infinite limit.[1]

The ideal LP filter consists in a network having the property that it transmits frequency components between $-f_c$ and $+f_c$ without modification except that they are delayed by a time interval t_d and that it entirely eliminates all frequencies of magnitude greater than f_c, that is,

$$W(f) = e^{-j\omega t_d} \qquad -f_c < f < f_c$$
$$W(f) = 0 \qquad |f| > f_c \tag{2-46}$$

Then by substituting Eqs. (2-43) and (2-46) into Eq. (2-41c),

$$R(t) = E \int_{-f_c}^{f_c} \frac{1 - e^{-j\omega T_1}}{j\omega} e^{j\omega(t - t_d)} df$$

By symmetry this becomes

$$R(t) = E \int_0^{f_c} \frac{e^{j\omega(t-t_d)} - e^{-j\omega(t-t_d)} - e^{j\omega(t-T_1-t_d)} + e^{-j\omega(t-T_1-t_d)}}{2j\pi f} df$$
$$= \frac{E}{\pi} \int_0^{\omega_c} \left[\frac{\sin \omega(t - t_d)}{\omega} + \frac{\sin \omega(T_1 - t + t_d)}{\omega} \right] d\omega \tag{2-47}$$

Now the transcendental function defined by the expression

$$\int_0^x \frac{\sin u}{u} du$$

is called the "sine integral of x" and is abbreviated Si(x). The series

---

[1] In this chapter emphasis is being placed on the Fourier integral and the Fourier transform because it is believed that the student *at this stage* will better understand the philosophy of the interchangeability of time and real frequency by a Fourier interpretation. However, modern circuit analysis places greater dependence upon the Laplace transform, which extends the frequency idea into the complex plane, as, for that matter, will be done in this book in certain other applications. The Laplace transform eliminates many of the difficult convergence problems met with at the infinite limit in the case of the Fourier transform, for example, with the step function. The actual forms of both the Fourier transform and the Laplace transform are similar, and the same transform tables apply.

for this function can be obtained by integrating term by term,

$$\text{Si}(x) = \int_0^x \frac{\sin u}{u}\, du = \int_0^x \left(1 - \frac{u^2}{\underline{|3}} + \frac{u^4}{\underline{|5}} - \frac{u^6}{\underline{|7}} + \cdots \right) du$$

$$\text{Si}(x) = x - \frac{x^3}{3\underline{|3}} + \frac{x^5}{5\underline{|5}} - \frac{x^7}{7\underline{|7}} + \cdots$$

Values of this function are listed in a number of handbooks,[1] and a plot of the function is shown in Fig. 2-7.   As $x \to +\infty$, the value of $\text{Si}(x) \to \pi/2$. Equation (2-47) may be written

$$R(t) = \frac{E}{\pi}\{\text{Si}[\omega_c(t - t_d)] + \text{Si}[\omega_c(T_1 - t + t_d)]\} \qquad (2\text{-}48)$$

If now the value of T_1 is made to approach infinity so that, for any value

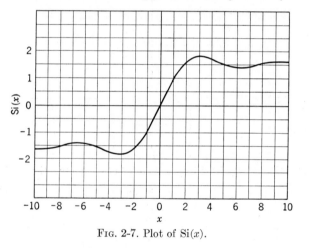

Fig. 2-7. Plot of $\text{Si}(x)$.

of $t - t_d$, T_1 is very much greater than $t - t_d$, then, no matter what the value of ω_c, Eq. (2-48) becomes

$$R(t) = \frac{E}{2} + \frac{E}{\pi}\,\text{Si}[\omega_c(t - t_d)] \qquad (2\text{-}49)$$

A plot of this expression, which is the transient response of the ideal LP filter to a step function, is shown in Fig. 2-8.

It is apparent that the effect of increasing the value of T_1 in the applied pulse to infinity is to introduce a d-c term $E/2$ into the expression.   The following facts may also be noted from Fig. 2-8:

1. The 50 per cent response point, $E/2$, occurs at a time t_d after $t = 0$. Furthermore, the response curve of Fig. 2-8 begins at $t = -\infty$.   This

[1] See, for example, E. Jahnke and F. Emde, "Tables of Functions," Dover Publications, New York, 1945.

would mean that the circuit has an anticipatory property and would start to respond *before* the driving function is applied. Clearly, this is an impossible situation and arises in this problem because the steady-state amplitude and delay (or phase) characteristics of the network were specified independently.

2. The "rise time," or steepness, of the response in the vicinity of $t = t_d$ is related to the cutoff frequency f_c of the filter. The two conclusions regarding delay and rise times may be carried over *qualitatively* to physical circuits.

Another qualitative rule may be derived in a similar manner by considering an LP filter in which the steady-state amplitude characteristic cuts off gradually rather than abruptly, as in Eqs. (2-46).[1] It may be

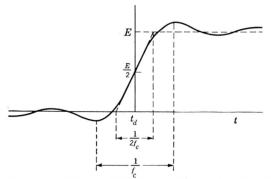

FIG. 2-8. Response of the ideal LP filter to the step function $EU(t)$.

shown that the overshoot, or peak in the transient response, is reduced by having a gradual cutoff characteristic.

It is of interest to note that, if the function of Eqs. (2-46) is introduced directly into Eq. (2-41a), the equation would be

$$e(f) = E \int_0^\infty e^{-j\omega t}\, dt$$

$$= -\left[\frac{Ee^{-j\omega t}}{j\omega}\right]_0^\infty \tag{2-50}$$

Direct substitution of the infinite limit in Eq. (2-50) does not give an answer, but by the analysis given above it is seen that the effect of the infinite limit is to produce a d-c term so that the spectrum will have a finite d-c term of value $E/2$ and a continuous spectrum of infinitesimals of value $E/j\omega$.

The complete response will then be obtained by adding the response to the d-c term to the response obtained by integrating the infinitesimals.

[1] See, for example, Colin Cherry, "Pulses and Transients in Communication Circuits," p. 169, Dover Publications, New York, 1950

2-10. Transient Response of an Ideal Bandpass (BP) Filter to a Step Function. In an ideal BP filter, only frequencies are transmitted between f_1 and f_2, the two cutoff frequencies, and, when expressions which also involve negative frequencies are used, between $-f_2$ and $-f_1$. There is also a delay t_d. No d-c term is involved, since it will not be transmitted.

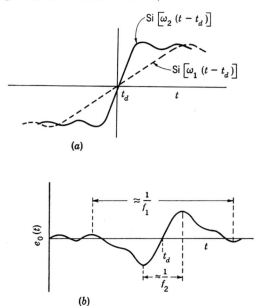

(a)

(b)

FIG. 2-9. Response of the ideal BP filter to $EU(t)$. (a) Sine integral components of the response. (b) General form of the response obtained by adding the two curves of a.

Then the output voltage will be given by Eq. (2-41c).

$$
\begin{aligned}
e_o(t) &= E \int_{-f_2}^{-f_1} \frac{e^{j\omega(t-t_d)}}{j\omega} \, df + E \int_{f_1}^{f_2} \frac{e^{j\omega(t-t_d)}}{j\omega} \, df \\
&= \frac{E}{\pi} \int_{f_1}^{f_2} \frac{\sin 2\pi f(t - t_d)}{f} \, df \\
&= \frac{E}{\pi} \{ \mathrm{Si}[\omega_2(t - t_d)] - \mathrm{Si}[\omega_1(t - t_d)] \}
\end{aligned}
\tag{2-51}
$$

The two functions $\mathrm{Si}[\omega_2(t - t_d)]$ and $\mathrm{Si}[\omega_1(t - t_d)]$ would then appear as in Fig. 2-9a. The output voltage is shown in Fig. 2-9b.

Note that the duration of the main response is inversely proportional to the lower cutoff frequency, while the rise time in the center is inversely proportional to the upper cutoff frequency. An accurate plot for the case $f_2 = 2f_1$ is shown in Fig. 2-10.

2-11. D-C Pulse of Duration T_1 Applied to an Ideal LP Filter. In this case the voltage of Eq. (2-45) is applied to an LP filter. If the

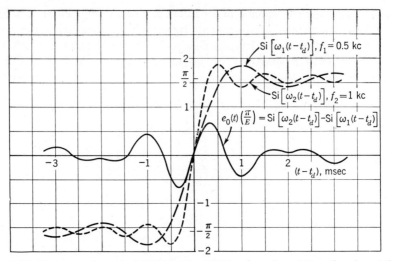

FIG. 2-10. Response of an ideal BP filter to $EU(t)$, where $f_1 = 500$ cycles, $f_2 = 1,000$ cycles. The response and its components are shown in normalized form.

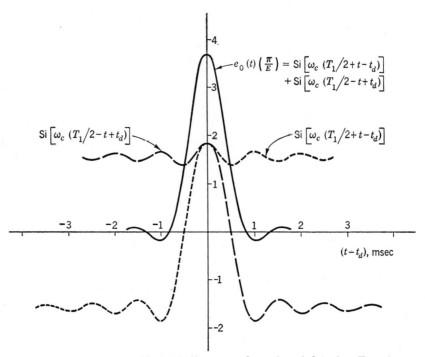

FIG. 2-11. Response of an ideal LP filter to a d-c pulse of duration $T_1 = 1$ msec (millisecond). The filter cutoff frequency is $f_c = 1$ kc. The response and its components are shown in normalized form.

conditions produced by an ideal filter are inserted in Eq. (2-41c), the expression would be

$$e_o(t) = \frac{E}{\pi} \int_0^{\omega_c} \frac{\sin \omega(T_1/2 - t + t_d) + \sin \omega(T_1/2 + t - t_d)}{f} \, df$$

$$= \frac{E}{\pi} \left\{ \text{Si} \left[\omega_c \left(\frac{T_1}{2} - t + t_d \right) \right] + \text{Si} \left[\omega_c \left(\frac{T_1}{2} + t - t_d \right) \right] \right\} \quad (2\text{-}52)$$

The two functions in Eq. (2-52) would then appear as in Fig. 2-11 for the case where $f_c = 1/T_1$. The function $e_o(t)$ is also shown in Fig. 2-11.

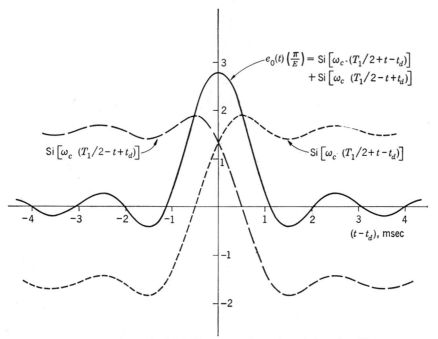

FIG. 2-12. Response of an ideal LP filter to a d-c pulse of duration $T_1 = 1$ msec. $f_c = 500$ cycles.

It will be observed that the solution of Eq. (2-52) is the same as would be obtained by superimposing two solutions of the type obtained in Eq. (2-49) with appropriate shifting of the time axis.

If f_c is equal to $1/2T_1$, the two functions and their sum would appear as in Fig. 2-12. If f_c is equal to $2/T_1$, the two functions and their sum would appear as in Fig. 2-13. Hence as the cutoff frequency is increased, the output voltage becomes more nearly like the input voltage. It is apparent that f_c should be at least equal to $1/2T_1$ in order to transmit a reasonable replica of the input pulse.

These facts permit certain conclusions to be drawn with regard to communication circuits. In machine telegraph circuits 7 intervals are allowed for each letter-code group, and in 5 of these intervals the voltage may or may not be applied during each interval, dependent upon the code of the letter to be transmitted. If 60 words are sent per minute and each word has 5 letters, then the number of possible pulses per minute would be

$$n = 60 \times 5 \times 7 = 2,100$$

or the number of pulses per second would be 35; hence $T_1 = \frac{1}{35}$. The

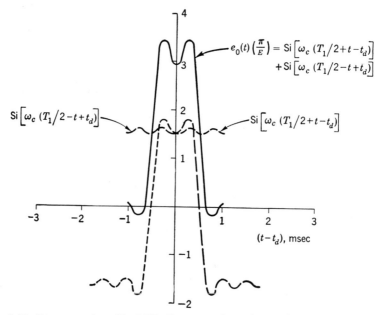

$$e_0(t)\left(\frac{\pi}{E}\right) = \text{Si}\left[\omega_c \left(T_1/2 + t - t_d\right)\right] + \text{Si}\left[\omega_c \left(T_1/2 - t + t_d\right)\right]$$

$\text{Si}\left[\omega_c \left(T_1/2 - t + t_d\right)\right]$

$\text{Si}\left[\omega_c \left(T_1/2 + t - t_d\right)\right]$

$(t - t_d)$, msec

FIG. 2-13. Response of an ideal LP filter to a d-c pulse of duration $T_1 = 1$ msec. $f_c = 2$ kc.

transmission system should then be designed to transmit frequencies up to 18 cycles, and preferably higher.

In television, on the other hand, it has been determined that the standards should permit a picture with a detail of about 250,000 dots to be sent 30 times per second. Therefore, the shortest pulse that should be recognized would have a time duration of approximately 1/7,500,000 sec. Hence the transmission system should be able to transmit up to a frequency of 3,750,000 cycles. The bandwidth in television transmission is specified to be 4 Mc.

2-12. Fourier Transforms, or Paired Functions. It has been stated previously that the network function $W(f)$ of physical circuits is a continuous function of frequency. In many instances this property leads to a simplified method of solving for the response by means of the Fourier integral.

In Eq. (2-41a) the expression is given for the analysis of any function of time into a function of frequency. It is convenient to set up tables to show on the one side sets of functions of time and corresponding to that on the other side the corresponding functions of frequency. These may be represented by the relations corresponding to Eqs. (2-41a) and (2-41c), $W(f)$ being taken as unity, i.e.,

$$g(f) = \int_{-\infty}^{\infty} f(t)e^{-pt}\, dt \tag{2-53}$$

$$f(t) = \int_{-\infty}^{\infty} g(f)e^{pt}\, df \tag{2-54}$$

where for convenience $p = j2\pi f$. In most cases if tables are constructed from Eq. (2-53), it will be necessary to use Eq. (2-54) only occasionally, since the correspondence of $g(f)$ to $f(t)$ may proceed in either direction.

Equations (2-53) and (2-54) are called the Fourier transforms.[1] The method of building up such a table will be shown. Consider the function

$$\begin{aligned} f(t) &= 0 && t < 0 \\ f(t) &= e^{-\beta t} && t > 0 \end{aligned} \tag{2-55}$$

Then Eq. (2-53) becomes

$$\begin{aligned} g(f) &= \int_{0}^{\infty} e^{-(p+\beta)t}\, dt \\ &= \frac{-e^{-(p+\beta)t}}{p+\beta} \end{aligned}$$

At the infinite limit, $e^{-(p+\beta)t} = 0$ if β has any positive real part, however small; therefore

$$g(f) = \frac{1}{p+\beta} \tag{2-55a}$$

and Eq. (2-55a) is the mate of Eq. (2-55). Furthermore since Eq. (2-55a) holds if β has any positive real part, no matter how small, it must be the limit as the real part is reduced to zero and hence must apply even if β is entirely imaginary. Therefore Eq. (2-55) is a general one so long as β does not have a *negative real* part.

The mates for the product of two functions may be obtained directly or by use of a relation which will now be developed. Let

$f_1(t)$ be the mate of $g_1(f)$
$f_2(t)$ be the mate of $g_2(f)$
$f(t)$ be the mate of $g_1(f)g_2(f)$, which is to be found

---

[1] In the case of the Laplace transform p is considered complex and is usually replaced by $p = \delta + j\omega$.

From Eq. (2-54)

$$f(t) = \int_{-\infty}^{\infty} g_1(f)g_2(f)e^{j2\pi ft}\, df \tag{2-56}$$

but by Eq. (2-53)

$$g_1(f) = \int_{-\infty}^{\infty} f_1(t)e^{-j2\pi ft}\, dt \tag{2-57}$$

Equation (2-57) cannot be substituted directly in Eq. (2-56) because there would be confusion of the time variable in the two separate integrations. However, Eq. (2-57) could also be written

$$g_1(f) = \int_{-\infty}^{\infty} f_1(\tau)e^{-j2\pi f\tau}\, d\tau \tag{2-57a}$$

and Eq. (2-57a) could be substituted directly in Eq. (2-56). This would give

$$\begin{aligned}
f(t) &= \int_{-\infty}^{\infty}\int_{-\infty}^{\infty} f_1(\tau)e^{-j2\pi f\tau}g_2(f)e^{j2\pi ft}\, d\tau\, df \\
&= \int_{-\infty}^{\infty} f_1(\tau)\left[\int_{-\infty}^{\infty} g_2(f)e^{j2\pi f(t-\tau)}\, df\right] d\tau
\end{aligned} \tag{2-58}$$

But by Eq. (2-54)

$$\int_{-\infty}^{\infty} g_2(f)e^{j2\pi f(t-\tau)}\, df = f_2(t-\tau)$$

$$f(t) = \int_{-\infty}^{\infty} f_1(\tau)f_2(t-\tau)\, d\tau \tag{2-59}$$

As an example of the application of Eq. (2-59), let

$$f_1(t) = e^{-\alpha t} \qquad f_2(t) = e^{-\beta t} \qquad t > 0$$

Then

$$g_1(f) = \frac{1}{p+\alpha} \qquad g_2(f) = \frac{1}{p+\beta}$$

The problem is to find the mate $f(t)$ of the function

$$g(f) = \frac{1}{(p+\alpha)(p+\beta)} \tag{2-60}$$

By the definition of $f_2(t)$ it has a value only when t is positive. Therefore $f_2(t-\tau)$ has a value only when τ is less than t. $f_1(\tau)$ has a value only when τ is greater than zero. Therefore, in substituting in Eq. (2-59) the infinite limits change to zero and t, and Eq. (2-59) for this case becomes

$$\begin{aligned}
f(t) &= \int_0^t e^{-\alpha\tau}e^{-\beta(t-\tau)}\, d\tau \\
&= e^{-\beta t}\int_0^t e^{-(\alpha-\beta)\tau}\, d\tau \\
&= e^{-\beta t}\left[\frac{-e^{-(\alpha-\beta)\tau}}{\alpha-\beta}\right]_0^t = \frac{-e^{-\alpha t}+e^{-\beta t}}{\alpha-\beta}
\end{aligned} \tag{2-60a}$$

Equation (2-60a) then gives the mate of the function of Eq. (2-60).

In the same way that Eq. (2-59) was derived to obtain the mate of $g_1(f)g_2(f)$ it can be shown that the mate of $f_1(t)f_2(t)$ is given by the expression

$$g(f) = \int_{-\infty}^{\infty} g_1(-x)g_2(f + x) \, dx \qquad (2\text{-}61)$$

where in this case x is the variable introduced for the purpose of integration.

It is apparent from the equations for the mates that, if $g_1(f)$ and $g_2(f)$ are the mates, respectively, of $f_1(t)$ and $f_2(t)$, $g_1(f) + g_2(f)$ is the mate of $f_1(t) + f_2(t)$. As an example of the application of this principle, consider the function

$$\cos at = \frac{e^{jat} + e^{-jat}}{2} \qquad t > 0$$

The mate of e^{jat} is $1/(p - ja)$, while that of e^{-jat} is $1/(p + ja)$. Therefore the mate of $\cos at$ is $\frac{1}{2}[1/(p - ja) + 1/(p + ja)] = p/(p^2 + a^2)$. Similarly the mate of $\sin at$ for $t > 0$ is $a/(p^2 + a^2)$.

Since a constant multiplier A does not affect the integration, if $f(t)$ and $g(f)$ are mates, $Af(t)$ and $Ag(f)$ are mates.

If the derivative of both sides of Eq. (2-54) is taken with respect to time, the following relation is obtained,

$$D_t f(t) = p \int_{-\infty}^{\infty} g(f)e^{j2\pi ft} \, df \qquad (2\text{-}62)$$

where D_t means "time derivative of." Therefore if $f(t)$ is the mate of $g(f)$, $D_t f(t)$ is the mate of $pg(f)$. Similarly $D_f g(f)$ is the mate of $-j2\pi tf(t)$. Furthermore, by integration,

$$\int_{-\infty}^{t} f_1(t) \, dt \text{ is the mate of } \frac{1}{p} g_1(f) \qquad (2\text{-}63)$$

$$\int_{-\infty}^{f} g_1(f) \, df \text{ is the mate of } -\frac{1}{j2\pi t} f_1(t) \qquad (2\text{-}64)$$

Some of the relations which have been derived above are summarized in Table 2-1. The most extensive table yet published is by G. B. Campbell, The Practical Application of the Fourier Integral, *Bell System Technical Journal*, vol. 7, p. 639, October, 1928. The tables of Laplace transforms published in many books may be used in the same manner.

2-13. Development by Partial Fractions. An alternative and very powerful method for the determination of mates is by the method of partial fractions. It is known from algebra that a fraction of the type

$$\frac{f(x)}{(x - a)(x - b)(x - c)^m \cdots (x - n)}$$

TABLE 2-1. FOURIER-TRANSFORM MATES

Pair	$g(f)$	$f(t)$
1	$\dfrac{1}{p}$	$U(t)$
2	$\dfrac{1}{p + \alpha}$	$e^{-\alpha t},\ t > 0$
3	$\dfrac{1}{p(p + \alpha)}$	$\dfrac{1 - e^{-\alpha t}}{\alpha},\ t > 0$
4	$\dfrac{1}{(p + \alpha)^2}$	$te^{-\alpha t},\ t > 0$
5	$\dfrac{1}{(p + \alpha)(p + \beta)}$	$\dfrac{e^{-\beta t} - e^{-\alpha t}}{\alpha - \beta},\ t > 0$
6	$\dfrac{p}{(p + \alpha)(p + \beta)}$	$\dfrac{\alpha e^{-\alpha t} - \beta e^{-\beta t}}{\alpha - \beta},\ t > 0$
7	$\dfrac{p}{p^2 + \omega^2}$	$\cos \omega t,\ t > 0$
8	$\dfrac{\omega}{p^2 + \omega^2}$	$\sin \omega t,\ t > 0$
9	$p g_1(f)$	$D_t f_1(t)$
10	$\dfrac{1}{p} g_1(f)$	$\displaystyle\int_{-\infty}^{t} f_1(t)\, dt$
11	$\displaystyle\int_{-\infty}^{f} g_1(f)\, df$	$-\dfrac{1}{j2\pi t} f_1(t)$

Note. $g_1(f)$ is the mate of $f_1(t)$.

can be expanded into the form

$$\frac{A}{x - a} + \frac{B}{x - b} + \frac{C_1}{x - c} + \frac{C_2}{(x - c)^2} + \cdots + \frac{C_m}{(x - c)^m}$$
$$+ \cdots + \frac{N}{x - n}$$

where $A,\ B,\ C_1,\ C_2,\ \ldots,\ C_m,\ \ldots,\ N$ are constants. The following rules apply:

1. To any factor of the first degree, as $x - a$ in the denominator, there corresponds a partial fraction of the form $A/(x - a)$

2. To any factor repeated m times, as $(x - c)^m$, in the denominator there corresponds a series of m partial fractions of the form

$$\frac{C_1}{x - c} + \frac{C_2}{(x - c)^2} + \cdots + \frac{C_m}{(x - c)^m}$$

The constants may be evaluated in the following way: When x is in the neighborhood of the value a, the value of the sum of the partial fractions is determined almost entirely by the term $A/(x - a)$. Therefore in this region

$$\frac{f(x)}{(x-a)(x-b)(x-c)^m \cdots (x-n)} \approx \frac{A}{x-a}$$

or

$$\frac{f(x)}{(x-b)(x-c)^m \cdots (x-n)} \approx A \qquad (2\text{-}65)$$

This approximation becomes closer and closer as x approaches a. Therefore in the limit, i.e., where x equals a, Eq. (2-65) becomes an identity and

$$\frac{f(a)}{(a-b)(a-c)^m \cdots (a-n)} = A \qquad (2\text{-}66)$$

$$\frac{f(b)}{(b-a)(b-c)^m \cdots (b-n)} = B \qquad (2\text{-}67)$$

and similar expressions apply to all the constants when $a, b, \ldots, n$ are different.

To show how this may be applied, let the problem be again to find the mate of $g(f) = 1/(p+\alpha)(p+\beta)$. Then

$$\frac{1}{(p+\alpha)(p+\beta)} = \frac{A}{p+\alpha} + \frac{B}{p+\beta}$$

Applying Eqs. (2-66) and (2-67),

$$A = \frac{1}{-\alpha+\beta}$$

$$B = \frac{1}{-\beta+\alpha}$$

Therefore

$$\frac{1}{(p+\alpha)(p+\beta)} = \frac{1}{\beta-\alpha}\left(\frac{1}{p+\alpha} - \frac{1}{p+\beta}\right)$$

Now the mate of $1/(p+\alpha)$ is $e^{-\alpha t}$, and the mate of $1/(p+\beta)$ is $e^{-\beta t}$. Therefore the mate of $\dfrac{1}{(p+\alpha)(p+\beta)}$ is $\dfrac{1}{\beta-\alpha}(e^{-\alpha t} - e^{-\beta t})$, which has previously been developed in Eq. (2-60a).

If there are two or more identical factors in the denominator, the procedure must be modified. Consider the fraction $\dfrac{f(x)}{(x-a)^m Q(x)}$, where $Q(x)$ has no factor $x-a$. Then

$$\frac{f(x)}{(x-a)^m Q(x)} = \frac{A}{(x-a)^m} + \frac{B}{(x-a)^{m-1}} + \cdots + \frac{M}{x-a} + \cdots \qquad (2\text{-}68)$$

As x approaches a, the right-hand side will be determined by the term $A/(x-a)^m$ and hence

$$A = \frac{f(a)}{Q(a)} \qquad (2\text{-}69)$$

The fraction can also be written

$$\frac{f(x)}{(x-a)^m Q(x)} = \frac{A}{(x-a)^m} + \frac{f(x) - AQ(x)}{(x-a)^m Q(x)} \tag{2-70}$$

Now the second term of the right-hand side of Eq. (2-70) must equal the sum of all the right-hand terms in Eq. (2-68) except the first. But these terms, if combined into a single fraction, would have $x - a$ only to the $(m - 1)$st power in the denominator. Hence $f(x) - AQ(x)$ has a factor $x - a$ which can be canceled in the second term of Eq. (2-70). Let the fraction $\dfrac{f(x) - AQ(x)}{(x-a)^m Q(x)}$ then be of the form $\dfrac{f_1(x)}{(x-a)^{m-1}Q_1(x)}$. By the same process used in the derivation of Eq. (2-69) the expression for B will be

$$B = \frac{f_1(a)}{Q_1(a)} \tag{2-71}$$

In the same way all the coefficients for the partial fractions may be obtained.

As an example consider the function

$$\frac{p+r}{(p+a)^2(p+c)} = \frac{A}{(p+a)^2} + \frac{B}{p+a} + \frac{C}{p+c}$$

By Eq. (2-69)

$$A = \frac{-a+r}{-a+c}$$

Then the second term on the right of Eq. (2-70) becomes

$$\begin{aligned}
\frac{f(p) - AQ(p)}{(p+a)^2 Q(p)} &= \frac{(p+r) - \dfrac{r-a}{c-a}(p+c)}{(p+a)^2(p+c)} \\[2mm]
&= \frac{(p+r)(c-a) - (r-a)(p+c)}{(p+a)^2(p+c)(c-a)} \\[2mm]
&= \frac{pc - pr - ar + ac}{(p+a)^2(p+c)(c-a)} \\[2mm]
&= \frac{(p+a)(c-r)}{(p+a)^2(p+c)(c-a)} \\[2mm]
&= \frac{c-r}{(p+a)(p+c)(c-a)}
\end{aligned}$$

Therefore

$$\frac{B}{p+a} + \frac{C}{p+c} = \frac{c-r}{(p+a)(p+c)(c-a)}$$

Then

$$B = \frac{c-r}{(-a+c)(c-a)} = \frac{c-r}{(c-a)^2}$$

$$C = \frac{c-r}{(-c+a)(c-a)} = \frac{r-c}{(c-a)^2}$$

and the original expression becomes

$$\frac{p + r}{(p + a)^2(p + c)} = \frac{r - a}{(c - a)(p + a)^2} + \frac{c - r}{(c - a)^2(p + a)} - \frac{c - r}{(c - a)^2(p + c)}$$

(2-72)

The mate of $1/(p + a)^2$ can be determined by the use of Eq. (2-59) and is te^{-at}. By the use of Eq. (2-72) the mate of $\dfrac{p + r}{(p + a)^2(p + c)}$ will be the sum of the mates of the functions on the right-hand side and will be

$$f(t) = \frac{r - a}{c - a}\, te^{-at} + \frac{c - r}{(c - a)^2}\,(e^{-at} - e^{-ct})$$

(2-73)

From these relations it is easy to make up most of the pairs of interest. Only a few of these were shown in Table 2-1.

As an example of the method by which these transforms may be applied to the solution of a typical transient problem, consider the case given by Fig. 2-14, where the switch is closed at time $t = 0$. Then the voltage function of time could be obtained from the table from pair 1. The same result may be obtained by setting $\beta = 0$ in pair 2 and multiplying both sides by the constant E. Hence the corresponding function of f will be

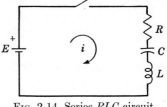

FIG. 2-14. Series RLC circuit.

$$Dr(f) = e(f) = \frac{E}{p} = \frac{E}{j2\pi f}$$

Now that the voltage has been obtained as a function of f, the current can be quickly determined also as a function of f. The impedance of Fig. 2-14 is

$$Z = R + j\omega L + \frac{1}{j\omega C}$$

$$= R + pL + \frac{1}{pC}$$

Hence the current as a function of f will be

$$i(f) = \frac{e(f)}{Z(f)} = \frac{E}{p(R + pL + 1/pC)}$$

$$= \frac{E}{L[p^2 + (R/L)p + 1/LC]}$$

This has the form of $g(f)$ of pair 5 in Table 2-1, where α and β are the negative of the roots of the equation $p^2 + Rp/L + 1/LC = 0$. Therefore

$$\alpha = \frac{R}{2L} - \sqrt{\frac{R^2}{4L^2} - \frac{1}{LC}}$$

$$\beta = \frac{R}{2L} + \sqrt{\frac{R^2}{4L^2} - \frac{1}{LC}}$$

Hence the current as a function of time is given by the $f(t)$ function in pair 5, that is,

$i(t)$

$$= \frac{E\,[\exp(-R/2L + \sqrt{R^2/4L^2 - 1/LC})\,t - \exp(-R/2L - \sqrt{R^2/4L^2 - 1/LC})t]}{2L\,\sqrt{R^2/4L^2 - 1/LC}}$$

where $\exp(x)$ stands for e^x. If $1/LC > R^2/4L^2$, this can be written

$$i = \frac{E}{L\,\sqrt{1/LC - R^2/4L^2}}\,e^{-Rt/2L}\,\sin\sqrt{\frac{1}{LC} - \frac{R^2}{4L^2}}\,t$$

$$= \frac{E}{\omega_1 L}\,e^{-Rt/2L}\,\sin\omega_1 t$$

where $\omega_1 = \sqrt{1/LC - R^2/4L^2}$, which is the solution desired.

2-14. Poles and Zeros. It has been shown that the transient and steady-state responses of a network are uniquely related through the Fourier integral. It will now be shown that the poles and zeros (to be defined later) of the network function uniquely determine both the transient and steady-state characteristics of a network except for a scale factor H. As a matter of convenience, the p notation of the last two sections will be adopted.

In physically realizable circuits the network function, or immittance, $W(p)$ of a lumped network may be expressed as a rational fraction,[1] i.e., as the ratio of two polynomials in p,

$$W(p) = \frac{a_1 p^m + a_2 p^{m-1} + \cdots + a_m}{b_1 p^n + b_2 p^{n-1} + \cdots + b_n} \tag{2-74}$$

Factoring out $a_1/b_1 = H$,

$$W(p) = H\,\frac{p^m + c_1 p^{m-1} + \cdots + c_m}{p^n + d_1 p^{n-1} + \cdots + d_n} \tag{2-74a}$$

where $c_k = a_k/a_1$
$\quad\quad d_k = b_k/b_1$

Now if the numerator in Eq. (2-74a) is equated to zero, the roots of the resulting equation may be designated p_{o1}, p_{o2}, . . . , p_{om} and the numerator may be written as the product of its factors $p - p_{ok}$. Similarly, the denominator may be written as the product of the factors $p - p_{xk}$, where p_{x1}, p_{x2}, . . . , p_{xn} are the roots of the denominator set equal to zero. Thus Eq. (2-74a) may be rewritten as

$$W(p) = H\,\frac{(p - p_{o1})(p - p_{o2}) \cdots (p - p_{om})}{(p - p_{x1})(p - p_{x2}) \cdots (p - p_{xn})} \tag{2-74b}$$

Now if p takes on any of the values p_{ok}, $W(p)$ becomes zero; hence,

[1] This point is covered in greater detail in Chaps. 4 and 14.

p_{o1}, p_{o2}, . . . , p_{om} are said to be *zeros* of $W(p)$. Similarly if p takes on any of the values p_{xk}, $W(p) \rightarrow \infty$; hence p_{x1}, p_{x2}, . . . , p_{xn} are said to be *poles* of $W(p)$. Both the poles and zeros may be either real, imaginary, or complex and, when complex, will appear in conjugate pairs of the general form $p_{a1} = \delta_a + j\omega_a$, $p_{a2} = \delta_a - j\omega_a$. In physical cases δ_a will be negative.

From Eq. (2-74b) it is apparent that if the zeros, poles, and scale factor H are specified, $W(p)$ is uniquely determined. It follows, then, that the behavior of a network may be specified by either (1) its steady-state response as a function of frequency, or (2) its response to a step function as a function of time, or (3) its poles, zeros, and scale factor.

It is of interest to note how the steady-state immittance, $W(\omega)$ or $W(f)$, may be obtained graphically by plots in the complex plane of $\delta + j\omega$. In general the factors in the numerator and denominator of Eq. (2-74b) are complex and may be written in polar form as

$$p - p_{ok} = \beta_k \underline{/\phi_k}$$
$$p - p_{xk} = \gamma_k \underline{/\theta_k} \tag{2-75}$$

Substituting into Eq. (2-74b),

$$W(p) = H \frac{\beta_1 \beta_2 \cdots \beta_m}{\gamma_1 \gamma_2 \cdots \gamma_n}$$
$$\underline{/(\phi_1 + \phi_2 + \cdots + \phi_m) - (\theta_1 + \theta_2 + \cdots + \theta_n)} \tag{2-74c}$$

A typical situation is illustrated in Fig. 2-15 for a circuit having two complex conjugate poles and a single negative, real zero. The zero and poles are plotted in the complex p plane. β_1, γ_1, and γ_2 are scaled from the diagram for a particular value of $\omega = \omega_1$; then

$$W(\omega_1) = H \frac{\beta_1}{\gamma_1 \gamma_2}$$

θ_1, θ_2, and ϕ_1 may also be measured, and the angle of $W(\omega_1)$ will be $\phi_1 - (\theta_1 + \theta_2)$. The student may observe that $W(\omega)$ may be obtained by letting the point ω_1 vary from $-\infty$ to $+\infty$ along the axis of real frequencies, which is the vertical axis in Fig. 2-15.

It is apparent from work earlier in the chapter that the poles and zeros of the network function also determine the network's response to any driving function. A simple extension of this work leads to a concept of fundamental importance in communication circuits, that the *character* of the response, i.e., oscillatory or nonoscillatory, is governed by the network poles.

Using the p notation of the last section, Eq. (2-41b) shows that the response of a network described by $W(p)$ will be

$$R(p) = W(p) Dr(p) \tag{2-76}$$

$Dr(t)$ may be a step function, say, of voltage, so that from pair 1 of Table 2-1 $Dr(p) = E/p$. As stated earlier, $W(p)$ is a rational fraction; hence $W(p)E/p$ will also be a rational fraction so that Eq. (2-76) may be written in the form of either Eq. (2-74a) or Eq. (2-74b). It should be noted that the denominator of these equations, expressed as a polynomial in p, will have *real* coefficients; therefore, the poles will be either real or

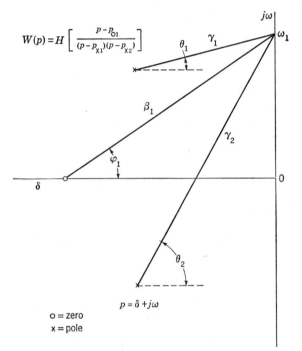

$$W(p) = H\left[\frac{p - p_{01}}{(p - p_{x1})(p - p_{x2})}\right]$$

$$p = \delta + j\omega$$

o = zero
x = pole

Fig. 2-15. Graphical determination of the steady-state characteristics at ω_1 from the pole and zero locations in the complex p plane.

complex conjugate pairs. Then if $R(p)$ is expanded by partial fractions, it will have the general form

$$R(p) = EH\left(\frac{A}{p - p_{x1}} + \cdots + \frac{F}{p - p_{xf}} + \frac{F}{p + p_{xf}^*} + \cdots\right) \quad (2\text{-}76a)$$

In this equation, the quotation p_{xf} and p_{xf}^* are complex conjugates. $R(t)$ may then be found by identifying each term with its mate in Table 2-1. It may be seen, then, that each real pole and each pair of complex conjugate poles of $R(p)$ contribute a corresponding time-varying term to $R(t)$, the former being exponential and the latter oscillatory. Since only the poles appear explicitly in Eq. (2-76a), it may be concluded that it is

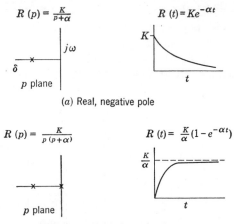

$$R(p) = \frac{K}{p+\alpha} \qquad\qquad R(t) = Ke^{-\alpha t}$$

(a) Real, negative pole

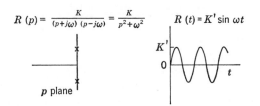

$$R(p) = \frac{K}{p(p+\alpha)} \qquad\qquad R(t) = \frac{K}{\alpha}(1-e^{-\alpha t})$$

(b) Real, negative pole + pole at zero

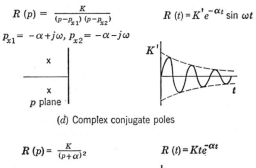

$$R(p) = \frac{K}{(p+j\omega)(p-j\omega)} = \frac{K}{p^2+\omega^2} \qquad R(t) = K' \sin \omega t$$

(c) Imaginary conjugate poles

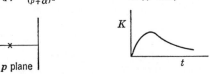

$$R(p) = \frac{K}{(p-P_{x1})(p-P_{x2})} \qquad\qquad R(t) = K'e^{-\alpha t} \sin \omega t$$

$$P_{x1} = -\alpha+j\omega, \; P_{x2} = -\alpha-j\omega$$

(d) Complex conjugate poles

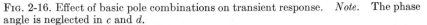
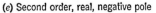

$$R(p) = \frac{K}{(p+\alpha)^2} \qquad\qquad R(t) = Kte^{-\alpha t}$$

(e) Second order, real, negative pole

FIG. 2-16. Effect of basic pole combinations on transient response. *Note.* The phase angle is neglected in *c* and *d*.

the poles of $R(p)$ which determine the character (i.e., exponential, sinusoid, damped-sinusoid) of the transient response. The zeros of $R(p)$ affect the amplitudes A, B, . . . of the several terms in $R(t)$. Some frequently encountered forms are shown in Fig. 2-16.

2-15. Responses of RC-coupled Amplifier. The broad-band RC-coupled amplifier, whose equivalent circuit is shown in Fig. 2-17a, will serve as a good example for the summarizing of the results of the foregoing sections and to show typical approximations that may be used in

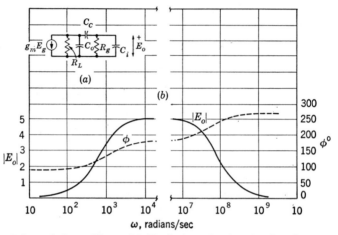

Fig. 2-17. RC-coupled amplifier. (a) Equivalent circuit. (b) Steady-state response curves. Note the break in the ω scale. $R_L = 1$ kilohm, $R_g = 100$ kilohms, $C_o = 6$ $\mu\mu$f, $C_i = 14$ $\mu\mu$f, $g_m E_g = -5$ ma, $C_c = 0.1$ μf.

calculating circuit responses. As will be explained in Chap. 15, typical values of the circuit parameters in Fig. 2-17a are

$$R_L = 1 \text{ kilohm} \qquad R_g = 100 \text{ kilohms}$$
$$C_i = 14 \ \mu\mu\text{f} \qquad C_o = 6 \ \mu\mu\text{f} \qquad C_c = 0.01 \ \mu\text{f}$$

It may be noted that the driving function is a current $g_m E_g$ and that the desired response is the output voltage E_o. It may be shown by the usual methods of steady-state analysis that the network function $W(\omega)$ is given by

$$W(\omega) = \frac{-j\omega C_c}{\dfrac{1}{R_L R_g} + j\omega\left(\dfrac{C_i + C_c}{R_L} + \dfrac{C_o + C_c}{R_g}\right) + (j\omega)^2[C_o C_i + C_c(C_o + C_i)]}$$

$$(2\text{-}77)$$

Now the engineer, in order to simplify his work, takes note of the relative magnitudes of the quantities involved in his calculations. Thus since $C_o < C_i \ll C_c$ ($<$ means "less than," $\ll$ means "very much less than"),

$$C_i + C_c \approx C_c \qquad C_o + C_c \approx C_c$$

and since $R_L \ll R_g$

$$\frac{C_i + C_c}{R_L} + \frac{C_o + C_c}{R_g} \approx C_c\left(\frac{1}{R_L} + \frac{1}{R_g}\right) \approx \frac{C_c}{R_L}$$

Furthermore, $C_oC_i \ll C_c(C_o + C_i)$; hence

$$C_oC_i + C_c(C_o + C_i) \approx C_c(C_o + C_i) = C_cC_s$$

where $C_s = C_o + C_i$. Therefore Eq. (2-77) may be simplified to

$$W(\omega) = \frac{-j\omega C_c}{1/R_LR_g + j\omega C_c/R_L + (j\omega)^2 C_cC_s} \qquad (2\text{-}78)$$

Factoring out $j\omega C_c/R_L$ from the denominator and rearranging the order of terms,

$$W(\omega) = \frac{-R_L}{1 + j(\omega C_s R_L - 1/\omega C_c R_g)} \qquad (2\text{-}78a)$$

The steady-state response to a sinusoidal current driving function will then be

$$E_o(\omega) = W(\omega)g_m E_g(\omega)$$

$$= -\frac{g_m R_L}{1 + j(\omega C_s R_L - 1/\omega C_c R_g)} \qquad (2\text{-}78b)$$

Equation (2-78b) may be used to calculate the steady-state response of the RC amplifier, subject, of course, to the approximations which have been made. Before doing this, however, it should be noted that different circuit components control the response in different ranges of frequency. Note that $\omega C_s R_L = 2 \times 10^{-8}\omega$, while $1/\omega C_c R_g = 10^3/\omega$. Hence, at very high frequencies $1/\omega C_c R_g \ll \omega R_L C_s$, and the response simplifies to

$$(E_o)_{\text{high}} = \frac{-g_m R_L}{1 + j\omega C_s R_L} \qquad (2\text{-}79a)$$

$$= \frac{g_m R_L}{\sqrt{1 + (\omega C_s R_L)^2}} \Big/\underline{-180° - \arctan \omega C_s R_L} \qquad (2\text{-}79b)$$

On the other hand, at very low frequencies, $\omega C_s R_L \ll 1/\omega C_c R_g$, and the response simplifies to

$$(E_o)_{\text{low}} = \frac{-g_m R_L}{1 - j/\omega C_c R_g} \qquad (2\text{-}79c)$$

$$= \frac{g_m R_L}{\sqrt{1 + (1/\omega C_c R_g)^2}} \Big/\underline{-180° + \arctan \frac{1}{\omega C_c R_g}} \qquad (2\text{-}79d)$$

At some particular frequency, $\omega_o/2\pi$, $\omega_o C_s R_L = 1/\omega_o C_c R_g$, and the response simplifies to

$$(E_o)_{mid} = -g_m R_L = g_m R_L \underline{/-180°} \qquad (2\text{-}79e)$$

As a practical matter, C_s and C_c have a negligible effect over a considerable range of frequencies which are often referred to as the "mid-frequency band" or simply "mid-band." The steady-state response of the amplifier in question with $g_m = 5 \times 10^{-3}$ mho and $E_g = -1$ volt is plotted in Fig. 2-17b. A more elegant presentation of this response in terms of normalized variables will be considered in Chap. 15.

Consider, next, the transient response of the RC amplifier shown in Fig. 2-17a. By replacing $j\omega$ by p and factoring out $C_s C_c$ from the denominator in Eq. (2-78), the network function becomes

$$W(p) = -\frac{p}{C_s \left(p^2 + p/R_L C_s + 1/R_L R_g C_s C_c\right)} \qquad (2\text{-}80)$$

In this case where the transient response is desired, let the driving current be a *negative* step function such that

$$\begin{aligned} i(t) &= 0 & t < 0 \\ i(t) &= -g_m E_g & t > 0 \end{aligned} \qquad (2\text{-}81)$$

(The negative sign is chosen in order that the response may be plotted as a positive function of time.) Then, from Table 2-1, $I(p) = -g_m E_g/p$. The output voltage will be

$$\begin{aligned} E_o(p) &= W(p) I(p) \\ &= \frac{g_m E_g}{C_s} \frac{1}{p^2 + p/R_L C_s + 1/R_L R_g C_s C_c} \end{aligned} \qquad (2\text{-}82)$$

Since the denominator is a second-degree polynomial, Eq. (2-82) will have two poles, say, p_{x1} and p_{x2}, and may be written

$$E_o(p) = \frac{g_m E_g}{C_s} \frac{1}{(p - p_{x1})(p - p_{x2})} \qquad (2\text{-}83)$$

Then by the mates of Table 2-1

$$e_o(t) = \frac{g_m E_g}{C_s(p_{x1} - p_{x2})} \left(e^{p_{x1}t} - e^{p_{x2}t}\right) \qquad (2\text{-}84)$$

The two poles may be evaluated by setting the denominator of Eq. (2-82) equal to zero and finding the roots of the resulting equation by the quadratic formula, thus:

$$\begin{aligned} \left.\begin{array}{c} p_{x1} \\ p_{x2} \end{array}\right\} &= -\frac{1}{2R_L C_s} \pm \sqrt{\left(\frac{1}{2R_L C_s}\right)^2 - \frac{1}{R_L R_g C_s C_c}} \\ &= -\frac{1}{2R_L C_s}\left(1 \mp \sqrt{1 - \frac{4R_L C_s}{R_g C_c}}\right) \end{aligned} \qquad (2\text{-}85)$$

Now, for the values given, $R_L \ll R_g$ and $C_s \ll C_c$; therefore $4R_LC_s/R_gC_c \ll 1$. The second term under the radical is therefore very small compared with 1, but it should not be neglected or the difference between the two poles and the nature of the response will be lost.

In a situation like this, slide-rule accuracy is inadequate, but resort may be made to the binomial expansion, viz.,

$$\sqrt{1 + a} = 1 + \frac{a}{2} - \frac{a^2}{4\lfloor 2} + \frac{3a^3}{8\lfloor 3} - \cdots$$

If $a \ll 1$, the series converges so rapidly that only the first two terms are significant and give an accuracy in numerical computation better than the slide rule. By applying this expansion to Eq. (2-85), the poles become

$$\left.\begin{array}{c} p_{x1} \\ p_{x2} \end{array}\right\} = -\frac{1}{2R_LC_s}\left[1 \mp \left(1 - \frac{2R_LC_s}{R_gC_c}\right)\right]$$

whence
$$p_{x1} = -\frac{1}{R_gC_s} = \frac{-1}{10^5 \times 10^{-8}} = -10^3$$

$$p_{x2} \approx -\frac{1}{R_LC_s} = -\frac{1}{10^3(0.2 \times 10^{-10})} = -5 \times 10^7 \qquad (2\text{-}85a)$$

Noting that $p_{x1} - p_{x2} \approx 1/R_LC_s$, Eq. (2-84) becomes

$$e_o(t) = g_mE_gR_L(e^{-10^3t} - e^{-5\times10^7t}) \qquad (2\text{-}86)$$

It is observed, then, that the response is proportional to the sum of the two exponentials. The general shape of Eq. (2-86) is shown in Fig. 2-18a, where it may be observed that the response consists of a build-up of relatively short duration followed by a long, slow decay. This comes about because of the great difference between the values of p_{x1} and p_{x2} and simplifies the work of plotting the actual response.

For values of t close to zero, say, of the order of 1 μsec or less, $e^{p_{x1}t} \approx 1$, and the "short-time" transient response may be expressed as

$$e_o(t)_{\text{short}} = g_mE_gR_L(1 - e^{-5\times10^7t}) \qquad (2\text{-}86a)$$

Since the leading edge of the applied step function occurs at $t = 0$, $e_o(t)_{\text{short}}$ is often called the "edge response." In this case of the RC amplifier the edge response has the form of an exponential build-up.

For larger values of time, say, of the order of 100 μsec or more, $e^{p_{x2}t} \approx 0$, and the "long-time" transient response simplifies to

$$e_o(t)_{\text{long}} = g_mE_gR_Le^{-10^3t} \qquad (2\text{-}86b)$$

This is the equation of an exponentially decaying function and results from the inability of the circuit to pass a d-c term because of the series capacitor C_c. Because of the shape of the exponential, $e_o(t)_{\text{long}}$ is often called the "sag." The transient response of Fig. 2-17a is plotted in Fig. 2-18.

It is of significance to note the following conclusions concerning the RC amplifier:

1. The steady-state response may be considered in three separate ranges of frequencies, or bands: the low, mid, and high. The low-band response depends upon the parameters R_g and C_c; the high-band response, on R_L and C_s.

2. The transient response may be considered in two separate time intervals: short (edge response) and long (sag). The edge response is

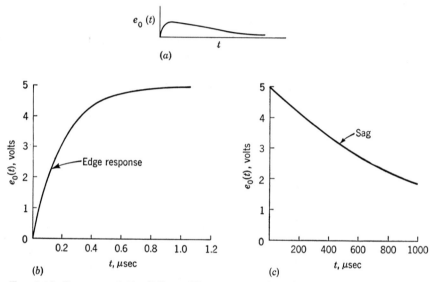

Fig. 2-18. Response of the RC amplifier to a step function. (a) General shape of $e_o(t)$. (b) The edge response for small values of t. (c) The sag response for large values of t. Note the change in time scale as compared with b.

governed by R_L and C_s and hence is related to the high-band steady-state characteristics. The sag is governed by R_g and C_c and hence is related to the low-band steady-state characteristics.

These ideas serve as important guides in considering the behavior of many communication circuits and illustrate quantitatively some of the conclusions reached qualitatively in Chap. 1.

PROBLEMS

2-1. Replace the inductor of Fig. 2-1 by a capacitor C. Find the complete solution for $i(t)$ and verify that integration with respect to time corresponds to multiplication by $1/j\omega$ in the frequency domain.

2-2. Sketch the steady-state impedance curves of a series RLC circuit in three different ways.

2-3. Calculate and sketch the transient response to $EU(t)$ of the circuit of Prob. 2-1.

2-4. Verify Eq. (2-16d).

2-5. (a) Calculate and sketch the frequency-spectrum envelope of a repetitive saw-tooth wave of amplitude E and period T. (b) Repeat for a single, nonrecurrent saw-tooth pulse of amplitude E and period T. (c) How are these two envelopes related?

2-6. A certain idealized filter has the following network function: $W(\omega) = A$, $-\omega_1 < \omega < +\omega_1$; $W(\omega)$ is linear between 0 at $-\omega_2$ and A at $-\omega_1$; $W(\omega)$ is linear between A at ω_1 and 0 at ω_2. The delay is t_d at all frequencies.

a. Derive an expression for the transient response to $EU(t)$.

b. Plot a curve of the response for $\omega_2 = 2\omega$, and compare with Fig. 2-8.

2-7. Calculate and plot the frequency spectrum of $U(t)$ which is shown in Fig. 2-4.

2-8. A single d-c current pulse of duration T_1 is applied to a shunt RC load. Let the cutoff frequency be defined by $f_c = 1/2\pi CR$.

a. Derive an expression for the voltage across the RC load as a function of time.

b. Calculate and plot $e_0(t)$ if $f_c = 2/T_1$.

2-9. A current step function $IU(t)$ is applied to a parallel combination of R, L, and C. Using the method of Fourier transforms, calculate the voltage across the parallel combination for the three cases $1/(2RC)^2$ greater than, equal to, and less than $1/LC$. Sketch the response for each case. Compare your results with the illustrative problem in Sec. 2-13.

CHAPTER 3

STEADY-STATE ANALYSIS
AND NETWORK THEOREMS

Kirchhoff's voltage and current laws are the basic working tools in solving network problems. Traditionally emphasis has been placed upon the voltage law and its natural consequence, the mesh, or loop, method of analyzing circuits, while the current law and the nodal method of analysis have been relegated to a secondary place. As a practical matter in dealing with communication networks it is the nodal analysis which often better fits the physical circuit. This is true for two primary reasons: (1) nodal analysis presumes current generators as sources, a condition closely matched in those circuits employing a pentode vacuum tube operated under linear class A conditions; (2) in correlating theoretical calculations with experimental measurements it is convenient to calculate those quantities which can be measured easily in the laboratory. A moment's reflection about electronic circuits in general shows that it is voltage, rather than current, which is the more easily measured quantity. In fact, in the plate circuit of a vacuum tube currents and voltages consist of two components: an alternating component superimposed on a d-c component. The measurement of the alternating component o-voltage is readily accomplished by means of an a-c vacuum-tube voltf meter, while no simple means are available for measuring the alternating component of current alone. Since the usual methods of analysis are concerned with alternating components only, it seems that one should solve for voltage, rather than current, as the quantity which can be checked directly by measurement. Certainly, then, at least as much emphasis should be given to the nodal analysis as to the more familiar mesh analysis. It will also be seen that in many cases a given circuit may be solved with fewer nodal equations than mesh equations. This is particularly true when the interelectrode capacitances of vacuum tubes must be taken into account.

An advantage is to be gained also from studying these two basic forms of analysis together. It will become apparent that a principle of general *duality* exists between certain networks, a principle that can be of considerable aid in the solution of network problems.

Because of their basic importance, it is advisable to review the application of the two laws of Kirchhoff as they are used in the steady-state analysis of circuits containing more than one mesh. Such a review will also make clear the concepts of general duality and equivalence.

3-1. Sign Conventions. In an a-c circuit current flows first in one direction and then in the other in every branch. However, in order to add and subtract their effect at junctions as is required by Kirchhoff's current law, it is essential that an *arbitrary* assignment be made of the direction of current flow that will be called positive. This is usually done by drawing an arrow → on the circuit diagram, the current then being considered positive when it is flowing in the direction of the arrow. It is of importance to note that the assignment of the arrow direction on the diagram is *arbitrary*, but, once assigned, it must be maintained throughout the analysis.

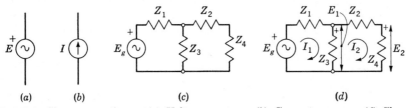

(a)   (b)   (c)   (d)

Fig. 3-1. Sign conventions. (a) Voltage source. (b) Current source. (d) Shows one possible set of assumed positive current directions and voltage polarities for network c.

The complex current itself may be designated in a number of ways, but throughout this book one form of single-subscript notation is used: the current is designated by I, followed by a single identifying subscript, I_g, I_1, I_3, ... The magnitude of the complex current, say, I_x, will be designated $|I_x|$. Similarly the potential difference between two points in an a-c network must be assigned an *assumed* positive direction which in this text will be indicated on circuit diagrams by a double-headed arrow with a + sign at one end. The two heads indicate the two points of the circuit across which the voltage is defined, and the voltage is considered positive when the end with the + sign is at a higher potential than the opposite end.

The complex voltage itself is identified by E followed by a single identifying subscript, E_g, E_1, E_x, and its magnitude by $|E_x|$.

The symbols used in this book for voltage and current generators are shown, respectively, in Fig. 3-1a and b.

The use of this notation may be clarified by considering the circuit shown in Fig. 3-1c. Before any solution is possible, assumed positive or arrow directions of current and voltage must be assigned. One possible set of these assumed directions is shown at d. Consider the problem of designating the voltage produced across Z_3 in terms of currents I_1 and I_2. The arrow direction of I_1 is such that positive current causes the upper end of Z_3 to be at a higher potential than the lower end; since the upper end of E_1 is marked $+$, the component of E_1 caused by I_1 is $+I_1Z_3$.

The arrow direction of I_2, however, is such that positive current causes the upper end of Z_3 to be at a lower potential than the lower end. Thus the component of E_1 caused by I_2 is $-I_2Z_3$. Then

$$E_1 = I_1Z_3 - I_2Z_3 = (I_1 - I_2)Z_3$$

3-2. Kirchhoff's Voltage Law; Mesh Analysis. Kirchhoff's voltage law may be stated as follows: *The algebraic sum of all the voltages around any closed loop in a network is zero.*

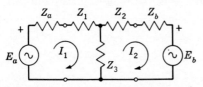

As a direct application of the law consider the circuit of Fig. 3-2. The current flowing through Z_2 is to be determined. Two loops, or meshes, that may be chosen for solving the network are those indicated by the currents I_1 and I_2. It should be stressed again that the arrow directions of current and assumed positive-voltage polarities have been assigned arbitrarily.

FIG. 3-2. Circuit for illustrating mesh analysis.

Application of the voltage law to the two loops yields

Mesh 1: $(Z_a + Z_1)I_1 + Z_3(I_1 - I_2) - E_a = 0$ (3-1)

Mesh 2: $(Z_2 + Z_b)I_2 + Z_3(I_2 - I_1) + E_b = 0$ (3-2)

The terms may now be collected and regrouped in a convenient manner. Since the two equations are linear, they may be solved readily by determinants; so the regrouping should place terms in an orderly fashion such that, on the left, vertical columns contain the same currents and all voltage sources appear on the right. Thus,

$$(Z_a + Z_1 + Z_3)I_1 \qquad\qquad -Z_3I_2 = E_a \qquad\qquad (3\text{-}3)$$
$$-Z_3I_1 + (Z_2 + Z_3 + Z_b)I_2 = -E_b \qquad\qquad (3\text{-}4)$$

Equations (3-3) and (3-4) are frequently simplified to the forms

$$Z_{11}I_1 + Z_{12}I_2 = E_1 \qquad\qquad (3\text{-}3a)$$
$$Z_{21}I_1 + Z_{22}I_2 = E_2 \qquad\qquad (3\text{-}4a)$$

where Z_{11} and Z_{22} are the sum of all the impedances in their respective meshes, that is,

$$Z_{11} = Z_a + Z_1 + Z_3 \qquad Z_{22} = Z_2 + Z_3 + Z_b$$
$$Z_{12} = Z_{21} = -Z_3$$

Then by Cramer's rule

$$I_2 = \frac{\begin{vmatrix} Z_{11} & E_1 \\ Z_{21} & E_2 \end{vmatrix}}{\begin{vmatrix} Z_{11} & Z_{12} \\ Z_{21} & Z_{22} \end{vmatrix}} = \frac{Z_{11}E_2 - Z_{21}E_1}{Z_{11}Z_{22} - Z_{21}Z_{12}} \tag{3-5}$$

$$= \frac{Z_3 E_a - (Z_a + Z_1 + Z_3)E_b}{(Z_a + Z_1)(Z_2 + Z_3 + Z_b) + Z_3(Z_2 + Z_b)} \tag{3-5a}$$

3-3. Generalization for a p-mesh Network. A multimesh network having B branches and N branch points, or nodes, can be shown to have p *independent* meshes, where $p = B - N + 1$. Such a network is often called a p-mesh network and can be described by a set of p simultaneous equations, each having the general form of Eqs. (3-3a) and (3-4a), namely,

$$\begin{aligned} Z_{11}I_1 + Z_{12}I_2 + Z_{13}I_3 + \cdots + Z_{1p}I_p &= E_1 \\ Z_{21}I_1 + Z_{22}I_2 + Z_{23}I_3 + \cdots + Z_{2p}I_p &= E_2 \\ \cdots\cdots\cdots\cdots\cdots\cdots\cdots\cdots\cdots\cdots\cdots \\ Z_{p1}I_1 + Z_{p2}I_2 + Z_{p3}I_3 + \cdots + Z_{pp}I_p &= E_p \end{aligned} \tag{3-6}$$

there being one equation for each of the p independent meshes. Each of the impedance coefficients appearing in the equations has a special significance. These will now be considered.

3-4. Mesh Impedance. Let the mesh to which the assumed current I_1 has been assigned be designated mesh 1. Then if all the meshes of the network but mesh 1 are open-circuited, all mesh currents but I_1 are zero and one has from the first equation

$$Z_{11} = \left(\frac{E_1}{I_1}\right)_{I_n=0} \qquad n = 2, 3, 4, \ldots, p \tag{3-7}$$

Thus Z_{11} is the impedance around mesh 1 *with all* other meshes open-circuited. Alternatively, Z_{11} is also the sum of all the impedances through which I_1 flows and is designated the "self," "loop," or "mesh" impedance of mesh 1. Similarly, Z_{22} is the mesh impedance of mesh 2, i.e., the mesh to which I_2 has been assigned arbitrarily, and is equal to $(E_2/I_2)_{I_n=0}$, $n = 1, 3, 4, \ldots, p$. In general Z_{mm} is the loop impedance of the mth mesh and is the sum of all the impedances in mesh m. As a specific example of this concept, in Fig. 3-3 $Z_{22} = Z_b + Z_c + Z_d + Z_e$.

3-5. Mutual Impedance. Let all the meshes but mesh 2 of the network described by Eqs. (3-6) be open-circuited. Then all the currents but I_2 will be zero, and one notes that the voltage *induced* in mesh 1, say, E_1', is $E_1' = Z_{12}I_2$, or

$$Z_{12} = \left(\frac{E_1'}{I_2}\right)_{I_n=0} \qquad n = 1, 3, 4, \ldots, p \tag{3-8}$$

Thus Z_{12} is the ratio of the voltage induced in mesh 1 to the current in mesh 2 *with all meshes but 2 open-circuited* and is called the "mutual impedance" between meshes 1 and 2. This induced voltage could be measured by connecting a voltmeter (theoretically of infinite impedance and capable of measuring phase as well as magnitude) in the first mesh and sending a current around the second mesh.

A similar definition holds for the remaining coefficients of the form Z_{mn} in Eqs. (3-6), each being the mutual impedance between meshes m and n. For instance, the mutual impedance between meshes 3 and 2 of

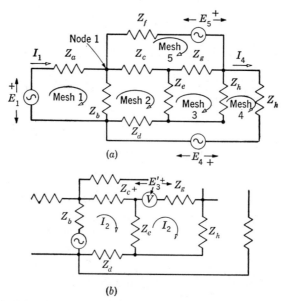

(a)

(b)

Fig. 3-3. A multimesh network. (b) Illustrates the method for determining the mutual impedance between the second and third meshes of a.

Fig. 3-3a could be measured in the manner shown in Fig. 3-3b and would be the ratio $Z_{32} = E_3'/I_2'$ measured by the voltmeter V.

The student will observe in Fig. 3-3b that $E_3' = -Z_e I_2$ or that

$$Z_{32} = -Z_e$$

Thus the mutual impedance Z_{mn} between the two meshes m and n may be seen also to be the sum of all the impedances through which both I_m and I_n flow in the original, unopen-circuited network. The mutual impedance is positive if the arrow directions of both currents are the same through the common impedance elements and negative if the arrow directions of current are opposite. It follows that, when a network contains only simple resistors, capacitors, and inductors, the mutual impedance is bilateral, that is, $Z_{mn} = Z_{nm}$.

In cases where the mutual impedance is due to mutual inductance particular care must be exercised in determining its sign because the winding polarity of the coils must be taken into account as well as the assumed positive directions of the mesh currents.

Where actual winding diagrams of the coil assembly are available as in Fig. 3-4a, no ambiguity is present; Lenz's law may be used to determine the sign associated with the mutual impedance. It is generally the case, however, that such a diagram is not available and some additional notation is required that gives the same information. To this end, winding terminals of the same polarity will be indicated in this book by a large dot as illustrated in Fig. 3-4b.[1] Once the dot locations are known,

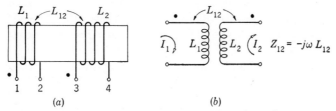

(a)   (b)

FIG. 3-4. Determination of the sign of the mutual impedance between two circuits coupled by mutual inductance.

the sign of the mutual impedance may be determined by the following rules:

1. The mutual inductance L_{mn} is always taken to be positive.

2. If the assumed arrow directions of I_m and I_n are both into (or out of) the dot terminals, the mutual impedance is positive, that is, $Z_{mn} = j\omega L_{mn}$. If the assumed positive directions of I_m and I_n are such that one flows into a dot terminal and the other out of a dot terminal, the mutual impedance is negative. To illustrate in Fig. 3-4b, the mutual impedance is $-j\omega L_{12}$.

3-6. Summary: Mesh Equations. The results of the foregoing paragraphs may be summarized into a set of rules for setting up the system of p simultaneous equations (3-6) which describe a p-mesh network. In the equation for the mth mesh:

1. The coefficient of I_m is the sum of all the impedances through which I_m flows and is designated Z_{mm}, the self-impedance of mesh m.

2. The coefficient of I_n, $n \neq m$, is the sum of all the impedances through which I_m and I_n flow and is designated Z_{mn}, the mutual impedance between meshes m and n. If I_m and I_n have the same arrow direction through the mutual elements, the mutual impedance is positive; if not, it is negative.

[1] An alternative method of marking polarities that is widely used in the Bell Telephone System numbers coil terminals in their winding sequence. Thus all odd-numbered terminals have the same polarities as do all even-numbered terminals.

3. Voltage sources in the mth mesh appear on the right-hand side of the equation, with a positive sign if their assumed polarity is such that they cause positive current to flow in the direction of the I_m arrow and with a negative sign if their assumed polarity causes positive current to flow in the opposite direction.

These rules may be applied to each mesh in turn to give the p equations (3-6). The student should observe that these rules permit Eqs. (3-3) and (3-4) to be written directly without the need of writing the preliminary equations (3-1) and (3-2) which result from the direct application of Kirchhoff's voltage law.

The unknowns in Eqs. (3-6) are the currents I_1, I_2, . . . , I_p, while the impedances and voltages are known. The problem, therefore, is to find one or more of the currents in terms of the impedances and voltages. Since the p simultaneous equations are linear, this may be done most conveniently by the use of determinants. Owing to space limitations the theory of determinants will not be treated here,[1] but the solutions for the equations may be given by means of a few definitions. The following notation will be used:

The impedance determinant D is obtained by including all the impedances in the form

$$D = \begin{vmatrix} Z_{11} & Z_{12} & \ldots & Z_{1p} \\ Z_{21} & Z_{22} & \ldots & Z_{2p} \\ Z_{31} & Z_{32} & \ldots & Z_{3p} \\ \cdot & \cdot & \cdot & \cdot \\ Z_{p1} & Z_{p2} & \ldots & Z_{pp} \end{vmatrix} \qquad (3\text{-}9)$$

As has been stated previously, in networks containing only linear bilateral elements, $Z_{mn} = Z_{nm}$; hence for such networks the determinant will exhibit symmetry about the principal diagonal from the upper left to the lower right corner. It may be stated also that in a number of communication networks, particularly those of the ladder type, several of the impedances Z_{mn} may be zero.

The minor M_{mn} is the determinant that is obtained by eliminating the mth row and nth column from D. The cofactor C_{mn} is defined in terms of the minor M_{mn} by the relationship $C_{mn} = (-1)^{m+n}M_{mn}$. Then, by the theory of determinants, the solution for the current in the mth mesh of the p-mesh network is

$$I_m = \frac{C_{1m}}{D} E_1 + \frac{C_{2m}}{D} E_2 + \cdots + \frac{C_{mm}}{D} E_m + \cdots + \frac{C_{pm}}{D} E_p \qquad (3\text{-}10)$$

It will be observed that the coefficient of each voltage on the right-hand

---

[1] The reader is referred to any good algebra text. See, for example, W. L. Hart, "College Algebra," D. C. Heath and Company, Boston, 1926, or E. A. Guillemin, "The Mathematics of Circuit Analysis," John Wiley & Sons, Inc., New York, 1949.

side of Eq. (3-10) is dimensionally an admittance; hence, adopting the definition

$$y_{mn} = \frac{C_{nm}}{D} \tag{3-11}$$

one notes that the solutions for all the unknown currents of the p-mesh network are given by

$$
\begin{aligned}
I_1 &= y_{11}E_1 + y_{12}E_2 + y_{13}E_3 + \cdots + y_{1p}E_p \\
I_2 &= y_{21}E_1 + y_{22}E_2 + y_{23}E_3 + \cdots + y_{2p}E_p \\
&\quad\cdots\cdots\cdots\cdots\cdots\cdots\cdots\cdots\cdots\cdots \\
I_m &= y_{m1}E_1 + y_{m2}E_2 + y_{m3}E_3 + \cdots + y_{mp}E_p \\
&\quad\cdots\cdots\cdots\cdots\cdots\cdots\cdots\cdots\cdots\cdots \\
I_p &= y_{p1}E_1 + y_{p2}E_2 + y_{p3}E_3 + \cdots + y_{pp}E_p
\end{aligned}
\tag{3-12}
$$

The several admittances appearing in the above equations all have physical significance and are given special names. These will now be considered in terms of the equation for the current in the mth mesh.

3-7. Mesh Driving-point Admittance, Impedance. Let all the meshes in the original network be closed and all generators but those in the mth mesh be replaced by their internal impedances. This condition effectively shorts out the generated voltages so that $E_n = 0$, $n \neq m$. Then one has from Eqs. (3-12)

$$I_m = y_{mm}E_m \qquad E_n = 0 \qquad n \neq m$$

or

$$y_{mm} = \left(\frac{I_m}{E_m}\right)_{E_n=0} \qquad n \neq m \tag{3-13}$$

This quantity is termed the "driving-point admittance of the mth mesh."

As an example, in Fig. 3-3a the driving-point admittance of the first mesh would be the ratio $y_n = I_1/E_1$, with the voltages E_4 and E_5 reduced to zero, but with all the meshes closed, i.e., connected as shown in the figure.

The reciprocal of y_{mm} is a useful quantity, the driving-point impedance of mesh m, and will be represented by the symbol z_{mm}. It should be observed that z_{mm} is *not* equal to the mesh impedance Z_{mm}. The driving-point admittance and impedance of any mesh may be calculated in terms of the original network impedance by means of Eq. (3-11).

These relationships may be made more clear by considering an example afforded by the circuit of Fig. 3-2. The driving-point impedance of mesh 1 or the driving-point impedance at the terminals of the generator E_1, namely, z_{11}, may be determined by inspection. The definition calls for E_2 to be reduced to zero; thus, replacing E_2 by a short circuit, one has by inspection

$$z_{11} = Z_a + Z_1 + \frac{Z_3(Z_2 + Z_b)}{Z_3 + Z_2 + Z_b} \tag{3-14}$$

It is suggested that the student verify this result by means of determinants, using Eq. (3-5) as a check on his work.

It may be noted further that, in special cases where only one generator is connected to the circuit, the driving-point impedance at the generator terminals is often called the "input impedance" and its reciprocal the "input admittance." The notation remains the same or is sometimes designated Z_{in} or Y_{in} as the case may be.

3-8. Mesh Transfer Admittance and Impedance. The remaining admittances in Eqs. (3-12) are of the general form y_{nm}. Following the method of the last section, let all the meshes in the network be closed and all generators but E_m be replaced by their internal impedances. Under these conditions one obtains from Eqs. (3-12)

$$I_n = y_{nm}E_m \qquad E_n = 0 \qquad n \neq m$$

or
$$y_{nm} = \left(\frac{I_n}{E_m}\right)_{E_n=0} \qquad n \neq m \qquad (3\text{-}15)$$

This quantity is termed the "mesh transfer admittance" between meshes m and n. For example in Fig. 3-3a the mesh transfer admittance between the first and fourth meshes would be $y_{41} = I_4/E_1$, with voltages E_4 and E_5 reduced to zero, but with all meshes closed as in the figure. The reciprocal of y_{nm} is the "mesh transfer impedance" and will be symbolized by z_{nm}. The values of these two quantities may be determined in terms of the original network impedances by means of Eq. (3-11). It should be noted that the mesh transfer impedance z_{nm} is *not* equal to the mutual impedance Z_{nm}. Again the circuit of Fig. 3-2 may be used to illustrate the concept for, letting E_2 become zero in Eq. (3-5), one has

$$z_{21} = \frac{E_1}{I_2} = \frac{(Z_a + Z_1)(Z_2 + Z_3 + Z_b) + Z_3(Z_2 + Z_b)}{Z_3} \qquad E_2 = 0 \quad (3\text{-}16)$$

The reciprocal is y_{21}.

3-9. Summary. The results of the foregoing paragraphs may be summarized as follows: If Kirchhoff's voltage law is applied to each mesh in turn of a network having p independent meshes, p linear simultaneous equations result, each having the general form

$$Z_{m1}I_1 + Z_{m2}I_2 + \cdots + Z_{mm}I_m + \cdots + Z_{mp}I_p = E_m$$

Z_{mm} is the self-impedance of mesh m, and the other impedances appearing in the equation are the *mutual* impedances between mesh m and the other meshes in the network.

The p voltage equations may be solved in turn for each of the mesh currents, in each case the current being expressed by an equation of the form

$$I_m = y_{m1}E_1 + y_{m2}E_2 + \cdots + y_{mm}E_m + \cdots + y_{mp}E_p$$

In this current equation y_{mm} is the driving-point admittance of mesh m, and the other admittances are the mesh *transfer* admittances between mesh m and the remaining meshes in the network.

In communication systems multimesh networks are ordinarily used to connect a generator to a load. As a result, two currents are of particular interest: the current in the generator and the current in the load. In such cases the two impedances of primary concern are the driving-point impedance of the input mesh and the mesh transfer impedance between the input and output meshes, for these quantities relate the desired currents to the applied generator voltage.

3-10. Current Generators. While the methods of mesh analysis may be used to solve any network problem, the nodal method is often easier to employ and may be more useful in a given problem. In this latter method it is convenient to work with current generators rather than with voltage generators.

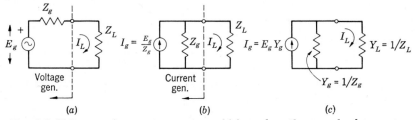

Fig. 3-5. Voltage and current generators which produce the same load current.

Current generators are seldom encountered in practice except when pentode vacuum tubes are used. Any voltage generator, however, may be replaced for purposes of analysis by a current generator that causes the same conditions in the load. For example, Fig. 3-5a shows a voltage generator with generated voltage E_g and series internal impedance Z_g connected to a load Z_L. At b the voltage generator has been replaced by a current generator which consists of a current source of value $I_g = E_g/Z_g$ *shunted* by the original generator impedance Z_g. The student may easily verify that both generators give the same value of current, I_L, in Z_L provided the values of Z_g and E_g remain unchanged.

In nodal analysis one generally uses admittances rather than impedances as a matter of convenience. Figure 3-5c shows the current-generator circuit with each impedance replaced by its corresponding admittance. The value of I_L is unchanged in all three circuits shown in the figure.

3-11. Kirchhoff's Current Law; Nodal Analysis. Kirchhoff's current law may be stated as follows: *The algebraic sum of all the currents at a node (or junction) in a network is zero.*

As a direct application of the law, consider the circuit of Fig. 3-6. The voltage across the admittance Y_c is to be determined in terms of the known currents I_x and I_y and the known admittances. The circuit is redrawn at b to show one possible choice of nodes and to show one possible set of assumed positive polarities for voltages between nodes 1 and

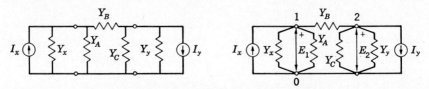

FIG. 3-6. Circuit for illustrating nodal analysis.

2 and the reference node identified as 0. Then application of the current law to nodes 1 and 2 yields

Node 1: $\quad (Y_x + Y_A)E_1 + Y_B(E_1 - E_2) - I_x = 0 \qquad$ (3-17)

Node 2: $\quad (Y_C + Y_y)E_2 + Y_B(E_2 - E_1) + I_y = 0 \qquad$ (3-18)

The terms may now be collected and regrouped for convenient solution by determinants. Thus

$$(Y_x + Y_A + Y_B)E_1 \qquad\qquad -Y_BE_2 = I_x \qquad (3\text{-}19)$$
$$-Y_BE_1 + (Y_B + Y_C + Y_y)E_2 = -I_y \qquad (3\text{-}20)$$

The last two equations are frequently simplified to the forms

$$Y_{11}E_1 + Y_{12}E_2 = I_1 \qquad\qquad (3\text{-}19a)$$
$$Y_{21}E_1 + Y_{22}E_2 = I_2 \qquad\qquad (3\text{-}20a)$$

where Y_{11} and Y_{22} are the sum of all the admittances directly connected to their respective nodes and Y_{12} is the sum of the admittances connected between these two nodes, i.e.,

$$Y_{11} = Y_x + Y_A + Y_B \qquad Y_{22} = Y_B + Y_C + Y_y$$
$$Y_{12} = Y_{21} = -Y_B$$

Then by Cramer's rule, the desired voltage E_2 is given by

$$E_2 = \frac{\begin{vmatrix} Y_{11} & I_1 \\ Y_{21} & I_2 \end{vmatrix}}{\begin{vmatrix} Y_{11} & Y_{12} \\ Y_{21} & Y_{22} \end{vmatrix}} = \frac{Y_{11}I_2 - Y_{21}I_1}{Y_{11}Y_{22} - Y_{12}Y_{21}}$$

$$= \frac{Y_BI_x - (Y_x + Y_A + Y_B)I_y}{(Y_x + Y_A)(Y_B + Y_C + Y_y) + Y_B(Y_C + Y_y)} \qquad (3\text{-}21)$$

3-12. Generalization for a $(p + 1)$-node Network. It can be shown that a multinode network having, say, $(p + 1)$ nodes all *conductively coupled* can be described by a set of p independent nodal equations.

Therefore, one node may be chosen arbitrarily as the "common," or "reference," node and the p equations set up in terms of the voltages between all other nodes and this reference. Each of these equations will have the general form of Eqs. (3-19a) and (3-20a), and the set of p equations will appear as

$$Y_{11}E_1 + Y_{12}E_2 + Y_{13}E_3 + \cdots + Y_{1p}E_p = I_1$$
$$Y_{21}E_1 + Y_{22}E_2 + Y_{23}E_3 + \cdots + Y_{2p}E_p = I_2$$
$$Y_{31}E_1 + Y_{32}E_2 + Y_{33}E_3 + \cdots + Y_{3p}E_p = I_3 \qquad (3\text{-}22)$$
$$\cdots\cdots\cdots\cdots\cdots\cdots\cdots\cdots\cdots\cdots\cdots$$
$$Y_{p1}E_1 + Y_{p2}E_2 + Y_{p3}E_3 + \cdots + Y_{pp}E_p = I_p$$

Each of the admittance coefficients appearing in the equations has a special significance. These will now be considered.

3-13. Node Admittance. In Eqs. (3-22) E_1 is the assumed potential difference between node 1 and the reference node, E_2 is the assumed potential difference between node 2 and reference, and so on. Then if all the nodes but 1 are shorted to the reference node, all the voltages but E_1 are zero and one has from the first of Eqs. (3-22)

$$Y_{11} = \left(\frac{I_1}{E_1}\right)_{E_n=0} \qquad n = 2, 3, 4, \ldots, p \qquad (3\text{-}23)$$

Thus Y_{11} is the total admittance between node 1 and the reference node, *with all other nodes shorted to the reference.* Inspection of Fig. 3-6b shows Y_{11} to be $Y_x + Y_A + Y_B$; hence Y_{11} may also be seen to be the *sum of all the admittances connected directly to node 1.* This quantity is designated the "self-admittance" of node 1. Similarly, Y_{22} is the self-admittance of node 2 and is the sum of all the admittances directly connected to node 2. In general Y_{mm} is the self-admittance of node m. As a specific example, the self-admittance of the node labeled 1 in Fig. 3-3a is $Y_{11} = 1/Z_a + 1/Z_b + 1/Z_c + 1/Z_f$.

3-14. Nodal Mutual Admittance. Let all the nodes except node 2 of the network described by Eqs. (3-22) be shorted to the reference node. Then all the node voltages but E_2 become zero, and the current flowing from node 1 to node 2, say, I_1', is $Y_{12}E_2$. Hence Y_{12}, the "nodal mutual admittance" between nodes 2 and 1, is the ratio of I_1' to E_2, *all nodes but node 2 being shorted to the reference node.* This concept is illustrated in Fig. 3-7, where the reference node is labeled 0. The original network is shown at a, and the circuit is redrawn at b to show nodes 1 and 3 shorted to the reference node. The current I_1' flowing from node 1 to node 2 as a result of E_2 could be measured by a millimeter (theoretically of zero impedance and also capable of measuring phase) in the branch Y_4, and the nodal mutual admittance would be the ratio $Y_{12} = -I_1'/E_2$.

The student will observe in Fig. 3-6b that $I_1' = -Y_4E_2$ or that

$$Y_{12} = -Y_4$$

Thus for the case where the network contains only simple resistances, inductances, and capacitances the nodal mutual admittance between any two nodes m and n may be seen also to be the *sum of all the admittances which connect the two nodes directly*. The nodal mutual admittance is positive if the two node voltages have *opposite* assumed positive polarities relative to the reference node and negative if the two node voltages have the same assumed positive polarities. It follows that the nodal mutual admittance between the nodes is bilateral, that is, $Y_{mn} = Y_{nm}$, if the network contains only simple resistors, inductors, and capacitors. When vacuum tubes or transistors are used in their linear range, similar analyses may be applied but Y_{mn} will not then equal Y_{nm}.

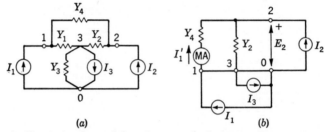

FIG. 3-7. Circuit for determining the mutual admittance between two nodes.

3-15. Summary of Nodal Equations. As was the case in mesh analysis, the final equations, (3-22), for the $(p + 1)$-node network may be written by inspection without the need of first applying the current law directly to each node in turn and then regrouping terms into the desired orderly form. For example, a little practice shows that Eqs. (3-19a) and (3-20a) may be written at once without first writing the preliminary equations (3-19) and (3-20). This is done by applying to each node in turn the following rules, which summarize the foregoing work. In the equation for the mth node:

1. The coefficient of E_m is the sum of all the admittances connected directly to the mth node and may be designated Y_{mm}, the self-admittance of the mth node.

2. The coefficient of E_n, $n \neq m$, is the sum of all the admittances directly joining nodes m and n and is designated Y_{mn}, the mutual admittance between nodes m and n. (This does not apply when $Y_{mn} \neq Y_{nm}$ as in vacuum tubes and transistors unless they are reduced to so-called equivalent circuits.) The nodal mutual admittance is negative if E_m and E_n have the same assumed positive polarities relative to the reference node; if not, it is positive.

3. Current sources connected to node m appear on the right-hand side of the equation with a positive sign if their arrow directions are into the node and with a negative sign if their arrow directions are away from the node.

The admittances and currents in Eqs. (3-22) are presumed to be known quantities while the several node voltages are unknown. These latter may be evaluated by means of determinants. The admittance determinant D' is obtained by including all the admittances in the form

$$D' = \begin{vmatrix} Y_{11} & Y_{12} & \cdots & Y_{1p} \\ Y_{21} & Y_{22} & \cdots & Y_{2p} \\ \cdots & \cdots & \cdots & \cdots \\ Y_{p1} & Y_{p2} & \cdots & Y_{pp} \end{vmatrix}$$

The minors and cofactors are determined from D' in the same manner as were the minors and cofactors from D, the impedance determinant in mesh analysis. Where the possibility of confusion between impedance and admittance is present, they will be designated C'_{mn} or M'_{mn}, the primes indicating that they are derived from the admittance determinant D'. In any given problem where no such chance of confusion is present, the primes may be omitted.

Solution of Eqs. (3-22) for E_m by determinants yields the equation

$$E_m = \frac{C'_{1m}}{D'} I_1 + \frac{C'_{2m}}{D'} I_2 + \cdots + \frac{C'_{mm}}{D'} I_m + \cdots + \frac{C'_{pm}}{D'} I_p \quad (3\text{-}24)$$

It will be observed that the coefficient of each current on the right-hand side of Eq. (3-24) is an impedance dimensionally; hence, adopting the definition,

$$z'_{mn} = \frac{C'_{nm}}{D'} \quad (3\text{-}25)$$

one notes that the solutions for all the unknown voltages of the $(p + 1)$-node network are given by

$$E_1 = z'_{11} I_1 + z'_{12} I_2 + z'_{13} I_3 + \cdots + z'_{1p} I_p$$
$$E_2 = z'_{21} I_1 + z'_{22} I_2 + z'_{23} I_3 + \cdots + z'_{2p} I_p$$
$$\cdots \cdots \cdots \cdots \cdots \cdots \cdots \cdots \cdots \cdots$$
$$E_m = z'_{m1} I_1 + z'_{m2} I_2 + z'_{m3} I_3 + \cdots + z'_{mp} I_p \qquad (3\text{-}26)$$
$$\cdots \cdots \cdots \cdots \cdots \cdots \cdots \cdots \cdots \cdots$$
$$E_p = z'_{p1} I_1 + z'_{p2} I_2 + z'_{p3} I_3 + \cdots + z'_{pp} I_p$$

The several impedances appearing in these equations all have physical significance and are given special names. These will now be considered in terms of the equation for E_m.

3-16. Nodal Driving-point Impedance, Admittance. In the general network described by Eqs. (3-22), let all current generators but I_m be replaced by their internal admittances alone. This condition is obtained by open-circuiting each current source but I_m so that $I_n = 0$, $n \neq m$. Then from Eqs. (3-26) one has

$$E_m = z'_{mm} I_m \qquad I_n = 0 \qquad n \neq m$$

or
$$z'_{mm} = \left(\frac{E_m}{I_m}\right)_{I_n=0} \qquad n \neq m \tag{3-27}$$

This quantity is termed the "nodal driving-point impedance" between node m and reference node.

As an example, the nodal driving-point impedance between node 1 and the reference node in Fig. 3-7a would be the ratio $z'_{11} = E_1/I_1$ with the branches containing I_2 and I_3 open.

The reciprocal of z'_{mm} is a useful quantity, the "nodal driving-point admittance" between node m and reference, and will be represented by the symbol y'_{mm}. It should be noted that y'_{mm} is *not* equal to the self-admittance of the node, Y_{mm}. z'_{mm} and y'_{mm} may be calculated in terms of the original network admittances by means of Eq. (3-25).

To clarify these relationships, consider the circuit of Fig. 3-6a. The nodal admittance between node 1 and the reference node can be determined by inspection: open-circuiting the I_y branch, one has by inspection

$$y'_{11} = Y_x + Y_A + \frac{Y_B(Y_C + Y_y)}{Y_B + Y_C + Y_y} \tag{3-28}$$

The student should verify this result by determinants.

3-17. Nodal Transfer Impedance, Admittance. The remaining impedances in Eqs. (3-26) are of the general form z'_{nm}. These may be interpreted by open-circuiting all current sources but I_m (with the generator admittances left in place). Under this condition, one has from the equations

$$E_n = z'_{nm} I_m \qquad I_n = 0 \qquad n \neq m$$

or
$$z'_{nm} = \left(\frac{E_n}{I_m}\right)_{I_n=0} \qquad n \neq m \tag{3-29}$$

This quantity is the "nodal transfer impedance" between nodes m and n. For example, in Fig. 3-7, the nodal transfer impedance between nodes 1 and 2 would be the ratio $z'_{21} = E_2/I_1$ with the branches containing I_2 and I_3 open. The reciprocal of z'_{21} is the "nodal transfer admittance" between nodes 1 and 2 and will be symbolized by y'_{21}. y'_{21} is not equal to Y_{21}, the mutual admittance between nodes 1 and 2.

The circuit of Fig. 3-6 may also be used to illustrate this concept, for letting I_y become zero in Eq. (3-21) one obtains

$$y_{21} = \frac{I_x}{E_2} = \frac{(Y_x + Y_A)(Y_B + Y_C + Y_y) + Y_B(Y_C + Y_y)}{Y_B} \qquad (3\text{-}30)$$

3-18. Summary. The results of the preceding paragraphs may be summarized as follows: Application of the nodal form of analysis to a network containing $p + 1$ conductively connected nodes results in p linear simultaneous equations each having the general form

$$Y_{m1}E_1 + Y_{m2}E_2 + \cdots + Y_{mm}E_m + \cdots + Y_{mp}E_p = I_m$$

Y_{mm} is the self-admittance of node m, and the other admittances that appear in the equation are the mutual admittances between node m and the other nodes in the network.

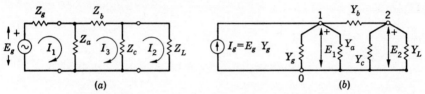

(a)   (b)

FIG. 3-8. Circuit for comparing mesh and nodal analysis.

Solution of the p current equations by determinants or other means yields equations for the unknown voltages between nodes and the reference node. Each of these will be of the form

$$E_m = z'_{m1}I_1 + z'_{m2}I_2 + \cdots z'_{mm}I_m + \cdots + z'_{mp}I_p$$

where z'_{mm} is the nodal driving-point impedance between node m and reference and the other impedances are nodal transfer impedances between node m and the remaining nodes.

3-19. Example. It is obvious that any given network may be solved by either the mesh or nodal equations, irrespective of the type of generator, but values computed directly may not always be the final characteristics desired. As an example consider the case of a Π network connecting a generator to a load Z_L. The diagram for the mesh analysis is shown in Fig. 3-8a. Since there are three meshes, three equations will be set up. Note that the sequence of meshes 1, 2, 3 is arbitrary. It is quite common to designate mesh 1 as the input mesh and mesh 2 as the output mesh. The set of three mesh equations will be

$$(Z_g + Z_a)I_1 \qquad + 0 \qquad - Z_aI_3 = E_g$$
$$0 + (Z_c + Z_L)I_2 \qquad - Z_cI_3 = 0$$
$$-Z_aI_1 \qquad - Z_cI_2 + (Z_a + Z_b + Z_c)I_3 = 0$$

The mesh transfer admittance between the input and output meshes will be by Eq. (3-15)

$$y_{21} = \frac{I_2}{E_g}$$

$$= \frac{Z_a Z_c}{(Z_g + Z_a)(Z_c + Z_L)(Z_a + Z_b + Z_c) - Z_a^2(Z_c + Z_L) - Z_c^2(Z_g + Z_a)}$$

and the mesh transfer impedance z_{21} will equal $1/y_{21}$.

For nodal analysis the corresponding circuit will be that shown in Fig. 3-8b. The only change is that the constant-voltage generator E_g in series with its impedance Z_g has been replaced by its equivalent constant-current generator I_g in parallel with the admittance Y_g (where $Y_g = 1/Z_g$ of Fig. 3-8a) and for convenience the network branches have been designated by their corresponding admittances. Since there are only two nodes other than the reference node, only two equations will be needed. They are

$$(Y_g + Y_a + Y_b)E_1 - \qquad\qquad Y_b E_2 = I_g$$
$$- Y_b E_1 + (Y_b + Y_c + Y_L)E_2 = 0$$

The nodal transfer impedance z'_{21}, will be given by Eq. (3-29),

$$z'_{21} = \frac{E_2}{I_g} = \frac{Y_b}{(Y_g + Y_a + Y_b)(Y_b + Y_c + Y_L) - Y_b^2}$$

and the nodal transfer admittance y'_{21} will equal $1/z'_{21}$.

Notice that the solution for the nodal transfer impedance does not give the current through the load, but rather the voltage across it for a given current from the generator source. There is however a relation between the mesh and nodal transfer impedances for this circuit which may be derived as follows:

$$I_g = E_g Y_g$$
$$E_2 = \frac{I_L}{Y_L} = \frac{I_2 \text{ (of Fig. 3-8a)}}{Y_L}$$
$$z'_{21} = \frac{E_2}{I_g} = \frac{I_2}{E_g Y_g Y_L} = \frac{1}{z_{21} Y_g Y_L}$$
$$z'_{21} z_{21} = Z_g Z_L$$

It is left to the student to show that the sets of equations in this example are consistent.

3-20. General Duality, Dual Networks.   Comparison of Eqs. (3-6) and (3-22) reveals that a formal symmetry exists between the mesh and nodal forms of analysis, and important use may be made of this fact in studying certain classes of circuits.

When two networks exhibit the property whereby the nodal equations of one network are similar, term by term, to the mesh equations of the other, voltage being interchanged with current and impedance being interchanged with admittance, the two circuits are said to exhibit the property of *general duality*. It will be found that such circuits display similar properties in so far as impedance is concerned on the one hand and as admittance is concerned on the other. The circuits of Figs. 3-2 and 3-6 are two such networks. The former is described by the mesh equations (3-3) and (3-4) and the latter by the nodal equations (3-19) and (3-20). These pairs of equations are seen to be identical term by term provided admittance is interchanged with impedance and current with voltage.

One frequently has need for considering passive dual networks, for example, the T and the II structures. The former is that portion of the network between the terminals indicated in Fig. 3-2. Letting Z_a and Z_b be zero in order to consider the four-terminal T structure alone, one has the mesh equations

$$\begin{aligned}(Z_1 + Z_3)I_1 &\quad - Z_3I_2 = E_a \\ -Z_3I_1 &+ (Z_2 + Z_3)I_2 = E_b\end{aligned} \tag{3-31}$$

A II structure is that portion of the network between the terminals indicated in Fig. 3-6. Letting Y_x and Y_y be zero in order to consider the II structure alone, one has the nodal equations

$$\begin{aligned}(Y_A + Y_B)E_1 &\quad - Y_BE_2 = I_x \\ -Y_BE_1 &+ (Y_B + Y_C)E_2 = I_y\end{aligned} \tag{3-32}$$

It can be seen at once that Eqs. (3-31) and (3-32) are similar, term by term, with the following interchanges:

$$\begin{aligned}Y_A &\text{ for } Z_1 & E_a &\text{ for } I_x \\ Y_C &\text{ for } Z_2 & E_b &\text{ for } I_y \\ Y_B &\text{ for } Z_3 & &\end{aligned} \tag{3-33}$$

Thus the T and II networks satisfy the condition for general duality. A direct consequence of this statement may now be demonstrated. Consider the mesh driving-point impedance $(z_{11})_T$ of the T network and the nodal driving-point admittance $(y'_{11})_{II}$ of the II network. $(z_{11})_T$ may be determined by solving the mesh equations for the ratio E_a/I_1, $E_b = 0$. It is instructive, however, to evaluate this quantity by inspection: it consists of Z_1 in series with the shunt combination of Z_2 and Z_3 (E_b being reduced to zero),

or
$$(z_{11})_T = Z_1 + \frac{Z_2Z_3}{Z_2 + Z_3} \tag{3-34}$$

Similarly, $(y'_{11})_{II}$ of the II network is I_x/E_1, $I_2 = 0$, or by inspection it is Y_A shunted by the series combination of Y_B and Y_C,

$$(y'_{11})_{II} = Y_A + \frac{Y_BY_C}{Y_B + Y_C} \tag{3-35}$$

One result of the T and Π networks being general duals is immediately apparent from Eqs. (3-34) and (3-35). $(y'_{11})_Π$ may be derived from the expression for $(z_{11})_T$ if the substitutions indicated in (3-33) are made.

Another example of this principle is afforded by comparing $(z_{12})_T$ and $(y'_{21})_Π$. For the former, one has by solution of Eqs. (3-31)

$$(z_{12})_T = \frac{E_2}{I_1} \qquad E_1 = 0$$
$$= \frac{Z_1Z_2 + Z_2Z_3 + Z_1Z_3}{Z_3} \qquad (3\text{-}36)$$

Then, utilizing the principle of general duality and the substitutions (3-33), one has for $(y'_{21})_Π$

$$(y'_{21})_Π = \frac{Y_AY_C + Y_AY_B + Y_CY_B}{Y_B} \qquad (3\text{-}37)$$

It is recommended that the student verify the last two equations. It will be found that the principle of general duality can greatly simplify the study of impedance-matching networks.

In certain instances two networks which satisfy the conditions of general duality may further exhibit the property whereby inductance, capacitance, and resistance in one circuit are replaced, respectively, by capacitance, inductance, and conductance in the other. In such cases the two are said to be *dual networks* or, simply, *duals*. Use is made of the properties of dual networks in the chapters on equalizers and filters.

3-21. Network Theorems. While Ohm's and Kirchhoff's laws are the fundamental working tools in solving network problems, much time can often be saved by making use of certain theorems. By means of these theorems, an answer to some specific problems can be secured with such increased facility that they may be considered the machine tools of network theory. The use of only Ohm's and Kirchhoff's laws in their simplest forms may be compared to the exclusive use of a file and a hack saw where a lathe might be applied.

There are many things in common life which are equivalent to each other, and when they have been mentally listed as similar situations, experience which has been secured in handling one case can be quickly applied to treating the equivalent problems. It is the ability to recognize new setups, to which old procedures can be applied, which enables some individuals to accomplish so much more in life than others.

In the same way, if there are certain fundamental similarities between new complicated structures and other simpler networks, it is not necessary to start from the beginning each time a new problem presents itself. The theorems studied in this chapter establish these similarities. Perhaps the most important of these theorems is that of superposition.

3-22. Superposition Theorem.   This principle states that: *In any network consisting of linear impedances, the current flowing at any point is the sum of the currents that would flow if each generator were considered separately, all other generators being replaced at the time by impedances equal to their internal impedances.*

This theorem may be proved rigorously on the basis of the foregoing sections.   Consider a multimesh circuit where the number of independent meshes is p.   Then, no matter how complicated, the network is described by the p simultaneous equations (3-6).   Furthermore, by Eq. (3-10) the current in *any* mesh m is

$$I_m = \frac{C_{1m}E_1}{D} + \frac{C_{2m}E_2}{D} + \cdots + \frac{C_{mm}E_m}{D} + \cdots + \frac{C_{pm}E_p}{D}$$

This solution constitutes a proof of the superposition theorem as each term on the right gives the contribution of an individual voltage to the total current I_m in terms of a mesh driving point or mesh transfer admittance of the network and shows that this contribution is independent of the effect of the other voltages.   It is left as an exercise for the student to prove the dual form of the superposition theorem, viz.: In any network consisting of current generators and linear admittances, the voltage between any node and the reference node is the sum of the voltages that would appear between the two nodes if each current generator were considered separately, each other current generator being replaced at the time by an admittance equal to its internal admittance.

The use of the superposition theorem permits the solution of networks without setting up a large number of simultaneous equations because only one generator at a time need be considered.   Another advantage of the superposition theorem is that, if new voltages are introduced into the system, it is not necessary to solve the network from the beginning.   An example, where new voltages not ordinarily accounted for may be introduced, is that of a telephone line exposed to inductive interference.

If voltages of different frequencies are introduced, the superposition theorem permits a solution to be obtained for each individual frequency, these solutions being independent of each other.   Therefore the currents of each frequency flow as though the other frequencies were absent if the impedances in the network are linear.

Other typical applications of the principle of superposition will be illustrated in the proofs of some of the following network theorems.

3-23. Reciprocity Theorem.   *In any system composed of linear, bilateral impedances if a voltage E is applied between any two terminals and the current I due to E is measured in any branch, their ratio (the transfer impedance) will be equal to the ratio obtained if the positions of E and I are interchanged.*
The proof of this theorem follows directly from the results of the previous

sections. A linear bilateral network contains only linear self and mutual R, L, and C elements; hence the two transfer impedances

$$z_{mn} = \frac{D}{C_{nm}} \quad \text{and} \quad z_{nm} = \frac{D}{C_{mn}}$$

are equal.

In the application of the reciprocity theorem it should be noticed that no impedances are interchanged in the transfer of E and I. The theorem does not apply to the interchange of a generator with internal impedance and a load impedance unless these two impedances are equal.

An important conclusion from this theorem is that it proves that a network of bilateral impedances transmits with equal effectiveness in both directions, when generator and load have the same impedance.

3-24. Compensation (Alteration) Theorem. *In a linear network if any impedance Z through which a current I flows is modified by an amount ΔZ, the current increment produced thereby at any point in the network is equal to the change in current at that point that would be produced by a generator of emf $I \, \Delta Z$ placed in series with the altered impedance.*

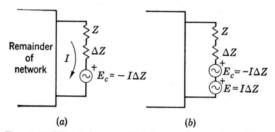

(a)   (b)

Fɪɢ. 3-9. Circuit for proof of the compensation theorem.

Consider the network of Fig. 3-9, one branch of which is shown in detail. Let a compensating emf $E_c = -I \, \Delta Z$ be introduced simultaneously with ΔZ as shown at a. Then the current I in this branch remains unchanged as will the currents at all other points in the circuit.

Now let a second emf $E = +I \, \Delta Z$ be introduced as at b. Then the current at every point in the circuit will be modified in accordance with the superposition theorem. However, $E + E_c = 0$; therefore the impedance change ΔZ alone must produce the same effect as $E = I \, \Delta Z$ acting in the branch containing Z, ΔZ, and $E_c = -I \, \Delta Z$. Since E_c exactly cancels the drop in ΔZ, the theorem is proved.

This theorem greatly simplifies a study of the effect of impedance tolerances in network design.

The use of the compensation theorem in handling network tolerances may be illustrated by a simple d-c example. It is desired to calculate the change in I_1 in

Fig. 3-10 when the right-hand resistance increases 20 per cent.   In the original circuit,

$$I_2 = {}^{10}\!\!/_{150} \times \tfrac{1}{2} = \tfrac{1}{30} \text{ amp}$$

At b, the resistance is increased to 120 ohms, and by the compensation theorem a voltage $E = I_2 \Delta R = \tfrac{2}{3}$ volt is added in series.   Then, by the superposition theorem,

$$\Delta I = \tfrac{2}{3} \times \tfrac{1}{170} \times \tfrac{1}{2} = \tfrac{1}{510} \text{ amp}$$

The student may verify this result by direct application of Kirchhoff's laws.

A simpler and more general form of the theorem is covered in the next section and will be designated the compensation theorem A.   It is introduced because of its application in Chap. 9.

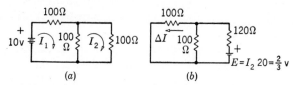

FIG. 3-10. Circuit for illustrating the use of the compensation theorem.

3-25. Compensation Theorem A.   *Any impedance in a network (either linear or nonlinear) may be replaced by a generator of zero internal impedance, whose generated voltage at every instant is equal to the instantaneous potential difference produced across the replaced impedance by the current flowing through it.*

Consider the network of Fig. 3-11.   In Fig. 3-11a, one branch of impedance, Z, through which a current I is flowing is considered separately from the rest of the system.   The equations of Kirchhoff's laws completely determine all the currents and potentials in the system.   These

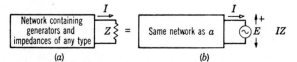

FIG. 3-11. Equivalent networks demonstrating the compensation theorem A.

equations, summing up the voltage around any mesh or the current at any point, will not be altered if the network is changed from Fig. 3-11a to Fig. 3-11b, and therefore this change cannot affect the current flowing anywhere in the system.

It should be noticed, in applying the compensation theorem A, that if any part of the network is later changed, the value of E must be changed. Observe also that there is no restriction in this theorem on the types of impedances in the network: they may be bilateral or unilateral, and they may be linear or nonlinear.

3-26. Current-division Theorem. *In a passive two-branch circuit the ratio of either branch current to the total current equals the impedance of the other branch divided by the sum of the branch impedances.* Proof of the theorem consists in writing E of Fig. 3-12 in terms of the currents and impedances by Ohm's law:

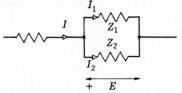

$$E = I \frac{Z_1 Z_2}{Z_1 + Z_2} = I_1 Z_1 = I_2 Z_2$$

whence

FIG. 3-12. Circuit for proving the current-division theorem.

$$\frac{I_1}{I} = \frac{Z_2}{Z_1 + Z_2} \qquad \frac{I_2}{I} = \frac{Z_1}{Z_1 + Z_2} \quad (3\text{-}38)$$

The current-division theorem simplifies the analysis of a number of circuits, particularly those of linear vacuum-tube amplifiers.

3-27. Equivalent Passive Networks. It is often true that the analysis of a circuit problem may be simplified by replacing some portion of that circuit by an *equivalent* network whose behavior is already known or readily calculable.

By definition:

An equivalent network is a network which, under certain conditions of use, may replace another network without substantial effect on electrical performance. *Note.* If one network can replace another network in any system whatsoever without altering in any way the electrical operation of that portion of the system external to the networks, the networks are said to be "networks of general equivalence." If one network can replace another network only in some particular system without altering in any way the electrical operation of that portion of the system external to the networks, the networks are said to be "networks of limited equivalence." Examples of the latter are networks which are equivalent only at a single frequency, over a single band, in one direction only, or only with certain terminal conditions (such as H or T networks). (ASA C42 65.06.500.)

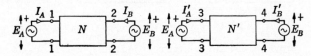

FIG. 3-13. Networks N and N' are equivalent if $I_A' = I_A$ and $I_B' = I_B$.

Thus two linear, passive networks may be said to be *equivalent* if, when identical voltages (of any value) are applied to corresponding terminals of the two networks, identical currents flow at corresponding terminals of the networks. This concept of equivalence is illustrated in Fig. 3-13. The networks N and N' are *equivalent* if

$$I_A = I_A' \qquad \text{and} \qquad I_B = I_B'$$

when the voltages E_A and E_B, of any value whatsoever, are applied to both networks. If this condition is satisfied, network N' may be substituted for N without disturbing any remaining portions of a circuit of which N may be a part.

In the following sections the conditions for equivalence will be considered for two-, three-, or four-terminal networks.

3-28. Two-terminal Equivalent Passive Networks. The simplest example of network equivalence is the two-terminal network shown in Fig. 3-14a. It is desired to construct a network having the impedance Z_{in} of a network a. One might first consider the question of how many complex impedance elements are required to synthesize Z_{in} *at a single frequency*. This question is answered by considering how many conditions must be satisfied. In general if Z_{in} is complex, the number of conditions is two: one must design for a given magnitude $|Z_{in}|$ and a given angle θ_{in} or, alternatively, for a given real part R_{in} and a given imaginary

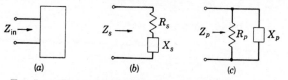

Fig. 3-14. Equivalent passive two-terminal networks.

part X_{in}; therefore the unknown must at least have a resistance and a reactance. In turn these two components may be connected in series as at b or in parallel as illustrated at c. The values of the series form may be evaluated as follows: Z_s must be equal to Z_{in}; so

$$Z_s = R_s + jX_s = Z_{in}/\theta_{in} = |Z_{in}|(\cos \theta_{in} + j \sin \theta_{in})$$

whence $\qquad R_s = |Z_{in}| \cos \theta_{in} \qquad X_s = Z_{in} \sin \theta_{in} \qquad (3\text{-}39)$

The shunt network of Fig. 3-14c can be handled most easily by working in admittance form; hence one notes that Y_p must be equal to $1/Z_{in}$; so

$$Y_p = \frac{1}{R_p} - \frac{j}{X_p} = \frac{1}{|Z_{in}|}/{-\theta_{in}} = \frac{1}{|Z_{in}|}(\cos \theta_{in} - j \sin \theta_{in})$$

whence $\qquad R_p = \frac{|Z_{in}|}{\cos \theta_{in}} \qquad X_p = \frac{|Z_{in}|}{\sin \theta_{in}} \qquad (3\text{-}40)$

Lest the student think of Eqs. (3-39) and (3-40) as "formulas" to be memorized, it is well to work out a typical example that frequently occurs in the laboratory.

A test is to be made on an artificial line which must be terminated in the impedance $500 - j153.5$ ohms at a frequency of 796 cycles. The elements available for synthesizing the impedance are a decade resistance box of range 1 to

1,000 ohms and a decade capacitor covering the range 0.001 to 1 μf. Then the series form of the impedance will be

$$\omega = 2\pi f = 2\pi \times 796 = 5{,}000 \text{ radians/sec}$$
$$Z_s = 500 - j153.5$$
$$= R_s - \frac{j}{\omega C_s}$$

Thus the required series elements are

$$R_s = 500 \text{ ohms}$$
$$C_s = \frac{1}{\omega \times 153.5} = \frac{1}{5 \times 10^3 (1.535 \times 10^2)} = 1.3 \ \mu f$$

Since the value of C_s is greater than that available from the decade capacitor, the parallel form of network should be considered.

$$Y_p = \frac{1}{Z} = \frac{1}{523/-17.1°} = 1.911 \times 10^{-3}/17.1°$$
$$= (1.827 + j0.561) \times 10^{-3}$$
$$= \frac{1}{R_p} + j\omega C_p$$

Then the required shunt components are

$$R_p = \frac{10^3}{1.827} = 534 \text{ ohms}$$
$$C_p = \frac{0.561 \times 10^{-3}}{5 \times 10^3} = 0.1121 \ \mu f$$

This set of values is quite satisfactory since they may be set up to three significant figures on the available decade units.

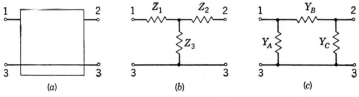

FIG. 3-15. Equivalent passive three-terminal networks.

In general since the reactance component varies with frequency, equivalence for any given set of components will hold only at a single frequency. The synthesis of some complex impedance over a wide range of frequencies is a complicated problem and will usually require more than the two elements used in the foregoing example.

3-29. Three-terminal Equivalent Passive Networks. Another commonly encountered configuration is the so-called three-terminal network shown in Fig. 3-15a, a network having two pairs of terminals with a common lead joining one terminal of each pair. It may now be shown that the basic definition of equivalence places certain restrictions on the mesh driving point and transfer impedances of the two networks that are to be equivalent; thus let N and N' of Fig. 3-13 be three-terminal networks. Then for network N one may write

$$I_A = \frac{E_A}{z_{11}} + \frac{E_B}{z_{12}} \qquad I_B = \frac{E_A}{z_{21}} + \frac{E_B}{z_{22}} \qquad (3\text{-}41)$$

and for network N'

$$I'_A = \frac{E_A}{z_{33}} + \frac{E_B}{z_{34}} \qquad I'_B = \frac{E_A}{z_{43}} + \frac{E_B}{z_{44}} \qquad (3\text{-}42)$$

Then if corresponding currents are to be equal in order to establish equivalence, it must be true that

$$z_{11} = z_{33} \qquad z_{22} = z_{44} \qquad (3\text{-}43)$$
$$z_{12} = z_{34} \qquad z_{21} = z_{43} \qquad (3\text{-}44)$$

Inasmuch as the networks are linear and bilateral

$$z_{12} = z_{21} \qquad z_{34} = z_{43}$$

and Eqs. (3-44) may be replaced by the single condition

$$z_{12} = z_{34} \qquad (3\text{-}45)$$

It follows from Eqs. (3-43) and (3-45) that *the two networks will also be equivalent if they have identical mesh driving-point and mesh transfer imped-ances.* This is a necessary and sufficient condition for equivalence; hence an equivalent network may be calculated if these three impedances are known for the original network.

Say that a three-terminal network is to be designed so that it is equiv-alent to the original network of Fig. 3-15a. In the interests of economy the equivalent network should contain the smallest number of elements possible. This minimum number may be arrived at quite simply by two methods of reasoning. First, for equivalence to be established, three design conditions must be satisfied (two driving-point and one transfer impedance); hence, three independent elements are required in the unknown network. In general the specified impedances are all complex; so the three unknown elements will also be complex. Second, if the student tries to interconnect three terminals with impedance elements, he will find that only three can be used without placing two or more elements in series or in parallel. He will also find that the three elements can be arranged either as a T or a Π as shown at b and c in Fig. 3-15. In power applications these are termed "star" and "delta," respectively. Thus either the T or the Π network may be designed to be equivalent to the original network.

The design of an equivalent T or Π network on this basis is of particular advantage when the internal structure of the original network is known,

for then the unknown elements may be calculated in terms of the impedance determinant and cofactors of the original network.[1]

By way of illustration say the original network has p meshes, and let the
meshes be numbered so that mesh 1 includes the input and mesh 2 the
output terminals. Then the circuit is described by Eqs. (3-6) except
that all the voltages but E_1 and E_2 are zero, the network itself being
passive. Then the input and output currents will be by Eq. (3-10)

$$
\begin{aligned}
I_1 &= \frac{C_{11}}{D} E_1 + \frac{C_{12}}{D} E_2 = \frac{E_1}{z_{11}} + \frac{E_2}{z_{12}} \\
I_2 &= \frac{C_{12}}{D} E_1 + \frac{C_{22}}{D} E_2 = \frac{E_1}{z_{12}} + \frac{E_2}{z_{22}}
\end{aligned}
\tag{3-46}
$$

Then if the Π network of Fig. 3-15c is to be made equivalent to the
original network, one may write

$$
\begin{aligned}
I_1 &= (Y_A + Y_B)E_1 + Y_B E_2 \\
I_2 &= +Y_B E_1 + (Y_B + Y_C)E_2
\end{aligned}
\tag{3-47}
$$

and one finally has

$$
Z_A = \frac{1}{Y_A} = \frac{D}{C_{11} - C_{12}} \qquad Z_C = \frac{1}{Y_C} = \frac{D}{C_{22} - C_{12}} \qquad Z_B = \frac{1}{Y_B} = \frac{D}{C_{12}}
\tag{3-48}
$$

The student should consult the reference for an extension of these ideas.

In communication work three-terminal networks may be of considerable physical length, terminals 1 and 3 being located some distance from
the other pair, 2 and 3. For this reason end-to-end impedance measurements on networks are often not feasible; hence if one wishes to construct
an equivalent network from *measurements* on the original network, he
must find some other value to replace the transfer impedance.

The impedances that are most easily measured are the open- or short-
circuit driving-point impedances at each pair of terminals. In this book
these impedances will be designated by the following symbols because
of their wide adoption:

Z_{o1} = input impedance at end 1 with the terminals at end 2 open-
circuited

Z_{o2} = input impedance at end 2 with the terminals at end 1 open-
circuited

Z_{s1} = input impedance at end 1 with the terminals at end 2 short-
circuited

Z_{s2} = input impedance at end 2 with the terminals at end 1 short-
circuited.

[1] M. B. Reed, General Formulas for "T" and "Π" Network Equivalents, *Proc.
IRE*, vol. 33, No. 12, p. 897, December, 1945.

One method of approach to synthesizing a T section that is equivalent to the original three-terminal network would be to ascertain whether the mesh transfer impedance z_{12} is specified uniquely in terms of Z_{o1}, Z_{o2}, Z_{s1}, and Z_{s2}. A simpler and more direct approach is to determine whether the elements of the T section itself may be evaluated in terms of these four measured impedances. Thus, reading from Fig. 3-15b,

$$Z_{o1} = Z_1 + Z_3 \tag{3-49}$$

$$Z_{s1} = Z_1 + \frac{Z_2 Z_3}{Z_2 + Z_3} \tag{3-50}$$

$$Z_{o2} = Z_2 + Z_3 \tag{3-51}$$

$$Z_{s2} = Z_2 + \frac{Z_1 Z_3}{Z_1 + Z_3} \tag{3-52}$$

Then the impedance elements of the equivalent T section must be as follows: Rearranging Eqs. (3-49) and (3-51),

$$Z_1 = Z_{o1} - Z_3 \tag{3-53}$$
$$Z_2 = Z_{o2} - Z_3 \tag{3-54}$$

Substitute Eqs. (3-53) and (3-54) into Eq. (3-50).

$$Z_{s1} = \frac{Z_{o1}Z_{o2} - Z_{o1}Z_3 - Z_{o2}Z_3 + Z_3{}^2 + Z_{o1}Z_3 - Z_3{}^2 + Z_{o2}Z_3 - Z_3{}^2}{Z_{o2}}$$

All but two of the terms in the numerator will cancel, and so by clearing of fractions

$$Z_{s1}Z_{o2} = Z_{o1}Z_{o2} - Z_3{}^2$$
$$Z_3 = \pm \sqrt{Z_{o2}(Z_{o1} - Z_{s1})} \tag{3-55}$$

Equations (3-53) to (3-55) complete the design of the equivalent T section except for an ambiguity of sign.

It is of interest to consider the products $Z_{o1}Z_{s2}$ and $Z_{o2}Z_{s1}$. From Eqs. (3-49) to (3-52)

$$Z_{o1}Z_{s2} = Z_1 Z_2 + Z_2 Z_3 + Z_1 Z_3$$
$$Z_{o2}Z_{s1} = Z_1 Z_2 + Z_2 Z_3 + Z_1 Z_3 \tag{3-56}$$

Therefore
$$Z_{o1}Z_{s2} = Z_{o2}Z_{s1} \tag{3-57}$$

Equation (3-57) shows that only three of the four impedances Z_{o1}, Z_{o2}, Z_{s1}, and Z_{s2} are unique and leads to an alternative expression for Z_3 of the equivalent T,

$$Z_3 = \pm \sqrt{Z_{o1}(Z_{o2} - Z_{s2})} \tag{3-58}$$

A similar procedure may be used to evaluate the components of the Π network that will be equivalent to the original network in Fig. 3-15. Once again work with the Π section is best carried out in terms of admittances; thus from Fig. 3-15c

$$Y_{o1} = Y_A + \frac{Y_B Y_C}{Y_B + Y_C} \qquad Y_{o2} = Y_C + \frac{Y_A Y_B}{Y_A + Y_B} \qquad (3\text{-}59)$$
$$Y_{s1} = Y_A + Y_B \qquad\qquad Y_{s2} = Y_C + Y_B$$

whence the design equations of the equivalent Π section, except for an ambiguity of sign, become

$$Y_A = Y_{s1} - Y_B \tag{3-60}$$
$$Y_C = Y_{s2} - Y_B \tag{3-61}$$
$$Y_B = \pm\ \sqrt{Y_{s2}(Y_{s1} - Y_{o1})} = \pm\ \sqrt{Y_{s1}(Y_{s2} - Y_{o2})} \tag{3-62}$$

Comparison of the design equations for the T and Π networks shows, once again, the general duality that exists between these two networks. It will be observed that the interchange of Y_A for Z_1, Y_C for Z_2, and Y_B for Z_3, plus the interchange of open-circuit admittance for short-circuit impedance, allows the design of the Π section from the equations of the T section.

Inspection of the foregoing design equations for an equivalent T or Π section in terms of the open- and short-circuit impedances of the original network shows that an ambiguity is present in the sign of Z_3 or Y_B. This indicates that the design equations can give two T's or two Π's but only one of each pair can be *equivalent* to the original network. To resolve this difficulty, additional information is required about the original network. In a large class of problems a knowledge of the phase angle between I_1 and I_2 with the network terminated in a specified load provides the necessary information. This situation is illustrated in the following example:

Measurements on a three-terminal network at 1 kc yield the following data: $Z_{o1} = 10 + j50$ ohms, $Z_{o2} = 5 + j0$ ohms, $Z_{s1} = 510 + j50$ ohms. I_2 lags I_1 when end 2 is terminated in a pure resistive load. Design the equivalent T section.

$$\pm Z_3 = \pm\ \sqrt{Z_{o2}(Z_{o1} - Z_{s1})} = \pm\ \sqrt{5\underline{/0°}\ 500\underline{/-180°}} = \mp j50 \text{ ohms}$$

Solution A. Choosing the positive sign,

$$Z_3 = +j50 \text{ ohms}$$
$$Z_1 = Z_{o1} - Z_3 = 10 + j0 \text{ ohms}$$
$$Z_2 = Z_{o2} - Z_3 = 5 - j50 \text{ ohms}$$

These values give the T section shown in Fig. 3-16a.

Solution B. Choosing the negative sign,

$$Z_3 = -j50 \text{ ohms}$$
$$Z_1 = 10 + j100 \text{ ohms}$$
$$Z_2 = 5 + j50 \text{ ohms}$$

which values yield the T section shown in Fig. 3-16b.

The phasor diagrams of the two networks are also drawn in the figure. Since network B provides the required sign of phase angle between I_1 and I_2, B rather than A is the equivalent network.

3-30. Physical Realizability of Equivalent Sections. It should be recognized that the arms of the *equivalent* T sections of physical structures are not necessarily *physically realizable*. It is quite possible for an individual arm to have a negative-resistance component, i.e., the impedance may lie in any of the four quadrants. If the network which it represents is physical, the total I^2R of all arms will be positive, although that due to an individual arm may be negative. The presence of nega-

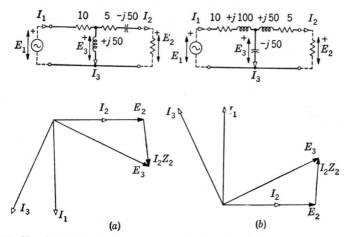

Fig. 3-16. Circuits having the same open- and short-circuit impedances but providing different phase shifts.

tive resistances in an arm of the equivalent network does not prevent its use in computation, since on paper a negative resistance presents no difficulty. The equivalent structure may also be set up physically if the arm with negative resistance is in series or in shunt with an external impedance whose resistance may be combined with the negative-resistance arm to make an impedance whose total resistance is positive.

3-31. Equivalence of T and Π Networks. In the preceding sections both the T and Π sections were designed to be equivalent to the same original three-terminal network. Then by the familiar axiom, "Things equal to the same thing are equal to each other," one might conclude that a Π section may be designed to be equivalent to a given T, and vice versa. The equations relating the impedance elements of a T and the elements of its equivalent Π are known as the "T-Π transformations."

In one respect, these transformations have already been derived, for given a T, it is possible to find Y_{o1}, Y_{o2}, and Y_{s1} and to evaluate the Π components from them by Eqs. (3-60) to (3-62). It is desirable, however, to have these transformations explicitly in terms of the component elements, and they may be derived by manipulation of the foregoing equations. Another approach, which utilizes the original definition of equivalence, will be used, however, to illustrate a different means of working the problem.

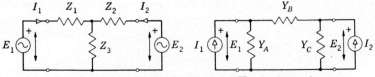

Fig. 3-17. Circuits for deriving the T-Π transformations.

The T and Π networks of Fig. 3-17 are to be made equivalent. Let the voltages E_1 and E_2 be applied to both networks as shown in the figure. Then

$$(Y_A + Y_B)E_1 \qquad - Y_BE_2 = I_1$$
$$- Y_BE_1 + (Y_B + Y_C)E_2 = I_2$$

and by Cramer's rule

$$E_1 = \frac{\begin{vmatrix} I_1 & -Y_B \\ I_2 & Y_B + Y_C \end{vmatrix}}{\begin{vmatrix} Y_A + Y_B & -Y_B \\ -Y_B & Y_B + Y_C \end{vmatrix}} = \frac{Y_B + Y_C}{Y_T{}^2} I_1 + \frac{Y_B}{Y_T{}^2} I_2 \qquad (3\text{-}63)$$

$$E_2 = \frac{Y_B}{Y_T{}^2} I_1 + \frac{Y_A + Y_B}{Y_T{}^2} I_2 \qquad (3\text{-}64)$$

where $Y_T{}^2 = Y_AY_B + Y_BY_C + Y_AY_C$ (3-65)
The mesh equations for the T network are

$$(Z_1 + Z_3)I_1 + Z_3I_2 = E_1 \qquad (3\text{-}66)$$
$$Z_3I_1 + (Z_2 + Z_3)I_2 = E_2 \qquad (3\text{-}67)$$

Now by definition, if the two networks are equivalent, corresponding voltages and corresponding currents are equal; hence coefficients of corresponding terms in Eqs. (3-63) and (3-66) and in (3-64) and (3-67) must be equal. Thus solving for the Z's one obtains the Π-T transformations

$$Z_1 = \frac{Y_C}{Y_T{}^2} \qquad Z_1 = \frac{Z_AZ_B}{Z_T}$$

$$Z_2 = \frac{Y_A}{Y_T{}^2} \qquad Z_2 = \frac{Z_BZ_C}{Z_T} \qquad (3\text{-}68)$$

$$Z_3 = \frac{Y_B}{Y_T{}^2} \qquad Z_3 = \frac{Z_AZ_C}{Z_T}$$

$$Y_T{}^2 = Y_AY_B + Y_BY_C + Y_AY_C \qquad Z_T = Z_A + Z_B + Z_C$$

The student may show that the corresponding T-Π transformations are

$$Y_A = \frac{Z_2}{Z_T{}^2}$$

$$Y_B = \frac{Z_3}{Z_T{}^2} \qquad Z_T{}^2 = Z_1 Z_2 + Z_2 Z_3 + Z_1 Z_3 \qquad (3\text{-}69)$$

$$Y_C = \frac{Z_1}{Z_T{}^2}$$

3-32. Equivalent Four-terminal Networks. A four-terminal network or two-terminal pair (Fig. 3-18) may lack the common lead of the three-terminal network but is indistinguishable from the latter in so far as equivalence is concerned, *provided no additional connection exists between the input and output generators through a third conductor such as ground.* This follows because measurements of the impedances Z_{o1}, Z_{o2}, Z_{s1}, and Z_{s2} are made only at one end or the other of the network. To determine

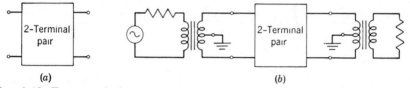

(a)   (b)

FIG. 3-18. Four terminal networks or two-terminals pairs. A balanced-to-ground connection is shown at b.

the presence or absence of a common lead *within* the network requires an additional end-to-end impedance measurement.   It may be concluded, then, that a T or a Π network may be designed to be equivalent to a two-terminal pair.

The student should know that certain types of communication networks, e.g., telephone lines, are purposely "balanced to ground." This means that both sides of the network have equal shunt admittances to ground and equal series impedances. Networks of this type operate between generators that are three-terminal devices, one terminal being connected to ground (in actual practice perhaps only by stray capacitances) as shown in Fig. 3-18b. If a T or a Π network is substituted for a network operated between two terminals of such three-terminal end devices, the third terminal being grounded, the common lead of the T or Π network destroys the balance. To make a *balanced* equivalent of the two-terminal pair, it is necessary only to divide Z_1 and Z_2 of the T network equally between the upper and lower series arms, giving a balanced T or H network as shown in Fig. 3-19a. A balanced Π or O network results from dividing the series impedance of the Π network equally between the upper and lower arms as shown in Fig. 3-19b. It should be apparent that such modifications of the original structures leave unaf-

fected the open- and short-circuit impedances and the design equations
of the T and II networks.

3-33. Lattice Network.   One of the commonest four-terminal networks
encountered in practice is the lattice, or bridge, network shown in Fig.
3-20.   The lattice-T transformation will now be derived in terms of the

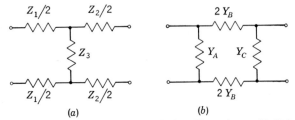

Fig. 3-19. Balanced networks.   (a) Balanced T or H section.   (b) Balanced II or O
section.

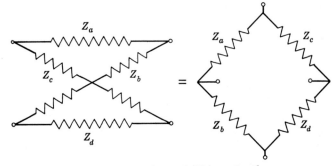

Fig. 3-20. Lattice, or bridge, network.

component impedances.   If the notation adopted in the previous sections is applied to Fig. 3-20, the following relations will be obtained:

$$Z_{o1} = \frac{(Z_a + Z_b)(Z_c + Z_d)}{Z_a + Z_b + Z_c + Z_d} \tag{3-70}$$

$$Z_{o2} = \frac{(Z_a + Z_c)(Z_b + Z_d)}{Z_a + Z_b + Z_c + Z_d} \tag{3-71}$$

$$Z_{s1} = \frac{Z_a Z_b Z_c + Z_a Z_c Z_d + Z_a Z_d Z_b + Z_b Z_c Z_d}{(Z_a + Z_c)(Z_b + Z_d)} \tag{3-72}$$

$$Z_{s2} = \frac{Z_a Z_b Z_c + Z_a Z_c Z_d + Z_a Z_b Z_d + Z_b Z_c Z_d}{(Z_a + Z_b)(Z_c + Z_d)} \tag{3-73}$$

Then $$Z_{o1} - Z_{s1} = \frac{(Z_b Z_c - Z_a Z_d)^2}{(Z_a + Z_b + Z_c + Z_d)(Z_a + Z_c)(Z_b + Z_d)} \tag{3-74}$$

Insert the results of Eqs. (3-74) and (3-71) in Eq. (3-55) to obtain one
of the equivalent T-section arms,

$$Z_3 = \pm \sqrt{\frac{(Z_b Z_c - Z_a Z_d)^2}{(Z_a + Z_b + Z_c + Z_d)^2}} \tag{3-75}$$

It is of interest to note that, in the special case where $Z_d = 0$, the lattice structure becomes a Π section and so Eq. (3-75) should reduce to the Π-T transformations. Therefore the positive root will be used, and Eq. (3-75) becomes

$$Z_3 = \frac{Z_b Z_c - Z_a Z_d}{Z_a + Z_b + Z_c + Z_d} \tag{3-76}$$

By inserting Eqs. (3-75), (3-70), and (3-71) in Eqs. (3-53) and (3-54)

$$Z_1 = \frac{Z_a Z_c + 2Z_a Z_d + Z_b Z_d}{Z_a + Z_b + Z_c + Z_d} \tag{3-77}$$

$$Z_2 = \frac{Z_a Z_b + 2Z_a Z_d + Z_c Z_d}{Z_a + Z_b + Z_c + Z_d} \tag{3-78}$$

Lattice structures are sometimes used in preference to ladder structures (T or Π networks). These are rather special applications, and so the relations for the design of a lattice structure will be discussed in a later chapter after the relations in repeated, or iterative, structures have been developed.

3-34. Equivalent Active Networks.   While the discussion of equivalence thus far has been restricted to passive networks, corresponding ideas may be set up for circuits containing voltage or current sources, but a new definition of equivalence is required for these active circuits: *Two active networks are said to be equivalent if, for any value of load impedance connected to the terminals of both circuits, they both produce the same value of load current.* Two theorems covering the equivalence of active circuits will be presented.

3-35. Thévenin's Theorem.   *The current in any impedance Z_R, connected to two terminals of a network, is the same as if Z_R were connected to a simple generator, whose generated voltage is the open-circuited voltage at the terminals in question and whose impedance is the impedance of the network looking back from the terminals, with all generators replaced by impedances equal to the internal impedances of these generators.*

In Fig. 3-21 the upper part is a diagrammatic representation of Thévenin's theorem. E_{oc} is the voltage measured at terminals 1, 2 with Z_R removed, and Z_g is the impedance measured back from terminals 1, 2. In measuring this impedance it is assumed that the generators have stopped generating; i.e., they are replaced by impedances equal to their internal impedances.

The network can be reduced to the simple network of Fig. 3-21c with three impedance elements and one generator. If there is more than one generator, then, by the superposition theorem, each could be considered separately in the proof. When each had been reduced to the simple network at the right, the generated voltages would all be connected in series and could be replaced by a single generator.   The proof holds, therefore, for any number of generators in the network.

In Fig. 3-21c a solution of the T network gives

$$I_2 = \frac{EZ_3}{Z_1Z_2 + Z_2Z_3 + Z_1Z_3 + Z_R(Z_1 + Z_3)} \qquad (3\text{-}79)$$

Equation (3-79) can be rearranged so that Z_R will appear in the denominator *only and be alone.*

$$I_2 = \frac{EZ_3/(Z_1 + Z_3)}{\dfrac{Z_1Z_2 + Z_2Z_3 + Z_1Z_3}{Z_1 + Z_3} + Z_R} \qquad (3\text{-}80)$$

This current is the same as would flow for any value of Z_R, if Z_R were connected to a generator whose generated voltage is $EZ_3/(Z_1 + Z_3)$ and whose internal impedance is $(Z_1Z_2 + Z_2Z_3 + Z_1Z_3)/(Z_1 + Z_3)$.

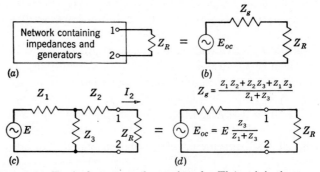

FIG. 3-21. Equivalent networks as given by Thévenin's theorem.

If Z_R is removed, the voltage at the terminals 1, 2 of the T network will be

$$E_{oc} = E\frac{Z_3}{Z_1 + Z_3} \qquad (3\text{-}81)$$

and if Z_R is removed and E is replaced by a short circuit, the impedance at the terminals 1, 2 will be

$$Z_g = Z_2 + \frac{Z_1Z_3}{Z_1 + Z_3} = \frac{Z_1Z_2 + Z_2Z_3 + Z_1Z_3}{Z_1 + Z_3} \qquad (3\text{-}82)$$

By comparing Eqs. (3-80) to (3-82), it will be seen that Eq. (3-80) gives the current which will flow if a generator whose emf is given by Eq. (3-81) and whose internal impedance is given by Eq. (3-82) is connected to the load Z_R.   This proves Thévenin's theorem.

While Thévenin's theorem as stated at the beginning of the section can be applied quite readily when the internal components of the generator and their configuration are known, another case often is encountered that requires some ingenuity in addition to the theorem. Say some generator is available in the laboratory, such as an audio oscillator. One wishes to determine its Thévenin's equivalent circuit in order to predict its behavior when serving as the voltage source for some complicated network. What measurements can be made on the oscillator which will allow one to synthesize the equivalent generator? Remember, one must also be sure the source is behaving as a linear network.

Two quantities must be determined, as may be seen from Fig. 3-21d: $|E_{oc}|$ (only the magnitude is required since the phase may be assumed zero) and Z_g. Feedback is employed in many typical oscillators; hence the internal emf cannot be made zero readily without changing the equivalent internal impedance; hence the determination of Z_g by a bridge measurement is not feasible Accurate a-c current measurements are difficult to make; so the problem resolves into: How many *voltage* measurements need be made? Since there are three unknowns, three voltage measurements will be required. The different values of voltage are obtained for different load conditions.

1. E_{oc} can be obtained by direct measurement under no-load conditions, i.e., with $Z_R = \infty$.

2. Let $Z_R = R_1 + jX_1$; then the voltage across the load will be

$$E_1 = E_{oc} \frac{R_1 + jX_1}{(R_g + R_1) + j(X_g + X_1)} \tag{3-83}$$

Taking magnitudes, squaring, and rearranging,

$$(R_g + R_1)^2 + (X_g + X_1)^2 = \left|\frac{E_{oc}}{E_1}\right|^2 (R_1^2 + X_1^2) \tag{3-84}$$

3. Let $Z_R = R_2 + jX_2$; then in a similar manner

$$(R_g + R_2)^2 + (X_g + X_2)^2 = \left|\frac{E_{oc}}{E_2}\right|^2 (R_2^2 + X_2^2) \tag{3-85}$$

Subtracting Eq. (3-85) from (3-84) and expanding,

$$R_g^2 + 2R_gR_1 + R_1^2 + X_g^2 + 2X_gX_1 + X_1^2 - R_g^2 - 2R_gR_2 - R_2^2$$
$$- X_g^2 - 2X_gX_2 - X_2^2 = \left|\frac{E_{oc}}{E_1}\right|^2 (R_1^2 + X_1^2) - \left|\frac{E_{oc}}{E_2}\right|^2 (R_2^2 + X_2^2)$$
$$\tag{3-86}$$

$$2(R_1 - R_2)R_g + 2(X_1 - X_2)X_g$$
$$= (R_1^2 + X_1^2)\left(\left|\frac{E_{oc}}{E_1}\right|^2 - 1\right) - (R_2^2 - X_2^2)\left(\left|\frac{E_{oc}}{E_2}\right|^2 - 1\right) \tag{3-87}$$

Now it is desirable to minimize the amount of calculation necessary in finding R_g and X_g; thus one tries to choose the loads intelligently. If one chooses $X_1 = X_2$, Eq. (3-87) may be solved for R_g in terms of known quantities. Then X_g may be determined from either Eq. (3-84) or Eq. (3-85). Notice, however, that both these equations are quadratics and there will be ambiguity in the sign of X_g.

If, on the other hand, one chooses $R_1 = R_2$, Eq. (3-87) may be solved for X_g with no ambiguity of sign.

$$X_g = \frac{(R_1{}^2 + X_1{}^2)(|E_{oc}/E_1|^2 - 1) - (R_1{}^2 + X_2{}^2)(|E_{oc}/E_1|^2 - 1)}{2(X_1 - X_2)} \tag{3-87a}$$

R_g may then be determined from either Eq. (3-84) or Eq. (3-85), and the choice of sign is no problem since R_g must be positive. Thus R_g, X_g (with proper sign), and $|E_{oc}|$ may be determined in terms of the three measured voltages.

Even further simplification results if $|E_1|$ and $|E_2|$ are measured with purely capacitive loads, making $R_1 = R_2 = 0$. Under these conditions

$$X_g = \frac{X_1{}^2(|E_{oc}/E_1|^2 - 1) - X_2{}^2(|E_{oc}/E_2|^2 - 1)}{2(X_1 - X_2)} \tag{3-88}$$

and from Eq. (3-84)

$$R_g{}^2 = \left|\frac{E_{oc}}{E_1}\right|^2 X_1{}^2 - (X_g + X_1)^2 \tag{3-89}$$

it being understood that X_1 and X_2 are *negative* quantities. A similar reduction in Eq. (3-87) cannot be obtained for inductive loads because the condition $R_1 = R_2 = 0$ cannot be satisfactorily approximated with physical inductors.

A familiar example of an application of Thévenin's theorem is the equivalent-plate-circuit theorem of electronics whereby the plate circuit of a vacuum tube operating under linear class A conditions is replaced by an equivalent generator μE_g in series with the dynamic plate resistance of the tube. These two equivalent series components may be used to calculate the a-c plate current flowing in the load. Use of the theorem allows the complicated structure of the vacuum tube to be replaced by an equivalent generator and series impedance, in so far as the calculation of a-c load current is concerned.

3-36. Norton's Theorem. A theorem suggested by E. L. Norton of the Bell Telephone Laboratories is: *The current in any impedance Z_R, connected to two terminals of a network, is the same as if Z_R were connected to a constant-current generator whose generated current is equal to the current which flows through the two terminals when these terminals are short-circuited, the constant-current generator being in shunt with an impedance equal to the impedance of the network looking back from the terminals in question.*

This theorem is simply the dual of Thévenin's theorem. It is illus-

trated by Fig. 3-22.   If one starts with Thévenin's theorem, it is apparent
from Fig. 3-22b that

$$I_R = \frac{E_{oc}}{Z_g + Z_R}$$

(3-90)

On short circuit the current would be

$$I_{sc} = \frac{E_{oc}}{Z_g}$$

(3-91)

In Fig. 3-22c the current through Z_R would be

$$I_R = \frac{I_{sc}Z_g}{Z_g + Z_R}$$

(3-92)

Combining Eqs. (3-91) and (3-92),

$$I_R = \frac{E_{oc}}{Z_g + Z_R}$$

(3-93)

which shows the equivalence of b and c in Fig. 3-22, and hence the equivalence of c to a.

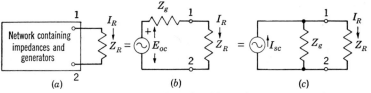

FIG. 3-22. Equivalent networks as given by Norton's theorem. (Compare with
Fig. 3-5.)

One of the commonest applications of Norton's theorem is the shunt
form of the equivalent plate circuit of a vacuum tube operated under
linear class A conditions.   Here the plate circuit of the tube is replaced
by a current generator $g_m E_g$ shunted by the dynamic plate resistance,
in so far as the calculation of a-c load current is concerned.   Another
use of the theorem was covered in Sec. 3-10.

3-37. Limitation on Thévenin's and Norton's Theorems.   The student
should pay particular care to note the wording of the two foregoing
theorems.   The equivalence afforded by Thévenin's or Norton's equivalent circuit holds for the *load current* and not for conditions within the
generator itself.   Failure to recognize the limitations of these theorems,
as well as of any other theorem, can lead to ridiculous results.

To illustrate this point, it will be shown that the power loss within the
generator of Fig. 3-21c is not the same as the power loss within the
equivalent generator of d.

Let all the impedances be pure resistances to simplify the calculations. Then in the former circuit under no-load conditions, that is, $Z_R \to \infty$, the power loss within the generator is $P_g = E^2/(R_1 + R_3)$, whereas the power loss within the Thévenin's equivalent generator under the same no-load conditions is zero.   Neither Thévenin's nor Norton's equivalent circuit can be used to calculate circuit efficiencies.

3-38. Other Theorems.   Other theorems will be developed in later chapters as subsequent theory is introduced.   Important examples are Foster's reactance theorem and the theorems governing the maximum transfer of power.

3-39. Special Properties of T and II Networks.   The amount of space that has been devoted to T and II networks indicates that they assume important status in the analysis of communication networks.   Because of their importance certain special properties that they exhibit will be investigated, properties that are primarily concerned with their impedance characteristics: the iterative, image, and characteristic impedances.

3-40. Asymmetrical T and II Networks.   The first impedance of the asymmetrical T network to be considered is the *iterative* impedance.   By definition: "The iterative impedance of a transducer is that impedance which, when connected to one pair of terminals, produces a like impedance at the other pair of terminals."   (ASA C42 65.08.387.)   By applying this definition to the asymmetrical T section, i.e., where $Z_1 \neq Z_2$, of Fig. 3-23, by definition if $Z_R = Z_{it}$, then $Z_{in} = Z_{it}$, and one may calculate Z_{it} in terms of the known components of the network.   Thus

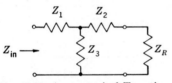

FIG. 3-23. Asymmetrical T section used for calculating Z_{it}.

$$Z_{in} = Z_1 + \frac{Z_3(Z_2 + Z_{it})}{Z_2 + Z_3 + Z_{it}} = Z_{it} \qquad (3\text{-}94)$$

Cross multiplying,

$$Z_1(Z_2 + Z_3 + Z_{it}) + Z_3(Z_2 + Z_{it}) = Z_{it}(Z_2 + Z_3 + Z_{it})$$
$$Z_{it}^2 + (Z_2 - Z_1)Z_{it} - (Z_1Z_2 + Z_2Z_3 + Z_1Z_3) = 0 \qquad (3\text{-}95)$$

and by the quadratic formula

$$Z_{it} = \frac{Z_1 - Z_2}{2} \pm \sqrt{\frac{(Z_1 - Z_2)^2}{4} + (Z_1Z_2 + Z_2Z_3 + Z_1Z_3)}$$

or $\qquad Z_{it} = \dfrac{Z_1 - Z_2}{2} \pm \sqrt{\dfrac{(Z_1 + Z_2)^2}{4} + (Z_1 + Z_2)Z_3} \qquad (3\text{-}96)$

As a general rule the choice of the sign in front of the radical is governed by the physical realizability of Z_{it}.   If the latter is to be built up as a passive physical structure, its real part must be positive, a condition that is usually satisfied by using the positive sign.

The student should observe that the value of Z_{it} given by Eq. (3-96) applies only when Z_1 is on the *input* side of the T section. If the T section is reversed, putting Z_2 on the input side, the new value of Z_{it} will differ from Eq. (3-96). The derivation of this new value is left as an exercise for the student.

The usefulness of Z_{it} as a concept in circuit analysis will become evident in the study of iterative networks, which are discussed in Chap. 6.

The iterative impedance of an asymmetrical Π section, i.e., one in which $Z_A \neq Z_C$, may be found in a similar manner, or one may utilize the principle of general duality between the T and Π networks and write for the iterative admittance, Y_A being on the input end,

$$Y_{it} = \frac{Y_A - Y_C}{2} \pm \sqrt{\frac{(Y_A + Y_C)^2}{4} + (Y_A + Y_C)Y_B} \qquad (3\text{-}97)$$

Another pair of impedances, the *image* impedances, also are characteristic of an asymmetrical four-terminal passive network. By definition: "The image impedances of a transducer are the impedances which will simultaneously terminate all of its inputs and outputs in such a way that at each of its inputs and outputs the impedances in both directions are equal." (ASA C42 65.08.390.)

More specifically for three- or four-terminal structures, such as the T and Π networks, the two image impedances, Z_{I1} and Z_{I2} are two values of impedance such that, if end 1 of the network is terminated in Z_{I1}, the input impedance at end 2 is Z_{I2}; and if end 2 is terminated in Z_{I2}, the input impedance at end 1 is Z_{I1}. From this definition their values can be determined in terms of the components of a T section as in Fig. 3-24.

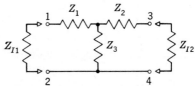

FIG. 3-24. Asymmetrical T section illustrating the image impedances.

The input impedance at terminals 1, 2, when Z_{I2} is connected between terminals 3, 4, is by definition, Z_{I1}. Therefore

$$Z_{I1} = Z_1 + \frac{(Z_2 + Z_{I2})Z_3}{Z_2 + Z_3 + Z_{I2}} \qquad (3\text{-}98)$$

Similarly, when Z_{I1} is connected to terminals 1, 2, the input impedance into terminals 3, 4 is Z_{I2}. Therefore

$$Z_{I2} = Z_2 + \frac{(Z_1 + Z_{I1})Z_3}{Z_1 + Z_3 + Z_{I1}} \qquad (3\text{-}99)$$

Solving these two equations simultaneously yields

$$Z_{I1} = \sqrt{\frac{Z_1 + Z_3}{Z_2 + Z_3} (Z_1Z_2 + Z_2Z_3 + Z_1Z_3)} \qquad (3\text{-}100)$$

$$Z_{I2} = \sqrt{\frac{Z_2 + Z_3}{Z_1 + Z_3} (Z_1Z_2 + Z_2Z_3 + Z_1Z_3)} \qquad (3\text{-}101)$$

The student may recognize the factors within the radical as the open- and short-circuit impedances of the T network. Hence alternative expressions for the image impedances of the T are

$$\begin{aligned} Z_{I1} &= \sqrt{Z_{o1}Z_{s1}} \\ Z_{I2} &= \sqrt{Z_{o2}Z_{s2}} \end{aligned} \qquad (3\text{-}102)$$

Corresponding equations for the image admittances of the asymmetrical Π network may be derived by the principle of general duality. It will be found that the concept of the image impedances of a network is of particular use in the design of impedance matching networks, Chap. 11.

3-41. Symmetrical T and Π Networks. The *symmetrical* T section is one in which the two series arms are equal, that is $Z_2 = Z_1$. Under this condition, from Eq. (3-96),

$$Z_{it} = \sqrt{Z_1^2 + 2Z_1Z_3} \qquad (3\text{-}103)$$

and from Eqs. (3-100) and (3-101)

$$Z_{I1} = Z_{I2} = \sqrt{Z_1^2 + 2Z_1Z_3} \qquad (3\text{-}104)$$

It may be observed from these equations that the image and iterative impedances of the symmetrical T network coalesce into a single value which is given a special designation, the *characteristic impedance*, Z_o. The same situation holds true for the symmetrical Π, where $Y_A = Y_C$.

It is the usual practice to adopt a special notation when one is dealing with the symmetrical T section. The two equal series arms are each designated $Z_1/2$ and the shunt arm Z_2 as shown in Fig. 3-25. It is convenient to derive expressions for the characteristic impedance in terms of this new notation; thus the characteristic impedance Z_o will be that value of impedance which, when it terminates the network, causes Z_{in} to be equal to Z_o. To state this mathematically, if the section of Fig. 3-25 is terminated in Z_o,

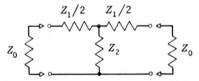

FIG. 3-25. Symmetrical T network illustrating the characteristic impedance.

$$Z_{in} = Z_o = \frac{Z_1}{2} + \frac{Z_2(Z_1/2 + Z_o)}{Z_1/2 + Z_2 + Z_o} \qquad (3\text{-}105)$$

Clearing and taking the square root,

$$Z_o = \sqrt{Z_1 Z_2 + \frac{Z_1{}^2}{4}} \qquad (3\text{-}106)$$

Equation (3-106) permits calculation of Z_o when Z_1 and Z_2 are known. It is not in optimum form for handling complex impedances, however. The rearranged form

$$Z_o = \sqrt{\frac{Z_1}{2}\left(2Z_2 + \frac{Z_1}{2}\right)} \qquad (3\text{-}106a)$$

is much better for this purpose, a fact that may be verified by working a numerical example.

Frequently the problem arises in the laboratory of determining the characteristic impedance of a symmetrical unknown network, i.e., one where Z_1 and Z_2 are not known. For such a situation the open- and short-circuit impedances of the network can be measured. Because of symmetry in the network

$$Z_{o1} = Z_{o2} = Z_{oc}$$
and
$$Z_{s1} = Z_{s2} = Z_{sc}$$

Then, since Z_o and the image impedances of a symmetrical network are identical,

$$Z_o = \sqrt{Z_{oc} Z_{sc}} \qquad (3\text{-}107)$$

Equation (3-107) applies to the symmetrical T section as well as to an unknown symmetrical network. It is suggested that the student verify this statement by evaluating Z_{oc} and Z_{sc} in terms of Z_1 and Z_2 to show the identity of Eqs. (3-106) and (3-107).

It follows, then, that the components of a symmetrical T section may be calculated in terms of the open- and short-circuit impedances. Using the new notation, Eqs. (3-53) to (3-55) reduce to

$$\frac{Z_1}{2} = Z_{oc} - Z_2 \qquad (3\text{-}108)$$
$$Z_2 = \sqrt{Z_{oc}(Z_{oc} - Z_{sc})}$$

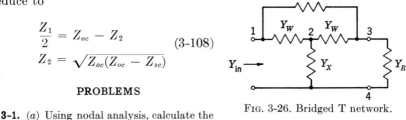

FIG. 3-26. Bridged T network.

PROBLEMS

3-1. (a) Using nodal analysis, calculate the input admittance between terminals 1, 4 of the bridged T network of Fig. 3-26.   (b) What is the input impedance between the same two terminals?   (c) What is the nodal transfer admittance between terminals 1, 4 and 3, 4?

3-2. Repeat Prob. 3-1, using mesh analysis.

3-3. (a) A two-terminal impedance consists of a 1,000-ohm resistance shunted by a 450-mh inductance. Calculate the components of an equivalent series network at 159 cycles. (b) Will the two networks be equivalent at 796 cycles?

3-4. An unknown network with two terminal pairs yields the following measurements, and I_2 lags I_1 when the load is resistive:

$$Z_{o1} = 0 \qquad\qquad Z_{o2} = +j200 \text{ ohms}$$
$$Z_{s1} = -j50 \text{ ohms} \qquad Z_{s2} = \infty$$

a. Calculate the components of an equivalent T network.

b. Repeat for an equivalent II network.

3-5. Reduce the bridged T network of Fig. 3-26 to an equivalent II network, and verify the results of Prob. 3-1a.

3-6. Construct a network involving eight resistance elements, and then reduce this network to an equivalent T section and an equivalent II section.

3-7. Construct a network involving eight impedance elements, each element to contain resistance and reactance, and then reduce this network to an equivalent T and an equivalent II section.

3-8. A four-terminal network that is known to be balanced to ground and to have inductive series arms yields the following data:

$$Z_{o1} = 10 + j10 \text{ ohms} \qquad Z_{s2} = 10 + j10 \text{ ohms}$$
$$Z_{s1} = 10 - j10 \text{ ohms}$$

Calculate the components of a *balanced* equivalent T section.

3-9. A transformer has two input and two output terminals with the following measurements:

$$Z_{o1} = 400 + j4,000 \qquad Z_{o2} = 100 + j1,000 \qquad Z_{s2} = 38 + j380$$

Determine the equivalent T and II sections.

3-10. A generator with a generated voltage of 1 volt and an internal impedance of $1,200 + j1,900$ ohms is connected to the input terminals of the transformer of Prob. 3-9. Determine from Thévenin's theorem the equivalent generator which can replace the network and actual generator as far as the load current is concerned.

3-11. It is desired to investigate I_L as a function of frequency in Fig. 3-27. This may be simplified if the network is reduced to an equivalent series circuit.

a. Derive the components of the equivalent series circuit as far as I_L is concerned.

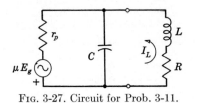

FIG. 3-27. Circuit for Prob. 3-11.

b. If the reactance of C is negligibly small as compared with r_p, what simplification can be made in the equivalent circuit?

c. What is the value of I_L, in polar form, under the conditions of (b)?

3-12. Show that the T-II transformations give circuits that are equivalent at all frequencies, provided that the T is constructed of inductances alone or capacitances alone.

3-13. The following data are obtained for an unknown generator at a frequency of 1 kc: (1) The open-circuit voltage is 10 volts. (2) The voltage across a 500-ohm-resistance load is 5.25 volts. (3) The voltage across a 250-ohm-resistance load is 3.46 volts.

a. Determine the components of the Thévenin equivalent generator.

b. Determine the components of the Norton equivalent generator.

3-14. (a) By calculating the power loss within the two equivalent generators calculated in Prob. 3-13, show that the equivalence does not hold within the generators: (b) By calculating the power dissipated in a 400-ohm resistive load, show that the equivalence does hold for the load.

3-15. Calculate the iterative and image impedances of a T network in which

$$Z_1 = 30 + j7.5 \text{ ohms} \qquad Z_3 = -j3{,}220 \text{ ohms}$$
$$Z_2 = 50 + j10 \text{ ohms}$$

3-16. For a certain network

$$Z_{o1} = Z_{o2} = 100 - j7.2 \text{ ohms}$$
$$Z_{s1} = 90 + j22 \text{ ohms}$$

Derive the components of the equivalent balanced T section at $\omega = 5{,}000$ radians/sec.

CHAPTER 4

RESONANCE

In the networks used in power-distribution systems, resistance and inductive reactance play the major role, while capacitive reactances are of only minor importance. This restricted use of capacitive reactances is due to the large size and cost of capacitances which could handle a reasonable number of volt-amperes at commercial frequencies.

Inductive reactances increase and capacitive reactances decrease as the frequency is raised; therefore even the inductive reactance or capacitive susceptance of a length of wire connecting two elements cannot be neglected at high frequencies. Use is therefore made of the fact that a capacitive susceptance can be neutralized by an inductance in parallel, or a series inductive reactance can be nullified by a series capacitive reactance of the same value. This phenomenon is called "resonance."

Because of the fact that one type of reactance increases with frequency while the other decreases, the total reactance or susceptance can be reduced to zero at only one frequency. This gives an important use of resonance, in that, by its means, circuits can be designed which will transmit freely certain frequencies and greatly impede others. This enables the use of a single medium, such as a telephone line or free space, for the transmission of several messages simultaneously, selective circuits at the receivers picking out those bands of frequencies associated with a given message for routing to its proper destination.

Two types of resonance have been referred to: (1) series resonance, or the neutralization of series *reactance*, and (2) parallel resonance, or the neutralization of parallel *susceptance*. Parallel resonance is often and preferably called "antiresonance" to distinguish it from series resonance. Either or both types of resonance may occur at different frequencies one or more times in a given network, the number of such resonant points depending on the number and character of the meshes.

4-1. Series Resonance. The simplest type of resonant circuit is a series circuit consisting of resistance, inductance, and capacitance as shown in Fig. 4-1. In such a series circuit *resonance* is defined to be the condition that obtains when the total net reactance is zero. The resonant frequency f_r is that value of frequency at which resonance occurs.

Phasor diagrams of the series resonant circuit are also drawn in this figure for the three cases where the frequency is less than, equal to, and greater than the resonant frequency. It will be seen that, when the reactance of the inductor is equal to the reactance of the capacitor, the phasor sum of the voltage drops across the inductor and the capacitor is zero. The total voltage, which is the phasor sum of the individual drops, is then a minimum for a given current and equal to the drop due to the resistance. If the frequency is increased above resonance, the total reactance will increase, so that for a given current the voltage will be greater. Likewise, if the frequency is decreased below resonance, the total reactance and voltage will increase again.

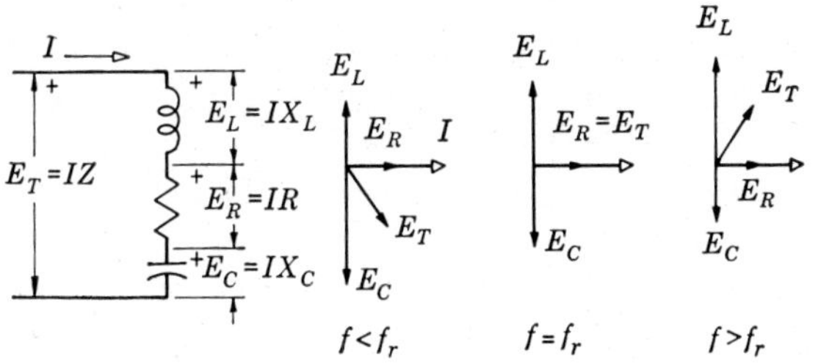

Fig. 4-1. Resonance in a series circuit.

The total impedance of a series circuit can be determined by adding the individual impedances in the complex form

$$Z = R + j\left(\omega L - \frac{1}{\omega C}\right) \tag{4-1}$$

It can be seen by inspection that $|Z|$ is a minimum when

$$\omega L = \frac{1}{\omega C} \tag{4-2}$$

or the resonant frequency is

$$f_r = \frac{1}{2\pi \sqrt{LC}} \tag{4-3}$$

At this frequency the reactive term, which is the only one which varies with frequency, disappears. At resonance, therefore,

$$Z_r = R \tag{4-4}$$

and the circuit has unity power factor. At lower frequencies $1/\omega C > \omega L$, and the total reactance is capacitive, while at frequencies higher than resonance $\omega L > 1/\omega C$, and the circuit is inductive. In determining how the reactance of such a circuit varies with frequency, use can be made of sketches showing the way each individual element behaves.

4-2. Reactance Curves. A curve is drawn in Fig. 4-2a, showing the variation with frequency of the reactance of a capacitor. This is the hyperbola $X_C = -1/\omega C$. Figure 4-2b is the corresponding curve for the reactance of an inductor, which is the straight line $X_L = \omega L$. In Fig. 4-2c these are combined and added to get the total reactance X_T. The frequency at which the curve crosses the abscissa is the point of resonance.

In actual circuits pure reactances are not present, the resistance R being largely a part of the inductor, but the general considerations are the same, except that the voltage measured across any physical element would be the phasor sum of its IX and IR drops.

The curves of Fig. 4-2 may be presented in another form to give a handy nomogram for the calculation of reactance and resonant frequency.

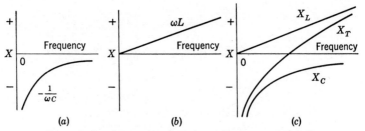

FIG. 4-2. Reactance sketches of a series resonant circuit.

This nomogram is derived by plotting the reactance vs. frequency curves on log-log paper. Consider the reactance of the inductor L,

$$X_L = \omega L = 2\pi L f \tag{4-5}$$

and taking logarithms

$$\log X_L = \log 2\pi L + \log f \tag{4-6}$$

Eq. (4-6) can be seen to plot as a straight line with unit slope and with y intercept equal to $\log 2\pi L$. In a similar manner the reactance of the capacitor C is[1]

$$X_C = \frac{-1}{\omega C} = \frac{-1}{2\pi C f} \tag{4-7}$$

---

[1] In accordance with the recommendations of the ASA the symbol X_C is used here to designate the capacitive reactance, $-1/\omega C$. There is variance in the past literature on this point, in many cases the usage being $X_C = +1/\omega C$. The student in reading the literature should make a practice of checking which sign is used by each author.

X_L is defined to be $+\omega L$. A general reactance X carries its own sign. The reactance of an inductance and capacitance in series is written $X = X_L + X_C$. Correspondingly $B_L = -1/\omega L$ and $B_C = +\omega C$. The susceptance of an inductance and capacitance in parallel is $B = B_L + B_C$.

and taking logarithms of the magnitudes

$$\log |X_C| = \log \frac{1}{2\pi C} - \log f \qquad (4\text{-}8)$$

Equation (4-8) also plots as a straight line with negative unit slope and with y intercept equal to $\log (1/2\pi C)$. If, now, Eqs. (4-6) and (4-8)

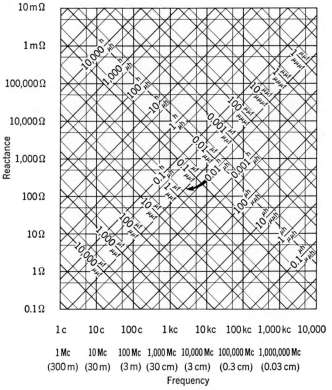

FIG. 4-3. Reactance chart. Always use corresponding, i.e., upper or lower, scales. (*General Radio Company*.)

are plotted on log-log paper for different values of L and C, the family of straight lines of Fig. 4-3 results. This nomogram may be used for determining reactance and resonant frequency as well, for Eq. (4-2) is represented on the figure by the intersection of the two curves representing the particular values of L and C involved.

4-3. Loci of Impedances and Admittances of Series Circuit. The locus of the terminal point of the impedance phasor, as the frequency is changed, is a straight line as illustrated in Fig. 4-4a. Since

$$Z = R + j\left(\omega L - \frac{1}{\omega C}\right)$$

this locus will be parallel to the reactance axis at a distance R. As the frequency is raised, the impedance phasor will be represented successively by Z_1, Z_2, Z_3, Z_4, Z_5, . . . and will extend from the origin to points on the vertical locus through R.

The locus of the corresponding admittance will now be determined. The derivation will be carried out on a geometrical basis and then will be related to the electrical circuit. In Fig. 4-4b the circle $OBGO$ is constructed to that its diameter $OG = 1/OR$. It is desired to find the relationship between any point X on the vertical line through R, and a point

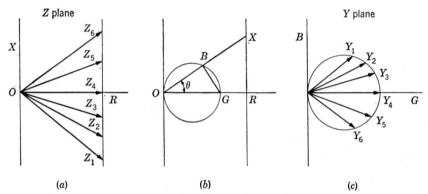

(a)   (b)   (c)

Fig. 4-4. Impedance and admittance loci of a series resonant circuit.

B, which is the point of intersection of the straight line OX and the circle. The angle OBG, being inscribed in a semicircle, is 90°. Then because the triangles OBG and ORX are similar

$$\frac{OB}{OG} = \frac{OR}{OX} \qquad (4\text{-}9)$$

But by the construction of the circle

$$OG = \frac{1}{OR} \qquad \text{or} \qquad OG \cdot OR = 1 \qquad (4\text{-}10)$$

Therefore

$$OB = \frac{1}{OX} \qquad (4\text{-}11)$$

Since X is *any* point on the vertical line, it may be concluded that the transformation [Eq. (4-11)] maps the vertical line, point by point, into the circle.

These geometrical results may now be applied to electrical circuits. For any two-terminal network, the impedance and admittance are related by

$$Y = \frac{1}{Z} \qquad \text{or} \qquad |Y|\underline{/\theta_y} = \frac{1}{|Z|\underline{/\theta_z}}$$

whence

$$Y = \frac{1}{|Z|} \qquad \theta_y = -\theta_z \qquad (4\text{-}12)$$

Since the electrical circuit requires a change of sign in the angle θ, the lower half of the impedance line maps into the upper half of the admittance circle and the upper half of the impedance line maps into the lower semicircle.

Now, the variation of Z with frequency for the series resonant circuit is given by a vertical line in the Z plane representing a constant value of R and a varying value of X. Thus the corresponding admittance will be represented by a circle of diameter $G = 1/R$ lying along the real axis of the admittance plane. This situation is shown at a and c in Fig. 4-4, where corresponding values of Z and Y are represented by corresponding subscripts. This circle diagram has important applications in electromechanical impedances such as telephone receivers, piezoelectric crystals, and magnetostriction oscillators, where resonant mechanical systems reflect their characteristics back into the electrical networks, and in the analysis of induction and synchronous rotating machinery. The transformation $Y = 1/Z$ is also of aid in the study of transmission lines.

The principle that has just been illustrated, whereby the straight line representing Eq. (4-1) in the complex Z plane is mapped into a circle in the complex Y plane by the transformation $Y = 1/Z$, is but one example of the so-called linear transformation of complex-variable theory. This transformation

$$y = \frac{\alpha + \beta z}{\gamma + \delta z} \tag{4-13}$$

where α, β, γ, and δ are complex constants, maps circles in the complex z plane into circles of the complex y plane, it being understood that straight lines are circles of infinite radius. If α, β, and γ be set equal to zero and δ equal to unity, Eq. (4-13) reduces to the special case specified by Eq. (4-12).

4-4. Quality Factor Q. The equations that govern resonance may be simplified by introducing the quality factor Q of the resonant circuit. This quantity will now be defined.

Basically Q is defined as the quality factor of an inductor and as such is a measure of the efficiency of energy storage in the inductor when an alternating current is passed through the inductor. Mathematically, the definition is

$$Q = 2\pi \, \frac{\text{max energy stored}}{\text{energy dissipated/cycle}} \tag{4-14}$$

or, multiplying numerator and denominator by f, the frequency of the current,

$$Q = \omega \, \frac{\text{max energy stored}}{\text{avg power dissipated}} \tag{4-14a}$$

In this book, the Q of an inductor will be designated by the subscript

L. Q_L may be expressed in terms of the resistive and inductive components of the inductor and in terms of the frequency of the current. To illustrate this, let a current of rms value I and of frequency f flow through the inductor represented in Fig. 4-5a. R and L are, respectively, the

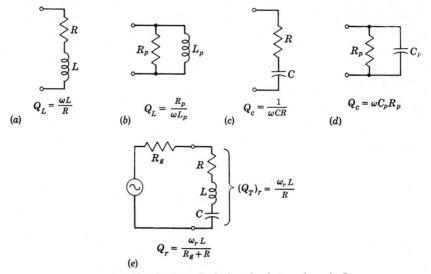

FIG. 4-5. Circuits for calculating the figure of merit Q.

series resistance and inductance of the inductor at frequency f. Then

$$\text{Max energy stored/cycle} = \frac{L}{2}\hat{I}^2$$

$$= \frac{L}{2}|\sqrt{2}\,I|^2 = L|I|^2 \tag{4-15}$$

and

$$\text{Avg power dissipated} = |I|^2R \tag{4-16}$$

Substitution of Eqs. (4-15) and (4-16) into Eq. (4-14a) reduces the quality factor of the inductor to

$$Q_L = \frac{\omega L}{R} \tag{4-17}$$

It should be noticed that Q_L depends upon frequency, and hence a numerical value of Q_L has meaning only when the corresponding value of frequency is known. It might seem from Eq. (4-17) that Q_L varies linearly with f. This is not generally true, however, because L and R also vary with frequency in physical inductors. The reasons for this variation are discussed later in the chapter.

At any frequency an inductor may also be specified in terms of its effective *shunt* resistive and inductive components, R_p and L_p, as shown in Fig. 4-5b. It is left as an exercise for the student to show that the expression for Q_L in terms of these shunt components is

$$Q_L = \frac{R_p}{\omega L_p} \tag{4-18}$$

While the concept of Q was originally applied to inductors, it may be extended so that the efficiency of energy storage in a capacitor, or in any two-terminal network for that matter, may be expressed in terms of the circuit components and frequency. Thus, for example, if the series resistance and capacitance of a capacitor are, respectively, R and C as in Fig. 4-5c, evaluation of Eq. (4-14a) when an rms current $|I|$ of frequency f flows through the capacitor shows the quality factor of the capacitor to be

$$Q_C = \frac{1}{\omega C R} \tag{4-19}$$

On the other hand, if the capacitor is represented by its *shunt* components R_p and C_p, the quality factor becomes

$$Q_C = \omega C_p R_p \tag{4-19a}$$

In practice, Q_C is often replaced by its reciprocal, the *dissipation factor*.

A further extension of the definition of Q to a two-terminal network containing both L and C is often of aid in the analysis of communication circuits. Thus in Fig. 4-5e it is possible to determine the quality factor Q_T of the circuit comprising R, L, and C in series. It should be noticed, however, that Eq. (4-14a) involves the *maximum* energy stored per cycle; hence Q_T will be expressed in terms of either L or C depending upon whether the frequency of the current is greater than or less than the resonant frequency of the combination. This is illustrated in the following example:

In the series resonant circuit of Fig. 4-5e the maximum energy stored per cycle in the capacitance is

$$(W_c)_m = \frac{|\hat{E}_c|^2 C}{2} = |E_c|^2 C = \frac{|I|^2}{\omega^2 C}$$

and the maximum energy stored per cycle in the inductance is

$$(W_L)_m = |I|^2 L$$

at frequencies below resonance $f < f_r$ and $\omega L < 1/\omega C$. Hence

$$(W_c)_m > (W_L)_m$$

Thus below resonance, by Eq. (4-14a),

$$Q_T = \frac{1}{\omega C R} \qquad f < f_r$$

On the other hand, above resonance $(W_C)_m < (W_L)_m$, and the circuit quality factor becomes

$$Q_T = \frac{\omega L}{R} \qquad f > f_r$$

At the resonant frequency the maximum energy stored is the same for both the inductance and capacitance, and the quality factor may be expressed in terms of either L or C as

$$(Q_T)_r = \frac{\omega_r L}{R} = \frac{1}{\omega_r C R} \tag{4-20}$$

In certain cases the quality factor of a complete circuit including the generator resistance in Fig. 4-5e is required.   In such a case the resistance used is the net series resistance in the circuit, or, for the figure,

$$Q_r = \frac{\omega_r L}{R_g + R} \tag{4-21}$$

This in turn may be related to the Q_T of Eq. (4-20) by dividing numerator and denominator by R to give

$$Q_r = \frac{\omega_r L/R}{1 + R_g/R} = \frac{(Q_T)_r}{1 + R_g/R} \tag{4-22}$$

Several applications of the concept of inductor or circuit Q in the study of resonance will be apparent in the next section.   Methods for measuring the quality factor will be discussed later in the chapter.

4-5. Sharpness of Resonance.   It has been shown in a previous section that the admittance of the series resonant circuit as a function of frequency plots as a circle in the complex Y plane.   An alternative and very useful representation may be obtained by plotting $|Y|$ and θ_y as a function of frequency in rectangular coordinates as in Fig. 4-6.   The ordinate of Fig. 4-6a is also a plot of current magnitude if the voltage is assumed to be constant.   If the resistance of the series circuit is increased, the admittance will be decreased at all frequencies, but much more markedly in the neighborhood of the resonant frequency.   A flatter curve will be obtained under these conditions.   In Fig. 4-6 curve 2 is drawn for a combination with higher resistance than curve 1.   Curve 1 will discriminate more in favor of frequencies in the region of the resonant frequency and therefore is called a "more selective" circuit.

In order to specify the degree of sharpness, it is customary to compute the frequency band within which the admittance or current exceeds a certain proportion of the maximum.   This proportion may be arbitrarily assumed; it is only necessary in comparing different curves that the same basis be used for each curve.   The most convenient limiting points to assume are those where the reactance has increased from its value of zero at resonance to a magnitude equal to the resistance. This will occur at two frequencies, one above and the other below the resonant frequency. At these points since $|X| = R$ and $Z = \sqrt{R^2 + X^2}$, $Z = \sqrt{2}\,R$, the admittance is 70.7 per cent of its maximum value and the power $|I|^2R$ for a given voltage is one-half the value at resonance. These two frequencies, which shall be designated f_1 and f_2, are termed the lower- and upper-half-power frequencies, respectively.

In most radio-frequency (rf) circuits, the reactances of the inductor and capacitor are individually much larger than the value of the resistance, so that, in the neighborhood of resonance, the reactance is a small difference between two relatively large quantities. It is preferable and convenient in the region of resonance to calculate this difference directly.

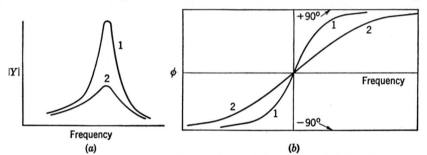

(a)   (b)

FIG. 4-6. Resonance curve of a circuit containing R, L, and C in series.

In Fig. 4-2a the slope of the reactance curve for the capacitance is

$$\frac{dX_c}{df} = + \frac{1}{2\pi f^2 C} \tag{4-23}$$

In Fig. 4-2b the slope of the reactance curve for the inductance is

$$\frac{dX_L}{df} = 2\pi L \tag{4-24}$$

At the resonant frequency

$$2\pi f_r L = \frac{1}{2\pi f_r C}$$

or

$$2\pi L = \frac{1}{2\pi f_r^2 C} \tag{4-25}$$

Therefore, from Eqs. (4-23) to (4-25), at the resonant frequency

$$\left(\frac{dX_c}{df}\right)_r = \left(\frac{dX_L}{df}\right)_r \tag{4-26}$$

which means that, if a change of frequency Δf is made in the neighborhood of resonance, the capacitive reactance will increase *algebraically* in a positive direction the same amount as the inductive reactance. Since the capacitive reactance is negative, its *absolute* value will *decrease* by the amount that the inductive reactance increases. The increase in inductive reactance of an inductance when the frequency is increased by an amount Δf is

$$\Delta X_L = 2\pi \, \Delta f \, L$$

Therefore, the change in the reactance of a series circuit in the region of resonance, for a change in frequency Δf, is *twice* the increase in inductive reactance alone, and so

$$\Delta X = 4\pi \, \Delta f \, L \qquad (4\text{-}27)$$

This expression will simplify computations of selectivity.

In the case where the frequency band is to be determined, within which the power is equal to, or greater than, one-half the maximum power, let f_1 equal the lower frequency at which the power dissipated is one-half the value at resonance. Let f_2 equal the higher frequency at which the power dissipated is one-half the value at resonance. Let f_r be the frequency at resonance. It has been explained that at resonance the reactance will be zero and at f_1 and f_2 the reactance will be equal to the resistance. Furthermore $\Delta f = f_r - f_1 = f_2 - f_r$. Then by Eq. (4-27)

$$4\pi(f_r - f_1)L = R$$
$$4\pi(f_2 - f_r)L = R$$

Therefore
$$f_2 - f_1 = \frac{R}{2\pi L} \qquad (4\text{-}28)$$

The sharpness of resonance in a circuit is therefore dependent on the ratio R/L and may be related to the quality factor of the series resonant circuit.

Let
$$BW = f_2 - f_1 = \text{half-power bandwidth} \qquad (4\text{-}28a)$$

Divide both sides of Eq. (4-28) by f_r. Since BW is the difference between the two half-power points,

$$\frac{BW}{f_r} = \frac{f_2 - f_1}{f_r} = \frac{R}{2\pi f_r L} = \frac{1}{Q_r} \qquad (4\text{-}29)$$

The *percentage* frequency discrimination of a resonant circuit BW/f_r is therefore inversely proportional to the quantity Q_r.

At times it is desirable to examine the variation in *voltage* across individual components. For example, if the grid circuit of a vacuum tube is connected across the capacitor, the voltage across the capacitor would determine the current in the plate circuit. Figure 4-7 shows the resonance curve for the three variables $|E_L|$, $|E_C|$, and $|I|$ of Fig. 4-1. It will be observed that the three curves have practically the same sharpness, the two voltage curves being tipped slightly from the current curves. All three curves check Eq. (4-29) for sharpness of resonance.

It will be observed from Fig. 4-7 that $|E_L|$ and $|E_C|$ maximize at practically the resonant frequency, a phenomenon that has been termed the "resonance rise of voltage." It may be shown that this maximum value

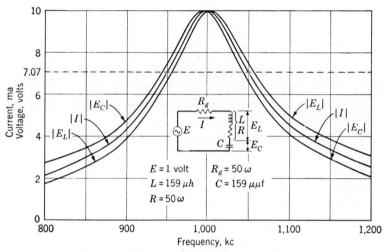

Fig. 4-7. Resonance curves of a series circuit.

of voltage is determined by the circuit Q and the applied voltage. At resonance

$$I = \frac{E}{R_g + R} = \frac{E}{R_t} \tag{4-30}$$

and the voltage across the capacitor will have the magnitude

$$|E_C| = \frac{|I|}{\omega C} = \frac{|E|}{\omega C R_t} \tag{4-31}$$

But at resonance $\omega_r L = 1/\omega_r C$. Therefore

$$|E_C| = |E|\frac{\omega_r L}{R_t} = |E|Q_r \tag{4-32}$$

A similar *approximation* holds for the voltage across the inductor. Remembering that any physical inductor has resistance, say, R as in Fig. 4-7, one may write for the voltage magnitude across the inductor at resonance

$$|E_L| = \frac{|E|}{R_t} \sqrt{R^2 + X_L{}^2} \tag{4-33}$$

Now if the quality factor of the inductor at f_r satisfies the inequality

$$Q_L = \frac{X_L}{R} \geq 10 \qquad f = f_r \qquad (4\text{-}34)$$

Eq. (4-33) becomes approximately

$$|E_L| \approx |E| \frac{X_L}{R_t} = |E|Q_L \qquad (4\text{-}35)$$

Equations (4-32) and (4-35) may be used to verify the data of Fig. 4-7.

4-6. Effect of Source Impedance. For purposes of comparison with curves which will be shown later in connection with the discussion of antiresonance, Fig. 4-8 shows the same three variables for the extreme condition where the generator is a constant-current one. In a constant-

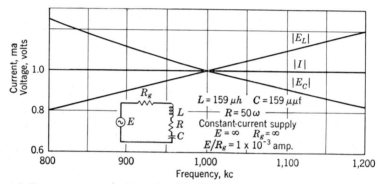

Fig. 4-8. Resonance curves of a series circuit driven by a constant-current generator.

current supply the generated voltage is infinite, and the internal resistance is also infinite, but the ratio of generated voltage to the internal resistance is finite and equal to the current supplied. It will be seen that in Fig. 4-8 the series circuit does not provide any frequency discrimination whatever under this condition.

4-7. The Universal Resonance Curve. Figure 4-6 shows the selectivity curves for two series resonant circuits having different values of Q. While the curves exhibit different peak values and different values of selectivity, still they have the same *shape*. This must be true because they both are described by the same basic equation

$$I = \frac{E}{R + j(\omega L - 1/\omega C)}$$

where R is the total series resistance of the circuit, including the generator, and it can be made easier to see if the basic equation is reduced to *normalized* form. Thus if current is divided by its peak or resonant value, and if frequency is divided by the resonant frequency, both these quantities will be reduced to a dimensionless, "per unit" basis and a normalized equation will result that is applicable to *all* series resonant circuits. The process of normalization may be carried out as follows:

Factor out R from the denominator of the basic equation.

$$I = \frac{E}{R} \frac{1}{1 + j(1/R)(\omega L - 1/\omega C)} \tag{4-36}$$

Factor out $\omega_r L$ from the second term in the denominator.

$$I = \frac{E}{R} \frac{1}{1 + j(\omega_r L/R)(\omega/\omega_r - 1/\omega \omega_r LC)} \tag{4-37}$$

But

$$\frac{E}{R} = I_r \qquad \frac{\omega_r L}{R} = Q_r \qquad \frac{1}{LC} = \omega_r{}^2 \tag{4-38}$$

Substituting Eqs. (4-38) into Eq. (4-37), and dividing through by I_r, there results

$$\frac{I}{I_r} = \frac{1}{1 + jQ_r(f/f_r - f_r/f)} \tag{4-39}$$

Equation (4-39) is in the desired normalized form and may be used for slide-rule calculations of both the magnitude and the phase of the current ratio. It should be noticed that the derivation of the equation assumes R to be independent of frequency in the vicinity of resonance. Actually R is frequency-dependent, but the use of the circuit Q defined at resonance eliminates R from the equation so that, in effect, the assumption is made that the circuit quality factor remains constant at its resonant frequency value. The validity of this latter assumption is discussed subsequently in the chapter.

While Eq. (4-39) is in a form that yields to ready calculation by the slide rule, it is of interest to reduce it formally into polar form, viz.,

$$\left| \frac{I}{I_r} \right| = \frac{1}{\sqrt{1 + [Q_r(f/f_r - f_r/f)]^2}} \tag{4-40a}$$

and

$$\theta = -\arctan Q_r \left(\frac{f}{f_r} - \frac{f_r}{f} \right) \tag{4-40b}$$

If Eq. (4-40a), giving the normalized current response of the series resonant circuit, is plotted with f/f_r as the independent variable, it will be found that the resulting curve displays *geometric symmetry*, that is to say, $|I/I_r|$ will have the same value at two frequencies, f_a and f_b, whose geometric mean is f_r, the resonant frequency. This may be demonstrated as follows:

Let two frequencies be chosen such that

$$f_a f_b = f_r{}^2 \tag{4-41}$$

Then the quantity $f_a/f_r - f_r/f_a$ is equal to

$$\left(\frac{f_a}{f_r} - \frac{f_r}{f_a}\right)^* = \frac{f_r^2}{f_b f_r} - \frac{f_r f_b}{f_r^2} = -\left(\frac{f_b}{f_r} - \frac{f_r}{f_b}\right)^* \qquad (4\text{-}42)$$

It follows at once, because of the identity between the two quantities marked with an asterisk, that $|I/I_r|$ in Eq. (4-40a) will have the same

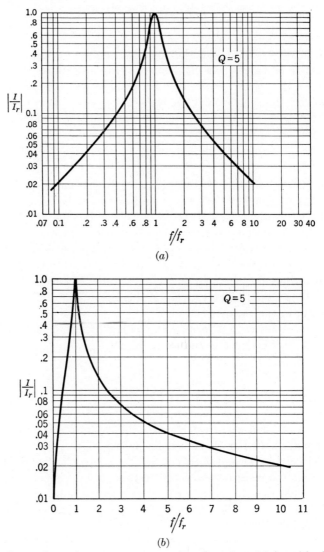

Fig. 4-9. Comparison of resonance curves plotted against (a) logarithmic and (b) linear frequency scales.

value at f_a and f_b; the property of geometric symmetry has been proved. It should be noticed also that, at f_a and f_b, any two frequencies whose geometric mean is f_r, θ will have the same magnitude but opposite sign.

One of the principal consequences of geometric symmetry is that Eq. (4-40a) displays mirror symmetry when plotted against a *logarithmic* frequency scale. This is illustrated in Fig. 4-9a, where Eq. (4-40a) is plotted for $Q_r = 5$. The same data are plotted against a linear frequency scale at b in the figure to show the asymmetry that results when a curve having geometric symmetry is plotted against a linear frequency scale. It should be mentioned that both curves are plotted with a logarithmic ordinate scale to allow the convenient presentation of the almost 100-to-1 range of values present. Such a procedure does not affect the symmetry along the horizontal axis, for more or less obvious reasons.

If, however, the second curve is inspected closely, it will be observed that *in the vicinity of resonance*, i.e., for values of f/f_r nearly equal to 1, *the curve appears to be symmetrical*, as near as the eye can tell. Use is made of this fact to derive a simplified approximation of the universal resonance curve [Eq. (4-39)], which may be used for calculations *near resonance*. This approximate form will now be derived, and it will be shown over what range of frequency it is valid.

Let δ be defined as the fractional deviation from resonance, i.e.,

$$\delta = \frac{f - f_r}{f_r} \tag{4-43}$$

Then, adding 1 to both sides of the equation,

$$1 + \delta = 1 + \frac{f - f_r}{f_r} = \frac{f}{f_r} \tag{4-44}$$

whence
$$\frac{f}{f_r} - \frac{f_r}{f} = 1 + \delta - \frac{1}{1 + \delta} = \frac{1 + 2\delta + \delta^2 - 1}{1 + \delta}$$

$$= \delta \frac{2 + \delta}{1 + \delta} \tag{4-45}$$

If, then, the frequency is restricted to values near resonance so that $|\delta| \ll 1$, one has the approximation

$$\frac{f}{f_r} - \frac{f_r}{f} \approx 2\delta \tag{4-46}$$

and the previous exact equation (4-39) becomes

$$\frac{I}{I_r} \approx \frac{1}{1 + j2Q_r\delta} \tag{4-47}$$

and the polar components of I/I_r become

$$\left| \frac{I}{I_r} \right| \approx \frac{1}{\sqrt{1 + (2Q_r\delta)^2}} \tag{4-48}$$

$$\theta \approx - \arctan 2Q_r\delta \tag{4-49}$$

Equation (4-48) displays *arithmetic* symmetry, i.e., at any two frequencies f_a and f_b, such that $f_r - f_a = f_b - f_r$, $|I/I_r|$ has the same value. The proof of this proposition is left as an exercise for the student.

Equations (4-48) and (4-49) are plotted in Fig. 4-10 to give the universal resonance curves. It should be noticed that $Q_r\delta$, rather than δ alone,

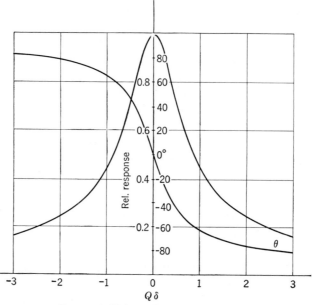

FIG. 4-10. Universal resonance curves.

is used as the independent variable so that the curves are independent of the specific value of Q_r. It must be stressed again that the curves are based on the assumption that $|\delta| \ll 1$.

A brief explanation about the sign of θ in Fig. 4-10 and Eq. (4-49) may be helpful. From the equation it is seen that θ is the angle of I relative to I_r. If θ is negative, I lags I_r. But at resonance current and applied voltage are in phase; thus *negative* θ implies current lagging the applied voltage, or a *positive* phase angle in the circuit.

4-8. Approximate Form Errors. Some idea of the magnitude of the errors introduced by use of the approximate equation (4-48) may be obtained from Fig. 4-11, where the exact and approximate equations have been plotted for a Q_r of 5 and of 10. The following facts may be observed from the curves: (1) The approximate curves are tipped to the left about the point of maximum response so that for any given response the frequencies given by the approximate equation are lower than those given by the exact equation.   (2) The difference between the exact and approximate frequencies decreases as resonance is approached.   (3) The difference between the exact and approximate frequencies decreases as Q_r is raised.   These points may be verified analytically from the work that follows.

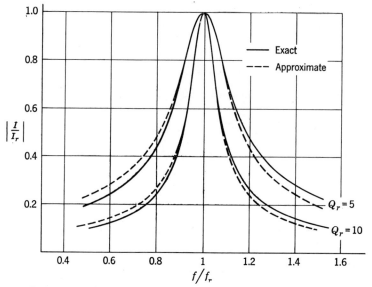

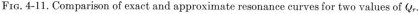

FIG. 4-11. Comparison of exact and approximate resonance curves for two values of Q_r.

Interestingly enough the approximate equation may be used to determine the bandwidth, say, $(\Delta f)_a$, between the two frequencies at which the normalized response has the value $1/a$.   From Eq. (4-40a)

$$\frac{Q_r}{f_r}\left(f_a - \frac{f_r^2}{f_a}\right) = \frac{Q_r}{f_r}(\Delta f)_a = \sqrt{a^2 - 1}$$

whence $(\Delta f)_a = \dfrac{f_r}{Q_r}\sqrt{a^2 - 1} = (BW)\sqrt{a^2 - 1}$ exact   (4-50a)

From the approximate form, Eqs. (4-43) and (4-48),

$$\frac{2Q_r}{f_r}(f_a - f_r) = \frac{Q_r}{f_r}(\Delta f)_a = \sqrt{a^2 - 1}$$

$$(\Delta f)_a = (BW)\sqrt{a^2 - 1}   \text{approximate}   (4\text{-}50b)$$

Since Eqs. (4-50a) and (4-50b) are identical, the statement is proved.

If, however, the actual frequencies at which the normalized response is $1/a$ are required, then the approximate, arithmetic symmetry form does introduce an error, the error being a function of Q_r and the value of normalized response.   Let

f'_b = exact frequency *below* resonance at which relative response is $1/a$

f_b = approximate frequency *below* resonance at which relative response is $1/a$

Let it be required to find the value of Q_r for which the difference between these two frequencies does not exceed $100k$ per cent.   That is,

$$\frac{f'_b - f_b}{f'_b} \le k \qquad \text{or} \qquad \frac{f_b}{f'_b} = y \ge 1 - k$$

Then from Eq. (4-40a)

$$Q_r \left(\frac{f'_b}{f_r} - \frac{f_r}{f'_b} \right) = - \sqrt{a^2 - 1}$$

the negative sign being chosen because $f'_b/f_r < f_r/f'_b$.   Then

$$f'_b = f_r \left(- \frac{\sqrt{a^2 - 1}}{2Q_r} \pm \sqrt{\frac{a^2 - 1}{4Q_r^2} + 1} \right)$$

The positive sign must be chosen for f'_b to be positive.   Expanding the second radical by the binomial expansion,

$$f'_b \approx f_r \left(- \frac{\sqrt{a^2 - 1}}{2Q_r} + 1 + \frac{a^2 - 1}{8Q_r^2} \right) \tag{4-51}$$

In a similar manner from Eqs. (4-43) and (4-48) one obtains

$$2Q_r \frac{(f_b - f_r)}{f_r} = - \sqrt{a^2 - 1}$$

or
$$f_b = f_r \left(1 - \frac{\sqrt{a^2 - 1}}{2Q_r} \right) \tag{4-52}$$

Then substituting for y in terms of f'_b and f_b and solving for Q_r,

$$Q_r = \frac{\sqrt{a^2 - 1}}{4} \left(1 \pm \sqrt{1 + \frac{2}{1/y - 1}} \right) \tag{4-53}$$

where the positive sign will be chosen to minimize the error introduced by using only the first two terms of the binomial expansion in Eq. (4-51).

By the hypothesis, $y \ge 1 - k$.   Substituting into Eq. (4-53), one finally obtains

$$Q_r \ge \frac{\sqrt{a^2 - 1}}{4} \left(1 + \sqrt{1 + \frac{2}{k}} \right) \tag{4-54}$$

Equation (4-54) is plotted in Fig. 4-12 for $k = 0.01$ and 0.03.   For example, if Q_r is 25, frequencies determined by the approximate equation are correct to 1 per cent within the $\frac{1}{10}$ relative response points.

4-9. Tuning: Series Resonance with Variable Capacitance.   In the foregoing discussion of resonance it has been assumed that the circuit parameters remained fixed while the frequency of the applied voltage was varied to give a selectivity curve. Resonance was said to occur when the frequency had a value such that $X_L = -X_C$.

In practice, resonance may be obtained in another manner. If the amplitude and frequency of the applied voltage are held constant, the circuit parameters may be varied to satisfy the resonant condition, viz., that $X_L = -X_C$. This procedure is known as *tuning*, and resonance is generally brought about by varying the circuit capacitance.

In case capacitance is used as the abscissa of a resonance curve, it is again easiest to specify the sharpness in terms of the variation between half power points, i.e., the change in capacitance necessary to increase

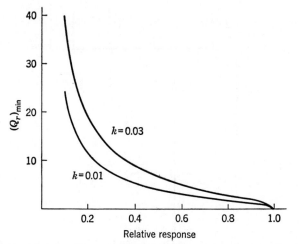

FIG. 4-12. Curves showing the error between the exact and approximate resonance curves. The error between the two forms is $100k$ per cent.

the current from $0.707I_{max}$ to I_{max} and reduce it again to $0.707I_{max}$. At each end point the total reactance will equal the resistance in magnitude. Let

C_1 = capacitance at lower half power point
C_2 = capacitance at upper half power point
C_r = capacitance at resonance

$$\frac{1}{\omega C_1} - \omega L = R$$

$$\omega L - \frac{1}{\omega C_2} = R$$

$$\frac{1}{\omega C_1} - \frac{1}{\omega C_2} = 2R$$

$$\frac{C_2 - C_1}{\omega C_1 C_2} = 2R$$

Now C_r^2 nearly equals $C_1 C_2$, and if ΔC is the change in capacitance between the two half power points,

$$\frac{C_2 - C_1}{\omega C_1 C_2} = \frac{\Delta C}{\omega C_r^2} = 2R$$

$$\frac{\Delta C}{C_r} = 2R\omega C_r = \frac{2R}{\omega L} = \frac{2}{Q} \tag{4-55}$$

Equation (4-55) is very similar to Eq. (4-29); so measurement of the sharpness of resonance by either the variation of frequency or the variation of capacity may be used to find Q and the resistance of the circuit.

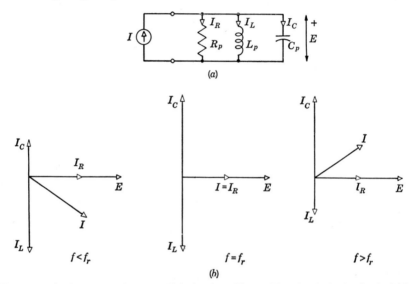

(a)

$f<f_r$ $f=f_r$ $f>f_r$

(b)

FIG. 4-13. Antiresonance in a parallel circuit. *Note.* The circuit is the dual of Fig. 4-1.

4-10. Parallel Resonance. In parallel resonance (antiresonance) two equal and opposite susceptances oppose each other, so that the admittance, instead of the impedance, is a minimum at the resonant frequency.

This situation is represented in Fig. 4-13. The total admittance of the shunt circuit can be determined by adding the individual admittances in complex form

$$Y = G_p + j\left(\omega C_p - \frac{1}{\omega L_p}\right) \tag{4-56}$$

Comparison of this equation, describing the shunt circuit of Fig. 4-13a, and Eq. (4-1) of the series circuit shows that these two circuits are exact duals, i.e., they are identical term by term except for the interchange of impedance and admittance. Thus admittance for the shunt circuit behaves in exactly the same manner when frequency is varied as does the impedance of the series circuit. Hence by the principle of duality one may immediately sketch the admittance and impedance loci of the shunt circuit as shown in Fig. 4-14. The susceptance curves are also shown in the figure.

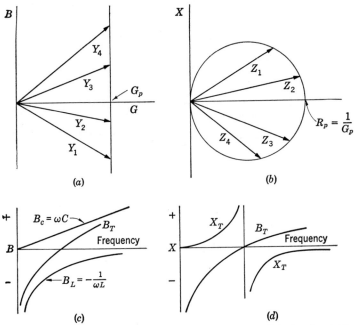

FIG. 4-14. Admittance and susceptance curves for the parallel circuit of Fig. 4-13.

The equation for the voltage drop across the shunt elements is

$$E = \frac{I}{Y} = \frac{I}{G_p + j(\omega C_p - 1/\omega L_p)} \qquad (4\text{-}57)$$

and again by the principle of duality it follows at once that E and Z (since I is constant) obey the universal resonance curve. This follows at once since Eq. (4-57) may be reduced to the normalized form

$$\frac{E}{E_r} = \frac{1}{1 + jQ_r(f/f_r - f_r/f)} \approx \frac{1}{1 + j2Q_r\delta} \qquad (4\text{-}58)$$

It should be observed, however, that in this case, where $R_p (=1/G_p)$ is in shunt with L_p, the circuit quality factor is given by Eq. (4-18), namely, $Q_r = R_p/\omega_r L_p$, and since at antiresonance $\omega_r L_p = 1/\omega_r C_p$, one may also write

$$Q_r = \omega_r C_p R_p \qquad (4\text{-}59)$$

At this point the student may object that the shunt form of the antiresonant circuit which has just been discussed is not the "usual" antiresonant circuit with which he is familiar; R should be in series with L rather than in shunt. In reply, it may be stated that the behavior of most antiresonant circuits at rf can be described equally well by both the shunt and the more conventional representations. At best, they are both only first-order approximations to the physical circuit. The reasons for this statement will be discussed later. For the moment the student's objection will be recognized. Consider the more familiar form of the antiresonant circuit that is shown in Fig. 4-15.

In this diagram it will be seen that the capacitive component of susceptance neutralizes the inductive component at the resonant frequency. If there were no resistance, there would be no total current and the admittance would be zero. At this frequency the power factor is unity. This

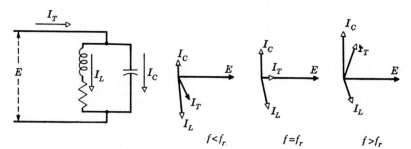

FIG. 4-15. Antiresonance in a parallel circuit of modified form.

will be discussed shortly under the algebraic solution. At frequencies below resonance, the circuit is inductive and above resonance it is capacitive, which is the reverse of the series-resonance case.

It is often desirable in circuits which are composed largely of reactive elements to determine the approximate manner in which the reactance varies with frequency. This can be done if the resistive components are neglected and sketches are drawn for the variation of the reactive components with frequency. Several examples of reactance sketching will be discussed in this chapter. A practical application of the use of these sketches will occur in the discussion of filters and Foster's reactance theorem.

Then, if R of Fig. 4-15 is neglected, the susceptances of that circuit are identical to those of the shunt circuit (Fig. 4-14a) and the curves of Fig. 4-14c and d apply here as well. In all reactance curves where resistance is neglected it should be noted that the *slope is positive* at all frequencies.

To solve algebraically for the impedance of Fig. 4-15, the procedure is to add the two admittances.

Let Y = total admittance.

$$Y = Y_L + Y_C = \frac{1}{R + jX_L} + \frac{1}{jX_C}$$

$$= \frac{R + j(X_L + X_C)}{(R + jX_L)jX_C} \tag{4-60}$$

$$Z = \frac{1}{Y} = \frac{-X_L X_C + jRX_C}{R + j(X_L + X_C)} \tag{4-61}$$

Rationalizing,

$$Z = \frac{RX_C{}^2}{R^2 + (X_L + X_C)^2} + j\frac{X_C{}^2 X_L + X_C X_L{}^2 + R^2 X_C}{R^2 + (X_L + X_C)^2} \tag{4-62}$$

4-11. Condition for Unity Power Factor in Parallel Resonant Circuit.
In order to make Z_T a pure resistance, the imaginary part of Eq. (4-62) should equal zero.

Therefore for unity power factor

$$X_C{}^2 X_L + X_C X_L{}^2 + R^2 X_C = 0$$
$$R^2 = -X_L(X_C + X_L) \tag{4-63}$$

It will be noticed that for unity power factor the criterion is not quite the same for series and parallel resonance, as in the former $-X_C$ must equal X_L. Where, as is often the case in radio circuits, the quality factor Q_r is high, say, greater than 10, $X_L \gg R$, and Eq. (4-63) nearly reduces to the equation.

$$X_L = -X_C \tag{4-64}$$

For example, let
$$X_L = 1{,}000 \text{ ohms}$$
$$R = 20 \text{ ohms}$$
Then to find X_C for unity power factor, change Eq. (4-63) to

$$X_C = -\left(X_L + \frac{R^2}{X_L}\right)$$
$$= -(1{,}000 + 0.4) = -1{,}000.4 \tag{4-65}$$

whose magnitude is almost equal to X_L.

Where the resistance is appreciable in comparison with the reactance, the inductive reactance should not be equal to the capacitive reactance and the currents I_L and I_C will have a definite ratio different from unity. This can be used to set the circuit for unity power factor if an ammeter is placed in each branch. This ratio is computed as follows: From Eq. (4-63)

$$R^2 + X_L{}^2 = -X_L X_C$$
$$\frac{R^2 + X_L{}^2}{X_C{}^2} = -\frac{X_L}{X_C}$$

Substituting Eq. (4-65) for $-X_C$,

$$\frac{R^2 + X_L{}^2}{X_C{}^2} = \frac{X_L{}^2}{X_L{}^2 + R^2}$$

But $|I_C/I_L| = \sqrt{R^2 + X_L{}^2}/|X_C|$. Therefore for unity power factor

$$\left|\frac{I_C}{I_L}\right| = \frac{X_L}{\sqrt{X_L{}^2 + R^2}} \tag{4-66}$$

Radio-transmitter circuits are sometimes tuned to resonance by making use of Eq. (4-66).

4-12. Conditions for Maximum Impedance in Parallel Resonant Circuit. It may be that, instead of desiring *unity power factor* from the adjustments of the parallel circuit, *maximum impedance* is required. In making the adjustments, the capacitance, frequency, or inductance may be varied. It is usual to adjust the capacitance in any resonant circuit, as this can most readily be made variable by the physical construction. Equation (4-61) is the simplest to find when the absolute value of Z is a maximum. Since the interest lies in the absolute value, the square of the impedance is most readily handled. This will eliminate square roots and when $|Z|^2$ is a maximum, $|Z|$ will be, also.

From Eq. (4-61), by finding the absolute value of numerator and denominator

$$|Z|^2 = \frac{(R^2 + X_L{}^2)X_C{}^2}{R^2 + (X_L + X_C)^2} \tag{4-67}$$

Equation (4-67) is simpler to apply than the use of the square root of the sum of the squares of the components in Eq. (4-62).

To maximize with respect to X_C,

$$\frac{\partial|Z|^2}{\partial X_C} = \frac{(R^2 + X_L{}^2)\{2X_C[R^2 + (X_L + X_C)^2] - 2X_C{}^2(X_L + X_C)\}}{[R^2 + (X_L + X_C)^2]^2} = 0$$
$$R^2 + X_L{}^2 + 2X_L X_C + X_C{}^2 - X_L X_C - X_C{}^2 = 0$$
$$R^2 = -X_L(X_C + X_L) \tag{4-68}$$

It will be seen that Eqs. (4-68) and (4-63) are identical, and therefore, when the capacitor is adjusted so that the impedance is a maximum, the circuit of Fig. 4-13 will also have unity power factor.

If the physical inductance of Fig. 4-13 is adjusted, the resistance may vary with the inductance. The nearest approximation is to assume they will vary proportionately; i.e., in varying the inductance, the magnitude of Z_L will vary but not its angle. Now

$$|Z_L|^2 = R^2 + X_L{}^2$$
$$X_L = |Z_L| \sin \theta$$

Equation (4-67) may be written

$$|Z|^2 = \frac{|Z_L|^2 X_C{}^2}{|Z_L|^2 + 2|Z_L| X_C \sin \theta + X_C{}^2} \qquad (4\text{-}69)$$

in which $|Z_L|$ represents the absolute magnitude of the impedance of the inductive branch. To maximize with respect to $|Z_L|$

$$\frac{\partial |Z|^2}{\partial |Z_L|} =$$

$$\frac{X_C{}^2[2|Z_L|(|Z_L|^2 + 2|Z_L| X_C \sin \theta + X_C{}^2) - |Z_L|^2(2|Z_L| + 2X_C \sin \theta)]}{(|Z_L|^2 + 2|Z_L| X_C \sin \theta + X_C{}^2)^2} = 0$$

$$|Z_L|^2 + 2|Z_L| X_C \sin \theta + X_C{}^2 - |Z_L|^2 - |Z_L| X_C \sin \theta = 0$$

$$-X_C = |Z_L| \sin \theta = X_L \qquad (4\text{-}70)$$

Therefore the way to make $|Z|$ a maximum, as $|Z_L|$ is varied, is to make the capacitive and inductive reactances have equal magnitudes. It has been shown that, when the resistance is small, this is practically the same as the criterion for unity power factor.

The maximum value of impedance may be found by substituting Eq. (4-70) into Eq. (4-61), thus:

$$Z_m = -\frac{X_L X_C}{R} + j\frac{R X_C}{R} = -X_C(Q_r - j) \qquad (4\text{-}71)$$

Taking magnitudes,

$$|Z_m| = |X_C| \sqrt{Q_r{}^2 + 1} \qquad (4\text{-}72)$$

and again, if Q_r is large with respect to 1, to a good approximation

$$|Z_m| = |X_C| Q_r = \frac{L}{RC} \qquad (4\text{-}73)$$

In a similar way the condition may be found for maximum impedance when the frequency is varied. It will be found that, when Q_r is large, Eq. (4-64) gives a high degree of approximation and hence the antiresonant frequency is approximately

$$f_r = \frac{1}{2\pi \sqrt{LC}} \qquad (4\text{-}74)$$

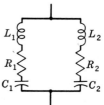

FIG. 4-16. Parallel-resonant circuit containing R, L, and C in both branches.

4-13. Resonance for Inductance and Capacitance in Both Branches. The derived equations can also be applied to the circuit shown in Fig. 4-16, provided that the term X_L applies to the total reactance in one branch and X_C applies to the total reactance in the other branch. In order to secure parallel resonance, one branch must have its inductive greater than its capacitive reactance, and the reverse must be the case in the other branch.

In Fig. 4-17 is shown a circuit in which taps are brought out from

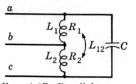

intermediate points on the inductance. The condition which must be met to secure resonance between a and c is that the inductive reactance of one branch is equal to the magnitude of the capacitive reactance of the other branch, or

$$\omega(L_1 + L_2 + 2L_{12}) = \frac{1}{\omega C} \qquad (4\text{-}75)$$

This is the same as saying that the total reactance measured *around* the loop L_1L_2C (including the effect of mutual inductance between L_1 and L_2) is zero.

To secure resonance between b and c, the inductive reactance of L_2 must equal the capacitive-reactance magnitude through L_1C, namely, $-[\omega(L_1 + 2L_{12}) - 1/\omega C]$. Therefore

$$\omega L_2 = \frac{1}{\omega C} - \omega(L_1 + 2L_{12}) \qquad (4\text{-}76)$$

But Eqs. (4-75) and (4-76) are identical, and therefore, if resonance is secured between two points at any frequency in a parallel circuit, the circuit will be resonant at the same frequency between any other two points.

It should be remembered that, if the capacitance between the leads a and c is appreciable in comparison with C, the movement of the tap from a to b may have an effect on the resonant frequency.

While the resonant frequency has not been changed by altering the connection of the lead from a to b, the impedance will be less than the impedance between a and c. It may be shown that

$$Z_{ac} = \frac{1}{\omega_r C} \left[\frac{\omega_r(L_1 + L_2 + 2L_{12})}{R_1 + R_2} - j \right]$$
$$\approx \frac{[\omega_r(L_1 + L_2 + 2L_{12})]^2}{R_1 + R_2} \qquad (4\text{-}77)$$

provided that

$$\frac{\omega_r(L_1 + L_2 + 2L_{12})}{R_1 + R_2} \gg 1$$

and

$$Z_{bc} = R_2 + j\omega_r L_2 - \left\{ \frac{R_2^2 - [\omega_r(L_2 + L_{12})]^2 + j2R_2\omega_r(L_1 + L_{12})}{R_1 + R_2} \right\}$$
$$\approx \frac{[\omega_r(L_2 + L_{12})]^2}{R_1 + R_2} \qquad (4\text{-}78)$$

provided that

$$\frac{\omega_r L_2}{R_2} \gg 1$$

where Z_{ac} = impedance at resonance between points a and c
$\quad\quad Z_{bc}$ = impedance at resonance between points b and c

4-14. Sharpness of Resonance in Parallel Circuit. It is apparent that, when a parallel combination of inductance and capacitance is con-

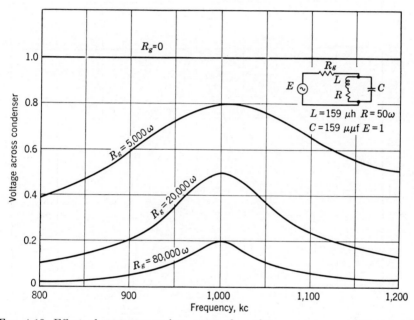

Fig. 4-18. Effect of generator resistance on the voltage across a parallel resonant circuit.

nected to a generator with a zero internal impedance, the voltage across the combination will not vary with frequency. On the other hand, if the generator has a high impedance, the voltage drop in this impedance will be a minimum at the antiresonant frequency where the current is a minimum. Therefore, the voltage across the combination will be a maximum at this frequency and will drop off as the frequency is increased or decreased from this value. The current through either branch will be a maximum at approximately the frequency where the voltage is a maximum. As the resistance of the generator is increased, this curve will become more peaked, because the drop in the generator impedance increases more at the off-resonant frequencies than at resonance. Figure 4-18 shows how the voltage across the capacitor varies with frequency and with different generator resistances for some assumed parallel combination.

In order to compare the sharpness of resonance for the curves of Fig. 4-18, they have been replotted in Fig. 4-19 with the following modification: As the resistance of the generator was increased, the generated voltage was also increased so as to bring all the curves to a common peak. This is often approximated in practice, for higher generated voltages are usually associated with higher internal resistances, both in vacuum tubes

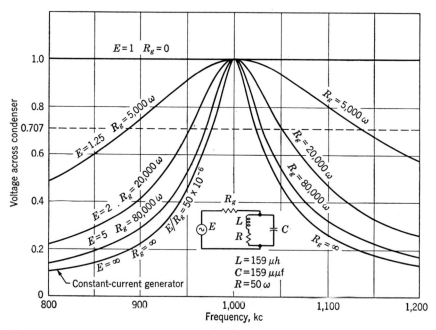

FIG. 4-19. Resonance curves of Fig. 4-18 with generator voltages modified to give a common peak.

and in electromagnetic generators.   It is also possible in Fig. 4-19 to include the case for a constant-current generator and show that, unlike the series-resonance case, the constant-current generator gives the most selective curve of all.

In order to make a comparison of the change, with frequency, of the different variables in the series and parallel resonant cases, Figs. 4-20 and 4-21 have been drawn.   In Fig. 4-20 the parallel circuit matches the generator resistance of 20,000 ohms at antiresonance.   This should be compared with the series case of Fig. 4-7, where the same R, L, and C in series match the generator resistance of 50 ohms at resonance.   It will be seen that, except for a different scale of ordinates, the curves of Fig. 4-7 can be superimposed on the curves of Fig. 4-20.   However, the

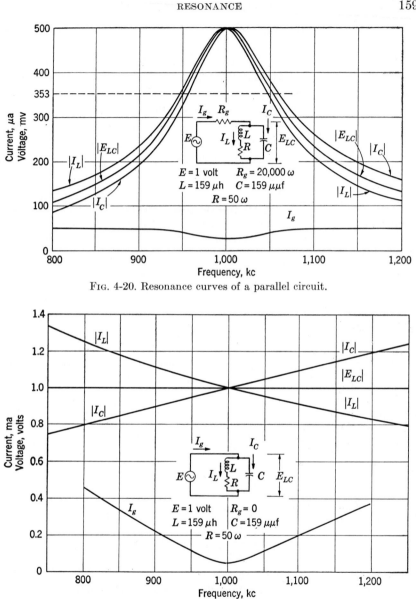

FIG. 4-20. Resonance curves of a parallel circuit.

FIG. 4-21. Resonance curves of a parallel circuit driven by a zero-resistance generator.

curve of common current of Fig. 4-7 corresponds in shape to the curve of common voltage of Fig. 4-20; the voltage across the capacitor in Fig. 4-7 corresponds to the current through the inductor of Fig. 4-20; and the voltage across the inductor in Fig. 4-7 corresponds to the current through the capacitor of Fig. 4-20.

As a further comparison Fig. 4-21 has been drawn for the case where the generator has zero internal impedance. The curves are of the same character as those shown for the constant-current supply of the series circuit shown in Fig. 4-8; they could be superimposed on each other with the same correspondences as between Figs. 4-7 and 4-20.

It can thus be seen that, to secure sharpness of resonance with a low-impedance generator, series resonance should be used, while, to secure sharpness with a high-impedance generator or supply network, a parallel combination must be used. As most of the generators in communication circuits have a high impedance, parallel resonance is used much more extensively than series resonance.

4-15. Universal Resonance Curve. In previous sections it has been shown how duals in the series and parallel resonant circuits behave in the same manner. It may now be demonstrated that the previously derived universal resonance curves may be applied to the parallel resonant circuit, provided that Q is properly evaluated. Thus consider the circuit of Fig. 4-22a. Application of Norton's theorem to the generator

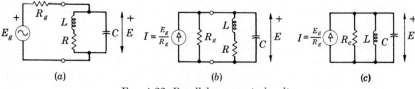

Fig. 4-22. Parallel resonant circuits.

produces the equivalent circuit shown at b. It is convenient to reduce this to the equivalent circuit c.

Thus, changing the RL branch into equivalent shunt form,

$$Y = \frac{1}{R + j\omega L} = \frac{R - j\omega L}{R^2 + (\omega L)^2}$$

Then if Q_L of the inductor is 10 or greater, $(\omega L)^2 \gg R^2$ or

$$Y \approx \frac{R}{(\omega L)^2} - \frac{j}{\omega L} \tag{4-79}$$

This of course corresponds to a shunt resistance $(\omega L)^2/R$ and a shunt inductance L. The net effective shunt resistance R_e, as depicted at c, will be the parallel combination of $(\omega L)^2/R$ and R_g,

$$R_e = \frac{R_g(\omega L)^2/R}{R_g + (\omega L)^2/R} = \frac{(\omega L)^2}{R + (\omega L)^2/R_g} \tag{4-80}$$

Since R_e and L are in *parallel*, the circuit Q becomes at resonance

$$Q_e = \frac{R_e}{\omega_r L} = \frac{\omega_r L}{R + (\omega_r L)^2/R_g} = \frac{(Q_L)_r}{1 + (\omega L)^2/R_g R} = \frac{(Q_L)_r}{1 + (Q_L)_r \omega_r L/R_g} \tag{4-81}$$

The last step is obtained by dividing numerator and denominator of the expression by R.

Then for the final circuit (Fig. 4-22c)

$$E = \frac{I}{Y} = \frac{I}{1/R_e + j(\omega C - 1/\omega L)} \tag{4-82}$$

Multiplying numerator and denominator by R_e and factoring out $1/\omega_r L$ from the parentheses,

$$E = \frac{IR_e}{1 + (R_e/\omega_r L)(\omega\omega_r LC - \omega_r/\omega)}$$

Noting that $IR_e = E_r$, the voltage at antiresonance, and substituting for known quantities,

$$\frac{E}{E_r} = \frac{1}{1 + jQ_e(f/f_r - f_r/f)} \tag{4-83}$$

This expression is identical to I/I_r for the series resonant circuit; therefore the universal resonance curves of Fig. 4-10 also apply to normalized voltage in the antiresonant circuit. This fact will be of particular use in the study of tuned amplifier circuits in Chap. 15.

Inasmuch as the circuit under consideration is the dual of the series resonant circuit, one may expect a resonance rise of current in each branch. This may be proved as follows: The current through the capacitor in Fig. 4-22c will be, at resonance,

$$|I_C| = \frac{E_r}{|X_C|} = \frac{IR_e}{X_L} = IQ_e \tag{4-84}$$

If the left-hand member of Eq. (4-83) is multiplied by I_r/I, the equation is seen to give the normalized impedance of the antiresonant circuit

$$\frac{Z}{Z_{ar}} = \frac{1}{1 + jQ_e(f/f_r - f_r/f)} \tag{4-83a}$$

Equation (4-83a) may be evaluated to give the equivalent series impedance of the antiresonant circuit, as shown in Fig. 4-23. The curves are plotted for the arithmetic symmetry approximations.

4-16. Design of an Antiresonant Circuit. A problem which frequently presents itself is that of designing a parallel circuit which will convert a branch resistance into a definite higher resistance at antiresonance. The usual circuit which is used is that shown in Fig. 4-15. From Eq. (4-62) the impedance at antiresonance will be a pure resistance given by

$$R_{ar} = \frac{RX_C^2}{R^2 + (X_L + X_C)^2} \tag{4-85}$$

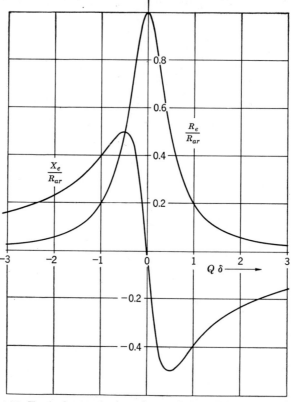

FIG. 4-23. Equivalent series impedance of a parallel resonant circuit.

From Eq. (4-63) $(X_L + X_C)^2 - R^4/X_L^2$. Introduce this in Eq. (4-85).

$$R_{ar} = \frac{X_C{}^2 X_L{}^2}{R(R^2 + X_L{}^2)} \tag{4-86}$$

Also from Eq. (4-63) $-X_L X_C = R^2 + X_L^2$. Therefore

$$R_{ar} = \frac{R^2 + X_L{}^2}{R}$$

$$X_L = \sqrt{R(R_{ar} - R)} \tag{4-87}$$

$$-X_L X_C = R_{ar} R$$

$$X_C = \frac{R_{ar} R}{X_L} = -R_{ar} \sqrt{\frac{R}{R_{ar} - R}} \tag{4-88}$$

One of the principal applications of such an antiresonant circuit is as the tuned plate load of a class C amplifier. In that application the relatively small resistance load R is transformed into the large value R_{ar} required for proper loading of the vacuum tube. The tuned circuit serves another important function in this application in that its selectivity characteristic discriminates against the high-order harmonics that are present in the plate current. Satisfactory suppression of these unwanted harmonics requires a inductor Q_L of 10 or more. This restriction brings up an important question in design because there are only two adjustable parameters in the network, X_L and X_C. Consequently it is impossible to design for three arbitrary values, R, R_{ar}, and Q_L. It will be shown that, if Q_L is specified, the impedance transformation ratio

$$n = \frac{R_{ar}}{R} \tag{4-89}$$

must be greater than a specified value. By definition $Q_L = X_L/R$. Introducing Eq. (4-87),

$$Q_L = \sqrt{\frac{R_{ar} - R}{R}} = \sqrt{n - 1}$$

whence
$$n = Q_L^2 + 1 \tag{4-90}$$

Equation (4-90) may be applied to (4-87) and (4-88) to give

$$X_C = -\frac{R_{ar}}{Q_L}$$

and
$$X_L = X_C \frac{Q_L^2}{Q_L^2 + 1} \tag{4-91}$$

Thus if Q_L is to be 10 or greater, the transformation ratio must be at least 101:1, and to a good approximation $X_L = -X_C$.

If this ratio causes R_{ar} to be too large, a satisfactory load for the tube may be obtained by tapping down on the coil as discussed in Sec. 4-13.

4-17. Circuit Components at Radio Frequency. In the foregoing treatment of resonant circuits it has been assumed that the circuit parameters, R, L, and C, are independent of frequency, and they have been thought of as circuit *constants*. Actually this may not be true; all three parameters vary with frequency, and their variation may become quite significant in rf work. These phenomena will now be considered.

4-18. Inductors. It is customary to think of the equivalent electrical circuit of an inductance coil as a constant inductance L in series with a constant resistance R. Actually at higher frequencies such a naïve equivalent circuit is not adequate. If the student thinks of the physical construction of a coil carefully, he will realize that all three types of impedance elements are present: inductance due to the flux linkages when current flows in the coil; resistance due to the finite conductivity of the wire that makes up the coil; and capacitance distributed throughout the entire structure, between turns and from end to end.

The effective wire resistance increases with frequency because of skin effect and the proximity effect.   In the former it may be shown that increasing frequency changes the current distribution within the cross-sectional area of the wire conductor, causing the current to crowd toward the surface of the conductor.   The resultant decrease in effective cross-sectional area causes a change in effective resistance proportional to the square root of frequency.

Further, the change in resistance is also affected by the flow of current in nearby conductors.   In an inductor this means that the distribution of current in any given turn is affected by the current in the other turns, causing a further change in the effective cross-sectional area.   The resulting increase in resistance has been termed the *proximity effect*.

It can be seen readily that the construction of an exact equivalent circuit for an inductor is a complicated procedure, and resort is generally made to a first-order approximation to the actual circuit.   This sim-

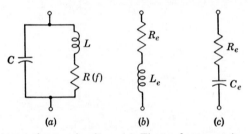

FIG. 4-24. Equivalent inductor circuits.   (*a*) First-order approximation.   (*b*) Below antiresonant frequency.   (*c*) Above antiresonant frequency.

plified equivalent circuit is shown in Fig. 4-24*a*.   It will be observed that the circuit is precisely the antiresonant circuit that has been studied in earlier sections, and their results may be applied here.   In order to emphasize that resistance changes with frequency because of skin and proximity effects, the internal resistance of the inductor will be represented by $R(f)$.   The equivalent series impedance of the inductor may be determined from Eq. (4-62) and is plotted, *assuming $R(f)$ is constant*, in Fig. 4-23.   The curves show that the circuit is inductive below the self-resonant frequency of the inductor, $f_r = 1/2\pi \sqrt{LC}$, and is capacitive for $f > f_r$.   Thus if the inductor is to have an inductive reactance, its operation must be confined to frequencies *below* the self-resonant frequency.   It may be shown from Eq. (4-62) that the effective series inductance at frequencies well below f_r is given approximately by

$$L_e = \frac{L}{1 - (f/f_r)^2} \tag{4-92}$$

provided that $Q_L = \omega L/R \geq 10$ over the frequency range of interest. This inequality is usually satisfied by most inductors in the rf range.

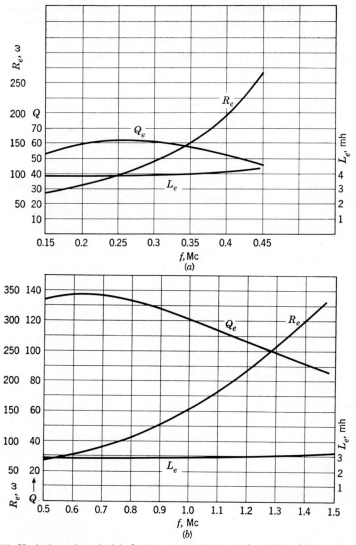

FIG. 4-25. Variation of typical inductor parameters as a function of frequency. (a) Air core. (b) Metal core.

In a similar fashion the effective series resistance at frequencies well below f_r may be shown to be

$$R_e = \frac{R(f)}{[1 - (f/f_r)^2]^2} \qquad (4\text{-}93)$$

where the variation of $R(f)$ with frequency is generally not known but will be something greater than $\sqrt{f}$.

Figure 4-25 shows the measured variation of R_e, L_e, and $Q_e = \omega L_e / R_e$

for two typical inductors.   It will be observed from these data that over
a given frequency range Q_e remains more constant than R_e, whose exact
behavior is difficult to predict.   It is for this reason that the universal-
resonance-curve equations are expanded in terms of Q at the resonant
frequency.

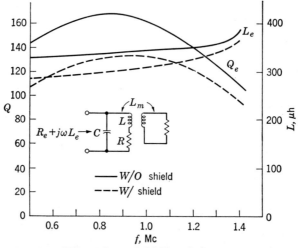

Fig. 4-26. Effect of metal shield on inductor parameters.

It is the usual practice in rf work to surround inductors with a grounded
aluminum shield to minimize both the magnetic and the electric coupling
to nearby units.   Such a shield adds further complication to the inductor's behavior because the shield acts like a secondary circuit of inductance and resistance coupled by mutual inductance to the inductor.
The first-order approximate circuit of a shielded inductor is shown at
the inset in Fig. 4-26.   The student may verify, at least in a qualitative

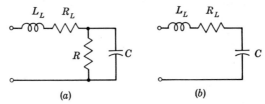

Fig. 4-27. Equivalent capacitor circuits.

fashion, that the shield acts to lower L_e and raise R_e.   Measured data
for L_e and Q_e as a function of frequency are plotted in Fig. 4-26 for a
typical inductor, with and without a shield.

4-19. Capacitors.   The first-order-approximation equivalent circuit of a
capacitor is shown in Fig. 4-27. R represents the losses of the capacitor
dielectric, and L_L and R_L represent the lead inductance and resistance,

respectively. For good air or mica dielectric capacitors R may be assumed infinite, giving the series resonant equivalent circuit of b. In this case the lead inductance may become of appreciable importance at frequencies in the vicinity of 100 Mc or more. In that range the inductance of a single lead is given to a good approximation by

$$L = 0.00508l \left(\ln \frac{4l}{d} - 1 \right) \quad \mu h \qquad (4\text{-}94)$$

where l = lead length, in.
$ d$ = lead diameter, in.
Thus if a 100-$\mu\mu$f capacitor has 1-in. leads of No. 22 copper wire on each end, the inductive reactance of the leads is 26 ohms. Considering that the reactance of C alone is -16 ohms at the same frequency, one notes that at 100 Mc the whole structure is *inductive* with a reactance of 10 ohms!

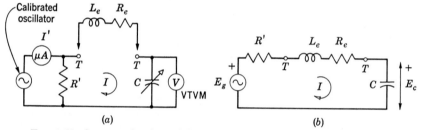

(a)   (b)

FIG. 4-28. Q-meter circuit used for measuring parameters of an inductor.

4-20. Measurement of Circuit Parameters. The results of the two preceding sections show that the design of circuits at radio frequencies is difficult because circuit parameters are not constants as they can be assumed to be in the lower power frequencies. This is particularly true when operation is extended into the very-high-frequency (vhf) (30- to 300-Mc) and ultrahigh-frequency (uhf) (300- to 3,000-Mc) ranges. At these high frequencies the best procedure is to determine the effective parameters by direct measurement at the desired operating frequencies. The series parameters of an inductor may be determined quite readily at rf by means of a number of devices which are known commercially as "Q meters." The operation of one such device will now be explained since it is an excellent practical application of series resonance. The basic circuit is given in Fig. 4-28a, the equivalent circuit in Fig. 4-28b. The current I', furnished by a calibrated oscillator, is held constant by suitable controls and a thermocouple current instrument. Application of Thévenin's theorem yields the equivalent circuit at the right. With the unknown coil connected to the terminals T, the variable capacitor is adjusted until a maximum voltage is indicated on the vacuum-tube voltmeter.   This maximum value of $|E_C|$ occurs at resonance, where

$$I = \frac{E_g}{R' + R_e} \tag{4-95}$$

So
$$|E_C| = I|X_C| = \frac{E_g|X_C|}{R' + R_e} \tag{4-96}$$

But resonance is defined by equal values of X_L and $|X_C|$; therefore

$$|E_C| = |E_g| \frac{X_L}{R' + R_e} \tag{4-97}$$

In a typical commercial version of the instrument R' is 0.04 ohm and for the usual case may be considered negligible with respect to R_e; thus

$$|E_C| = |E_g|Q_e \tag{4-98}$$

If, therefore, I', and so E_g, is set to a fixed, known value, then the vacuum-tube voltmeter may be calibrated directly in Q_e.   The effective inductance is given by

$$L_e = \frac{1}{\omega_r{}^2 C} \tag{4-99}$$

The above description covers only two of the many measurements that can be made with the Q meter.   The other properties of resonance may be applied for the measurement of the distributed capacitance of inductors and the like.   While the Q meter may be used to determine the quality factor of an inductive circuit, it cannot determine the Q_r of a resonant circuit at the resonant frequency.   This is because at f_r the series resonant circuit has a series impedance that is a pure resistance. This difficulty may be overcome by measuring Q_r by means of the half-power-bandwidth method.   For example in the circuit of Fig. 4-5e the frequency of the applied voltage may be varied to f_1 and f_2, at which the current drops to 70.7 per cent of its resonance value.   Then by Eq. (4-29) the Q_r of the entire circuit including the generator impedance at f_r will be $Q_r = f_r/(f_2 - f_1)$.

On the other hand, if it is required to find the quality factor of the resonant circuit $R\ L\ C$ alone, one can obtain the desired result from impedance measurements, for the total reactance is

$$X = X_L + X_C = \omega L - \frac{1}{\omega C}$$

Differentiating with respect to f,

$$\frac{dX}{df} = 2\pi L + \frac{1}{2\pi C f^2}$$

But at the resonant frequency the derivative has the value

$$\left(\frac{dX}{df}\right)_r = 2\pi L + \frac{1}{2\pi C f_r{}^2} = 4\pi L \qquad (4\text{-}100)$$

Then from the derived form for Q_r and Eq. (4-100)

$$(Q_L)_r = \frac{\omega_r L}{R} = \frac{f_r}{2R}\left(\frac{dX}{df}\right)_r \qquad (4\text{-}101)$$

Inasmuch as R and $(dX/df)_r$ can be determined from impedance measurements, Eq. (4-101) may be used to determine $(Q_L)_r$ from laboratory data. The equation also is of value in determining the Q of resonant sections of transmission lines.

The quality factor of an antiresonant circuit may be determined in a similar manner. The two half-power frequencies f_1 and f_2 may be found as the frequencies at which the voltage across the antiresonant circuit drops to 0.707 times its resonance value. Then Eq. (4-29) gives the quality factor, at the antiresonant frequency, of the entire circuit including the generator impedance.

The Q of the antiresonant circuit alone may be determined from admittance measurements, and by duality the necessary relationship may be shown to be

$$Q = \frac{R_p f_r}{2}\left(\frac{dB}{df}\right)_r = \frac{f_r}{2G_p}\left(\frac{dB}{df}\right)_r \qquad (4\text{-}102)$$

where G_p is the equivalent conductance of the network at the antiresonant frequency.

4-21. Multiple Resonance. It is possible for a network to be resonant at one frequency and antiresonant at another; in fact a network is limited in the number of its resonant and antiresonant frequencies only by the number of its capacitive and inductive elements. Circuits that have more than one resonant or antiresonant frequency are said to exhibit *multiple resonance.*

An example of the use of a circuit which is resonant at one frequency and antiresonant at another is the case where a parallel combination of inductance and capacitance is inserted in an antenna circuit to present a high impedance to an interfering signal. Such a combination is called a "wave trap." At the same time the circuit as a whole is tuned to resonance to accept a desired signal.

It is often the practice, where such networks become rather complicated, to analyze their behavior on the assumption that only pure reactances are present, i.e., the small resistances representing the power losses in the reactance elements are neglected or assumed to be zero. As has been explained previously, this practice greatly simplifies the work involved and means are available to correct the results for the resistive components.

Subject to this simplifying assumption, a great deal can be learned about a multiple-resonant circuit from its reactance or susceptance curves similar to Figs. 4-2 and 4-14c and d. The method of using these curves may be demonstrated by working the example shown in Fig. 4-29.

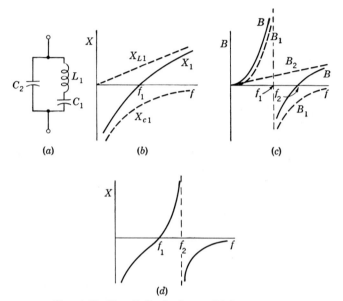

FIG. 4-29. Circuit displaying multiple resonance.

At b the reactances of L_1 and C_1 are added to get their total reactance X_1 as a function of frequency. Since the two branches L_1C_1 and C_2 are in parallel, they may be handled most readily as susceptances. Thus at c, B_1 is the reciprocal of X_1 and is added graphically to $B_2 = \omega C_2$. The reciprocal of their sum is plotted at d. This is the reactance of the combination of the three elements.

Inspection of d shows that at f_1 the over-all impedance is zero, indicating series resonance; therefore f_1 is a series resonant frequency, or a *zero*. Furthermore, the total impedance is infinite (remember, lossless elements have been assumed) at f_2; thus f_2 is an antiresonant frequency, or a *pole*.

The frequencies at which the zero and pole occur may be determined by setting up the equation for Z, the driving-point impedance.

$$Z = \frac{(-j/\omega C_2)j(\omega L_1 - 1/\omega C_1)}{j(\omega L_1 - 1/\omega C_1 - 1/\omega C_2)}$$

Factoring out L_1/ω from the numerator and denominator,

$$Z = -\frac{j}{\omega C_2} \frac{\omega^2 - 1/L_1 C_1}{\omega^2 - \dfrac{1}{L_1 C_1 C_2/(C_1 + C_2)}} \tag{4-103}$$

It is clear that, at $\omega^2 = 1/L_1 C_1$, $Z = 0$, defining a zero, or resonant frequency. Thus, adopting the previous notation,

$$\omega_1^2 = \frac{1}{L_1 C_1} \qquad \omega_1 = \frac{1}{\sqrt{L_1 C_1}} \tag{4-104}$$

Similarly at $\omega^2 = \dfrac{1}{L_1 C_1 C_2/(C_1 + C_2)}$, $Z \to \infty$, defining the pole, or anti-resonant frequency.

So $\qquad \omega_2^2 = \dfrac{1}{L_1 C_1 C_2/(C_1 + C_2)} \qquad \omega_2 = \dfrac{1}{\sqrt{L_1 C_1 C_2/(C_1 + C_2)}} \tag{4-105}$

By introducing Eqs. (4-104) and (4-105), Eq. (4-103) may be simplified to

$$Z = \frac{-j}{\omega C_2}\left[\frac{(\omega^2 - \omega_1^2)}{(\omega^2 - \omega_2^2)}\right] \tag{4-106}$$

The circuit of Fig. 4-30 may be analyzed in a similar manner to give

$$Z = j\omega L_0 \left[\frac{(\omega^2 - \omega_2^2)}{(\omega^2 - \omega_1^2)}\right] \tag{4-107}$$

where ω_1 is a pole of value

$$\omega_1^2 = \frac{1}{L_1 C_1} \tag{4-108}$$

and ω_2 is a zero of value

$$\omega_2^2 = \frac{1}{L_0 L_1 C_1/(L_0 + L_1)} \tag{4-109}$$

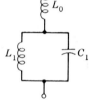

FIG. 4-30. Circuit whose impedance is given by Eq. (4-107).

The subscripts of the ω's are chosen to show the order of their values, that is, $\omega_2 > \omega_1$.

It will be observed that Eqs. (4-106) and (4-107) are quite similar in form, differing only in the coefficient preceding the bracket and in the subscripts of the ω's. This similarity represents a general principle which may be obtained by extrapolating these results. Thus the driving-point impedance of *any* lossless, two-terminal network will have the form

$$Z = x \frac{(\omega^2 - \omega_{o1}^2)(\omega^2 - \omega_{o2}^2)(\omega^2 - \omega_{o3}^2) \cdots (\omega^2 - \omega_{on}^2)}{(\omega^2 - \omega_{x1}^2)(\omega^2 - \omega_{x2}^2)(\omega^2 - \omega_{x3}^2) \cdots (\omega^2 - \omega_{xm}^2)} \tag{4-110}$$

where $x = j\omega H$ or $x = H/j\omega$.

The student should note that the foregoing sentence is stated without proof. The above results merely show that *two* circuit configurations of lossless elements have driving-point impedances of the specified form. The general proof is available in more advanced texts.

4-22. Foster's Reactance Theorem. In Eq. (4-110) each frequency $\omega_{ok}/2\pi$ is a zero, for if $f = f_{ok}$, $Z = 0$. Further, these values of frequency are known as *internal* zeros, meaning simply that they are finite and different from zero frequency. Similarly, each frequency $\omega_{xk}/2\pi$ is an *internal* pole; if $f = f_{xk}$, $Z \to \infty$ and f_{xk} will always be finite and different from zero frequency. With these definitions and Eq. (4-110) one may state Foster's reactance theorem: *The driving-point impedance of any two-terminal, lossless network is uniquely specified by its internal poles and zeros, which occur at real frequencies, and a scale factor H.* This follows because H and the internal singularities are the only constants in Eq. (4-110).

Two corollaries are of importance here.

Corollary 1. *The poles and zeros of a two-terminal lossless network must alternate along the frequency scale.* This is known as the *separation property* of such networks and may be proved by differentiating Eq. (4-110). It will be found that $dZ/j \, d\omega > 0$, that is, the reactance curves will always have positive slopes. (This is also apparent from the fact that both the reactance and susceptance curves of all lossless components have positive slope.) Then since Z can change sign at only a pole or a zero, the separation property is proved.

A consequence of the separation property is that the number of *internal* zeros, z, and the number of *internal* poles, p, can never differ by more than 1.

In working a numerical example, it is convenient to have the subscripts on the internal singularities ordered so that $\omega_1 < \omega_2 < \omega_3 \cdots$. It is therefore desirable to expand Eq. (4-110) into two alternative forms corresponding to the two possible forms of the external factor x.

If $x = j\omega H$, $\omega = 0$ and $Z = 0$ at direct current. Then by virtue of the separation property, the next higher (or first internal) singularity must be a pole, with zeros and poles alternating above that. Thus, for $x = j\omega H$, Eq. (4-110) may be written

$$Z = j\omega H \frac{(\omega^2 - \omega_2^2)(\omega^2 - \omega_4^2) \cdots (\omega^2 - \omega_{2z}^2)}{(\omega^2 - \omega_1^2)(\omega^2 - \omega_3^2) \cdots (\omega^2 - \omega_{2z\pm1}^2)} \qquad (4\text{-}110a)$$

On the other hand, if $x = H/j\omega$, $Z \to \infty$ at $\omega = 0$, indicating an external pole at direct current. By the separation property the first internal singularity must be a zero, with poles and zeros alternating with increasing frequency. Thus for $x = H/j\omega$ Eq. (4-110) may be written

$$Z = \frac{H}{j\omega} \frac{(\omega^2 - \omega_1^2)(\omega^2 - \omega_3^2) \cdots (\omega^2 - \omega_{2p+1}^2)}{(\omega^2 - \omega_2^2)(\omega^2 - \omega_4^2) \cdots (\omega^2 - \omega_{2p}^2)} \qquad (4\text{-}110b)$$

Corollary 2. *There are only four possible types of reactance curves that may be obtained with two-terminal, lossless networks.* This corollary may be proved by noting the possibilities inherent in Eqs. (4-110a) and (4-110b), namely, z and p may be equal or may differ by 1. Since there

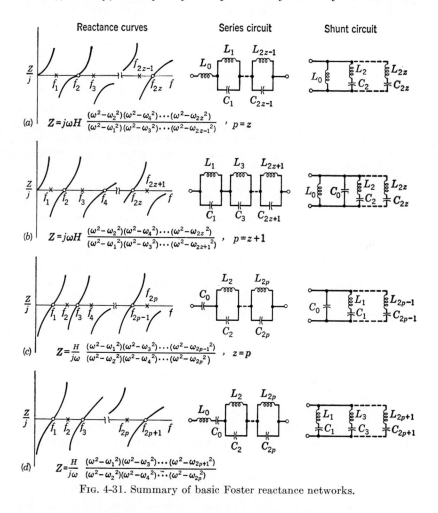

FIG. 4-31. Summary of basic Foster reactance networks.

are two equations each having two possible relationships between z and p, Z has four possible forms. These are illustrated in Fig. 4-31.

Consider a specific example, say, $x = j\omega H$ and $z = p$. As previously explained, an external zero occurs at direct current. Then an equal number of internal singularities alternate, beginning with a pole and ending with a zero. By the separation property an external pole occurs at infinite frequency. The last statement may also be verified from Eq.

(4-110a).   Factoring out ω^2/ω^2 and taking the limit as $\omega \to \infty$;

$$\lim_{\omega \to \infty} Z = \lim_{\omega \to \infty} j\omega H \frac{[1 - (\omega_2/\omega)^2][1 - (\omega_4/\omega)^2] \cdots [1 - (\omega_{2z}/\omega)^2]}{[1 - (\omega_1/\omega)^2][1 - (\omega_3/\omega)^2] \cdots [1 - (\omega_{2z-1}/\omega)^2]}$$

This case is illustrated in Fig. 4-31a.   In the diagram zeros are indicated by a small circle and poles by a small cross.

Two of the possible circuit configurations that give the specified reactance curve are also shown in the figure.   It is of interest to note how these circuits may be checked from physical considerations.   Thus, continuing the previous example, which is shown at a in the figure, consider the behavior of the series form circuit.   At direct current there is a direct short through the inductances $L_0, L_1, L_3, \ldots, L_{2z-1}$, giving $Z = 0$ at direct current.   At infinite frequency the reactance of L_0 is infinite. Since L_0 is in series with the remainder of the network, $Z \to \infty$ at infinite frequency.   Thus the two *external* singularities of the reactance curve have been verified: a zero at direct current and a pole at infinite frequency. Furthermore, since the several antiresonant loops such as L_1C_1 are all in series, the total impedance must be infinite at the antiresonant frequency of each of these loops; hence the number of antiresonant loops must correspond to the number of *internal* poles on the reactance curve.

The shunt circuit may be checked in a similar fashion. L_0 contributes the external zero at direct current.   Since each of the shunt branches contains a series inductance, Z is infinite at infinite frequency.   The number of series resonant branches must equal the number of *internal* zeros on the reactance curve for, at each resonant frequency, the total impedance goes to zero.

The other three possibilities are also shown in Fig. 4-31 and may be checked by the same methods used in analyzing Fig. 4-31a.

4-23. Canonic Forms.   The student should take particular note of the fact that, in each of the Foster networks shown in Fig. 4-31, the total number of elements is one more than the sum of internal poles and zeros and is the *minimum* number of elements that may be used to synthesize a given reactance curve.   It is for this reason that the Foster networks are referred to as fundamental, or *canonic*, circuit forms.   The value of these canonic forms in designing a minimum-element structure to give a specified reactance curve will become apparent when the synthesis of these reactive networks is considered.

4-24. Synthesis of Foster Networks.   The components of a Foster network to provide a given reactance frequency curve may be determined by expanding Eq. (4-110) with the proper number of pole and zero factors, by *partial fractions*, as described in Sec. 2-13.   Such an expansion reduces the equation into a series of terms each of which may be identified with a capacitance and inductance in parallel, or an antiresonant circuit. This procedure may best be illustrated by working a typical example.

It is required to synthesize a reactive network which will give a response as shown in Fig. 4-31b, having two internal poles, ω_1 and ω_3, and one internal zero, ω_2. For this case, then, Eq. (4-110) reduces to

$$Z = j\omega H \frac{(\omega^2 - \omega_2{}^2)}{(\omega^2 - \omega_1{}^2)(\omega^2 - \omega_3{}^2)} \tag{4-111}$$

The degree of ω in the numerator is 3, and in the denominator 4. Thus Z is a *proper* rational fraction, and the partial-fraction expansion[1] in terms of ω^2 is

$$Z = j\omega H \left[\frac{A}{(\omega^2 - \omega_1{}^2)} + \frac{B}{(\omega^2 - \omega_3{}^2)} \right] \tag{4-112}$$

Since the two equations (4-111) and (4-112) must be identical, one may evaluate A and B by equating the terms within the brackets.

$$\frac{A}{(\omega^2 - \omega_1{}^2)} + \frac{B}{(\omega^2 - \omega_3{}^2)} = \frac{(\omega^2 - \omega_2{}^2)}{(\omega^2 - \omega_1{}^2)(\omega^2 - \omega_3{}^2)}$$

Reducing to a common denominator,

$$A(\omega^2 - \omega_3{}^2) + B(\omega^2 - \omega_1{}^2) = (\omega^2 - \omega_2{}^2)$$

Let $\omega = \omega_1$.

$$A(\omega_1{}^2 - \omega_3{}^2) = (\omega_1{}^2 - \omega_2{}^2)$$

or

$$A = \frac{(\omega_1{}^2 - \omega_2{}^2)}{(\omega_1{}^2 - \omega_3{}^2)} \tag{4-113}$$

Let $\omega = \omega_3$.

$$B(\omega_3{}^2 - \omega_1{}^2) = (\omega_3{}^2 - \omega_2{}^2)$$

or

$$B = \frac{(\omega_3{}^2 - \omega_2{}^2)}{(\omega_3{}^2 - \omega_1{}^2)} \tag{4-114}$$

Thus, given the values of the poles and the zero, one may obtain numerical values for A and B. Then Eq. (4-112) becomes

$$Z = \frac{j\omega H A}{(\omega^2 - \omega_1{}^2)} + \frac{j\omega H B}{(\omega^2 - \omega_3{}^2)} \tag{4-115}$$

Since the total impedance of two networks in series is the *sum* of their individual impedances, Eq. (4-115) represents two impedance combinations in series. Each combination may be identified from Fig. 4-32, where a number of basic reactance combinations are tabulated. Thus each term of Eq. (4-115) is a shunt LC combination, and the components

[1] See, for example, W. L. Hart, "College Algebra," D. C. Heath and Company, Boston, 1926.

of the first term may be calculated. From Eq. (4-115) and Fig. 4-32

$$C_1 = \frac{1}{|HA|}$$

and

$$L_1 = \frac{1}{\omega_1{}^2 C_1}$$

(4-116)

The components of the remaining parts of the network are calculated in a similar manner, and it will be noticed that the series-form network of Fig. 4-31b has been derived.

	Element	Z	Y	Internal singularity
a	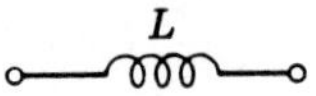 L	$j\omega L$	$\dfrac{1}{j\omega L}$	None
b	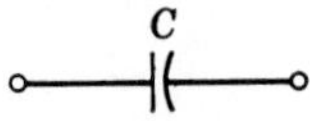 C	$\dfrac{1}{j\omega C}$	$j\omega C$	None
c	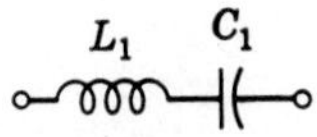 $L_1 \quad C_1$	$j\dfrac{L_1}{\omega}(\omega^2 - \omega_1{}^2)$	$\dfrac{\omega}{jL_1(\omega^2 - \omega_1{}^2)}$	$\omega_1{}^2 = \dfrac{1}{L_1 C_1}$
d	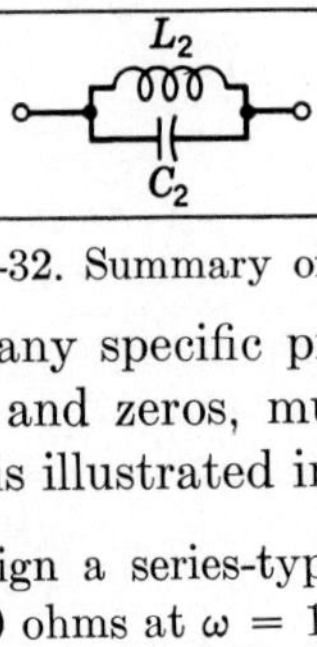 $\begin{matrix} L_2 \\ C_2 \end{matrix}$	$\dfrac{\omega}{jC_2(\omega^2 - \omega_2{}^2)}$	$\dfrac{jC_2(\omega^2 - \omega_2{}^2)}{\omega}$	$\omega_2{}^2 = \dfrac{1}{L_2 C_2}$

FIG. 4-32. Summary of basic elements for synthesizing Foster reactance networks.

In any specific problem one additional piece of data, other than the poles and zeros, must be specified in order that H may be evaluated. This is illustrated in the following numerical example:

Design a series-type Foster network to give a driving point impedance of $+j100$ ohms at $\omega = 1$ megaradian/sec. There is to be a zero at 3 megaradians/sec, and poles at 2 and 4 megaradians/sec. Following the previous notation of ordering the subscripts, let

$\omega_1 = 2$ megaradians/sec

$\omega_2 = 3$ megaradians/sec

$\omega_3 = 4$ megaradians/sec

To find H, substitute $\omega = 1$ megaradian/sec into Eq. (4-111).

$$j100 = j(1 \times 10^6)H \frac{(1 \times 10^6)^2 - (3 \times 10^6)^2}{[(1 \times 10^6)^2 - (2 \times 10^6)^2][(1 \times 10^6)^2 - (4 \times 10^6)^2]}$$

(4-110a)

$$= -jH\frac{8 \times 10^{-6}}{45}$$

or $$H = -\frac{45 \times 10^2}{8 \times 10^{-6}} = -5.63 \times 10^8$$

From Eq. (4-113)

$$A = \frac{(\omega_1{}^2 - \omega_2{}^2)}{(\omega_1{}^2 - \omega_3{}^2)} = \frac{(4 - 9) \times 10^{12}}{(4 - 16) \times 10^{12}} = +0.416$$

From Eq. (4-114)

$$B = \frac{(\omega_3{}^2 - \omega_2{}^2)}{(\omega_3{}^2 - \omega_1{}^2)} = \frac{(16 - 9) \times 10^{12}}{(16 - 4) \times 10^{12}} = +0.584$$

From Eq. (4-116)

$$C_1 = \frac{1}{|HA|} = \frac{1}{(5.63 \times 10^8)(0.416)} = 4{,}250 \ \mu\mu f$$

$$L_1 = \frac{1}{\omega_1{}^2 C_1} = 58.7 \ \mu h$$

$$\text{and } C_3 = \frac{1}{|HB|} = \frac{1}{(5.63 \times 10^8)(0.584)} = 3{,}040 \ \mu\mu f$$

$$L_3 = \frac{1}{\omega_3{}^2 C_3} = 20.5 \ \mu h$$

L_1 and C_1 are in parallel. C_3 and L_3 are in parallel. The two parallel combinations are in series. This completes the design of the required network.

The student might well wonder how the equivalent shunt Foster network of Fig. 4-31b is derived. In that form a number of branches are in parallel; hence a good approach to the problem would be to work in terms of admittance, rather than impedance, because admittances in parallel add directly. Thus, to get the shunt equivalent of the previously derived network, one need only invert the impedance equation (4-111) and expand by partial fractions. (Notice the similarity here to the procedure used in the last chapter to design equivalent shunt-form two-terminal impedances.) Thus, inverting Eq. (4-111),

$$Y = \frac{1}{j\omega H} \frac{(\omega^2 - \omega_1{}^2)(\omega^2 - \omega_3{}^2)}{(\omega^2 - \omega_2{}^2)} \tag{4-117}$$

As in the previous example the partial-fraction expansion is to be carried out in terms of ω^2; so it is convenient to multiply through by ω/ω, giving

$$Y = \frac{\omega}{jH} \frac{(\omega^2 - \omega_1{}^2)(\omega^2 - \omega_3{}^2)}{\omega^2(\omega^2 - \omega_2{}^2)} \tag{4-117a}$$

Now Y includes an *improper* rational fraction whose degree of ω in the numerator is not less than the degree of ω in the denominator; thus one divides through once by the denominator to give the partial-fraction expansion in ω^2.

$$Y = \frac{\omega}{jH} \left(1 + \frac{C}{\omega^2} + \frac{D}{\omega^2 - \omega_2{}^2} \right)$$

$$= \frac{\omega}{jH} + \frac{C}{jH\omega} + \frac{\omega D}{jH(\omega^2 - \omega_2{}^2)} \tag{4-118}$$

Remembering that H, C, and D may be positive or negative depending upon the specific values of the singularities, one can, by comparing each term with the basic forms of Fig. 4-32, identify them as

$$\frac{\omega}{jH}: \qquad \text{A capacitance of value } C_0 = \frac{1}{|H|} \qquad (4\text{-}119)$$

$$\frac{C}{jH\omega}: \qquad \text{An inductance of value } L_0 = \frac{|H|}{|C|} \qquad (4\text{-}120)$$

$$\frac{\omega D}{jH(\omega^2 - \omega_2{}^2)}:$$

A series resonant circuit with resonant frequency f_2, where

$$L_2 = \left|\frac{H}{D}\right| \text{ and } C_2 = \frac{1}{\omega_2{}^2 L_2} \qquad (4\text{-}121)$$

These three branches are all connected in parallel to give the shunt Foster form of Fig. 4-31b. It should be apparent that the two constants C and D are evaluated in the same manner as were A and B of the series-type circuit.

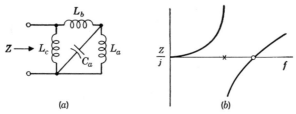

(a)   (b)

FIG. 4-33. A redundant network. Figure 4-30 gives the same impedance function with a minimum number of elements.

4-25. Simplifying Redundant Networks. It has been pointed out (but not proved) that Foster networks are *canonic* in that they synthesize a given reactance curve with the minimum number of reactive elements. This fact may be utilized to simplify a redundant network. Repeated addition of reactance and susceptance curves shows that the reactance of the circuit of Fig. 4-33 exhibits one internal pole and one internal zero as shown at *b*. Then, since the network has four elements, rather than three as is the case with canonic forms, the original network is redundant; it has more than the minimum number of required elements. A Foster network may therefore be designed which will require only three elements. One such possible network is shown in Fig. 4-30. As a matter of fact, whenever in a network the number of inductors differs from the number of capacitors by more than one, there are redundant elements. However, there can also be such elements when this is not the situation, and a resort to reactance plots is one of the simplest methods to discover redundancy.

4-26. Cauer Networks. The student must not think that the Foster forms of Fig. 4-31 are the only types of canonic networks. Other configurations are possible; for example, where only four internal singularities are needed, a dead-end bridged T structure may be used (see Prob. 4-15). In any case, regardless of the number of poles and zeros a Cauer network may be used in place of a Foster network. These Cauer structures are ladder networks and have the form shown in Fig. 4-34a. They are derived by expanding the impedance function into a *continued fraction*, rather than a partial fraction. The expansion of the driving-point impedance of a two-terminal ladder network into a continued fraction may be demonstrated for the generalized ladder structure of Fig. 4-34a. The series elements of the network are written as impedances, and the shunt

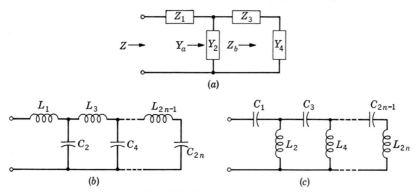

FIG. 4-34. Cauer networks.

elements as admittances, for convenience in the expansion which begins at the right-hand end of the network.

The driving-point impedance of the last two elements may be obtained by inverting Y_4 and adding it to Z_3.

$$Z_b = Z_3 + \frac{1}{Y_4}$$

The driving-point admittance of the last three elements may be obtained by inverting Z_b and adding it to Y_2.

$$Y_a = Y_2 + \frac{1}{Z_3 + 1/Y_4}$$

Then the driving-point impedance of the entire array is

$$Z = Z_1 + \frac{1}{Y_2 + 1/(Z_3 + 1/Y_4)} \tag{4-122}$$

Equation (4-122) is in the form of a continued fraction and is often written as

$$Z = Z_1 + \frac{1}{\left| Y_2 \right.} + \frac{1}{\left| Z_3 \right.} + \frac{1}{\left| Y_4 \right.} \qquad (4\text{-}122a)$$

where the symbol $\left\lceil \right.$ is a space-saving notation for the continued fraction.

In general any driving-point impedance function may be synthesized by two alternative Cauer networks, the series-L type of Fig. 4-34b, and the series-C type of Fig. 4-34c. For the series-L type the continued-fraction form of Z will be

$$Z = j\omega L_1 + \frac{1}{\left| j\omega C_2 \right.} + \frac{1}{\left| j\omega L_3 \right.} + \frac{1}{\left| j\omega C_4 \right.} + \cdots \qquad (4\text{-}123)$$

This form may be obtained by arranging the analytical expression for Z in *descending* powers of ω and carrying out a process of repeated long division, the remainder being inverted after each division. The resulting expression will have the form of Eq. (4-123), but the coefficient of each $j\omega$ term will have a numerical value. Then each element of the network may be identified with its corresponding term in the continued fraction and so may be evaluated.

For the series-C Cauer network the continued-fraction form of Z will be

$$Z = \frac{1}{j\omega C_1} + \frac{1}{\left| 1/j\omega L_2 \right.} + \frac{1}{\left| 1/j\omega C_3 \right.} + \frac{1}{\left| 1/j\omega L_4 \right.} + \frac{1}{\left| 1/j\omega C_5 \right.} + \cdots \qquad (4\text{-}124)$$

In contrast to the series-L case the numerical form of Eq. (4-124) is obtained by arranging the analytical expression for Z in *ascending* powers of ω before carrying out the process of repeated long division. These methods will be illustrated later by numerical examples.

The study of Foster-type networks earlier in the chapter showed that only four types of impedance curves can be obtained from lossless two-terminal networks. It was also shown that the character of the external singularities placed certain restrictions on the elements in the network. Since Cauer networks are also two-terminal lossless structures, similar restrictions apply to them. Knowledge of these restrictions can guide the algebraic manipulation that must be carried out in the synthesizing process.

Consider these restrictions for the series-L type (Fig. 4-34b). If the impedance is to be zero at direct current, C_{2n} must be shorted out so that a continuous path from terminal to terminal is provided through inductances alone. Furthermore, if a zero is to occur at infinite frequency, L_1 must be shorted out so that a purely capacitive path connects terminal to terminal. This latter fact may be verified by Eq. (4-123). If L_1 is different from zero, $Z \to \infty$ at infinite frequency; if L_1 is shorted out, $Z = 0$ at infinite frequency.

A similar set of restrictions may be set up for the series-C network of Fig. 4-34c. If the impedance is to be zero at direct current, C_1 must be shorted out so that L_2 may provide the required short-circuit path between terminals at direct current. This fact may be verified from Eq. (4-124). Furthermore, L_{2n} must be shorted out if a zero is to occur at infinite frequency.

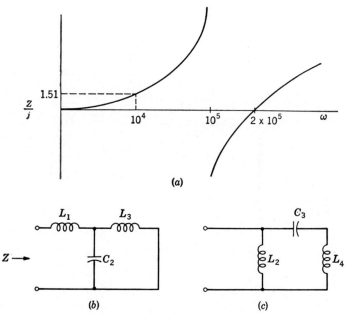

Fig. 4-35. Examples of two Cauer networks and their impedance curve.

With these restrictions established, the process of synthesizing Cauer networks to give a specified impedance function may be illustrated.

Design a two-terminal lossless network to meet the following specifications: $Z = j1.51$ ohms at 1.59 kc, and there shall be only two internal singularities, a pole at 15.9 kc and a zero at 31.8 kc.

From the specifications it may be predicted that the reactance frequency curve has the form shown in Fig. 4-35a. Since the curve exhibits a zero at direct current, the factor x in Eq. (4-110) is $j\omega H$. Further from Eq. (4-110) the expression for Z must be

$$Z = j\omega H \frac{(\omega^2 - \omega_2^2)}{(\omega^2 - \omega_1^2)}$$

where $\omega_2 = 2\pi(31.8 \times 10^3) = 2 \times 10^5$ radians/sec.
$\omega_1 = 2\pi(15.9 \times 10^3) = 1 \times 10^5$ radians/sec.
and one may predict that the form of the network will be that shown in Fig. 4-35b. The value of H may be determined by substituting in the equation for

$\omega = 2\pi(1.59 \times 10^3) = 1 \times 10^4$ radians/sec. Thus

$$H = j\frac{1.51}{j10^4}\frac{10^8 - 10^{10}}{10^8 - 4 \times 10^{10}} = 0.375 \times 10^{-4}$$

Hence the analytical expression for the required impedance function is

$$Z = j\omega(0.375 \times 10^{-4})\frac{\omega^2 - 4 \times 10^{10}}{\omega^2 - 10^{10}}$$

The series-L type Cauer network will be designed first; hence the numerator is multiplied out and the terms arranged in *descending* powers of ω.

$$Z = \frac{(0.375 \times 10^{-4})j\omega^3 - (1.5 \times 10^6)j\omega}{\omega^2 - 10^{10}}$$

Then by long division

$$\begin{array}{r} 0.375 \times 10^{-4}j\omega \\ \omega^2 - 10^{10}\overline{)(0.375 \times 10^{-4})j\omega^3 - (1.5 \times 10^6)j\omega} \\ \overline{)(0.375 \times 10^{-4})j\omega^3 - (0.375 \times 10^6)j\omega} \\ - 1.125 \times 10^6 j\omega \end{array}$$

or $$Z = (0.375 \times 10^{-4})j\omega - \frac{(1.125 \times 10^6)j\omega}{\omega^2 - 10^{10}}$$

To get the continued-fraction form, the remainder, or second term, is inverted and the process of long division carried out again.

$$\begin{array}{r} (0.889 \times 10^{-6})j\omega \\ -(1.125 \times 10^6)j\omega\overline{)\omega^2 - 1 \times 10^{10}} \\ \omega^2 \\ \overline{- 1 \times 10^{10}} \end{array}$$

or $$Z = (0.375 \times 10^{-4})j\omega + \frac{1}{\lfloor(0.889 \times 10^{-6})j\omega} + \frac{10^{10}}{\lfloor 1.125 \times 10^6 j\omega}$$

Rearranging the remainder,

$$Z = (0.375 \times 10^{-4})j\omega + \frac{1}{\lfloor(0.889 \times 10^{-6})j\omega} + \frac{1}{\lfloor(1.125 \times 10^{-4})j\omega}$$

But, from Fig. 4-35b, Z in terms of the circuit elements must be

$$Z = j\omega L_1 + \frac{1}{\lfloor j\omega C_2} + \frac{1}{\lfloor j\omega L_3}$$

Then, comparing coefficients in the last two equations, one has

$$L_1 = 0.375 \times 10^{-4} = 37.5\ \mu h$$
$$C_2 = 0.889 \times 10^{-6} = 0.889\ \mu f$$
$$L_3 = 1.125 \times 10^{-4} = 112.5\ \mu h$$

This completes the design of the series-L-type Cauer network. It should be observed that the number of circuit elements is 1 greater than the number of internal singularities; hence the structure is canonic. The student will observe that for this case the Cauer and series-type Foster networks are identical. When more than two internal singularities are required, this is no longer true.

To illustrate further the method of continued fractions, let a series-C network be designed to give the same impedance function. This is done by first arranging the analytical expression for Z in *ascending* powers of ω.

$$Z = \frac{(1.5 \times 10^6)j\omega - (0.375 \times 10^{-4})j\omega^3}{10^{10} - \omega^2}$$

It has already been determined that a zero occurs at direct current; hence C_1 in the network must be zero, and one predicts that the network will have the form shown in Fig. 4-35c. Since the reactance of C_1 must be zero, one inverts the equation for Z and begins the process of long division, the remainder being inverted each time as has been demonstrated above. The resulting expression is

$$Z = \cfrac{1}{\cfrac{0.667 \times 10^4}{j\omega}} + \cfrac{1}{\cfrac{2 \times 10^6}{j\omega}} + \cfrac{1}{\cfrac{0.75}{(0.375 \times 10^{-4})j\omega}}$$

But from the figure

$$Z = \cfrac{1}{1/j\omega L_2} + \cfrac{1}{1/j\omega C_3} + \cfrac{1}{1/j\omega L_4}$$

Then by equating corresponding terms

$$L_2 = \frac{1}{0.667 \times 10^4} = 150 \ \mu\text{h}$$

$$C_3 = \frac{1}{2 \times 10^6} = 0.5 \ \mu\text{f}$$

$$L_4 = \frac{0.375 \times 10^{-4}}{0.75} = 50 \ \mu\text{h}$$

This completes the design of the series-C Cauer structure, which, once again, is canonic, the number of elements exceeding the number of internal singularities by 1.

4-27. Choosing Canonic Forms. The results thus far indicate that for any given impedance function at least four possible canonic networks may be designed—two Foster and two Cauer types. Theoretically, at least, all four give identical behavior, and the student might well wonder why all four types have been considered when any one will do the job. Aside from pedagogic reasons, the answer lies in the practical problems of building a network that has been designed.

For example, as has been seen, all inductors inevitably have some shunt capacitance. The effect of this capacitance is to cause undesirable changes in the effective inductance, especially when the frequency of operation approaches the self-resonant frequency of the inductor. On this basis alone, then, the series Foster circuit seems preferable, for its design calls for a capacitance, say, C, shunted across each inductance, save possibly one. This capacitance may be used to "wash out" the stray capacitance associated with the coil, that is, C may be adjusted so that its value plus the strays equals the design value. Such a procedure cannot be used in the shunt Foster forms, but these latter permit the use of a common ground connection.

Another practical consideration is the size and cost of the components required by each of the equivalent networks. In general each of the four possible circuits requires a different set of values. Thus that design having the most economical set may be chosen. In this regard one may note the following facts about low-level circuit components used at low voltages and currents.

Fixed capacitors are generally made with three types of dielectrics: paper, ceramics, and mica in that order of increasing cost. The nominal ranges of capacitance available with these dielectrics are:

$$
\begin{array}{ll}
\text{Ceramic} \dots \dots & 1 \ \mu\mu\text{f}-0.01 \ \mu\text{f} \\
\text{Mica} \dots \dots \dots & 5 \ \mu\mu\text{f}-0.01 \ \mu\text{f} \\
\text{Paper} \dots \dots \dots & 500 \ \mu\mu\text{f}-1 \quad \mu\text{f}
\end{array}
$$

As a general rule cost and physical size go up with capacitance. The paper dielectric gives the greatest losses, and its values drift more with time and temperature. Thus where possible it is desirable to use capacitance values not exceeding 0.01 μf with either ceramic or mica as the dielectric.

Variable capacitors which may be used for trimming the parameters to the proper value are generally available with three types of dielectric. The nominal ranges are:

$$
\begin{array}{ll}
\text{Ceramic} \dots \dots \dots & 50 \ \mu\mu\text{f max,} \ \ 7{:}1 \ \text{ratio} \\
\text{Air} \dots \dots \dots \dots & 500 \ \mu\mu\text{f max,} \ \ 10{:}1 \ \text{ratio} \\
\text{Mica} \dots \dots \dots \dots & 0.001 \ \mu\text{f} \ \ \text{max,} \ \ 10{:}1 \ \text{ratio}
\end{array}
$$

In regard to inductors those having inductances up to approximately 100 μh are often self-supporting and may be adjusted over a small range by slight changes in the between-turns spacing. In another type of construction the coils are wound on a supporting tube of treated paper or ceramic with a movable slug inside the tube. Slugs of high-permeability materials such as powdered iron alloys or magnetic ceramics (ferrites) increase the effective inductance as they are centered in the coil winding. Slugs consisting of a shorted turn of silver-plated copper decrease the effective inductance as they are centered in the coil winding. In general, positioning of the slug proves a 2 or 3 to 1 change in effective inductance. The high-permeability-type slug increases inductance more than effective coil resistance with the result that Q's of the order of 100 or more may be obtained.

In the millihenry range the single-layer type of winding is usually replaced by groups of narrow-width multiple-layer coils. In the 100-mh and greater range resort is often made to winding the coils on closed cores of high-permeability materials.

4-28. Reactance Frequency Curves for Dissipative Networks. The reactance curves shown thus far are for ideal elements of zero resistance.

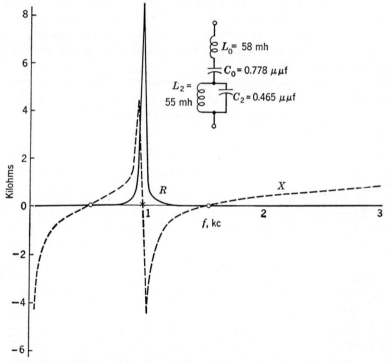

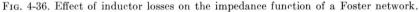

FIG. 4-36. Effect of inductor losses on the impedance function of a Foster network.

They show the reactances reversing through infinity at the antiresonant frequencies. Such ideal elements do not exist, and furthermore nature does not deal in infinities. Therefore, the actual reactance must reverse by passing through zero at antiresonance. This has been shown in Fig. 4-23. Because of the behavior of the real part of the impedance, the *magnitude* of the impedance goes through a large, but finite, maximum at the pole. How these effects show up in a physical Foster network is illustrated in Fig. 4-36.

The network was designed to the following specifications: $Z = +j400$ ohms at 2 kc; internal zeros at 500 cycles and 1.5 kc; internal pole at 1 kc. Design values of inductance, namely, $L_0 = 58.2$ mh, $L_2 = 54.6$ mh, were set to only two significant figures on decade inductors. The inductor quality factors were $Q_0 = 90$, $Q_2 = 81$, both measured at 1 kc.

The measured value of Z at 2 kc was $14.1 + j405$ ohms. Poles and zeros checked the design values to less than 3 per cent, which is within the accuracy of the frequency calibration of the oscillator and of the impedance-measuring equipment.

Measured values of resistance were less than 20 ohms from 0 to 590 cycles and above 1.7 kc. The student should notice that, even though X passes through zero at the pole, $|Z|$ is large, approximately 8,500 ohms, because of the sharp rise in the resistive component.

4-29. Resonant Circuits as Impedance-transforming Networks. Section 4-16 has shown how a parallel resonant circuit can transform a low resistance *in one of its branches* to match a high-resistance generator. It will be shown later in Chap. 11 how a parallel resonant circuit can be used to match any two impedances external to itself, a function which it is peculiarly able to perform in the narrow h-f bands used in radio communication, where the constants necessary to build an efficient transformer of inductances alone cannot be attained.

PROBLEMS

4-1. Draw a log-log reactance vs. frequency chart for the following values of inductance and capacitance: 1, 2, 6, 8, and 10 mh; 0.01, 0.02, 0.04, 0.06, 0.08, and 0.1 μf. Cover the frequency range from 10 cycles to 1 Mc.

4-2. By geometrical inversion derive the admittance locus of a series circuit consisting of constant L in series with R that varies from 0 to ∞.

4-3. Repeat Prob. 4-2 for a circuit of constant C in series with R that varies from 0 to ∞.

4-4. A 53-ohm resistor is in series with an inductance coil. The parallel inductance of the coil is 100 μh and the parallel resistance 56.5 kilohms.

a. Reducing the network to an equivalent series circuit, find Q_L and Q at 1 Mc.

b. Verify your results for Q by using the basic definition in terms of stored and dissipated energy.

4-5. An inductance of 200 μh has a Q of 50, which is to be assumed independent of frequency. This inductance is connected in series with a capacitance of 100 $\mu\mu$f to a generator with a generated voltage of 1 volt. The generator has a constant internal resistance equal to the resistance of the coil at resonance. Construct a table from which the curves of current, voltage across the capacitor, and voltage across the inductance as a function of frequency may be determined.

4-6. Verify the results of Prob. 4-5, using the universal resonance curves.

4-7. Using Eq. (4-48), verify that $BW = f_r/Q$.

4-8. A radio antenna has an effective series resistance of 25 ohms and an induced voltage of 250 μv. The antenna is connected to a series coil and variable capacitor. The coil has inductance $L = 270$ μh, and its Q varies as

f, kc......	550	800	1,000	1,200	1,400	1,600
Q........	60	81	92	99	100	94

a. Plot a curve of C_r vs. f, where C_r is the value of capacitance required to produce resonance.

b. Plot a curve of $|E|_C$ vs. f.

4-9. Verify Eq. (4-83) by reducing the circuit of Fig. 4-22a into an equivalent series circuit. This may be done by applying Thévenin's theorem to all the circuit lying to the left of the capacitor.

4-10. An inductance of 200 μh has a constant Q_L of 50 and is shunted by a 100-$\mu\mu$f capacitor. The shunt combination is connected to the terminals of a generator whose internal resistance is equal to the antiresonant impedance of the tuned circuit. The generated voltage is 100 volts. Plot a curve of voltage across the tuned circuit vs. frequency in the neighborhood of the antiresonant frequency.

4-11. A class C amplifier is to work into a resistive load of 10 kilohms at 500 kc. The physical load of 72 ohms, pure resistance, is placed in series with an inductance L whose resistance is negligible. This combination is shunted by a capacitance C to form the tuned tank circuit.

a. Calculate the required values of L and C.

b. What is the Q of the tuned load?

c. It is found that the fundamental and second-harmonic components of plate current have relative amplitudes of 0.325 and 0.26, respectively. Calculate their relative amplitudes in the 72-ohm resistance. What is the percentage reduction of second harmonic to fundamental?

4-12. An inductance of 200 μh has a Q of 100. Two capacitors are connected in series across its terminals. A generator with an internal resistance of 10,000 ohms is connected across one of the capacitors. What should be the capacitances of the two capacitors, in order that the load presented by the parallel circuit to the generator shall be a resistance of 10,000 ohms? What will be the generator current and the current in each branch in this case? $f = 1,000,000$ cycles.

4-13. The d-c inductance of a coil is 20 μh, and the coil is self-resonant at 20.5 Mc.

a. Calculate the effective series inductance at 10 Mc.

b. Up to what frequency does the series inductance remain within 1 per cent of its d-c value?

c. What is the shunt capacitance of the coil?

4-14. A Q meter has a fixed frequency oscillator that operates at 1 Mc. The capacitance C is variable from 30 to 450 $\mu\mu$f.

a. Draw a calibration curve to show how the capacitor may be calibrated to read effective series inductance directly. Is any advantage to be gained by using a log-log plot of L vs. C? Explain.

b. What should be the oscillator frequency to have the C scale direct reading from 0.1 to 1.5 mh?

4-15. The dead-end bridged T network shown in Fig. 4-37 has the values

$$L_1 = L_2 = 100 \ \mu h$$
$$C_1 = C_2 = C_3 = 100 \ \mu\mu f$$

a. Calculate the internal poles and zeros of the network.

b. Sketch the curves of driving-point reactance vs. frequency.

c. Is the network canonic, i.e., does it have the minimum possible number of elements?

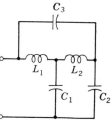

Fig. 4-37. Dead-end bridged T network.

4-16. Synthesize a series-type Foster network that has the same input impedance as in Prob. 4-15.

4-17. Synthesize a shunt-type Foster network to give the Z of Eq. (4-110a).

4-18. The circuit of Fig. 4-33a has a pole at $\omega_1 = 10^6$ radians/sec and a zero at $\omega_2 = 1.5 \times 10^6$ radians/sec. The input impedance is $+j1,000$ ohms at 0.8×10^6 radians/sec. Design a series-type Foster network that is equivalent to the original network.

4-19. Design a Cauer network to synthesize the impedance

$$Z = \frac{2 \times 10^{10} - 9.5 \times 10^{-5}\omega^2 + 2.5 \times 10^{-20}\omega^4}{j\omega - 3.5 \times 10^{-15}j\omega^3}$$

CHAPTER 5

BRIDGE NETWORKS

An important class of networks often encountered in communication engineering comprises the null, or bridge, networks. These circuits usually take the form of a two-terminal pair whose elements are so arranged that at some particular frequency both the nodal and mesh transfer impedances between the terminal pairs become infinite. Use may be made of this property to measure voltage transfer ratios, impedance, and frequency. The property of infinite transfer impedance may also be used to separate two signals originating at different points but traversing a common network, e.g., two telegraph or telephone messages passing along a transmission line in opposite directions. Three basic types of null networks and some of their more important applications will be considered: the a-c Wheatstone bridge, the parallel-T, and the bridged-T networks. A number of applications of bridge networks which employ mutual inductance will also be considered.

5-1. A-C Wheatstone Bridge. Figure 5-1 shows the components of a Wheatstone bridge for measuring impedances. A source of alternating voltage is impressed between the points a and b, and a detector is connected between the points c and d. In the af band this detector is usually a pair of telephone receivers, but it may be another indicator such as a vacuum-tube voltmeter. The detector may incorporate an amplifier to make it more sensitive. It is

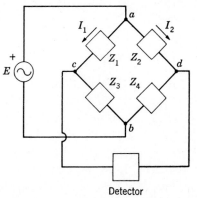

Fig. 5-1. Wheatstone bridge for measurement with alternating currents.

desirable that this amplifier be tunable to the frequency being measured. A sensitive harmonic analyzer makes an almost ideal bridge detector.

When the bridge is balanced, the points c and d are at the same potential and no current will flow in the detector circuit, no matter what its impedance. Then one may write *at balance*

$$I_1 Z_1 = I_2 Z_2 \tag{5-1}$$

and

$$I_1 Z_3 = I_2 Z_4 \tag{5-2}$$

Therefore *at balance*

$$\frac{Z_1}{Z_3} = \frac{Z_2}{Z_4} \quad \text{or} \quad Z_1 Z_4 = Z_2 Z_3 \tag{5-3}$$

Equation (5-3) is the *equation of balance* of the a-c Wheatstone bridge, i.e., if the four impedances satisfy Eq. (5-3), no current flows in the detector, the transfer impedance between terminals a, b and c, d is infinite, and the bridge is said to be balanced.

In the general case all the four impedances are complex; thus the equation of balance imposes two requirements on the circuit, one condition on the impedance magnitudes, and one on their angles, for Eq. (5-3) may be written:

$$\frac{|Z_1|\underline{/\theta_1}}{|Z_3|\underline{/\theta_3}} = \frac{|Z_2|\underline{/\theta_2}}{|Z_4|\underline{/\theta_4}} \tag{5-4}$$

whence

$$\frac{|Z_1|}{|Z_3|} = \frac{|Z_2|}{|Z_4|} \quad \text{and} \quad \theta_1 - \theta_3 = \theta_2 - \theta_4 \tag{5-5}$$

A similar set of conditions on the real and imaginary components of the impedances may also be derived.

When the bridge is used for impedance measurement, it is customary to make Z_1 and Z_2 pure resistances. For this condition Eq. (5-3) simplifies to

$$\frac{R_1 + j0}{R_3 + jX_3} = \frac{R_2 + j0}{R_4 + jX_4} \tag{5-6}$$

Inverting the equation,

$$\frac{R_3}{R_1} + j\frac{X_3}{R_1} = \frac{R_4}{R_2} + j\frac{X_4}{R_2} \tag{5-7}$$

For Eq. (5-7) to be satisfied, the real components of both sides of the equation must be equal and so must be the imaginary components. Thus, if Z_3 is the unknown impedance, its components may be determined as follows:

Equating reals,

$$\frac{R_3}{R_1} = \frac{R_4}{R_2} \quad \text{or} \quad R_3 = \frac{R_1}{R_2} R_4 \tag{5-8}$$

Equating imaginaries,

$$\frac{X_3}{R_1} = \frac{X_4}{R_2} \quad \text{or} \quad X_3 = \frac{R_1 X_4}{R_2} \tag{5-9}$$

Or alternatively one may find from Eqs. (5-4) and (5-5) that

$$|Z_3| = \frac{R_1}{R_2}|Z_4| \qquad (5\text{-}10a)$$

and
$$\theta_3 = \theta_4 \qquad (5\text{-}10b)$$

Equations (5-10) state that the polar coordinates of the impedances must balance, and Eqs. (5-8) and (5-9) show that this is equivalent to saying that the rectangular coordinates must balance. Either pair of equations proves that, in general, two adjustments must be made on any a-c bridge to secure a balance. This is in contrast to a d-c bridge, where one adjustment only is necessary (although the ratio arm may be adjusted roughly to bring the reading within the limits set by the range of the variable arm).

5-2. Adjustment of Wheatstone Bridges. Physical adjustments may correspond to the satisfying of a balance in either polar coordinates or rectangular coordinates. For example, in Fig. 5-1, let the impedance Z_3 be the unknown. Suppose that a variable reactance in series with a variable resistance is provided for Z_4. Within quite a wide range, then, R_1 and R_2 may be fixed, so that, if they are adjustable, their variations usually occur in big steps. The value of the variable reactance X_4 is then adjusted to satisfy Eq. (5-9) and the value of the variable resistance R_4 (plus any resistance inherent in the reactive element) is adjusted to satisfy Eq. (5-8). This is, then, a balancing of rectangular coordinates.

It is easier to construct resistances variable over a wide range than variable reactances. Frequently, therefore, for a-f measurements the reactive standard X_4 is fixed in magnitude. Under these conditions a balance may be obtained if one of the ratio arms R_1 or R_2 in addition to R_4 is continuously adjustable, or else its increments should be small enough to fall within the accuracy required in the measurements. The adjustments required are, first, to make resistance R_4 such that the power factor or angle of Z_4 is equal to that of the unknown Z_3, thereby satisfying Eq. (5-10b), and, second, to adjust one of the ratio arms R_1 or R_2 until Eq. (5-10a) is satisfied. The actual controls, therefore, individually obtain a balance for each of the two polar coordinates.

In practice, it is not feasible to balance one coordinate exactly before balancing the other. In either type of adjustment (polar or rectangular) one control should be changed until the tone in the receivers or any other indication which may be used is an approximate minimum; then the other control should be varied until the tone is further reduced. By alternating from one control to the other, successive approximations will finally secure an exact balance. The number of alternations required will decrease with experience.

This "sliding balance" may be thought of in terms of a man who is constrained to walk in either the north-south directions or the east-west directions, trying to reach the bottom of a lopsided bowl-shaped valley. Starting at any given point in the bowl, he walks east or west until he is at a minimum elevation at that latitude (adjustment of R). He then walks north or south until he finds the lowest altitude on that longitude (adjustment of X), then east or west again, and so on, until he finally reaches the bottom.

It has sometimes been suggested, in discussions of the bridge, that the resistances should be first balanced on direct current. This operation is of no value in most cases, as the effective resistance of the majority of networks or impedance elements will vary with frequency. This change in effective resistance with frequency (and similar changes in effective inductance or capacitance) also introduces a difficulty in bridge balances if the source of alternating voltage is not a pure sine wave, for when a balance is reached for the fundamental, the harmonics will not be balanced and so a tone remains in the detector. When using the telephone receiver as the indicator, the operator must concentrate his attention on this fundamental, and, with practice, he can distinguish it and notice when it disappears, if the harmonics are not too strong. If a selective circuit in the detector is used, the same effect is achieved by electrically or mechanically concentrating the attention on the fundamental.

The fact that the balance of bridges for a particular configuration depends upon frequency may be used as a means of determining an unknown frequency. In this case the variable arm may be calibrated directly in terms of frequency. The bridge may also be used as a harmonic analyzer.

Since inductors cannot be wound with zero resistance, there will be times when, in order to secure a balance, resistance must be added to the unknown Z_3 instead of the standard Z_4. An example of this would be, in a balance of polar coordinates, when the power factor of the unknown is less than that of the standard inductance. Inductance standards must be wound with air cores to prevent saturation effects, and their power factor is therefore high in comparison with inductors which have cores of ferrous materials.

5-3. Sensitivity of Bridge. It is possible to select a wide variety of combinations of Z_1 and Z_2 which will give a balance for the bridge of Fig. 5-1, if Z_4 is also adjustable. It is desirable to select an order of magnitude for these impedances which will give the most sensitive balance.[1] Assume, in Fig. 5-1, that Z_1, Z_2, Z_3, and Z_4 are initially in balance. Assume that Z_3 is the unknown and that Z_4 is then changed by a small factor p. Then the impedance in this arm will be $(1 + p)Z_4$. The

---

[1] The student is referred to the catalogue of the General Radio Company for an alternative treatment of bridge sensitivity.

sensitivity can be computed by determining the voltage which appears between the points c and d when the detector is disconnected. Let this voltage be ΔE. The value of I_1 will be

$$I_1 = \frac{E}{Z_1 + Z_3} \tag{5-11}$$

and of I_2

$$I_2 = \frac{E}{Z_2 + (1 + p)Z_4}$$

$$\Delta E = I_1 Z_1 - I_2 Z_2$$

$$\frac{\Delta E}{E} = \frac{Z_1}{Z_1 + Z_3} - \frac{Z_2}{Z_2 + (1 + p)Z_4}$$

$$= \frac{Z_1 Z_4 + p Z_1 Z_4 - Z_2 Z_3}{(Z_1 + Z_3)(Z_2 + Z_4 + p Z_4)} \tag{5-12}$$

From Eq. (5-3), $Z_1 Z_4 = Z_2 Z_3$. If p is small, $p Z_4$ may be neglected in the denominator of Eq. (5-12). Then

$$\frac{\Delta E}{E} = \frac{p Z_1 Z_4}{(Z_1 + Z_3)(Z_2 + Z_4)} \tag{5-12a}$$

Let

$$\frac{Z_3}{Z_1} = \frac{Z_4}{Z_2} = r$$

$$\frac{Z_1 + Z_3}{Z_1} = \frac{Z_2 + Z_4}{Z_2} = 1 + r$$

Then Eq. (5-12a) becomes

$$\frac{\Delta E}{E} = \frac{p Z_1 Z_4}{(1 + r)^2 Z_1 Z_2} = \frac{pr}{(1 + r)^2} \tag{5-12b}$$

where all the quantities are complex. The problem now is to determine the value of r that makes $|\Delta E/E|$, and hence the sensitivity, a maximum. Thus, taking magnitudes,

$$\left| \frac{\Delta E}{E} \right| = \frac{|p| \cdot |r|}{|1 + r|^2} \tag{5-13}$$

For convenience let

$$r = |r|\underline{/\theta} = |r| \cos \theta + j|r| \sin \theta$$

Then

$$|1 + r|^2 = (1 + |r| \cos \theta)^2 + |r|^2 \sin^2 \theta$$
$$= 1 + 2|r| \cos \theta + |r|^2 \tag{5-14}$$

Substituting into Eq. (5-13),

$$\left| \frac{\Delta E}{E} \right| = \frac{|p| \cdot |r|}{1 + 2|r| \cos \theta + |r|^2}$$

Then differentiating with respect to $|r|$ and equating to zero to find the maximum,

$$\frac{d|\Delta E/E|}{d|r|} = |p|\frac{1 + 2|r|\cos\theta + |r|^2 - (2\cos\theta + 2|r|)|r|}{(1 + 2|r|\cos\theta + |r|^2)^2} = 0 \quad (5\text{-}15)$$

and $\qquad |r| = 1$ $\hfill (5\text{-}16)$

This shows that for maximum sensitivity the impedance Z_1 should be of the same order of magnitude as Z_3, and, hence, Z_2 should be of the same order of magnitude as Z_4. In other words, if an impedance of the order of 1,000 ohms is to be measured, known impedance arms of the order of 1,000 ohms will give the most sensitive bridge, while if the unknown has an impedance of the order of 1 megohm, the other arms should also be of the same order.

If the detector has a finite impedance and its indication is dependent on the *power* delivered to it, the optimum impedance of the detector may be readily found. Applying Thévenin's theorem, the open-circuited voltage of the network supplying the detector will be given by Eq. (5-12b). If the generator impedance is negligible, the impedance of the network looking back into the terminals c, d will be

$$Z_{cd} = \frac{Z_1 Z_3}{Z_1 + Z_3} + \frac{Z_2 Z_4}{Z_2 + Z_4}$$

In case the impedance arms are all of the same magnitude, Z_{cd} will equal the impedance of a single arm. Therefore, the detector should have a magnitude of the same order as the unknown. If the detector responds to voltage only and not power, then its impedance should be as high as possible.

5-4. Wagner Earth. In setting up any circuits to operate at af or rf, circuit elements are frequently introduced which are not indicated on the circuit diagram. The most important of these are the capacitances of the various elements to each other and to ground. In balancing a bridge at af it will frequently be found that the apparent balance shifts as the observer moves around, particularly if the detector is a pair of telephone receivers on the observer's head. This is due to the stray capacitances of the detector to ground. If the detector were at ground potential, this effect would not occur. The best way of securing this result is to make use of a separate balancing arm as shown in Fig. 5-2. In this case it is desirable to make the ratio arms pure resistances so that the

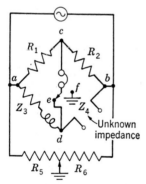

FIG. 5-2. Use of Wagner earth to eliminate disturbance of stray capacitances to ground in the balance of a bridge.

auxiliary balance may also be secured with pure resistance. The bridge is first balanced in the usual manner with the two-pole switch connected to point e. The switch is then thrown to f and the resistances R_5 and R_6 adjusted for a balance so that $R_5/R_6 = R_1/R_2$. The point c will then be at ground potential. The resistors R_5 and R_6 should be low enough so that their admittance is large in comparison with that of any stray capacitances between the points a and b and ground. After making this Wagner-earth balance, the switch should be returned to e and the bridge rebalanced. It may be necessary to repeat the process of balancing the Wagner earth again, but this is uncommon.

5-5. Maxwell Bridge. Another bridge of importance is shown in Fig. 5-3. Since it has the same general configurations as Fig. 5-1, Eq. (5-3) will apply. The student may verify that at balance the components of the unknown arm are given by

$$R_4 = \frac{R_2R_3}{R_1} \tag{5-17a}$$

$$L_4 = R_2R_3C_1 \tag{5-17b}$$

The equations indicate that the balance is independent of frequency, a condition which will be true, however, only if the impedance elements themselves are independent of frequency.

The Maxwell bridge is especially convenient for the measurement of large inductances, because it is readily possible to make the impedance of the four arms of the same order of magnitude. This is in contrast to the case encountered with the basic circuit of Fig. 5-1, where the standard inductor should be air-cored, and these are not ordinarily available in sizes above 1 henry.

This bridge also affords one of the best means for measuring the typically large *incremental* inductance of an audio transformer, i.e., the inductance with a direct current flowing through the transformer

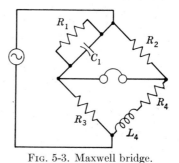

FIG. 5-3. Maxwell bridge.

winding. Such a direct current may be introduced by a d-c supply in series with the oscillator or in the detector arm, since the balance is independent of the impedance in these arms.

5-6. The Wien Bridge. Thus far in the discussion of the Wheatstone bridge it has been tacitly assumed that the equation of null is used to find an unknown impedance. This need not be the case, however; for example, bridges may be used for the measurement of frequency.

The Maxwell bridge would be unsatisfactory for this purpose, of course, for its conditions of balance are independent of frequency. One simple frequency-sensitive bridge could be obtained by making Z_1, Z_2, and Z_3 pure resistances, and by making Z_4 a series resonant circuit in Fig. 5-1. The capacitor in Z_4 could be adjusted for a null in the detector; then the frequency of the applied signal would be

$$f = \frac{1}{2\pi \sqrt{L_4 C_4}} \tag{5-18}$$

It is interesting to consider what the primary frequency range of such a frequency bridge would be.   Assuming L_4 to be constant, the frequency range would depend upon the capacitance range of the adjustable capacitor C_4.   In general, variable air dielectric capacitors have a ratio of maximum to minimum capacitance of approximately 10:1.   Thus the primary frequency range of this bridge is $\sqrt{10}:1$ approximately.

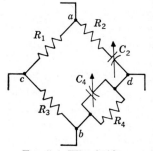

FIG. 5-4. Wien bridge.

This reduction in frequency range as compared with the range of the variable element may be eliminated by using a Wien bridge, shown in Fig. 5-4.   Since the basic configuration is the same as that of Fig. 5-1, one may apply Eq. (5-3); thus $Z_1 Z_4 = Z_2 Z_3$, and, substituting in terms of the impedance elements,

$$R_1 \frac{R_4}{1 + j\omega C_4 R_4} = R_3 \frac{1 + j\omega C_2 R_2}{j\omega C_2} \tag{5-19}$$

Cross multiplying,

$$j\omega C_2 R_1 R_4 = R_3[(1 - \omega^2 C_4 R_4 C_2 R_2) + j\omega(C_4 R_4 + C_2 R_2)]$$

Equating reals,

$$f = \frac{1}{2\pi \sqrt{C_4 R_4 C_2 R_2}} \tag{5-20a}$$

Equating imaginaries,

$$C_2 R_1 R_4 = R_3(C_4 R_4 + C_2 R_2) \tag{5-20b}$$

Now let $R_2 = R_4$ and $C_2 = C_4$; then

$$f = \frac{1}{2\pi C_4 R_4} \tag{5-21}$$

and $R_1 = 2R_3$

Equations (5-21) indicate that, if the two capacitances, C_2 and C_4, are always equal and each has a range of 10:1, then the frequency range is also 10:1.   The desired result is accomplished.

The Wien bridge designed to satisfy Eqs. (5-21) is particularly convenient in that 10:1 capacitances allow the capacitance dials to be calibrated in decades of frequency. The switching of decades may be accomplished by changing the values of R_1 and R_3 by a factor 10. Such an arrangement is often used in feedback audio oscillators where the Wien bridge is used as the frequency-determining element. The student must note, however, that the use of the Wien bridge does not give something for nothing. The price paid for making the frequency and capacitance ranges identical is the cost of an additional variable capacitor, C_2, that must be "ganged" to C_4 (i.e., connected to C_4 so that the two capacitors may be adjusted simultaneously by a common control).

5-7. Substitution Methods. In the foregoing discussion of bridge circuits the measurement of impedance is absolute in that a single balance is obtained and the unknown determined in terms of the equation of balance and the known impedances Z_1, Z_2, and Z_3. When measurements are made in the rf range, such a procedure invariably introduces a number of residual errors due to stray capacitances, and the like. To overcome these effects, resort is made to a substitution method of measurement whereby the bridge is balanced twice, once with the unknown, and once with the unknown shorted out. By this means the residual errors tend to cancel out, and the unknown is determined in terms of the *change* in the values of the bridge elements. The substitution method may be illustrated by the bridge circuit shown in Fig. 5-5. It shows the basic circuit used in the General Radio type 916-A impedance bridge. In the commercial model of the instrument an elaborate shielding system is used. This is omitted in the diagram, for the shielding has no effect on the equations of balance. Since the bridge has the same form as Fig. 5-1, one may determine the equation of balance by substituting the element values in Eq. (5-3). The balance will be considered first with the unknown Z_x in place, and the values of the two variables C_a and C_p will

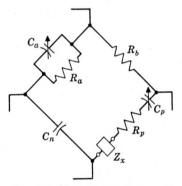

FIG. 5-5. Basic circuit of General Radio Company 916-A impedance bridge, which uses the substitution method of measurement.

be identified by the subscript 2. Thus, substituting into Eq. (5-3), $Z_1Z_4 = Z_2Z_3$.

$$\frac{R_a(jX_{a2})}{R_a + jX_{a2}} [(R_p + R_x) + j(X_x + X_{p2})] = R_b(jX_n) \qquad (5\text{-}22)$$

Canceling j and cross multiplying,

$$(R_p + R_x)R_aX_{a2} + j(X_x + X_{p2})R_aX_{a2} = R_aR_bX_n + jX_{a2}R_bX_n \qquad (5\text{-}23)$$

Equating reals,

$$R_p + R_x = R_b \frac{X_n}{X_{a2}} \tag{5-24}$$

Equating imaginaries,

$$X_x + X_{p2} = \frac{R_b}{R_a} X_n \tag{5-25}$$

The balance condition with Z_x shorted out will now be considered. The corresponding values of the variable elements are denoted by the subscript 1. Thus from Eqs. (5-24) and (5-25), if $Z_x = 0$,

$$R_p = R_b \frac{X_n}{X_{a1}} \tag{5-26}$$

$$X_{p1} = \frac{R_b}{R_a} X_n \tag{5-27}$$

Subtracting Eq. (5-26) from Eq. (5-24),

$$R_x = R_b X_n \left(\frac{1}{X_{a2}} - \frac{1}{X_{a1}} \right) = \frac{R_b}{C_n} (C_{a2} - C_{a1}) \tag{5-28}$$

Equating Eqs. (5-25) and (5-27),

$$X_x = X_{p1} - X_{p2} = \frac{1}{\omega} \left(\frac{1}{C_{p2}} - \frac{1}{C_{p1}} \right) \tag{5-29}$$

The last two equations indicate that the unknown is determined by the *difference* of two readings on the variable standard capacitors C_a and C_p.

It is highly desirable in an instrument of this sort to have dials calibrated to read the unknowns, R_x and X_x, directly. This may be effected in the following manner: In the actual bridge C_a and C_p are shunted by small trimmer capacitors (not shown in the diagram) which are adjustable by means of "initial-balance" controls independent of C_a and C_p. Thus with the unknown shorted out, the *dials* of C_a and C_p are set to read zero. The balance is then obtained with the trimmers. This procedure, in effect, makes $C_{a1} = 0$ and $1/C_{p1} = 0$. Effectively, then, the equations of balance become

$$R_x = \frac{R_b}{C_n} \frac{1}{C_{a2}}$$
$$X_x = \frac{1}{\omega C_{p2}} \tag{5-30}$$

The trimmers are left unchanged, the unknown is inserted, and a second balance is obtained with C_a and C_p. By virtue of Eq. (5-30), then, the dial of C_a may be calibrated to read resistance directly in ohms. The same may be done for the dial of C_p with one exception. Inasmuch as the X_x balance condition is frequency-dependent, the dial may be calibrated correctly in ohms for one frequency only, say 1 Mc. If measurements are made at some other frequency, the reactance reading must then be corrected by the factor f_{Mc}.

5-8. Use of Mutual Inductance in Bridge Circuits. In some applications of the bridge it is not practicable to apply the voltage between the points a and b of Fig. 5-1. It is possible to balance a bridge in which the voltage is applied between any two of the points a, b, c, or d, provided *mutual inductance* is introduced to couple two adjacent branches. An example of this is the ordinary three-wire single-phase distribution system shown in two forms in Fig. 5-6.

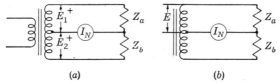

(a) (b)

Fig. 5-6. Balance in three-wire single-phase distribution system.

In Fig. 5-6a the transformer is provided to produce the two voltages E_1 and E_2 in phase with each other. If the impedances Z_a and Z_b are adjusted to have the relation $E_1/E_2 = Z_a/Z_b$, there will be no current in the neutral. It is not necessary to have a two-winding transformer, for an autotransformer can be used in the same way, as shown in Fig. 5-6b. In this latter illustration the meter I_N may be considered as the detector, and the two halves of the transformer and two impedances Z_a and Z_b will constitute the four arms of a bridge. In this bridge it will be observed that the voltage E is impressed across one of the four arms, but the mutual inductance or transformer action permits the balance to be obtained.

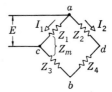

Fig. 5-7. A-c bridge which uses mutual impedance.

In Fig. 5-7 is shown a general arrangement of a bridge with a mutual impedance between the two arms Z_1 and Z_3. The voltage E is applied to two branches, one branch consisting of the three arms Z_2, Z_4, and Z_3 in series, and the other branch being Z_1 alone. Between branches Z_1 and Z_3 there is a mutual impedance Z_m, usually a mutual inductance. The mutual impedance will cause the current in one branch to induce a voltage in the opposite branch. Adding up the voltage drops and induced voltages in each of the two branches will give the following relations:

Z_1 branch:

$$E = I_1 Z_1 - I_2 Z_m \qquad (5\text{-}31)$$

$Z_2 Z_4 Z_3$ branch:
$$E = I_2(Z_2 + Z_3 + Z_4) - I_1 Z_m \qquad (5\text{-}32)$$

Multiply Eq. (5-31) by Z_m/Z_1.

$$E\frac{Z_m}{Z_1} = I_1 Z_m - I_2 \frac{Z_m{}^2}{Z_1} \tag{5-31a}$$

Add Eq. (5-31a) to Eq. (5-32).

$$E\left(1 + \frac{Z_m}{Z_1}\right) = I_2\left(Z_2 + Z_3 + Z_4 - \frac{Z_m{}^2}{Z_1}\right)$$

$$I_2 = E\frac{Z_1 + Z_m}{Z_1(Z_2 + Z_3 + Z_4) - Z_m{}^2} \tag{5-33}$$

For a balance the potential of d with respect to c must be zero, i.e.,

$$I_2 Z_2 = E \tag{5-34}$$

Substitute Eq. (5-34) in Eq. (5-33).

$$\frac{I_2(Z_1 + Z_m)Z_2}{Z_1(Z_2 + Z_3 + Z_4) - Z_m{}^2} = I_2$$

$$Z_1 Z_2 + Z_m Z_2 = Z_1 Z_2 + Z_1 Z_3 + Z_1 Z_4 - Z_m{}^2$$

The equation for balance is therefore

$$Z_1 Z_3 + Z_1 Z_4 = Z_2 Z_m + Z_m{}^2 \tag{5-35}$$

If the mutual impedance is a pure mutual inductance, then $Z_m = j\omega L_m$. If Z_1 and Z_3 are two windings on a transformer, in which practically all the flux of one coil links with that of the other, then

$$Z_1 Z_3 \approx Z_m{}^2 \tag{5-36}$$

By applying this to Eq. (5-35), the latter becomes

$$Z_1 Z_3 + Z_1 Z_4 = Z_2 \sqrt{Z_1 Z_3} + Z_1 Z_3$$

$$\sqrt{\frac{Z_1}{Z_3}} = \frac{Z_2}{Z_4} \tag{5-37}$$

But if the resistances of Z_1 and Z_3 can be neglected in comparison with their reactances and if n_1/n_3 is the transformer turns ratio,

$$\frac{Z_1}{Z_3} = \frac{n_1{}^2}{n_3{}^2}$$

and a balance may be obtained, if

$$\frac{Z_2}{Z_4} = \frac{n_1}{n_3} \tag{5-37a}$$

5-9. Measurement of Phase Shift by Mutual-inductance Bridge. The bridge may be used to measure the ratio of two voltages in both phase and magnitude. An example of this would be to measure the phase shift on a filter or artificial line. This is illustrated in Fig. 5-8 by a typical circuit.

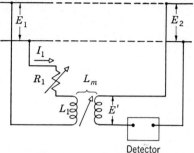

$$I_1 = \frac{E_1}{R_1 + j\omega L_1}$$

$$E' = j\omega L_m I_1 = \frac{j\omega L_m E_1}{R_1 + j\omega L_1}$$

If R_1 and L_m are adjusted until there is no indication in the detector $E' = E_2$,

$$\frac{E_2}{E_1} = \frac{j\omega L_m}{R_1 + j\omega L_1} \quad (5\text{-}38)$$

Fig. 5-8. Measurement of the complex ratio of two voltages by means of a mutual-inductance bridge.

Since the mutual inductance may be made either positive or negative by rotation, the complex ratio E_2/E_1 may be measured in any of the four quadrants.

5-10. Applications Other than Measurement. Thus far in the chapter the application of bridge circuits has been confined to the field of measurements. The null, or infinite transfer impedance property of the bridge circuit, has many other useful and interesting applications in the general field of communications. These have to do primarily with either the

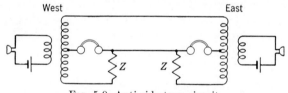
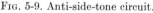

Fig. 5-9. Anti-side-tone circuit.

separation or the combination of two signals in a common transmission medium. A number of these applications will now be discussed, first in telephony and telegraphy, and then in radio.

5-11. Anti-side-tone Circuits. In a number of telephone applications it is desirable that the sound introduced in the transmitter should not be heard in the local receiver. In noisy surroundings this is particularly true, as the local sound tends to mask out the desired message from the distant point. A circuit which will prevent the transmitter from producing a response in the local receiver is called an "anti-side-tone" circuit. An instance of its application is the telephone set. It has the added advantage of causing the user to speak loudly since he cannot hear himself so well through the receiver.

Figure 5-9 shows one of the many possible combinations based on the bridge circuit of Figs. 5-6 and 5-7. The impedance Z should equal, in phase and magnitude, the input impedance of the telephone line, including the effect of the termination at the other end. The design of such networks is considered at the end of Chap. 8. The accuracy with which Z should be adjusted depends upon the particular application. In a telephone set it is made only approximate, and so the anti-side-tone effect is not complete.

When the transmitter at the east end is energized, it will produce no effect in the receiver at that end but will impress a voltage on the line which will affect the receiver at the opposite end. Similarly, the operation of the transmitter at the west end will produce a sound in the east receiver but none in the west instrument.

Half the energy available will be dissipated in the local impedance Z, but this is counterbalanced by the fact that there will be no loss in the local receiver. With the proper value of transmitter and receiver resistance there will also be no loss in Z at the other end of the line, and so the efficiency will be as great as for a set with side tone. The balancing conditions will be considered more in detail in the discussion of telephone repeaters, where an exact balance is very important.

5-12. Duplex Circuits. It would be possible, in a circuit similar to that of Fig. 5-9, to have two one-way messages transversing the line simultaneously in opposite directions. One person at the west could talk continuously to an individual listening to a receiver at the east end, while a similar combination was operating in the opposite direction. Commercial circuits, however, must provide for two-way conversations, and so this circuit is used in telephone work, not to permit simultaneous conversations, but only to eliminate extraneous local noises from the local receiver.

In telegraph work, on the other hand, a message is usually transmitted continuously and the reply sent back at some later time. Under these conditions it is feasible to operate in two directions simultaneously, the only requirement being that good operators (or machines), who do not require repeats in the message, except at rare intervals, shall be used. The bulk of modern telegraphic traffic is handled by machines, which can be adjusted to operate at uniform speed and make a negligible number of mistakes. Under these conditions transmission of at least two messages on a wire simultaneously will greatly reduce the cost of the outside plant. When two telegraph messages are sent in opposite directions at the same time, the system is called a "duplex telegraph."

The balance for a telegraph circuit may be obtained in either of two ways, both shown in Fig. 5-10.

In Fig. 5-10a the balance is obtained by a differentially wound relay. The artificial line, AL, must match in impedance, over the range of frequencies required for telegraphy, the input impedance of the line. This artificial network usually consists of a variable resistance and capacitor in parallel. There are four possible combinations of the two keys. The relay at the west end should operate only under the control of the east key, and vice versa. The four combinations are:

Condition 1. Neither key depressed. No current will flow and so neither relay will be operated.

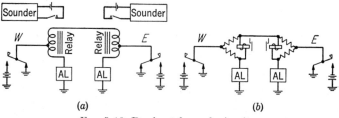

FIG. 5-10. Duplex telegraph circuits.

Condition 2. Key *E* depressed; key *W* open. The current will divide equally in the east relay, one-half going into the physical line and the other into the artificial line. The magnetomotive force (mmf) produced in the east relay by current in one branch will balance that due to the current in the other branch, and so the east relay will not operate. At the west end the line current will flow through one-half of the relay winding to ground at the key and so will operate that relay.

Condition 3. Key *W* depressed, key *E* open. This condition is the reverse of condition 2, and so the east relay will be operated while the west relay will not.

Condition 4. Both keys depressed. The two ends of the physical line will be at equal potentials, and so no current will flow over the line or through the relay windings connected to it. Current from the local battery flows through the other winding of each relay, operating it, and so both relays are operated.

Examination of the four conditions shows that the requirements for transmission of signals simultaneously in both directions are met.

The circuit of Fig. 5-10*b* will operate in a similar manner, the balance being obtained electrically instead of magnetically.

Under changing line conditions, such as a decrease in insulation resistance incident to wet weather, the balance may be upset, and the circuit become inoperative until the artificial line is readjusted.

If the relays are of the polar type, i.e., act for mmfs in one direction but not the other, then the balance required of the artificial line need not be so exact and the circuit can operate under greater variations in line conditions. For this reason most duplex telegraph circuits use such polar relays, and the key reverses the potential of the battery, instead of connecting it and disconnecting it as it does in the two circuits of Fig. 5-10.

5-13. Phantom Circuits. Any means by which the number of communication channels carried by a given number of wires can be increased tends to reduce the relative cost of outside plant, a major charge against long-distance transmission. An extremely simple method by which this can be done is the use of "phantom" circuits. A phantom circuit gives an additional telephone channel for each four wires, thereby increasing the carrying capacity 50 per cent. It works on a balancing principle similar to that of a bridge circuit. The terminal equipment required is very simple, consisting only of a pair of repeating coils (or transformers) at each end of the phantom. The connection is shown in Fig. 5-11.

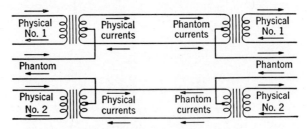

FIG. 5-11. Phantom telephone circuits.

The standard two-wire circuits are usually called "physical," or "side," circuits. The terminals of both physicals and phantoms are brought in to jacks on the long-distance board, so that the operator does not need to treat a phantom circuit any differently from a physical.

By the principle of superposition the signals may be considered one at a time. A voltage impressed on the phantom circuit at the west end of Fig. 5-11 will cause a current to enter at the mid-tap of the secondary winding of each repeating coil. *If the impedances of the two line wires of the physicals* are equal to each other, the current will divide equally and so produce mmfs which cancel each other in each repeating coil. The currents due to the signal impressed on the phantom terminals will flow in the same direction in the two wires of physical 1 and in the opposite direction in the two wires of physical 2. At the far end the two currents will again produce equal and opposing mmfs in the repeating coils, so that no flux will be produced. This absence of flux, due to the currents resulting from the phantom signal, prevents this signal from being transferred to the substations connected to the physicals. It also means that the effective inductance of the repeating coils is negligible for phantom currents. Three conversations, one on each physical and one on the phantom, can therefore be carried on simultaneously without interference.

The directions of the currents at some instant due to the several signals are shown by the arrows in Fig. 5-11.

In order to make sure that the mmfs completely cancel each other, the leakage flux must be made negligible. This is accomplished by winding the two halves of the secondary winding with wires which are adjacent to each other, as illustrated in Fig. 5-12. Toroidal cores are also used to reduce leakage flux.

It is extremely important that the impedances of the two sides of each physical line be made as nearly identical as possible. If this is not done, the phantom currents in the two sides will not be identical and so a mmf will be set up in the repeating coils. This will result in "cross talk," or interference between the unbalanced physical and the phantom. If both physicals should be un-balanced, the phantom would provide a path so that cross talk could also occur between the two physicals, as well as between each physical and the phantom.

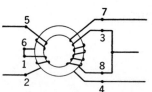

FIG. 5-12. Windings of the repeating coils for use in phantom circuits.

The transmission on the phantom is actually better than on the physicals. Since the phantom uses two wires in parallel for each conductor, the line impedance is cut in half.

In order to prevent the currents flowing in one pair of wires in a cable from inducing a voltage in another pair, the pairs are twisted continuously along their length. On open-wire lines the two wires are transposed at regular intervals for the same purpose.

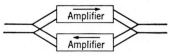

FIG. 5-13. Two-way telephone repeater which will not operate because of "singing."

When two pairs are phantomed, each pair individually must also be treated as a single conductor and the two pairs twisted with each other in a cable or transposed with each other on an open-wire line. Cables in which this is done are called "quadded" cables. Owing to the greater effective separation of the sides of a phantom circuit, its susceptibility to inductive interference is greater.

5-14. Telephone Repeaters. One of the most important applications of a bridge balance is in the two-way repeater on telephone lines. As the length of a telephone circuit is increased, the line losses will reach a limit at which the transmission will no longer be commercially feasible. Beyond this point it is necessary to introduce amplification to make up for the line losses. The transmission of a telephone circuit should be the same in both directions. Therefore the amplifier must operate in both directions. The first idea which would occur to the experimenter is to connect two amplifiers side by side as shown in Fig. 5-13, one to operate in one direction and the second to amplify in the opposite direction. The circuit of Fig. 5-13 would not work, because it would oscillate, or "sing."

The output of one amplifier would be impressed on the input of the other, and the amplified output of the second would be reintroduced to the input of the first. It is necessary, therefore, to isolate the output of one amplifier from the input of the other, and also to separate the signals passing in one direction along the line for amplification by one amplifier, while those propagated in the opposite direction are acted upon by the second amplifier. This can be done by the same principle which was applied in the anti-side-tone circuit of Fig. 5-9. The two-way repeater circuit is shown in Fig. 5-14. This is called a "22-type repeater circuit," the digits standing for "two-way, two-element."

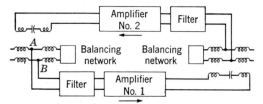

FIG. 5-14. 22-type telephone repeater.

The transformer is called a "hybrid coil." The output of one vacuum-tube amplifier induces a voltage in the secondary, which impresses equal voltages upon the line and the balancing network. If the impedance of the balancing network[1] equals that of the line, over the range of frequencies which are to be amplified, there will be no voltage between the points A and B, due to the output of the vacuum-tube amplifier 2, just as none was impressed across the receiver of Fig. 5-9, due to the local transmitter. Under this condition the output of one amplifier is isolated from the input of the other. A voltage impressed by the line, on the other hand, will be transferred to the grid of the tube whose input circuit is connected between AB. This will be amplified and half of the output energy delivered to the far line, the other half being dissipated in the balancing network.

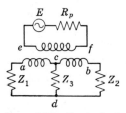

FIG. 5-15. Equivalent circuit for analysis of a telephone repeater.

5-15. Impedance Relations in 22-type Repeaters. The analysis of the bridge circuit of Fig. 5-14 can be made most readily by considering the two-winding transformer of Fig. 5-15. This can be done because the only purpose of the third winding in Fig. 5-14 is to keep the line balanced to ground.

The generator and impedance R_p in Fig. 5-15 represent the effect of the vacuum-tube output circuit. Z_1 represents the input impedance of

[1] Balancing networks for typical lines are discussed in Chap. 8.

the line, Z_2 that of the balancing network, and Z_3 that of the input circuit of the vacuum-tube amplifier.

In order to prevent singing, no current should flow in Z_3 due to the voltage E. In order to accomplish this, if ac and cb are identical windings, the following relation is necessary:

$$Z_1 = Z_2$$

It is desirable to make the transfer of power from the tube to the line as efficient as possible. This can be done by adjusting the turns ratio of the transformer. Let n_1 represent the number of the turns on winding ef, and n_2 the number on the winding ab. Since $Z_1 = Z_2$, the load on the secondary is $2Z_1$. If the line is terminated at the distant end in its characteristic impedance Z_o, then $Z_1 = Z_o$, as will be shown in Chap. 6. (If a line is not so terminated, undesirable reflections occur). Then the correct turns ratio will be

$$\frac{n_1}{n_2} = \sqrt{\frac{R_p}{2Z_o}} \tag{5-39}$$

It is desirable that the input impedance, looking into the repeater at the terminals a, d, should be Z_o, so as to prevent any reflection of a signal arriving at the repeater. This can be done by a proper selection of the impedance Z_3.

Consider for the moment that Z_2 is disconnected. Looking into the terminals a, b of the transformer, the impedance will be $2Z_o$ if Eq. (5-39) is satisfied. Looking into the terminals a, c the impedance would be $Z_o/2$, since the impedance is proportional to the *square* of the number of turns. If Z_2 is disconnected, the value of Z_3 which would make the impedance between a and d equal to Z_o would be

$$Z_3 = \frac{Z_o}{2} \tag{5-40}$$

The voltage drop between a and c would then be equal to the voltage drop between c and d. The power arriving would be divided into two equal parts, one half being dissipated in Z_3 and the other half in R_p. Since the power is cut in half in both the input and the output circuit, the power output of the repeater is one-quarter of that which would be obtained if corresponding amplifiers were used in one direction only. The current flowing in the winding ac would induce a voltage in the other half of the secondary cb, which would be equal to the voltage ac, if the transformer were 100 per cent efficient. In an actual case the voltage between c and b would be practically that between a and c. But since $E_{ac} = E_{cd}$ and $E_{ac} = E_{cb}$, the voltage between b and d will be zero: $E_{bd} = 0$.

Therefore, it makes no difference whether Z_2 is connected or not when a signal is applied by the line to the terminals a, d, since no voltage is induced across it, and the deductions obtained for Z_2 when disconnected also hold when it is connected. The principal deduction is that, to prevent reflection if Eq. (5-39) is true, then Eq. (5-40) should be satisfied.

If both networks become unbalanced, the 22-type repeater will sing, or oscillate. Since it is not possible to secure a perfect balance at all frequencies, the gain of a repeater is usually limited, the tendency to sing increasing with increased gain. In order to prevent singing at a frequency outside the range necessary for speech transmission, a filter is introduced to provide attenuation at the higher frequencies. The cut-off frequency of this filter is usually set at the highest frequency which it is desirable to transmit.

5-16. Two-way One-element Repeaters. It is possible to construct a repeater in which the line itself acts as the balancing network. Only one amplifier is necessary in order to act in both directions. This is called a 21-type, or two-way, one-element repeater. Its circuit is shown in Fig. 5-16.[1]

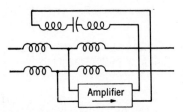

FIG. 5-16. 21-type telephone repeater.

A 21-type repeater can be used only between two lines of similar characteristics. Furthermore, it sends half the amplified energy back toward the sending station and therefore produces a very strong echo. This feature prevents its use on a long line where more than one repeater is required.

5-17. Four-wire Repeaters. In the 22-type repeater of Fig. 5-14 the signals traveling in opposite directions are separated. Each amplifier element might be replaced by a long-cable circuit with a succession of one-way amplifiers. Then the hybrid coils and balancing networks need be provided only at the terminals. One cable pair is necessary for transmission in one direction and the other pair in the opposite direction, so that a four-wire circuit is used. The advantage of such a circuit lies in the higher gain which can be obtained with one-way repeaters, both because of the absence of loss in balancing circuits and the impossibility of singing in a single, properly designed, one-way repeater. The number of repeater points can then be decreased or the size of conductor reduced, or both. Most long-cable circuits operate on this principle.

---

[1] The comparative simplicity of the 21-type repeater has made its use desirable in a number of military applications. For example, the EE 89-A is a Signal Corps 21-type repeater for use in field telephone systems. As used in typical field systems, its introduction into a line gives an increase of 30 to 50 per cent in the useful distance of transmission, depending upon the particular type of line used.

5-18. Bridge Circuits for Radio-frequency Amplifiers. Another use for bridge circuits is to make a vacuum tube a true one-way device; i.e., the bridge can prevent energy in the plate circuit from being fed back to the grid circuit.

For example, one of the principal problems of a tuned rf amplifier employing a triode vacuum tube is its tendency to oscillate. This tend-ency is due to the feedback path afforded by the grid-plate interelectrode capaci-tance C_{gp}. The basic a-c circuit of such an amplifier is shown in Fig. 5-17a. Because of C_{gp}, the tube does not function as a true one-way, or unilateral, device; the plate voltage can produce a voltage be-tween grid and cathode. The immediate problem, then, is to *neutralize* the effect of C_{gp}. This may be done by modifying the circuit as shown at b in the figure.

Inspection of the redrawn circuit at c shows that the tuned plate load, C_{gp}, and the neutralizing capacitor C_N form a bridge circuit with mutual inductance coupling between two arms as in Fig. 5-7. C tunes the inductance to resonance, and the large circulating current also helps to make the voltage across ad in phase with the volt-age between d and b. Hence, proper ad-justment of C_N can bring the bridge into balance. Then the output voltage appear-ing between a and d can have no effect on the grid voltage between c and d because the transfer impedance between these two terminal pairs is infinite.

Other variations of the neutralizing circuit differ in form from Fig. 5-17, but the principle is the same. In each case the circuitry is forced into bridge form

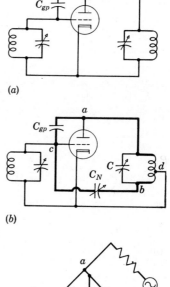

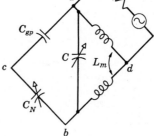

Fig. 5-17. Bridge circuit for neu-tralizing a tuned-triode vacuum-tube amplifier.

so that the null condition prevents the feedback of energy from the plate to the grid circuit.

5-19. Adding Two Signals. It is frequently necessary in communica-tion work to have two separate generators deliver power to a common load impedance without having any interaction between the generators. While this result may be accomplished by using the isolating properties of vacuum tubes, it may also be effected by a passive bridge network as shown in Fig. 5-18. If $R_1 = R_2$ and $X_3 = X_4$, the bridge is balanced and E_A can produce no current through E_B and E_B can produce no current through E_A. Thus the two generators are isolated from each other; yet both simultaneously deliver power to R_1 and R_2. It should be noticed that if X_3 and X_4 comprise single, identical reactors the balance is independent of frequency.

The circuit just described has an interesting application in television broadcasting. The transmission of a complete television program requires two transmitters, one amplitude-modulated for the picture signal and a second frequency-modulated for the associated sound signal. Generally these two transmitters, operating at different frequencies, must feed a common radiating system which involves two antennas at right angles to each other. Thus in Fig. 5-18 E_A could represent, say, the picture transmitter, and E_B the sound.

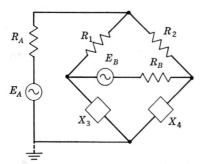

FIG. 5-18. Circuit for adding signals from two generators without mutual interaction.

Then both units could deliver power simultaneously to the two antennas, R_1 and R_2, without interacting upon each other.

5-20. Twin-T Null Circuit. Another basic form of null circuit, other than the Wheatstone bridge, is the twin- or parallel-T circuit. First the equation of balance for the basic circuit shown in Fig. 5-19a will be determined. Then the behavior of the twin-T network with a specific set of components will be considered.

Consider the basic circuit at Fig. 5-19a. If the network is to give a null, the output voltage E_2 must be zero. The equation of balance may be determined by setting up the circuit equations in nodal form and finding the condition that makes $E_2 = 0$. Applying Kirchhoff's current law, one has

$$
\begin{array}{llll}
(Y_g + Y_1 + Y_3)E_1 & +0 & -Y_3E_3 & -Y_1E_4 & = I \\
0 & +(Y_L + Y_2 + Y_4)E_2 & -Y_4E_3 & -Y_2E_4 & =0 \quad (5\text{-}41) \\
-Y_3E_1 & -Y_4E_2 & +(Y_3 + Y_4 + Y_5)E_3 & +0 & =0 \\
-Y_1E_1 & -Y_2E_2 & +0 & +(Y_1 + Y_2 + Y_6)E_4 & =0
\end{array}
$$

Then for a null to occur, one may write $E_2 = IC'_{12}/D' = 0$. Then the null condition is satisfied if the cofactor $C'_{12} = 0$. Thus, substituting from Eq. (5-41),

$$
Y_3Y_4(Y_1 + Y_2 + Y_6) + Y_1Y_2(Y_3 + Y_4 + Y_5) = 0 \qquad (5\text{-}42)
$$

Equation (5-42) is the equation of balance for the basic twin-T structure. In common with the a-c Wheatstone bridge, its balance condition is independent of the generator and load admittances. If Y_L represents a detector, the circuit may be used as an impedance or frequency bridge in a manner similar to that described earlier in the chapter. For measurements in the rf ranges a substitution method is usually employed (see Prob. 5-12).

The twin-T circuit exhibits a selectivity curve which may closely resemble that of the antiresonant circuit, and interestingly enough this

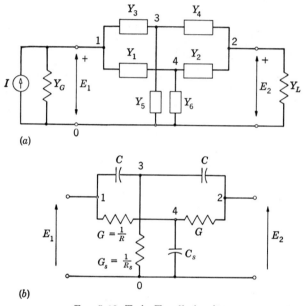

(a)

(b)

FIG. 5-19. Twin-T null circuits.

curve may be obtained without the use of inductance. Furthermore, the effective Q can be made much greater than that obtainable in the usual antiresonant circuit.

This selective property of the twin-T network is used so often in practice that it is well worth investigating. It is usual in this application to use equal resistances for the Y_1 and Y_2 elements, equal capacitances for Y_3 and Y_4, resistance for Y_5, and capacitance for Y_6. Thus, for the circuit of Fig. 5-19b,

$$Y_1 = Y_2 = G \qquad Y_3 = Y_4 = j\omega C$$
$$Y_5 = G_s \qquad Y_6 = j\omega C_s \qquad (5\text{-}43)$$

Then, substituting into the equation of null [(5-42)],

$$-(\omega_0 C)^2(2G + j\omega_0 C_s) + G^2(j2\omega_0 C + G_s) = 0 \qquad (5\text{-}44)$$

where ω_0 is 2π times the null frequency. Then, equating reals,

$$2(\omega_0 C)^2 G = G^2 G_s \qquad (5\text{-}45)$$

and imaginaries

$$(\omega_0 C)^2 \omega_0 C_s = 2\omega_0 C G^2 \qquad (5\text{-}46)$$

Hence, from the last two equations, the null frequency may be determined for

$$\omega_0{}^2 = \frac{GG_s}{2C^2} = \frac{2G^2}{C_s C} \qquad (5\text{-}47)$$

Thus, given the circuit components, it is possible to determine the frequency at which the null occurs.

How would one go about designing the RC twin-T circuit to give a specified f_0? One must choose the four component values to satisfy Eq. (5-47). In order to simplify the procedure, it is convenient to define a design parameter n in the following manner: Rearranging the two right-hand members of Eq. (5-47),

$$n = \frac{G_s}{2G} = \frac{2C}{C_s} \qquad (5\text{-}48)$$

Then $\omega_0{}^2$ becomes

$$\omega_0{}^2 = \frac{GG_s}{2C^2} = \frac{G}{2C^2} 2G_n = n \frac{G^2}{C^2}$$

or

$$\omega_0 = \frac{\sqrt{n}}{RC} \qquad (5\text{-}49)$$

Thus if one is interested in designing for a specified f_0 only, any two of the three unknowns, R, C, and n, may be chosen at will and the third calculated from Eq. (5-49). Equation (5-48) may then be used to determine C_s and R_s.

5-21. Selectivity. Actually it may be shown that the value of the design parameter n controls the network selectivity in much the same manner as does Q in the antiresonant circuit. Investigation of the selectivity, then, allows one to choose n intelligently and removes one degree of arbitrariness in the design of the RC twin-T network.

Some simplification of the work results from noting that the twin-T structure when used as a selective network is normally used between two vacuum pentodes. In this type of service, Y_g, the source impedance, is $1/r_p$ of the driving tube. In general r_p will be very large compared with the network impedances, so that Y_g may be assumed to be negligible in Eq. (5-41). Similarly, since Y_L is the reciprocal of the input impedance of a vacuum tube, it, too, may be assumed negligible. Further simplification of the work results from expressing the unknowns in terms of G, ω_0, and n; thus from Eq. (5-49)

$$C = \sqrt{n} \, \frac{G}{\omega_0} \qquad (5\text{-}50)$$

and from Eq. (5-48)

$$C_s = \frac{2C}{n} = \frac{2G}{\sqrt{n}\,\omega_0} \tag{5-51}$$

and
$$G_s = 2nG \tag{5-52}$$

Substitution of these values into Eqs. (5-41) yields the circuit determinant.

$$
\begin{vmatrix}
G + j\sqrt{n}\,G\,\dfrac{\omega}{\omega_0} & 0 & -j\sqrt{n}\,G\,\dfrac{\omega}{\omega_0} & -G \\[2ex]
0 & G + j\sqrt{n}\,G\,\dfrac{\omega}{\omega_0} & -j\sqrt{n}\,G\,\dfrac{\omega}{\omega_0} & -G \\[2ex]
-j\sqrt{n}\,G\,\dfrac{\omega}{\omega_0} & -j\sqrt{n}\,G\,\dfrac{\omega}{\omega_0} & j2\sqrt{n}\,G\,\dfrac{\omega}{\omega_0} + 2nG & 0 \\[2ex]
-G & -G & 0 & 2G + j\dfrac{2G}{\sqrt{n}}\,\dfrac{\omega}{\omega_0}
\end{vmatrix}
$$

By definition the network *transfer function* is E_2/E_1. But in terms of the cofactors and network determinant

$$E_2 = I\,\frac{C_{12}'}{D'} \qquad \text{and} \qquad E_1 = I\,\frac{C_{11}'}{D'}$$

whence $E_2/E_1 = -M_{12}'/M_{11}'$. Evaluation of the two minors, M_{12}' and M_{11}', leads to the following result for the transfer function:

$$\frac{E_2}{E_1} = \frac{1 - (f/f_0)^2}{[1 - (f/f_0)^2] + j2(\sqrt{n} + 1/\sqrt{n})(f/f_0)} \tag{5-53}$$

This, then, is the basic equation whose magnitude gives the selectivity and whose angle gives the phase shift of the twin-T-network transfer function.

Equation (5-53) is by no means in optimum form for slide-rule calculation. For the latter, the best form is $1/[1 + jaf(f)]$. To obtain this form, one divides the numerator and denominator of Eq. (5-53) by $1 - (f/f_0)^2$, giving

$$\frac{E_2}{E_1} = \frac{1}{1 + j\dfrac{2(\sqrt{n} + 1/\sqrt{n})f/f_0}{1 - (f/f_0)^2}} = \frac{1}{1 - j2\dfrac{\sqrt{n} + 1/\sqrt{n}}{f/f_0 - f_0/f}} \tag{5-54}$$

By comparing these results with Eq. (4-39) it is observed that the transfer function displays geometric symmetry about f_0 in frequency and about 1 in n. In illustration of the latter statement the values of $n = 2$ and $n = \frac{1}{2}$ will give the same selectivity curve. This may be proved quite readily by the student.

It is now possible to determine what value of n gives the most selective curve. Figure 5-20 shows typical selectivity curves of the RC twin-T network for two values of n. The solid curve is sharper and hence more selective. The criterion for the most selective curve, then, is that it has

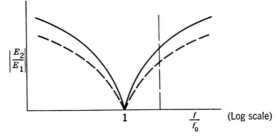

FIG. 5-20. Selectivity curves for the twin-T null network.

the maximum value of $|E_2/E_1|$, at any frequency different from f_0. Then if the *magnitude* of E_2/E_1, in Eq. (5-54), is differentiated with respect to n and the derivative set equal to zero, it is found that $n = 1$ gives the most selective curve.

Selectivity curves for a typical RC twin-T network are shown in Fig. 5-21. The network is designed for a null frequency at 5 kc and with

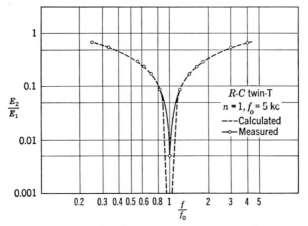

FIG. 5-21. Measured and calculated curves of the transfer function of a twin-T network.

$n = 1$; the results are plotted as $|E_2/E_1|$ on a logarithmic scale. The small circles indicate measured results that were obtained in the laboratory. It will be observed that there is excellent agreement between the actual and measured results except in the vicinity of the null frequency. This discrepancy is caused by three primary factors. First, the oscillator used to measure the curves has some harmonic content.

Thus, when it is set for 5 kc, some small 10- and 15-kc components are present that give a finite, though small, output voltage.   Second, a perfect null cannot be obtained because the physical network has stray capacitances that are not taken into account in the theoretical analysis. These circuit strays become more important as the operating frequency is raised.   For example, if a similar network were designed for a null at 50 kc, the discrepancy between the measured and theoretical response curves would be even greater.   Third, the actual bridge components were set to two significant figures only.

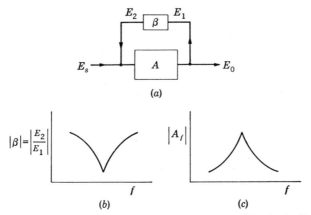

Fig. 5-22. Feedback amplifier employing a twin-T network in the feedback loop.

In general the RC twin-T network is most useful as a null network in the lower af because it provides an effective Q greater than that obtainable with LC circuits at low frequencies.   Furthermore, it has an economic advantage in that it is constructed of components which are less expensive than inductors of large inductances.

At higher af, where smaller values of L may be used, the twin-T network is not in such a favorable position.   At still higher frequencies its common ground lead presents a possible advantage again over the a-c Wheatstone bridge, although special care must be exercised to minimize the effects of stray capacitance.

5-22. Typical Application.   It is well known in the study of electronics that, if the amplifier in Fig. 5-22a has a large amplification $|A|$, the over-all gain with feedback will be

$$A_f = -\frac{1}{\beta}$$

where β is the response of the feedback network.   Then if a twin-T network having a transfer function as shown at b is used as the β network, the amplitude response of the over-all amplifier will be proportional to

$|E_1/E_2|$ or the reciprocal of Eq. (5-54) as shown at c. It follows, therefore, that a virtual tuned-amplifier characteristic may be obtained by using the twin-T structure as the feedback network. A feedback amplifier of this type may be used to good advantage with the detector on an impedance bridge. The sharp selectivity characteristic minimizes the effect of oscillator harmonics, and a more nearly perfect null may be obtained. The common ground lead of the twin T is of particular value in this application. Further, the resultant response gives a large value of effective $Q = f_0/(f_2 - f_1)$.

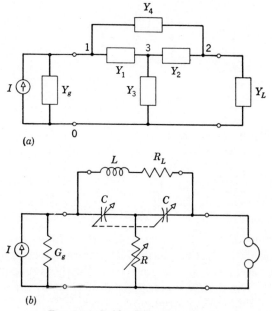

FIG. 5-23. Bridged T null networks.

5-23. Bridged T Network. A third type of commonly used null network is the bridged T network whose basic form is shown in Fig. 5-23. The method of handling the circuit to determine the equation of null and the selectivity is identical to that of the twin-T circuit and the bridged T network shares the feature of the common ground lead with that circuit.

PROBLEMS

5-1. Prove that if, at balance, the generator and detector in a bridge are interchanged the balance remains unaffected.

5-2. A modification of Fig. 5-3 would be to connect R_1C_1 in series, in which case the bridge is called a "Hay bridge." Derive the equation of balance for the Hay bridge.

5-3. A Wien bridge is to be designed to cover the frequency range 1 to 10 kc. A two-section variable capacitor is available, each section of which covers 40 to 400 $\mu\mu$f. A value of 1,000 ohms is to be used for R_3. Determine the remaining resistances in the circuit.

5-4. The circuit of Fig. 5-24 may be used to measure the complex propagation constant, γ, of the network N, which is defined by $e^\gamma = E_1/E_2$. Assuming L and R have been adjusted to give a null in the detector, derive an equation for determining γ in complex form.

5-5. A "simplex telegraph" system is obtained by operating a telegraph channel between ground and a balanced-to-ground telephone line. Draw a schematic of the

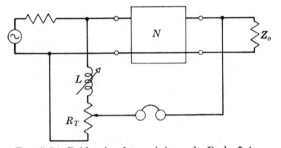

FIG. 5-24. Bridge for determining γ in Prob. 5-4.

simplex system, and show that the telegraph and telephone channels operate without mutual interference. It may be assumed that two repeating coils are available.

5-6. A two-wire telephone line is to be connected to a radio transmitter and a radio receiver. The telephone line must carry two-way conversations. The transmitter and receiver can each handle only one-way communication. Devise a suitable system, using a hybrid coil, to effect the required two-wire to four-wire transition.

5-7. In the neutralizing circuit of Fig. 5-17 the plate-tank-circuit coil is tapped up 30 per cent from the bottom of the coil. Under this condition the coefficient of coupling between the two parts of the coil is 0.48. The self-inductance of the upper part L_{ad} is 20 μh; of the lower part L_{bd}, 6 μh. If C_{gp} is 8.6 $\mu\mu$f, what nominal value of C_N should be chosen for neutralization at $\omega = 10^6$ radians/sec?

5-8. In the circuit of Fig. 5-18 derive an equation for the phase relationship between the two components of voltage produced across R_1 by the generators E_A and E_B.

5-9. (a) Calculate the components of the twin-T section that gives the selectivity curve of Fig. 5-21. Use $R = 1.5$ kilohms. (b) Repeat a for $f_0 = 5$ kc and with $n = 0.25, 0.5, 2,$ and 4. Plot the selectivity curves for these four networks.

5-10. (a) Following the general method used for the twin-T network, determine the selectivity curve for the Wien bridge of Fig. 5-4 in terms of f/f_0. Use d as the reference node, a as node 1, c as node 2, and b as node 3. Assume zero admittance for the generator and load. (b) Does the selectivity depend upon the value of R_1 or R_3? (c) Compare the merits of the twin-T circuit and the Wien bridge as a feedback network for a selective amplifier. (d) Which of the two circuits can be made more selective?

5-11. Transform the twin-T circuit of Fig. 5-19b into an equivalent Π section, and show that Z_b of the equivalent Π contains virtual inductance at $f < f_0$.

5-12. Figure 5-25 shows the circuit of the General Radio type 821-A impedance-measuring set. The circuit may be identified as a twin-T structure. C_b and C_g are variable, and the substitution method is used. Determine equations for G_x and B_x at the null frequency in terms of the bridge parameters.

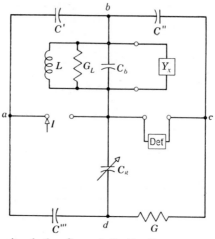

FIG. 5-25. Basic circuit of the General Radio Company type 821-A impedance measuring set.

5-13. (a) Derive the equation of null for the bridged T network of Fig. 5-23a.   (b) Is it possible to get a null if the network contains only resistance and capacitance and if $Y_1 = Y_2$?

5-14. It is desired to check L, R_L, and Q_L of a number of production coils at a frequency of 1.59 kc with the bridged T circuit of Fig. 5-23b.

    a. What are the equations for L, R_L, and Q_L at the null frequency?

    b. If the mean values of the coils are $L = 100$ mh and $Q_L = 25$, what mean values of C and R are required in the network?

    c. Which dials, if any, may be calibrated directly in terms of the unknowns?

CHAPTER 6

ITERATIVE NETWORKS

A group of networks frequently encountered in communication engineering consists of *iterative* circuits, i.e., a number of identical, passive stages all connected in cascade, or tandem, between a generator and a load as shown in Fig. 6-1. Typical examples of this network are the artificial line and the wave filter. For a general termination Z_R the calculation of voltage and current at any one of the junctions in the cascade can be handled by direct application of the methods of Chap. 3, but this can be a tedious process. For example, if, in Fig. 6-1, there are 20 iden-

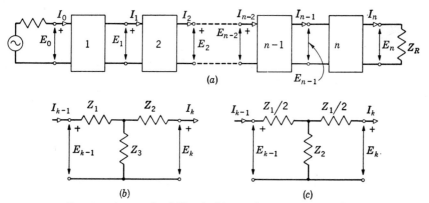

(a)

(b)   (c)

FIG. 6-1. A cascade of identical lumped-constant networks.

tical T sections in the cascade, 21 simultaneous mesh equations would have to be set up and solved to evaluate any one of the currents. If, however, and this is the often-encountered case, Z_R is equal to the *iterative impedance* of each of the stages, the behavior of each stage may be calculated *independently* of the remaining stages. This results in great simplification of the problem.

In Chap. 3 it was found that, if a network such as that of Fig. 6-1b is terminated in its iterative impedance, the input impedance of the network is also the iterative value. When this idea is applied to the cascade, it is apparent that, if $Z_R = Z_{it}$, every stage in the cascade is terminated in Z_{it} and every stage behaves in exactly the same manner.

It is apparent that this is true no matter how many sections there may be. If there is any dissipation whatever in the network, as the number of sections becomes larger and larger the effect of the terminating impedance becomes less and less. Thus for a sequence involving an infinite number of sections the input impedance will always be the iterative impedance. It is also apparent that, no matter what the termination may be, as the number of sections of a finite sequence is increased, the input impedance will approach asymptotically (although perhaps in an oscillatory manner) the iterative impedance.

If the component stages are symmetrical, as in Fig. 6-1c, the iterative impedance is usually given the special designation of *characteristic impedance*. Since, in a cascade of asymmetrical networks terminated in Z_{it}, the only difference from a cascade of symmetrical sections is in the two ends, a study of the symmetrical case gives also the key to the analysis of the asymmetrical one. Therefore the analysis of the symmetrical case will be developed.

6-1. The Complex Propagation Constant. Consider a typical symmetrical component T stage of the cascade as shown in Fig. 6-1c. Let a voltage E_{k-1} be applied to the input terminals, and *let the section be terminated in its characteristic impedance* Z_{oT}. Then the currents I_{k-1} and I_k will flow, the latter producing the output voltage E_k across Z_{oT}. In the general case, Z_1 and Z_2 will be complex; hence I_{k-1} will differ from I_k, and E_{k-1} will differ from E_k in both magnitude and phase. Then, reading from the diagram, by the current division theorem, the complex current ratio will be

$$\frac{I_{k-1}}{I_k} = \frac{Z_1/2 + Z_2 + Z_{oT}}{Z_2} \tag{6-1}$$

By the definition of the characteristic impedance Z_{oT} the input impedance of the T section is also Z_{oT}; hence

$$E_{k-1} = I_{k-1}Z_{oT} \tag{6-2}$$

and
$$E_k = I_kZ_{oT} \tag{6-3}$$

Dividing Eq. (6-2) by (6-3) and introducing Eq. (6-1),

$$\frac{E_{k-1}}{E_k} = \frac{I_{k-1}}{I_k} = \frac{Z_1/2 + Z_2 + Z_{oT}}{Z_2} \tag{6-4}$$

Since every component stage in the cascade behaves in the same manner when $Z_R = Z_{oT}$, Eq. (6-4) may be generalized to give the current and voltage ratios along the entire iterative structure; thus

$$\frac{E_0}{E_1} = \frac{E_1}{E_2} = \frac{E_2}{E_3} = \cdots = \frac{E_{n-1}}{E_n}$$
$$= \frac{I_0}{I_1} = \frac{I_1}{I_2} = \frac{I_2}{I_3} = \cdots = \frac{I_{n-1}}{I_n} = \frac{Z_1/2 + Z_2 + Z_{oT}}{Z_2} \tag{6-5}$$

Equation (6-5) shows that the *ratio* of input to output current for each of the T sections is the same. This comes about because an equal *proportion*, rather than an equal amount, of current is drained off by the shunt arm in each section; consequently it is convenient to express the current and voltage ratios of Eq. (6-5) logarithmically. This may be done by defining a *complex propagation constant*, γ, such that

$$e^\gamma = \frac{I_{k-1}}{I_k} = \frac{E_{k-1}}{E_k} = \frac{Z_1/2 + Z_2 + Z_{oT}}{Z_2} \tag{6-6}$$

Inasmuch as the right-hand member of Eq. (6-6) is complex, γ will also be complex; thus let

$$\gamma = \alpha + j\beta \tag{6-7}$$

It is now possible to determine the rectangular coordinates of γ. Let the complex ratio of Eq. (6-6) be expressed in polar form, say, $|I_{k-1}/I_k| \underline{/\phi}$; then

$$e^\gamma = \left| \frac{I_{k-1}}{I_k} \right| \underline{/\phi}$$

or

$$e^{\alpha+j\beta} = \left| \frac{I_{k-1}}{I_k} \right| e^{j\phi} \tag{6-8}$$

Taking natural logarithms,

$$\alpha + j\beta = \ln \left| \frac{I_{k-1}}{I_k} \right| + j\phi \tag{6-9}$$

Equating reals,

$$\alpha = \ln \left| \frac{I_{k-1}}{I_k} \right| = \ln \left| \frac{Z_1/2 + Z_2 + Z_{oT}}{Z_2} \right| \quad \text{nepers/section} \tag{6-10}$$

Equating imaginaries,

$$\beta = \phi = \arg \frac{Z_1/2 + Z_2 + Z_{oT}}{Z_2} \quad \text{radians/section} \tag{6-11}$$

where "arg" stands for "argument," which in turn means "angle of."

From Eq. (6-10) it is seen that α, the real part of the complex propagation constant, is a measure of the change in *magnitude* of the current or voltage in each T section; it is known as the *attenuation constant*.

It is apparent that β is a measure of the difference in *phase* between the input and output currents or voltages. β is designated the network *phase-shift constant, delay constant,* or *wavelength constant.* β will be positive when the output current lags the input current.

The value of the complex propagation constant as an aid in solving iterative-structure problems where $Z_R = Z_{it}$ may now be seen. Say that it is required to find the current output of the kth stage in Fig. (6-1a). Then

$$\frac{I_0}{I_k} = \frac{I_0}{I_1} \frac{I_1}{I_2} \frac{I_2}{I_3} \cdots \frac{I_{k-2}}{I_{k-1}} \frac{I_{k-1}}{I_k} \tag{6-12}$$

But from Eqs. (6-5) and (6-6)

$$\frac{I_0}{I_k} = (e^\gamma)^k = e^{k\gamma} \tag{6-13}$$

or the total attenuation loss of k sections in the cascade is $k\alpha$ nepers, and the corresponding phase shift will be $k\beta$ radians. The corresponding voltage ratio E_0/E_k is also given by $e^{k\gamma}$. It must be stressed that these relationships are valid only if the cascade is terminated such that $Z_R = Z_{oT}$ (or $Z_R = Z_{it}$ for asymmetrical component sections). If Z_R differs from this value, reflections occur and the foregoing treatment no longer holds. The subject of reflection is discussed in Chap. 9.

The following facts should be noted concerning the dimensions of α, β, and γ: Since all exponents must be dimensionless, $k\gamma$ as in Eq. (6-13) must be dimensionless. Since k is the number of sections, the dimensions of α, β, and γ are "per section." The student will observe that α is given as nepers per section and β as radians per section in Eqs. (6-10) and (6-11). The terms "neper" and "radian," even though they are dimensionless, serve primarily as reminders that the natural, or napierian, logarithm has been used. This designation is necessary as well as convenient, for as will be seen, α may also be expressed in terms of another dimensionless unit, the decibel, which is derived from the common logarithm to the base 10. Also, β may be expressed in degrees to simplify computations.

6-2. Related Sections. While Eqs. (6-10) and (6-11) have been derived for a ladder structure made up of symmetrical T sections, it may be shown quite readily that they also apply to a ladder of symmetrical Π sections, provided that the T and Π sections are assembled from the same basic L section.

Consider the basic L section shown in Fig. 6-2a. If two such L sections are connected in cascade with shunt arms adjoining, the two shunt arms each of value $2Z_2$ combine to give a value Z_2 and the symmetrical T section of Fig. 6-2b results. If, on the other hand, two of the basic L sections are cascaded with the series arms adjoining, the two series arms each of value $Z_1/2$ combine to give a value Z_1 and the symmetrical Π section of Fig. 6-2c results.

It must be stressed that the symmetrical T and Π networks of Fig. 6-2 are not equivalent but are *related* networks in that they are assembled from the same basic L section; they do not have the same open- and short-circuit impedances.

If, now, a number of related T sections are connected in cascade, the series arms may be combined to give the iterative ladder structure of Fig. 6-2d. Similarly if a number of the related Π sections are cascaded, adjacent shunt arms may be combined to give the *same* ladder structure (Fig. 6-2d).

Since a network of T's, no matter how long, could differ from a network of the same number of related Π sections by only the arrangement of the terminating L sections, and since the effect of these on the over-all current ratio could be made negligibly small by making the lines long enough, the propagation constant must be the same for related T and Π sections.

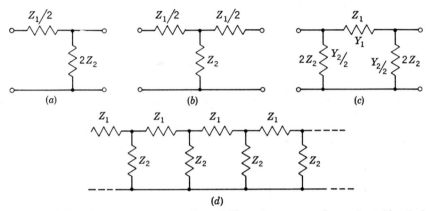

Fig. 6-2. Related sections. The L, T, and Π sections are made up from identical values of Z_1 and Z_2.

It may be concluded that the complex propagation constant for both a symmetrical T section and its related Π section is given by Eq. (6-6) or

$$\gamma = \ln \frac{Z_1/2 + Z_2 + Z_{oT}}{Z_2} \qquad (6\text{-}14)$$

where $Z_{oT} = Z_o$ of the symmetrical T section

$$= \sqrt{Z_1 Z_2 + Z_1{}^2/4}$$

The student may wish to determine the dual form of Eq. (6-14) from the related Π section, which is

$$\gamma = \ln \frac{Y_2/2 + Y_1 + Y_{o\Pi}}{Y_1} \qquad (6\text{-}14a)$$

where $Y_{o\Pi} = \sqrt{Y_1 Y_2 + Y_2{}^2/4}$, and prove they give the same value of γ.

6-3. Impedance Relationships in Related Networks. Inasmuch as the open- and short-circuit impedances differ for the related T and Π networks, the two networks will have different values of characteristic impedance. Let Z_{oT} symbolize the characteristic impedance of the T section, $Z_{o\Pi}$ the characteristic impedance (and $Y_{o\Pi}$ the characteristic admittance) of the related Π section. Then by Eq. (3-106)

$$Z_{oT} = \sqrt{Z_1 Z_2 + \frac{Z_1{}^2}{4}} \qquad (6\text{-}15)$$

By the principle of general duality the characteristic admittance of the II section is

$$Y_{o\text{II}} = \sqrt{Y_1 Y_2 + \frac{Y_2^2}{4}} \tag{6-16}$$

or, substituting for admittances in terms of corresponding impedances,

$$\frac{1}{Z_{o\text{II}}} = \sqrt{\frac{1}{Z_1 Z_2} + \frac{1}{4Z_2^2}} = \frac{1}{Z_1 Z_2}\sqrt{Z_1 Z_2 + \frac{Z_1^2}{4}} \tag{6-17}$$

or

$$Z_{o\text{II}} Z_{o\text{T}} = Z_1 Z_2$$

This interrelationship between $Z_{o\text{T}}$, $Z_{o\text{II}}$, and the basic Z_1 and Z_2 elements has special significance in that the basic L section can transform

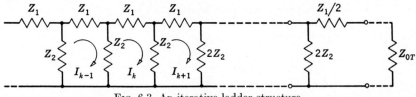

Fig. 6.3. An iterative ladder structure.

$Z_{o\text{T}}$ to $Z_{o\text{II}}$, and vice versa. To illustrate this principle, let the shunt-arm side of the L section (Fig. 6-2a) be terminated in $Z_{o\text{II}}$. Then the input impedance at the series-arm end is

$$Z_{in} = \frac{Z_1}{2} + \frac{2Z_2 Z_{o\text{II}}}{2Z_2 + Z_{o\text{II}}}$$

Substituting for $Z_{o\text{II}}$ from Eq. (6-17),

$$Z_{in} = \frac{Z_1}{2} + \frac{2Z_2 Z_1 Z_2 / Z_{o\text{T}}}{2Z_2 + Z_1 Z_2 / Z_{o\text{T}}}$$

Reducing to a common denominator and clearing,

$$Z_{in} = Z_{o\text{T}} \tag{6-17a}$$

It may be proved in a similar manner that, if the series-arm end of the L section is terminated in $Z_{o\text{T}}$, the input impedance at the shunt-arm end is $Z_{o\text{II}}$. These impedance-transforming properties of the L section will be of particular use in the study of wave filters (Chap. 7). An immediate application of this property may be seen by considering the problem of terminating the iterative ladder structure. If the ladder structure is built up of symmetrical II sections, then the far end of the line will terminate in a shunt arm of value $2Z_2$ as shown in Fig. 6-3. Then if the structure is to be properly terminated so that Eq. (6-6) or (6-7) is valid, Z_R must be $Z_{o\text{T}}$.

It may happen that the resistance and reactance elements required to build up $Z_{o\Pi}$ do not have values as convenient as those necessary to build up Z_{oT}. If, then, an additional half section, i.e., a basic L, is added to the end of the line, as illustrated in Fig. 6-3, the termination of $Z_R = Z_{oT}$ becomes proper and Eqs. (6-6) and (6-7) may be used for the calculation of voltage and current.

6-4. γ in Terms of Hyperbolic Functions. Equation (6-14) expresses γ in terms of the natural logarithm of a complex impedance ratio. Other expressions for γ may be derived in terms of hyperbolic functions. These alternative forms are often of considerable use in the study of wave filters and transmission lines. One of these alternative forms may be derived by setting up a "difference equation" for the kth loop in Fig. 6-3. Applying Kirchhoff's voltage law to the kth mesh,

$$-Z_2 I_{k-1} + (Z_1 + 2Z_2) I_k - Z_2 I_{k+1} = 0 \qquad (6\text{-}18)$$

Dividing through by $-I_k/2Z_2$,

$$\frac{I_{k-1}}{2I_k} - \frac{Z_1 + 2Z_2}{2Z_2} + \frac{I_{k+1}}{2I_k} = 0$$

But $e^\gamma = I_{k-1}/I_k = I_k/I_{k+1}$; therefore

$$\frac{e^\gamma + e^{-\gamma}}{2} = 1 + \frac{Z_1}{2Z_2}$$

Introducing the definition of the hyperbolic cosine [Eq. (A-2)],[1]

$$\cosh \gamma = 1 + \frac{Z_1}{2Z_2} \qquad (6\text{-}19)$$

The student may be led to believe that Eq. (6-19) is easier to use than Eq. (6-14), but this is not necessarily true unless Z_1 and Z_2 are both real, or unless they are both imaginary as they may be considered to be in the study of wave filters. In either of these two cases $\cosh \gamma$ will be real, and the determination of the real and imaginary parts of γ is a relatively simple matter. If, on the other hand, Z_1 and Z_2 are complex, the determination of α and β is in general more difficult than if Eq. (6-14) is used. It may be shown after considerable manipulation (see Appendix) that α and β may be calculated from Eq. (6-19) by the following equations:

Let $1 + Z_1/2Z_2 = A + jB$, A and B being known. Then

$$\cosh \alpha = \frac{\sqrt{(1 + A)^2 + B^2} + \sqrt{(1 - A)^2 + B^2}}{2}$$

$$\cos \beta = \frac{\sqrt{(1 + A)^2 + B^2} - \sqrt{(1 - A)^2 + B^2}}{2} \qquad (6\text{-}20)$$

[1] Equations indicated by "A" are in the Appendix.

Since the right-hand members of these two equations are real numbers, α and β may be determined from tables of real hyperbolic and trigonometric functions.

Still another expression may be obtained for the complex propagation constant of a ladder network, this time in terms of the hyperbolic tangent rather than the hyperbolic cosine. From Eqs. (A-9) and (6-19)

$$\begin{aligned}
\sinh \gamma &= \sqrt{\cosh^2 \gamma - 1} \\
&= \sqrt{\left(1 + \frac{Z_1}{2Z_2}\right)^2 - 1} = \sqrt{\frac{Z_1}{Z_2} + \left(\frac{Z_1}{2Z_2}\right)^2} \\
&= \frac{1}{Z_2}\sqrt{Z_1 Z_2 + \frac{Z_1^2}{4}} = \frac{Z_{oT}}{Z_2}
\end{aligned} \tag{6-21}$$

Dividing Eq. (6-21) by (6-19),

$$\tanh \gamma = \frac{\sinh \gamma}{\cosh \gamma} = \frac{Z_{oT}}{Z_2 + Z_1/2}$$

But for the T section, $Z_{oc} = Z_1/2 + Z_2$, and from Eq. (3-107), $Z_{oT} = \sqrt{Z_{oc}Z_{sc}}$. Therefore

$$\tanh \gamma = \sqrt{\frac{Z_{sc}}{Z_{oc}}} \tag{6-22}$$

While Eq. (6-22) has a form that is easy to remember, it presents the same problem as does Eq. (6-19) when α and β are to be determined. In general Z_{sc} and Z_{oc} are complex impedances; so $\tanh \gamma$ is complex, and equal, say, to $C + jD$. It may be shown (see Appendix) that α and β may be found independently by the equations

$$\begin{aligned}
\tanh 2\alpha &= \frac{2C}{1 + C^2 + D^2} \\
\tan 2\beta &= \frac{2D}{1 - (C^2 + D^2)}
\end{aligned} \tag{6-23}$$

Equations (6-23) are desirable but are by no means essential for the solution of α and β from Eq. (6-22) in a numerical example. Resort may be made to reducing the hyperbolic tangent to exponential form as illustrated in the following example:

Find α and β for a symmetrical four-terminal network whose open- and short-circuit impedances are

$$Z_{oc} = 552\underline{/-59.5^\circ} \text{ ohms} \qquad Z_{sc} = 501\underline{/-14.1^\circ} \text{ ohms}$$

Calculations are to be carried to slide-rule accuracy. By Eqs. (6-23) and (A-3)

$$\tanh \gamma = \frac{e^\gamma - e^{-\gamma}}{e^\gamma + e^{-\gamma}} = \frac{e^{2\gamma} - 1}{e^{2\gamma} + 1} = \sqrt{\frac{Z_{sc}}{Z_{oc}}}$$

$$= \sqrt{\frac{501/-14.1°}{552/-59.5°}} = \sqrt{0.909/45.4°}$$

$$= 0.953/22.7° = 0.779 + j0.368$$

$$e^{2\gamma} - 1 = (0.779 + j0.368)(e^{2\gamma} + 1)$$

$$e^{2\gamma} = \frac{1.779 + 0.368}{0.221 - j0.368} = \frac{1.814/11.7°}{0.429/-59.0°} = 4.24/70.7°$$

Then $\alpha = \frac{1}{2} \ln 4.24 = 1.442/2 = 0.721$ neper/section and $\beta = 70.7/2 = 35.4°$/section.

These results may be checked by Eqs. (6-23).

$$C = 0.779 \qquad D = 0.368$$

Substituting,

$$\tanh 2\alpha = \frac{2(0.779)}{1 + (0.779)^2 + (0.368)^2} = \frac{1.558}{1 + 0.606 + 0.136}$$

$$= \frac{1.558}{1.742} = 0.893$$

$$\alpha = \frac{1.44}{2} = 0.72 \text{ neper/section}$$

and

$$\tan 2\beta = \frac{2(0.368)}{1 - (0.606 + 0.136)} = \frac{0.736}{0.258} = 2.85$$

$$\beta = \frac{70.7}{2} = 35.4°/\text{section}$$

6-5. Design of the T Section. The need often arises in practice to design an iterative ladder structure to give specified values of characteristic impedance and complex propagation constant. It is convenient to derive equations giving the T elements directly in terms of the specified quantities, and, further, such a derivation shows one application for the equation for γ in hyperbolic form.

It has been shown in Chap. 3 that the elements of a T section can be expressed in terms of the open- and short-circuit impedances. It is therefore desirable to have γ and Z_o expressed in terms of Z_{oc} and Z_{sc}. Of the three equations that have been derived for γ, then, Eq. (6-22) is the most useful for the immediate problem. Squaring Eq. (6-22),

$$\frac{Z_{sc}}{Z_{oc}} = \tanh^2 \gamma \tag{6-24}$$

and from Eq. (3-107)

$$Z_{sc}Z_{oc} = Z_o^2 \tag{6-25}$$

Multiplying Eqs. (6-24) and (6-25) and solving for Z_{sc},

$$Z_{sc} = Z_o \tanh \gamma \tag{6-26}$$

Dividing Eq. (6-25) by (6-24) and solving for Z_{oc},

$$Z_{oc} = \frac{Z_o}{\tanh \gamma} \tag{6-27}$$

The design of the symmetrical T section may be completed by applying Eqs. (3-108).

$$Z_2 = \sqrt{Z_{oc}(Z_{oc} - Z_{sc})} = \sqrt{Z_o \frac{\cosh \gamma}{\sinh \gamma} \left(Z_o \frac{\cosh \gamma}{\sinh \gamma} - Z_o \frac{\sinh \gamma}{\cosh \gamma} \right)}$$

$$= \sqrt{Z_o^2 \frac{\cosh^2 \gamma - \sinh^2 \gamma}{\sinh^2 \gamma}}$$

$$Z_2 = \frac{Z_o}{\sinh \gamma} \tag{6-28}$$

Similarly,

$$\frac{Z_1}{2} = Z_{oc} - Z_2 = Z_o \frac{\cosh \gamma}{\sinh \gamma} - \frac{Z_o}{\sinh \gamma}$$

$$= \frac{Z_o(\cosh \gamma - 1)}{\sinh \gamma}$$

This may be simplified by the half-angle formulas.

$$\cosh \gamma - 1 = 2 \sinh^2 \frac{\gamma}{2} \tag{6-29}$$

$$\sinh \gamma = 2 \sinh \frac{\gamma}{2} \cosh \frac{\gamma}{2} \tag{6-30}$$

Then, substituting and clearing,

$$\frac{Z_1}{2} = Z_o \tanh \frac{\gamma}{2} \tag{6-31}$$

The required T section may then be designed to give the specified values of Z_o and γ by means of Eqs. (6-28) and (6-31).

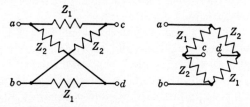

FIG. 6-4. Lattice network. The arrangement at b simplifies the calculation of the open- and short-circuit impedances.

6-6. The Lattice Network. Thus far in the chapter it has been assumed that the iterative structure is composed of T or Ⅱ sections. This is by no means necessary; for example, iterative structures may be encountered in practice that are made up of symmetrical-lattice sections. A typical symmetrical lattice is illustrated in Fig. 6-4. Since the network is symmetrical, its iterative and image impedances are identical to Z_o, and by virtue of Eq. (3-107) $Z_o = \sqrt{Z_{oc}Z_{sc}}$. From Fig. 6-4

$$Z_{oc} = \frac{Z_1 + Z_2}{2} \tag{6-32}$$

$$Z_{sc} = 2\,\frac{Z_1 Z_2}{Z_1 + Z_2} \tag{6-33}$$

whence

$$Z_o{}^2 = Z_1 Z_2 \tag{6-34}$$

The complex propagation constant may be determined in terms of Z_1 and Z_2 by Eq. (6-22).

$$\tanh \gamma = \sqrt{\frac{Z_{sc}}{Z_{oc}}} = \frac{2Z_1 Z_2}{Z_1 + Z_o} \tag{6-35}$$

Introducing Eq. (6-34) and the definition of the hyperbolic tangent [Eq. (A-3)],

$$\frac{e^{2\gamma} - 1}{e^{2\gamma} + 1} = \frac{2Z_o}{Z_1 + Z_o{}^2/Z_1} = \frac{2Z_o Z_1}{Z_1{}^2 + Z_o{}^2}$$

Solving for $e^{2\gamma}$,

$$e^{2\gamma} = \left(\frac{Z_1 + Z_o}{Z_1 - Z_o}\right)^2$$

whence

$$e^\gamma = \pm\,\frac{Z_1 + Z_o}{Z_1 - Z_o} = \frac{1 + Z_1/Z_o}{1 - Z_1/Z_o} \tag{6-36}$$

In the last step the negative sign is chosen from physical considerations.

Since γ and Z_o are known for the lattice section, current and voltage along an iterative structure composed of such sections may be determined by

$$\frac{E_0}{E_k} = \frac{I_0}{I_k} = e^{k\gamma}$$

provided that the structure is terminated properly in Z_o.

6-7. Wave Motion. In a cascade of networks, if a driving voltage or current is impressed suddenly on the input, the effect is not immediately observable at the output but occurs at a later time. This gives rise to the notion of waves.

The word *wave* has a dual meaning in the technical press. In its most general sense a wave is a function of both time and space, such that a disturbance at a point p, at a time t, is related in a definite manner to what occurs at distant points at later times. (A wave is not necessarily repetitive, as, for example, a tidal wave.) In a distortionless wave the disturbances at distant points are exact replicas (except for changes in magnitude and delay in time) of the disturbance at the original point.

In a special sense the word wave is also used to represent a disturbance as a function of time at a particular point, as, for example, a *voltage wave* or a *current wave*. These can be shown on an oscillograph. The reader can generally tell from the context which type of wave a writer or speaker is referring to.

This chapter will be interested in the wave which is a function of both time and space. An illustration of such a wave is provided by the dachshund.

> There was a dachshund once so long
> He hadn't any notion
> How long it took to notify
> His tail of an emotion.
>
> And so it was that though his eyes
> Were filled with woe and sadness
> His little tail went wagging on
> Because of previous gladness.

Mathematically a wave may be recognized if a relation such as

$$y = f_1(x)f_2(x - vt) \tag{6-37}$$

is observed, where x is any space variable, not necessarily a rectangular coordinate. Such a function indicates that, except for a change in magnitude with x which is independent of time, what happens at a point x_0 at time t_0 is repeated at all values $x_0 + \Delta x$ at a time $t_0 + \Delta x/v$, no matter what the value of Δx, be it large or small. The velocity with which the disturbance would propagate would be v. An example of such a wave would be

$$y = Ae^{-\alpha x} \cos \omega \left(\frac{x}{v} - t\right) \tag{6-38}$$

A more complex wave might be represented by the summation

$$y = \sum_{k=1}^{n} B_k e^{-\alpha_k x} \cos \omega_k \left(\frac{x}{v_k} - t\right) \tag{6-38a}$$

If n is allowed to go to ∞, and successive values of ω_k are taken sufficiently close, equation (6-38a) can describe a wave of any shape. Such a wave would preserve its form or shape if α_k and v_k were the same for all values of k.

Since measurements are usually most conveniently made with sinusoidal signals, it is useful to analyze the behavior of a network first at a single frequency and then as a function of frequency.

It may now be shown that a signal applied to the input terminals of a cascade of lumped networks terminated in Z_o is propagated along the cascade as a wave. Say the input voltage is $e_0 = \hat{E}_0 \cos \omega t$, which may, of course, be written as $e_0 = \text{Re} \{\hat{E}_0 e^{-j\omega t}\}$. Then, by the methods developed earlier in the chapter, the voltage appearing across the output terminals of the xth section will be

$$e_x = \text{Re} \{\hat{E}_0 e^{j\omega t} e^{-\gamma x}\} = \text{Re} \{\hat{E}_0 e^{-\alpha x} e^{j(\omega t - \beta x)}\}$$
$$= \hat{E}_0 e^{-\alpha x} \cos (\omega t - \beta x) \qquad (6\text{-}39)$$

where x, being the number of sections, can take on only integral values: 1, 2, 3, ... (In Chap. 8 it will be shown that the same equation applies to a transmission line where x can have *any* value up to the total length of the line.) Equation (6-39) may also be written as

$$e_x = \hat{E}_0 e^{-\alpha x} \cos \omega \left(t - \frac{\beta x}{\omega} \right) \qquad (6\text{-}39a)$$

Since this has the exact form of Eq. (6-38) (remember $\cos -\phi = \cos \phi$), it has been shown that a sinusoidal input signal is propagated as a wave along a properly terminated cascade.

6-8. Phase Velocity, Phase Delay. By comparison of Eqs. (6-39a) and (6-38) it is apparent that the velocity with which a signal of single frequency propagates through the structure is

$$v_p = \frac{\omega}{\beta} \text{ sections/sec} \qquad (6\text{-}40)$$

This is called the *phase velocity* of the network at the particular frequency $\omega/2\pi$.

Since, at any finite frequency, v_p will be finite if β differs from zero, it might be expected that the signal, after traveling x sections, lags the input signal by some interval of time, say, τ_p. From Eq. (6-39a) it may be seen that the term $\beta x/\omega = x/v_p$ has the dimensions of time and represents the *delay* introduced on a point of constant phase as the signal passes through x sections of the cascade; it may be designated the *phase delay* introduced by x sections. Thus,

$$\tau_p = \frac{x}{v_p} = \frac{\beta x}{\omega} \qquad (6\text{-}40a)$$

and Eq. (6-39a) may be written as

$$e_x = \hat{E}_0 e^{-\alpha x} \cos \omega(t - \tau_p) \qquad (6\text{-}39b)$$

6-9. Wave Motion on Cascade of Dissipationless Sections. As an example, consider the network shown in Fig. 6-5, a T section of pure reactances,

$$Z_1 = j\omega L$$

$$Z_2 = \frac{1}{j\omega C}$$

$$Z_o = \sqrt{\frac{L}{C} - \frac{\omega^2 L^2}{4}}$$

If $L/C > \omega^2 L^2/4$, Z_o will be a pure resistance. When the T section is terminated in such a resistance, the ratio of current will be, from Eq. (6-1),

$$\frac{I_{k-1}}{I_k} = \frac{\sqrt{L/C - \omega^2 L^2/4} + j(\omega L/2 - 1/\omega C)}{1/j\omega C} \tag{6-41}$$

The absolute value of $(I_{k-1}/I_k)^2$ will be obtained by adding the squares of the real and imaginary components in Eq. (6-41),

$$\left|\frac{I_{k-1}}{I_k}\right|^2 = \frac{\dfrac{L}{C} - \dfrac{\omega^2 L^2}{4} + \dfrac{\omega^2 L^2}{4} - \dfrac{L}{C} + \dfrac{1}{\omega^2 C^2}}{1/\omega^2 C^2} = 1 \tag{6-42}$$

It will be seen, then, that the magnitude of the current ratio is unity. This would be expected if the characteristic impedance is a pure resistance, for a change in current would mean a loss of power and the pure reactance elements cannot dissipate any energy.

There is, however, a shift in phase, the output current and voltage lagging the input current and voltage by β. Then if the iterative structure consists of a large number of lossless T sections in cascade and is terminated in Z_o, the phasor diagram for the currents has the form shown in Fig. 6-6. It will be observed that the locus

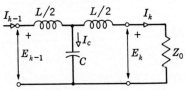

FIG. 6-5. Lossless T section.

of the several phasors representing the currents between sections is a circle and the value of the current at any junction k is

$$I_k = I_0 \underline{/-k\beta} \tag{6-43}$$

where I_0 is the current at the input of the entire iterative structure. The phase of I_0 is arbitrarily taken to be zero.

In order to show graphically the character of the wave motion, the voltage and/or current should be plotted as a function of x and t. Of course, a network with a large number of sections per wavelength would be desirable in order to have enough points to show the wave motion well. In order to show a function of both time and space on two-dimensional plots, it is convenient to make a series of plots of $|E|$ vs. x at uniform intervals of time. This is done in Fig. 6-7 for intervals of $\frac{1}{8}$ cycle.

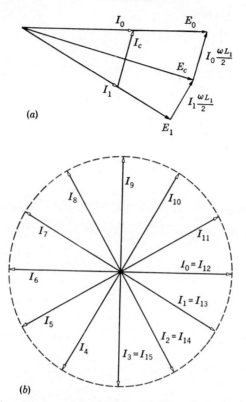

Fig. 6-6. Phasor diagrams for a cascade of lossless T sections terminated in Z_o. (a) One section. (b) Locus of currents along the cascade.

The distance between two adjacent positive maxima would be termed a *wavelength* and would be equal to the number of sections which produce a lag of 2π radians. If n_λ is the number of sections for 1 wavelength,

$$n_\lambda\beta = 2\pi$$
$$n_\lambda = \frac{2\pi}{\beta} \tag{6-44}$$

The wave should proceed at a phase velocity of 1 wavelength/cycle, and therefore

$$v_p = n_\lambda f = \frac{\omega}{\beta}$$

which checks Eq. (6-40).

6-10. Wave Motion on Cascade with Dissipative Sections. If the sections had resistance in either branch, there would be a loss in power and the output voltage and current of each section would necessarily be less than the input voltage and current. This is shown in the phasor

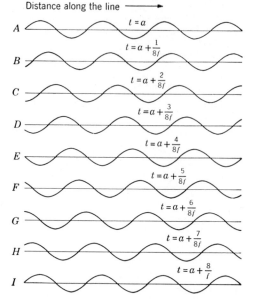

FIG. 6-7. Instantaneous distribution of current and voltage along a resistanceless cascade terminated in its characteristic impedance.

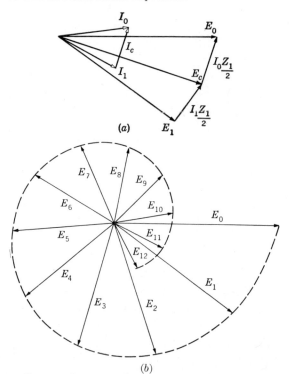

FIG. 6-8. Phasor diagrams for a cascade of T sections having dissipation and terminated in Z_o. (a) One section. (b) Locus of voltages along the cascade.

diagram of Fig. 6-8a. There would also be a difference in phase, and so the voltage and current at the different instants would be similar to the curves of Fig. 6-9. A phasor diagram for voltages along the line would be similar to that of Fig. 6-8b.

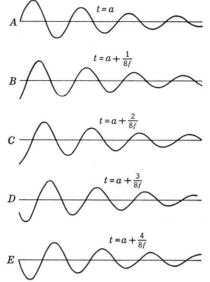

If an ammeter or voltmeter (which reads effective rather than instantaneous values) were connected at various points along the line, they would all have the same reading in the dissipationless case. For the case with dissipation the reading of an ammeter would be $I_x = I_0 e^{-\alpha x}$. These two cases are shown in Fig. 6-10.

6-11. Wave Motion with Signal Involving More than One Frequency: Distortion. Results thus far have been concerned with single-frequency signals. Consider what happens when a more complicated wave is involved, i.e., one including two or more frequencies, which, as mentioned earlier, may be expressed as

FIG. 6-9. Instantaneous distribution of current or voltage along a line with dissipation, terminated in its characteristic impedance.

$$e_x = \sum_{k=1}^{n} (\hat{E}_0)_k e^{-\alpha_k x} \cos \omega_k (t - \tau_{pk}) \tag{6-45}$$

If this signal is to be propagated without distortion, its *shape*, or form, must remain unchanged as it moves along the cascade, i.e., the *relative*

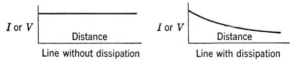

FIG. 6-10. Envelope of readings obtained with an ammeter or voltmeter at junctions along a cascade for the cases illustrated in Figs. 6-7 and 6-9.

amplitudes of all its frequency components must remain the same, and all its frequency components must undergo the same delay in time. It follows, then, that this complicated signal will be propagated without distortion if the cascade is such that α_k and τ_{pk} have the same values for all the frequencies comprising the signal.

If α_k is not constant over this band of frequencies, the cascade is said to introduce *frequency distortion*, i.e., the amplitudes of the several frequency components in the signal undergo different amounts of attenuation.

If τ_{pk} is not constant over this frequency band, the cascade is said to introduce *delay distortion*, i.e., the several frequency components undergo different amounts of delay in passing through the cascade.

By the definition of τ_p [Eq. (6-40a)] $\tau_p = \beta x/\omega$. Thus if β is directly proportional to frequency over the band of frequencies comprising the signal, τ_p will be constant and no delay distortion will occur. By the same token, $v_p = \omega/\beta$ will also be constant over the required frequency band.

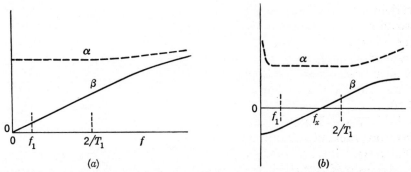

(a)   (b)

FIG. 6-11. Transmission of a repetitive pulse through a network. (a) Transmission characteristics of a typical dissipative LP structure. (b) Transmission characteristics of a quasi-LP structure. *Note.* Characteristics are plotted against a linear frequency scale.

As an example of these ideas, consider that a repetitive pulse of duration T_1 and fundamental repetition frequency $f_1 = 1/T$ as shown in Fig. 2-6 is applied to a cascaded structure. The frequency spectrum of this wave was calculated in Sec. 2-8 and plotted in Fig. 2-6.

It is apparent from that plot that α and τ_p would have to be constant over an infinite band of frequencies for the pulse to be transmitted free of all distortion. As a practical matter, however, the frequency spectrum of Fig. 2-6 shows that the frequency components higher than $2/T_1$ have relatively small amplitudes. Thus if α is independent of frequency and β is directly proportional to frequency from direct current to $2/T_1$ as in Fig. 6-11a, the wave would be transmitted with negligible frequency and phase-delay distortion, for then α, τ_p, and v_p would all be constant over the significant frequency band. The response curves shown in Fig. 6-11a are typical of so-called "dissipative low-pass (LP) structures."

6-12. Group Velocity and Delay. Another basic type of structure, the "quasi-LP" type, has α and β characteristics of the general form indicated in Fig. 6-11b. [The student should compare these curves with those of the RC amplifier (Fig. 2-17)]. If the repetitive pulse of Fig. 2-6 is applied to such a quasi-LP structure (either singly or in cascade), will the waveform of the signal be maintained at the output? Consider first the question of frequency distortion. It will be observed from Fig. 6-11b that α is constant for all the significant a-c components of the signal. The d-c component will not be passed by the network but may be restored by a process known as "clamping"; thus no frequency distortion will be introduced.

As to phase-delay distortion, however, it will be observed that, while β is *linear* with f, it is not *directly proportional to f;* therefore τ_p and v_p are not constant over the required band. In fact the characteristics shown in Fig. 6-11b indicate that frequencies between f_1 and f_x have negative phase velocities, those between f_x and $2/T_1$ have positive phase velocities, and f_x has infinite phase velocity.

These facts notwithstanding, it may be shown that the characteristics of Fig. 6-11b will allow the repetitive pulse to be transmitted without a change in waveform. To do this, it is necessary to introduce the concepts of *group velocity* and *group delay.* These concepts can best be understood by considering a simple case, that of the propagation of two frequencies in a cascade of networks where the phase velocity varies with frequency.

If one plots at a given instant the sum of two waves of slightly different frequency as a function of space, the envelope of the sum would show a beating effect, as illustrated in Fig. 6-12. The maxima of the envelope occur at the positions where the two waves are in phase. If, now, as time passes, the two waves move in space at the same phase velocity, the envelope of their sum will also move in space at exactly the same velocity. If, on the other hand, the two waves move at different phase velocities, it will be found that the envelope will move in space at a velocity which is in general different from the phase velocity of either component wave. A plot showing two such waves of different frequency and phase velocity and their sum is shown in Fig. 6-12 for two different times, t_1 and t_2 (in this case without attenuation).

Consider the case of two waves of frequencies $\omega/2\pi$ and $(\omega + \Delta\omega)/2\pi$ with respective phase shifts per section of β and $\beta + \Delta\beta$. They can be represented by equations

$$y_1 = A_1 f_1(x) \cos (\omega t - \beta x) \tag{6-46a}$$
$$y_2 = A_2 f_2(x) \cos [(\omega + \Delta\omega)t - (\beta + \Delta\beta)x] \tag{6-46b}$$

These two waves are in phase for a combination of t_1 and x_1 defined by the relation

$$\omega t_1 - \beta x_1 = (\omega + \Delta\omega)t_1 - (\beta + \Delta\beta)x_1$$

or

$$\Delta\omega \, t_1 = \Delta\beta \, x_1 \tag{6-47a}$$

At some later time t_2 the position of in-phaseness will have moved to

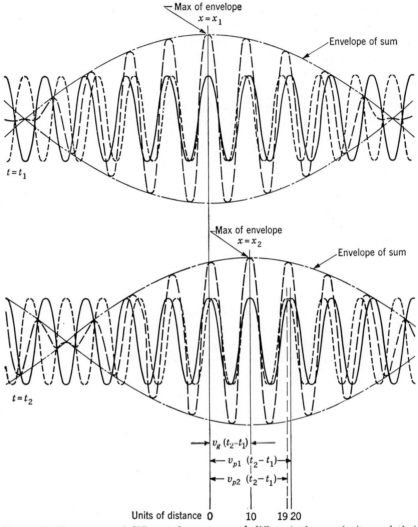

Fig. 6-12. Two waves of different frequency and different phase velocity and their sum as a function of space at two instants of time, t_1 and t_2. The solid line is wave 1, the dotted line is wave 2, and the dashed line is their sum.

a position x_2 corresponding to the relation

$$\omega t_2 - \beta x_2 = (\omega + \Delta\omega)t_2 - (\beta + \Delta\beta)x_2$$

or
$$\Delta\omega\, t_2 = \Delta\beta\, x_2 \qquad\qquad (6\text{-}47b)$$

Since the maximum of the envelope is determined by the positions at which the two waves are in phase, the envelope will travel a distance $x_2 - x_1$ in time $t_2 - t_1$. Hence the velocity of the *envelope*, called the *group velocity* and designated by v_g will be

$$v_g = \frac{x_2 - x_1}{t_2 - t_1}$$

From Eqs. (6-47a) and (6-47b)

$$\Delta\omega \, (t_2 - t_1) = \Delta\beta \, (x_2 - x_1)$$

or

$$v_g = \frac{\Delta\omega}{\Delta\beta} \qquad\qquad (6\text{-}48)$$

Figure 6-12 has been drawn for a case where the ratio of the two frequencies is $f_2/f_1 = {}^{19}\!/_{18}$ and the ratio of the two phase velocities is $v_{p1}/v_{p2} = {}^{19}\!/_{20}$.

Hence, since $v_p = \omega/\beta$, $\omega_2\beta_1/\omega_1\beta_2 = {}^{19}\!/_{20}$. Also,

$$\frac{\omega_2 - \omega_1}{\omega_1} = \frac{19 - 18}{18} = \frac{1}{18}$$

and

$$\frac{\beta_1}{\beta_2} = \frac{\omega_1 v_{p2}}{\omega_2 v_{p1}} = \frac{18}{19}\frac{19}{20} = \frac{9}{10}$$

$$\frac{\beta_2 - \beta_1}{\beta_1} = \frac{10 - 9}{9} = \frac{1}{9}$$

Then

$$\frac{v_g}{v_{p1}} = \frac{\omega_2 - \omega_1}{\beta_2 - \beta_1}\frac{\beta_1}{\omega_1} = \frac{1}{18} \times 9 = \frac{1}{2}$$

Hence the group velocity for this case should be one-half the phase velocity of the lower frequency. The diagram shows that, while the lower frequency wave has traveled two of its wavelengths, the envelope has traveled only half as far.

More specifically the group velocity is usually defined in terms of the limit as $\Delta\omega$ approaches zero and is therefore given a meaning at a particular frequency, say, ω_1. For this case

$$v_g = \left(\frac{d\omega}{d\beta}\right)_{\omega_1} \qquad\qquad (6\text{-}48a)$$

and a group, or envelope, delay τ_g may be defined by

$$\tau_g = \frac{x}{v_g} = \frac{d\beta}{d\omega}\,x \qquad\qquad (6\text{-}49)$$

The group velocity and group delay, as well as the phase velocity and phase delay, are functions of frequency, and these functions are in general all different, except for the special case where v_p is independent of frequency, and then $v_g = v_p$ and $\tau_g = \tau_p$.

These results may now be applied to the example of Fig. 6-11b. Since, as shown by the β characteristic, $d\beta/d\omega$ is constant over the band of important frequencies comprising the repetitive pulse (the pulse being the envelope of all the components), that train of pulses will be transmitted along the cascade without a change in the waveform of the envelope even though τ_p and v_p are not constant.

This apparent discrepancy in the criterion for no delay or phase distortion may be resolved quite readily. If τ_g is constant in the frequency band of interest, βx, by integration of Eq. (6-49), is

$$\beta x = \tau_g \omega + \beta_0$$

where β_0 is a constant of integration. There are an infinity of possible βx curves that satisfy this relationship, a few of which are shown in Fig. 6-13. For any of these curves, Eq. (6-45) reduces to

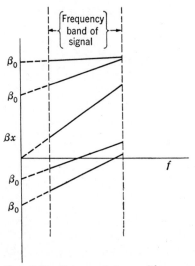

$$e_x = \sum_{k=1}^{n} (\hat{E}_0)_k e^{-\alpha_k x} \cos (\omega t - \beta x)$$

$$= \sum_{k=1}^{n} (\hat{E}_0)_k e^{-\alpha_k x} \cos [\omega(t - \tau_g) + \beta_0]$$

and the signal will be transmitted without a change in waveform (provided that α is constant) even though v_p and τ_p are not constant. It may be concluded, therefore, that, in so far as the absence of delay distortion of the signal is concerned, $d\beta/d\omega$ rather than β/ω should be constant. For true LP structures, $\beta_0 = 0$ and $d\beta/d\omega =$ constant corresponds to β proportional to ω.

Fig. 6-13. Curves of βx vs. f for constant group delay.

Similar analyses would apply to bandpass (BP) and high-pass (HP) structures; in fact, the quasi-LP structure is actually a BP network.

It may be shown that the group velocity of any physical network and the group time delay are always positive and finite. This checks with the intuitive feeling that any response at the output of a physical network must occur after the driving force has been applied. If any assumptions are made in a network which violate this, such as those in Chap. 2 regarding so-called ideal filters, it is apparent that the network cannot be realized physically.

It is therefore frequently stated that the *energy* is propagated through a network at the group velocity, although this is only even approximately true when the important components contributing to the energy lie within the range where the group velocity is substantially independent of frequency and hence can be given a definite value for the energy pulse.

6-13. Transmission Units. Thus far in the chapter the unit used for attenuation constant, which is a measure of the change in magnitude of current and voltage on an iterative structure terminated in its characteristic impedance, has been the neper. It has also been stated that an alternative, dimensionless attenuation unit is the decibel. The origin and interrelationship between these units will now be considered.

The attenuating character of any network could be represented in terms of the number of standard T sections of arbitrarily chosen characteristics which would give the same attenuation. It may be convenient in specifying this standard section to give definite physical configurations to Z_1 and Z_2 or to specify the base and exponent that give the ratio $|I_{k-1}/I_k|$. Both these methods have been used.

The so-called "mile of standard cable" was the first standard extensively used for telephonic transmission. It consisted of physical values of 88 ohms resistance for Z_1 and 0.054 μf capacitance for Z_2. It originally corresponded to a commonly used cable of 19-gauge copper, but modern 19-gauge cable has a different capacitance.

Such a standard cable varies, with frequency, in its attenuating characteristics. It served the purpose when talking tests were used for measurement, and the majority of actual circuits produced distortion similar to the standard, but its use has now been discarded for units which represent the same attenuation at all frequencies.

During the years when the standard cable was the unit of transmission, the attenuation of a large number of pieces of apparatus and network combinations was expressed in this unit. In looking for a new unit it was desirable that it should, in most practical instances, have nearly the same value as the old unit. If a single frequency standard must be used, the attenuation of speech transmission is most nearly like the attenuation of a frequency of 800 to 1,000 cycles. Formerly the unit most widely used was the "800-cycle mile"; i.e., current or power ratios were expressed in terms of the number of miles of standard cable which would cause the same ratio at 800 cycles. The attenuation of 886 cycles on a mile of standard cable is such that

$$\frac{P_1}{P_2} = \left|\frac{E_1 I_1}{E_2 I_2}\right| = 10^{0.1} \tag{6-50}$$

This ratio gave a convenient value which could be expressed in terms of common logarithms and was adopted as a standard for all frequencies. This unit was first labeled the "transmission unit." Later its name was changed to "decibel" and abbreviated "db." The number of such units of attenuation produced by any network is expressed by the relation

$$\frac{P_1}{P_2} = 10^{0.1N} \tag{6-51}$$

$$N_{\text{db}} = 10 \log \frac{P_1}{P_2} \tag{6-52}$$

This unit is approximately the same as the 800-cycle mile, the mile being about 5 per cent higher.

The unit "bel" is seldom used as such but is equal to 10 db, and the number of bels is the common logarithm of the power ratio. The name was selected in honor of the inventor of the telephone, Alexander Graham Bell.

The most common use of the decibel as a unit is to express quantitatively the increase or decrease in power due to the insertion or substitution of a new element in a network. As an example, suppose that the current in the terminal impedance at the end of a line is initially 1 ma. Let any piece of apparatus be inserted at some point in the network such that the current is reduced to 0.3 ma as a result of the change. Since the terminal impedance has not been changed,

$$\frac{P_1}{P_2} = \left(\left|\frac{I_1}{I_2}\right|\right)^2 = \left(\frac{1.0}{0.3}\right)^2 = 11.11$$

The number of decibels loss caused by the introduction of the new unit will be

$$N_{db} = 10 \log 11.11$$
$$= 10 \times 1.046$$
$$= 10.46 \text{ loss}$$

On the other hand, suppose an amplifier is inserted which causes the current in the terminal load to increase from 1 to 5 ma. Then the so-called "loss" would be computed from Eq. (6-52) as before.

$$N_{db} = 10 \log \frac{P_1}{P_2} = 10 \log \left(\frac{1}{5}\right)^2$$
$$= 10(-1.400)$$
$$= -14.00$$

A "loss" of -14.00 db represents an increase in power since the answer is negative and so is interpreted as a "gain" of 14.00 db.

Since the logarithm of any number is equal to the negative of the logarithm of the reciprocal of that number, in using Eq. (6-52) it is possible to use the higher power always in the numerator as P_1, and if this higher power occurs after the change, the result is interpreted as a gain. In the example just given

$$\log \frac{1}{25} = -\log_{10} 25 = -1.400$$

It is also simple to find the power ratio if the decibels are given. For example, if the loss due to any change is 18.06 db, then

$$\log_{10} \frac{P_1}{P_2} = 1.806$$

$$\frac{P_1}{P_2} = \text{antilog } 1.806 = 64$$

$$\frac{I_1}{I_2} = \sqrt{64} = 8$$

While the decibel is primarily a unit of *power* ratio, it is apparent that *if the receiving-end impedance is constant* during the power change Eq. (6-52) may also be written

$$N_{db} = 10 \log\left(\left|\frac{I_1}{I_2}\right|\right)^2 = 20 \log\left|\frac{I_1}{I_2}\right| = 20 \log\left|\frac{E_1}{E_2}\right| \qquad (6\text{-}53a)$$

On the other hand, if the power change is wholly or partially due to a change in the receiving impedance, Eq. (6-53a) *cannot* be used.

It is apparent that there is a direct relation between a loss expressed in nepers and one expressed in decibels. Since $\ln x = 2.30 \log x$,

$$\text{nepers} = 2.30 \log\left|\frac{I_1}{I_2}\right|$$

$$= \frac{2.3}{20} N_{db} = 0.115 N_{db}$$

Therefore 1 db equals 0.115 neper, or 1 neper represents 8.686 db.

Equation (6-52) may be used apart from its original derivation to represent the ratio of any two powers, whether they are in the same networks or not. It should be noticed that the decibel is fundamentally a unit of *power ratio* and not of power. When referred to some arbitrary level, the decibel is often used as a unit of absolute value of power; e.g., in telephone testing the zero level is 1 milliwatt (mw), and other powers are referrred to it. Positive values represent higher powers and negative values lower powers. Thus +30 db would be a power 1,000 times the standard, or 1 watt, and −30 db would be a power 1/1,000 times the zero level, or 1 microwatt (μw).

For testing in radio systems, including telephone lines feeding them, a zero level of 6 mw has been adopted as standard. In sound measurements the zero level is taken as 10^{-16} watt/sq cm, which is approximately the threshold of audibility at 1,000 cycles.

6-14. Weber–Fechner Law. Another reason for the use of logarithmic transmission units is that the human senses perceive such units as approximately equal intervals. An important law in psychology is the Weber-Fechner law, which states that "the minimum change in stimulus necessary to produce a perceptible change in response is proportional to the stimulus already existing." This means that the senses perceive proportional rather than absolute changes in the intensity or character of stimuli, such as sound or light waves. As discussed in Chap. 2, one of the most easily recognized intervals in music is the octave. Each octave on the musical scale represents a frequency ratio of 1:2; i.e., the interval is a proportional rather than an absolute change. Similarly, a change in loudness is interpreted in terms of the sound already present; a cricket in the country may increase the surrounding noise by many times and therefore represent a change of a number of decibels, while in a city street it would be inaudible and would represent a negligible percentage increase in acoustic power. The absolute difference of intensity of the lights and shadows of the image projected on a screen by a motion-picture projector is the same, whether the screen is in bright daylight or a darkened room, but the eye, perceiving relative intensity, sees the contrasts much better when the surroundings are dark. For a similar reason time passes more swiftly for adults than for children: A year to a child of ten is one-tenth of the total time that he has observed; from birthday to birthday seems a long interval, while to the adult of forty the period between leap years seems no longer.

A change in acoustic power of 1 db is approximately the minimum recognizable by the average human ear and therefore becomes a very useful unit of acoustic, as well as electric, power ratio. Absolute acoustic power is also often specified in decibels, and a reference level sometimes used is the threshold of audibility; i.e., a sound which can be just heard when other sounds are absent. This reference level varies with frequency (see Fig. 1-13). An acoustic level of 20 db would be a pressure ten times that at the threshold of audibility. This would be greater absolute power at 200 cycles than it would be at 1,000 cycles, because the threshold is higher in the former case. The zero level now preferred is a power density of 10^{-16} watt/sq cm at all frequencies.

6-15. Losses in a Transmission Network. The results of the preceding sections show that if an iterative structure is terminated in its iterative or characteristic impedance, then the *attenuation* loss of the first k sections will be

$$\text{Attenuation loss} = 20 \log \left| \frac{I_0}{I_k} \right| = 20 \log \left| \frac{E_0}{E_k} \right|$$
$$= 8.686 k\alpha \quad \text{db} \tag{6-54}$$

where α is still in nepers per section. It is of interest to note that this loss may also be expressed in terms of the input power to the first section and the output power of the kth section. From Eq. (6-4)

$$\frac{E_0}{E_k} = \frac{I_0}{I_k} \tag{6-55}$$

or

$$\left|\frac{I_0}{I_k}\right| = \left|\frac{E_0 I_0}{E_k I_k}\right|^{\frac{1}{2}}$$

From the definition of power

$$\begin{aligned} P_0 &= |E_0 I_0| \cos \theta_0 \\ P_k &= |E_k I_k| \cos \theta_k \end{aligned} \tag{6-56}$$

Now since a termination $Z_R = Z_o$ causes the input impedance of each section to be Z_o, $\theta_0 = \theta_k$, whence

$$\frac{P_0}{P_k} = \left|\frac{E_0 I_0}{E_k I_k}\right| = \left|\frac{I_0}{I_k}\right|^2 \tag{6-57}$$

Then combining Eqs. (6-54) and (6-57), an alternative expression for the attenuation loss is,

$$\text{If } Z_R = Z_o, \text{ attenuation loss} = 10 \log \frac{P_0}{P_k} \quad \text{db} \tag{6-58}$$

The equations given above presume an idealized situation, viz., that the iterative structure is properly terminated. This ideal situation is the exception rather than the rule, however; in the general case where $Z_R \neq Z_o$ current and voltage at the kth section can no longer be determined by Eq. (6-6) because reflections occur, a subject covered in Chap. 9. Where reflections do occur, $10 \log (P_0/P_R)$ does not give the "attenuation loss," and two other losses have been defined to give a measure of circuit performance, the *transmission loss* and the *insertion loss*.

The transmission loss is defined as follows: "In communication, transmission loss (frequently abbreviated 'loss') is a general term used to denote a decrease in power in transmission from one point to another. Transmission loss is usually expressed in decibels." (ASA C42 65.08.060.)

Then, applying this definition to the iterative structure not terminated in Z_o,

$$\text{If } Z_R \neq Z_o, \text{ transmission loss} = 10 \log \frac{P_1}{P_2} \quad \text{db} \tag{6-59}$$

The student will probably object that Eqs. (6-58) and (6-59) are identical. This is true, but he should observe that, with an improper termination, Z_o is no longer the input impedance of each section in the cascade; thus

$$\text{If } Z_R \neq Z_{it}, \frac{E_0}{E_k} \neq \frac{I_0}{I_k}$$

and

$$\text{Transmission loss} \neq 20 \log \left|\frac{I_0}{I_k}\right| \neq 20 \log \left|\frac{E_0}{E_k}\right|$$

$$\neq 8.686 k\alpha \quad \text{db}$$

Still another quantity is defined which, while it is not a loss in the usual sense, has been called the *insertion loss* of a network.

Frequently it is necessary to determine how the power delivered to a fixed load is changed by the insertion of some network in cascade, connecting a source to a load. The corresponding loss in power is called the insertion loss of the network and may be defined as follows: "The insertion loss resulting from the insertion of a transducer in a transmission system is the ratio of power delivered before the insertion to that part of the system following the transducer to the power delivered to that same part after the insertion." (ASA C42 65.08.087.)

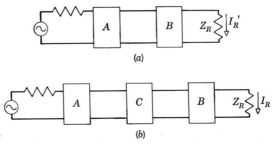

FIG. 6-14. Circuits for calculating the *insertion* loss of network C.

For example, in Fig. 6-14a, let I'_R be the *load* current when the load is fed through the cascade AB. Then the power delivered to the load is

$$P'_R = |I'_R|^2 R_R \qquad (6\text{-}60)$$

Upon introduction of the network C between networks A and B, as in Fig. 6-14b, a new value of load current, I_R, flows and produces a load power

$$P_R = |I_R|^2 R_R \qquad (6\text{-}61)$$

Then by definition

$$\text{Insertion loss} = 10 \log \frac{P'_R}{P_R} \qquad (6\text{-}62)$$

$$= 20 \log \left| \frac{I'_R}{I_R} \right| \quad \text{db}$$

$$= \ln \left| \frac{I'_R}{I_R} \right| \quad \text{nepers} \qquad (6\text{-}62a)$$

The student should take care to notice the difference between Eqs. (6-59) and (6-62) despite their similarity in form. He should also prove as an exercise that, for a given network with $Z_R = Z_o$, all three losses—attenuation, transmission, and insertion—become one and the same.

It should also be observed that the insertion loss of a two-terminal-pair network depends upon where it is inserted and so is not a definite value which can be assigned to the network. The transmission loss similarly depends upon the termination. The attenuation loss, on the other hand, is a specific value for any particular two-terminal pair or any group of identical pairs in cascade. Further work in Chap. 9 will show the inter-relationship between insertion and attenuation loss.

6-16. Cascade of Dissimilar Sections with Identical Characteristic Impedances. Thus far in the chapter the equations such as (6-54) for the total attenuation loss of k sections in a cascade structure presume all the sections to be identical. The case often arises, particularly in the analysis of wave filters, where the several sections in the cascade have the same value of Z_o, but different values of γ, say, $\gamma_1, \gamma_2, \ldots$. The student may show quite easily that when such a system of dissimilar sections is terminated in Z_o

$$\frac{I_0}{I_n} = \frac{I_0}{I_1}\frac{I_1}{I_2} \cdots \frac{I_{n-1}}{I_n}$$

$$= e^{\gamma_1}e^{\gamma_2} \cdots e^{\gamma_n} \tag{6-63}$$

and

$$\text{Attenuation loss} = \alpha_1 + \alpha_2 + \cdots + \alpha_n \tag{6-64}$$

$$\text{Total phase shift} = \beta_1 + \beta_2 + \cdots + \beta_n \tag{6-65}$$

PROBLEMS

6-1. A line is composed of T sections of pure resistance. The series resistances of the T sections are 50 ohms each, and the shunt resistances are 5,000 ohms each. Compute the characteristic impedance and the attenuation constant.

6-2. A line composed of 100 sections, similar to those of Prob. 6-1, is terminated in its characteristic resistance. A generator whose emf is 1 volt and whose internal resistance is 200 ohms is connected at the sending end. What will be the current at the sending and receiving ends of the line?

6-3. Plot a curve of current vs. distance along the line of Prob. 6-2, taking points at intervals of 20 sections. Plot also a curve of the logarithm of current vs. distance. Compute and plot similar curves of voltage distribution.

6-4. A symmetrical T section is made up of the following components: $R_1 = 20$ ohms, $L_1 = 3$ mh, $C_2 = 0.1$ μf. Evaluate α, β, and Z_o at $\omega = 5,000$ radians/sec.

6-5. Repeat Prob. 6-4, but evaluate Z_o from Z_{oc} and Z_{sc} and γ by means of Eq. (6-22).

6-6. A cascade of six identical Π sections is terminated in its characteristic impedance. $\gamma = 0.1 + j\pi/6$. $E_0 = 5$ volts. Plot a polar diagram of the voltages along the cascade.

6-7. Design a symmetrical T section to have $Z_o = 600$ ohms and $\gamma = 0 + j\pi/4$.

6-8. Repeat Prob. 6-7 for a symmetrical Π section.

6-9. A T section has a total series resistance of 200 ohms and a shunt branch consisting of a 0.1-μf capacitor. It is terminated in its characteristic impedance.

a. Plot α, v_p, and v_o at intervals of one octave from 200 to 3,200 cycles.

b. State your conclusions regarding the distortion introduced by the network.

6-10. What will be the current in the load if the generator and load of Prob. 6-2 are connected directly? What is the loss in decibels introduced by the line of Prob. 6-2 when it is connected between the load and generator?

6-11. A T section has a total series resistance of 200 ohms and a shunt branch of 100 ohms. Calculate the attenuation, transmission, and insertion losses for the following conditions:

    a. $E_g = 10$ volts, $R_g = R_R = 173.2$ ohms.

    b. $E_g = 10$ volts, $R_g = 500$ ohms, $R_R = 173.2$ ohms.

    c. $E_g = 10$ volts, $R_g = R_R = 500$ ohms.

Compare the losses for the three cases.

CHAPTER 7

WAVE FILTERS

In communication systems it frequently becomes desirable to discriminate between frequency bands, accepting one group and rejecting others in a particular branch of the network. Combinations which accomplish this purpose are called "wave filters." They differ from simple resonant circuits in providing a substantially constant transmission over the band which they accept, this band lying between any limits which the designer may select.

Ideally, filters should produce no attenuation in the band desired and should provide an infinite attenuation at all other frequencies. These bands are referred to as the "transmission," or "pass- ," and "attenuation," or "stop," bands, respectively. Actual filters fall short of this ideal, the undesired frequencies being attenuated by a finite amount. This attenuation may be made as large as necessary if a sufficient number of meshes of proper design are used. Commercial filters are designed to meet the technical requirements with a minimum cost and therefore a minimum number of meshes which will give the required attenuation in any particular application.

The student should be aware that two different philosophies of design are used in the synthesis of filter circuits. For lack of standard terms these may be called the "classical" and "modern" points of view. In the classical system, which is based largely on the work of O. J. Zobel and G. A. Campbell, a given class of networks is analyzed so that their attenuation and phase characteristics as a function of frequency are known and tabulated. Then, given a desired attenuation characteristic, the designer can choose that particular network whose attenuation characteristic most closely approximates the desired form. No attempt is made in the classical approach to design for both attenuation and phase (or delay) characteristics simultaneously. α is the design criterion, and the designer must accept the β characteristic associated with it. In systems used for the transmission of speech such a procedure is generally satisfactory since phase or delay distortion is not readily discernible by the human ear.

More recent interest in picture transmission as in facsimile or television systems has shown that delay distortion is fully as important as frequency distortion. In these systems delay must be considered.

In contrast to the older theory of filter synthesis, in the modern approach the designer starts with the desired responses of both α and β and then sets about designing the necessary network, whose configuration is unknown at the beginning of the design process. As a practical matter it is usually impossible exactly to satisfy both responses, and the designer is content to approximate them. This latter method, while more powerful than the classical, requires mathematical tools that are beyond the scope of this book. The work in this chapter, then, will follow the classical method and so will be concerned primarily with analyzing the behavior of two basic filter structures, the ladder and lattice networks. As a matter of convenience certain properties of any symmetrical lossless network will be investigated first.

7-1. Characteristic Impedance of Networks of Pure Reactances. As stated above, a filter ideally should have zero attenuation in the passband, a condition which may be satisfied only if the elements of the filter are dissipationless and which cannot be realized in practice. If, however, the components are inductors and capacitors of high quality factor, their effective resistance will be low and the losses in the passband will be small. For this reason, wave filters are designed on the assumption of lossless circuit elements, i.e., the design is based on purely reactive elements. The following discussion will proceed on this basis.

It was shown in Chap. 3 that the characteristic impedance of a symmetrical four-terminal network is

$$Z_o = \sqrt{Z_{oc}Z_{sc}} \tag{7-1}$$

If the elements of a network are pure reactances, there are four possible combinations of signs for Z_{oc} and Z_{sc}:

Condition 1. $Z_{oc} = +jX_a$, $Z_{sc} = -jX_b$.
Condition 2. $Z_{oc} = -jX_a$, $Z_{sc} = +jX_b$.
Condition 3. $Z_{oc} = +jX_a$, $Z_{sc} = +jX_b$.
Condition 4. $Z_{oc} = -jX_a$, $Z_{sc} = -jX_b$.

Here X_a and X_b are positive real numbers.

If either condition 1 or condition 2 exists,

$$Z_o = \sqrt{-j^2X_aX_b} = \pm \sqrt{X_aX_b} \tag{7-2}$$

and the *characteristic impedance is a pure resistance*. Only the positive root corresponds to a physically realizable passive termination. If, on the other hand, either condition 3 or condition 4 holds,

$$Z_o = \sqrt{+j^2X_aX_b} = \pm j \sqrt{X_aX_b} \tag{7-3}$$

and the *characteristic impedance is a pure reactance*. In other words if

the impedances are reactances of opposite sign, the characteristic impedance is a pure resistance, while if they are of the same sign, the characteristic impedance is a pure reactance.

As the frequency changes, the value, or even the character, of Z_{oc}
and Z_{sc} may change. Over one range of frequencies Z_o may be a pure
resistance, while over another it may be a pure reactance.

7-2. Absorption of Power by Terminated Network of Pure Reactances.
If the characteristic impedance of a cascade of sections is a pure resistance
and each section is made up of pure reactances, then power can readily be
absorbed from a generator by this cascade if it is terminated in its characteristic impedance Z_o. Since the elements of the filter cannot absorb
any power, all the power must be delivered to the termination. If no
power is lost and the characteristic impedance is a pure resistance, $|E_1I_1|$
must equal $|E_2I_2|$. Also, in a line terminated in Z_o, $E_1/E_2 = I_1/I_2$. As
a result of these two equalities $|E_1| = |E_2|$ and $|I_1| = |I_2|$ and there will
be zero attenuation.

If the characteristic impedance of the cascade of sections is a pure
reactance, then a line terminated in Z_o will absorb no power from the
generator and the current and voltage will be 90° out of phase at all points.
It would be physically possible for such a line to have attenuation, since
a decrease in voltage and current does not involve a dissipation of power
when E and I are 90° out of phase with each other.

7-3. Propagation Constant of Network of Pure Reactances. It was
shown in Eq. (6-22) that the propagation constant of a symmetrical network is given by the equation

$$\tanh \gamma = \sqrt{\frac{Z_{sc}}{Z_{oc}}} \tag{7-4}$$

If either condition 1 or condition 2 holds,

$$\tanh \gamma = \sqrt{-\frac{X_b}{X_a}} = j\sqrt{\frac{X_b}{X_a}} \tag{7-5}$$

while if either condition 3 or condition 4 holds,

$$\tanh \gamma = \sqrt{+\frac{X_b}{X_a}} = \sqrt{\frac{X_b}{X_a}} \tag{7-6}$$

This shows that, if the characteristic impedance is a pure resistance,
the hyperbolic tangent of the propagation constant is a pure imaginary,
while if Z_o is a pure reactance, $\tanh \gamma$ is a real number. Now

$$\tanh \gamma = \tanh (\alpha + j\beta) = \frac{\sinh \gamma}{\cosh \gamma} = \frac{\sinh \alpha \cos \beta + j \cosh \alpha \sin \beta}{\cosh \alpha \cos \beta + j \sinh \alpha \sin \beta}$$

Rationalize the denominator by multiplying the numerator and denominator by the conjugate of the latter, and simplify.

$$\tanh \gamma = \frac{\sinh \alpha \cosh \alpha + j \sin \beta \cos \beta}{\sinh^2 \alpha + \cos^2 \beta} \tag{7-7}$$

If $\tanh \gamma$ is a pure imaginary, then Eq. (7-7) shows that

$$\sinh \alpha \cosh \alpha = 0 \tag{7-8}$$

Since this is possible only for $\alpha = 0$, there will be zero attenuation when Z_o is a pure resistance, a conclusion which was also reached in a previous paragraph.

If $\tanh \gamma$ is a real number, then, from Eq. (7-7),

$$\sin \beta \cos \beta = 0 \tag{7-9}$$

Hence, if $\tanh \gamma$ has a value, $\sinh \alpha \cosh \alpha$ must have a value greater than zero and there must be attenuation. This is the case when Z_o is a pure reactance. These principles may be summarized in the following theorem:

In a symmetrical network of pure reactances, if the characteristic impedance is a pure resistance, the attenuation constant is zero, while if the characteristic impedance is a pure reactance, there must be a value for the attenuation constant.

If a cascade of pure reactance networks is terminated in some value other than the characteristic impedance, the input impedance will differ from Z_o only to the extent that the reflected wave can interfere with the initial wave at the input terminals, as discussed in Chap. 9. *If the attenuation is large, the load impedance has little effect on the input impedance and the latter will be practically Z_o.* Therefore, if the series of sections made of pure reactances has a characteristic impedance which is a pure reactance, then, even if it is terminated in a pure resistance, the input impedance will still be almost entirely reactive since attenuation is present. Hence, in this case very little power will be absorbed by the cascade from the generator, and so very little can be delivered to the load, even though the cascade cannot dissipate power. This is the primary principle of filter action, viz., in the attenuation band of frequencies relatively little power can be absorbed from the supply network at the input terminals of the filter. Since the filter structure is assumed to be constructed of pure reactive elements, all the power absorbed at the input end at any frequency is delivered to the load.

7-4. Determination of Transmission and Attenuation Bands of Filter Networks. If a reactance sketch of the open- and short-circuited reactances of a filter section is made, the type of the filter and the location of all transmission and attenuation bands may be readily determined. In any range of frequencies where the reactances are of opposite sign, the attenuation will be zero. This is illustrated by the reactance sketches of Fig. 7-1 for some hypothetical network. The critical frequencies which correspond to zeros and poles of either Z_{oc} or Z_{sc} are labeled f_1, f_2, etc. It is apparent that there will be zero attenuation between frequencies f_1 and f_4 and for any frequencies above f_5 because in these ranges Z_{oc} and Z_{sc} are opposite types of reactance. The frequencies which mark the boundary between transmission and attenuation bands are called *cutoff* frequencies. In the illustrations, f_1, f_4, and f_5 are cutoff

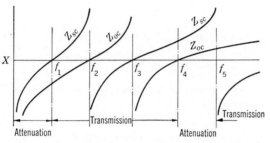

Fig. 7-1. Determination of transmission and attenuation bands of a filter network from its open- and short-circuited reactance curves.

frequencies. It is apparent from Fig. 7-1 that cutoff frequencies occur when there is a critical frequency for either curve which does not coincide with a critical frequency of the other curve. When two critical frequencies coincide, they do not mark cutoff points. These critical points are useful in controlling the magnitude of the characteristic impedance or the attenuation constant in the various bands.

Usually it is not very convenient to work with the open- and short-circuited impedances. Any two factors into which the characteristic impedance may be factored may be used in the same way as the open- and short-circuited impedances.

7-5. Ladder Networks as Filters. The ladder structure is one of the commonest forms of filter network that is considered under the classical theory of wave filters. Both the T section and its *related* II section are grouped under this common heading owing to the configuration of a long cascade of such sections. The characteristic impedances of these related T and II sections are derived in Chap. 6 and are repeated here for reference.

$$Z_{oT} = \sqrt{Z_1 Z_2 + \frac{Z_1^2}{4}} \qquad (6\text{-}15)$$

$$Z_{oII} = \frac{Z_1 Z_2}{\sqrt{Z_1 Z_2 + Z_1^2/4}} = \frac{Z_1 Z_2}{Z_{oT}} \qquad (6\text{-}16)$$

The characteristic impedance of the T section is sometimes called the *mid-series iterative impedance*, while that of the Π section has a corresponding term: *mid-shunt iterative impedance*. These terms are applied because in a long line of T sections the input point is in the middle of the series impedance Z_1, while in a long line of Π sections the input would be at a point where the initial shunt admittance was one-half the value of other shunt admittances.

In Eq. (6-15) the part under the radical could be divided into two factors, as follows:

$$Z_{oT} = \sqrt{Z_1\left(Z_2 + \frac{Z_1}{4}\right)} \qquad (7\text{-}10)$$

The characteristic impedance would be a pure resistance if the reactance of Z_1 is opposite in sign to the reactance of $Z_2 + Z_1/4$, while it would be reactive if Z_1 and $Z_2 + Z_1/4$ were of the same sign. Hence, if reactance curves of these two factors are drawn, they can be used to determine the location of transmission and attenuation bands in the same way as the open- and short-circuited impedance curves shown in Fig. 7-1. The cutoff frequencies would occur when critical frequencies of Z_1 and $Z_2 + Z_1/4$ do not occur at the same frequency. This would be the case if

$$Z_1 = 0 \qquad Z_2 \neq 0 \text{ or } \infty \qquad (7\text{-}11)$$

or

$$Z_2 + \frac{Z_1}{4} = 0 \qquad Z_1 \neq 0 \text{ or } \infty \qquad (7\text{-}12)$$

or

$$Z_2 = \infty \qquad Z_1 \neq 0 \text{ or } \infty \qquad (7\text{-}13)$$

The case of $Z_1 = \infty$ would make $Z_2 + Z_1/4 = \infty$ and so would make two critical frequencies coincide and would not give a cutoff frequency.

Equations (7-11) to (7-13) can be combined into the relations

$$\frac{Z_1}{4Z_2} = 0 \qquad \text{or} \qquad \frac{Z_1}{4Z_2} = -1$$

Another way to state this is that the ratio $Z_1/4Z_2$ must lie between the value 0 and -1 in the transmission band. Therefore, to make Z_o real,

$$-1 < \frac{Z_1}{4Z_2} < 0 \qquad (7\text{-}14)$$

Since Z_1Z_2 is a real number when Z_1 and Z_2 are pure reactances, it is apparent from Eq. (6-16) that Z_{oII} will be resistive when Z_{oT} is resistive, and reactive when Z_{oT} is reactive. Therefore, the transmission and attenuation bands are identical whether Z_1 and Z_2 are arranged in T or Π sections.

7-6. Attenuation of Ladder Network. To emphasize the fact that attenuation occurs when $Z_1/4Z_2$ does not lie within the limits specified by the inequality (7-14), the ratio of input to output currents for a section terminated in Z_o will be computed. Equation (6-4) gives the ratio of input to output currents for a T section. It is repeated here for convenience.

$$\frac{I_1}{I_2} = \frac{Z_1/2 + Z_2 + Z_o}{Z_2} = 1 + \frac{Z_1}{2Z_2} + \frac{Z_o}{Z_2} \qquad (7\text{-}15)$$

The possible values of $Z_1/4Z_2$ may be divided into the three cases listed below under cases A, B, and C.

Case A. Equation (7-14) is satisfied. $-1 < Z_1/4Z_2 < 0$.

In this case Z_o is real, and the numerator of Eq. (7-15) will be a *complex number.* In order to make Z_o a pure resistance, Z_1 must be an inductive reactance and $Z_1/4 + Z_2$ must be a capacitive reactance, or vice versa. It follows that Z_2 must be the same type of reactance as $Z_1/4 + Z_2$.

Let

$$Z_1 = +jX_a \qquad \text{and} \qquad Z_2 = -jX_b$$

or let

$$Z_1 = -jX_a \qquad \text{and} \qquad Z_2 = +jX_b$$

Then from Eq. (7-15),

$$\frac{I_1}{I_2} = \frac{\sqrt{X_a X_b - X_a^2/4} \pm j(X_a/2 - X_b)}{\pm jX_b} \qquad (7\text{-}16)$$

The absolute value of the numerator of Eq. (7-16) will be the square root of the sum of the squares of the real and imaginary portions.

$$\left|\frac{I_1}{I_2}\right| = \frac{\sqrt{X_a X_b - X_a^2/4 + X_a^2/4 - X_a X_b + X_b^2}}{X_b} \qquad (7\text{-}17)$$

$$\left|\frac{I_1}{I_2}\right| = 1 \qquad (7\text{-}18)$$

This proves the conclusion previously obtained that if Z_o is a pure resistance there will be zero attenuation. Because of the difference in the angles of the numerator and denominator of Eq. (7-16), there will be a *shift in phase* of the current, and hence of the voltage, in passing through the section. The magnitude of this shift will depend on the numerical values of Z_1 and Z_2.

Case B. $Z_1/4Z_2 > 0$, that is, $Z_1/4Z_2$ is any positive number.

In this case Z_1 and Z_2 are reactances of the same type, and Z_o is also a pure reactance. Because of the fact that actual values of Z_1 and Z_2 have some slight resistance, the only physically realizable value of Z_o is a reactance of the same type as Z_1 and Z_2. Then, either

$$Z_1 = +jX_a \qquad \text{and} \qquad Z_2 = +jX_b$$

or

$$Z_1 = -jX_a \qquad \text{and} \qquad Z_2 = -jX_b$$

and Eq. (7-15) becomes

$$\frac{I_1}{I_2} = 1 + \frac{X_a}{2X_b} + \sqrt{\frac{X_a}{X_b} + \frac{X_a{}^2}{4X_b{}^2}} \qquad (7\text{-}19)$$

This ratio is always greater than 1 and is a pure number, because the j's cancel out, and hence there must be attenuation but no phase shift.

Case C. $Z_1/4Z_2 < -1$.

In this case Z_1 and Z_2 are opposite types of reactance, but $|Z_1| > |4Z_2|$. Then, either

$$Z_1 = +jX_a \qquad Z_2 = -jX_b \qquad \text{and} \qquad \frac{Z_1}{4} + Z_2 = +jX_c$$

$$\text{or} \qquad Z_1 = -jX_a \qquad Z_2 = +jX_b \qquad \text{and} \qquad \frac{Z_1}{4} + Z_2 = -jX_c$$

where X_a, X_b, and X_c may have any value between zero and infinity. In the first case $Z_o = +j\sqrt{X_aX_c}$, and in the second case

$$Z_o = -j\sqrt{X_aX_c}$$

Then Eq. (7-15) becomes

$$\frac{I_1}{I_2} = 1 - \frac{X_a}{2X_b} - \frac{\sqrt{X_aX_c}}{X_b} \qquad (7\text{-}20)$$

If $|Z_1| > |4Z_2|$ then $X_a/2X_b > 2$, and the right side of Eq. (7-20) will be a negative real number whose absolute value is greater than 1. Therefore, $|I_1/I_2|$ will be greater than 1, and there must be attenuation. The significance of the negative value of the ratio is that such a section will shift the current through an angle of exactly 180°.

Equations (7-19) and (7-20) again substantiate the argument previously advanced that, if the characteristic impedance is a pure reactance, there *must* be attenuation.

On a long cascade, the only difference between a series of related Π sections and a series of related T sections is in the terminating half sections, as explained in Chap. 6. Since the half sections could not greatly affect the total attenuation of a *long* cascade, and since the attenuation per section is the total attenuation divided by the number of sections, it is apparent that the attenuation of a Π section is the same as for a T section with the same values of Z_1 and Z_2, and the arguments just upheld may be applied to either type. This is further verified by γ being the same for related T and Π sections, as proved in Chap. 6.

7-7. Classification of Filter Operation by Hyperbolic Functions. It is possible to verify the characteristics of the three cases by considering an expression for γ in terms of hyberbolic functions. From Eq. (6-19) $\cosh \gamma = 1 + Z_1/2Z_2$. This may be changed to a more useful form by applying Eq. (A-11), yielding

$$\sinh \frac{\gamma}{2} = \sqrt{\frac{Z_1}{4Z_2}} \qquad (7\text{-}21)$$

If Z_1 and Z_2 are both pure imaginary values, their ratio and hence $Z_1/4Z_2$ will be a pure real number. Since Z_1 and Z_2 may be anywhere in the range of from $-j\infty$ to $+j\infty$, $Z_1/4Z_2$ may also have any real value between the infinite limits. Then $\sinh(\gamma/2) = \sqrt{Z_1/4Z_2}$ will also have infinite limits but may be either real or imaginary depending upon whether $Z_1/4Z_2$ is positive or negative. One must now determine how these facts affect the components of γ, namely α and β, for in general one would expect γ to be complex. It will be shown that α and β take on different values depending upon the range of $Z_1/4Z_2$.

By Eq. (A-15)

$$\sinh \frac{\gamma}{2} = \sinh\left(\frac{\alpha}{2} + j\frac{\beta}{2}\right) = \sinh\frac{\alpha}{2}\cos\frac{\beta}{2} + j\cosh\frac{\alpha}{2}\sin\frac{\beta}{2}$$

$$= \sqrt{\frac{Z_1}{4Z_2}} \qquad (7\text{-}21a)$$

Consider, first, the case where $Z_1/4Z_2$ is negative, making $\sqrt{Z_1/4Z_2}$ imaginary and equal, say, to $\pm jx$. Then substituting into Eq. (7-21a) and equating reals,

$$\sinh \frac{\alpha}{2}\cos\frac{\beta}{2} = 0 \qquad (7\text{-}22a)$$

and, equating imaginaries,

$$\cosh \frac{\alpha}{2}\sin\frac{\beta}{2} = \pm x \qquad (7\text{-}22b)$$

Both these equations must be satisfied by α and β. Equation (7-22a) may be satisfied either if $\alpha = 0$ or if $\beta = \pm\pi$. These two possible solutions will be considered separately.

If $\alpha = 0$, Eq. (7-22a) is satisfied and $\cosh(\alpha/2) = 1$. Then from Eq. (7-22b)

$$\sin \frac{\beta}{2} = \pm x \qquad (7\text{-}23)$$

But the sine can have a maximum value of 1; therefore this solution is valid only for $Z_1/4Z_2$ negative and having maximum magnitude of unity. This may be identified as case A and may be summarized as follows:

Case A. $-1 \le Z_1/4Z_2 \le 0$, $\alpha = 0$,

$$\beta = 2 \arcsin x = 2 \arcsin \sqrt{\left|\frac{Z_1}{4Z_2}\right|}.$$

The second possible solution of Eqs. (7-22) is for $\beta = \pm\pi$. Then

$\sin (\beta/2) = \pm 1$, and Eq. (7-22b) gives

$$\pm \cosh \frac{\alpha}{2} = \pm x$$

or
$$\cosh \frac{\alpha}{2} = x \qquad (7\text{-}24)$$

Since $\cosh (\alpha/2) \geq 1$, this solution is valid for $Z_1/4Z_2$ negative and having magnitude greater than or equal to unity and may be identified as case C.

Case C. $-\infty \leq Z_1/4Z_2 \leq -1$, $\beta = \pm \pi$,

$$\alpha = 2 \operatorname{arccosh} x = 2 \operatorname{arccosh} \sqrt{\left| \frac{Z_1}{4Z_2} \right|}.$$

(Note that there is no physical difference between $\beta = +\pi$ and $\beta = -\pi$.)

On the other hand, it is conceivable that $Z_1/4Z_2$ may be positive, so that $\sqrt{Z_1/4Z_2}$ is real and equal, say, to $\pm x$. Then substituting into Eq. (7-21a) and equating reals,

$$\sinh \frac{\alpha}{2} \cos \frac{\beta}{2} = \pm x \qquad (7\text{-}25)$$

and, equating imaginaries,

$$\cosh \frac{\alpha}{2} \sin \frac{\beta}{2} = 0 \qquad (7\text{-}26)$$

Once again, α and β must satisfy both these equations. Inasmuch as $\cosh (\alpha/2) \geq 1$ for any real α, Eq. (7-26) can be satisfied only by $\beta/2 = 0$, $\pm \pi$, or $\beta = 0$. (Note that there is no physical difference between $\beta = 0$ and $\beta = 2\pi$.) Then $\cos (\beta/2) = \pm 1$, and Eq. (7-25) reduces to

$$\sinh \frac{\alpha}{2} = x \qquad (7\text{-}27)$$

Physical considerations require α to be positive always.

This solution may be identified as case B.

Case B. $0 \leq Z_1/4Z_2 \leq \infty$, $\beta = 0$,

$$\alpha = 2 \operatorname{arcsinh} x = 2 \operatorname{arcsinh} \sqrt{\frac{Z_1}{4Z_2}}.$$

It will be seen that the three limits of cases A, B, and C are mutually exclusive, and therefore, as soon as the value of Z_1/Z_2 is known, it is possible to determine immediately which case applies to the filter. Z_1 and Z_2 are made of different types of reactances or combinations of reactances so that, as the frequency changes, a filter may pass from one case to another. Case A is the transmission band, while both cases B and C are attenuating bands.

The following tabular form shows the various cases:

Case	$\dfrac{Z_1}{4Z_2}$	α	β	Character of Z_o	Band
A	-1 to 0	0	$2\arcsin\sqrt{\left\|\dfrac{Z_1}{4Z_2}\right\|}$	Pure resistance	Pass-
B	0 to $+\infty$	$2\operatorname{arcsinh}\sqrt{\dfrac{Z_1}{4Z_2}}$	0	Pure reactance	Stop
C	$-\infty$ to -1	$2\operatorname{arccosh}\sqrt{\left\|\dfrac{Z_1}{4Z_2}\right\|}$	$\pm\pi$	Pure reactance	Stop

The foregoing results will now be applied to one general type of ladder filters, the constant-k structures.

7-8. Constant-k Ladder Filters.[1] A ladder network is said to be of the constant-k type if Z_1 and Z_2 of the network are *inverse*, i.e., if

$$Z_1Z_2 = R^2 = k \tag{7-28}$$

Equation (7-28) states that Z_1 and Z_2 are *inverse* if their product is a constant, independent of frequency. The construction of inverse impedances is covered in more detail in Chap. 14. For the purpose of this chapter it suffices to note two particular combinations of inverse structures. If $Z_1 = j\omega L_1$ and $Z_2 = 1/j\omega C_2$, then

$$Z_1Z_2 = \frac{L_1}{C_2} = R^2 \tag{7-29}$$

which is independent of frequency; therefore an inductive reactance and a capacitive reactance can be inverse impedances. Further if $Z_1 = j(\omega L_1 - 1/\omega C_1)$, a lossless series resonant circuit, and

$$Z_2 = \frac{1}{j(\omega C_2 - 1/\omega L_2)}$$

a lossless antiresonant circuit, then

$$Z_1Z_2 = \frac{\omega L_1 - 1/\omega C_1}{\omega C_2 - 1/\omega L_2} = \frac{L_2}{C_1}\frac{\omega^2 L_1 C_1 - 1}{\omega^2 L_2 C_2 - 1} \tag{7-30}$$

Equation (7-30) may be made independent of frequency if $L_1C_1 = L_2C_2$. Therefore a lossless series resonant circuit and a lossless antiresonant circuit are inverse, *provided that* the resonant frequency of the one coincides with the antiresonant frequency of the other and if $L_2/C_1 = L_1/C_2 = R^2$.

---

[1] The analysis used here in terms of a normalized frequency variable follows the method of E. A. Guillemin, "Communication Networks," vol. II, John Wiley & Sons, Inc., New York, 1935.

The defining relationship of constant-k ladder filters, viz., Eq. (7-28) may be combined with the results of the last section to give universal curves of α and β for all such filters. By virtue of Eq. (7-28)

$$\frac{Z_1}{4Z_2} = \frac{Z_1^2}{4R^2}$$

or

$$\sqrt{\frac{Z_1}{4Z_2}} = \pm\frac{Z_1}{2R} = \pm j\frac{X_1}{2R} = \pm jx \tag{7-31}$$

where x may be identified with the same parameter of cases A and C of the last section. Then one can use the results of the foregoing table to draw the universal curves of Fig. 7-2.

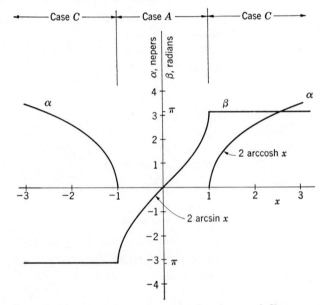

Fig. 7-2. Universal curves of α and β for constant-k filters.

The quantity R of Eqs. (7-28) and (7-31) has a special significance which may be seen by considering the characteristic impedance of the ladder network.

$$Z_{oT} = \sqrt{Z_1 Z_2 + \frac{Z_1^2}{4}} = \sqrt{Z_1 Z_2}\sqrt{1 + \frac{Z_1}{4Z_2}}$$

Substituting the constant-k condition from Eq. (7-28),

$$Z_{oT} = R\sqrt{1 + \frac{Z_1^2}{4R^2}} \tag{7-32}$$

Thus R is seen to be the value of Z_{oT} at that frequency at which $Z_1 = 0$ and is known as the *nominal impedance* of the network.

The universal curves of Fig. 7-2 and the concept of nominal impedance may be used to design the four types of constant-k ladder filters.

7-9. Low-pass Constant-k Ladder Filter. By definition, an LP filter is one which passes without attenuation all frequencies up to a cutoff frequency f_c and attenuates all frequencies greater than f_c. The α vs. frequency curve of an ideal, or perfect, LP filter, then, would have the form shown in Fig. 7-3a. This ideal curve cannot be realized and is approached only approximately by the constant-k LP section.

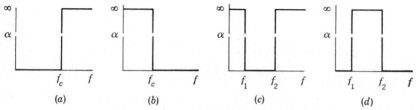

(a) (b) (c) (d)

FIG. 7-3. Attenuation characteristics of four basic types of ideal filters. (a) Low-pass. (b) High-pass. (c) Bandpass. (d) Band elimination.

To design this section, one notes that in Fig. 7-2 a LP section can be obtained if x is allowed to range only from 0 to ∞ with a cutoff occurring at $x = 1$. x is a normalized frequency variable; hence the problem is to choose X_1 so that, as frequency goes from 0 to ∞, x goes from 0 to ∞.

If the student considers the problem, he will realize that if X_1 is chosen to be ωL_1, then x varies from 0 to ∞ as f covers the same range; the desired condition is satisfied. Then given f_c and the nominal impedance R, one may design the required LP constant-k network provided that at f_c, $x = +1$. Then, substituting into Eq. (7-31),

$$\frac{2\pi f_c L_1}{2R} = 1$$

whence

$$L_1 = \frac{R}{\pi f_c} \qquad (7\text{-}33)$$

Z_2 may be obtained because in the constant-k structure Z_1 and Z_2 are inverse; thus from Eq. (7-29)

$$Z_1 Z_2 = \frac{L_1}{C_2} = R^2$$

whence

$$C_2 = \frac{1}{\pi R f_c} \qquad (7\text{-}34)$$

Equations (7-33) and (7-34) complete the design of the LP section, which is shown in Fig. 7-4.

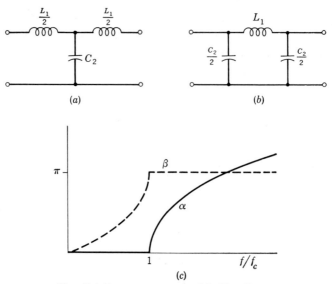

Fig. 7-4. Low-pass constant-k ladder filters.

The curves of α and β may be determined as a function of normalized frequency by reducing x in terms of f/f_c. Thus from Eq. (7-31)

$$x = \frac{\omega L_1}{2R} = \frac{2\pi f}{2R} \frac{R}{\pi f_c} = \frac{f}{f_c} \qquad (7\text{-}35a)$$

Thus from Fig. 7-2

$$\alpha = 0 \qquad \beta = 2 \arcsin \frac{f}{f_c} \qquad \text{for } f < f_c \qquad (7\text{-}35b)$$

$$\alpha - 2 \operatorname{arccosh} \frac{f}{f_c} \qquad \beta = \pi \qquad \text{for } f > f_c \qquad (7\text{-}35c)$$

and

$$f_c = \frac{1}{\pi \sqrt{L_1 C_2}} \qquad (7\text{-}35d)$$

These results are shown in Fig. 7-4c.

It is suggested that the student verify the transmission and attenuation bands by sketching reactance curves of the filter.

7-10. High-pass Constant-k Ladder Filter. By definition, an HP filter is one which attenuates all frequencies up to a cutoff frequency f_c and passes without attenuation all frequencies greater than f_c. The attenuation characteristic of an ideal HP structure is shown at b in Fig. 7-3. Again the constant-k ladder structure only approximates the ideal behavior and is designed in a manner analogous to that used in the last section.

Reference to Fig. 7-2 shows that the range of x corresponding to HP action is from $-\infty$ to 0. The problem, then, is to choose the components of X_1 so that, as f varies from 0 to $+\infty$, x varies from $-\infty$ to 0, that is, X_1 must provide an inverse relationship between x and f. This condition is satisfied if X_1 is the reactance of a capacitor. From Fig. 7-2 cutoff occurs at $x = -1$. Then, substituting into Eq. (7-31) for the cutoff condition,

$$-\frac{1}{2R(2\pi f_c)C_1} = -1$$

whence
$$C_1 = \frac{1}{4\pi R f_c} \qquad (7\text{-}36)$$

The corresponding design equation for Z_2 of the ladder section is determined by Eqs. (7-28) and (7-29). Thus for Z_1 and Z_2 to be inverse,

$$Z_2 = j\omega L_2 = \frac{R^2}{Z_1} \qquad L_2 = R^2 C_1$$

or
$$L_2 = \frac{R}{4\pi f_c} \qquad (7\text{-}37)$$

Again x may be shown to be a normalized frequency variable, for, substituting for X_1 in Eq. (7-31),

$$x = -\frac{1}{2R\omega C_1}$$

and, eliminating C_1 by Eq. (7-36),

$$x = -\frac{1}{2R(2\pi f)} 4\pi R f_c = -\frac{f_c}{f} \qquad (7\text{-}38)$$

and from cases A and C

$$\alpha = 2 \operatorname{arccosh} \frac{f_c}{f} \qquad \beta = -\pi \qquad \text{for } f < f_c$$

$$\alpha = 0 \qquad \beta = -2 \arcsin \frac{f_c}{f} \qquad \text{for } f > f_c \qquad (7\text{-}39)$$

and
$$f_c = \frac{1}{4\pi \sqrt{L_2 C_1}}$$

The constant-k HP structure and its response curves are shown in Fig. 7-5.

7-11. Bandpass Constant-k Ladder Filter. A BP filter is one which attenuates all frequencies below a lower cutoff frequency f_1 and above an upper cutoff frequency f_2. Frequencies lying between f_1 and f_2 comprise the passband and are transmitted with zero attenuation. The attenuation characteristic of an ideal BP is shown in Fig. 7-3c.

To design a BP constant-k ladder filter, one chooses Z_1 to be a lossless series resonant circuit, or $X_1 = \omega L_1 - 1/\omega C_1$. Then as frequency varies from 0 to $+\infty$, x varies from $-\infty$ to $+\infty$ as may be seen from Eq.

(7-31).   Thus the BP filter includes the entire x range in Fig. 7-2, the lower cutoff frequency f_1 corresponds to $x = -1$, and the upper cutoff frequency f_2 corresponds to $x = +1$.   These facts are used to design the BP filter.

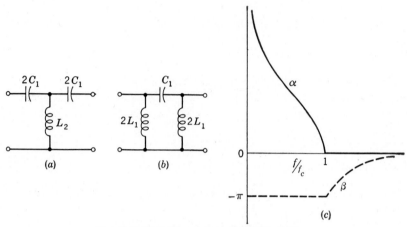

Fig. 7-5. High-pass constant-k ladder filters.

Substituting the upper cutoff condition into Eq. (7-31) at ω_2,

$$x = \frac{\omega_2 L_1 - 1/\omega_2 C_1}{2R} = 1 \tag{7-40}$$

Similarly at ω_1,

$$x = \frac{\omega_1 L_1 - 1/\omega_1 C_1}{2R} = -1 \tag{7-41}$$

The last two simultaneous equations may be solved for L_1 to give

$$L_1 = \frac{R}{\pi(f_2 - f_1)} \tag{7-42}$$

and for C_1 to give

$$C_1 = \frac{f_2 - f_1}{4\pi R f_1 f_2} \tag{7-43}$$

From previous work it is known that the inverse shunt element Z_2 will be a lossless antiresonant circuit consisting of L_2 and C_2 in shunt.

Furthermore, for Z_1 and Z_2 to be inverse structures

$$\frac{L_2}{C_1} = \frac{L_1}{C_2} = R^2 \tag{7-44}$$

and

$$L_1 C_1 = L_2 C_2 \tag{7-45}$$

Then solving for L_2 and C_2,

$$L_2 = \frac{R(f_2 - f_1)}{4\pi f_1 f_2} \tag{7-46}$$

$$C_2 = \frac{1}{\pi R(f_2 - f_1)} \tag{7-47}$$

Equation (7-45) states that the resonant frequency of Z_1 must be the same as the antiresonant frequency of Z_2 in order for the two impedances to be inverse, i.e.,

$$\omega_r{}^2 = \frac{1}{L_1 C_1} = \frac{1}{L_2 C_2} \tag{7-48}$$

If one substitutes for the four circuit elements, he finds that

$$f_r{}^2 = f_1 f_2 \tag{7-49}$$

indicating that the response of the BP filter probably displays geometric symmetry about the resonant frequency f_r. This is verified by reducing x to normalized frequency form. From Eq. (7-31)

$$x = \frac{X_1}{2R} = \frac{\omega L_1 - 1/\omega C_1}{2R} = \frac{\omega^2 L_1 C_1 - 1}{2R\omega C_1} \tag{7-50}$$

Introducing Eq. (7-49) and eliminating L_1 and C_1,

$$x = \frac{f_r}{f_2 - f_1}\left(\frac{f}{f_r} - \frac{f_r}{f}\right) \tag{7-51}$$

From cases A and C, then, the response of the BP filter will be given by

$$\alpha = 0 \qquad \beta = 2\arcsin\frac{f_r}{f_2 - f_1}\left(\frac{f}{f_r} - \frac{f_r}{f}\right) \qquad \text{for } f_1 \leq f \leq f_2$$

$$\alpha = 2\operatorname{arccosh}\left|\frac{f_r}{f_2 - f_1}\left(\frac{f}{f_r} - \frac{f_r}{f}\right)\right| \qquad \beta = -\pi \text{ for } f < f_1 \tag{7-52}$$

$$\alpha = 2\operatorname{arccosh}\frac{f_r}{f_2 - f_1}\left(\frac{f}{f_r} - \frac{f_r}{f}\right) \qquad \beta = +\pi \text{ for } f > f_2$$

The student may verify that the cutoff frequencies may be determined from the circuit elements by

$$f_2 = \frac{1}{2\pi}\left(\frac{1}{\sqrt{L_1 C_2}} + \sqrt{\frac{1}{L_1 C_2} + \frac{1}{L_1 C_1}}\right) \tag{7-53a}$$

$$f_1 = \frac{1}{2\pi}\left(-\frac{1}{\sqrt{L_1 C_2}} + \sqrt{\frac{1}{L_1 C_2} + \frac{1}{L_1 C_1}}\right) \tag{7-53b}$$

Figure 7-6 shows the constant-k BP filter and its response curves.

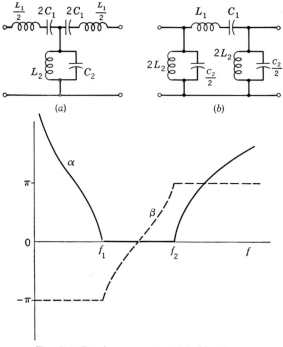

Fig. 7-6. Bandpass constant-k ladder filters.

7-12. Low-pass–Bandpass Analogy. The design of the three basic filter sections in the preceding paragraphs has been based on the general curves of Fig. 7-2. For example, for the LP network Z_1 was chosen such that the range of real frequencies corresponds to $0 \leq x \leq +\infty$, while for the BP network Z_1 was chosen so that the real frequency range corresponds to $-\infty \leq x \leq +\infty$. This suggests a close analogy between the LP and BP cases. In fact, given the LP design equations, it is possible to derive those of the BP filter by making a suitable change in variables. One notes the following corresponding quantities in the two filters:

L_1 in the LP section is replaced in the BP section by L_1 and C_1 in series, where $\omega_r{}^2 = \omega_1\omega_2 = 1/L_1C_1$.

C_2 in the LP section is replaced in the BP section by L_2 and C_2 in parallel, where $\omega_r{}^2 = \omega_1\omega_2 = 1/L_2C_2$.

The bandwidth, which is equal to f_c in the LP case, is made equal to the bandwidth $f_2 - f_1$ in the BP case, and $f_r = \sqrt{f_1f_2}$.

Figure 7-7 shows an example of such an analog. Figure 7-7a is a LP filter designed for $R = 600$ ohms and $f_c = 3,000$ cycles. Figure 7-7b is the analogous BP filter with $R = 600$ ohms, $f_1 = 1,000$ cycles, and $f_2 = 4,000$ cycles, showing that L_1 and C_2 are identical for the two designs.

7-13. Band-elimination Constant-k Ladder Filter. A band-elimination filter is one which passes without attenuation all frequencies less than the lower cutoff frequency f_1 and greater than the upper cutoff frequency f_2. Frequencies lying between f_1 and f_2 comprise the stop band and are attenuated. The ideal case is shown in Fig. 7-3d.

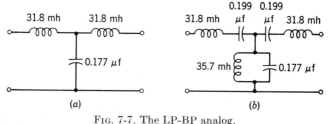

Fig. 7-7. The LP-BP analog.

The band-elimination filter is designed in much the same manner as is the BP filter. The derivation of the necessary equations is left as an exercise for the student. The student may also set up an analogue between the HP and band-elimination sections.

7-14. Variation of Characteristic Impedance with Frequency. At the cutoff frequency defined by Eq. (7-12),

$$Z_1 + 4Z_2 = 0$$
$$Z_{oT} = 0$$
$$Z_{o\text{II}} = \infty$$

In passing from the transmission to the attenuating band at this frequency the characteristic impedance of the T section must drop to zero while that of the II section must rise to infinity. These are the only values through which Z_o could pass continuously from a real to an imaginary value.

The variation of the characteristic impedance within the passband of a constant-k ladder filter may be derived. From Eq. (7-31)

$$\frac{Z_1}{4Z_2} = -x^2$$

and, substituting into Eq. (7-32),

$$Z_{oT} = R\sqrt{1 - x^2} \tag{7-54}$$

For the mid-shunt impedance

$$Z_{o\text{II}} = \frac{Z_1 Z_2}{Z_{oT}}$$

but $Z_1 Z_2 = R^2$; therefore

$$Z_{o\text{II}} = \frac{R}{\sqrt{1 - x^2}} \tag{7-55}$$

Equations (7-54) and (7-55) are plotted in Fig. 7-8 for $0 \le |x| \le 1$, that is, for the passband. In the stop band where $|x| > 1$, both Z_{oT} and $Z_{o\text{II}}$ become imaginary. It is apparent that such a section cannot be terminated properly throughout the passband by a single resistance. If the load is adjusted for the lower frequencies, bad reflection will occur at

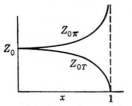

the upper range, and vice versa, if the load is matched at the higher frequencies. Under these conditions the transmission loss is not equal to the attenuation loss. Therefore it is desirable to seek a filter section which will have a smaller variation in Z_o over a considerable portion of the passband, and this will be done later in the chapter.

FIG. 7-8. Variation of the characteristic impedance with frequency in the LP constant-k filter.

7-15. Variation of Attenuation with Frequency. It has been mentioned that the attenuation throughout the attenuating band is finite and therefore does not present a perfect barrier to the transmission of power at frequencies within this band. The attenuating characteristics of the simple LP section are shown in Fig. 7-9a.

It is usually desirable to have high attenuation near the cutoff frequency, as well as at other points. In Fig. 7-9b is shown another type

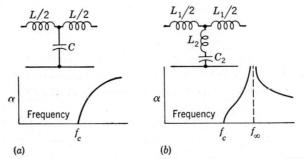

FIG. 7-9. Variation of attenuation with frequency in two types of LP filters.

of LP filter. This filter has very high attenuation at the frequency where Z_2 becomes resonant and shunts a zero reactance across the line. By properly selecting L_2 and C_2, this frequency of infinite attenuation, which will be designated as f_∞, can be placed anywhere in the attenuating band.

7-16. m-Derived T Sections. It would be highly desirable if different filter sections of the general type of Fig. 7-9b could be joined together, each section to have an f_∞ at a different point in the attenuating band, so that a high value of α might be maintained throughout the entire region.

In order to join together filter sections without reflection, it would be necessary that their characteristic impedances be equal to each other at all frequencies. If their characteristic impedances matched at all frequencies, they would also have the same transmission band, since in this band, and this band only, Z_o is a pure resistance. In Fig. 7-10 are shown two T sections related in a definite manner.

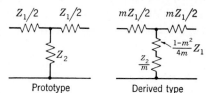

The characteristic impedance of the one called the prototype is $Z_{oT} = \sqrt{Z_1 Z_2 + Z_1^2/4}$. In the derived type let the new branches be called Z_1' and Z_2' and its characteristic impedance Z_{oT}'.

Fig. 7-10. T sections which have identical characteristic impedances.

Imagine that Z_1 and Z_1' are related by the equation

$$Z_1' = mZ_1 \qquad (7\text{-}56)$$

The problem is then to find a configuration of Z_2' such that

$$Z_{oT} = Z_{oT}' \qquad (7\text{-}57)$$

If Eqs. (7-56) and (7-57) hold,

$$Z_1 Z_2 + \frac{Z_1^2}{4} = Z_1' Z_2' + \frac{(Z_1')^2}{4} = mZ_1 Z_2' + \frac{m^2 Z_1^2}{4}$$

$$Z_2' = \frac{Z_2}{m} + \frac{(1 - m^2)Z_1}{4m} \qquad (7\text{-}58)$$

Hence, if Z_2 is given the configuration specified by Eq. (7-58) and illustrated in Fig. 7-10b, the characteristic impedances and the cutoff frequencies of both structures in Fig. 7-10 will be identical. Such sections can be joined together without reflection.

It is interesting to note what would be the effect if, instead of making the assumption of Eq. (7-56), the following assumption were made in an effort to find two filter sections with the same characteristic impedance:

$$Z_2' = mZ_2 \qquad (7\text{-}56a)$$

The problem is then to endeavor to find a proper configuration for Z_1' such that $Z_{oT} = Z_{oT}'$. If Eqs. (7-57) and (7-56a) hold,

$$Z_1 Z_2 + \frac{Z_1^2}{4} = Z_1' Z_2' + \frac{(Z_1')^2}{4} = mZ_1' Z_2 + \frac{(Z_1')^2}{4}$$

Solve for Z_1'.

$$Z_1' = -2mZ_2 \pm \sqrt{m^2 Z_2^2 + 4Z_1 Z_2 + Z_1^2} \qquad (7\text{-}58a)$$

Equation (7-58a) does not give a physical configuration for Z_1' which can hold for all frequencies. Therefore the mathematical experiment which was attempted in Eq. (7-56a) resulted in failure, while the one attempted in Eq. (7-56) gave success. This is usually the case in engineering developments: many experiments both physical and mathematical are attempted, and some result in failure, while others are successful. In the literature only the successful experiments are reported, and the student often obtains an erroneous impression of the methods by which such derivations are originally obtained. Usually the failures greatly outnumber the successes, but one success is worth the effort involved in making the experiments which failed.

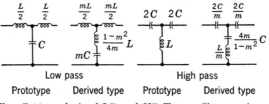

Low pass — Prototype — Derived type — High pass — Prototype — Derived type

Fig. 7-11. m-derived LP and HP T-type filter sections.

By using Eq. (7-58) and varying the value of m, any number of sections, each differing from the other in certain respects but each having the same mid-series characteristic impedance, can be constructed and joined together to form a complete filter.

Figure 7-11 shows the application of this principle to the design of LP and HP filters. It is usual to take the simplest (constant-k) type as the prototype and derive other types from it.

In order to have the portion of the shunt impedance represented by $(1 - m^2)Z_1/4m$ maintain this relation at all frequencies, it is necessary that this reactance be of the same type as Z_1. This limits the physical structure to values of m such that $1 - m^2$ is positive, or[1] $m < 1$.

The behavior of α and β for the m-derived T sections will now be investigated.

7-17. α and β for m-derived Sections. The analysis of the prototype, or constant-k, sections was simplified by the use of a parameter x defined by Eq. (7-31), namely, $\pm jx = \sqrt{Z_1/4Z_2}$. Similar simplification results for the m-derived sections by defining an analogous parameter x_m,

$$\pm jx_m = \sqrt{\frac{Z_1'}{4Z_2'}} \tag{7-59}$$

or, squaring,

$$x_m{}^2 = -\frac{Z_1'}{4Z_2'} \tag{7-59a}$$

[1] The restriction that $m < 1$ does not apply if mutual inductance between the two halves of the series arm Z_1 is utilized (see Prob. 7-11).

That x_m is related to x may be shown by substituting for Z_1' and Z_2' from Eqs. (7-56) and (7-58).

$$x_m{}^2 = \frac{-mZ_1}{4[Z_2/m + (1 - m^2)Z_1/4m]} = -m^2 \frac{Z_1}{4Z_2} \frac{1}{[1 + (1 - m^2)Z_1/4Z_2]}$$

$$= \frac{m^2x^2}{1 - (1 - m^2)x^2} \tag{7-60}$$

Note that when x equals ± 1 or 0, $x = x_m$, irrespective of the value of m.

Then as a direct analog of Eq. (7-21a), one may write for the m-derived sections

$$\sinh \frac{\gamma}{2} = \sinh \frac{\alpha}{2} \cos \frac{\beta}{2} + j \cosh \frac{\alpha}{2} \sin \frac{\beta}{2}$$

$$= \sqrt{\frac{Z_1'}{4Z_2'}} = \pm jx_m \tag{7-61}$$

This equation may be handled in the same manner as was Eq. (7-21) to yield the following cases:

Case A.   Passband. $-1 \le x \le +1$.

$$\alpha = 0$$

$$\beta = 2 \arcsin x_m = 2 \arctan \frac{mx}{\sqrt{1 - x^2}} \tag{7-62}$$

Case B.   Attenuation band. $1 < |x| < 1/\sqrt{1 - m^2}$.

$$\alpha = 2 \operatorname{arccosh} \frac{mx}{\sqrt{1 - (1 - m^2)x^2}} \tag{7-63}$$

$$\beta = \pm \pi$$

Case C.   Attenuation band. $|x| > 1/\sqrt{1 - m^2}$.

$$\alpha = 2 \operatorname{arcsinh} \left| \frac{mx}{\sqrt{1 - (1 - m^2)x^2}} \right| \tag{7-64}$$

$$\beta = 0$$

These results are plotted in Fig. 7-12.   It should be noticed that, in the regions corresponding to case A, the sign of β is chosen so that the β curve has positive slope.

Comparison of Figs. 7-2 and 7-12 shows that the m-derived sections have the same transmission and attenuation bands as their prototypes. This is to be expected since the m-derived design is based on both types of sections having the same characteristic impedance.   It has been shown previously that the bands are uniquely determined by the character, i.e., whether real or imaginary, of Z_o.

7-18. Frequencies of Infinite Attenuation. Figure 7-12 also shows that the m-derived sections provide infinite attenuation at certain frequencies, corresponding to $|x| = 1/\sqrt{1 - m^2}$. This relationship may be

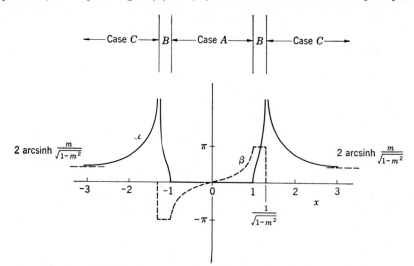

Fig. 7-12. Universal curves of α and β for the m-derived sections.

used to select m to cause f_∞ to lie at any desired point within the attenuation band. For example, from Eq. (7-35) for the LP filter $x = f/f_c$. Then at $f = f_\infty$

$$|x| = \frac{f_\infty}{f_c} = \frac{1}{\sqrt{1 - m^2}}$$

or

$$m = \sqrt{1 - \left(\frac{f_c}{f_\infty}\right)^2} \qquad (7\text{-}65)$$

The student should notice from Fig. 7-11 that the infinite attenuation occurs as the result of the shunt arm of the m-derived section going into resonance, causing a short circuit across the network.

Corresponding expressions may be derived for the three remaining basic filter types.

The student should observe that, as m is made smaller, f_∞ approaches f_c, the cutoff frequency, making for a more abrupt cutoff attenuation characteristic in the m-derived section. It may be shown from Eq. (7-64) that a decrease in m lowers α at high values of x. For this reason m-derived sections are seldom used alone, but usually in cascade with one or more prototype sections. Such a combination of different sections is known as a composite filter and is discussed later.

7-19. Terminating T Sections. All the T sections discussed this far, both the prototype and the m-derived, have a characteristic impedance

Z_{oT} given by Eq. (7-54) and plotted in Fig. 7-8. It will be observed that in the passband Z_{oT} is a pure resistance *whose value varies with frequency.* Therefore it is difficult to terminate these sections properly; it would be desirable to use a fixed resistance as a termination. This difficulty may be reduced by using a half or L section as an impedance-transforming device.

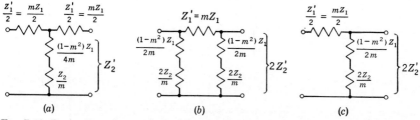

FIG. 7-13. Derivation of an m-derived terminating L or half section. (a) m-derived T section. (b) Related II section. (c) Basic L or half section.

Figure 7-13a shows an m-derived T section. At b the same impedance elements are rearranged to give the *related* II section, whose characteristic impedance will be designated Z'_{oII}. The behavior of Z'_{oII} will now be investigated. From Eq. (6-17)

$$Z'_{oII} = \frac{Z'_1 Z'_2}{Z_{oT}}$$

Then substituting for Z'_1, Z'_2, and Z_{oT} from Eqs. (7-56), (7-58), and (7-54).

$$Z'_{oII} = \frac{mZ_1[Z_2/m + (1 - m^2)Z_1/4m]}{R\sqrt{1 - x^2}}$$
$$= \frac{Z_1 Z_2[1 + (1 - m^2)Z_1/4Z_2]}{R\sqrt{1 - x^2}} \qquad (7\text{-}66)$$

But $Z_1 Z_2 = R^2$ and $Z_1/4Z_2 = -x^2$; therefore

$$Z'_{oII} = \frac{R[1 - (1 - m^2)x^2]}{\sqrt{1 - x^2}} \qquad (7\text{-}66a)$$

By introducing Eq. (7-55), Z'_{oII} may be rewritten as

$$Z'_{oII} = Z_{oII}[1 - (1 - m^2)x^2] \qquad (7\text{-}66b)$$

The student is reminded that Z_{oII} refers to the related *prototype* II section, whereas Z'_{oII} refers to the related *m-derived* II section. It is desirable to see how Z'_{oII} varies with x as a function of the parameter m. This may be done by plotting the family of curves shown in Fig. 7-14. As a matter of convenience the curves are plotted in normalized form with the dependent variable $Z'_{o\text{II}}/R$ *inverted*. Use of the inverted variable limits most of the curves to finite values and makes their comparison simpler. Inspection of the curves shows that for $m = 0.6$, $Z'_{o\text{II}}$ remains within

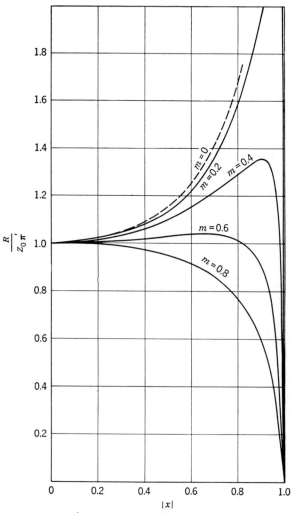

FIG. 7-14. Variation of $Z'_{o\text{II}}$ of the related Π section of an m-derived T section.

4 per cent of the fixed nominal impedance R for almost 90 per cent of the passband. This is used as a satisfactory solution to the terminating problem. Any of the T sections, whether prototype or m-derived, may be joined to a terminating half section with $m = 0.6$. A final termination of a resistance of R ohms is used. Then by the impedance-transforming properties of the half section that were described in Sec. 6-3, the T sec-

tion will have *almost* the correct termination of Z_{oT} for roughly 90 per cent of the passband. Figure 7-15 shows the actual impedance presented to the T section by the half section terminated in R. It will be observed that the real part of the impedance closely approximates Z_{oT} and the imaginary part is small.

In the attenuation band the value of terminating impedance for the T sections is not important so long as the attenuation is high. This will be explained further in Chap. 9, Reflection.

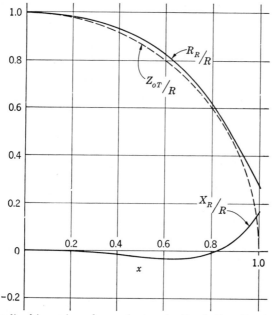

FIG. 7-15. Normalized input impedance of a terminating half section terminated in R. $m = 0.6$.

7-20. Composite Filters. A single filter section seldom provides enough attenuation for most practical purposes. If a number of sections are joined together and if their characteristic impedances match, the total attenuation at any frequency will be the sum of the attenuations of the individual sections and by this means a filter may be built up to meet any required conditions. If all the sections were similar to Fig. 7-9a, the total attenuation would not be very high at frequencies just above cutoff but would be very large at higher frequencies. On the other hand, if all the sections were like Fig. 7-9b, the attenuation would rise rapidly above cutoff until f_∞ were reached and then would fall and continue to drop at high frequencies. For most purposes it is desirable that the attenuation be high throughout the entire attenuating band. This can most conveniently be accomplished by the use of individual sections with the same cutoff frequencies and characteristic impedances, but with different frequencies of infinite attenuation. The use of m-derived sections, each with a different value of m, makes this possible, as they can be joined together without reflection.

Further, the use of terminating half sections with $m = 0.6$ transforms Z_{oT} into essentially a fixed resistance R, the nominal characteristic impedance. A composite filter, then, will usually have the following components: (1) one or more prototype sections; (2) one or more m-derived

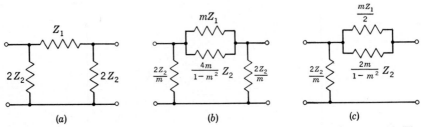

(a)   (b)   (c)

Fig. 7-16. (a, b) Π sections which have identical characteristic impedances. (c) The half section of b.

sections, m being chosen to provide the required frequencies of infinite attenuation; (3) two terminating half sections with $m = 0.6$. The design of a typical composite filter will be considered later.

7-21. m-derived Π Sections. Thus far in the discussion the m-derived sections have been T sections that were designed on the basis of matching the mid-series characteristic impedance Z_{oT}. It is also possible to design m-derived Π sections so that $Z_{oΠ}$ is the same for the prototype and derived sections. These sections are frequently called *mid-shunt* m-derived filters and are shown in Fig. 7-16. The proof of the identity of the characteristic impedances of the protoptype and derived types follows the same method as for the T section and is left to the student. It is most convenient to use admittances. In this case the assumption $Y'_2 = mY_2$ gives a physically realizable structure, while the assumption $Y'_1 = mY_1$ will not. The student may also show that the α and β characteristics of the m-derived Π sections are given by Eq. (7-11) by noting that the parameter x_m is the direct analog of Eq. (7-59a), viz.,

$$x_m{}^2 = -\frac{Z'_1}{4Z'_2} = -\frac{Y'_2}{4Y'_1}$$

$$= -\frac{mY_2}{4[Y_1/m + (1 - m^2)Y_2/4m]} = \frac{m^2x^2}{1 - (1 - m^2)x^2} \qquad (7\text{-}67)$$

7-22. Composite Filter of Derived Π Sections. The derived Π sections of Fig. 7-16 can also be used in constructing a composite filter. In this

case a nearly uniform impedance match over the passband may be secured
by terminating in a half T section, whose values have been derived from
the relations of Fig. 7-16 and whose m is again equal to 0.6.

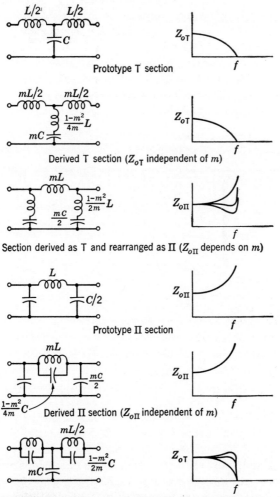

FIG. 7-17. Summary of the characteristic impedances of simple prototype and derived
LP filter sections as a function of frequency.

7-23. Summary of Design Procedure.   The fundamental data required
for a filter are the passband (or the cutoff frequency for an LP or HP
filter) and the nominal characteristic impedance into which it is to work.
From these data the components of the prototype section are calculated
from Eqs. (7-33) and (7-34), (7-36) and (7-37), or (7-42), (7-43), (7-46),

and (7-47), depending on the type of filter desired. Construct one or more intermediate sections by the relations in Fig. 7-10 or 7-16. The number of sections needed will be determined by the attenuation requirements outside the passband, and the m's will be selected to arrange the values of infinite-attenuation frequencies properly. If a sharp cutoff is required, a small value of m must be used for one section. The end of the filter should then be terminated in a half section of $m = 0.6$. The shunt arm of the terminating half section should have twice the impedance of the shunt arm of the T section, since the shunt arm of a II section is $2Z_2$. This means that the inductances should be twice, and the capacitances half, the value of the shunt arm of the derived T section.

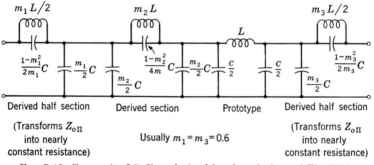

Fig. 7-18. Composite LP filter derived by the relations of Fig. 7-16.

It should be noticed that, in the type of design developed in detail, the prototype was selected as the simplest T section for the type of filter chosen, other T sections were derived which would have the same characteristic impedance as the T prototype, and the terminating half sections had their Z_1 and Z_2 arms derived by the equations of Fig. 7-10. It would also be possible to start with a simple II prototype, derive other II sections which would match by the equations of Fig. 7-16, and then use two half sections with the Z_1 and Z_2 arms derived by the equations of Fig. 7-16 to change the impedance of the structure into the same type. A summary of the different types of sections and their characteristic impedance is shown in Fig. 7-17.

A filter derived by the relations of Fig. 7-16 would have the general configuration of Fig. 7-18, where the capacitances of adjacent sections are usually combined into a single capacitor. A choice between the design of Fig. 7-18, based on II's, or Fig. 7-19, based on T's, might be made on the basis of which gave the most convenient size or type of elements or upon the effect of the input impedance upon the transmission system as a whole. For instance, the input terminals of an LP filter of the type of Fig. 7-19 could not be placed in parallel with the input terminals of an HP filter which was intended to pass frequencies above

1,000 cycles, because the first shunt arm is resonant at 1,250 cycles and so would short-circuit the input of the HP filter at that frequency which it is intended to pass. The filter of Fig. 7-18 could be used more effectively because its input impedance would be very high at that frequency

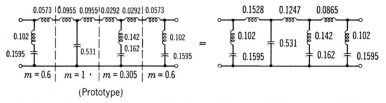

(Prototype)

Fig. 7-19. Composite 600-ohm LP filter with a cutoff frequency of 1 kc.

since the first series arm would be antiresonant. However, in many cases more complicated design formulas are necessary when filters are to operate in parallel, in order to attain the proper impedance relations.

As an example of the calculation of a composite LP filter, one will be designed to have a cutoff frequency of 1,000 cycles and to operate into a 600-ohm line. In order to give a sharp cutoff, one value of f_∞ will be selected equal to 1,050 cycles. The terminating half sections with $m = 0.6$ will also, by Eq. (7-65), give a value of f_∞ 25 per cent above the cutoff frequency, or at 1,250 cycles. T sections will be used. The values for the prototype will be, by Eqs. (7-33) and (7-34),

$$L = \frac{600}{\pi 1,000} = 0.1910 \text{ henry}$$

$$C = \frac{1}{\pi 1,000 \times 600} = 0.531 \times 10^{-6} \text{ farad}$$

For the section with $f_\infty = 1,050$ cycles, by Eq. (7-65),

$$m = \sqrt{1 - \left(\frac{1,000}{1,050}\right)^2} = 0.305$$

$$\frac{1 - m^2}{4m} = \frac{0.907}{1.22} = 0.743$$

$$\frac{mL}{2} = \frac{0.305 \times 0.1910}{2} = 0.0292 \text{ henry}$$

$$\frac{1 - m^2}{4m} L = 0.743 \times 0.1910 = 0.142 \text{ henry}$$

$$mC = 0.305 \times 0.531 = 0.162 \ \mu\text{f}$$

For the terminating half section $m = 0.6$,

$$\frac{mL}{2} = 0.0573 \text{ henry}$$

$$\frac{1 - m^2}{4m} L = 0.2665 \times 0.191 = 0.051 \text{ henry}$$

$$mC = 0.6 \times 0.531 = 0.319 \ \mu\text{f}$$

The complete filter will be that shown in Fig. 7-19.

Inasmuch as there is no need to preserve the identity of inductors in series, adjacent inductors in the series arm are combined to give the final form shown at b in the figure. This procedure reduces the number of elements required and in general raises the quality factor of the series inductive elements.

7-24. Attenuation of Filter Sections. A reasonable estimate of the filter response may be obtained by directly applying the theory of iterative structures. Subject to two assumptions, viz., that the filter elements are lossless and that the section is properly terminated at all frequencies, one notes that the total transmission loss is the sum of the α's of each section and that the total phase shift is the sum of the individual β's.

Practically speaking, neither of these two assumptions is satisfied, thereby introducing discrepancies between calculated and measured results. These discrepancies will now be considered.

If dissipation is present, the use of Eq. (7-21) will in general require the use of tables or charts of inverse hyperbolic functions or formulas such as are found in the Appendix. However, the points at which the dissipation produces the greatest variation from the ideal values will be at the cutoff and *infinite-attenuation* frequencies. At these frequencies simplifications may be made. The dissipation of the capacitors is usually negligible in comparison with that of the inductors. At f_∞ the dissipation of importance will be that of the inductor of the shunt arm.

Let $Q_2 =$ quality factor of this inductor

$$= \frac{\omega(1 - m^2)}{4m} \frac{L_1}{R}$$

Then for the m-derived T LP filter of the type shown in Fig. 7-11, at f_∞

$$Z_1' = jm\omega_\infty L_1$$

$$Z_2' = \frac{1 - m^2}{4m} \frac{\omega_\infty L_1}{Q_2}$$

Hence

$$\frac{Z_1'}{4Z_2'} = j\frac{m^2 Q_2}{1 - m^2} = \frac{m^2 Q_2}{1 - m^2} \underline{/90^\circ} \qquad (7\text{-}68)$$

or

$$\sqrt{\frac{Z_1'}{4Z_2'}} = \sqrt{\frac{m^2 Q_2}{2(1 - m^2)}} (1 + j) \qquad (7\text{-}68a)$$

Then from Eq. (7-21a)

$$\sinh\frac{\alpha}{2}\cos\frac{\beta}{2} = \cosh\frac{\alpha}{2}\sin\frac{\beta}{2} = \sqrt{\frac{m^2 Q_2}{2(1 - m^2)}} \qquad (7\text{-}69)$$

But α is large; therefore

$$\sinh\frac{\alpha}{2} \approx \cosh\frac{\alpha}{2} \approx \frac{e^{\alpha/2}}{2} \qquad (7\text{-}70)$$

and $\beta \approx 90°$. From Eqs. (7-69) and (7-70)

$$\frac{e^{\alpha/2}}{2\sqrt{2}} \approx \sqrt{\frac{m^2 Q_2}{2(1 - m^2)}}$$

or

$$\alpha \approx \ln \frac{4m^2 Q_2}{1 - m^2} \qquad (7\text{-}71)$$

Equation (7-71) may be given in terms of the ratio f_∞/f_c by using Eq. (7-65),

$$\alpha \approx \ln 4Q_2 \left[\left(\frac{f_\infty}{f_c} \right)^2 - 1 \right] \qquad (7\text{-}71a)$$

At the cutoff frequency the dissipation of both inductances is important. For this case

$$Z_1' = \left(\frac{1}{Q_1} + j \right) m\omega_c L_1 \qquad (7\text{-}72)$$

$$Z_2' = \left(\frac{1}{Q_2} + j \right) \frac{1 - m^2}{4m} \omega_c L_1 - \frac{j}{\omega_c m C_2}$$

But from Eqs. (7-33) and (7-34)

$$\frac{1}{C_2} = (\pi f_c)^2 L_1 = \frac{\omega_c^2 L_1}{4}$$

Therefore $\quad Z_2' = \frac{1 - m^2}{4mQ_2} + j\left(\frac{1 - m^2}{4m} - \frac{1}{4m} \right) = \left(\frac{1 - m^2}{Q_2} - jm^2 \right) \frac{\omega_c L_1}{4m}$

$$(7\text{-}73)$$

In this case it is convenient to find γ in terms of the hyperbolic cosine; thus from Eq. (6-22)

$$\cosh \gamma = 1 + \frac{Z_1'}{2Z_2'}$$

So one requires the ratio

$$\frac{Z_1'}{2Z_2'} = \frac{2m^2(1/Q_1 + j)}{(1 - m^2)/Q_2 - jm^2}$$

$$= 2m^2 \frac{\left(\dfrac{1 - m^2}{Q_1 Q_2} - m^2 \right) + j\left(\dfrac{1 - m^2}{Q_2} + \dfrac{m^2}{Q_1} \right)}{\left(\dfrac{1 - m^2}{Q_2} \right)^2 + m^4}$$

But if Q_1 and Q_2 are both large, terms involving $1/Q_2^2$ or $1/Q_1 Q_2$ are negligible. Further, assuming $Q_1 \approx Q_2 = Q$,

$$\frac{Z_1'}{2Z_2'} \approx 2\left(-1 + \frac{j}{m^2 Q} \right) \qquad (7\text{-}74)$$

Then, substituting into Eq. (6-19),

$$\cosh \gamma = \cosh \alpha \cos \beta + j \sinh \alpha \sin \beta = 1 + \frac{Z_1}{2Z_2}$$

$$= -1 + j \frac{2}{m^2 Q} \tag{7-75}$$

$$\cosh \alpha \cos \beta = -1 \tag{7-76}$$

$$\sinh \alpha \sin \beta = \frac{2}{m^2 Q} \tag{7-77}$$

If α is small, β must be nearly equal to π and the following approximations may be made: Let

$$\beta = \pi - \Theta, \text{ where } \Theta \text{ is small}$$

$$\cos \beta = -\cos \Theta = \frac{\Theta^2}{2} - 1, \text{ using two terms in cosine series}$$

$$\sin \beta = \sin \Theta = \Theta$$

$$\cosh \alpha = 1 + \frac{\alpha^2}{2}$$

$$\sinh \alpha = \alpha$$

Then Eqs. (7-76) and (7-77) become

$$\left(1 + \frac{\alpha^2}{2}\right)\left(\frac{\Theta^2}{2} - 1\right) = -1 \tag{7-76a}$$

$$\alpha\Theta = \frac{2}{m^2 Q} \tag{7-77a}$$

From Eq. (7-76a),

$$\frac{\Theta^2}{2} - \frac{\alpha^2}{2} + \frac{\alpha^2 \Theta^2}{4} = 0$$

If α and Θ are small, $\alpha^2 \Theta^2/4$ may be neglected, which gives $\Theta = \alpha$. Insert this in Eq. (7-77a).

$$\alpha = \frac{1}{m}\sqrt{\frac{2}{Q}} \tag{7-78}$$

Equations (7-71a) and (7-78) show that, as m is reduced and f_∞ is made to approach f_c, the attenuation at the cutoff frequency is increased, while that at the frequency of infinite attenuation is reduced. This places a practical limit on the use of m-derived sections to give a sharp rise in attenuation near cutoff, because too low a value of m will increase the attenuation in the transmission band near the cutoff frequency. The higher the value of Q, the sharper is the rise in attenuation which may be secured. The general effect of dissipation on the attenuation of a filter section is shown in Fig. 7-20.

The foregoing discussion relates to the *attenuation* of a filter. The student is reminded that the insertion loss corresponds to the attenuation loss only if the sections are properly terminated in their characteristic impedance. It has been shown, however, that a terminating

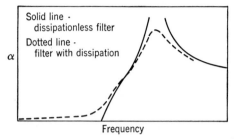

FIG. 7-20. Effect of dissipation on attenuation of an *m*-derived filter section.

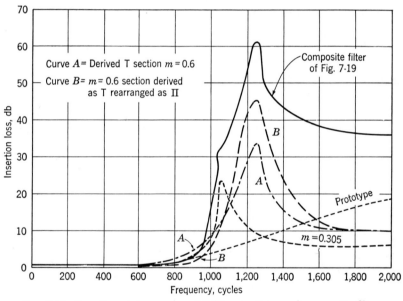

FIG. 7-21. Experimental curves on LP filter sections and composite filter.

half section does not transform the fixed nominal impedance R into Z_o exactly; hence the actual response of the filter will not correspond to the sum of the α's of the component sections.

To circumvent this difficulty, filter response is usually calculated or measured as the *insertion loss* [Eq. (6-62)]. The insertion loss is in general higher than the loss due to attenuation as a result of the mismatch in impedance near the cutoff frequency. Figure 7-21 shows experimental curves of the filter designed in Fig. 7-19, together with the insertion loss

of individual sections.   The inductors used were wound on powdered
permalloy toroidal cores and tapped in decade steps.   Since the whole
coil was not in use, the characteristics are not so close to the ideal as
could be secured with coils made especially for the filter designed.   One
point of interest is a comparison of the curves for the $m = 0.6$ section
in its original derived T form and in the rearranged Π form.   Because of
the improved impedance characteristics the latter form shows a much
sharper cutoff.   It is also of interest to note the characteristic of the
simple prototype which makes it unsuitable for use by itself as a filter
which must produce a sharp cutoff.

7-25. Repeated Derivations.   It has been shown previously that the
use of an m-derived half section greatly simplifies the problem of properly
terminating the composite filter.   By adding one additional shunt element to the prototype structure one obtains control of the $Z'_{o\text{II}}$ characteristic in terms of a parameter m.   Figure 7-14 shows that $m = 0.6$
gives a good compromise in maintaining $Z'_{o\text{II}}$ reasonably constant.   Thus
if the mid-shunt end of the half section is terminated in a fixed resistance
of value R, the nominal impedance, the mid-series impedance closely
matches $Z_{o\text{T}}$ of the rest of the filter over most of the passband.

The addition of still more elements to the basic section gives even
greater control over the $Z'_{o\text{II}}$ characteristic so that the new section provides an even better match to the fixed value R.   The new section is
obtained by m-deriving an m-derived section and is known as a double-
m-derived section.

While it is beyond the scope of this text to investigate this problem
of *repeated derivation*, an outline of the method used in deriving the sections will be given.   For further details the reader is referred to the
works of Zobel and Shea.

One is tempted to derive the new section, whose elements will be denoted Z''_1
and Z''_2, by letting $Z''_1 = m_2 Z'_1$, following the procedure for the mid-series m-
derived section.   This leads to a useless result where the m of Eqs. (7-56) and (7-58)
is replaced by mm_2.   Since the product mm_2 is a constant, it is equivalent to a
single parameter in these equations.

A more useful approach is to find a mid-shunt double-m-derived section which
has the same $Z'_{o\text{II}}$ as a mid-series single m-derived section.   Again work is simplified by using admittances.   For $Z'_{o\text{II}}$ or $Y'_{o\text{II}}$ to be the same for both sections,

$$Y'_1 Y'_2 + \frac{(Y'_2)^2}{4} = Y''_1 Y''_2 + \frac{(Y''_2)^2}{4}$$

Let $Y''_2 = m_2 Y'_2$, or $Z''_2 = Z'_2/m_2$.   Then, substituting and solving,

$$Y''_1 = \frac{Y'_1}{m_2} + \frac{(1 - m_2{}^2) Y'_2}{4 m_2}$$

or

$$\frac{1}{Z''_1} = \frac{1}{m_2 Z'_1} + \frac{1}{4 m_2 Z'_2 / (1 - m_2{}^2)}$$

It will be observed from the last equation that the new series arm Z_1'' has two elements in parallel. Substitution for Z_1' and Z_2' from Eqs. (7-56) and (7-57) yields the half section shown in Fig. 7-22. The student should remember that in the last half section the series arm has the value $Z_1''/2$ and the shunt arm $2Z_2''$.

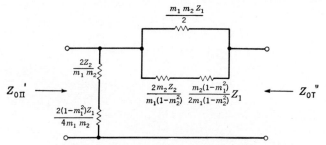

FIG. 7-22. Double m-derived half section.

The student may show (though not without considerable algebraic manipulation) that Z_{oT}'' of the double-m-derived section is given by

$$Z_{oT}'' = \frac{R\sqrt{1 - x^2}\,[1 - (1 - m_1^2)x^2]}{1 - (1 - m_1^2 m_2^2)x^2} \qquad (7\text{-}79)$$

Since Eq. (7-79) involves two parameters, m_1 and m_2, it is not an easy matter to find their optimum values by graphical analysis inasmuch as a large number of curves is required. One alternative approach involves the location of the maximum and minimum values of Z_{oT}'' by differentiation with respect to x^2. m_1 and m_2 may then be chosen to give equal deviations of these maximum and minimum values from R. Other methods are also possible that give slightly different values for the m's. Zobel has recommended $m_1 = 0.723$ and $m_2 = 0.4134$. The deviation between Z_{oT}'' and R for these values is plotted in Fig. 7-23. The corresponding data for Z_{oII}' of a single m-derived section with $m = 0.6$ are also plotted in the same figure for comparison. The improvement afforded by the double-m-derived section is quite apparent. It holds Z_{oT}'' to within roughly ± 2 per cent of R for over 95 per cent of the passband.

7-26. Lattice Networks as Filters. Thus far in the chapter attention has been restricted to filters of the ladder type. The "classical" theory of filters also deals with lattice networks. The basic lattice structure is depicted in Fig. 6-4 and from Eqs. (6-34) and (6-36).

$$Z_o = \sqrt{Z_1 Z_2} \qquad (6\text{-}34)$$

$$e^\gamma = \frac{1 + \sqrt{Z_1/Z_2}}{1 - \sqrt{Z_1/Z_2}} \qquad (6\text{-}36)$$

or

$$\tanh\frac{\gamma}{2} = \sqrt{\frac{Z_1}{Z_2}} \qquad (7\text{-}80)$$

The pass- and stop bands may be determined in the same manner as for ladder structures.

From Eq. (6-34) it is apparent that, if Z_1 and Z_2 are reactances of opposite sign, Z_o will be resistive, while if they are of the same sign, Z_o will be reactive. Therefore, if reactance curves of Z_1 and Z_2 are drawn similar to the Z_{oc} and Z_{sc} curves of Fig. 7-1, the same criteria may be applied to determine the transmission and attenuation bands. The values of α and β for any frequency may be computed from Eq. (6-36) or Eq. (7-80).

Since Z_o is a function of the product Z_1Z_2 alone, and γ is a function of the ratio Z_1/Z_2, Z_o and γ may be chosen *independently* in the lattice filter. This is in contrast to ladder filters, where Z_o depends upon $Z_1(Z_2 + Z_1/4)$ and γ depends on Z_1/Z_2. For this reason the lattice provides a more flexible basis for design than the ladder.

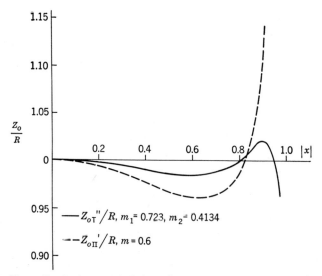

Fig. 7-23. Normalized characteristic-impedance curves for m-derived and double m-derived sections.

Foster's reactance theorem can be utilized to good advantage in the study of lattice filters. On the assumption that only lossless elements are used, Z_1 and Z_2 may be expressed by Eqs. (4-110a) or (4-110b), no matter how complicated they are in structure. By way of example, let Z_1 consist of four nonredundant elements and Z_2 of five. Further, let their reactance curves be those shown in Fig. 7-24. Then by Foster's theorem the two impedances could be written as

$$Z_1 = j\omega H_1 \frac{(\omega^2 - \omega_3{}^2)}{(\omega^2 - \omega_1{}^2)(\omega^2 - \omega_4{}^2)} \tag{7-81}$$

$$Z_2 = \frac{H_2}{j\omega} \frac{(\omega^2 - \omega_1{}^2)(\omega^2 - \omega_3{}^2)}{(\omega^2 - \omega_2{}^2)(\omega - \omega_4{}^2)} \tag{7-82}$$

The curves show that Z_1 is positive for $\omega < \omega_1$; hence by Eq. (7-81) H_1 is negative. H_2 may be shown to be positive in a similar manner.

Substituting into Eq. (6-34), one obtains

$$Z_o = j \; \frac{\sqrt{|H_1 H_2|}}{\sqrt{(\omega^2 - \omega_2{}^2)}} \frac{(\omega^2 - \omega_3{}^2)}{(\omega^2 - \omega_4{}^2)} \tag{7-83}$$

For $\omega < \omega_2$

$$Z_o = \frac{\sqrt{H_1 H_2}}{\sqrt{(\omega_2{}^2 - \omega^2)}} \frac{(\omega_3{}^2 - \omega^2)}{(\omega_4{}^2 - \omega^2)} \tag{7-84}$$

Since this is real, $\omega < \omega_2$ defines a transmission band, confirming the data of Fig. 7-24.

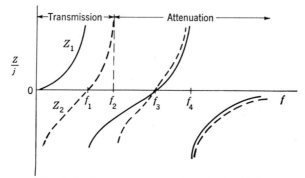

Fig. 7-24. Reactance curves for a lattice filter.

By the same token if $\omega > \omega_2$, Eq. (7-83) shows Z_o to be imaginary, defining an attenuation band. Thus the structure is an LP filter. The same results may be confirmed by substituting Eqs. (7-81) and (7-82) into Eq. (7-79) and solving for α and β.

The student should particularly note from Eq. (7-84) that the variation of Z_o from a constant value is determined by the poles and zeros of Z_1 and Z_2 which lie in the attenuation band. The proper choice of their values is not an easy problem, and methods have been suggested by Cauer, Bode, and others.

It may also be shown from Eqs. (7-80) to (7-82) that in the attenuation band

$$\tanh \frac{\gamma}{2} = -\omega \sqrt{\left| \frac{H_1}{H_2} \right|} \frac{\sqrt{(\omega^2 - \omega_2{}^2)}}{(\omega^2 - \omega_1{}^2)} \tag{7-85}$$

showing that the α characteristic is determined by the zeros and poles of Z_1 and Z_2 which lie in the transmission band. These facts verify the earlier statement that Z_o and γ of the lattice filter may be adjusted independently.

7-27. All-pass Lattice. It is of interest to observe what happens in the lattice filter if Z_1 and Z_2 are made inverse structures as they were for constant-k ladder sections. For this situation, one has from Eq. (6-34) $Z_o = \sqrt{Z_1 Z_2} = R$ or, more explicitly, the zeros of Z_1 [Eq. (7-81)] are the same as the poles of Z_2 [Eq. (7-82)], and vice versa, so that $Z_o = \sqrt{H_1 H_2}$. Since Z_o is a positive real constant independent of frequency, the entire frequency range from zero to infinity is the passband and the structure is known as an "all-pass" structure. As such, the network is useless as a filter but has important applications as a phase equalizer (Chap. 14).

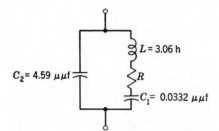

FIG. 7-25. Equivalent circuit of a piezo-electric crystal. Values are for a series resonant frequency of 500 kc. Crystal dimensions are 2.5 cm square by 0.545 cm thick.

7-28. Lattice-to-ladder Conversion. As a practical matter, lattice filters are not often used, principally because a lattice structure requires more elements than an equivalent ladder structure. Nevertheless, the concepts used in the design of lattice filters are of fundamental importance. A typical design procedure that the student might encounter would involve the synthesis of a lattice section to meet certain specifications. This section would then be transformed into an equivalent T or Π section, neither of which would in general be of the constant-k or m-derived type. The student should consult the literature for further discussion of the methods used to obtain the necessary transformations (see Probs. 7-15 and 7-16).

7-29. Piezoelectric Crystals as Filter Elements. Certain advantages are to be gained by using piezoelectric crystals as circuit elements in the construction of filters. These may be seen from the equivalent electrical circuit of these crystals which is discussed in Chap. 16, Electromechanical Coupling, and is reproduced here in Fig. 7-25 for convenience. The Q at the series resonant frequency varies from 2,000 to 30,000, which is far in excess of values obtainable with an inductor. By mounting the crystal in an evacuated enclosure the damping of the mechanical vibrations is reduced, producing the higher Q values just cited.

Neglecting R, one notes that the crystal has three reactive elements. From the study of Foster's reactance theorem this means that the crystal exhibits one internal zero and one internal pole, which are given by

$$\omega_o{}^2 = \frac{1}{LC_1} \tag{7-86}$$

and

$$\omega_x{}^2 = \frac{1}{LC_1 C_2/(C_1 + C_2)} \tag{7-87}$$

C_2, which is due to the crystal holder, exceeds $100C_1$; so the two singularities are very close together. Thus if the crystal is used in a filter, extremely sharp cutoff characteristics can be obtained. Furthermore, since the crystal can serve either as a resonant or as an antiresonant element, it can be used to good advantage in either BP or band-elimination filters with extremely narrow pass- or stop bands. If wider bands are required, the crystal characteristic can be modified with a series inductor, but not without a modification of the other arm (see Prob. 7-18).

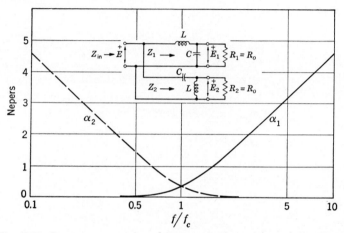

Fig. 7-26. Crossover network and its attenuation vs. frequency curves.

7-30. Crossover Filter. The filtering action of the reactive networks covered this far in the chapter is based on the behavior of their characteristic impedances as a function of frequency. At certain frequencies Z_o becomes reactive; so no power can be absorbed from the generator, and a stop band results. Another basic type of filter, the crossover network, operates on a somewhat different basis. Two loads are provided, as shown in Fig. 7-26, and the input power is shared by them in a ratio depending upon the frequency.

From physical considerations it may be seen that all of the input power is delivered to R_1 at direct current. As the frequency is raised, less and less power is delivered to R_1 and more and more to R_2 until, at infinite frequency, all the input power goes to R_2. Hence, as viewed between the input terminals and R_1, the structure behaves as an LP filter, R_2 serving as a dissipating resistor. On the other hand, the structure appears as an HP filter as viewed between the input terminals and R_2, R_1 serving as a dissipating resistor. If L and C are chosen properly, the input impedance remains resistive and equal to R_o at all frequencies. This will now be shown.

Reading from the diagram,

$$Z_1 = j\omega L + \frac{R_o}{1 + j\omega C R_o} = \frac{R_o(1 - \omega^2 LC) + j\omega L}{1 + j\omega C R_o} \tag{7-88}$$

$$Z_2 = \frac{1}{j\omega C} + \frac{j\omega L R_o}{R_o + j\omega L} = \frac{R_o(1 - \omega^2 LC) + j\omega L}{-\omega^2 LC + j\omega C R_o} \tag{7-89}$$

$$Y_{in} = \frac{1}{Z_1} + \frac{1}{Z_2} = \frac{1}{R_o} \frac{(1 - \omega^2 LC) + j2\omega C R_o}{(1 - \omega^2 LC) + j\omega L/R_o} \tag{7-90}$$

Then if Z_{in} is to be made equal to R_o, and independent of frequency, the following condition must apply: $2CR_o = L/R_o$, or

$$\frac{L}{C} = 2R_o{}^2 \tag{7-91}$$

Another equation is required to design the network, preferably one relating L and C to the crossover frequency, f_c, at which equal powers are delivered to R_1 and R_2. From Eqs. (7-88) and (7-89)

$$G_1 = \mathrm{Re}\left\{\frac{1}{Z_1}\right\} = \frac{R_o}{R_o{}^2(1 - \omega^2 LC)^2 + (\omega L)^2} \tag{7-92}$$

$$G_2 = \mathrm{Re}\left\{\frac{1}{Z_2}\right\} = \frac{(\omega^2 LC)^2 R_o}{R_o{}^2(1 - \omega^2 LC)^2 + (\omega L)^2} \tag{7-93}$$

Now, at f_c, G_1, and G_2 must be equal for equal powers to be delivered to the loads; hence

$$\omega_c = \frac{1}{\sqrt{LC}} \tag{7-94}$$

Equations (7-91) and (7-94) may be used to design the network for given values of f_c and R_o.

The LP and HP attenuation constants α_1 and α_2, respectively, may be determined readily. By definition,

$$e^{\alpha_1} = \left|\frac{E}{E_1}\right| = \left|\frac{R_o(1 - \omega^2 LC) + j\omega L}{R_o}\right|$$

Introducing Eqs. (7-91) and (7-94) and taking natural logarithms,

$$\alpha_1 = \ln\left|1 - \left(\frac{f}{f_c}\right)^2 + j\sqrt{2}\,\frac{f}{f_c}\right| \tag{7-95}$$

Similarly

$$\alpha_2 = \ln\left|1 - \left(\frac{f_c}{f}\right)^2 - j\sqrt{2}\,\frac{f_c}{f}\right| \tag{7-96}$$

It may be seen that Eqs. (7-95) and (7-96) give identical results except for the inversion of the normalized frequency variable; hence α_1 and α_2

display geometric symmetry about f_c with respect to each other. For this reason they are plotted against a logarithmic normalized frequency scale in Fig. 7-26.

While the crossover network may be used as either an HP or an LP filter as explained previously, its chief application is in sound-reproducing systems where both attenuation characteristics are utilized simultaneously.

The difficulties are so great in building a single loudspeaker to reproduce sound efficiently over an audio range extending from 30 cycles to 15 kc that it is often the practice to employ two different speakers rather than one.[1] One of 12 in. or greater diameter, termed the "woofer," is designed to give efficient reproduction below some frequency selected in the 400- to 1,000-cycle range. The second, smaller speaker is designed to work efficiently at the higher frequencies and is called a "tweeter." When these two units are fed from a single audio amplifier, the problem is to direct the different frequency components to the proper speaker. The crossover network (or "frequency divider") serves this purpose admirably. R_1 of Fig. 7-26 is replaced by the woofer voice coil and R_2 by the tweeter voice coil, and the filtering action is provided by the crossover network.

In practice the speaker impedances vary with frequency; hence the input impedance will vary to some extent from the theoretical value of R_o. The α characteristics of the network may be made more or less steep than those in Fig. 7-26 by using variations of the basic circuit.[2]

PROBLEMS

7-1. Compute the constants of a composite LP filter, to operate into a load of 600 ohms and have a cutoff frequency of 1,200 cycles. In addition to the terminating half sections and one section of the prototype, there shall be one section with a value of $f_\infty = 1,250$ cycles.

7-2. Compute the constants of a composite HP filter to operate into a load of 600 ohms and have a cutoff frequency of 1,200 cycles. One of the intermediate sections is to have a value $f_\infty = 1,100$ cycles.

7-3. Compute the constants of a composite BP filter to operate into a load of 600 ohms and have cutoff frequencies of 800 and 2,000 cycles. In addition to the terminating sections and one section of the prototype, there shall be one section with one value of $f_\infty = 2,100$ cycles.
What will be the other frequency of infinite attenuation?

7-4. Arrange various configurations of reactances as the shunt and series arms of a T filter section. Sketch the reactance curves, and determine the number of attenuating and transmission bands.

[1] It is possible, of course, in a more elaborate system to use three or more speakers, each one operating in a different portion of the audio range. In such cases, two or more crossover networks may be used in combination to provide the required power-dividing action as a function of frequency.

[2] See, for example, F. E. Terman, "Radio Engineers' Handbook," McGraw-Hill Book Company, Inc., New York, 1943. See also Prob. 7-21.

7-5. For a LP prototype T section, with a cutoff frequency of 1,000 cycles and a value of $\sqrt{Z_1Z_2}$ equal to 600 ohms, compute and plot the characteristic impedance vs. frequency curve from 0 to 2,000 cycles.

Compute the constants of an m-derived T section, $m = 0.6$, from the prototype specified above, and plot its characteristic impedance vs. frequency curve over the same range. Repeat for $m = 0.8$ and $m = 0.4$.

Rearrange the constants of the three T sections just designed into Π sections where the impedances of the two shunt arms of the Π section each equals twice the value for the shunt arm of the T section. Compute and plot curves of characteristic impedance vs. frequency over the same range.

7-6. Compute and plot a curve of the attenuation of the two filter sections specified in Prob. 7-5, over a range of 0 to 2,000 cycles.

7-7. For coils with $Q = 100$ compute the attenuation of the m-derived T section of Prob. 7-5 at 500 and 1,000 cycles and at f_∞. Sketch the approximate values of α for the range of 0 to 2,000 cycles.

7-8. A single-T-section constant-k LP filter is inserted between a generator of internal impedance R_g, and a resistive load, R, equal to the filter's nominal impedance.

a. Derive an equation for the decibels insertion loss of the filter in terms of x ($= f/f_c$) and R_g/R.

b. Plot curves of the insertion loss vs. x for $R_g/R = 0$, 0.5, 1, and 2. Cover the range $0 \leq x \leq 2$, using increments of 0.2.

c. From the results recommend the value of R_g that gives the best LP characteristic.

7-9. A common configuration for a band-elimination filter is an inductance and capacitance in parallel for Z_1 and an inductance and capacitance in series for Z_2. For such a filter derive the fundamental design equations, and design a 600-ohm filter to eliminate the band between 800 and 2,000 cycles.

7-10. (*a*) Set up the HP–band-elimination analog. (*b*) Design the filter of Prob. 7-9 by means of the analog.

7-11. (*a*) Show that the presence of L_m in Fig. 7-27 effectively places negative inductance in series with C_b. (This may be done by replacing the inductance combination $L_aL_mL_a$ by an equivalent inductive T section.) This condition permits the design of an LP section with $m > 1$. (*b*) Derive design equations for L_a, L_m, and C_b in terms of the prototype components for this m-derived section.

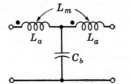

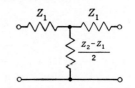

FIG. 7-27. Circuit for Prob. 7-11.   FIG. 7-28. T section for Prob. 7-15.

7-12. Verify Eq. (7-79).

7-13. Prove that the pass- and stop bands of a lattice filter remain unchanged if Z_1 and Z_2 are interchanged.

7-14. (*a*) Starting with reactance curves, derive the circuit configurations for two possible *minimum-element* lattice filters for each of the LP, HP, BP, and band-elimination types. Tabulate your results, giving equations for the cutoff frequencies in each case. (*b*) What advantages, if any, would result from replacing the sections by nonminimum-element lattice structures?

7-15. Prove that the T section of Fig. 7-28 and the lattice section of Fig. 6-4 are equivalent.

7-16. (a) Z_1 and Z_2 are both series resonant arms in a lattice filter. What type of α characteristic does it have? (b) By means of Prob. 7-15 transform the lattice into an equivalent T structure. (c) What restrictions on the components L_1, L_2, C_1, and C_2 of the original lattice are necessary if the T section is to be physically realizable? (d) Is the equivalence independent of frequency?

7-17. Two of the crystals of Fig. 7-25 are used as the Z_1 elements of a lattice filter. Inductances of value L_2 are used as the Z_2 elements.

 a. Determine the type of filter by means of reactance curves.

 b. Evaluate the cutoff frequencies.

 c. Explain briefly why the cutoff frequencies are independent of L_2.

 d. What simple expedient will give a decrease in the width of the stop band?

7-18. Z_1 of Prob. 7-17 is modified by adding inductance L_1 in series with the crystal. The type of filter is to remain unchanged.

 a. What Z_2 elements are required?

 b. What critical frequency remains the same as in Prob. 7-17?

 c. Is the other critical frequency raised or lowered by L_1?

 d. What is the equation for the critical frequency of Z_2?

7-19. Calculate the values of L and C in Fig. 7-26 for a crossover frequency of 450 cycles for use with a woofer-tweeter system. Both voice coils have a nominal impedance of 8 ohms resistive.

7-20. Consider the network of Fig. 7-26 with the two elements shunting R_1 and R_2 removed.

 a. What L and C are required for Z_{in} to equal R_o at all frequencies?

 b. Derive an equation for the cutoff frequency.

 c. Calculate and plot α_1 and α_2. Compare with Fig. 7-26.

7-21. Compare α_1 of Fig. 7-26 in the higher-frequency range well above cutoff with α of the constant-k and m-derived LP filters. Of what significance is the difference?

7-22. Sketch the circuit diagram for a crossover network system for use with three different speakers, each of which works over a different portion of the audio band. Derive the necessary design equations in terms of two crossover frequencies f_{c1} and f_{c2}. Assume the same nominal resistance for all three speakers.

CHAPTER 8

THE INFINITE LINE

When two pieces of apparatus are connected together in the laboratory by a short pair of leads as in Fig. 8-1, the student whose experience is confined to audio would expect equal input and output currents I_i and I_o frequencies. Furthermore for negligible lead resistance he would expect E_i and E_o to be equal. Experience at radio frequencies shows that, when the lead length is an appreciable portion of a wavelength at the frequency of operation, neither of these equalities is realized: E_o differs from E_i and I_o differs from I_i in both magnitude and phase.

Fig. 8-1. A generator and load connected by a pair of wires.

A similar situation exists on telephone lines that carry af signals. On such lines whose length is an appreciable portion of a wavelength (say, $> 0.1\lambda$) at the operating frequencies, current and voltage undergo changes of amplitude and phase along the length of the line. On such "long lines" it is not sufficient to consider the wires as conductors exhibiting only resistance and perhaps inductance and having no electrical connection between them along their lengths. The correct picture of their behavior requires an equivalent circuit containing all three types of circuit elements, viz., resistance, inductance, and capacitance. This equivalent circuit is discussed in the sections that follow. Once the circuit is established, the behavior of the transmission line when electrical signals are applied may be predicted.

8-1. Distributed Parameters. The equivalent circuit of a transmission line may be developed by considering a basic type of such a line which consists of two straight parallel wires of uniform size, separated by air, and is called the "parallel-wire" line. Inasmuch as the wires are formed of some conducting material, usually copper or aluminum, they will have resistance. Because the wires have uniform size, this resistance will be *uniformly distributed* along their entire lengths.

294

At radio frequencies energy may possibly be radiated from the transmission line in the form of electromagnetic waves. This loss in energy may be taken into account by considering the line resistance to be increased by the "radiation resistance," a fictitious resistance whose value is the radiated power divided by the square of the line-current magnitude. The possibility of radiation from a parallel-wire line is precluded by keeping the line spacing small, say, much less than one-tenth of a wavelength. In this book it will be assumed that no radiation takes place from the line so that the effective increase in line resistance due to radiation may be neglected.

Furthermore, when current flows through the wires, a magnetic field is established about them. This field links the wire current; hence inductance is present, once again *distributed uniformly* along the entire wire length. This resulting inductance caused by the flux linkages impedes the flow of current and so is effectively in series with the distributed line resistance.

The fact that the input and output currents of the line differ leads one to realize that there is *admittance* between the wires even though there is no apparent connection between them. This shunt admittance consists of two components. First, capacitance is present because the line consists of two conductors separated by a dielectric. Second, for between-the-wire dielectrics that are not perfect insulators, conduction current will flow between the wires. This conduction, or leakage, path may be represented by shunt resistance or, more conveniently, by a conductance between the wires. As was the case for the series resistance and inductance, the shunt conductance and capacitance are *uniformly distributed* over the entire length of the line. For the latter reason it is impossible to draw an accurate equivalent circuit of the line, for no symbols are available for representing *distributed* circuit parameters. A rough approximation is shown in Fig. 8-2; the student must think of the transmission line as a limiting case where the small line length Δx approaches zero and the line parameters are uniformly distributed, rather than being lumped as in the approximate diagram.

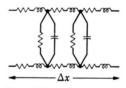

FIG. 8-2. Approximate equivalent circuit of a length Δx of transmission line.

It is convenient in the study of transmission lines to state the numerical values of these distributed parameters for a unit length of line, the unit of length being 1 mile, 1 m, or whatever length is most convenient for the particular problem under investigation. Since the series elements of inductance and resistance are present on both sides of the line, the line resistance, for example, is defined as the resistance of *both* wires for a unit line length and is denoted by the symbol R. Thus by definition

R = loop resistance per unit length of line

= sum of resistance of *both* wires for unit line length

Similarly, L is defined to be

L = loop inductance per unit length of line

= sum of inductance of *both* wires for unit line length.

The line conductance and capacitance are present *between* the two wires, and the "loop" notation is unnecessary. Thus by definition

G = shunt conductance between wires per unit line length

C = shunt capacitance between wires per unit line length

In the work that follows use will be made of Z, the loop impedance per unit line length, and Y, the shunt admittance per unit length. These quantities are defined by

$$Z = R + j\omega L \tag{8-1}$$
$$Y = G + j\omega C \tag{8-2}$$

The student should take particular care to note that the units of the four line parameters all involve reciprocal length, for example, Z is not expressed in ohms as is the usual case but in ohms per mile, ohms per foot, or ohms per meter, as the case may be. He should also observe that the symbols Z and Y have special significance in the study of transmission lines and that $Z \neq 1/Y$.

8-2. Transmission-line Types. In the last section a pair of parallel wires was used as an example to develop the equivalent circuit of a transmission line. Many other configurations are also used for transmission lines. A few of the more common types will be described.

One of the commonest forms of transmission line is the coaxial cable. This type consists of a hollow, cylindrical conductor surrounding a coaxial center conductor of circular cross section. Where a rigid line may be used, the center conductor is often supported by a number of insulating disks spaced at intervals that are very small compared with a wavelength at the operating frequency. The outer conductor then takes the form of a copper pipe that is grounded. A principal advantage of this type of construction is that the electric and magnetic fields produced by the electrical signals are confined wholly to the region enclosed by the outer conductor.

Where mechanical requirements rule out the use of a rigid coaxial line, a flexible line may be formed in this manner: The center conductor is formed of thin, uninsulated conductors twisted together, the whole being embedded in an extruded polyethylene plastic of circular cross section. This plastic serves as spacer and dielectric for the line. The plastic in turn is covered by a flexible conducting braid. The entire cable is often covered with a protecting sheath of polyvinyl plastic. This type of construction allows the entire cable to have a reasonable degree of mechanical flexibility.

Inasmuch as the outer conductor of the flexible coaxial cable is not a solid, continuous conducting sheet, the electric and magnetic fields may not be confined to the region surrounded by the outer braid and leakage fields may be present outside the cable, particularly at uhf and above. This condition results from the incomplete shielding by the outer conductor and may be minimized by adding a second grounded shield braid outside the cable. This results in a so-called "shielded coaxial cable."

The common telephone cable consists of a number of wire pairs, insulated with paper and twisted together. The several pairs are also twisted over the entire cable length to minimize cross talk that results from magnetic and capacitive coupling between adjacent pairs. The whole group of pairs is surrounded by a protective outer coating of lead or of corrugated aluminum covered with plastic. The telephone cable and other common transmission-line types are illustrated in Fig. 8-3.

8-3. Calculation of Line Parameters. While the concepts of the per unit length line parameters R, L, G, and C, were developed for the parallel-wire line, they are by no means peculiar to that configuration. All transmission lines exhibit all four of the line parameters to some extent, though in certain cases one or two of them may be of negligible magnitude. This is notably demonstrated by the common telephone cable. Since each wire pair is twisted and currents flow in opposite directions in the two conductors comprising the pair, the flux linkages are so small that the inductance per unit length, L, may be neglected in a number of calculations. Furthermore, the paper serves as an excellent insulator so that G, the shunt conductance, is of neglible magnitude. The effect of neglecting L and G in calculations for the telephone cable will be illustrated later in the chapter.

Cable and transmission-line manufacturers publish tables giving the four line parameters of their products. Typical values are listed in Table 8-1. For simple line configurations, such as those of the parallel-wire or coaxial type, R, L, and C may be calculated from a knowledge of the line geometry and the properties of the materials from which they are made. The necessary equations may be derived by direct application of field theory. They will not be derived[1] here but are summarized in Table 8-2.

8-4. The Infinite Line, Z_o. Since the equivalent circuit of a length Δx of a transmission line and the means of evaluating its components R, L, G, and C have been covered in previous sections, it is now possible to predict the behavior of a line when electrical signals are applied to it. Using the equivalent-circuit idea, let the line be considered as being made up of a large number of incremental lengths, Δx. Each such length of line then exhibits series loop inductance $L \Delta x$, series loop resistance $R \Delta x$,

---

[1] See, for example, E. C. Jordan, "Electromagnetic Waves and Radiating Systems," Prentice-Hall, Inc., New York, 1950.

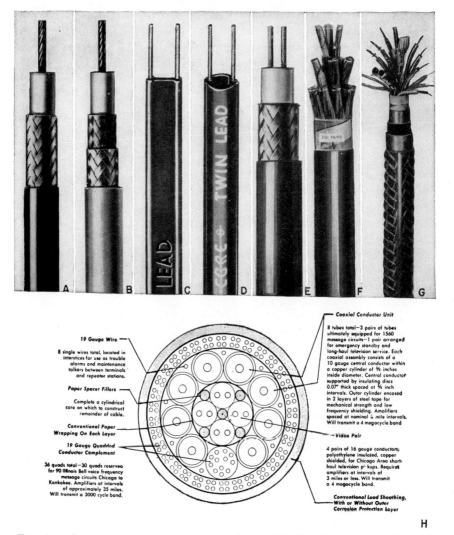

H

Fig. 8-3. Common types of transmission line. (*A*) Flexible coaxial cable. (*B*) Shielded coaxial cable. (*C*) Twin lead. (*D*) Air-core twin lead. (*E*) Shielded pair. (*F*) Telephone cable. (*G*) Cable showing construction of coaxial elements and pairs. (*H*) Cross section of Chicago–Terre Haute cable. [(*A–E*) *American Phenolic Corporation.* (*F–H*) *Illinois Bell Telephone Co.*]

shunt conductance $G \Delta x$, and shunt capacitance $C \Delta x$. The corresponding series impedance and shunt admittance will be, then, by Eqs. (8-1) and (8-2)

$$Z \Delta x = (R + j\omega L) \Delta x \qquad (8\text{-}3)$$
$$Y \Delta x = (G + j\omega C) \Delta x \qquad (8\text{-}4)$$

As a matter of convenience these elements may be arranged in a symmetrical T configuration *so that the entire line may be considered as the limiting case as $\Delta x \to 0$ of a number of symmetrical T sections in cascade,* each T having the elements defined by Eqs. (8-3) and (8-4). On this basis the results of Chap. 6 may be used to calculate the variation of

TABLE 8-1*

Type	Gauge, mils	Spacing, in.	Loop constants/mile			
			R, ohms	L, mh	C, μf	G, μmhos
Open-wire lines						
Open-wire...........	104	12	10.15	3.66	0.00837	0.29
Open-wire phantom..	104	12	5.08	2.23	0.01409	0.58
Open-wire...........	104	18	10.15	3.93	0.00797	0.29
Open-wire...........	165	12	4.11	3.37	0.00915	0.29
Open-wire phantom..	165	12	2.06	2.08	0.01514	0.58
Open-wire...........	165	18	4.11	3.64	0.00863	0.29
Paper-insulated cable pairs						
Side................	19†	..	85.8	1	0.062	1.5
Side................	16†	..	42.1	1	0.062	1.5
Phantom............	19†	..	42.9	0.7	0.1	2.4
Phantom............	16†	..	21.0	0.7	0.1	2.4

For coaxial cable, $d_2 = 0.375$ in., $d_1 = 0.1004$ in.
* From Amer. Tel. and Tel. Co.
† A.W.G.

steady-state current and voltage along a uniform line, provided that it is terminated in Z_o. Expressions will first be derived for γ and Z_o in terms of the line constants. Then equations will be derived for voltage and current as a function of distance along the line.

8-5. Characteristic Impedance. Corresponding to Z_1 of the symmetrical lumped iterative structure, one has $Z \Delta x$ for the line and, corresponding to Z_2, $1/Y \Delta x$. Thus from Eq. (6-15)

$$Z_o = \sqrt{Z_1 Z_2 + \frac{Z_1{}^2}{4}} = \sqrt{Z_1 Z_2 \left(1 + \frac{Z_1}{4 Z_2}\right)}$$

Substituting for Z_1 and Z_2, one has for the uniform line

$$Z_o = \lim_{\Delta x \to 0} \sqrt{\frac{Z}{Y}\left[1 + \frac{ZY(\Delta x)^2}{4}\right]}$$

$$= \sqrt{\frac{Z}{Y}} = \sqrt{\frac{R + j\omega L}{G + j\omega C}} \tag{8-5}$$

TABLE 8-2. LINE PARAMETERS FOR PARALLEL-WIRE LINE AND
COAXIAL CABLE

Parallel-wire line:

$$L = \underbrace{\frac{\mu_c}{4\pi}}_{\substack{\text{due to} \\ \text{flux link-} \\ \text{ages within} \\ \text{conductors}}} + \underbrace{\frac{\mu_d}{\pi}\ln\frac{s}{r}}_{\substack{\text{due to} \\ \text{flux linkages} \\ \text{outside} \\ \text{conductors}}} \quad \text{henrys/m}$$

$$C = \frac{\pi\epsilon_0}{\text{arccosh}\dfrac{s}{2r}} \quad \text{farads/m}$$

$$\approx \frac{\pi\epsilon_0}{\ln\dfrac{s}{r}} \quad \text{farads/m} \quad \text{for } s > 5r$$

$$R_{dc} = \frac{2}{\pi r^2 \sigma} \quad \text{ohms/m}$$

$$R_{ac} = \frac{R_{dc}r}{2}\sqrt{\pi f \mu_c \sigma} \quad \text{ohms/m}$$

Coaxial line:

$$L = \underbrace{\frac{\mu_d}{2\pi}\ln\frac{r_2}{r_1}}_{\substack{\text{due to flux} \\ \text{linkages between} \\ \text{conductors}}} + \underbrace{\frac{\mu_c}{8\pi}\left[\frac{4r_3^4}{(r_3^2 - r_2^2)^2}\ln\frac{r_3}{r_2} - \frac{2r_3^2}{r_3^2 - r_2^2}\right]}_{\substack{\text{due to flux linkages} \\ \text{within conductors}}} \quad \text{henrys/m}$$

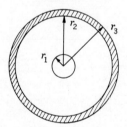

Coaxial line:

$$C = \frac{2\pi\epsilon_d}{\ln\dfrac{r_2}{r_1}} \quad \text{farads/m}$$

$$R_{dc} = \frac{1}{\pi\sigma}\left(\frac{1}{r_1^2} + \frac{1}{r_3^2 - r_2^2}\right) \quad \text{ohms/m}$$

$$R_{ac} = \sqrt{\frac{f\mu_c}{4\pi\sigma}}\left(\frac{1}{r_1} + \frac{1}{r_2}\right) \quad \text{ohms/m}$$

where ϵ_d = dielectric permittivity
     = $\kappa\epsilon_0$
     ϵ_0 = $10^{-9}/36\pi$ mks
     μ_c = conductor permeability
     = $(\mu_r)_c\mu_0$
     μ_d = dielectric permeability
     = $(\mu_r)_d\mu_0$
     μ_0 = $4\pi \times 10^{-7}$ mks
     σ = conductivity of conductors

8-6. Complex Propagation Constant. The complex propagation constant $\gamma_{\Delta x}$ for the equivalent section of length Δx may be obtained in a similar manner. Applying Eq. (6-6) to the element of line of length Δx, one has

$$e^{\gamma_{\Delta x}} = \frac{Z_1/2 + Z_2 + Z_o}{Z_2} = 1 + \frac{Z_1}{2Z_2} + \sqrt{\frac{Z_1}{Z_2}\left(1 + \frac{Z_1}{4Z_2}\right)}$$

Substituting for Z_1 and Z_2,

$$e^{\gamma_{\Delta z}} = 1 + \frac{ZY(\Delta x)^2}{2} + \sqrt{ZY}\,\Delta x\,\sqrt{1 + \frac{ZY(\Delta x)^2}{4}} \qquad (8\text{-}6)$$

Now the problem is to evaluate γ in terms of Z and Y. This may be done by expanding both sides of Eq. (8-6) into an infinite series. For example, the left-hand member may be expanded as the power series

$$e^{\theta} = 1 + \theta + \frac{\theta^2}{\lfloor 2} + \frac{\theta^3}{\lfloor 3} + \cdots \qquad (8\text{-}7)$$

The right-hand member may be developed in the desired form by expanding the radical of the third term by means of the binomial series

$$(1 + a)^{\frac{1}{2}} = 1 + \frac{a}{2} - \frac{a^2}{8} + \frac{a^3}{16} - \cdots \qquad (8\text{-}8)$$

The application of these expansions to Eq. (8-6) and neglecting of higher-order terms yield

$$1 + \gamma_{\Delta x} + \frac{\gamma_{\Delta x}^2}{2} + \cdots + = 1 + \sqrt{ZY}\,\Delta x + \frac{ZY(\Delta x)^2}{2} \qquad (8\text{-}9)$$

Therefore
$$\gamma_{\Delta x} = \sqrt{ZY}\,\Delta x$$

The $\gamma_{\Delta x}$ thus derived is for a section of length Δx. For n such sections the propagation constant would be n times as great. In a unit length there would be $1/\Delta x$ such sections, and therefore for such a unit length $\gamma = \gamma_{\Delta x}/\Delta x$.

$$\gamma = \sqrt{ZY} = \sqrt{(R + j\omega L)(G + j\omega C)} = \alpha + j\beta \qquad (8\text{-}10)$$

8-7. Current and Voltage. As a matter of convenience, let the applied voltage and current at the input, or *sending*, end of the line be designated E_S and I_S, respectively. Then by direct analogy to Eq. (6-13) the current I_x at a distance x from the sending end will be related to I_S by

$$\frac{I_S}{I_x} = e^{\gamma x} \qquad (8\text{-}11)$$

and
$$\frac{E_S}{E_x} = e^{\gamma x} \qquad (8\text{-}12)$$

If γ is known, the attenuation constant and wavelength constant can be derived by performing the operation of extracting the square root of ZY in the polar form and reducing the result to the rectangular form. By Eq. (8-10) the real part of γ will be the attenuation constant, and the imaginary part will be the wavelength constant. Equation (6-44) can be applied, except that the value of n_λ will be in the length units used in computing γ and is generally written

$$\lambda = \frac{2\pi}{\beta} \qquad (8\text{-}13)$$

Similarly Eq. (6-40) is written

$$v_p = \lambda f = \frac{\omega}{\beta} \tag{8-14}$$

The units of α are called *nepers per unit length*. Sometimes the term "hyperbolic radians per unit length" is used. If Z and Y are given in ohms and mhos per mile, respectively, α will be in nepers per mile. Similarly β is obtained in radians per unit length, and, for Z and Y units in miles, β would be given in radians per mile.

In the foregoing sections the line equations have been derived by considering the uniform line as the limiting case of a cascade of symmetrical and identical T sections. An alternative approach based on the differential equations for line current and voltage is given below.

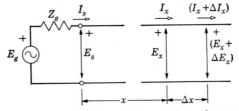

Fig. 8-4. Notation for setting up the differential equations of current and voltage on a transmission line.

Consider the element of line of length Δx and located a distance x from the sending end as shown in Fig. 8-4. The input, or sending-end, voltage and current are E_S and I_S, respectively. The average value of current flowing along the element will be $I_x + \Delta I_x/2$; thus, applying Kirchhoff's voltage law to the element, one has

$$E_x - (E_x + \Delta E_x) = Z \, \Delta x \left(I_x + \frac{\Delta I_x}{2} \right) \tag{8-15}$$

Dividing through by Δx and taking the limit as $\Delta x \to 0$, one obtains for the space derivative of voltage

$$\frac{dE_x}{dx} = -Z I_x \tag{8-16}$$

The average value of voltage along the element is $E_x + \Delta E_x/2$. Then, applying Kirchhoff's current law to the element,

$$I_x - (I_x + \Delta I_x) = Y \, \Delta x \left(E_x + \frac{\Delta E_x}{2} \right)$$

and, dividing through by Δx and taking the limit as $\Delta x \to 0$,

$$\frac{dI_x}{dx} = -Y E_x \tag{8-17}$$

Equations (8-16) and (8-17) show, as may well be expected, that current and voltage at any point on the line are interrelated. It is convenient, however, to eliminate I_x from Eq. (8-16) and E_x from Eq. (8-17) so that each equation involves only one independent variable. This may be brought about by differentiating Eq. (8-16),

$$\frac{d^2 E_x}{dx^2} = -Z \frac{dI_x}{dx}$$

Substituting from Eq. (8-17),

$$\frac{d^2 E_x}{dx^2} = ZY E_x \tag{8-18}$$

In a similar fashion

$$\frac{d^2 I_x}{dx^2} = ZY I_x \tag{8-19}$$

The last two equations are linear differential equations with constant coefficients whose solutions are

$$E_x = A_1 e^{\sqrt{ZY}x} + A_2 e^{-\sqrt{ZY}x} \tag{8-20}$$
$$I_x = B_1 e^{\sqrt{ZX}x} + B_2 e^{-\sqrt{ZY}x} \tag{8-21}$$

where the A's are constants with the dimension of voltage and the B's are constants with the dimension of current. It may be expected, then, that the A's and B's are interrelated. This may be verified by substituting Eqs. (8-20) and (8-21) into Eq. (8-16),

$$\sqrt{ZY}\, A_1 e^{\sqrt{ZX}x} - \sqrt{ZY}\, A_2 e^{-\sqrt{ZY}x} = -Z(B_1 e^{\sqrt{ZY}x} + B_2 e^{-\sqrt{ZY}x})$$

Equating coefficients of corresponding powers of e,

$$\sqrt{ZY}\, A_1 = -ZB_1 \qquad B_1 = -\sqrt{\frac{Y}{Z}}\, A_1 \tag{8-22}$$

$$\sqrt{ZY}\, A_2 = ZB_2 \qquad B_2 = \sqrt{\frac{Y}{Z}}\, A_2 \tag{8-23}$$

Hence Eq. (8-21) may be rewritten as

$$I_x = -\sqrt{\frac{Y}{Z}}\, A_1 e^{\sqrt{ZY}x} + \sqrt{\frac{Y}{Z}}\, A_2 e^{-\sqrt{ZY}x} \tag{8-21a}$$

Now Eqs. (8-20) and (8-21a) are quite general in that no stipulation has been made concerning the termination of the line. Thus any termination may be handled by substituting in appropriate boundary conditions to evaluate A_1 and A_2. In this chapter the *infinite line* is being considered; thus, at $x = \infty$, $E_x = 0$, and, from Eq. (8-20), $A_1 = 0$. Furthermore, at $x = 0$, $E_x = E_S$, and, from Eq. (8-20), $A_2 = E_S$, whence

$$E_x = E_S e^{-\sqrt{ZY}x} \tag{8-24}$$

and, from Eq. (8-21a),

$$I_x = \sqrt{\frac{Y}{Z}}\, E_S e^{-\sqrt{ZY}x}$$

But, at $x = 0$, $I_x = I_S$; therefore

$$I_S = \sqrt{\frac{Y}{Z}}\, E_S \qquad\qquad (8\text{-}25a)$$

and

$$I_x = I_S e^{-\sqrt{ZY}x} \qquad\qquad (8\text{-}25)$$

One notes that the input impedance of the infinite line, namely, Z_o, is E_S/I_S; thus from Eq. (8-25a)

$$Z_o = \sqrt{\frac{Z}{Y}}$$

Further, if γ is used for $\sqrt{ZY}$, these results are entirely consistent with those obtained by the previous method.

As an exercise, the student should carry out the solution for a line of finite length l terminated in Z_o. The results should, of course, be identical with those for the infinite line (see Prob. 8-5).

The results of the foregoing sections will be applied to solve an illustrative example.

The attenuation and wavelength constants will be determined for an open-wire line. One of the standard lines in use consists of copper wires 0.104 in. in diameter and spaced 12 in. apart. The distributed constants of such a line are

$R = 10.4$ ohms/mile
$L = 3.67$ mh/mile
$C = 0.00835$ μf/mile
$G = 0.8$ μmho/mile

The determination will be made at a frequency of 796 cycles, i.e., $\omega = 5,000$. This value of frequency approximates, as far as a single frequency can, the average of the voice wave and so is commonly used in measuring or computing attenuation. The value of G given above is, of course, an approximation, as it is dependent largely on weather conditions for the case of an open-wire line.

$$Z = R + j\omega L = 10.4 + j5,000 \times 3.67 \times 10^{-3}$$
$$= 10.4 + j18.35 = 21.08\underline{/60.45°}$$
$$Y = G + j\omega C = (0.8 + j5,000 \times 0.00835) \times 10^{-6}$$
$$= (0.8 + j41.75) \times 10^{-6} = 41.76\underline{/88.916°} \times 10^{-6}$$

$$Z_o = \sqrt{\frac{Z}{Y}} = \sqrt{\frac{21.08\underline{/60.45°}}{41.76 \times 10^{-6}\underline{/88.916°}}} = \sqrt{\frac{21.08 \times 10^6}{41.76}}\,\underline{/\frac{60.45° - 88.916°}{2}}$$

$$Z_o = 711\underline{/-14.233°} = 689 - j175$$

$$\gamma = \sqrt{ZY} = \sqrt{21.08\underline{/60.45°} \times 41.76 \times 10^{-6}\underline{/88.916°}}$$

$$= \sqrt{21.08 \times 41.76 \times 10^{-6}}\,\underline{/\frac{60.45° + 88.916°}{2}}$$

$$= 0.0297\underline{/74.683°} = 0.00785 + j0.0287$$

The attenuation constant is the real part of γ, and the wavelength constant is the imaginary component.

$$\alpha = 0.00785 \text{ neper/mile}$$
$$\beta = 0.0287 \text{ radian/mile}$$

The wavelength is therefore

$$\lambda = \frac{2\pi}{\beta} = 219 \text{ miles}$$

The phase velocity is

$$v_p = f\lambda = \frac{\omega}{\beta} = \frac{5,000}{0.0287} = 174,300 \text{ miles/sec}$$

As an example of the use of these constants, consider an open-wire line 300 miles long. Let a generator, with an internal impedance which is a pure resistance of 600 ohms and which has a generated voltage of 2 volts, be connected to the sending end. At the receiving end the line is terminated in its characteristic impedance. What will be the voltage, current, and power at the receiving end?

Since the line is terminated in its characteristic impedance, the input impedance of the line at the sending end will also be the characteristic impedance. The input current when connected to the generator will then be

$$I_1 = \frac{2}{600 + 689 - j175} = \frac{2}{1,289 - j175} = \frac{2}{1,300 \underline{/-7.734^\circ}} = 0.001539 \underline{/7.734^\circ}$$

From Eq. (8-11)

$$I_2 = I_1 e^{-\gamma l} = I_1 e^{-\alpha l} e^{-j\beta l}$$

Now

$$e^{-\alpha l} = e^{-300 \times 0.00785} = e^{-2.355} = \frac{1}{e^{2.355}} = \frac{1}{10.55} = 0.0948$$

But

$$e^{-j\beta l} = e^{-j(300 \times 0.0287)} = e^{-j8.61}$$

will simply rotate the numerical value through an angle of -8.61 radian and will not change its magnitude, for

$$e^{j\Theta} = \cos\Theta + j\sin\Theta$$

Therefore

$$e^{-\gamma l} = 0.0948 \underline{/-8.61 \text{ radians}}$$
$$= 0.0948 \underline{/-493^\circ}$$

The current at the receiving end will then be

$$I_2 = 0.001539 \underline{/7.734^\circ} \times 0.0948 \underline{/-493^\circ}$$
$$= 0.0001458 \underline{/-485.267^\circ}$$

This current is therefore lagging the input current by more than a cycle. The voltage across the terminating impedance will be

$$E_2 = I_2 Z_o = 0.0001458 \underline{/-485.267^\circ} \times 711 \underline{/-14.233^\circ}$$
$$= 0.1036 \underline{/-499.5^\circ}$$

The power derived to the load will be

$$P = |E_2| |I_2| \cos\Theta = 0.1036 \times 0.0001458 \times \cos 14.233^\circ$$
$$= 14.6 \times 10^{-6} \text{ watt}$$

or the following expression may be used:

$$P = |I_2|^2 R_R = (0.0001458)^2 \times 689$$
$$= 14.6 \times 10^{-6} \text{ watt}$$

8-8. Nominal-T Section. The need often arises in practice of testing in the laboratory various types of transmission apparatus such as telephone repeaters or telegraph relays under conditions that simulate those in the field. Such tests might investigate the response of the apparatus when it is connected between two sections of telephone cable, each being of several miles length. When such a test is required, it is inconvenient to use the necessary lengths of actual cable because of their physical size and the desirability of having some lumped constant network which simulates their behavior is quite evident. Lumped constant networks which duplicate the behavior of an actual transmission line are usually termed "artificial lines."

To the engineer who is concerned with the transmission of electrical power over long lines the design of an artificial power line is quite straightforward because his is a single-frequency problem; equivalence of the artificial and actual lines is required only at the transmission frequency, nominally 60 cycles. In this case a single T section can be designed that is equivalent to any predetermined length l of transmission line at 60 cycles. For example, knowledge of the line parameters R, L, G, and C permits the calculation of γ and Z_o at 60 cycles. Then by Eqs. (6-28) and (6-31) the T components may be calculated:

$$Z_2 = \frac{Z_o}{\sinh \gamma l} \tag{6-28}$$

$$\frac{Z_1}{2} = Z_o \tanh \frac{\gamma l}{2} \tag{6-31}$$

For the communication engineer, however, who is concerned with the transmission of signals that cover a broad band of frequencies, single-frequency equivalence between the artificial and actual lines is not sufficient. His problem is that Z_o and γ are both frequency-dependent in the last two equations; hence it would appear that no single set of lumped impedance elements comprising Z_1 and Z_2 could give exact equivalence over a band of frequencies. The use of proper design techniques, however, can make *approximate* equivalence hold over the required bandwidth.

In the theory of real hyperbolic functions it is well known that if θ is small, say, less than 0.1 radian,

$$\sinh \theta \approx \tanh \theta \approx \theta$$

If θ is complex, a similar approximation holds true. This may be illustrated by considering the real and imaginary parts of θ independently. Thus let $\theta = \gamma l = \alpha l + j\beta l$. Then

$$
\begin{array}{llll}
\text{If } \alpha l \text{ is small,} & \cosh \alpha l \approx 1 & \sinh \alpha l \approx \alpha l \\
\text{If } \beta l \text{ is small,} & \cos \beta l \ \approx 1 & \sin \beta l \ \approx \beta l
\end{array}
\tag{8-26}
$$

Then, if both αl and βl are small,

$$
\begin{aligned}
\sinh \gamma l &= \sinh (\alpha l + j\beta l) \\
&= \sinh \alpha l \cos \beta l + j \cosh \alpha l \sin \beta l \\
&\approx \alpha l + j\beta l = \gamma l
\end{aligned}
\tag{8-27}
$$

Similarly

$$
\begin{aligned}
\cosh \gamma l &= \cosh (\alpha l + j\beta l) \\
&= \cosh \alpha l \cos \beta l + j \sinh \alpha l \sin \beta l \\
&\approx 1 + j(\alpha l)(\beta l) \approx 1
\end{aligned}
$$

so that

$$
\tanh \frac{\gamma l}{2} = \frac{\sinh (\gamma l/2)}{\cosh (\gamma l/2)} \approx \frac{\gamma l}{2}
\tag{8-28}
$$

Hence, if αl and βl are both small, the components of the equivalent T section become

$$
Z_2 \approx \frac{Z_o}{\gamma l} = \sqrt{\frac{Z}{Y}} \frac{1}{\sqrt{ZY}\, l} = \frac{1}{Yl}
\tag{8-29}
$$

$$
\frac{Z_1}{2} \approx Z_o \frac{\gamma l}{2} = \sqrt{\frac{Z}{Y}} \sqrt{ZY} \frac{l}{2} = \frac{Zl}{2}
\tag{8-30}
$$

Thus if the length of line l is chosen *small* enough to make the approximations of Eqs. (8-27) and (8-28) valid over the desired frequency range, the T section that is equivalent to that line length is obtained by setting the series-arm impedance Z_1 equal to the loop series impedance and the shunt-arm admittance $1/Z_2$ equal to the shunt admittance of the line section. A T section designed in this manner from Eqs. (8-29) and (8-30) is known as a "nominal-T" section. Any length of physical line may then be replaced by the appropriate number of nominal T's.

As an example of the design of an artificial line, consider the nominal-T section of the open-wire line of the last illustrative example. The frequency range of equivalence is to be 30 to 5,500 cycles.

It will be shown in the next section that α and β both increase with frequency for a transmission line; hence the design will be carried out for the highest frequency of interest, namely, 5.5 kc, where α and β have their *largest* values. This will allow the determination of l to satisfy the approximations that αl and βl both be small. Now

$$
\gamma = \sqrt{ZY} = (R + j\omega L)(G + j\omega C)
$$

At $f = 5.5$ kc, $\omega = 2\pi(5.5 \times 10^3) = 3.455 \times 10^4$ radians/sec, and

$$\gamma =$$
$$\sqrt{[10.4 + j(3.455 \times 10^4)(3.67 \times 10^{-3})][8 \times 10^{-7} + j(3.455 \times 10^4)(8.35 \times 10^{-9})]}$$
$$= \sqrt{(10.4 + j126.9)(0.08 + j28.82) \times 10^{-5}}$$
$$= \sqrt{(127\underline{/83.05°})(2.882 \times 10^{-4}\underline{/90°})}$$
$$= 0.1915\underline{/86.53°}$$

$$\alpha + j\beta = 0.01149 + j0.191 \text{ per mile}$$

Then if βl is to be small, say, less than 0.1, the required section length is

$$l < \frac{0.1}{0.191} = 0.524 \text{ mile}$$

As a matter of convenience let l be taken as 0.5 mile. This is conservative since both αl and βl will be less than 0.1. Then the components of the nominal-T section will be

$$\frac{Z_1}{2} = \frac{Zl}{2} = \frac{(R + j\omega L) \times 0.5}{2} = \frac{R}{4} + j\frac{\omega L}{4}$$

$$Z_2 = \frac{1}{Yl} = \frac{1}{(G + j\omega C) \times 0.5} = \frac{1}{G/2 + j\omega C/2}$$

The nominal-T section is shown in Fig. 8-5. Then

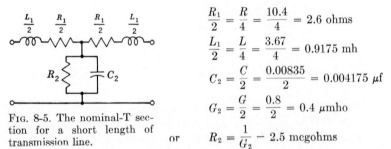

$$\frac{R_1}{2} = \frac{R}{4} = \frac{10.4}{4} = 2.6 \text{ ohms}$$

$$\frac{L_1}{2} = \frac{L}{4} = \frac{3.67}{4} = 0.9175 \text{ mh}$$

$$C_2 = \frac{C}{2} = \frac{0.00835}{2} = 0.004175 \text{ } \mu f$$

$$G_2 = \frac{G}{2} = \frac{0.8}{2} = 0.4 \text{ } \mu mho$$

Fig. 8-5. The nominal-T section for a short length of transmission line.

or

$$R_2 = \frac{1}{G_2} - 2.5 \text{ megohms}$$

Each such T section is the equivalent, to an excellent approximation, of $\frac{1}{2}$ mile of the open-wire line up to a frequency of 5.5 kc. Ten such sections in cascade would simulate the behavior of 5 miles of the line up to that frequency. The design restriction that αl, $\beta l < 0.1$ is more conservative than is usually necessary; a commonly used artificial line is considered in Prob. 8-7.

8-9. Line Distortion. The student knows from the results of Chap. 6 that, if a complicated wave is to be transmitted *without distortion*, the waveform at the line receiving end must be the same as the waveform of the original input signal. This condition requires that α and v_g of the line must be independent of frequency. As was shown in Chap. 6, the requirement on v_g specifies that β shall be linear with frequency.

It is of interest, then, to determine whether or not the transmission line satisfies the requirements for distortionless propagation. This may be done by formally solving Eq. (8-10) for α and β. Squaring both sides of Eq. (8-10), one obtains

$$(\alpha + j\beta)^2 = (R + j\omega L)(G + j\omega C)$$
$$(\alpha^2 - \beta^2) + j2\alpha\beta = (RG - \omega^2 LC) + j\omega(LG + RC) \tag{8-31}$$

Equating reals,

$$\alpha^2 - \beta^2 = RG - \omega^2 LC \tag{8-32}$$

Equating imaginaries,

$$2\alpha\beta = \omega(LG + RC) \tag{8-33}$$

Squaring Eq. (8-33) and substituting into the result for α^2 from Eq. (8-32) yield the biquadratic in β,

$$\beta^4 + (RG - \omega^2 LC)\beta^2 - \frac{\omega^2}{4}(LG + RC)^2 = 0$$

whence

$$\beta = \sqrt{\frac{\omega^2 LC - RG + \sqrt{(RG - \omega^2 LC)^2 + \omega^2(LG + RC)^2}}{2}} \tag{8-34}$$

Substitution of Eq. (8-34) into Eq. (8-32) and solution for α yield

$$\alpha = \sqrt{\frac{RG - \omega^2 LC + \sqrt{(RG - \omega^2 LC)^2 + \omega^2(LG + RC)^2}}{2}} \tag{8-35}$$

Inspection of the last two equations shows that, in general, the value of α does vary with frequency and therefore the line will introduce frequency distortion. β does not vary directly with frequency; hence the line also introduces delay distortion. The next section shows what relationships are required between the line parameters for distortionless propagation to take place.

8-10. Distortionless Line. It is desirable to know the conditions on the line parameters that permit distortionless propagation, for that knowledge can be of aid in designing new lines or modifying old ones to minimize distortion. The necessary conditions may be determined by considering either frequency or delay distortion. Say, for example, that α is to be made independent of frequency to eliminate frequency distortion. Careful inspection of Eq. (8-35) shows that the condition will be satisfied if $R = G = 0$, in which case $\alpha = 0$, or, barring this possibility, if the ω^2 term resulting from extraction of the inner square root is equal to the $\omega^2 LC$ term under the outer radical, for then only terms that are independent of ω will remain. This may be stated mathematically

$$\sqrt{(RG - \omega^2 LC)^2 + \omega^2(LG + RC)^2} = K + \omega^2 LC \tag{8-36}$$

where K is some constant to be evaluated. Squaring,

$$(RG)^2 - 2RGLC\omega^2 + (LC)^2\omega^4 + \omega^2[(LG)^2 + 2RGLC + (RC)^2]$$
$$= K^2 + 2KLC\omega^2 + (LC)^2\omega^4$$

or

$$(RG)^2 + \omega^2[(LG)^2 + (RC)^2] = K^2 + 2KLC\omega^2$$

For the identity to hold true, coefficients of corresponding powers of ω on both sides of the equation must be equal; hence,

$$\omega^0: \qquad\qquad\qquad\qquad K = RG \qquad\qquad\qquad (8\text{-}37)$$

$$\omega^2: \qquad\qquad\qquad (LG)^2 + (RC)^2 = 2KLC$$

Substituting for K from Eq. (8-37),

$$(LG)^2 - 2RGLC + (RC)^2 = 0$$

whence $\qquad\qquad LG - RC = 0 \qquad$ or $\qquad \dfrac{L}{C} = \dfrac{R}{G} \qquad\qquad (8\text{-}38)$

Substitution of Eq. (8-38) into Eq. (8-35) shows that α reduces to

$$\alpha = \sqrt{RG} = \sqrt{\frac{C}{L}}\, R \qquad\qquad (8\text{-}39)$$

Furthermore, β becomes from Eq. (8-34)

$$\beta = \omega \sqrt{LC} = \omega L \sqrt{\frac{G}{R}} \qquad\qquad (8\text{-}40)$$

and $\qquad\qquad\qquad Z_o = \sqrt{\frac{Z}{Y}} = \sqrt{\frac{R}{G}} = \sqrt{\frac{L}{C}} \qquad\qquad (8\text{-}41)$

$$v_p = \frac{\omega}{\beta} = \frac{1}{\sqrt{LC}} \qquad\qquad (8\text{-}42)$$

$$v_g = \frac{d\omega}{d\beta} = \frac{1}{\sqrt{LC}} \qquad\qquad (8\text{-}43)$$

It will be seen that, in the case where the condition specified by Eq. (8-38) is fulfilled, the attenuation, phase and group velocities, and characteristic impedance are independent of frequency, and the last is a pure resistance. When such a line is terminated in its characteristic impedance and fed from a generator whose internal impedance is a pure resistance, there will be no frequency or delay distortion.

This derivation has assumed that the so-called "line constants" R, L, G, and C are really constant. Actually, owing primarily to skin effect, they change with frequency, and so even a line with the relations of Eq. (8-38) at some one frequency would have some distortion.

8-11. Line of Low Distortion. Actually to fulfill Eq. (8-38) is not feasible in physical lines. In well-maintained cable, G is very small, and an extremely large value of L would be necessary. It is not desirable to increase G, for by Eq. (8-39) this would cause a much greater attenuation. Fortunately it is not necessary to increase the inductance to the value required by Eq. (8-38) to reduce distortion to a small amount.

Consider the case where ωL is very much greater than R and ωC is very much greater than G. Now $Z = R + j\omega L$, $Y = G + j\omega C$, and Z

and Y would both have angles nearly equal to $\pi/2$ for this case. The absolute value of Z is nearly equal to ωL, and the absolute value of Y is nearly ωC. If any angle θ is small, then the following relation will be very nearly true, $\theta = \sin \theta = \tan \theta$, while if it is nearly equal to $\pi/2$, $\cos \theta = \cot \theta = \dfrac{\pi}{2} - \theta$ or $\theta = \pi/2 - \cot \theta$. Therefore in polar coordinates, since the angles of Z and Y will nearly equal $\pi/2$ for the conditions specified,

$$Z = \omega L \left/ \frac{\pi}{2} - \frac{R}{\omega L} \right. \tag{8-44}$$

$$Y = \omega C \left/ \frac{\pi}{2} - \frac{G}{\omega C} \right. \tag{8-45}$$

$$\gamma = \sqrt{ZY} = \omega \sqrt{LC} \left/ \frac{\pi}{2} - \frac{1}{2}\left(\frac{R}{\omega L} + \frac{G}{\omega C}\right) \right. \tag{8-46}$$

The angle of $\sqrt{ZY}$ is one-half the sum of the angles of Z and Y. Since this angle θ is nearly $\pi/2$, the sine can be assumed as unity while the cosine is equal to $\pi/2 - \theta$, or

$$\cos \theta = \frac{1}{2}\left(\frac{R}{\omega L} + \frac{G}{\omega C}\right)$$

Equation (8-46) can then be reduced to the rectangular form

$$\alpha + j\beta = |\gamma| \cos \theta + j|\gamma| \sin \theta$$

From Eq. (8-46) $|\gamma| = \omega \sqrt{LC}$. Therefore

$$\alpha + j\beta = \frac{1}{2}\left(\frac{R}{\omega L} + \frac{G}{\omega C}\right)\omega \sqrt{LC} + j\omega \sqrt{LC}$$

$$\alpha = \frac{1}{2}\left(R \sqrt{\frac{C}{L}} + G \sqrt{\frac{L}{C}}\right) \tag{8-47}$$

$$\beta = \omega \sqrt{LC} \tag{8-48}$$

$$v_p = v_g = \frac{\omega}{\beta} = \frac{1}{\sqrt{LC}} \tag{8-49}$$

From Eqs. (8-44) and (8-45)

$$Z_o = \sqrt{\frac{Z}{Y}} = \sqrt{\frac{L}{C}} \left/ \frac{1}{2}\left(\frac{G}{\omega C} - \frac{R}{\omega L}\right) \right. \qquad \text{radians} \tag{8-50}$$

It will be seen that, for this case also, except for the elements neglected in the approximation, the attenuation and velocity are independent of frequency, if R, L, C, and G do not change with frequency. The magnitude of the characteristic impedance is also independent of frequency, and its angle will be very small; that is, Z_o is nearly a pure resistance.

Combining Eqs. (8-50) and (8-47), the latter may be rewritten

$$\alpha = \frac{1}{2}\left(\frac{R}{|Z_0|} + G|Z_0|\right) \tag{8-51}$$

If, as is often the case, G is negligible, Eq. (8-51) becomes

$$\alpha = \frac{R}{2}\sqrt{\frac{C}{L}} = \frac{R}{2|Z_0|} \tag{8-51a}$$

8-12. Cables. Telephone cables find wide application in the field of communications, and it is of interest to investigate their behavior as a special case. Inspection of the data of Table 8-1 shows that in common cables the inductance and conductance are very small so that over the range of frequencies used in telephony $\omega L \ll R$ and $G \ll \omega C$. Thus at least to slide-rule accuracy one may use the approximations

$$Z \approx R \qquad Y \approx j\omega C \tag{8-52}$$

Then
$$\gamma = \sqrt{ZY} = \sqrt{j\omega CR} = \sqrt{\omega CR / 90°}$$
$$= \sqrt{\omega CR} / 45° = \sqrt{\omega CR}\,(\cos 45° + j \sin 45°)$$

$$\gamma = \alpha + j\beta = \sqrt{\frac{\omega CR}{2}} + j\sqrt{\frac{\omega CR}{2}}$$

$$\alpha = \sqrt{\frac{\omega CR}{2}} \tag{8-53}$$

$$\beta = \sqrt{\frac{\omega CR}{2}} \tag{8-54}$$

$$v_p = \frac{v_g}{2} = \frac{\omega}{\beta} = \sqrt{\frac{2\omega}{CR}} \tag{8-55}$$

$$Z_o = \sqrt{\frac{Z}{Y}} = \sqrt{\frac{R}{j\omega C}} = \sqrt{\frac{R}{\omega C}} / -45° \tag{8-56}$$

Combining Eqs. (8-53) and (8-54), it is also possible to write

$$\alpha = 0.707 \frac{R}{|Z_0|} \tag{8-57}$$

It will be seen that the higher frequencies travel faster and are attenuated more than the lower ones.

8-13. Loading. It is quite apparent from the foregoing equations that both delay and frequency distortion are introduced by a cable, a fact that may be verified by inspecting the magnitudes of typical cable parameters in the light of earlier sections. For example from Table 8-1 for the 16-gauge cable

$$\frac{L}{C} = \frac{10^{-3}}{0.062 \times 10^{-6}} = 16.12 \times 10^3 \qquad \frac{R}{G} = \frac{42.1}{1.5 \times 10^{-6}} = 28.1 \times 10^6$$

Therefore
$$\frac{L}{C} \ll \frac{R}{G}$$

If, then, the cable is to be modified so that it more nearly approximates the distortionless ideal, four methods of approach are available:

1. Reduce R. To do this to a significant extent requires the use of much larger conductors, which in turn causes an increase in cable size and cost. Reduction of R also lowers $|Z_o|$.

2. Decrease C. This requires an increase of spacing between conductors, again with increase of cable size and cost. Decreasing C raises $|Z_o|$ and lowers α.

3. Increase G. This may be effected by lowering the quality of conductor insulation, a poor solution because it increases losses. Increasing G also lowers $|Z_o|$.

4. Increase L. This has the primary effect of raising $|Z_o|$ and lowering α and offers the best approach to the improvement of cable response.

Increasing the inductance of the line to reduce attenuation is called "loading" and was first suggested by Oliver Heaviside. Pupin developed the theory of lumped constants, which made loading practicable.

It can easily be shown physically why raising the characteristic impedance of a line will increase its efficiency and hence reduce the attenuation. If the conductance is negligible, the loss in any section will depend on the square of the current flowing along the line. In power systems the lines are usually a small fraction of a wavelength long, and therefore the input impedance of a line is determined largely by the terminating impedance connected to it. To transmit at high voltage and low current at commercial power frequencies, it is necessary only to connect transformers at either end between the line and actual terminating equipment.

In a communication line the frequencies are higher, and the attenuation and length (in wavelengths) are also much greater. Under these conditions, the *input impedance* of the line is largely determined by the *constants of the line, rather than its termination*. This is particularly true when the total attenuation is high. The ratio of input voltage to input current is, therefore, nearly equal to the characteristic impedance, and, for a given amount of power, both current and voltage are definitely fixed. *To transmit the same power at a lower current, it is necessary to increase the characteristic impedance of the line*, and this can be done by increasing the inductance or lowering the capacitance.

If the leakage is appreciable, then the loss in the leakage resistances will be proportional to the square of the voltage, which in turn will increase with the characteristic impedance. This shows why, in Eq. (8-51), the second term $G|Z_o|$ has the characteristic impedance in the numerator. This term is never as great as the first term $R/|Z_o|$ in actual lines. If Z_o alone is varied, without changing R or G, then the attenuation is a minimum when the two components of Eq. (8-51) are equal.

As an example showing the effect of adding loading, consider the case where loading coils, whose inductances are 246 mh each and whose resistances are 7.3

ohms apiece, are added at the standard intervals of 7.88 miles. This would be an addition of 246/7.88 mh/mile if the effect of lumping is neglected, as it can be at the lower af. The other constants of the line will be assumed to be the same as in the previous problem. (Sec. 8-7).

Then the impedance per mile will be

$$Z = 10.4 + j18.35 + \frac{7.3 + j5,000 \times 0.246}{7.88}$$

$$= 11.32 + j174.35 = 174.35\underline{/86.30°}$$

$$Y = 41.76 \times 10^{-6}\underline{/88.92°}$$

$$Z_o = \sqrt{\frac{Z}{Y}} = 2,038\underline{/-1.32°}$$

$$\gamma = \sqrt{ZY} = 0.0850\underline{/87.60°} = 0.0036 + j0.0850$$

$$\alpha = 0.0036 \text{ neper/mile}$$

$$\beta = 0.0850 \text{ radian/mile}$$

$$\lambda = \frac{2\pi}{0.0850} = 74 \text{ miles}$$

$$v_p = \frac{\omega}{\beta} = 58,800 \text{ miles/sec}$$

Compare these values with the results obtained from approximate equations of Eqs. (8-47) to (8-50).

$$L = \left(3.67 + \frac{246}{7.88}\right) \text{mh} = 0.03487 \text{ henry/mile}$$

From Eq. (8-50)

$$Z_o = \sqrt{\frac{0.03487}{0.00835 \times 10^{-6}}} \bigg/ \frac{1}{2}\left(\frac{0.8}{41.75} - \frac{11.32}{174.35}\right)$$

$$= 2,041 \bigg/ -\frac{0.0458}{2} \text{ radian} = 2,041\underline{/-1.32°}$$

From Eq. (8.47) or (8.51)

$$\alpha = \frac{1}{2}\left(\frac{11.32}{2,041} + 0.8 \times 2,041 \times 10^{-6}\right)$$

$$= \frac{1}{2}(0.00555 + 0.00163)$$

$$= 0.00359 \text{ neper/mile}$$

It is apparent that the attenuation due to the series resistance is still 555/163 times as great as that due to the conductance.

From Eq. (8-48)

$$\beta = \omega \sqrt{LC} = 5,000 \sqrt{0.03487 \times 0.00835 \times 10^{-6}}$$

$$\beta = 0.0853 \text{ radian/mile}$$

From Eq. (8-49)

$$v_p = \frac{1}{\sqrt{LC}} = 58,600 \text{ miles/sec}$$

It is apparent that in the case of the loaded line the approximate relations check very closely.

The reduction in the attenuation constant from 0.00785 to 0.0036, due to the addition of the loading coils, means that a loaded line $^{785}\!/_{360}$, or 2.18, times the length of an unloaded one would give the same attenuation. The improvement is much more marked for cables, where the initial self-inductance is negligible. In the case of cable a reduction in attenuation to one-third to one-fifth the value for unloaded cable is secured in commercial systems.

It is possible to increase the inductance uniformly along a line by wrapping it with a tape of some ferrous material, such as iron or permalloy. This treatment is expensive, and the amount of inductance which can be economically provided is small. Such a loading is, at present, used only on submarine cables where the difficulty of adding lumped loading is great. On land lines and cables, inductance is added in lumps at regular intervals. Under these conditions the performance will be modified from that obtained when the inductance is distributed, as a series of lumped inductances and capacitances constitute a filter whose attenuation rapidly increases when the frequency exceeds a certain value. This effect of loading will be discussed more fully later in the chapter. Because of this LP filter action, cables with carrier systems are not loaded.

Unfortunately, it is not possible to increase the inductance without increasing the resistance, because of the wire used in winding the coils. It is apparent, therefore, that an indefinite increase in inductance would not continue to produce an economic gain in transmission. Furthermore, the effective resistance of the loading coils will vary somewhat with frequency, owing to hysteresis and eddy-current losses, and the system, aside from the filter effect referred to, will not be entirely distortionless.

Nevertheless, the improvement in reduced attenuation, frequency distortion, and delay distortion is very marked when loading is added to a cable, as will be seen by comparing the foregoing results. For the cable, α, v_g, and Z_o all vary as the square root of the frequency, while, in the case where ωL is large in comparison with the resistance, α, v_g, and Z_o are independent of frequency.

8-14. Campbell's Formula for Loaded Line.[1] In the case of loaded lines the circuit is a combination of lumped and distributed constants. The cable, or line, is supplemented by lumped inductances inserted in series at intervals. To find the effect of such a combination, the line between loading points should be reduced to a T section, after which the impedance of one-half the loading coil should be inserted in each series

---

[1] This section is included primarily to illustrate a method of analysis which may be used where the circuit contains both lumped and distributed parameters.

arm. From this new T section the over-all characteristic impedance and attenuation constant may be computed. For many purposes the section of line between loading points will be so short that Eqs. (8-29) and (8-30) will apply. In the interests of generality, however, the general equations for the equivalent T section of a line will be used, viz., Eqs. (6-28) and (6-31),

$$Z_2 = \frac{Z_o}{\sinh \gamma l}$$

$$\frac{Z_1}{2} = Z_o \frac{\cosh \gamma l - 1}{\sinh \gamma l}$$

where Z_o = characteristic impedance of cable

γ = propagation constant of cable

Then the last equation gives the series arm of a section of cable *between two adjacent loading coils*.

Let the loading coil impedance be denoted Z_L. Then the equivalent series arm including the loading coil will be

$$\frac{Z_1'}{2} = \frac{Z_L}{2} + Z_o \frac{\cosh \gamma l - 1}{\sinh \gamma l} \tag{8-58}$$

The shunt arm of the section will be the equivalent arm of the cable alone, since the loading coil does not introduce any additional admittance. The value of this shunt arm is given by Eq. (6-28). Equation (6-19) can now be used to determine the propagation constant of the cable with loading included. Let γ' be the value of this propagation constant. Then by Eq. (6-19), since the section is taken as the unit of length, that is, $l = 1$:

$$\cosh \gamma' = 1 + \frac{Z_1'}{2Z_2}$$

$$\cosh \gamma' = 1 + \frac{\dfrac{Z_L}{2} + Z_o \dfrac{\cosh \gamma l - 1}{\sinh \gamma l}}{Z_o/(\sinh \gamma l)}$$

$$\cosh \gamma' = 1 + \frac{Z_L}{2Z_o} \sinh \gamma l + \cosh \gamma l - 1$$

$$\cosh \gamma' = \cosh \gamma l + \frac{Z_L}{2Z_o} \sinh \gamma l \tag{8-59}$$

This equation was first developed by G. A. Campbell and bears his name.

8-15. Loaded Cable as a Filter. When a cable is loaded by inserting inductors at intervals, the combination of cable capacitance and lumped inductance has the configuration of a "lossy" LP filter. The attenuation is reduced by the loading for frequencies below the cutoff value given by Eq. (7-35) but rises rapidly above that point. The values used in Eq. (7-35) for the computation of a loaded circuit are L, the inductance of the loading coil, and C, the capacitance of the cable *between two adjacent loading coils*. The cutoff frequency may be raised by decreasing the inductance per coil, or by spacing the coils closer together, or both. Decreasing the inductance per coil will, of course, raise the attenuation in the transmission band. Spacing the coils closer together increases the cost, because the cost depends more upon the number of coils installed than on the size of these inductances.

In the design of loading coils it is important that saturation and stray fields be avoided. For this reason the coils are wound on toroidal cores. These cores are manufactured of permalloy, ground to dust and then held together by a binder so that there is a large number of small air gaps to reduce the possibility of saturation. If saturation should occur, non-linear distortion would result and new frequencies would be introduced because of the nonlinearity of the circuit constants.

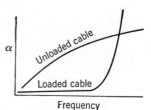

FIG. 8-6. Attenuation in cable circuits.

Figure 8-6 shows the way in which attenuation varies with frequency on loaded and unloaded cables.

The advantage of loading is not so great on open-wire lines, which have an appreciable inductance of their own and so have much less distortion than cable. As a result the practice of loading open-wire lines has been abandoned.

Table 8-3 shows the values of attenuation, characteristic impedance, phase velocity, and cutoff frequency for several types of loading under the assumption that the inductance of the loading coil is *uniformly* distributed. Actual values of α, Z_o, v_p, and f_c calculated by Campbell's formula will differ from those shown in the table, but the latter show the qualitative effect of the loading inductance and the spacing between the load coils. The table gives values for both phantomed (see Chap. 5) and nonphantomed circuits.

The type of loading in Table 8-3 is specified in terms of the Bell System nomenclature. The first letter gives the spacing between adjacent coils, namely, H denotes 6,000 ft, or 1.135 miles, and B 3,000 ft, or 0.568 mile. The digits specify the load-coil inductance in millihenrys. The last letter designates the type of circuit: S side, P phantom, N non-phantom, or physical. Thus H-21-S indicates a 21-mh coil, spaced at 6,000-foot intervals on a side circuit. Formerly the terms heavy and medium loading were used, but the medium-loading spacing of 1.66 miles has now been abandoned because of the lower cutoff frequency it produces.

A side circuit is a pair of conductors used for one side of a phantom group. A physical circuit is a pair not associated with a phantom group.

TABLE 8-3. CHARACTERISTICS OF LOADED CABLE AT 1,000 CYCLES, LOADING ASSUMED TO BE UNIFORMLY SPACED*

Gauge	Type	Type of loading	Load-coil spacing, miles	Load-coil constants		Line constants per mile					Z_o		v_p, miles/sec	Cutoff frequency, kc
				R, ohms	L, mh	R, ohms	L, mh	C, μf	G, μmhos	α, nepers/mile	Ohms	Deg		
19 A.W.G.	Side	None	.....	....	..	85.8	1	0.062	1.5	0.1249	470.1	−42.80	46,930	6.700
19 A.W.G.	Side	H-31-S	1.135	2.7	31	88.2	28	0.062	1.5	0.0643	710.0	−13.20	20,555	3.997
19 A.W.G.	Side	H-88-S	1.135	7.3	88	92.2	78	0.062	1.5	0.0418	1,131	−5.22	14,319	5.655
19 A.W.G.	Side	B-88-S	0.568	7.3	88	98.7	156	0.062	1.5	0.0322	1,590	−2.76	17,882	6.700
16 A.W.G.	Side	None	.....	....	..	42.1	1	0.062	1.5	0.0842	330.7	−40.65	64,506	3.997
16 A.W.G.	Side	H-31-S	1.135	2.7	31	44.5	28	0.062	1.5	0.0334	682.5	−6.99	23,818	5.655
16 A.W.G.	Side	H-88-S	1.135	7.3	88	48.5	78	0.062	1.5	0.0224	1,124	−2.71	14,365	6.959
16 A.W.G.	Side	B-88-S	0.568	7.3	88	54.9	156	0.062	1.5	0.0185	1,587.4	−1.49	10,165	3.738
19 A.W.G.	Phantom	None	.....	....	..	42.9	0.7	0.100	2.4	0.1106	262.1	−41.97	51,525	5.936
19 A.W.G.	Phantom	H-18-P	1.135	1.4	18	44.1	17	0.100	2.4	0.0529	428.8	−11.11	23,781	6.959
19 A.W.G.	Phantom	H-63-P	1.135	6.1	63	48.3	56	0.100	2.4	0.0331	751.8	−3.80	13,334	3.738
19 A.W.G.	Phantom	B-50-P	0.568	3.7	50	49.4	89	0.100	2.4	0.0273	945.2	−2.41	10,590	5.936
16 A.W.G.	Phantom	None	.....	....	..	21	0.7	0.100	2.4	0.0746	184.8	−38.98	70,604	11.276
16 A.W.G.	Phantom	H-18-P	1.135	1.4	18	22.2	17	0.100	2.4	0.0273	416.7	−5.76	24,129	11.276
16 A.W.G.	Phantom	H-63-P	1.135	6.1	63	26.4	56	0.100	2.4	0.0185	749.4	−2.04	13,354	
16 A.W.G.	Phantom	B-50-P	0.568	3.7	50	27.5	89	0.100	2.4	0.0157	943.9	−1.30	10,597	
19 A.W.G.	Physical	B-22	0.568	1.28	22	88.1	40	0.062	1.5	0.0546	826.8	−9.55	19,790	
16 A.W.G.	Physical	B-22	0.568	1.25	22	44.3	40	0.062	1.5	0.0281	809.4	−4.89	20,010	

* From Amer. Tel. and Tel. Co.

8-16. Shunt-loaded Line. A case of considerable theoretical interest because of its analogy to wave guides is a line with shunt distributed inductance. In particular this case is of interest because of the effect on group and phase velocity. Such a line could not be realized practically, but it could be approximated by shunt lumped inductive loading at sufficiently close intervals. Let L_1 be the series inductance per unit length and L_2 the shunt inductance per unit length. The equivalent circuit for a short length Δx would be that shown in Fig. 8-7.

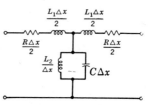

FIG. 8-7. The equivalent T section of a length Δx of line having shunt inductance loading.

Consider the case where $R \ll \omega L_1$ and $G = 0$.

$$Z = R + j\omega L_1 = \omega L_1 \bigg/ \frac{\pi}{2} - \frac{R}{\omega L_1}$$

$$Y = j\left(\omega C - \frac{1}{\omega L_2}\right) = \omega C\left(1 - \frac{1}{\omega^2 L_2 C}\right)\bigg/ \frac{\pi}{2}$$

$$\gamma = \sqrt{ZY} = \omega\sqrt{L_1 C\left(1 - \frac{1}{\omega^2 L_2 C}\right)}\bigg/ \frac{\pi}{2} - \frac{R}{2\omega L_1} \qquad (8\text{-}60)$$

$$Z_o = \sqrt{\frac{L_1}{C}\frac{\omega^2 L_2 C}{\omega^2 L_2 C - 1}}\bigg/ -\frac{R}{2\omega L_1}$$

Now if $\omega < \sqrt{1/L_2 C}$, the value under the radicals in the expressions for γ and Z_o will be negative, i.e., the radical will become imaginary, γ will then have a small angle and be largely attenuation, while Z_o will have an angle nearly $\pi/2$ and will have a large reactive component.

For $\omega > \sqrt{1/L_2 C}$ the values of the radical will be real, γ will be largely imaginary (small α and large β), and Z_o will be nearly a pure resistance. Hence the line will behave like an HP filter. Unlike the case in series loading this filter action is not due to the effect of the lumpiness of the loading but would be present even if distributed inductance could be added.

Above the cutoff frequency ($\omega > \sqrt{1/L_2 C}$), by derivations similar to those of Eqs. (8-47) to (8-49),

$$\alpha = \frac{R}{2}\sqrt{\frac{C}{L_1}\left(1 - \frac{1}{\omega^2 L_2 C}\right)} \qquad (8\text{-}61)$$

Therefore shunt loading, like series lumped loading, decreases the attenuation in the passband but restricts the width of the passband.

$$\beta = \omega \sqrt{L_1 C \left(1 - \frac{1}{\omega^2 L_2 C}\right)}$$

$$v_g = \frac{d\omega}{d\beta} = \sqrt{\frac{1}{L_1 C} \left(1 - \frac{1}{\omega^2 L_2 C}\right)} \qquad (8\text{-}62)$$

$$v_p = \frac{\omega}{\beta} = \frac{1}{\sqrt{L_1 C (1 - 1/\omega^2 L_2 C)}}$$

Plots of β, v_g, and v_p are shown in Fig. 8-8 for the case where R is negligible. Note that $v_p > v_g$ at all frequencies and

$$v_p v_g = \frac{1}{L_1 C} = \text{phase or group velocity of unloaded line}$$

Hence, as the frequency is increased above the cutoff value, the phase velocity will decrease while the group velocity will increase, their product being equal to the square of the velocity of a similar line without shunt loading. It will be shown later that the phase velocity of an unloaded line is generally close to the velocity of light, and so the phase velocity of the shunt-loaded line may be much greater than that of light, while the group velocity, which is the velocity with which a pulse would be transmitted, will always be less than that of light. As has been mentioned, wave guides have similar properties with respect to their group and phase velocities and also behave as HP filters.

8-17. Lines of Low Loss. As the frequency of the signals applied to a line is raised, the imaginary part of the loop series impedance,

$$Z = R + j\omega L$$

increases faster than does the real part, which because of skin effect increases as the square root of frequency (see Table 8-2). Thus at some high frequency $\omega L \gg R$. In typical lines, G is so small that it may be neglected with respect to ωC. Subject to these conditions, one may write

$$Z = R + j\omega L \qquad R \ll \omega L$$
$$Y = j\omega C$$

Then
$$Z_o = \sqrt{\frac{Z}{Y}} = \sqrt{\frac{L}{C} + \frac{R}{j\omega C}} = \sqrt{\frac{L}{C}} \sqrt{1 - j\frac{R}{\omega L}}$$

The second radical may be expanded into a series by means of the binomial expansion; thus

$$\sqrt{1 - j\frac{R}{\omega L}} = 1 - j\frac{1}{2}\frac{R}{\omega L} + \frac{1}{8}\left(\frac{R}{\omega L}\right)^2 + j\frac{3}{48}\left(\frac{R}{\omega L}\right)^3 + \cdots$$

By the hypothesis $R/\omega L \ll 1$; hence the series converges very rapidly,

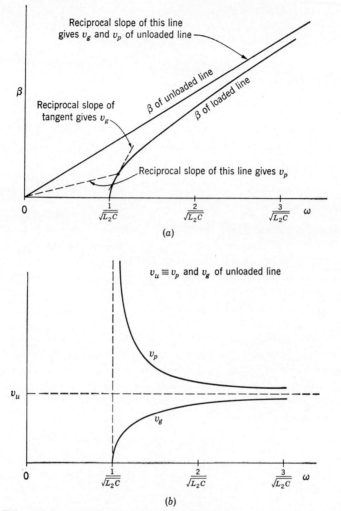

FIG. 8-8. Effect of shunt loading on a line of low dissipation. (a) β as a function of ω. (b) Relative phase and group velocities as a function of ω.

and only the first two terms need by retained;[1] thus

$$Z_o = \sqrt{\frac{L}{C}}\left(1 - j\,\frac{R}{2\omega L}\right) \tag{8-63}$$

$$= \sqrt{\frac{L}{C}}\,\sqrt{1 + \left(\frac{R}{2\omega L}\right)^2}\Big/-\arctan\frac{R}{2\omega L} \tag{8-63a}$$

[1] The student should observe that, if, say, $R = 0.01\omega L$, use of the first two terms of the series will give results more accurate than can be obtained by direct use of the slide rule.

Again, since $R/\omega L \ll 1$, Z_o is slightly capacitive and its magnitude to all intents and purposes is $\sqrt{L/C}$.

The complex propagation constant is handled in a similar manner.

$$\gamma = \sqrt{ZY} = \sqrt{(R + j\omega L)j\omega C} = \sqrt{(j\omega)^2 LC + j\omega CR}$$
$$= j\omega \sqrt{LC} \sqrt{1 - j\frac{R}{\omega L}}$$

In this case, since one is concerned with both α and β, the first four terms of the binomial expansion of the second radical are retained.

$$\gamma = \alpha + j\beta$$
$$= j\omega \sqrt{LC} \left[1 - j\frac{1}{2}\frac{R}{\omega L} + \frac{1}{8}\left(\frac{R}{\omega L}\right)^2 + j\frac{1}{16}\left(\frac{R}{\omega L}\right)^3 + \cdots \right]$$
$$= \frac{R}{2}\sqrt{\frac{C}{L}}\left[1 - \frac{1}{8}\left(\frac{R}{\omega L}\right)^2 \right] + j\omega\sqrt{LC}\left[1 + \frac{1}{8}\left(\frac{R}{\omega L}\right)^2 \right] \quad (8\text{-}64)$$

Hence $\alpha = \dfrac{R}{2}\sqrt{\dfrac{C}{L}}\left[1 - \dfrac{1}{8}\left(\dfrac{R}{\omega L}\right)^2 \right]$ \hfill (8-64a)

$$\beta = \omega\sqrt{LC}\left[1 + \frac{1}{8}\left(\frac{R}{\omega L}\right)^2 \right] \quad (8\text{-}64b)$$

In general the second term of both these equations will be so small as to be negligible. The student should observe the similarity between these equations and those of the line of low distortion.

8-18. Lossless Line. At frequencies even higher than those considered in the last section, R may be completely neglected relative to ωL, and one has the approximations

$$Z \approx j\omega L$$
$$Y \approx j\omega C$$
$$Z_o = \sqrt{\frac{L}{C}} \qquad \alpha = 0 \qquad \beta = \omega\sqrt{LC} \quad (8\text{-}65)$$
$$v_p = v_g = \frac{1}{\sqrt{LC}} \quad (8\text{-}66)$$

This case is designated the "lossless line" and will be of considerable use in subsequent chapters.

8-19. Division of Energy between Electric and Magnetic Fields of Lossless Line. It is interesting to note that, where $\omega L \gg R$, the energy in the wave is divided equally between the electromagnetic and electrostatic fields. The maximum energy stored per unit length in the inductance of the wire as the wave passes is

$$W_L = \frac{LI^2}{2} \quad (8\text{-}67)$$

while the maximum energy stored per unit length in the capacitance is

$$W_C = \frac{CE^2}{2} \tag{8-68}$$

But it has been shown by Eq. (8-65) that for this case

$$Z_o = \frac{E}{I} = \sqrt{\frac{L}{C}}$$

and this can be rewritten

$$CE^2 = LI^2$$

Therefore $$W_L = W_C \tag{8-69}$$

8-20. Maximum Velocity. In case R and G are negligible, it is interesting to see what will be the maximum phase and group velocity which can be obtained on a transmission line. In this case it has been shown by Eq. (8-66) that

$$v_g = v_p = \frac{1}{\sqrt{LC}} \tag{8-66}$$

For a two-wire line when the separation is large compared with the radius of the wire, the inductance in *millihenrys* per mile of *line* is

$$L = 1.481 \log \frac{s}{r} + L' \tag{8-70}$$

where s is the separation between wires and r is the radius of the wires. L' is the inductance due to the linkage of flux and current within the conductor. It is equal to 0.1609 millihenry/mile for low frequencies, but as the frequency increases and the current is concentrated more near the surface of the wire, this factor approaches zero at high frequencies.

The capacitance between two wires for $s \gg r$, in *microfarads* per mile of *line* is

$$C = \frac{0.01941}{\log (s/r)} \tag{8-71}$$

In Eq. (8-66) the L and C are in henrys per unit length and farads per unit length, respectively. Therefore

$$LC = (1.481 \times 10^{-3})(0.01941 \times 10^{-6}) + \frac{0.01941 \times 10^{-6}L'}{\log (s/r)} \tag{8-72}$$

The second term in Eq. (8-72) becomes small in comparison with the first as either the separation between wires or the frequency is increased. The first term is a constant and is the minimum possible value which

LC can have. Substituting this term in Eq. (8-66),

$$v_{g,\max} = v_{p,\max} = \frac{1}{\sqrt{1.481 \times 0.01941 \times 10^{-9}}}$$
$$= 186{,}300 \text{ miles/sec}$$

This is the maximum velocity waves can have on such a transmission line and is equal to the velocity of light. In an actual line the effect of resistance and conductance, and the term L' in Eq. (8-70), is to reduce the velocity below that of light, but this reduction is only a few per cent on an unloaded open-wire line.

Increasing the inductance of a line by loading will always reduce the velocity of propagation, as it increases the value of β. On loaded *cables* the velocity becomes quite low and is usually of the order of 10,000 to 20,000 miles/sec.

In telegraphic communication the *speed of signaling* is proportional to the maximum number of dots which can be transmitted without undergoing such distortion that an individual dot becomes confused (by the receiving equipment) with the one preceding or succeeding it. It is interesting to note that loading a cable (since it reduces the distortion) increases the speed of signaling at the same time it reduces the group velocity. Telegraphic pulses are ideally square in form and so include a fairly wide range of frequencies. If the group velocity is not constant but increases with frequency, the higher frequencies will arrive at the receiving station sooner than the lower frequencies and individual pulses will drag out into the time assigned to the succeeding pulse. If this distortion is sufficient, the receiving equipment will not respond properly to individual pulses and the only solution for a given line would be to send more slowly. On the other hand, in a cable of low distortion, even though, because of a low group velocity, pulses may be introduced into the input before preceding ones have emerged from the output, no difficulty will be experienced by the receiving equipment in properly interpreting the individual pulses as they arrive at the termination.

8-21. Proper Termination of Transmission Line. In order to secure the maximum transfer of energy between two connecting networks, it will be shown in Chap. 11 that, if their angles are not adjustable, the relation should be $|Z_1| = |Z_2|$. It is apparent, therefore, that, if a generator had an impedance Z_g, it would be desirable to connect it to a load of the same absolute value. This could be done if the line were long, by selecting a line whose characteristic impedance was equal to Z_g or by connecting a transformer between the generator and line so that the impedances would match. At the receiving end the generator and line could, by Thévenin's theorem, be considered as a new generator whose generated voltage was equal to the open-circuited voltage and whose internal impedance would be equal to the impedance looking back into the line, which in this case would be equal to the characteristic impedance. Therefore the load receiving the most power from the line would have a magnitude equal to the characteristic impedance. It is thus seen that terminating a long line in its characteristic impedance at both sending and receiving ends will give the most efficient transfer of energy, if the angles cannot be modified, as is usually the case. It will be shown in Chap. 9, Reflection, why such a termination is desirable from the standpoint of distortion, and therefore most long lines are terminated in this manner.

8-22. Balancing Networks. In the study of telephone repeaters in Chap. 5 it was found that their proper operation depends upon the presence of a *balancing network* whose input impedance is equal, or very nearly

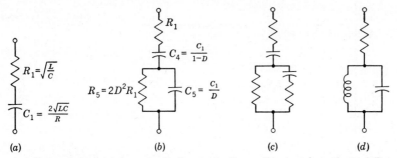

Fig. 8-9. Balancing networks. (*a, b*) Open-wire line. See text for values of R_1 and C_2. (*c*) Unloaded cable. (*d*) Loaded cable.

so, to the characteristic impedance of a line at all frequencies of interest. In designing balancing networks the basic problem is to satisfy this condition with a minimum number of lumped-circuit elements. Typical configurations of these networks for three common types of line are shown in Fig. 8-9. Given these networks, the next step is to evaluate their components.

By way of example, let the elements of Fig. 8-9*a* be evaluated for an open-wire line. For such a line G may be neglected with respect to ωC except at the lowest frequencies. Then

$$Z_o = \sqrt{\frac{Z}{Y}} \approx \sqrt{\frac{R + j\omega L}{j\omega C}} = \sqrt{\frac{L}{C}}\left(1 + \frac{R}{j\omega L}\right)^{\frac{1}{2}} \qquad (8\text{-}73)$$

Then, in the frequency range where $\omega L \gg R$, the factor in the parentheses may be replaced by the first two terms of its binomial expansion, giving

$$Z_o \approx \sqrt{\frac{L}{C}}\left(1 + \frac{R}{j2\omega L}\right) = \sqrt{\frac{L}{C}} + \frac{R}{j2\omega\sqrt{LC}} \qquad (8\text{-}74)$$

This has the same form as the impedance of Fig. 8-9a,

$$Z_1 = R_1 + \frac{1}{j\omega C_1} \tag{8-75}$$

Hence by equating real and imaginary terms one obtains

$$R_1 = \sqrt{\frac{L}{C}} \qquad C_1 = \frac{2\sqrt{LC}}{R} \tag{8-76}$$

where, of course, R, L, and C are the line parameters.

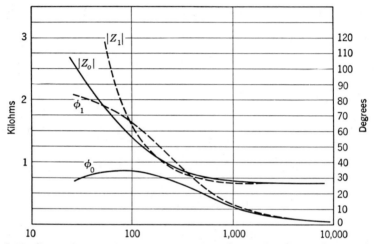

FIG. 8-10. Comparison of the characteristic impedance of a line and an equivalent balancing network of the form shown in Fig. 8-9a.

From the foregoing, one would expect that Z_o and Z_1 are nearly equal at high frequencies but tend to differ at low frequencies because the two inequalities used in the derivation are not satisfied. This is verified in Fig. 8-10, where Z_o and Z_1 are plotted for an open-wire line having the parameters $R = 10.4$ ohms/mile, $L = 3.67$ mh/mile, $G = 0.8$ μmhos/ mile, and $C = 0.00835$ μf/mile. A closer approximation to Z_o over a wider band may be obtained by using more elements in the balancing network, for example, the circuit of Fig. 8-9b may be used (see Prob. 8-18). The components of balancing networks for the loaded and unloaded cable may be evaluated in a similar manner, but the work is more complicated.[1]

[1] See R. S. Hoyt, Impedance of Smooth Lines, and Design of Simulating Networks, *Bell System Tech. J.*, vol. 2, no. 2, p. 1, April, 1923, and Impedance of Loaded Lines, and Design of Simulating and Compensating Networks, *Bell System Tech. J.*, vol. 3 no. 7, p. 414, July, 1924.

PROBLEMS

8-1. Neglecting all losses and flux linkages within the conductors, derive equations for Z_o, γ, and v_p for an air dielectric coaxial cable.

8-2. Repeat Prob. 8-1 for a parallel-wire transmission line. *Note.* For SLS^γ component of L due to flux linkages outside the conductors is $(\mu d/\pi)$ arc cosh $s/2r$.

8-3. Compute, for a frequency of 796 cycles, the characteristic impedance, attenuation constant, wavelength constant, velocity of propagation, and wavelength for the cables and open-wire lines of Table 8-1. The constants given are for a length of 1 mile and are equally distributed.

8-4. The 19-gauge cable is terminated in Z_o and fed from a generator of internal impedance Z_o and with an internal emf of 10 volts. Plot the loci of the current and voltage phasors for 10 miles, beginning at the input terminals. $f = 796$ cycles.

8-5. A line of finite length l is terminated in Z_o. Starting with Eqs. (8-20) and (8-21a), evaluate A_1 and A_2, and show that the equations for E_x and I_x are identical to those of a line of infinite length.

8-6. (a) Design a nominal-T section corresponding to 3,000 ft of 19-gauge cable. (b) Assuming the inductance and conductance are negligible, sketch a diagram of a *balanced* nominal-T section. This section is frequently used in laboratories for an artificial cable. (c) Check Z_o and γ for the nominal-T section against the actual cable at 5,000 cycles.

8-7. A commonly used artificial line is made up of T sections having the following components:

$$R_1 = 80 \text{ ohms} \qquad L_1 = 29.2 \text{ mh} \qquad C_2 = 0.064 \text{ } \mu\text{f} \qquad G_2 = 0$$

Each section corresponds to 7.88 miles of a standard transmission line.

a. Calculate the per mile parameters of the line.

b. Compare Z_o and γ for the artificial and actual lines at 796 cycles.

8-8. Compute by the exact relations the same constants for the cables of Prob. 8-3 if a loading coil whose inductance is 0.175 henry and whose resistance is 10.6 ohms is introduced at intervals of 1.66 miles. Assume that at the frequency given the inductance can be considered as distributed. Compute the characteristics by the approximate relations for $\omega L \gg R$ and $\omega C \gg G$, and compare with the exact results.

8-9. For the 19-gauge cable compute and plot a curve of attenuation constant vs. frequency, phase velocity vs. frequency, and characteristic impedance magnitude vs. frequency over a range of 500 to 3,000 cycles at intervals of 500 cycles.

8-10. Repeat Prob. 8-9 with the loading coils of Prob. 8-8 added.

8-11. Repeat Prob. 8-10, but consider the loading coils as being lumped.

8-12. One hundred miles of 19-gauge cable are terminated in their characteristic impedance. A generator whose internal resistance is 600 ohms and whose emf is 1 volt is connected at the sending end. What will be the current at each end and the power received by the load? $\omega = 5,000$ radius/sec.

8-13. What will be the power received by the load if the cable of Prob. 8-12 has loading coils inserted as in Prob. 8-8? The load is changed to equal the new characteristic impedance.

8-14. What will be the gain in decibels caused by the changes introduced in Prob. 8-13?

8-15. Draw a phasor diagram of sending and received current and voltage for the cases given by Probs. 8-12 and 8-13.

8-16. What will be the current through, and voltage across, a 600-ohm resistance which is dissipating 1 milliwatt? Compute the value of voltage and current if the power dissipated in the 600-ohm resistance is 5, 10, 15, and 20 decibels above and below 1 milliwatt (mw).

8-17. A line is one wavelength long and has a characteristic impedance of 600 ohms pure resistance. The attenuation is negligible. At each end of the line a generator with an internal resistance of 600 ohms is connected. The generated voltages are equal to 1 volt and in phase with each other. By means of the principle of superposition draw a phasor diagram of the voltage and current due to each generator and the resultant sums at intervals of one-eighth wavelength along the line.

8-18. Evaluate the components of the balancing network of Fig. 8-9b for the line whose Z_o is shown in Fig. 8-10. Use $D = 0.5$. Plot curves of Z_o and the balancing network impedance over the range from 30 cycles to 8 kc. Compare your results with Fig. 8-10.

8-19. Derive equations for the components of a nominal II section of a section of transmission line having length l.

8-20. Repeat Prob. 8-17 with the exception that the two generated voltages are 180° out of phase.

8-21. Repeat Probs. 8-17 and 8-20 for the case where $e^{\alpha l} = 2$ and the generated voltage at one end of the line is one-half that at the other.

Note. Problems 8-17, 8-20, and 8-21 bring out important principles in the theory of reflection, as they show the effect of two waves traveling on a line at the same time. They should be solved before proceeding to the next chapter.

CHAPTER 9

REFLECTION

9-1. Approximate Solution of General Line. By means of the analysis given in the preceding chapter, the current and voltage can be determined anywhere along a line terminated in its characteristic impedance. If the line is long enough, the input impedance of the line will be almost equal to the characteristic impedance even though it is not terminated in Z_o. For instance, if the value of αl is equal to 2.3 or more, the input impe-

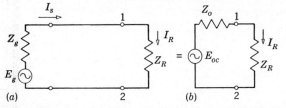

FIG. 9-1. Approximation of the conditions at the receiving end of a long line by the use of Thévenin's theorem.

dance of a line will be within 2 per cent of the characteristic impedance, even for the extreme terminations of short or open circuits. If the termination is nearly equal to the characteristic impedance, the line may be quite short and still the input impedance will be approximately equal to Z_o.

For such a long line an approximate solution is available when the line is not terminated in Z_o. Consider the case of Fig. 9-1. At the receiving end the receiving current can be analyzed in terms of Thévenin's theorem. If the approximation discussed in the previous paragraph holds, the impedance, looking back from the terminals 1, 2, will equal Z_o. Since a solution of the problem has been given for the special case where the terminating impedance Z_R equals Z_o, it is easy to determine the value of the open-circuited voltage at the terminals 1, 2. In the previous chapter it was shown that, if $Z_R = Z_o$,

$$I_S = \frac{E_g}{Z_g + Z_o} \tag{9-1}$$

$$|I_R| = |I_S|e^{-\alpha l} = \frac{E_g e^{-\alpha l}}{|Z_g + Z_o|} \tag{9-2}$$

Now by the analysis shown in Fig. 9-1, if $Z_R = Z_o$,

$$|I_R| = \left| \frac{E_{oc}}{2Z_o} \right| \tag{9-3}$$

Equate the right-hand sides of Eqs. (9-2) and (9-3), and solve for E_{oc}.

$$|E_{oc}| = \left| \frac{2Z_o E_g e^{-\alpha l}}{Z_g + Z_o} \right| \tag{9-4}$$

This value of E_{oc} is exactly twice the value of the terminal voltage at the end of the line when the latter is terminated in Z_o.

Since the open-circuit voltage is independent of the termination, Eq. (9-4) may be used directly in the circuit of Fig. 9-1b to determine the received current for any termination,

$$|I_R| = \left| \frac{E_{oc}}{Z_R + Z_o} \right| = \frac{2|Z_o| E_g e^{-\alpha l}}{|Z_g + Z_o| \, |Z_R + Z_o|} \tag{9-5}$$

Equation (9-5) is an exact solution if either $Z_g = Z_o$ or $Z_R = Z_o$, for then no approximations are involved. The nearer these equalities exist, or the greater the value of αl, the closer will be the approximation of Eq. (9-5). Under the same conditions Eq. (9-1) is a good approximation for I_S.

9-2. Exact Equations for Line Terminated in an Impedance Different from Z_o. If a line is terminated not in its characteristic impedance but in an impedance of some other value, it is possible to consider this termination Z_R as made up of two parts, one of which is the characteristic impedance Z_o and the other is the difference between Z_R and Z_o, which will be referred to as Z_R'. Then

$$Z_R = Z_o + Z_R' \tag{9-6}$$

Since Z_R may be greater or less than Z_o and may have any phase relation with it, Z_R' is an impedance phasor which may lie in *any of the four quadrants* and therefore may not be physically realizable. This does not affect the validity of the treatment.

Similarly the generator impedance may be divided into two parts, one equal to Z_o and the remainder, which will be referred to as Z_g', such that

$$Z_g = Z_o + Z_g' \tag{9-7}$$

A line which has a generator at the sending end with an internal impedance Z_g and a receiving-end impedance Z_R will correspond to Fig. 9-2.[1]

---

[1] Attention is called to the method of measuring distances in Fig. 9-2. x indicates distance measured from the sending end and y distance from the receiving end of the line. At any point on the line $y = l - x$. The voltage at that point is designated by either E_x or E_y and the current by I_x or I_y. The two systems of notation are used to simplify the equations for current and voltage. For example, in certain cases it is convenient to express solutions in terms of receiving-end quantities. Where this is true it is convenient to use y rather than $l - x$.

By compensation theorem A, it is possible to replace any impedance in a network by a generator which has a zero internal impedance and a voltage equal to the potential drop across the impedance. By an application of this theorem the impedances Z_g' and Z_R' may be replaced by generators of zero impedance, whose generated voltages will be, respectively, $-I_S Z_g'$ and $-I_R Z_R'$. The negative sign indicates that the action of the impedance, or its equivalent generator, is in the opposite direction to the assumed positive direction of current. The use of this theorem

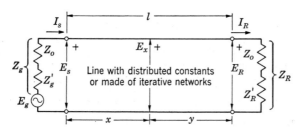

Fig. 9-2. Analysis of a line not terminated in Z_o.

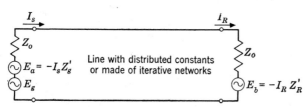

Fig. 9-3. Circuit equivalent to the network of Fig. 9-2.

reduces the line to the case of one terminated in its characteristic impedance at both ends, and the superposition theorem can now be conveniently applied, for the line terminated in Z_o represents a rather simple problem. The situation is illustrated in Fig. 9-3.

9-3. Wave Motion on Line Not Terminated in Z_o. It has been shown that a generator applied to a transmission line initiates a wave which travels in one direction, if the line is infinite, or is terminated in its characteristic impedance. It is apparent from Fig. 9-3 that the action of Z_R', that is, a termination other than Z_o, is to set up a reflected wave which will start at the receiving end and travel back towards the sending end. In the general case the voltage and current on a transmission line will be the resultant of *two* waves. If the resultant phasor voltage at any distance x from the sending end is designated by E_x and the voltage of the wave traveling in the positive direction, i.e., from left to right in Fig. 9-3, is called E_x', while the voltage traveling in the negative direction is E_x'', then at any point the phasor relation will be

$$E_x = E_x' + E_x'' \tag{9-8}$$

E'_x will be due to the two generators E_g and E_a, while E''_x will be caused by the generator E_b. It has been shown that a wave traveling in the positive x direction can be represented by the relation

$$E'_x = A_2 e^{-\gamma x} = A_2 e^{-\alpha x - j\beta x} \qquad (9\text{-}9)$$

so that a wave in the negative direction will be represented by the equation

$$E''_x = A_1 e^{\gamma x} = A_1 e^{\alpha x + j\beta x} \qquad (9\text{-}10)$$

and therefore Eq. (9-8) becomes

$$E_x = A_2 e^{-\gamma x} + A_1 e^{\gamma x} \qquad (9\text{-}11a)$$

Similarly it may be shown that the current I_x at any point of the line is given by the equation

$$I_x = B_2 e^{-\gamma x} + B_1 e^{\gamma x} \qquad (9\text{-}11b)$$

The student will observe that Eqs. (9-11a) and (9-11b) are identical to Eqs. (8-20) and (8-21), which were derived in the last chapter by setting up the differential equations for the voltage and current along the line. The solution given here is offered with the thought that it presents a better physical picture of the nature and cause of reflection.

9-4. Current in Initial and Reflected Waves. The general solution of Figs. 9-2 and 9-3 in terms of the line, generator, and load constants will now be obtained. Let

I'_S be the component of the sending-end current due to E_g and E_a (initial, or incident, wave)

I'_R be the component of the receiving-end current due to E_g and E_a (initial, or incident, wave)

I''_R be the component of the receiving-end current due to E_b (reflected wave)

I''_S be the component of the sending-end current due to E_b (reflected wave)

I'_S and I'_R are due to the initial wave traveling from left to right in Fig. 9-3, and I''_R and I''_S are due to the reflected wave traveling from right to left. Then

$$I_S = I'_S + I''_S \qquad (9\text{-}12a)$$
$$I_R = I'_R + I''_R \qquad (9\text{-}12b)$$

$$I'_S = \frac{E_g + E_a}{2Z_o} = \frac{E_g - I_S Z'_g}{2Z_o} = \frac{E_g - (Z_g - Z_o)I_S}{2Z_o}$$

$$I'_R = I'_S e^{-\gamma l} = \frac{E_g - (Z_g - Z_o)I_S}{2Z_o} e^{-\gamma l}$$

$$I''_R = \frac{E_b}{2Z_o} = -\frac{I_R Z'_R}{2Z_o} = -\frac{I_R(Z_R - Z_o)}{2Z_o} \qquad (9\text{-}13)$$

$$I''_S = I''_R e^{-\gamma l} = -\frac{I_R(Z_R - Z_o)e^{-\gamma l}}{2Z_o}$$

It would be of interest to determine the ratio of the currents in the initial and reflected waves at the point of reflection. From Eqs. (9-12b) and (9-13)

$$\frac{I''_R}{I_R} = \frac{-Z'_R}{2Z_o} = \frac{Z_o - Z_R}{2Z_o} = \frac{I''_R}{I'_R + I''_R}$$

Now from the theory of proportions, if $a/b = c/d$, then

$$\frac{a}{b-a} = \frac{c}{d-c}$$

Therefore

$$\frac{I''_R}{I'_R} = \frac{Z_o - Z_R}{2Z_o - (Z_o - Z_R)} = \frac{Z_o - Z_R}{Z_o + Z_R} \qquad (9\text{-}14)$$

It will be seen that this ratio becomes zero when $Z_o = Z_R$ and reflection is eliminated.

In the same way that the current is analyzed by the principle of superposition, it is possible to divide the voltage at any point on the line into two components: (1) the voltage in the initial wave set up by the generators E_g and E_a and traveling from left to right in Fig. 9-3; (2) the voltage in the reflected wave set up by the generator E_b and traveling from right to left in Fig. 9-3.

Let

E'_S be the component of the sending-end voltage due to E_g and E_a (initial wave)

E'_R be the component of the receiving-end voltage due to E_g and E_a (initial wave)

E''_R be the component of the receiving-end voltage due to E_b (reflected wave)

E''_S be the component of the sending-end voltage due to E_b (reflected wave)

Then

$$E_S = E'_S + E''_S \qquad (9\text{-}12c)$$
$$E_R = E'_R + E''_R \qquad (9\text{-}12d)$$

Let the voltage be assumed as positive when the upper wire of Fig. 9-2 is at a higher potential than the lower and the current be assumed as positive when it flows in the upper wire from left to right. Then, when the voltage in the initial wave is positive, it will tend to set up a positive current flowing from left to right in the upper wire, while when the voltage in the reflected wave is positive, it will tend to set up a current in the upper wire flowing from right to left, i.e., a negative current. This is also apparent from the fact that the initial wave represents a flow of energy from left to right, while the reflected wave is due to a flow of energy in the opposite direction. Therefore

$$\frac{E'_S}{I'_S} = \frac{E'_R}{I'_R} = -\frac{E''_R}{I''_R} = -\frac{E''_S}{I''_S} = Z_o \qquad (9\text{-}15)$$

This may be used with Eq. (9-14) to determine the ratio of voltages in the initial and reflected waves at the receiving end.

$$\frac{E_R''}{E_R'} = -\frac{I_R''}{I_R'} = \frac{Z_R - Z_o}{Z_R + Z_o} = \rho = |\rho|\underline{/\varphi} \tag{9-16}$$

The ratio $(Z_R - Z_o)/(Z_R + Z_o)$ is called the *reflection coefficient* and is designated by the symbol ρ.*

Equations (9-14) to (9-16) and the relations

$$I_R' = I_S' e^{-\gamma l} \qquad I_S'' = I_R'' e^{-\gamma l}$$
$$E_R' = E_S' e^{-\gamma l} \qquad E_S'' = E_R'' e^{-\gamma l}$$

are sufficient to solve almost any long-lines problem. They are so simple they can be quickly memorized, and the problems can be readily solved on a slide rule in a series of natural steps which anyone can remember. Assume that in Fig. 9-3 the following data are given: E_g, Z_S, Z_R, and the constants and length of the line. The steps are as follows:

Step 1. Determine Z_o, α, and β for the line.

Step 2. *Assume* an arbitrary voltage for E_S', say, 1 volt. Let the additional subscript 1 refer to all values obtained for this assumption.

Step 3. Find E_{R1}' from the relation $E_{R1}' = E_{S1}' e^{-\gamma l}$.

Step 4. Find E_{R1}'' from Eq. (9-16).

Step 5. Find E_{S1}'' from the relation $E_{S1}'' = E_{R1}'' e^{-\gamma l}$.

Step 6. Find I_{S1}', I_{R1}', I_{S1}'', and I_{R1}'' from Eq. (9-15).

Step 7. Find E_{S1}, E_{R1}, I_{S1}, and I_{R1} by adding their components as indicated by Eqs. (9-12).

Step 8. Determine the input impedance Z_{in} of the line from the ratio of E_{S1} to I_{S1}. When this input impedance is known, the *actual* sending-end voltage can be determined by the relation

$$E_s = \frac{E_g Z_{in}}{Z_g + Z_{in}}$$

Step 9. Multiply the values of E_{S1}, E_{R1}, I_{S2}, and I_{R1} obtained in step 7 (on the assumption of step 2 that E_S' equals 1 volt) by the ratio E_S/E_{S1} to obtain actual values of current and voltage.

If several problems are solved by this step-by-step method, the student will obtain a better understanding of the effects of reflection, attenuation, and phase shift than he will by merely substituting values in formulas.

* ASA Y10.9–1953. Prior to the adoption of this standard, Γ or $\mathbf{K}$ were frequently used, ρ being reserved for standing wave ratio. In reading the literature the student should exercise care to avoid confusing symbols used before and after the adoption of the standard.

As an example of this method of solution consider the case of a 100-mile line whose characteristics are the same as in the illustrative problem of the preceding chapter, i.e.,

$$Z_o = 689 - j175 = 711\underline{/14.23°}$$
$$\alpha = 0.00785 \text{ neper/mile}$$
$$\beta = 0.0287 \text{ radian/mile}$$

Let the terminal impedance in this case have a value

$$Z_R = 500\underline{/45°} = 353.5 + j353.5$$

The problem will be to find the voltage, current, and power in the terminating impedance. The generator will again have an induced voltage of 2 volts and an internal impedance of 600 ohms pure resistance.

$$\alpha l = 0.785 \text{ neper}$$
$$e^{\alpha l} = 2.192$$
$$\beta l = 2.87 \text{ radians} = 164.33°$$

Assume

$$E'_{S1} = 1\underline{/0} \text{ volt}$$

Then

$$E'_{R1} = \frac{1}{2.192}\underline{/-164.33°} = 0.456\underline{/-164.33°} = -0.440 - j0.123$$

$$E''_{R1} = E'_{R1} \frac{Z_R - Z_o}{Z_R + Z_o}$$

$$E''_{R1} = 0.456\underline{/-164.33°} \times \frac{353.5 + j353.5 - 689 + j175}{353.5 + j353.5 + 689 - j175}$$

$$= 0.456\underline{/-164.33°} \times \frac{626\underline{/122.43°}}{1,059\underline{/9.7°}}$$

$$= 0.456\underline{/-164.33°} \times 0.591\underline{/112.73°}$$

$$= 0.270\underline{/-51.6°} = 0.168 - j0.211$$

$$E''_{S1} = \frac{0.270\underline{/-51.6°}}{2.192\underline{/-164.33°}} = 0.123\underline{/-215.93°} = -0.100 + j0.072$$

$$I'_{S1} = \frac{1}{711\underline{/-14.23°}} = 1.407 \times 10^{-3}\underline{/14.23°} = (1.364 + j0.347) \times 10^{-3}$$

$$I''_{S1} = \frac{0.123\underline{/-215.93°} \times 1\underline{/180°}}{711\underline{/-14.23°}} = 0.173 \times 10^{-3}\underline{/-21.7°}$$

$$= (0.161 - j0.064) \times 10^{-3}$$

$$E_{S1} = 1 - 0.100 + j0.072 = 0.900 + j0.072 = 0.900\underline{/4.58°}$$

$$I_{S1} = (1.364 + j0.347 + 0.161 - j0.064) \times 10^{-3}$$

$$= (1.525 + j0.283) \times 10^{-3} = 1.55 \times 10^{-3}\underline{/10.5°}$$

$$E_{R1} = (-0.440 - j0.123 + 0.168 - j0.211) = (-0.272 - j0.334)$$

$$= 0.431\underline{/230.87°}$$

$$Z_{in} = \frac{0.900\underline{/4.58°}}{1.55 \times 10^{-3}\underline{/10.5°}} = 580\underline{/-5.92°} = 576 - j60$$

The actual value of E_S may now be determined.

$$|E_S| = \frac{2 \times 580}{|600 + 576 - j60|} = \frac{2 \times 580}{1.176} = 0.986$$

Since the original assumption ($E'_{S1} = 1$) gave a value $E_{S1} = 0.900$, the values of all computed quantities should be corrected by the ratio $0.986:0.900$ (if absolute values only are needed).

$$|E_R| = \frac{0.431 \times 0.986}{0.900} = 0.472 \text{ volt}$$

$$|I_R| = \left|\frac{E_R}{Z_R}\right| = \frac{0.472}{500} = 0.944 \times 10^{-3} \text{ amp}$$

$$P_R = |E_R| \, |I_R| \cos \theta_R = 0.472 \times 0.944 \times 0.707 \times 10^{-3}$$
$$= 0.315 \times 10^{-3} \text{ watt}$$

It would be interesting to compare the value just obtained with the approximate solution which can be obtained from Eq. (9-5).

$$|Z_g + Z_o| = |1{,}289 - j175| = 1{,}300$$
$$|Z_R + Z_o| = |1{,}042 + j178| = 1{,}059$$
$$|I_R| = \frac{2 \times 711 \times 2}{1{,}300 \times 1{,}059 \times 2.192} = 0.945 \times 10^{-3} \text{ amp}$$

This check, of course, is much better than would ordinarily be expected, but it does indicate that the approximate equation will give a very good idea of the magnitudes involved.

It is possible to set up single equations to obtain the sending and receiving currents. This can be done by substituting the values derived in Eq. (9-13) into Eqs. (9-12a) and (9-12b).

$$I_S = I'_S + I''_S = \frac{E_g - (Z_g - Z_o)I_S - I_R(Z_R - Z_o)e^{-\gamma l}}{2Z_o} \qquad (9\text{-}17a)$$

$$I_R = I'_R + I''_R = \frac{[E_g - (Z_g - Z_o)I_S]e^{-\gamma l} - I_R(Z_R - Z_o)}{2Z_o} \qquad (9\text{-}17b)$$

Solve for I_R and I_S by treating Eqs. (9-17a) and (9-17b) as simultaneous equations. Then

$$I_R = \frac{2E_g Z_o}{(Z_o + Z_R)(Z_g + Z_o)e^{\gamma l} + (Z_o - Z_R)(Z_g - Z_o)e^{-\gamma l}} \qquad (9\text{-}18a)$$

$$I_S = \frac{E_g[(Z_o + Z_R)e^{\gamma l} + (Z_o - Z_R)e^{-\gamma l}]}{(Z_o + Z_R)(Z_g + Z_o)e^{\gamma l} + (Z_o - Z_R)(Z_g - Z_o)e^{-\gamma l}} \qquad (9\text{-}18b)$$

9-5. Differential-equation Solution. It is interesting to see how the foregoing results may be checked from the differential equations which were set up for the transmission line in Chap. 8. Equations (8-20) and (8-21a) were perfectly general, having been derived with no stipulation concerning the termination at the receiving end of the line. They are repeated here for convenience with Z and Y eliminated in terms of γ and Z_o:

$$E_x = A_1 e^{\gamma x} + A_2 e^{-\gamma x} \tag{8-20}$$

$$I_x = -\frac{A_1}{Z_o} e^{\gamma x} + \frac{A_2}{Z_o} e^{-\gamma x} \tag{8-21a}$$

Since the term $A_1 e^{\gamma x}$ represents a voltage wave traveling in the negative x direction, A_1 may be identified as E_S'', the magnitude of the reflected wave, while A_2 is E_S', the magnitude of the incident wave, both at the sending end of the line. Their values in terms of known quantities may be obtained from the boundary conditions as given in Fig. 9-2.

At $x = 0$, $E_x = E_S = E_g - I_S Z_g$, $I_x = I_S$. Substituting into Eqs. (8-20) and (8-21),

$$A_1 + A_2 = E_g - I_S Z_g \qquad -\frac{A_1}{Z_o} + \frac{A_2}{Z_o} = I_S$$

Eliminating I_S and collecting terms,

$$(Z_o - Z_g)A_1 + (Z_o + Z_g)A_2 = E_g Z_o \tag{9-19}$$

At the receiving end of the line $x = l$, and

$$E_x = E_R = I_R Z_R \qquad \text{and} \qquad I_x = I_R$$

Substituting into Eqs. (8-20) and (8-21),

$$A_1 e^{\gamma l} + A_2 e^{-\gamma l} = Z_R \left(-\frac{A_1 e^{\gamma l}}{Z_o} + \frac{A_2 e^{-\gamma l}}{Z_o} \right)$$

Collecting terms,

$$(Z_o + Z_R)e^{\gamma l}A_1 + (Z_o - Z_R)e^{-\gamma l}A_2 = 0 \tag{9-20}$$

Equations (9-19) and (9-20) may be solved simultaneously for A_1 and A_2, giving

$$A_1 = \frac{E_g Z_o(Z_o - Z_R)e^{-\gamma l}}{d}$$

$$A_2 = \frac{-E_g Z_o(Z_o + Z_g)e^{\gamma l}}{d} \tag{9-21}$$

where $\qquad d = (Z_o - Z_g)(Z_o - Z_R)e^{-\gamma l} - (Z_o + Z_g)(Z_o + Z_R)e^{\gamma l}$

Substitution of Eqs. (9-21) into (8-20) and (8-21) yields

$$E_x = E_g Z_o \frac{(Z_o + Z_R)e^{\gamma(l-x)} - (Z_o - Z_R)e^{-\gamma(l-x)}}{(Z_o + Z_g)(Z_o + Z_R)e^{\gamma l} - (Z_o - Z_g)(Z_o - Z_R)e^{-\gamma l}} \tag{9-22}$$

$$I_x = E_g \frac{(Z_o + Z_R)e^{\gamma(l-x)} + (Z_o - Z_R)e^{-\gamma(l-x)}}{(Z_o + Z_g)(Z_o + Z_R)e^{\gamma l} - (Z_o - Z_g)(Z_o - Z_R)e^{-\gamma l}} \tag{9-23}$$

The quantity $l - x$ appearing in the exponents of the last two equations is simply the distance from the *receiving* end of the line to the point x and may be designated y as indicated in Fig. 9-2.

It is suggested that the student factor Eqs. (9-22) and (9-23) into the forms

$$E_x = E'_R e^{\gamma y} + E''_R e^{-\gamma y} \tag{9-22a}$$
$$I_x = I'_R e^{\gamma y} + I''_R e^{-\gamma y} \tag{9-23a}$$

and verify Eq. (9-15). Two points are of significance here. First, the incident wave "sees" an impedance Z_o at every point along the line, and the reflected wave "sees" an impedance $-Z_o$. The negative sign in the latter case is due to the assumed positive directions of current and voltage that are set up in Fig. 9-2. It will be observed that the arrow direction of I_x is to the right in the diagram while the reflected wave moves to the left.

The second point of interest is that the incident and reflected waves are mutually independent as they move along the line. This is to be expected since the transmission line is a linear system; the total current and voltage at any point along the line is the sum of the incident and reflected components in accordance with the principle of superposition.

9-6. Alternate Forms. Equations (9-22) and (9-23) give the current and voltage at any point along the line in terms of a known generator voltage E_g and its internal impedance Z_g. It often happens that other quantities are known rather than E_g and it is desirable to modify the equations accordingly. For example, the sending-end voltage E_S rather than E_g may be the known quantity. Thus if one considers Z_g to be zero, $E_g = E_S$ and the equations become

$$E_x = E_S \frac{(Z_o + Z_R)e^{\gamma y} - (Z_o - Z_R)e^{-\gamma y}}{(Z_o + Z_R)e^{\gamma l} - (Z_o - Z_R)e^{-\gamma l}} \tag{9-24}$$

$$I_x = \frac{E_S}{Z_o} \frac{(Z_o + Z_R)e^{\gamma y} + (Z_o - Z_R)e^{-\gamma y}}{(Z_o + Z_R)e^{\gamma l} - (Z_o - Z_R)e^{-\gamma l}} \tag{9-25}$$

On the other hand, measurements may be made at the *receiving* end of an actual system, in which case the equations should be stated in terms of receiving-end quantities. The necessary transformation may be brought about by letting $y = 0$ to get an expression for E_R and eliminating E_S from Eqs. (9-24) and (9-25). The student may show that the resulting equations may be written

$$E_x = \frac{I_R}{2}[(Z_o + Z_R)e^{\gamma y} - (Z_o - Z_R)e^{-\gamma y}] \tag{9-26}$$

$$I_x = \frac{I_R}{2Z_o}[(Z_o + Z_R)e^{\gamma y} + (Z_o - Z_R)e^{-\gamma y}] \tag{9-27}$$

While the foregoing line equations are quite adequate for the purposes of numerical computation, simplification of the study of certain line phenomena may result from having the equations in terms of hyperbolic functions of γy. (For discussion of hyperbolic functions refer to the

Appendix.) These may be obtained by collecting terms of Z_o and Z_R in Eqs. (9-26) and (9-27) and combining the exponentials to give

$$E_x = E_R \cosh \gamma y + I_R Z_o \sinh \gamma y \tag{9-28}$$

$$I_x = I_R \cosh \gamma y + \frac{E_R}{Z_o} \sinh \gamma y \tag{9-29}$$

9-7. Input and Transfer Impedances of Terminated Transmission Line.

In previous chapters it has been pointed out that two important properties of a four-terminal network (of which the transmission line is an example) are its input and mesh transfer impedances. These may be determined from the foregoing equations of the general line terminated in Z_R. $y = l$ defines the sending end of the line; hence from Eqs. (9-26), (9-27), and (9-16)

$$Z_{in} = \frac{E_S}{I_S} = Z_o \frac{1 + \rho e^{-2\gamma l}}{1 - \rho e^{-2\gamma l}} \tag{9-30}$$

$$Z_t = \frac{E_S}{I_R} = \frac{1}{2} [(Z_o + Z_R)e^{\gamma l} - (Z_o - Z_R)e^{-\gamma l}] \tag{9-31}$$

or in hyperbolic form

$$Z_{in} = Z_o \frac{Z_o \sinh \gamma l + Z_R \cosh \gamma l}{Z_o \cosh \gamma l + Z_R \sinh \gamma l} \tag{9-30a}$$

$$Z_t = Z_o \sinh \gamma l + Z_R \cosh \gamma l \tag{9-31a}$$

As an example of the use of the various equations that have been derived, the problem in Sec. 9-4 will be solved again, with equations first in the exponential and then in the hyperbolic form. Since generator quantities are specified, and receiving-end power, and hence E_R is required, Eq. (9-22) may be used by letting $x = l$.

$$E_R = \frac{2E_g Z_o Z_R}{(Z_o + Z_g)(Z_o + Z_R)e^{\gamma l} - (Z_o - Z_g)(Z_o - Z_R)e^{-\gamma l}}$$

From the given quantities

$Z_o + Z_g = 689 - j175 + 600 = 1{,}289 - j175 = 1{,}300/\underline{-7.74°}$

$Z_o + Z_R = 689 - j175 + 353.5 + j353.5 = 1{,}042.5 + j178.5 = 1{,}060/\underline{9.7°}$

$e^{\gamma l} = e^{\alpha l} /\underline{\beta l} = e^{0.785} \bigg/ \dfrac{\pi}{180} (2.87) = 2.192/\underline{164.2°}$

$(Z_o + Z_g)(Z_o + Z_R)e^{\gamma l} = (1.3 \times 10^3)/\underline{-7.74°} \ (1.06 \times 10^3)/\underline{9.7°} \ 2.192/\underline{164.2°}$

$\qquad = 3.02 \times 10^6/\underline{166.2°} = (-2.935 + j0.72)10^6$

$Z_o - Z_g = 689 - j175 - 600 = 89 - j175 = 196.8/\underline{-63.1°}$

$Z_o - Z_R = 689 - j175 - 353.5 - j353.5 = 335.5 - j528.5 = 626/\underline{-57.6°}$

$e^{-\gamma l} = 0.456/\underline{-164.2°}$

$(Z_o - Z_g)(Z_o - Z_R)e^{-\gamma l}$

$\qquad = (1.968 \times 10^2)/\underline{-63.1°} \ (6.26 \times 10^2)/\underline{-57.6°} \ 0.456/\underline{-164.2°}$

$\qquad = 5.64 \times 10^4/\underline{-284.9°} = (1.455 + j5.45)10^4$

$(Z_o + Z_g)(Z_o + Z_R)e^{\gamma l} - (Z_o - Z_g)(Z_o - Z_R)e^{-\gamma l}$

$\quad = (-2.935 + j0.72 - 0.01455 - j0.0545) \times 10^6 = (-2.95 + j0.665) \times 10^6$

$\qquad\qquad\qquad\qquad\qquad\qquad\qquad = 3.02 \times 10^6/\underline{167.2°}$

Substituting,

$$E_R = \frac{2(2)(7.11 \times 10^2)/-14.25°(5 \times 10^2)/45°}{3.02 \times 10^6/167.2°} = 0.471/-135.5° \text{ volts}$$

Then $\quad P_R = |E_R|^2 G_R = \dfrac{|E_R|^2 \cos \theta_R}{|Z_R|} = \dfrac{(0.471)^2(0.707)}{0.5 \times 10^3} = 0.314 \text{ mw}$

This checks the previous result.

The use of the hyperbolic forms may be demonstrated by deriving an equation, say, for I_R. Letting $x = l$ in Eq. (9-23) and collecting terms,

$$I_R = \frac{E_g}{(Z_g + Z_R) \cosh \gamma l + (Z_o + Z_g Z_R/Z_o) \sinh \gamma l}$$

From tables of circular and hyperbolic function of real numbers the following values are obtained:

$$\sinh \alpha l = \sinh 0.785 = 0.868$$
$$\cosh \alpha l = \cosh 0.785 = 1.324$$
$$\sin \beta l = \sin 164.33° = 0.270$$
$$\cos \beta l = \cos 164.33° = -0.963$$

From equations in the Appendix.

$$\begin{aligned}
\sinh \gamma l &= \sinh (\alpha l + j\beta l) \\
&= [0.868 \times (-0.963)] + j(1.324 \times 0.270) \\
&= -0.835 + j0.358 = 0.910/156.86° \\
\cosh \gamma l &= [1.324 \times (-0.963)] + j(0.868 \times 0.270) \\
&= -1.274 + j0.234 = 1.297/169.6°
\end{aligned}$$

Polar values can be obtained directly as shown in the Appendix. An alternative solution for $\sinh \gamma l$ and $\cosh \gamma l$ would be

$$\tan \beta l = \tan 164.33° = -\tan 15.67 = -0.0280$$
$$\tanh \alpha l = \tanh 0.785 = 0.656$$
$$\sinh \gamma l = \sqrt{(0.868)^2 + (0.270)^2} \Big/ \arctan \frac{-0.280}{0.656}$$
$$= 0.910/\arctan - 0.427$$

From a table of tangents running up to 90°

$$\arctan 0.427 = 23.13°$$

Since $\beta l = 164.33°$ is in the second quadrant, $\sinh \gamma l$ is in the second quadrant. Therefore

$$\sinh \gamma l = 0.910/156.87°$$

Similarly,

$$\cosh \gamma l = \sqrt{(0.868)^2 + (0.963)^2} \Big/ \arctan (-0.280 \times 0.656)$$
$$= 1.297/169.6°$$

Proceeding with the problem,

$$Z_R + Z_g = 353.5 + j353.5 + 600 = 953.5 + j353.5$$
$$= 1,046/\underline{20.3°}$$

$$Z_o + \frac{Z_R Z_g}{Z_o} = 689 - j175 + \frac{600/\underline{0°} \times 500/\underline{45°}}{711/\underline{-14.23°}}$$
$$= 902 + j190 = 923/\underline{11.88°}$$

Substituting,

$$I_R = \frac{2}{1,046/\underline{20.3°} \times 1.297/\underline{169.6°} + 923/\underline{11.88°} \times 0.910/\underline{156.87°}}$$

$$= \frac{2}{1,318/\underline{189.9°} + 838/\underline{168.75°}}$$

$$= \frac{2}{-1,300 - j229 - 822 + j164}$$

$$= \frac{2}{-2,122 - j65}$$

$$|I_R| = \frac{2}{2,123} = 0.944 \times 10^{-3}$$

$$|E_R| = |I_R| \, |Z_R| = 0.944 \times 10^{-3} \times 500 = 0.472 \text{ volt}$$

This agrees with the values obtained in the earlier solution.

9-8. Insertion Loss of Transmission Line. It was demonstrated in Chap. 6 that the insertion loss of a symmetrical four-terminal network differs from its attenuation loss unless the network is terminated in its characteristic impedance. This fact may be demonstrated for the transmission line and an interpretation given to the factors causing the difference.

Let the generator of Fig. 9-1a be connected directly to the load Z_R. Then the load current that would flow under this condition would be

$$I'_R = \frac{E_g}{Z_g + Z_R} \tag{9-32}$$

The actual load current with the line inserted between the generator and load would be found by setting $x = l$ in Eq. (9-23),

$$I_R = \frac{2E_g Z_o}{(Z_o + Z_g)(Z_o + Z_R)e^{\gamma l} - (Z_o - Z_g)(Z_o - Z_R)e^{-\gamma l}} \tag{9-33}$$

In general, if αl is large, say, at least 2.3, the second term in the denominator will be negligibly small in comparison with the first. (This was the case in the illustrative example of the last section and in the first section of this chapter.) Subject to this approximation, the insertion loss becomes by Eq. (6-62a)

$$\text{Insertion loss} = \ln \left| \frac{I'_R}{I_R} \right| = \ln \left(\frac{|Z_o + Z_g| \, |Z_o + Z_R|}{2|Z_o| \, |Z_g + Z_R|} e^{\alpha l} \right)$$

$$= \alpha l + \ln \frac{|Z_o + Z_g| \, |Z_o + Z_R|}{2|Z_o| \, |Z_g + Z_R|} \qquad \text{nepers} \tag{9-34}$$

If either Z_g or Z_R equals Z_o, the second term in Eq. (9-34) becomes zero and the insertion and attenuation losses become equal. One sees, then, that in general the insertion loss of the line differs from the line attenuation loss αl because of impedance mismatch at either the generator or the load.

These facts may be related to Eq. (9-34) by judiciously factoring its second term as in the next section.

9-9. Reflection Factor. When a line is terminated in Z_o, a wave traveling down the line is completely absorbed at the receiving end. If it is not so terminated, all the energy which arrives will not be absorbed but a return wave will be set up. Hence, a termination not equal to Z_o is said to set up reflection. This idea of reflection at a junction is carried over to any two impedances, one a supply and the other a load impedance.

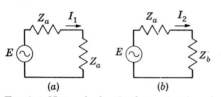

FIG. 9-4. Networks for the determination of reflection loss.

Consider Fig. 9-4. The two circuits have the same generated voltage. Circuit a shows the case where the impedances are identical, while b is for the case of a general load $Z_b \neq Z_a$. The current and volt-amperes delivered to the load of Fig. 9-4a will be

$$I_1 = \frac{E}{2Z_a}$$

$$(VA)_1 = I_1^2 Z_a = \frac{E^2}{4Z_a} \qquad (9\text{-}35)$$

The current and volt-amperes of Fig. 9-4b will be

$$I_2 = \frac{E}{Z_a + Z_b}$$

$$(VA)_2 = I_2^2 Z_b = \frac{E^2 Z_b}{(Z_a + Z_b)^2} \qquad (9\text{-}36)$$

The *transfer constant* of a properly terminated network is defined as one-half the natural logarithm of the ratio of the input and output volt-amperes. This "transfer constant" will be discussed in more detail in Chap. 11. By this definition the effect of the mismatch of Fig. 9-4b can also be expressed in terms of the transfer constant θ of a network which, when inserted between the generator and load of Fig. 9-4a, would produce the same drop in volt-amperes delivered as is produced by the mismatch. This would give

$$e^{-2\theta} = \frac{(VA)_2}{(VA)_1} = \frac{4Z_a Z_b}{(Z_a + Z_b)^2} \qquad (9\text{-}37)$$

The term *reflection factor* is applied to the ratio $e^{-\theta}$ and is designated here by the symbol k.*

$$k = e^{-\theta} = \frac{2\sqrt{Z_a Z_b}}{Z_a + Z_b} \qquad (9\text{-}38)$$

The insertion loss given by Eq. (9-34) can be written in terms of reflection factors. This equation may be rearranged as follows:

$$\text{Insertion loss} = \alpha l + \ln \left| \frac{Z_g + Z_o}{2\sqrt{Z_g Z_o}} \right| \left| \frac{Z_R + Z_o}{2\sqrt{Z_R Z_o}} \right| \left| \frac{2\sqrt{Z_g Z_R}}{Z_g + Z_R} \right|$$

$$= \alpha l + \ln \left| \frac{Z_g + Z_o}{2\sqrt{Z_g Z_o}} \right| + \ln \left| \frac{Z_R + Z_o}{2\sqrt{Z_R Z_o}} \right| - \ln \left| \frac{Z_g + Z_R}{2\sqrt{Z_g Z_R}} \right| \qquad (9\text{-}39)$$

Let k_s be the reflection factor at the sending end, k_r the reflection factor at the receiving end, and k_{sr} the reflection factor if the generator were connected directly to the load. Then

$$\text{Insertion loss} = \alpha l + \ln \left| \frac{1}{k_s} \right| + \ln \left| \frac{1}{k_r} \right| - \ln \left| \frac{1}{k_{sr}} \right| \text{ nepers} \qquad (9\text{-}40)$$

The term $\ln |1/k|$ is termed the *reflection loss*. In some cases $\ln |1/k|$ may be a negative number, in which case there is a *reflection gain*. From Eq. (9-39) it is apparent that, for the approximations used in deriving Eq. (9-34), the insertion loss of a cable in nepers equals the attenuation loss of the cable plus the reflection loss at the sending end, plus the reflection loss at the receiving end, minus the reflection loss which would occur if the generator were connected directly to the receiving load.

The actual power ratio for the two cases of Fig. 9-4 would *not* be given by the reflection factor or reflection loss. If the *power* ratio is desired

$$\frac{P_1}{P_2} = \frac{(VA)_1 \cos \theta_a}{(VA)_2 \cos \theta_b} = \frac{\cos \theta_a}{k^2 \cos \theta_b} \qquad (9\text{-}41)$$

where θ_a = angle of Z_a

θ_b = angle of Z_b

Hence, the loss in nepers introduced by changing a load impedance from Z_a to Z_b would be

$$N_{\text{nep}} = \ln \left| \frac{1}{k} \right| + \frac{1}{2} \ln \frac{\cos \theta_b}{\cos \theta_a} \qquad (9\text{-}42)$$

However, since the angles do not need to appear in the complete formula [Eq. (9-40)], the second term of Eq. (9-42) is not included in the definition of *reflection loss*.

* ASA Y10.9–1953 uses the symbol ρ for both reflection factor and reflection coefficient. To avoid confusion, in this text the reflection factor is designated k, ρ being reserved for the reflection coefficient [Eq. (9-16)].

If the approximations used in deriving Eq. (9-34) do not hold, then an additional term called the *interaction factor* must be introduced in Eq. (9-40). However, in this case it is usually more convenient to obtain the insertion loss by direct computation of the power delivered to the load with and without the network, and so this will not be treated here. The reader is referred to the works of Johnson and Shea for a treatment of this interaction factor.

9-10. Analogy of Electric Waves on Line and Water Waves in Canal. Equations (9-22a) and (9-23a) have been interpreted in terms of *traveling* electrical waves, the first term corresponding to the incident wave traveling from the generator to the load and the second term to a reflected wave initiated by reflection at Z_R and moving toward the sending end. These traveling waves have a counterpart in hydraulics, in the case of a very long, straight canal of water. If a disturbance is made at one end of the canal, waves will travel along and a set of bobs on the surface will give the instantaneous values similar to the instantaneous values of voltage and current shown in Fig. 6-7. If, however, the set of bobs is arranged so as to be moved up on rods in the water but, owing to friction, remain at the highest point of the wave after it has passed, so as to record *maximum* values, then a straight line will be obtained, similar to the values read by a voltmeter on the lossless infinite line as shown in Fig. 6-10a.

Suppose, instead of having the canal very long, a vertical dam is constructed so that the waves will strike it. There will then be a piling up of water at the dam which will start a wave back in the opposite direction.

In the same way, if the electric line is not infinitely long or terminated in its characteristic impedance but instead is open-circuited, then, when the wave strikes the end, it also will be reflected. The electric wave in traveling has half its energy stored in the magnetic field, due to the current, and half its energy stored in the electric field, due to voltage. When it strikes the open circuit, the magnetic field will collapse, for the current must become zero. But a changing magnetic field produces an electric field. It is upon this principle that all generators and transformers operate. The energy stored in the magnetic field will therefore be turned into energy in an electric field and added onto the existing field, so that the voltage at the open circuit will be increased. This increased voltage will start a wave traveling back in the opposite direction, and since there has been nothing to absorb any energy at the open circuit, the returning wave will be of the same magnitude as the original wave. As the electric field starts moving back, it will set up a magnetic field again and the energy will once more be divided equally between the two. As the electric field has simply been doubled at the instant of reflection, the voltage of the returning wave starts out in the same phase as the original wave, but the magnetic wave, and hence the current of the reflected wave, is in opposite phase to the incident wave at the open-circuited point. The total voltage and current at any point and any instant are therefore the sum of the voltages or currents of the incident and reflected waves. That the current has been reversed in phase is evident from the fact that the two current waves must add to zero at the point of open circuit and, since the two voltages are equal and do not add to zero, they must remain in phase.

This is also shown by rearranging Eq. (9-14) and substituting in the condition $Z_R = \infty$.

$$\frac{I_R''}{I_R'} = \frac{Z_o - Z_R}{Z_o + Z_R} = \frac{Z_o/Z_R - 1}{Z_o/Z_R + 1}$$

If $Z_R = \infty$,

$$\frac{I_R''}{I_R'} = -1$$

Similarly, from Eq. (9-16)

$$\rho = \frac{E_R''}{E_R'} = 1\underline{/0}$$

Now consider a periodic disturbance to be made at the mouth of the canal so that a steady state is reached with a continuous train of waves being propagated along the canal and being reflected at the dam. Then if the sliding bobs were arranged so that they would remain fixed at their highest points, it would be found that they would go through a succession of maxima and minima indicating a wave fixed in space, or simply a standing wave. The existence of standing waves on a transmission line will now be considered for the cases where Z_R corresponds to an open and a short circuit.

9-11. Open-circuited Line with Attenuation. The steady-state voltage along a transmission line is given by Eq. (9-22a), $E_x = E_R' e^{\gamma y} + E_R'' e^{-\gamma y}$. The instantaneous value of the incident component is given by

$$e_x'(y,t) = \text{Re}\ \{\hat{E}_R' e^{\gamma y} e^{j\omega t}\} = \hat{E}_R' e^{\alpha y} \cos\ (\omega t + \beta y) \qquad (9\text{-}43)$$

indicating a wave traveling in the negative y direction, and the reflected component by

$$e_x''(y,t) = \text{Re}\ \{\hat{E}_R'' e^{-\gamma y} e^{j\omega t}\} = \hat{E}_R'' e^{-\alpha y} \cos\ (\omega t - \beta y + \varphi) \qquad (9\text{-}44)$$

indicating a wave traveling in the positive y direction. If the line is terminated in an open circuit, $\rho = 1\underline{/0°}$, making E_R'' and E_R' equal and in phase. The two component waves are plotted in Fig. 9-5 for successive intervals of time for one half cycle. The second half cycle would be the same, except that all values of both the component and resultant waves would have reversed values. In Fig. 9-5F are shown the values of the resultant waves plotted on top of each other. The values which would be read by a voltmeter on the open-circuited line would correspond to the *envelope* of curve 9-5*F*, as the meter would read a value proportional to the *maximum* amplitude that ever occurs at each point. Since the maxima and minima remain fixed in position along the line, the voltmeter readings indicate the presence of a standing wave of voltage.

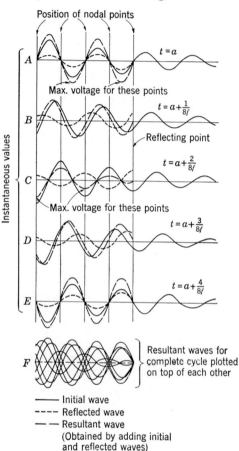

Fig. 9-5. Instantaneous distribution of voltage on a short-circuited line or current on an open-circuited line which has attenuation.

The equation for the standing wave may be derived readily from the line equations in hyperbolic form. For example, since $Z_R = \infty$ for the open-circuit termination, I_R must be zero and Eq. (9-28) reduces to

$$E_x = E_R \cosh \gamma y = E_R \cosh (\alpha y + j\beta y) \qquad (9\text{-}45)$$

Since a voltmeter reads a value proportional to the *magnitude* of the voltage, by Eq. (A-16a)

$$|E_x| = |E_R| \sqrt{\sinh^2 \alpha y + \cos^2 \beta y} \qquad (9\text{-}45a)$$

As y increases, the first term under the radical will increase continuously, while the second term will vary between the values $+1$ and 0. At first the $\cos^2$ term will predominate, but as the length is increased, the $\sinh^2$ term will become more and more important, this effect being

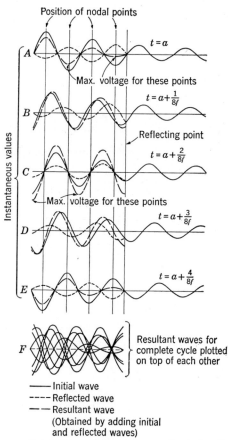

Fɪɢ. 9-6. Instantaneous distribution of current on a short-circuited line or voltage on an open-circuited line which has attenuation.

felt sooner if α is large. The fluctuation from maximum to minimum will therefore diminish as y becomes larger, as is shown on the plot B of Fig. 9-7.

If the wave is reversed by the reflection, as is the case for current on the open-circuited line, then the incident and reflected waves for one-half cycle will have the form shown in Fig. 9-6A to E. Figure 9-6F is the superposition of the resultant waves for instants differing by one-eighth cycle over a full cycle, and the effective current represented by these waves would be proportional again to the envelope of these curves, indicating a standing wave of current.   The student may obtain the expression for this envelope curve from Eqs. (9-29) and (A-15a).

It will be observed in both Figs. 9-5 and 9-6 that the instant at which the wave is a maximum at the nodes is displaced in *time* by one-fourth cycle from the instant at which the wave is a maximum at the antinodes.

In Fig. 9-7 is shown a plot of the *envelopes* of Figs. 9-5F and 9-6F to illustrate the way in which effective or maximum current and voltage will vary along the line with complete reflection.   Also plotted in this

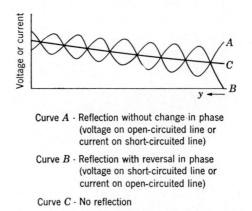

Curve *A* - Reflection without change in phase
(voltage on open-circuited line or
current on short-circuited line)

Curve *B* - Reflection with reversal in phase
(voltage on short-circuited line or
current on open-circuited line)

Curve *C* - No reflection

FIG. 9-7. Distribution of effective voltage and current along a line with attenuation.

figure is the exponential curve corresponding to the distribution for a line terminated in its characteristic impedance.   It will be seen that the fluctuations of current will behave in a manner similar to that of the voltage except that the maxima of current will be displaced one-quarter wavelength from the voltage maxima.

The input impedance of an open-circuited line will be designated by Z_{oc} and may be shown from Eqs. (9-30a), (A-3), (A-15a), and (A-16a) to be

$$Z_{oc} = Z_o \coth \gamma l \tag{9-46}$$

$$= Z_o \sqrt{\frac{\sinh^2 \alpha l + \cos^2 \beta l}{\sinh^2 \alpha l + \sin^2 \beta l}} \bigg/ \arctan (\tanh \alpha l \tan \beta l) - \arctan \frac{\tan \beta l}{\tanh \alpha l}$$
$$\tag{9-46a}$$

It will be seen that the magnitude will pass through minimum values approximately when $\cos^2 \beta l = 0$ and $\sin^2 \beta l = 1$ and will pass through maximum values approximately when $\cos^2 \beta l = 1$ and $\sin^2 \beta l = 0$.   These minimum values correspond to odd-quarter wavelengths, i.e., when

$$\beta l = (2n + 1) \frac{\pi}{2}$$

while the maximum values correspond to even-quarter wavelengths, i.e., when $\beta l = 2n\pi/2$. At lengths where either $\sin^2 \beta l = 0$ or $\cos^2 \beta l = 0$, that is, at all integral quarter wavelengths corresponding to maxima and minima of $|Z_{oc}|$,

$$\arctan \left(\tanh \alpha l \tan \beta l\right) = \arctan \frac{\tan \beta l}{\tanh \alpha l} = 0 \text{ or } \infty$$

and the angle of the hyperbolic cotangent (and hyperbolic tangent) as given in Eq. (9-46a) will be zero. The angle of Z_{oc} is then the same as that of the characteristic impedance.

9-12. Short-circuited Line with Attenuation. Equations (9-43) and (9-44) also apply to the short-circuited line provided, of course, that the proper relationship is established between E''_R and E'_R. Since $Z_R = 0$,

$$\rho = \frac{Z_R - Z_o}{Z_R + Z_o} = -1 \qquad E''_R = -E'_R \qquad I''_R = I'_R$$

Hence Fig. 9-6 applies to the voltage, and Fig. 9-5 to the current distribution on the short-circuited line. The student may derive expressions for $|E_x|$ and $|I_x|$ for the short-circuit termination as an exercise and relate the results to Fig. 9-7.

By Eq. (9-30a), Z_{sc}, the input impedance of the short-circuited line, will be

$$Z_{sc} = Z_o \tanh \gamma l = \frac{Z_o}{\coth \gamma l} \tag{9-47}$$

On comparing this to Eq. (9-46) it will be seen that the hyperbolic cotangent factor has been moved to the denominator; hence the lengths or frequencies which correspond to $|Z_{oc}|$ maxima become minima of $|Z_{sc}|$, and vice versa.

9-13. Phasor Diagram of Line Terminated in a Reactance. If the line is terminated in a pure reactance instead of a short or open circuit, there still can be no absorption of energy from the wave and total reflection will occur for this case as well. Under these circumstances both voltage and current will shift in phase on reflection, the total shift of the two being 180°, but the division of shift will depend upon the magnitude of the reactance and whether it is inductive or capacitive.

In Fig. 9-8 is shown a progressive phasor diagram for the case where the line has attenuation and is terminated in a pure reactance. The case is one where the line is less than one-fourth wavelength, and for convenience the characteristic impedance is taken as a pure resistance, that is, $\omega L/R = \omega C/G$. If, as is usually the case, the characteristic impedance has a capacitive reactance component, the current phasor in each case will be leading the voltage.

In Fig. 9-8a the voltage and current of the initial wave at a point y_1 less than one-fourth wavelength from the end are shown. In Fig. 9-8b the voltage and current in the initial wave are shown upon arriving at the end. In Fig. 9-8c are shown the shifts in voltage and current due to reflection by the reactance, this reflection being of such an amount that the phasor current and voltage due to the sum of the initial and reflected waves will have the proper ratio and phase relation as determined by the impedance of the terminating reactance. The quantitative solution for

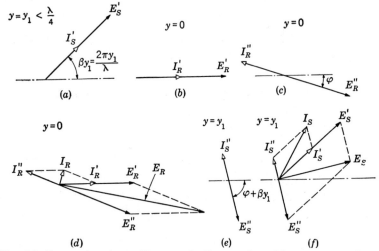

FIG. 9-8. Progressive phasor diagram of a line terminated in a pure capacitance.

the shift is given by Eq. (9-16). In Fig. 9-8d these currents and voltages at the end are added, showing that the shift assumed is for a capacitive reactance. The voltage and current of Fig. 9-8c will be retarded through an angle βy_1 and attenuated in passing back along the line until at the point y_1 they will correspond to Fig. 9-8e. In Fig. 9-8f are shown the resultant voltage and current at the point y due to the sums of the two waves obtained from Figs. 9-8a and 9-8e.

9-14. Instantaneous Voltage and Current on Terminated Line. In the hydraulic model mentioned earlier some of the energy would have been reflected and some would have gone on if, instead of having a dam to reflect the wave completely, a submerged board had been placed in the canal. The returning wave would therefore not be as strong as the original wave.

If two transmission lines of differing characteristics are joined together, or if the single line is terminated in something other than the characteristic impedance, reflection will also occur with the returning wave weaker than the incident wave. Standing waves will again be produced, but since the two waves can never cancel each other at any point, the current and voltage will never be reduced to zero even at the receiving end, but only to a minimum value.   Figure 9-9A to E shows a plot at different instants of instantaneous values of voltage for the case of partial

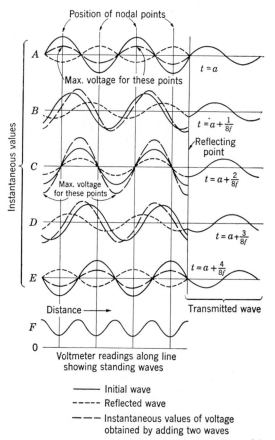

Fig. 9-9. Instantaneous distribution of voltage on a line terminated in a second line of greater characteristic impedance.   (Attenuation of lines assumed as negligible.)

reflection, where the return wave is half the magnitude of the original wave.   Figure 9-9F shows the plot of effective values of the voltage along the line and is obtained by examining curves A to E and determining the maximum voltage which ever occurs at each point of the line.   If the impedance of the termination is greater than the characteristic impedance but has the same angle, the minimum points of current and voltage will occur at the same points as the nodes of the open-circuited line, while if the terminating impedance is less than the characteristic impedance, the minimum points will correspond to the nodes of a short-circuited line. In both cases the minimum points of voltage will be maximum points of current, and vice versa.

9-15. Phasor Diagram of General Transmission Line. In Fig. 9-10 is shown the phasor diagram for the more general case of a line with attenuation, with a characteristic impedance having a capacitive component and a terminating impedance having both resistive and reactive components, not equal to the characteristic impedance. The various

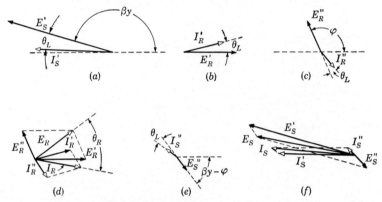

FIG. 9-10. Progressive phasor diagram of a line which has attenuation and is terminated in an impedance which has a resistive component.

steps are the same as those in Fig. 9-8. This diagram uses the data obtained from the illustrative problem which was solved earlier in the chapter.

The angle θ_L is the angle of the characteristic impedance, in this case $-14.25°$. In order to compare with other diagrams, the angle of E'_R was made equal to zero, and so the angles of Fig. 9-10 will be displaced by βy (164.33°) from the values obtained in the problem. The angle φ of Fig. 9-10c is the angle through which the voltage is rotated by reflection as obtained from Eq. (9-16) and is equal to 112.34°. The angle θ_R is the angle of the load impedance (45°).

9-16. Input Impedance vs. Frequency Characteristic of Transmission Line. In the line which has partial reflection, as the distance from the receiving end is increased, the impedance of the line will pass through maximum and minimum values at intervals of one-quarter wavelength as the reflected wave is alternately in and out of phase with the initial wave. The nearer the terminating impedance is (in both magnitude and phase) to the characteristic impedance, the smaller will be the variation in the input impedance of the line with increasing length. As in the case of total reflection, the effect of attenuation is also to reduce these variations as the length of the line is increased.

If the line is kept constant in physical length but the frequency is varied, then the electrical length, i.e., the distance measured in wavelengths, will vary and the phase relation of the incident and reflected wave will vary also. The characteristic impedance of a line changes with frequency as shown in Chap. 8, but this change progresses along a smooth

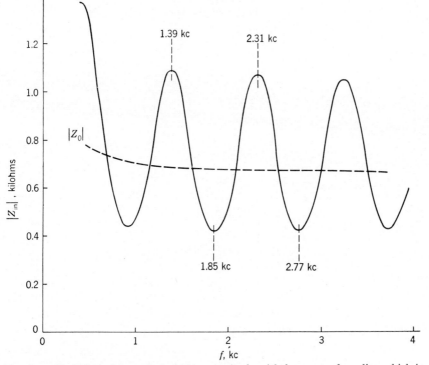

Fig. 9-11. Variation of input impedance magnitude with frequency for a line which is terminated in a short circuit.

curve. When there is reflection, however, the input impedance will fluctuate somewhat after the manner of Fig. 9-11, which is plotted for a typical open-wire line terminated in a short circuit.

9-17. Location of Unknown Reflecting Point on Transmission Line. The greater the degree of reflection and the less the attenuation between the reflecting point and the point at which the impedance is measured, the greater will be the magnitude of the impedance variation. The frequency difference between two successive maximum points is that which makes the distance to the reflection change by one-half wavelength. This impedance variation can be used to locate the distance to an irregularity such as a fault on a telephone line, if a measurement is made and a curve similar to Fig. 9-11 is plotted. Then let

f_1 = frequency for any maximum impedance point on the curve of
Fig. 9-11

f_2 = frequency for an adjacent maximum impedance point

Minimum points may be used in place of maximum points.

The difference between these two frequencies corresponds to a change in electrical length of one-half wavelength. If the distance in wavelengths for f_1 is $a\lambda_1$, then if v is the phase velocity and d the physical distance to the reflecting point,

$$d = a\lambda_1 = \frac{av_1}{f_1} \tag{9-48}$$

and also

$$d = \left(a + \frac{1}{2}\right)\lambda_2 = \left(a + \frac{1}{2}\right)\frac{v_2}{f_2} \tag{9-49}$$

From Eq. (9-48)

$$a = \frac{f_1 d}{v_1} \tag{9-50}$$

Substituting Eq. (9-50) in Eq. (9-49),

$$d = \left(\frac{f_1 d}{v_1} + \frac{1}{2}\right)\frac{v_2}{f_2}$$

$$v_1 f_2 d = v_2 f_1 d + \frac{v_1 v_2}{2}$$

$$d = \frac{v_1 v_2}{2(v_1 f_2 - v_2 f_1)} \tag{9-51}$$

If the phase velocity is substantially constant over the range from f_1 to f_2, then Eq. (9-51) becomes

$$d = \frac{v}{2(f_2 - f_1)} \tag{9-51a}$$

From Eq. (9-51) the distance to the reflecting point can be determined.

These impedance measurements give a method by which the time that a wave takes to travel to a reflecting point and return to the sending end can be accurately measured. If this time and the velocity of propagation are known, the distance to the irregularity can be determined. This corresponds to methods developed for the measurement of the height of an airplane above the surface of the earth, by using a frequency-modulated transmitter and detecting the beats between the initial and reflected waves at a receiver in the airplane.

9-18. Reflection a Cause of Distortion. Reflection may cause both frequency and delay distortion. It has been shown that the input impedance of the line will vary with frequency when an irregularity exists. This will cause a variation with frequency in the power absorbed by the line from the generator, and therefore in the power delivered by the line to the load, resulting in distortion. This variation will be greatest in long lines of low attenuation. The longer the line, the more rapidly the impedance varies with frequency, while, the lower the attenuation, the greater will be the magnitude of the variation. While long lines by themselves usually have a high attenuation, it is common practice to introduce repeaters, or amplifiers, which reduce the over-all attenuation in both directions and therefore give a reflected wave of the same order of magnitude as the initial wave.

Fig. 9-12. Photograph transmitted by wire over a line which was improperly terminated, showing the effect of echo or reflection.

Reflection also gives rise to delay distortion in the form of echoes. Both the group and phase velocity on loaded lines may be as low as 10,000 miles/sec, so that on a line 1,000 miles long $\frac{1}{10}$ sec is consumed in the passage of a signal from the sending to the receiving point. If the signal is reflected there, it will return to the starting point $\frac{1}{5}$ sec after it originally left. This interval is sufficient to cause considerable distortion of the nature of an echo, which is disconcerting to both parties conversing. Such an echo becomes visible when photographs or television signals are being sent over lines. A case of this kind is shown in the photograph of Fig. 9-12, which was sent over a line with improper termination. In the termination of a line, it is difficult to match the characteristic impedance at all frequencies, and so some reflection always occurs. It will be noticed that this type of distortion will also be most pronounced when the line is electrically long and yet has low attenuation, so that the reflected wave is appreciable in comparison with the initial wave. Because of the speed of signaling this condition may be present when a relatively long antenna leadin is mismatched at the input terminals of a television set. The light second image as shown in Fig. 9-12 is often referred to as a "ghost." However ghosts in television are more commonly due to reflections in the radio paths because of the longer distances involved.

On long lines it is now customary to place echo suppressors. In order to use vacuum-tube amplifiers on a telephone line, so that a gain will take place in both directions, it is necessary to introduce a bridge circuit which separates waves traveling in one direction from those progressing in the opposite way. This circuit was shown in Chap. 5. At such a point there exist two one-way paths, and it is possible to insert a voice-operated relay which short-circuits one path when the other is being used. This effectively suppresses any echoes.

9-19. Determination of Line Constants by Impedance Measurements. Since a reflected wave is altered by the path over which it has traveled, it might be expected that its condition upon its return would give a good deal of information upon the character of the route it has taken, just as returning travelers always have a tale to tell of the sights they have seen. This is the case if αl is not too large, and, by measuring the open- and short-circuited impedances of any length of line, the characteristics of the line can be determined.

Since

$$Z_{oc} = Z_o \coth \gamma l = \frac{Z_o}{\tanh \gamma l}$$

and

$$Z_{sc} = Z_o \tanh \gamma l$$

therefore

$$\sqrt{Z_{oc} Z_{sc}} = Z_o \tag{9-52}$$

This corresponds to Eq. (3-107) for a T section.

Similarly,

$$\tanh \gamma l = \sqrt{\frac{Z_{sc}}{Z_{oc}}} \tag{9-53}$$

If $\tanh \gamma l$ is known, γl and hence $\alpha l + j\beta l$ can be determined.

Since $\gamma = \sqrt{ZY}$ and $Z_o = \sqrt{Z/Y}$, if Z_o and γ are known, Z and Y can be determined.

$$Z_o \gamma = Z = R + j\omega L$$

$$\frac{\gamma}{Z_o} = Y = G + j\omega C$$

Solution of γ from Eq. (9-53) can be obtained by Eqs. (A-21) or may be handled in exponential form as has been demonstrated in the illustrative example in Sec. 6-4.

In computing β it must be remembered that the solution for β is multi-valued, i.e., if $\tan \beta$ is given, there will be a corresponding value for β in every alternate quadrant. For example if $\tan 2\beta = -1$, β may be $3\pi/8$,

$7\pi/8$, $11\pi/8$, ... Therefore it is necessary to know the approximate value of the phase velocity in order to select the proper quadrant for β. If this velocity is unknown, it can be determined by making a variable-frequency run similar to Fig. 9-11 and applying Eq. (9-51) with a known value of d.

Equation (A-21) is used in conjunction with Eq. (9-53) to find the value of γ from the open- and short-circuited readings, and from γ and Z_o to determine the value of the distributed constants on the line. In using Eq. (A-21) in this connection it is useful to remember from Eq. (9-53) that

$$C^2 + D^2 = \frac{|Z_{sc}|}{|Z_{oc}|}$$

As a numerical example of this method of determining the characteristics of a line from impedance measurements, let the values of a 50-mile length of line at a frequency of 796 cycles be

$$Z_{oc} = 328/-29.2°$$
$$Z_{sc} = 1{,}548/6.8°$$

Then
$$Z_o = \sqrt{Z_{oc}Z_{sc}} = 712/-11.2°$$

$$\tanh \gamma l = \sqrt{\frac{Z_{sc}}{Z_{oc}}} = 2.17/18°$$

$$\tanh \gamma l = 2.07 + j0.674$$

Then
$$C = 2.07$$
and
$$D = 0.674$$
$$C^2 + D^2 = 4.71$$

Substitute in Eq. (A-21).

$$\tanh 2\alpha l = \frac{4.14}{5.71} = 0.724$$

$$2\alpha l = 0.916$$
$$\alpha l = 0.458$$

$$\alpha = \frac{0.458}{50} = 0.00916 \text{ neper/mile}$$

and
$$\tan 2\beta l = \frac{1.348}{-3.71} = -0.364$$

This is an open-wire line with a velocity of the order of 176,000 miles/sec, and so the wavelength is of the order of 220 miles. Hence, for a 50-mile length, βl must be in the first quadrant. Therefore

$$2\beta l = 160°$$
$$\beta l = 80° = 1.40 \text{ radians}$$
$$\beta = \frac{1.40}{50} = 0.028 \text{ radian/mile}$$
$$\gamma = \alpha + j\beta = 0.00916 + j0.028 = 0.0295/71.8°$$
$$Z = Z_o\gamma = 712\backslash 11.2° \times 0.0295/71.8°$$

$$= 21\underline{/60.6°}$$
$$= 10.25 + j18.3$$
$$R = 10.25 \text{ ohms/mile}$$
$$L = \frac{18.3}{\omega} = 0.00366 \text{ henry/mile}$$
$$Y = \frac{\gamma}{Z_o} = \frac{0.0295\underline{/71.8°}}{712\overline{\rule{0pt}{1.5ex}\,11.2°}} = 41.4 \times 10^{-6}\underline{/83°}$$
$$= (5 + j41.1) \times 10^{-6}$$
$$G = 5 \times 10^{-6} \text{ mho/mile}$$
$$C = \frac{41.1 \times 10^{-6}}{\omega} = 0.00822\mu\text{f/mile}$$

While Eqs. (9-52) and (9-53) are true for any length of line, it is desirable to make measurements on a short enough section so that there is an appreciable difference between the open- and short-circuited impedances or accuracy will be lost in computing γl. If the reflected wave is so attenuated that it is negligible in comparison with the initial wave at the sending end, it is difficult to interpret its story.

PROBLEMS

9-1. A No. 19 A.W.G. cable (see Table 8-1) is 20 miles long. What will be the transmission loss of this cable at 796 cycles when inserted between a 600-ohm resistive load and a generator of 600 ohms internal resistance?

9-2. (a) Calculate the insertion loss for the generator, cable, and load of Prob. 9-1. Compute by the approximate method and by the use of initial and reflected waves. (b) Compare the values of transmission, insertion, and attenuation loss. Account for the differences.

9-3. A 20-section loaded cable has $C = 0.075$ µf/section. $R = 24.35$ ohms/ section. R of coils negligible while $L = 0.175$ henries/coil. Compute αl and βl at 1, and 3 kc by the use of Campbell's formula.

9-4. The loaded cable of Prob. 9-3 is connected between the generator and load of Prob. 9-1. Compute the insertion loss by the approximate method and by either the exponential or the hyperbolic form of line equations.

9-5. In Fig. 9-4 zero reflection loss does not necessarily specify the condition for maximum load power. Demonstrate this fact by assuming Z_b to be the conjugate of Z_a and plotting the reflection loss in decibels as a function of $\theta_a = \arctan (X_a/R_a)$.

9-6. An open-wire line 200 miles long has the following constants at 1 kc:

$$\alpha = 0.00695 \text{ neper/mile} \qquad Z_o = 731\underline{/-11.2°}$$
$$\beta = 0.036 \text{ radian/mile} \qquad Z_R = 731\underline{/0°}$$

a. Calculate and plot $|Z_{in}/Z_o|$ at 20-mile intervals.

b. At what approximate length will $|Z_{in}|$ settle down to $|Z_o|$?   Explain briefly.

9-7. Repeat Prob. 9-6 for $Z_R = 0$.

9-8. Draw phasor diagrams showing currents and voltages at the receiving end of a "lossy" line terminated in (a) a short circuit; (b) an open circuit.

9-9. Using the data of Fig. 9-11, determine the approximate distance between the fault and the sending end.   The value of β is known to be 0.07 radian/mile at 2 kc.

9-10. In the normal operating frequency range of unloaded telephone cables, $\alpha = \beta$.

a. At what values of βl is $|Z_{in}/Z_o|$ maximum if the cable is short-circuited at the receiving end?

b. Evaluate $|Z_{in}/Z_o|$ at the first two maxima and first two minima.

c. From the results of *b* what would be the shape of a curve of $|Z_{in}|$ vs. βl?

d. Explain why the technique of Prob. 9-9 could not be used to locate a fault on an unloaded cable.

9-11. It is desired to sketch the shape of $|Z_{in}|$ vs. frequency from 0.5 to 5 kc for 100 miles of the 104-mil 18-in.-spacing open-wire line of Table 8-1 terminated in an open circuit.

a. Plot the curve of $|Z_o|$, using 500-cycle increments.

b. Plot the envelope curve $|Z_{oc}|_{max}$.

c. Plot the envelope curve $|Z_{oc}|_{min}$.

d. Compute the frequencies at which $|Z_{in}|$ has the values of $|Z_{oc}|_{max}$, $|Z_o|$, and $|Z_{oc}|_{min}$, and sketch the required curve.

9-12. Explain qualitatively why no ghost results if the antenna leadin for a television set is matched in Z_o at *either* end, i.e., at the antenna or at the receiver input.

9-13. The open-circuited impedance at 796 cycles of a 5-mile length of loaded cable is

$$Z_{oc} = 1,930\underline{/68.8°} \text{ ohms}$$

The short-circuited impedance of the same 5-mile length is

$$Z_{sc} = 1,308\underline{/-76.2°} \text{ ohms}$$

Compute the value of Z_o, α, β, v_p, λ, R, L, C, and G by means of hyperbolic functions and by the direct application of the exponential form of the line equations.

Note. The approximate phase velocity is 10,000 miles/sec. This must be known in order to locate the quadrant of 2β after $\tan 2\beta$ is known.

CHAPTER 10

LINES OF LOW LOSS

The widespread use of television, radar, and other vhf and uhf services has greatly increased the interest in the behavior of transmission lines at these high frequencies. Above the audio spectrum the high losses of the telephone cable make it a poor transmission medium, and resort is generally made to open-wire lines, coaxial cables, or modifications of these types as illustrated in Fig. 8-3.

When the frequency of the signals applied to these lines becomes 50 Mc or more, the physical length of the line is usually short enough so that αl is very small, but βl, the electrical length (i.e., the number of wavelengths), may be long. This chapter considers the approximations that may be used when these conditions are satisfied. When αl is negligible, the line may be considered as lossless. When αl is very small, yet has a value which cannot be neglected, the line is considered to be of low loss. These two cases are considered in order. It is also interesting to note that at the low frequencies used in power systems (usually 60 cycles) the requirement of high power efficiency also dictates the use of lines with a low loss. Such lines are usually operated with short electrical lengths between terminal components, the longest never exceeding one-tenth of a wavelength.

10-1. The Lossless Line. The conditions for the lossless line may be stated as $R = 0$ and $G = 0$; thus from Eqs. (8-65)

$$Z = j\omega L \qquad\qquad Y = j\omega C$$

$$Z_o = R_o = \sqrt{\frac{L}{C}} \qquad \gamma = 0 + j\omega \sqrt{LC} \qquad\qquad (10\text{-}1)$$

Since $\alpha = 0$ for the lossless line, $\gamma = j\beta$ and the equations for voltage, current, and impedance may be expressed in terms of hyperbolic functions of $j\beta y$. These in turn may be reduced to circular functions of βy as described in the Appendix. Thus from Eqs. (9-28), (9-29), (9-30a), and (9-30)

$$E_x = E_R \cos \beta y + j I_R R_o \sin \beta y \qquad\qquad (10\text{-}2)$$

$$I_x = I_R \cos \beta y + j \frac{E_R}{R_o} \sin \beta y \qquad\qquad (10\text{-}3)$$

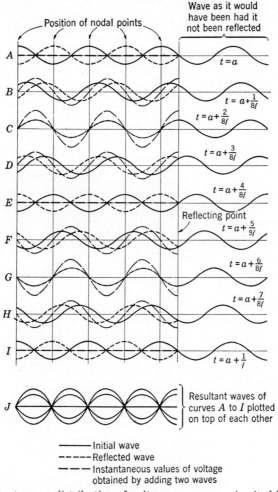

Fig. 10-1. Instantaneous distribution of voltage on an open-circuited line or current on a short-circuited line which has zero attenuation.

$$Z_{in} = R_o \frac{Z_R \cos \beta l + jR_o \sin \beta l}{R_o \cos \beta l + jZ_R \sin \beta l} \tag{10-4}$$

$$= R_o \frac{Z_R + jR_o \tan \beta l}{R_o + jZ_R \tan \beta l} \tag{10-4a}$$

$$= R_o \frac{1 + \rho e^{-i2\beta l}}{1 - \rho e^{-i2\beta l}} \tag{10-4b}$$

where y = distance measured from *receiving* end

$\quad\quad l$ = length of line

10-2. Lossless Open-circuited Line. When the line termination is an open circuit ($Z_R = \infty$), I_R must be zero and the equations for current

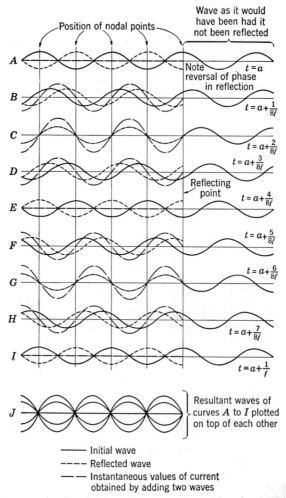

FIG. 10-2. Instantaneous distribution of current on an open-circuited line or voltage on a short-circuited line which has zero attenuation.

and voltage along the line become

$$E_x = E_R \cos \beta y = E_R \frac{e^{j\beta y} + e^{-j\beta y}}{2} \qquad (10\text{-}5)$$

$$I_x = j \frac{E_R}{R_o} \sin \beta y = \frac{E_R}{R_o} \frac{e^{j\beta y} - e^{-j\beta y}}{2} \qquad (10\text{-}6)$$

These equations show that once again the voltage and current at every point are the sum of the incident and reflected waves at that point. Furthermore the *magnitudes* of these components remain constant over the length of line and are equal to each other. The traveling voltage waves and their resultants are plotted for several successive time intervals in Fig. 10-1. The superposition of the resultant waves is shown at J, and the presence of a standing wave is again apparent.

The student may observe the close similarity between Figs. 9-5 and 10-1. They differ only in that the traveling waves maintain constant amplitude and the nodes of the standing wave have zero value for the lossless case. Similar curves are plotted for the current in Fig. 10-2.

It is apparent from Eqs. (10-6) and (10-5) that maxima of the voltage standing wave pattern are displaced one-quarter wavelength from the maxima of the current standing wave pattern since $|E_x|$ is proportional to $|\cos \beta y|$ and $|I_x|$ to $|\sin \beta y|$. It should also be noted that at every point current and voltage are in time quadrature (90° out of phase) as indicated by the factor j in the current equation. These facts are illustrated in Fig. 10-3. Since the magnitudes are shown, the upper curves of Fig. 10-1J are proportional to voltmeter

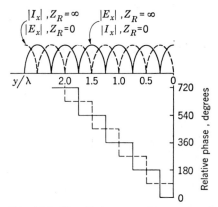

FIG. 10-3. Standing waves of current and voltage for the open- or short-circuited lossless line. Relative phase between voltage and current is shown in the lower part of the figure.

and ammeter readings along a line (voltmeter for open-circuited line, ammeter for short-circuited line.)

From Eq. (10-4) the input impedance of the lossless open-circuited line will be

$$Z_{oc} = \lim_{Z_R \to \infty} R_o \frac{1 + j(R_o/Z_R) \tan \beta l}{R_o/Z_R + j \tan \beta l} = -jR_o \cot \beta l \qquad (10\text{-}7)$$

Z_{oc} is plotted in Fig. 10-4. It will be observed that this quantity is always a pure reactance and that the line is resonant at odd-quarter wavelengths and antiresonant at even-quarter wavelengths. As explained in the last chapter, if, instead of varying the physical length of the line, it is kept constant and the frequency is varied, the electrical length of the line will be varied just as effectively as when the frequency is kept constant and the physical length of line is changed. Thus the impedance curves of Fig. 10-4 might have frequency instead of distance for their abscissa. It is possible, therefore, to obtain any reactance desired by varying either the length or the frequency.

10-3. Lossless Short-circuited Line. When the line is terminated in a short circuit, E_R must be zero and Eqs. (10-2) and (10-3) reduce to

$$E_x = jI_R R_o \sin \beta y \qquad (10\text{-}8)$$
$$I_x = I_R \cos \beta y \qquad (10\text{-}9)$$

Comparison of these equations with Eqs. (10-5) and (10-6) shows that the current on the short-circuited line behaves like voltage on the open-circuited line, and vice versa; hence Figs. 10-1 to 10-3 also apply to the short-circuited line provided that current and voltage are interchanged.

By letting $Z_R = 0$ in Eq. (10-4a), Z_{sc}, the input impedance of the short-circuited line, is found to be

$$Z_{sc} = jR_o \tan \beta l \tag{10-10}$$

and is plotted in Fig. 10-4.

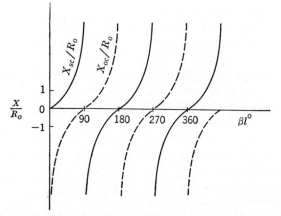

Fig. 10-4. Input impedance of an open- or short-circuited lossless line.

10-4. Standing Wave Ratio. An important quantity in the study of lossless transmission lines is the *standing wave ratio* of voltage or current along the line, which is defined as follows: "The standing wave ratio is the ratio of the amplitude of a standing wave at an anti-node to the amplitude at a node." (ASA C42 65.08.459.) It will be represented by the symbol S.* Stated more simply, the standing wave ratio is defined by the equation

$$S = \left| \frac{E'_{x,\text{max}}}{E_{x,\text{min}}} \right| \tag{10-11}$$

$|E_{x,\text{max}}|$ being the voltage magnitude at a maximum or antinode and $|E_{x,\text{min}}|$ the voltage magnitude at a minimum or node. Since the very existence of a standing wave depends upon reflection, it might be expected that S may be related to the reflection coefficient ρ, which is a measure of the degree of mismatch causing the reflection.

---

* Much of the past literature designates the standing wave ratio by ρ. This text uses S, reserving ρ for the reflection coefficient (Sec. 9-4) in accordance with ASA Y10.9–1953.

From earlier studies it is known that E_x is the sum of E'_x and E''_x. $|E_x|$ goes through successive maxima and minima because, at certain points which may be designated y_{max}, the two components add in phase to give a maximum $|E_{x,max}|$ and, at other points, say, y_{min}, they add in phase opposition to give a minimum $|E_{x,min}|$. This will now be demonstrated in a more precise fashion.

Setting $\alpha = 0$ in Eq. (9-22a) (for a *lossless* line is being considered),

$$E_x = E'_R e^{j\beta y} + E''_R e^{-j\beta y}$$

Introducing the reflection coefficient in polar form,

$$E_x = E'_R e^{j\beta y} + E'_R |\rho| e^{j\varphi} e^{-j\beta y}$$
$$= E'_R e^{j\beta y} [1 + |\rho| e^{j(\varphi - 2\beta y)}] \tag{10-12}$$
$$|E_x| = |E'_R| \, |1 + |\rho| e^{j(\varphi - 2\beta y)}| \tag{10-12a}$$

Now the voltage has a maximum magnitude when the two components are in phase, i.e., at values of $y = y_{max}$, where

$$\varphi - 2\beta y_{max} = \pm 2n\pi \qquad n = 0, 1, 2, 3, \ldots$$

or

$$y_{max} = \frac{\varphi \pm 2n\pi}{2\beta} \tag{10-13}$$

Hence *adjacent* maxima are separated by $\pi/\beta = \lambda/2$, or by a half wavelength, and have the magnitude

$$|E_{max}| = |E'_R|(1 + |\rho|) \tag{10-14}$$

Similarly the voltage has a minimum magnitude when the two components of Eq. (10-12a) are 180° out of phase, i.e., at values of $y = y_{min}$ where

$$\varphi - 2\beta y_{min} = \pm(2n + 1)\pi \qquad n = 0, 1, 2, 3, \ldots$$
$$y_{min} = \frac{\varphi \pm (2n + 1)\pi}{2\beta} \tag{10-15}$$

Thus voltage minima are spaced at intervals of $\lambda/2$ along the line, lie midway between voltage maxima, and have the value

$$|E_{min}| = |E'_R|(1 - |\rho|) \tag{10-16}$$

Then substituting Eqs. (10-14) and (10-16) into (10-11),

$$S = \frac{1 + |\rho|}{1 - |\rho|} \tag{10-17}$$

It should be observed that S is a real, rather than a complex, quantity and has a minimum value of unity.

The foregoing results may be used to check the standing wave of voltage for the open-circuited lossless line which is plotted in Fig. 10-3. For this case $Z_R = \infty$, and $\rho = 1\underline{/0^\circ}$ as may be seen from Eq. (9-16). Then, by Eq. (10-17), $S = \infty$. Furthermore the first voltage maximum occurs at

$$y_{max} = \frac{\varphi}{2\beta} = 0$$

and the first voltage minimum occurs at

$$y_{min} = \frac{\pi}{2\beta} = \frac{\pi}{2}\frac{\lambda}{2\pi} = \frac{\lambda}{4}$$

As exercises, the student may relate S to I'_R and I''_R and verify the standing current wave patterns for the open- and short-circuited cases.

The standing wave pattern along the transmission line may be determined experimentally by taking readings of voltage with a high-impedance vacuum-tube voltmeter. It will be shown in subsequent sections that sufficient information, namely, S and y_{max} or y_{min}, may be obtained from these measurements to determine the value of Z_R/R_o.

10-5. Lossless Line Terminated in Resistance. The previous discussions of the lossless line have been confined to an open- or short-circuit termination. To generalize these results, consider the case where the line is terminated in a pure resistance so that $Z_R = R_R + j0$, and let $R_R/R_o = r_r$. Then r_r is the value of R_R normalized with respect to the characteristic impedance R_o.

Before considering this case in detail it is instructive to make some predictions. First, if $r_r \neq 1$, that is, if $R_R \neq R_o$, reflection occurs at the termination and standing waves of current and voltage will exist along the line. Second, the standing wave ratio and the location of the voltage maxima and minima may be determined. By Eq. (9-16)

$$\rho = \frac{R_R/R_o - 1}{R_R/R_o + 1} \qquad Z_R = R_R + j0$$

Introducing r_r

$$\rho = \frac{r_r - 1}{r_r + 1} \qquad\qquad (10\text{-}18)$$

Two possibilities may be considered, depending upon whether r_r is greater than or less than unity.

If $r_r > 1$, or $R_R > R_o$, Eq. (10-18) may be written

$$\rho = \frac{r_r - 1}{r_r + 1}\underline{/0^\circ} \qquad\qquad (10\text{-}19)$$

therefore

$$\varphi = 0$$

and from Eq. (10-13) it is apparent that the first voltage maximum will be located at the receiving end or in general $y_{max} = n\lambda/2$. This result may be checked intuitively, for in the limit as $R_R \to \infty$, this case must reduce to the open-circuited line. Furthermore, substituting for $|\rho|$ from Eq. (10-19) into Eq. (10-17),

$$r_r > 1 \qquad S = r_r \qquad (10\text{-}20)$$

One concludes, therefore, that the standing wave ratio is equal to the normalized load resistance and a voltage maximum occurs at the load when a lossless line is terminated in a resistance greater than R_o.

On the other hand, if $R_R < R_o$, $r_r < 1$ and Eq. (10-18) may be written

$$\rho = -\frac{1 - r_r}{1 + r_r} = \frac{r_r - 1}{r_r + 1} \underline{/180°} \qquad \varphi = 180° \qquad (10\text{-}21)$$

Under this condition, Eq. (10-15) shows that a voltage minimum occurs at the load. Furthermore Eq. (10-17) shows the standing wave ratio to be

$$r_r < 1 \qquad S = \frac{1}{r_r} \qquad (10\text{-}22)$$

It follows, then, that, if the voltage standing wave pattern indicates a voltage maximum or minimum at the load, the termination is a pure resistance. If the load voltage is a maximum, $R_R = SR_o$, while if it is a minimum, $R_R = R_o/S$.

With these predictions completed it is of interest to consider the shape of the standing wave pattern along the line. Substituting

$$I_R R_o = E_R \frac{R_o}{R_R} = \frac{E_R}{r_r}$$

into Eq. (10-2),

$$E_x = E_R \left(\cos \beta y + j \frac{1}{r_r} \sin \beta y \right) \qquad (10\text{-}23)$$

or, taking magnitudes,

$$|E_x| = |E_R| \sqrt{\cos^2 \beta y + \frac{1}{r_r^2} \sin^2 \beta y} \qquad (10\text{-}23a)$$

Equation (10-23a) may be reduced into terms involving only constants and $\sin^2 \beta y$ to verify the predictions made above. A more useful approach, however, consists in plotting E_x/E_R in the complex plane such that the imaginary part of E_x/E_R is plotted against the real part with βy as the variable, to obtain the locus of the voltage ratio. (The student should observe that this is not a new technique; it corresponds to plotting the locus of an impedance in the complex plane. See Chap. 4.)

Thus let U and V be defined by

$$\frac{E_x}{E_R} = U + jV = \cos \beta y + j \frac{1}{r_r} \sin \beta y \qquad (10\text{-}23b)$$

Then
$$U = \cos \beta y \qquad r_r V = \sin \beta y$$

Squaring and adding,

$$U^2 + r_r{}^2 V^2 = 1$$

Rearranging,

$$\left(\frac{U}{1}\right)^2 + \left(\frac{V}{1/r_r}\right)^2 = 1 \tag{10-24}$$

Equation (10-24) plots as an ellipse, centered on the origin and with semiaxes 1 and $1/r_r$ as shown in Fig. 10-5a and b. It should be noted

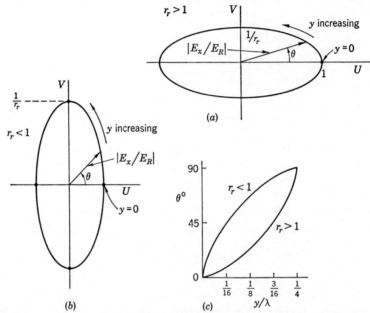

(a)

(b)   (c)

FIG. 10-5. Locus of E_x/E_R for a lossless line terminated in a pure resistance $R_R = r_r R_o$. (a) $r_r > 1$. (b) $r < 1$. (c) Angle of E_x/E_R.

that θ, the angle of E_x/E_R, whose tangent is V/U, is not a linear function of y but, rather, varies in the manner sketched in Fig. 10-5c. The actual standing wave pattern may be obtained by plotting the length of $|E_x/E_R|$ against y. Typical curves for $r_r - \frac{1}{2}$ and 2 are shown in Fig. 10-6. It will be observed that S has the same value in both cases. Figure 10-6 shows that the maximum rate of change of voltage in the standing wave pattern occurs near the voltage minima rather than the voltage maxima. For this reason, minima, being sharper, are easier to locate accurately with a voltmeter than are the maxima when standing wave measurements are made on the line.

This fact may also be verified by a careful consideration of the phasor diagrams of voltage along the line. As long as standing waves are present, i.e., if $r_r \neq 1$, $|E_R''| < |E_R'|$, and from Eq. (9-22)

$$E_x = E_R' e^{i\beta y} + E_R'' e^{-i\beta y}$$

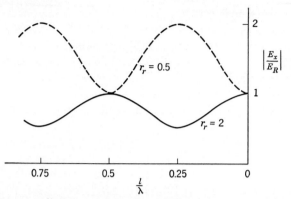

FIG. 10-6. Voltage standing wave pattern for a lossless line terminated in $r_r = R_R/R_o = 2$ and 0.5. The same value of E_R is assumed in both cases.

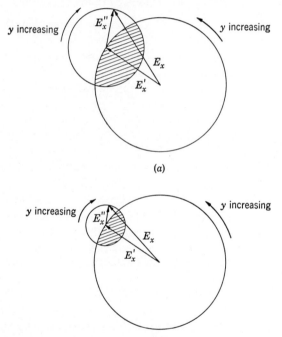

FIG. 10-7. Voltage phasor diagrams for the lossless line terminated in a pure resistance. r_r is smaller at b than in a.

Then, at some arbitrary point spaced y from the receiving end, the complex voltages will add as shown in Fig. 10-7a. As y changes, the component phasors will rotate in the directions indicated.

The unshaded sector of the smaller circle defines the condition $|E_x| > |E'_R|$ and so corresponds to a region of maximum voltage. On the other hand, the shaded sector corresponds to a region of minimum voltage.

Since the latter sector corresponds to a smaller change in y, the voltage minimum will be narrower, or "sharper," than the voltage maximum.

The phasors are drawn in Fig. 10-7b for a value of r_r nearer unity than in Fig. 10-7a. It may be seen that, while the voltage minimum is still sharper than the maximum, it is so to a lesser degree than in the first case. In the limit as $r_r = 1$, the small circle vanishes and there are no maxima and minima. As might be expected a "flat" line results because the termination is R_o.

10-6. Input Impedance with Resistive Termination. The input impedance for a lossless line terminated in a pure resistance of normalized value $r_r = R_R/R_o$ may be calculated from Eqs. (10-4a) and (10-4b). For example, if we let $Z_R = r_r R_o$, Eq. (10-4a) becomes

$$Z_{in} = R_o \frac{r_r + j \tan \beta l}{1 + j r_r \tan \beta l} \tag{10-25}$$

Thus in general Z_{in} will be complex except at certain lengths of line.

If $\tan \beta l = 0$, corresponding to electrical line lengths of $n\lambda/2$, Z_{in} becomes real and has the value $r_r R_o = R_R$. Furthermore, if $\tan \beta l \to \infty$, corresponding to electrical lengths of $(2n + 1)\lambda/4$, Z_{in} is real again and has the value $R_o/r_r = R_o^2/R_R$. From these data the student may verify that for a lossless line terminated in a pure resistance R_R: (1) impedance maxima occur at voltage maxima and are purely resistive with value SR_o; (2) impedance minima occur at voltage minima and are purely resistive with value R_o/S.

10-7. The Bicircular Impedance Chart. Rather than calculate the value of Z_{in} at other points along the line, it is convenient to show that the impedance locus as l varies from zero on up is a circle which may be used to compute Z_{in}. It is desirable, however, to divide Z_{in} by R_o so that the circle diagram will be in normalized form, which is applicable to any lossless line regardless of its characteristic impedance value. Small letters may be used to indicate normalized values so that

$$z_{in} = r_{in} + j x_{in} = \frac{Z_{in}}{R_o} \qquad z_r = r_r + j x_r = \frac{Z_R}{R_o}$$

The circle diagram for z_{in} will be derived graphically by the use of geometric inversion, which was described in Chap. 4. For this reason it is convenient to rearrange Eq. (10-25) in such a manner that the coefficient of $1/(1 + j r_r \tan \beta l)$ is a constant. This may be brought about by adding and subtracting $1/r_r$.

$$
\begin{aligned}
z_{in} &= \left(\frac{r_r + j \tan \beta l}{1 + j r_r \tan \beta l} - \frac{1}{r_r} \right) + \frac{1}{r_r} \\
&= \frac{r_r - 1/r_r}{1 + j r_r \tan \beta l} + \frac{1}{r_r}
\end{aligned} \tag{10-26}
$$

Now this equation in effect says to multiply the reciprocal of $1 + jr_r \tan \beta l$ by $r_r - 1/r_r$ and to add $1/r_r$ to the product. These steps are carried out in Fig. 10-8. For a fixed termination r_r is constant, and βl is variable; thus Fig. 10-8a shows $1 + jr_r \tan \beta l$. The student should remember that

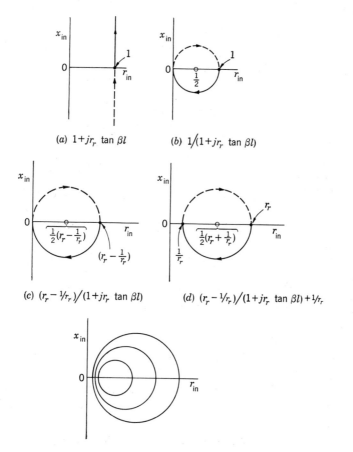

(a) $1+jr_r \tan \beta l$ (b) $1/(1+jr_r \tan \beta l)$

(c) $(r_r - 1/r_r)/(1+jr_r \tan \beta l)$ (d) $(r_r - 1/r_r)/(1+jr_r \tan \beta l) + 1/r_r$

(e) Family of constant-S curves

FIG. 10-8. Development of the curves of constant standing wave ratio for the bicircular chart. See text for explanation.

the tangent is periodic; hence, as l increases, the quantity will always move upward along the vertical line reaching ∞ at $\beta l = \pi/2$ and then returning from $-\infty$ to move upward again, reaching $+\infty$ again at $\beta l = 3\pi/2$, etc. The lower half of the line is dotted to enable the student to follow the changes of sign in the subsequent steps.

At b in the figure the reciprocal is formed by the process of geometric inversion. Steps c and d are self-explanatory, but it should be noticed that the center of the circle in d lies at

$$\frac{1}{2}\left(r_r - \frac{1}{r_r}\right) + \frac{1}{r_r} = \frac{1}{2}\left(r_r + \frac{1}{r_r}\right)$$

and the circle intersects the real axis at a maximum value of

$$\left(r_r - \frac{1}{r_r}\right) + \frac{1}{r_r} = r_r$$

and at a minimum value of $1/r_r$; hence the radius of the circle is

$$r = \frac{1}{2}\left(r_r - \frac{1}{r_r}\right)$$

The circle of Fig. 10-8d corresponds to a fixed value of r_r and hence to a fixed value of S, the standing wave ratio. Different terminating resistances correspond to different values of S and yield the family of constant-S circles sketched at e. By Eqs. (10-20) and (10-22)

$$S = r_r \text{ if } r_r \geq 1 \qquad \text{and} \qquad S = \frac{1}{r_r} \text{ if } r_r < 1$$

Hence the abscissa lying to the right of 1 provides a direct scale of standing wave ratios.

Now for these curves to be useful in the computation of input impedance, they must be calibrated in terms of line length l or βl, so that the input impedance corresponding to a specific length may be identified. It will now be demonstrated that loci of constant values of βl, with r_r as the variable, are also circles, but centered on the imaginary, rather than the real, axis. To do this, it is desirable to rearrange Eq. (10-25) so that the coefficient of $1/(1 + jr_r \tan \beta l)$ is again a constant in terms of a specified value of βl. This may be brought about by adding and subtracting $j/\tan \beta l$.

$$z_{tn} = \left(\frac{r_r + j \tan \beta l}{1 + jr_r \tan \beta l} + \frac{j}{\tan \beta l}\right) - \frac{j}{\tan \beta l}$$
$$= \frac{\tan \beta l + 1/\tan \beta l}{r_r \tan \beta l - j} - \frac{j}{\tan \beta l}$$

Again, the indicated steps are illustrated in Fig. 10-9. Figure 10-9a shows the plot of $r_r \tan \beta l - j$, r_r being the variable. The reciprocal is plotted by geometric inversion at b, the result multiplied by $\tan \beta l + 1/\tan \beta l$ at c, and $-j/\tan \beta l$ added at d.

As shown at d, the center of the semicircle lies on the imaginary axis at

$$\frac{1}{2}\left(\tan \beta l + \frac{1}{\tan \beta l}\right) - \frac{1}{\tan \beta l} = \frac{1}{2}\left(\tan \beta l - \frac{1}{\tan \beta l}\right) = -\frac{1}{\tan 2\beta l}$$

and the circle radius is

$$\frac{1}{2}\left(\tan \beta l + \frac{1}{\tan \beta l}\right) = \frac{1}{\sin 2\beta l}$$

The last two steps indicated may be proved by trigonometric identities. The circle of Fig. 10-9d corresponds to a fixed value of βl. Different values of βl will have similar circular loci; thus e shows the family of

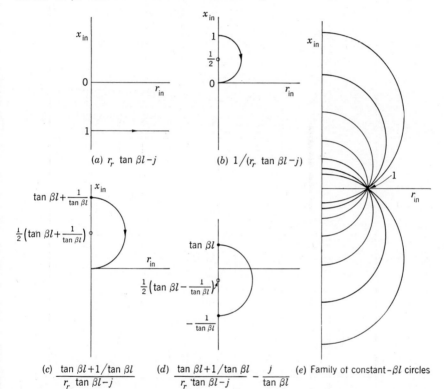

(a) $r_r \tan \beta l - j$

(b) $1/(r_r \tan \beta l - j)$

(c) $\dfrac{\tan \beta l + 1/\tan \beta l}{r_r \tan \beta l - j}$

(d) $\dfrac{\tan \beta l + 1/\tan \beta l}{r_r \tan \beta l - j} - \dfrac{j}{\tan \beta l}$

(e) Family of constant-βl circles

FIG. 10-9. Development of the curves of constant βl for the bicircular chart. See text for explanation.

curves from $\beta l = 0$ to $180°$. Since z_{in} is periodic at intervals of $180°$ of βl, additional curves are not required.

The two families of curves of Figs. 10-8e and 10-9e corresponding to constant S and constant βl, respectively, may be superposed on a set of rectangular z coordinates to give the so-called "bicircular chart" of Fig. 10-10.[1] This chart may be used to calculate the input impedance of a

[1] The student who is familiar with elementary field theory may recognize the two sets of orthogonal curves to be identical to one-half the field pattern around a pair of charged, long, parallel conductors. In this case the lines of electric potential correspond to the constant-S curves and the electric field intensity to the constant-βl curves.

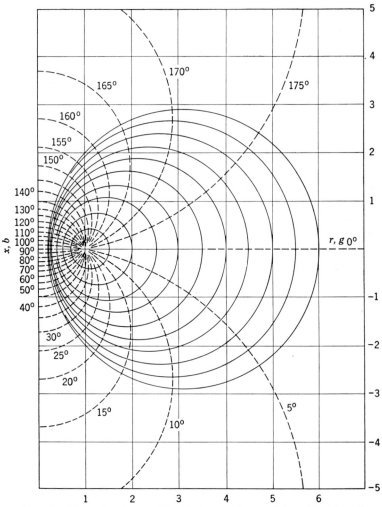

FIG. 10-10. The bicircular chart. The chart may be used for either impedance or admittance in solving lossless-line problems. (Solid constant-S curves are identified by their intersection with the horizontal axis.)

lossless line of any length terminated in a pure resistance, provided, of course, that the normalized values lie on the chart. This will now be demonstrated.

A lossless line of length 0.695 m is terminated in $Z_R = 250 + j0$ ohms, $R_o = 100$ ohms, and $\lambda = 10$ m. Find S, ρ, and Z_{in}.

Converting Z_R to normalized units,

$$z_r = \frac{Z_R}{R_o} = \frac{250 + j0}{100} = 2.5 + j0$$

Enter the chart at z_r. This point lies on the real axis at $r_r = 2.5$. Since $r_r > 1$, $S = r_r$.

ρ, the reflection coefficient, cannot be determined directly from the chart, but it may be calculated.

$$\rho = \frac{z_r - 1}{z_r + 1} = \frac{2.5 + j0 - 1}{2.5 + j0 + 1} = \frac{1.5\underline{/0°}}{3.5\underline{/0°}} = 0.429\underline{/0°}$$

Converting l to degrees,

$$\beta l = \frac{360}{\lambda} l = \frac{360 \times 0.695}{10} = 25°$$

Enter the chart at z_r, and rotate *clockwise* 25° on the $S = 2.5$ circle, and read $z_{in} = 1.3 - j1.05$. Converting to ohms

$$Z_{in} = R_o z_{in} = 130 - j105 \text{ ohms}$$

The next example illustrates how the chart may be used in conjunction with standing wave measurements made on the line.

Measurements are made on a parallel-wire line which is fabricated from copper tubing of $\frac{1}{4}$ in. radius, spaced 3.055 in. on centers. A voltage minimum occurs at the load, and the standing wave ratio is measured to be 3. The distance between adjacent voltage minima is 26 in., and the line is 9 ft long. Determine λ, Z_R, and Z_{in}.

Since adjacent minima are spaced a half wavelength apart,

$$\lambda = \frac{2 \times 26}{12} = 4.34 \text{ ft}$$

Locate the $S = 3$ circle. A voltage minimum corresponds to an impedance minimum; hence read z_r at the *left-hand* intersection of the circle and the real axis. Read $z_r = 0.333 + j0$. R_o is required to convert this to the unnormalized value. By Prob. 8-2

$$R_o = 276 \log \frac{s}{r} = 276 \log \frac{3.055}{0.25} = 276 \log 12.22$$
$$= 276 \times 1.088 = 300 \text{ ohms}$$

Then

$$Z_R = R_o z_r = 300(0.333 + j0) = 100 + j0 \text{ ohms}$$

To find Z_{in}, enter the chart at z_r, and rotate βl degrees on the $S = 3$ circle.

$$\beta l = \frac{360 l}{\lambda} = \frac{360 \times 9}{4.34} = 748°$$

Since the chart is periodic at intervals of 180°, subtract $4 \times 180 = 720°$, giving 28°. Therefore enter the chart at z_r, rotate clockwise to $90° + 28° = 118°$ on the $S = 3$ circle, and read $z_{in} = 0.43 + j0.3$. Convert to ohms.

$$Z_{in} = R_o z_{in} = 300(0.43 + j0.3) = 129 + j90 \text{ ohms}$$

It will be demonstrated later that the bicircular chart may also be used if Z_R is complex, rather than purely resistive.

10-8. Lossless Line Terminated in a Complex Impedance. When the lossless line is terminated in a complex impedance Z_R, different from R_o, reflection again occurs and the reflection coefficient ρ will be complex. The results of the previous sections may be used to determine the standing wave patterns along the line as will be demonstrated in an illustrative example later in the section. It should be noticed, however, that since

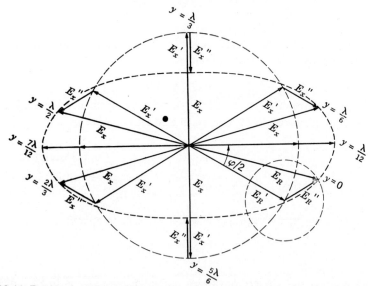

Fig. 10-11. Progressive phasor diagram for voltage along a lossless line terminated in a complex impedance Z_R. The locus is an ellipse whose major axis is inclined at an angle $\varphi = \arg \rho$ to the reference.

$\varphi (= \arg \rho)$ is not zero or 180° in this case, neither a voltage maximum nor a voltage minimum occurs at the receiving end.

It is of interest to obtain the locus of E_x in the complex plane for the general termination as y is varied. While it is possible to obtain an analytical expression for the locus by methods used in earlier sections, the shape of the curve may be obtained by drawing phasor diagrams of voltage for progressive points along the line, beginning at the termination. The method is illustrated in Fig. 10-11 where E_R' is chosen to be the reference and ρ is assumed to have the value $0.5 / 60°$. The student should note that the incident component $E_x' = E_R' e^{j\beta y}$ rotates counterclockwise with increasing y (motion toward the sending end), while the reflected component $E_x'' = E_R'' e^{-j\beta y}$ rotates clockwise with increasing y. The figure shows the locus to be an ellipse as it was for the resistive termination, but here the major axis is inclined $\varphi°(= \arg \rho)$ relative to the reference. The actual voltage standing wave pattern could be obtained by taking the length of $|E_x|$ on the ellipse and plotting it against a linear scale of y.

A lossless line is driven with a signal such that $\lambda = 1$ m. $E_R = 10/0°$ volts. $Z_R = 100 - j50 = 111.9/-26.58°$ ohms. $R_o = 300/0°$ ohms. Calculate data for sketching the current and voltage standing wave patterns.

By Eq. (9-16)

$$\rho = \frac{Z_R - R_o}{Z_R + R_o} = \frac{100 - j50 - 300}{100 - j50 + 300} = \frac{-200 - j50}{400 - j50}$$

$$= \frac{206/194.02°}{404/-7.12°} = 0.511/201.14° = -0.476 - j0.184$$

Find E'_R by letting $y = 0$ in Eq. (10-12).

$$E'_R = \frac{E_R}{1 + \rho} = \frac{E_R}{1 - 0.476 - j0.184} = \frac{E_R}{0.524 - j0.184}$$

$$= \frac{10/0°}{0.555/-19.38°} = 18.01/19.38° \text{ volts}$$

By Eq. (10-13) the first voltage maximum occurs at

$$y_{max} = \frac{\varphi}{2\beta} = \frac{\varphi\lambda}{2 \times 360} = \frac{201.14 \times 1}{2 \times 360} = 0.279 \text{ meter}$$

Successive voltage maxima will be spaced at intervals of a half wavelength from this value.

By Eq. (10-15) the first voltage minimum occurs at

$$y_{min} = y_{max} - \frac{\lambda}{4} = 0.279 - 0.25 = 0.029 \text{ meter}$$

By Eqs. (10-14) and (10-16)

$$|E_{max}| = |E'_R|(1 + |\rho|) = 18.01 \times 1.511 = 27.2 \text{ volts}$$
$$|E_{min}| = |E'_R|(1 - |\rho|) = 18.01 \times 0.489 = 8.8 \text{ volts}$$

By Eq. (10-17)

$$S = \frac{1 + |\rho|}{1 - |\rho|} = \frac{1.511}{0.489} = 3.09$$

The currents may be handled in a similar manner. By Eq. (9-15)

$$I'_R = \frac{E'_R}{R_o} = \frac{18.01/19.38°}{3 \times 10^2/0°} = 60/19.38° \text{ ma}$$

$$|I_x| = I'_R e^{j\beta y}(1 - |\rho|e^{j(\varphi - 2\beta y)})$$
$$|I_{max}| = |I'_R|(1 + |\rho|) = 60 \times 1.511 = 90.7 \text{ ma}$$
$$|I_{min}| = \frac{|I_{max}|}{S} = \frac{90.7}{3.09} = 29.35 \text{ ma}$$

The student may show that current minima occur at points of maximum voltage and that current maxima occur at points of minimum voltage and that E_x and I_x are in phase at these points.

10-9. Input Impedance with Complex Termination. It was demonstrated in Sec. 10-7 that the bicircular chart may be used to determine the input impedance of a lossless line terminated in a pure resistance. The question now arises: "Can the chart also be used if Z_R is complex rather than real?" This question may be answered by considering a specific problem.

A line of length l is terminated in an impedance of normalized value $z_r = 1.3 - j1.05$ as shown in Fig. 10-12a, and it is required to find the normalized input impedance z_{in}. Reference to the first illustrative example in Sec. 10-7 shows, however, that, if a line of length l_1, corresponding

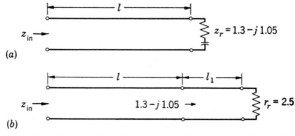

FIG. 10-12. The load z_r of a is replaced by a line of length l, terminated in a resistance, and whose normalized input impedance equals z_r of a.

to an electrical length $\beta l_1 = 25°$, is terminated in a pure resistance $r_r = 2.5$, its input impedance is $z_{in} = 1.3 - j1.05$. The thought then occurs that for purposes of analysis the actual terminating impedance in Fig. 10-12a may be replaced by the equivalent section of line terminated in $r_r = 2.5$ as shown at b. This is now a familiar problem: a line of length $l + l_1$ is terminated in a pure resistance, and the bicircular chart can be used to determine z_{in}.

Actually, once this concept has been established, it is no longer necessary to go through the intermediate step of replacing z_r by the equivalent line and resistance load. One need only enter the chart at z_r and rotate clockwise βl degrees on a circle of constant S and read z_{in}.

It may also be demonstrated that in cases where z_r is complex the chart may also be used to determine φ, the angle of the reflection coefficient ρ. By Eq. (10-13) the first voltage maximum occurs at

$$y_{max} = \frac{\varphi}{2\beta} \qquad \text{or} \qquad \varphi = 2\beta y_{max} \qquad (10\text{-}27)$$

Reference to Fig. 10-10 shows, however, that the circles of constant βl on the bicircular chart have fixed calibrations which may not coincide with the actual values of βl in a specific problem. This is shown more clearly in Fig. 10-13. At z_r, actual $\beta y = 0$, but the chart indicates a value, say, $(\beta y')_r$. Also, at the first maximum of voltage which corresponds to an impedance maximum, actual $\beta y = \beta y_{max}$, but the indicated value is $\beta y' = 0$. Thus, equating differences between actual and indicated values,

$$\beta y_{max} - 0 = 0 - (\beta y')_r$$

Substituting into Eq. (10-27),

$$\varphi = -2(\beta y')_r \tag{10-27a}$$

This point, along with the general use of the chart, will be illustrated in an example.

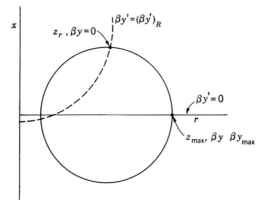

FIG. 10-13. Method of determining φ on the bicircular chart. Primed quantities refer to chart calibrations of βl.

Determine S, ρ, and Z_{in} for the following situation:

$$\lambda = 10 \text{ ft} \qquad R_o = 100 \text{ ohms}$$
$$l = 0.555 \text{ ft} \qquad Z_R = 140 - j120 \text{ ohms}$$

Normalize Z_R.

$$z_r = \frac{Z_R}{R_o} = 1.4 - j1.2$$

Convert l to degrees.

$$\beta l = \frac{360l}{\lambda} = \frac{360 \times 0.555}{10} = 20°$$

Enter the chart (Fig. 10-10) at z_r. Figure 10-14 illustrates the points and loci of interest. This point for z_r lies at the intersection of the $S = 2.8$ and $\beta l = 22.5°$ circles. Thus $S = 2.8$.

$$(\beta l')_r = 22.5° \qquad \varphi = -2(\beta l')_r = -45°$$

$|\rho|$ cannot be obtained from the chart directly; hence, calculating,

$$|\rho| = \frac{S - 1}{S + 1} = \frac{2.8 - 1}{2.8 + 1} = \frac{1.8}{3.8} = 0.474$$

To find z_{in}, enter the chart at z_r, and rotate *clockwise* 20°, or to an indicated value of $22.5 + 20 = 42.5°$, and read

$$z_{in} = 0.68 - j0.82$$

Then $$Z_{in} = R_o z_{in} = 68 - j82 \text{ ohms}$$

The student should observe that, in using the bicircular chart, motion

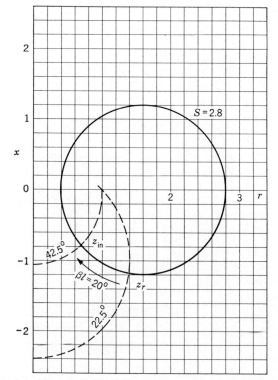

Fig. 10-14. A portion of the bicircular chart used in the illustrative example.

toward the generator, that is, l increasing, corresponds to *clockwise* rotation on a constant-S circle. By the same token, motion toward the load corresponds to *counterclockwise* rotation. The following problem indicates this principle:

The standing wave ratio on a lossless line is measured as 1.5 with the first voltage minimum lying 60 electrical degrees from the termination. Find the normalized value of terminating impedance.

The first voltage minimum corresponds to an impedance minimum which must be on the real axis of the chart between 0 and 1. Therefore enter the chart at the left-hand intersection of the real axis and the $S = 1.5$ circle. The indicated $\beta l'$ is 90°. Rotate *toward the load* (counterclockwise) 60° to an indicated value $\beta l' = 90° - 60° = 30°$, and read $z_r = 1.14 - j0.42$.

10-10. Input Admittance of Lossless Line. It is frequently convenient to work problems in terms of admittance rather than impedance. The necessary relationships for the lossless line will now be derived. Again small letters may be used for normalized values, so that

$$y = \frac{Y}{G_o} = YR_o = \frac{R_o}{Z} = \frac{1}{z}$$

Then substituting $z_{in} = 1/y_{in}$ and $z_r = 1/y_r$ into the normalized form of Eq. (10-4a), viz.,

$$z_{in} = \frac{z_r + j \tan \beta l}{1 + j z_r \tan \beta l} = r_{in} + j x_{in} \tag{10-28}$$

and solving for y_{in}, one obtains

$$y_{in} = \frac{y_r + j \tan \beta l}{1 + j y_r \tan \beta} = g_{in} + j b_{in} \tag{10-28a}$$

Since these two equations are identical in form and sign, it is evident that the bicircular chart may be used for the calculation of admittance in exactly the same manner as it was used for impedance except that the rectangular coordinates are interpreted in terms of g and b, rather than r and x.

10-11. Smith Impedance Chart. While the bicircular chart is very useful as a tool in calculating line impedances and admittances, it has a number of shortcomings which make its use cumbersome. Among these are the facts that the S and βl circles are not concentric, making interpolation difficult, and only a limited range of impedance values can be encompassed on a chart of reasonable size. P. H. Smith of the Bell Telephone Laboratories published another form of impedance chart in 1939[1] which does not have these shortcomings, and as a result his chart has largely superseded the bicircular chart. The Smith chart is designed on the basis of *concentric* circles of $|\rho|$ or S, and the necessary transformation is obtained by trading the rectangular impedance coordinates of the bicircular chart for orthogonal circular impedance coordinates. The derivation of the chart is carried out most easily by expressing the normalized input impedance of the lossless line in terms of the reflection coefficient as in Eq. (10-4b). Then replacing ρ by its polar form, $|\rho|/\underline{\varphi}$, and rearranging the equation,

$$|\rho|/\underline{\varphi} - 2\beta l = \frac{z_{in} - 1}{z_{in} + 1} \tag{10-29}$$

The student may note that the left-hand side of the equation represents a family of circles of radius $|\rho|$, centered on the origin as desired. The next step, then, is to find the form of the z coordinates. This may be

---

[1] Phillip H. Smith, Transmission Line Calculator, *Electronics*, January, 1939.

done by the use of geometric inversion; hence Eq. (10-29) should be arranged so that the coefficient of $1/(z_{in} + 1)$ is a constant. This may be accomplished by adding and subtracting 1 to the right-hand member.

$$|\rho|\underline{/\varphi - 2\beta l} = \left(\frac{z_{in} - 1}{z_{in} + 1} - 1\right) + 1$$

$$= \frac{-2}{z_{in} + 1} + 1 \qquad (10\text{-}30)$$

The step-by-step instructions indicated in Eq. (10-30) are carried out in

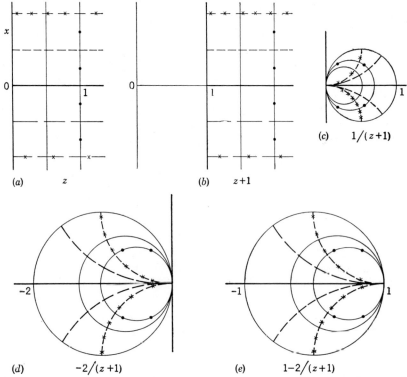

(a)   z

(b)   z+1

(c)   1/(z+1)

(d)   -2/(z+1)

(e)   1-2/(z+1)

FIG. 10-15. Development of the Smith-chart impedance coordinates. See text for details.

Fig. 10-15. Figure 10-15a shows the half z plane corresponding to complex impedances having positive resistive components. The vertical lines correspond to constant values of r and the horizontal lines to constant values of x. The individual lines are marked for easy identification in the remaining steps. At b the whole diagram is shifted to the right by one unit corresponding to $z + 1$. The inverted form, $1/(z + 1)$, is obtained by geometric inversion at c. The student should notice two

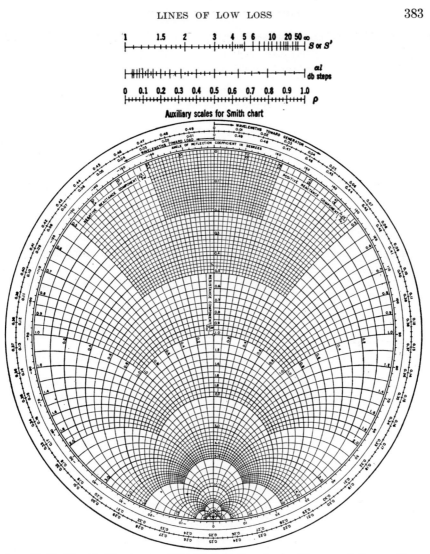

FIG. 10-16. The Smith chart. (*The Emeloid Co., Inc.*) The use of the auxiliary scales is explained in Sec. 10-14.

important consequences of this step. First, curves of negative reactance (positive susceptance) appear in the upper half circle and curves of positive reactance in the lower half circle. Second, the entire infinite range of z for positive values of r has been mapped to the region *inside the unit circle.*

In Fig. 10-15*d* the diagram of c is multiplied by -2 with another change in the location of the reactance curves. At e the circle becomes centered on the origin by adding $+1$. Inasmuch as the loci of constant values of $|\rho|$ or S are circles centered on the origin, they are not shown on the chart, whose usual form is shown in Fig. 10-16.[1]

Since at an impedance maximum $z_{in} = r_{in} + j0 = S$, for $r > 1$, the constant-S circles may be conveniently located by the intersections of the right-hand portion of the real axis and the constant-r circles. The value of $|\rho|$ for any given value of standing wave ratio may be determined by rearranging Eq. (10-17) to give

$$|\rho| = \frac{S - 1}{S + 1} \tag{10-31}$$

An auxiliary scale is plotted above the Smith chart in Fig. 10-16, giving the relationship between numerical values of $|\rho|$ and S.

It should be noticed that the chart is calibrated around its periphery in terms of wavelengths rather than in degrees of $2\beta l$. Also, the chart furnishes a direct calibration of the reflection coefficient angle φ in degrees.

The Smith chart is used in the same manner as the bicircular chart and in addition may be used for admittance calculations, except for a 180° shift in φ as indicated by the equation

$$|\rho|\underline{/\varphi - (2\beta l + \pi)} = \frac{y_{in} - 1}{y_{in} + 1} \tag{10-29a}$$

The use of the Smith chart will be illustrated by the following example:

A voltage minimum occurs 18 cm from the termination on a lossless line. Adjacent minima are 20 cm apart. $S = 2.5$, $l = 52$ cm. Find z_r and z_{in}.

$$\lambda = 2 \times 20 = 40 \text{ cm.}$$

Draw the $S = 2.5$ circle as shown in Fig. 10-17. A voltage minimum corresponds to an impedance minimum; therefore locate this point at the intersection of the $S = 2.5$ circle and $r = 1/S = 0.4$. The load is 18 cm away from this point. Converting to electrical length,

$$y_{min} = 18 \frac{\lambda}{40} = 0.45\lambda$$

Rotate 0.45λ *toward the load*, and read $z_r = 0.43 + j0.27$.

The input terminals are $52 - 18 = 34$ cm toward the generator from the point of minimum impedance, corresponding to an electrical length $34(\lambda/40) = 0.85\lambda$. Since once around the chart corresponds to an electrical length of 0.5λ, starting at the impedance minimum rotate $(0.85 - 0.5)\lambda = 0.35\lambda$, and read

$$z_{in} = 0.89 - j0.89.$$

10-12. Resonant Stubs. Short sections of open- or short-circuited transmission lines are often called stubs and can be used as impedance

---

[1] Copies of the Smith chart are available from The Emeloid Co., Inc., Hillside, N.J. The same company also manufactures a Smith chart calculator. The Smith charts in this book are reproduced with permission of The Emeloid Company.

elements in impedance-matching systems as explained in Chap. 12. When they have lengths that are integral multiples of a quarter wavelength at the fundamental operating frequency, they are referred to as "resonant stubs" and as such display the property of multiple resonance

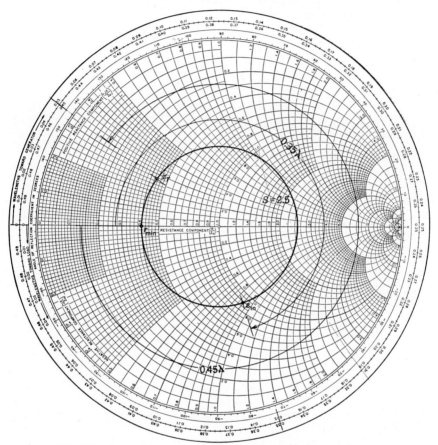

FIG. 10-17. The Smith chart, showing the solution of the illustrative example.

as a function of frequency and can be used as sharply tuned filters. For example, Fig. 10-18a shows a transmission line supported on quarter-wave stubs. The transmitter delivers a fundamental signal of frequency f_1 and an unwanted second harmonic of frequency f_2. Under the assumption that the stubs are virtually lossless, the phase velocity is independent of frequency so that $\lambda_2 = \lambda_1/2$. Consider the behavior of the system at the fundamental and second harmonic frequencies. At f_1 the stub length s is $\lambda_1/4$, and the stubs have almost infinite input impedance and so serve as insulating supports (or quarter-wave insulators) for the transmission line! Note that, the better the conductivity of the supports, the better the insulation. At f_2, however, the stub length becomes $\lambda_2/2$, and the stubs have very low input impedance and thereby throw a short circuit across the main transmission line. Thus power is delivered

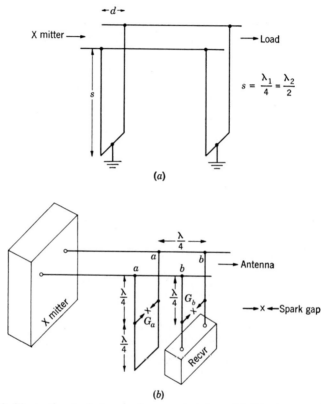

$$s = \frac{\lambda_1}{4} = \frac{\lambda_2}{2}$$

Fig. 10-18. Illustrating typical uses of resonant stubs. (a) Quarter-wave insulators. (b) A simple radar TR system.

to the load at f_1, but the power of the harmonic component is completely reflected to the generator, indicating a filtering or harmonic-suppressing action.

Resonant stubs are also used as components in radar transmit-receive (TR) systems. In typical radar sets a common antenna is used for both the transmitter and receiver as indicated in Fig. 10-18b. The transmitter sends out pulses of high amplitude and of durations of the order of 1 μsec at intervals of the order of milliseconds. The function of the TR system is to protect and isolate the receiver during the transmission of pulses and to isolate the transmitter from the system between pulses so that the small-amplitude echo signal is directed to the receiver. Consider how the system of Fig. 10-18b performs these functions.

The voltage during pulses is high enough to break down the spark gaps which then form an arc, virtually the equivalent of a short circuit. Thus the input impedance of the stub at aa is infinite. The spark gap G_b protects the receiver and also causes infinite stub impedance at bb. Under these conditions essentially all the transmitter energy is delivered to the antenna, provided that the latter is properly coupled to terminate the transmission line.

Between pulses, energy levels are too low to support conduction of the gaps so that G_a and G_b become open circuits. The stub impedance at aa becomes zero (being spaced a half wavelength from a short circuit). The impedance looking toward the transmitter at bb, being spaced a quarter wavelength from a short circuit, is infinite. Under this "receive" condition the returning energy is directed to the receiver.

10-13. Effect of Small Losses. In the foregoing sections standing wave patterns and input impedances have been determined for the high-frequency line by assuming that line losses are completely negligible. When one is concerned with the efficiency of power transmission along the line, however, this assumption ignores the very quantity which is most important; hence the assumption of zero line loss cannot be used. Furthermore, in determining the figure of merit Q of resonant stubs or in computing the input impedance of lines that are long physically, say, of lengths of 50 ft or more, line losses may not be considered negligible.

On this basis the student might assume that the general methods of Chap. 9 should be used. This is a possibility, but since the line losses are small, certain approximations may be used to simplify the calculations. The general equations for determining γ and Z_o for these low-loss lines have been considered in Chap. 8 and are summarized here for convenience.

$$Z_o = \sqrt{\frac{L}{C}}\left(1 - j\frac{R}{2\omega L}\right)$$

$$\alpha = \frac{R}{2}\sqrt{\frac{C}{L}}\left[1 - \frac{1}{8}\left(\frac{R}{\omega L}\right)^2\right] \approx \frac{R}{2R_o} \qquad R \ll \omega L$$

$$\beta = \omega\sqrt{LC}\left[1 + \frac{1}{8}\left(\frac{R}{\omega L}\right)^2\right]$$

10-14. Smith Chart for $\alpha l \neq 0$. It has been shown in Chap. 9 that as αl increases on a lossy line Z_{in} approaches Z_o, or, in normalized form, z_{in} approaches 1. It would seem, then, that the locus of z_{in} for a line not terminated in Z_o and with a value for α would appear as a spiral on the Smith chart. This locus would begin at z_r and spiral in toward the center of the chart. In contrast the locus of z_{in} for a lossless line is a circle.

Thus the circle of constant ρ of the lossless line is replaced by a spiral ρ' for the lossy line. The form of this spiral will now be derived, and its use with the Smith chart will be demonstrated.

By analogy to Eq. (10-29) ρ' will be defined by

$$|\rho'|\underline{/\varphi - 2\beta l} = \frac{z'_{in} - 1}{z'_{in} + 1} \tag{10-32}$$

where z'_{in} is the normalized input impedance of a lossy line which, by Eq. (9-30a), is

$$z'_{in} = \frac{\sinh \gamma l + z_r \cosh \gamma l}{\cosh \gamma l + z_r \sinh \gamma l}$$

Expanding $\sinh \gamma l$ and $\cosh \gamma l$ and dividing numerator and denominator by $\cosh \alpha l \cos \beta l$,

$$z'_{in} = \frac{(\tanh \alpha l + j \tan \beta l) + z_r(1 + \tanh \alpha l \tan \beta l)}{(1 + j \tanh \alpha l \tan \beta l) + z_r(\tanh \alpha l + j \tan \beta l)}$$

Collecting the $\tan \beta l$ terms,

$$z'_{in} = \frac{(z_r + \tanh \alpha l) + j(1 + z_r \tanh \alpha l) \tan \beta l}{(1 + z_r \tanh \alpha l) + j(z_r + \tanh \alpha l) \tan \beta l} \tag{10-33}$$

Substituting Eq. (10-33) into Eq. (10-32) and clearing,

$$|\rho'|\underline{/\varphi - 2\beta l} = \left(\frac{z_r - 1}{z_r + 1}\right)\left(\frac{1 - j \tan \beta l}{1 + j \tan \beta l}\right)\left(\frac{1 - \tanh \alpha l}{1 + \tanh \alpha l}\right) \tag{10-34}$$

It will be observed that the first factor in Eq. (10-34) is the reflection coefficient ρ and that the second factor is $1\underline{/-2\beta l}$; hence the equation may be written

$$|\rho'|\underline{/\varphi - 2\beta l} = |\rho|\underline{/\varphi - 2\beta l}\frac{1 - \tanh \alpha l}{1 + \tanh \alpha l} \tag{10-34a}$$

The quantity $|\rho|\underline{/\varphi - 2\beta l}$ is precisely the circular locus for a lossless line; hence $(1 - \tanh \alpha l)/(1 + \tanh \alpha l)$ may be designated the *spiral factor* $\mathfrak{F}$ caused by the presence of line losses.

While Eq. (10-34a) is quite adequate for determining the input impedance of a lossy line with the Smith chart, it is not convenient to use because a $|\rho|$ scale does not appear directly on the chart. Since the real axis calibration is identical to the standing wave ratio S for values greater than unity, it would be more convenient to relate the spiral factor to the standing wave ratio. Let S' be the standing wave ratio on the lossy line. Then by analogy to Eq. (10-17)

$$S' = \frac{1 + |\rho'|}{1 - |\rho'|} = \frac{1 + |\rho|\mathfrak{F}}{1 - |\rho|\mathfrak{F}} \tag{10-35}$$

To illustrate the spiral locus and the use of Eq. (10-35), consider the special case of a line one wavelength long having an attenuation loss of 1 db and terminated in the normalized impedance $z = 1 + j1$. From the Smith chart of Fig. 10-16 the locus of z_{in} if the line were lossless would be a circle corresponding to $S = 2.6$ or $|\rho| = 0.444$. The spiral locus which includes the effect of the line loss may be determined by calculating typical points as indicated below. $\mathfrak{F}$ is calculated from Eq. (10-34a) and S' by Eq. (10-35).

$\dfrac{l}{\lambda}$	αl, nepers	tanh αl	$1 -$ tanh αl	$|\rho|\mathfrak{F}$	$1 - |\rho|\mathfrak{F}$	S'
0.125	0.0144	0.0144	0.9856	0.431	0.569	2.52
0.25	0.0288	0.0288	0.9712	0.420	0.580	2.45
0.375	0.0432	0.0432	0.9568	0.406	0.594	2.37
0.50	0.0576	0.0576	0.9424	0.395	0.605	2.31
0.625	0.0720	0.0720	0.9280	0.384	0.616	2.22
0.75	0.0864	0.0864	0.9136	0.372	0.628	2.19
0.875	0.1008	0.1008	0.8992	0.358	0.642	2.11
1.00	0.1152	0.1150	0.8850	0.352	0.648	2.09

These points are shown connected by a spiral in Fig. 10-19. It should be observed that the normalized input impedance is $1.09 + j0.8$ as compared with $1 + j1$, which is obtained on the lossless assumption.

The foregoing problem illustrates that considerable calculation is entailed in using Eq. (10-35). To minimize calculation it is convenient to construct an alignment chart of S, αl, and $|\rho|$ for use with the chart. Since S is a function of the reflection coefficient magnitude, it is convenient to set $|\rho| = 1$ in constructing this scale. Then, substituting into Eq. (10-35) for $\mathfrak{F}$,

$$S' = \frac{1}{\text{tanh } \alpha l} \qquad (10\text{-}35a)$$

The alignment chart corresponding to this equation and Eq. (10-17) is plotted in Fig. 10-16. The use of the chart in determining the input impedance of a lossy line is illustrated in the next example. Since only Z_{in} is required, the actual spiral locus need not be determined.

An antenna is connected to a television receiver by 50 ft of 300-ohm twin-lead line. The input impedance of the receiver is 75 ohms resistive. Manufacturer's data on the line give the following: $Z_o = 300$ ohms resistive. Relative velocity $= 82$ per cent. Attenuation $= 2$ db/100 ft at 100 Mc. Find the impedance into which the antenna works at 100 Mc.

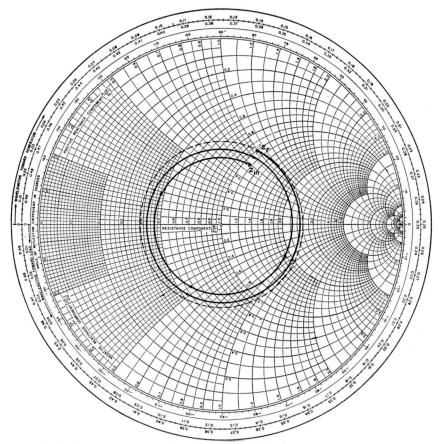

FIG. 10-19. Illustrating the effect of small line losses on the input impedance of a transmission line. The locus is a spiral rather than a circle as in the lossless case.

The relative velocity of 82 per cent means that $v_p = 0.82c$, where c is the velocity in free space; hence

$$\lambda = \frac{v_p}{f} = \frac{0.82(3 \times 10^8)}{10^8} = 2.46 \text{ m}$$

Since 1 m = 3.281 ft,

$$l = \frac{50}{3.281} \text{ m} = \frac{50}{3.281} \frac{\lambda}{2.46} = 6.19\lambda$$

$$\alpha l = 2 \times {}^{50}\!/_{100} = 1 \text{ db}$$

The normalized terminating impedance is

$$z_r = \frac{Z_R}{R_o} = \frac{75}{300} = 0.25$$

Enter the chart (Fig. 10-20) at z_r, rotate on a circle of constant S 6.19λ, and read the value of z_{in} on a lossless basis; thus $z_{in} = 1.32 + j1.7$. This value of z_{in}

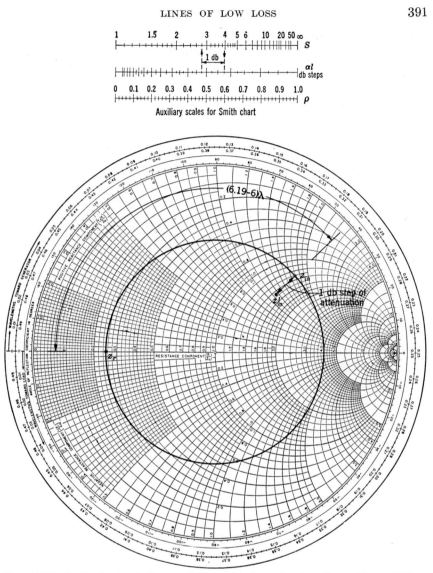

Fig. 10-20. Smith-chart solution of the example for a low-loss line. *Note.* Major divisions on the αl scale correspond to 1-db steps.

corresponds to $S = 4$. Transfer from the $S = 4$ to the αl scale; move 1 db to the left on the αl scale and back up to the S (now the S') scale, reading $S' = 2.8$. Move inward radially on the chart to a radius $S' = 2.8$, and read the actual input impedance, $z'_{in} = 1.49 + j1.22$.

Converting to ohms,

$$Z'_{in} = R_o z_{in} = 300(1.49 + j1.22) = 447 + j366 \text{ ohms}$$

10-15. Efficiency of Transmission. One powerful method of calculating the transmission efficiency of low-loss circuits is to compute the current distribution on the assumption there are *no* losses and then to compute the $|I|^2 R$ losses on the basis of this current distribution. Situations where this is useful include antennas, reactance networks with elements of high Q, and low-loss lines.

Consider the case of a low-loss line where the value of G is negligible and which is terminated in a pure resistance R_R, and as before let $r_r = R_R/R_o$.

Then the current ratio between the incident and reflected waves at the termination will be a real number

$$\frac{I_R''}{I_R'} = -\rho = \frac{1 - r_r}{1 + r_r}$$

Now at any point y the total current I_y will be $I_y = I_y' + I_y''$, and the phase shift between I_y' and I_y'' will be $2\beta y$ if ρ is positive ($r_r < 1$) and $2\beta y + \pi$ if ρ is negative ($r_r > 1$). The magnitudes of I_y' and I_y'' will not depend appreciably on y for lines of low loss. Hence $|I_y''| = \rho|I_y'|$.

The phase between the initial and reflected currents will depend on y. I_y will be a standing wave.

Now the magnitude of I_y can be obtained most easily by considering the component of I_y'' in phase with I_y', which will be $-\rho|I_y'| \cos 2\beta y$, and the component of I_y'' in quadrature with I_y', which will be $\rho|I_y'| \sin 2\beta y$. Hence

$$|I_y|^2 = |I_y'|^2[(1 - \rho \cos 2\beta y)^2 + (\rho \sin 2\beta y)^2]$$
$$= |I_y'|^2(1 + \rho^2 - 2\rho \cos 2\beta y) \tag{10-36}$$

Now let R = resistance per unit length of line. The power lost along the line will be

$$P_{\text{lost}} = \int_0^l |I_y|^2 R\, dy$$
$$= |I_y'|^2 \left(1 + \rho^2 - \rho \frac{\sin 2\beta l}{\beta l}\right) Rl \tag{10-37}$$

Rl equals the total series line resistance, and the power delivered to the load will be

$$P_{\text{out}} = |I_R|^2 R_R = |I_y'|^2(1 - \rho)^2 R_R \tag{10-38}$$
$$\frac{P_{\text{lost}}}{P_{\text{out}}} = \frac{[1 + \rho^2 - (\rho \sin 2\beta l)/\beta l]Rl}{(1 - \rho)^2 r_r R_o} \tag{10-38a}$$

On substituting for the value of ρ in terms of r_r, this equation becomes

$$\frac{P_{\text{lost}}}{P_{\text{out}}} = \frac{Rl}{2R_o}\left[r_r + \frac{1}{r_r} + \left(\frac{1}{r_r} - r_r\right)\frac{\sin 2\beta l}{2\beta l}\right] \tag{10-38b}$$

In order to make the power loss a minimum, r_r should be chosen such that

$$\frac{\partial \dfrac{P_{lost}}{P_{out}}}{\partial r_r} = \frac{Rl}{2R_o}\left[1 - \frac{1}{r_r{}^2} - \left(\frac{1}{r_r{}^2} + 1\right)\frac{\sin 2\beta l}{2\beta l}\right] = 0$$

whence
$$r_r = \sqrt{\frac{1 + (\sin 2\beta l)/2\beta l}{1 - (\sin 2\beta l)/2\beta l}} \qquad (10\text{-}39)$$

As βl gets larger and larger, $(\sin 2\beta l)/2\beta l$ goes through maxima and minima but approaches zero, so that *for long lines r_r should be unity for*

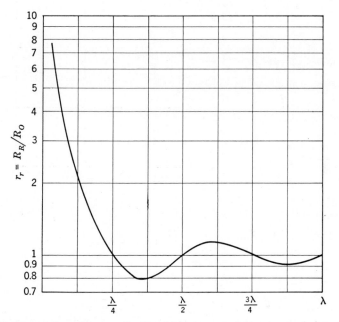

FIG. 10-21. Plot of the value $r_r = R_R/R_o$ which gives maximum transmission efficiency as a function of line length.

maximum efficiency. However for short values of line, say, much less than $\lambda/4$, the maximum efficiency will be obtained for large values of r_r. This is the case on the ordinary power transmission line where the maximum efficiency is obtained by using high voltages and low currents. This is accomplished by using step-up transformers at the sending end and a step-down transformer at the receiving end so that the load presented to the line is much higher than its characteristic impedance. However, on lines of long electrical length the standing wave effect means that, with a high impedance and hence low current at the receiving end, there will be a high current at some other points on the line and the reduction in loss due to low I^2R where the current is low is more than offset by a high I^2R at other points with a net increase in total loss.

A plot of Eq. (10-39) is shown in Fig. 10-21. If the optimum value of

r_r for each length of line as determined by Eq. (10-39) is substituted back into Eq. (10-38b), it is possible to see the effect of the losses caused by a

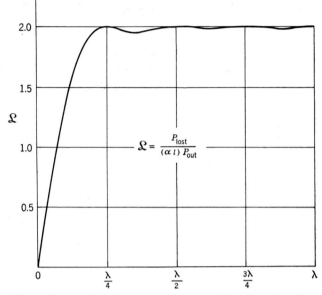

FIG. 10-22. Plot of the loss function $\mathcal{L}$ as a function of line length. For each length $r_r = R_R/R_o$ has the optimum value specified by Eq. (10-39) and Fig. 10-21.

standing wave. By Eq. (8-64a) $Rl/2R_o = \alpha l$; thus Eq. (10-38b) may be written

$$\frac{P_{\text{lost}}}{P_{\text{out}}} = (\alpha l)\mathcal{L} \qquad (10\text{-}38c)$$

where $\mathcal{L}$ is a standing wave loss function defined as

$$\mathcal{L} = r_r + \frac{1}{r_r} + \left(\frac{1}{r_r} - r_r\right)\frac{\sin 2\beta l}{2\beta l} \qquad (10\text{-}40)$$

$\mathcal{L}$ as a function of line length in terms of λ, always with the optimum value of r_r specified by Eq. (10-39), is shown in Fig. 10-22. This figure shows that for a given total line resistance and characteristic impedance, i.e., for a given αl, short lines which can be operated with high impedance termination are most efficient. For values of length greater than $\lambda/4$, $\mathcal{L}$ has a value nearly equal to 2, irrespective of the length, the line should be terminated in R_o,

$$\frac{P_{\text{loss}}}{P_{\text{out}}} = \frac{Rl}{R_o} = 2\alpha l$$

and the fractional loss is fundamentally only a function of the total series resistance and the characteristic impedance.

If the line is longer than about λ, the term in Eq. (10-40) involving βl becomes negligible and

$$\mathcal{L} \approx \frac{r_r{}^2 + 1}{r_r} \tag{10-40a}$$

For small deviations of r_r from unity the factor $(r_r{}^2 + 1)/r_r$ does not rise rapidly, increasing only from 2 to 2.5 when r_r changes from 1 to 2 or from 1 to $\frac{1}{2}$. Hence, the loss will not increase greatly if the ratio of R_R/R_o (and the standing wave ratio) are kept within the limits $\frac{1}{2}$ to 2. However, for large deviations $(r_r{}^2 + 1)/r_r$ nearly equals r_r, and the loss will be directly proportional to the value of r_r. Equations for calculating R_o for the parallel-wire and coaxial lines are given in Table 8-2.

10-16. Q of Quarter-wave Shorted Stub. The antiresonant circuit is often used as the tuned load in vacuum-tube-amplifier and oscillator circuits. As the frequency of operation is raised, the values of inductance and capacitance comprising the tuned circuit become so small that, at vhf and higher frequencies, lumped circuit parameters become impractical and resort is made to the resonant properties of transmission lines. Since the quarter-wave short-circuited stub behaves like an antiresonant circuit, it is often used as the plate load at these higher frequencies.

When the stub is used for this purpose, its Q and half-power bandwidth become important and the assumption of negligible line losses leads to the ridiculous results of infinite Q and zero bandwidth. A close approximation to the correct value may be obtained by using the assumptions of the last section. The current and voltage along the quarter-wave short-circuited line will be $I_y = I_R \cos \beta y$, $E_y = I_R R_o \sin \beta y$. At the input end $E_{in} = I_R R_o$. The average power lost will be

$$\begin{aligned} P_{\text{lost}} &= \int_0^{\lambda/4} |I_R|^2 \cos^2 \beta l R \, dl \\ &= \frac{|I_R|^2 R l}{2} \end{aligned} \tag{10-41}$$

The input impedance will be determined by the input voltage and the power lost, i.e.,

$$\begin{aligned} Z_{in} = R_{in} &= \frac{|E_{in}|^2}{P_{\text{lost}}} \\ &= \frac{2|I_R|^2 R_o{}^2}{|I_R|^2 R l} = \frac{2R_o{}^2}{R l} \end{aligned} \tag{10-42}$$

The maximum energy stored per cycle will be

$$\int_0^{\lambda/4} |I_R|^2 L \cos^2 \beta l \, dl = |I_R|^2 \frac{L l}{2} \tag{10-43}$$

The value of Q will be

$$Q = \omega \frac{\text{max energy stored per cycle}}{\text{avg power dissipated}}$$

Substituting from Eqs. (10-41) and (10-43),

$$Q = \frac{\omega L}{R} \qquad (10\text{-}44)$$

Therefore the Q of the quarter-wave section is identical to the Q of each infinitesimal length. At high frequencies R is proportional to the square root of frequency. Then, since ω is directly proportional to frequency, Eq. (10-44) shows that the Q of a shorted quarter-wave section is proportional to the square root of frequency.

10-17. Line Dimensions for Minimum-Loss Coaxial Line. The foregoing results may be used for determining the dimensions of a maximum-Q (or minimum-loss) coaxial line. For any given termination Eq. (10-38b) shows that the ratio of power lost to power output is proportional to Rl/R_o. Thus with a coaxial cable, if the diameter of the inner conductor is held constant, increasing the diameter of the outer conductor will increase R_o and decrease R and hence indefinitely decrease the loss. Unfortunately it will also indefinitely increase the cost of the coaxial line. On the other hand, if the diameter of the outside conductor, which largely determines the cost, is held constant while the diameter of the inside conductor is increased, R and R_o will both decrease. Hence one would expect that there is an optimum ratio for the diameters (or radii) of the two conductors. For convenience let the ratio of the two radii be $r_2/r_1 = x$.

From the data of Table 8-2 it may be seen that, at hf where the flux linkages *within* the conductors can be neglected, β ($= \omega \sqrt{LC}$) is independent of x at any given frequency. Thus for a given frequency and a line terminated in R_o (or any fixed value of r_r) $\mathcal{L}$ of Eq. (10-10) is constant and $P_{\text{lost}}/P_{\text{out}}$ may be minimized by minimizing $\alpha = R/2R_o$ with respect to x. Substituting from Table 8-2,

$$\alpha = \frac{K(x + 1)}{\ln x} \qquad K = \text{constant} \qquad (10\text{-}45)$$

Differentiating and setting the derivative equal to zero to find the minimum,

$$\frac{d\alpha}{dx} = K \frac{\ln x - (x + 1)/x}{\ln^2 x} = 0$$

$$\ln x = 1 + \frac{1}{x}$$

A transcendental equation of this form may be solved graphically by plotting $\ln x$, and $1 + 1/x$ vs. x. The solution of the equation is given by the intersection of the two curves and is found to be $x = 3.6$. Thus the coaxial line with a fixed outer-conductor diameter must have a ratio of outer- to inner-conductor radius of 3.6 in order to have minimum loss and maximum transmission efficiency. This value corresponds to a characteristic impedance $R_o = 138 \log 3.6 = 76.9$ ohms.

Not only is 3.6 the optimum ratio for transmission efficiency, but it also gives the maximum Q for a short-circuited stub.

10-18. Line Dimensions for Minimum-flashover Coaxial Line. The total amount of power which may be transmitted along a given coaxial line is limited by the flashover voltage, i.e., as the applied voltage is raised, the stress in the dielectric between the conductors is increased. If the voltage is raised beyond a critical value, the dielectric breaks down and sparking occurs between the conductors.

The application of field theory to the geometry of the coaxial cable shows that the maximum electric field intensity in the dielectric occurs at the surface of the inner conductor (radius r_1) and has the value

$$\mathcal{E} = \frac{E}{r_1 \ln (r_2/r_1)} \tag{10-46}$$

where E is the voltage drop between the conductors.

Then, for a constant-size outer conductor and fixed value of E, $\mathcal{E}$ and hence the danger of flashover may be minimized by proper choice of the ratio of the conductor radii, $x = r_2/r_1$. Thus

$$\mathcal{E} = \frac{E}{r_2} \frac{x}{\ln x} \tag{10-46a}$$

and

$$\frac{d\mathcal{E}}{dx} = \frac{E}{r_2} \frac{\ln x - 1}{(\ln x)^2} = 0 \tag{10-47}$$

or

$$x = e = 2.718$$

Therefore, the danger of flashover is minimized by choosing the ratio of diameters to be e. This ratio corresponds to a line characteristic impedance of 60 ohms.

10-19. An Engineering Compromise. The last two sections indicate that a single coaxial line cannot be designed to provide simultaneously maximum efficiency and minimum dielectric stress. How, then, shall a line be chosen? Shall emphasis be placed on efficiency of transmission, or shall the problem of dielectric stress be given major consideration? This problem is best considered by observing how these two quantities *vary* as the r_2/r_1 ratio (or R_o) is varied. To this end the curves of Fig. 10-23 have been plotted in normalized form from Eqs. (10-45) and (10-46a). It will be observed that both curves of $\alpha/\alpha_{\min}$ and $\mathcal{E}/\mathcal{E}_{\min}$ are relatively flat for R_o lying between 65 and 75 ohms. A reasonable compromise value would be around 70 ohms ($r_2/r_1 \approx 3.2$).

Figure 10-23 also shows a curve of normalized maximum transmitted power for the condition where the voltage gradient is just below the critical value for flashover (see Prob. 10-14). Consideration of these data

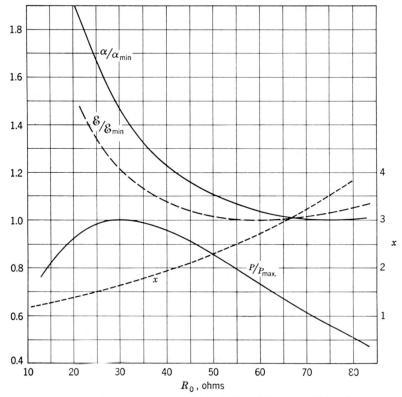

FIG. 10-23. Normalized curves showing the variation of line loss, dielectric stress, and maximum transmitted power as a function of R_o for coaxial cables.

dictates a compromise value of R_o lower than 70 ohms. In practice typical values lying in the range of 50 to 75 ohms are commonly used.

10-20. Contrast between Operation of Power and Communication Lines. The equations developed in this chapter are applicable to both power and communication lines, but it is interesting to note differences in the method of operation in the two cases. (See the table on page 399.)

In power operation constant voltage at the output terminals of the generator or the generator-transformer combination may be achieved by a voltage regulator. This gives the equivalent of a zero impedance source. At the receiving end of the line the voltage across the variable load may be kept constant in magnitude by an induction regulator (equiv-

Power operation	*Communication operation*
Single frequency	Wide band of frequencies
Line always electrically short ($l < 0.1\lambda$)	Line may be short or long
Line may be represented by nominal-T or Π section	Solution usually requires long-line equations
Negligible voltage variation must be maintained at load	Voltage at load must vary with signal
Variable impedance load	Constant impedance load
Impedance at termination usually much greater than Z_o	Impedance termination usually nearly equal to Z_o
Generator usually equivalent to low or zero impedance source with constant generated voltage	Generator usually has appreciable impedance, and voltage varies with signal

alent to a variable transformer ratio) or by using a synchronous capacitor. At major load centers the latter is preferred. The arrangement is illustrated in Fig. 10-24.

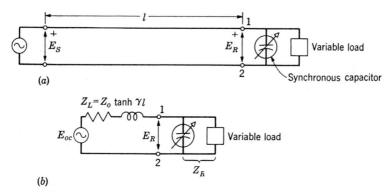

(a)

(b)

FIG. 10-24. Circuits for studying the voltage regulation of a power-transmission line. (a) Basic circuit. (b) The circuit to the left of terminals 1, 2 is replaced by the Thévenin equivalent circuit.

The situation at the receiving end can be represented by Thévenin's theorem. The open-circuited voltage will be given by $E_{oc} = E_S/\cosh \gamma l$. In practical lines $|\cosh \gamma l| = \sqrt{\sinh^2 \alpha l + \cos^2 \beta l}$ will always be less than unity, and so the open-circuited voltage will be greater than the sending-end voltage as a result of the standing wave.

The equivalent internal impedance looking back into the receiving terminals of the line will be the short-circuited impedance of the line $Z_o \tanh \gamma l$. Since power lines are electrically short, $Z_o \tanh \gamma l$ will always be inductive.

Hence the only problem is so to adjust the susceptance of the capacitor as the load is varied that the magnitude of the E_R is kept constant. Fortunately this is relatively simple, because any drop in $|E_R|$ means that the susceptance of the synchronous capacitor should be increased, and this merely requires an increase in the excitation of the synchronous machine. This is the same type of operation which is required in the synchronous generator at the sending end, and so the same type of regulator may be used. Furthermore, a so-called synchronous capacitor can be made to draw lagging current also.

In power systems branch lines are usually required as shown in Fig. 10-25. Note, however, that, if synchronous capacitors are used at each

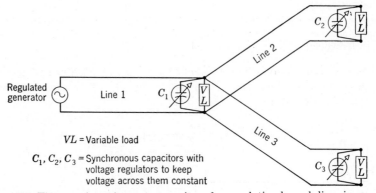

FIG. 10-25. The use of synchronous capacitors for regulating branch lines in a power-transmission system.

of the branch points, the sending-end voltage of each individual line may be kept constant and hence the supply of each line is equivalent to a zero-impedance generator. Hence each line is the equivalent of Fig. 10-24.

PROBLEMS

10-1. A vhf push-pull oscillator requires a tuned load to work at 50 Mc. The plate-to-plate capacitance is 20 $\mu\mu$f.

a. What lumped inductance is required in shunt with the 20-$\mu\mu$f capacitance?

b. How many meters of lossless 100-ohm (that is, $R_o = 100$ ohms) short-circuited line could replace this lumped inductance?

c. From physical considerations which load would have the higher Q (if the line actually has losses)?

10-2. (*a*) Show that the input reactance of a shorted lossless stub one-half wavelength long at f_o can be expressed as

$$X_{sc} = R_o \tan \frac{\pi \Delta f}{f_o} \qquad \Delta f = f - f_o$$

(*b*) Show that the reactance of a series inductance L_o and capacitance C_o, resonant at f_o, can be expressed for small values of Δf as

$$X = \omega_o L_o \frac{2 \Delta f}{f_o}$$

(*c*) Calculate and plot X_{sc}/R_o and $X/\omega_o L_o$ for $\pm \Delta f/f_o = 0.005$, 0.01, 0.05, and 0.1.

(d) From these results what value should R_o have for X_{sc} and X to be essentially equal over a ± 10 per cent change from the resonant frequency?

10-3. It is common practice in the vhf range to use a shorted stub one-eight wavelength long at f_o to replace a lumped inductance L_o.

a. Calculate and plot $X/\omega_o L_o$ and X_{sc}/R_o for the same values of $\Delta f/f_o$ specified in Prob. 10-2. For approximate equivalence over this band what R_o is required?

b. What line length would be required for X and X_{sc} to have equal values and equal slopes at f_o? Is this a practical solution?

c. If the line length is changed to $\lambda_o/16$, what R_o is required? What improvement over a results?

10-4. A lossless line is terminated in a pure reactance $\pm jaR_o$. a may have any value.

a. Does complete reflection occur? Why?

b. What is the standing wave ratio?

c. Can a voltage maximum or minimum occur at the receiving end? Explain.

d. By means of Eq. (10-2) predict and sketch the shape of the voltage standing wave pattern, using $a = 1$ for illustration.

e. Sketch the locus of $|E_x/E_R|$ in the complex plane.

10-5. For a line terminated in a pure resistance aR_o, derive expressions for y_{max}, y_{min}, $|Z_{in}|_{max}$, $|Z_{in}|_{min}$, and S by eliminating the $\cos^2 \beta y$ term in Eq. (10-23a).

10-6. Verify the elliptical locus of Fig. 10-5 by drawing phasor diagrams of voltage at several points over one wavelength of line beginning at $y = 0$. Assume

$$Z_R = aR_o + j0, a > 1.$$

10-7. For the conditions specified in Fig. 10-11 sketch progressive phasor diagrams and the locus of I_x. Verify that Z_{in} is real at lengths corresponding to y_{max} and y_{min}.

10-8. In Fig. 10-18a can the distance d be $(2n + 1) \lambda/4$?

10-9. A lossless stub is shorted on one end and open on the other. Its length is $\lambda_1/4$. A tap is made at the mid-point.

a. What is the input impedance at the tap?

b. If the tap points are used to support a transmission line, what sort of filtering action occurs at f_1, $2f_1$, $3f_1$, and $4f_1$?

10-10. The input impedance of a lossless line 140 electrical degrees long is $118 + j138$ ohms.

a. Find Z_R if $R_o = 100$ ohms.

b. What would be the value of Z_{in} at lengths corresponding to y_{max} and y_{min}?

10-11. (a) Find the relationship between Z_{in} and Z_R for a quarter-wave line by means of Eq. (10-4a). (b) From this result suggest a means of using the Smith chart for converting impedance to admittance, and vice versa.

10-12. An rf transmission line is constructed from No. 8 B. & S. copper (128.5 mils). It is to have an $R_o = 600$ ohms and is four wavelengths long at $f = 4 \times 10^6$ cycles. Determine the spacing of the line and the efficiency when properly terminated. Determine also its efficiency when it is terminated in a resistance of 73 ohms.

10-13. Derive the value of R_o for a parallel-wire line whose dimensions give maximum Q. Use the data of Table 8-2, assuming the flux linkages within the conductors to be negligible. It is not valid to assume $s > 5r$.

10-14. The maximum-power-handling capability of a lossless line occurs when the maximum electric field intensity equals the flashover value. Derive an expression for the transferred power of a coaxial line in terms of $x = r_2/r_1$. For what value of x is the power maximum? Correlate your results with Fig. 10-23.

10-15. Derive an expression for the Q of a low-loss short-circuited quarter-wave line by evaluating the derivative $(dB_{in}/d\omega)_{\omega_r}$. Note that, if αl is small, $\sinh \alpha l \approx \alpha l$ and $\cosh \alpha l \approx 1$.

10-16. (a) In Fig. 10-24b solve for $|E_{oc}/Z_L E_R|^2$ in terms of the admittances Y_L and Y_R. (b) If $Y_R = G_R + jB_R$ is the only variable, prove that Y_R plots as a circular locus in the complex plane. Explain briefly how the synchronous capacitor holds $|E_R|$ constant when the load proper is varied. (c) Sketch one such circular locus, being sure to locate the circle's center in the proper quadrant. (d) Derive equations for P and Q in terms of E_R and the load conductance and susceptance, where P and Q are the real and reactive components, respectively, of the load volt-amperes. Relate P and Q to the axes of parts b and c. *Note.* This problem is an introduction to Prob. 10-17.

10-17. A three-phase transmission line is 225 miles long and operates at 60 cycles. The line-to-line voltage at the receiving end is 275 kv. The line constants per phase are

$$R = 0.113 \text{ ohm/mile} \qquad L = 2 \text{ mh/mile}$$
$$C = 0.0136 \ \mu\text{f/mile} \qquad G = 0$$

The maximum customer load for all three phases is 120,000 kw at 0.9 power factor. Find the rating in kva of the synchronous capacitor at the load end and the sending-end voltage for minimum size of the synchronous capacitor. The minimum size corresponds to the case where the leading kva required by the synchronous capacitor at full load is equal to the lagging kva required at no load. This is found by graphical construction corresponding to Prob. 10-16 and experimentation with the radius of constant voltage ratio $|E_{oc}/Z_L E_R|$.

CHAPTER 11

IMPEDANCE TRANSFORMATION

In an over-all system for the transmission of communication signals it is often desirable, where possible, to adjust elements of the network so that the power delivered to the load will be a maximum. As a general rule, generators, or signal sources, are fixed-impedance devices; so the problem of designing for maximum power output is essentially one of choosing a proper load or of *transforming* a fixed impedance into a proper load for the signal source. The following theorems govern the choice of a load impedance to absorb maximum power from a known, fixed generator.

11-1. Maximum-power-transfer Theorem. *The maximum power will be absorbed by one network from another joined to it at two terminals, when the impedance of the receiving network is varied, if the impedances looking into the two networks at the junction are conjugates of each other.*

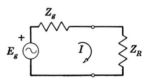

FIG. 11-1. Generator, with internal impedance, delivering power to a load.

To prove this, it will first be demonstrated that the maximum power is absorbed from a generator when the external impedance is the conjugate of the internal impedance. In Fig. 11-1 Z_R is the load impedance which is to be varied until the power is a maximum. Z_g is the internal impedance and is fixed. Consider first the case where Z_g and Z_R are pure resistances. Then

$$I = \frac{E_g}{R_g + R_R}$$

$$P = |I|^2 R_R = \frac{|E_g|^2 R_R}{(R_g + R_R)^2} \tag{11-1}$$

Differentiate Eq. (11-1) and equate to zero in order to find the relation for maximum power.

$$\frac{\partial P}{\partial R_R} = |E_g|^2 \frac{(R_g + R_R)^2 - 2R_R(R_g + R_R)}{(R_g + R_R)^4} = 0$$

$$R_g{}^2 + 2R_g R_R + R_R{}^2 - 2R_g R_R - 2R_R{}^2 = 0$$

Therefore $\qquad\qquad R_R = R_g \qquad$ for max power $\qquad$ (11-2)

If Z_g and Z_R have reactance, then Eq. (11-1) would become

$$P = \frac{|E_g|^2 R_R}{(R_g + R_R)^2 + (X_g + X_R)^2} \tag{11-3}$$

It can be seen by inspection that, as far as X_R is concerned, the power in Eq. (11-3) is a maximum when

$$X_R = -X_g \tag{11-4}$$

i.e., if Z_g is inductive, Z_R should be capacitive, and vice versa. If Eq. (11-4) is fulfilled, Eq. (11-3) reduces to Eq. (11-1) and therefore Eq. (11-2) will give the condition for maximum power. Combining the criteria of

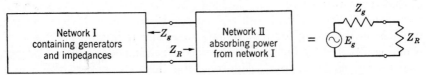

Fig. 11-2. Equivalence of networks supplying power to a load.

Eqs. (11-2) and (11-4) indicates that Z_R and Z_g should be equal in magnitude, but the angle of one should be the negative of the other; i.e., the impedances should be conjugates.

From Thévenin's theorem any network can be replaced by a generator with an internal impedance equal to the impedance looking back from the receiving terminals. In Fig. 11-2 is shown such a system, with network I replaced by a generator with an internal impedance Z_g and network II acting only as an absorber of power. Therefore, for the purposes under consideration, having only two terminals it can be replaced by a single impedance Z_R. The system is then the same as Fig. 11-1 and Eqs. (11-2) and (11-4) will hold for it also.

Corollary. The maximum power that can be absorbed from an active network equals $|E_g|^2/4R_g$, where E_g is the open-circuit voltage at the output terminals and R_g is the resistive component of the impedance looking back from the output terminals.

By Thévenin's theorem any supply network can be reduced to the equivalent of a simple generator. By the maximum-power-transfer theorem, the termination should be the conjugate of the internal impedance. Then

$$I = \frac{E_g}{R_g + R_g} = \frac{E_g}{2R_g}$$

$$P_{\text{max}} = |I|^2 R_g = \frac{|E_g|^2}{4R_g} \tag{11-5}$$

By means of Norton's theorem the student may show that the maximum power that can be absorbed from an active network may also be expressed as

$$P_{\max} = \frac{|I_g|^2}{4G_g} \qquad (11\text{-}5a)$$

where I_g = short-circuit current at output terminals

G_g = conductive component of admittance looking back from output terminals

Since $P_{\max}$ represents the maximum power available to a matched load from an active circuit or generator, the quantity represented by Eqs. (11-5) and (11-5a) is often called the *available power* of a generator.

11-2. Theorem. *If the magnitude of the load impedance may be varied, but not the angle, then the maximum power will be absorbed from a generator when the magnitude of the load impedance is equal to the magnitude of the impedance of the supply network.*

It is often possible in a system such as Fig. 11-1 to vary the *magnitude* of Z_R but impossible to change its *angle*. This can be done, for instance, by the use of transformers. To determine the best value for $|Z_R|$, Eq. (11-3) should be reduced to polar coordinates. Let θ be the angle of Z_R.

$$P = |I|^2 R_R = \frac{|E_g|^2 |Z_R| \cos\theta}{(R_g + |Z_R|\cos\theta)^2 + (X_g + |Z_R|\sin\theta)^2} \qquad (11\text{-}6)$$

Determine the condition for maximum power transfer in the same way as before.

$$\frac{\partial P}{\partial |Z_R|} =$$

$$|E_g|^2 \cos\theta \frac{\left\{ \begin{array}{c} (R_g + |Z_R|\cos\theta)^2 + (X_g + |Z_R|\sin\theta)^2 \\ -|Z_R|\,[2(R_g + |Z_R|\cos\theta)\cos\theta + 2(X_g + |Z_R|\sin\theta)\sin\theta] \end{array} \right\}}{[(R_g + |Z_R|\cos\theta)^2 + (X_g + |Z_R|\sin\theta)^2]^2} = 0$$

$$(R_g + R_R)^2 + (X_g + X_R)^2 = 2[R_R R_g + R_R{}^2 + X_g X_R + X_R{}^2]$$

$$R_g{}^2 + R_R{}^2 + X_g{}^2 + X_R{}^2 = 2(R_R{}^2 + X_R{}^2)$$

$$R_g{}^2 + X_g{}^2 = R_R{}^2 + X_R{}^2$$

The condition is then

$$|Z_R| = |Z_g| \qquad (11\text{-}7)$$

Therefore, if only the magnitude of Z_R can be varied, its value should be made equal to the magnitude of Z_g, in order to absorb the maximum amount of power. This will also apply to the network of Fig. 11-2.

In power work the matching of impedances to secure the greatest power in the receiving device is practically never done, as the over-all efficiency under these conditions is only 50 per cent. Furthermore, the voltage regulation is also 50 per cent, which would be much too great for most power loads. Power generators are usually rated on a full-load current which gives the maximum permissible heating, and this current is usually far below what would flow if the load equaled the generator impedance.

In communication networks, on the other hand, where the cost of power is small in proportion to the total expense and the currents are small, so that temperature rise is usually not a factor, extensive use is made of the fact that matching impedances will secure maximum power transfer. Regulation is not so important in these networks, for devices such as telephone receivers will operate satisfactorily over wide voltage variations.

11-3. Impedance-transforming Principle. The foregoing theorems give the optimum values of terminating impedance for a generator. Since typical loads do not necessarily match the generators from which they obtain their power, some method of transforming these impedances is desirable. Also, other occasions arise where the magnitude of the load is not at an optimum value, and an impedance-transforming network should be used.

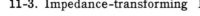
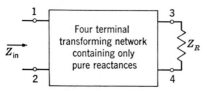

FIG. 11-3. Illustrating the principle of impedance transformation.

The principle of impedance transformation is illustrated in Fig. 11-3. This shows a network connecting a load impedance Z_R to two input terminals 1, 2. If this connecting network is made of pure reactances, any power delivered to the input terminals 1, 2 must in turn be transferred to the load Z_R. However, the resistive and reactive components of the input, or driving-point, impedance at 1, 2 will, in general, be different from the impedance Z_R connected to the output terminals 3, 4. Hence, the reactance network may be considered to be an "impedance-transforming" network changing the impedance Z_R into an impedance Z_{in}. By proper design it is possible to transform Z_R into any impedance which may be desired.

Where the chief concern is to deliver maximum power to the load Z_R, the network is designed so that Z_{in} "matches" the generator impedance in accordance with the foregoing theorems. In this case the network may be considered as an *impedance-matching* network.

If the network contains resistive components, then the output power would be less than the input power and this power loss would usually be undesirable. Therefore most transforming networks are made of reactances with the lowest possible resistance consistent with cost considerations and are *designed* on the assumption that only pure reactances are involved.

11-4. An Impedance-transforming Theorem. The design of lossless transforming networks is assisted by the following theorem first proposed in a previous edition of this book:

If a group of four-terminal networks containing only pure reactances are arranged in cascade to connect a generator to a load, then if at any junction there is a conjugate match of impedances, there will be a conjugate match of impedances at every other junction in the system. The term "conjugate match" means that, if in one direction from a junction the impedance has the dimensions $R + jX$, then in the opposite direction the impedance will have the dimensions $R - jX$.

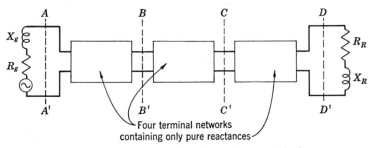

Fig. 11-4. Diagram for conjugate impedance-match theorem.

The theorem is illustrated by Fig. 11-4. If the dimensions of the network elements are such that there is a conjugate match at any one of the junctions AA', BB', CC', or DD', there must be a match at all the junctions. This follows immediately from the maximum-power-transfer theorem. If there is a conjugate match at AA', then the maximum possible power is being drawn from the generator with its internal impedance $R_g + jX_g$. Since the four-terminal networks contain only pure reactances, there can be no dissipation and all the power absorbed at the input terminals must be transferred to the output. If at any junction there should not be a conjugate match, then by adjusting the impedance beyond the junction an increased absorption of power could be obtained. This would require an increase in the power delivered by the generator, which is an impossibility. Therefore there must be a conjugate match at all junctions.

The theorem shows that in a cascade of matching networks it is necessary to match only at one junction if the networks are nondissipative. In actual practice, since there is usually some dissipation it is frequently desirable to adjust at more than one point. An example is a radio transmitter feeding a line which is in turn coupled to an antenna. If the line were nondissipative, it would be necessary to adjust the matching conditions at only one point, but it has been shown in the last chapter that an actual line whose length exceeds $\lambda/4$ has a minimum dissipation when it is terminated in its characteristic impedance. Hence the coupling network between the antenna and line is usually adjusted to give this termination, and the network coupling the transmitter to the line is adjusted to present the proper load to the vacuum tubes. A minor mismatch at either network can be compensated for by readjusting the other without appreciable increase in losses.

11-5. The L Matching Network. An example of the design of a lossless impedance-transformer, or *matching*, network is afforded by the following problem: A lossless structure is to be designed to transform a resistance R_{I1} to a resistance R_{I2} at a given frequency, the structure to contain the smallest possible number of elements.

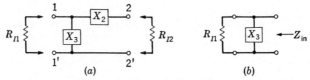

FIG. 11-5. The reactive L impedance-transforming section. The elements are numbered in accordance with a general treatment considered later in the chapter.

Since two design conditions are specified, viz., the values of R_{I1} and R_{I2}, the network must contain at least two adjustable elements. If these elements are connected in series or parallel, they are equivalent to a single reactance at the given frequency and a third element would be required. To avoid this redundancy, the two reactive elements may be arranged as an L section as shown in Fig. 11-5a. The behavior of the circuit may be observed by first considering the effect of shunting X_3 across R_{I1} as in Fig. 11-5b. The input impedance then will be

$$Z_{in} = j\,\frac{R_{I1}X_3}{R_{I1} + jX_3} = \frac{R_{I1}X_3{}^2 + jR_{I1}{}^2X_3}{R_{I1}{}^2 + X_3{}^2}$$

Hence the resistive component has been transformed from R_{I1} to the *smaller* value $R_{I1}X_3{}^2/(R_{I1}{}^2 + X_3{}^2)$. This may be made equal to R_{I2} by proper choice of X_3. Then the reactive component of Z_{in} may be canceled out by means of the series element X_2. Thus the design equations for X_3 and X_2 are

$$X_3 = \pm R_{I1}\sqrt{\frac{R_{I2}}{R_{I1} - R_{I2}}} \qquad X_2 = \mp \sqrt{R_{I2}(R_{I1} - R_{I2})} \quad (11\text{-}8)$$

The following points should be noted: First, X_3 may be either positive or negative (inductive or capacitive), but X_2 and X_3 must be of opposite sign. Second, from Eqs. (11-8), $R_{I1} > R_{I2}$ for X_2 and X_3 to be physically realizable and different from zero; thus *the shunt reactance is in parallel with the larger of the two resistances.* Third, the match occurs at a single frequency.

Since the network of Fig. 11-5a has been designed to provide a conjugate match at the terminals 2, 2′, by virtue of the impedance-transforming theorem of the last section, it will also provide a conjugate match at terminals 1, 1′. Hence if the network designed by Eqs. (11-8) were reversed and the resistance R_{I2} were connected at terminals 2, 2′, the impedance looking into terminals 1, 1′ would be equal to R_{I1}. Thus the L section may be used to step up or step down the value of resistance. The student should observe that, if X_2 is chosen to be inductive and X_3

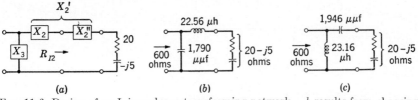

(a)   (b)   (c)

FIG. 11-6. Design of an L impedance-transforming network.   *b* results from choosing X_2 to be positive in Eqs. (11-8), *c* from choosing X_2 to be negative.

capacitive, the network is identical to the antiresonant circuit of Fig. 4-15. The student should check Eqs. (4-87) and Eq. (4-88) against Eqs. (11-8).

While Eqs. (11-8) have been derived for the case where the two impedances to be matched are pure resistances, this is not necessarily a restriction on the L network. If either (or both) of the impedances has a reactive component, it may be canceled out by an additional reactance or susceptance of opposite sign. This additional element may then be incorporated as part of the matching network. One procedure which may be used is illustrated in the following example:

A short antenna has an input impedance of $20 - j5$ ohms at

$$\omega = 5 \times 10^6 \text{ radians/sec.}$$

Design an L section to match the antenna to a 600-ohm transmission line. Add a "compensating" reactance $X_2'' = +5$ ohms in series with the antenna so that the L section is terminated in a pure resistance $R_{12} = 20$ ohms as shown in Fig. 11-6a. The input impedance is to be $R_{I1} = 600$ ohms. Then by Eqs. (11-8)

$$X_2 = \pm \sqrt{20(600 - 20)} = \pm \sqrt{20 \times 580} = \pm 107.8 \text{ ohms}$$

$$X_3 = \mp \sqrt{600 \frac{20}{600 - 20}} = \mp 600 \sqrt{\frac{20}{580}} = \mp 111.5 \text{ ohms}$$

Because of the choice of signs, two solutions are possible. Consider the case where X_2 is inductive, or positive. Combining X_2 and the compensating reactance into a single value, say, X_2',

$$X_2' = X_2 + X_2'' = 107.8 + 5 = 112.8 \text{ ohms}$$

or
$$L_2' = \frac{X_2'}{\omega} = \frac{112.8}{5 \times 10^6} = 22.56 \ \mu\text{henry}$$

and
$$C_3 = -\frac{1}{\omega X_3} = \frac{1}{5 \times 10^6(1.115 \times 10^2)} = 1{,}790 \ \mu\mu\text{f}$$

The resulting network is shown at b in Fig. 11-6.

Alternatively if X_2 is chosen to be capacitive, or negative, the combined value of X_2 and the compensating reactance will be

$$X_2' = X_2 + X_2'' = -107.8 + 5 = -102.8 \text{ ohms}$$

or
$$C_2' = -\frac{1}{\omega X_2'} = \frac{1}{5 \times 10^6(1.028 \times 10^2)} = 1{,}946 \ \mu\mu\text{f}$$

and
$$L_3 = \frac{X_3}{\omega} = \frac{115.8}{5 \times 10^6} = 23.16 \ \mu\text{h}$$

The resulting network is shown in Fig. 11-6c.

11-6. Graphical Design of L Network. In the interests of work that follows in the next chapter it is desirable to derive the design equations

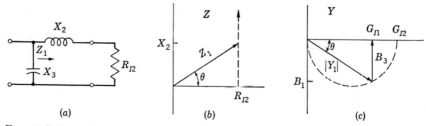

(a)   (b)   (c)

Fig. 11-7. Impedance and admittance loci of a reactive L impedance-transforming section.

of the last section by considering the impedance and admittance loci of the L matching network. As a specific application of this general method, say, R_{I2} is to be transformed into a larger resistance R_{I1} by the L section of Fig. 11-7a. The required values of X_2 and X_3 are to be determined.

The locus of $R_{I2} + jX_2$ as X_2 is increased is indicated by the dashed line at b. The corresponding locus of $1/(R_{I2} + jX_2)$ is shown by the dashed semicircle at c. The problem is to find the value of X_2 such that $1/(R_{I2} + jX_2) = Y_1$ lies directly below $G_{I1} = 1/R_{I1}$ in the Y plane. Then if a susceptance B_3 of value $+|B_1|$ is shunted across $R_{I2} + jX_2 = Z_1$, the input admittance will have the desired value G_{I1}.

From Fig. 11-7b

$$X_2 = |Z_1| \sin \theta = |Z_1| \sqrt{1 - \cos^2 \theta}$$

$$= |Z_1| \sqrt{1 - \frac{(R_{I2})^2}{|Z_1|^2}} = \sqrt{|Z_1|^2 - (R_{I2})^2} \qquad (11\text{-}9)$$

From Fig. 11-7c

$$B_1 = -|Y_1| \sin \theta = -|Y_1| \sqrt{1 - \cos^2 \theta}$$

$$= -|Y_1| \sqrt{1 - \frac{(G_{I1})^2}{|Y_1|^2}} = -\sqrt{|Y_1|^2 - (G_{I1})^2} \qquad (11\text{-}10)$$

Since θ has the same magnitude in both figures,

$$\cos \theta = \frac{R_{I2}}{|Z_1|} = \frac{G_{I1}}{|Y_1|}$$

or
$$R_{I1} R_{I2} = |Z_1|^2 = 1/|Y_1|^2 \qquad (11\text{-}11)$$

Noting that B_3 should have a value of $+|B_1|$, one has from Eqs. (11-9) to (11-11)

$$X_2 = + \sqrt{R_{I2}(R_{I1} - R_{I2})} \qquad B_3 = + \sqrt{\frac{R_{I1} - R_{I2}}{(R_{I1})^2 R_{I2}}}$$

These results are, of course, identical to Eqs. (11-8).

11-7. Frequency Response of L Section. Since the reactances of inductors and capacitors vary with frequency, it is apparent that Eqs. (11-8) can be satisfied, and hence maximum power will be delivered to the load, at one and only one frequency, if X_2 and X_3 each consists of a single reactive element. The transmission of intelligence, however, requires a finite band of frequencies; therefore it is important to consider the response of the

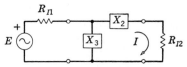

FIG. 11-8. Circuit for investigating the frequency response of the reactive L matching section.

matching network at frequencies on either side of the design value, f_d. To this end the circuit of Fig. 11-8 will be investigated. The load is assumed to be a pure resistance R_{I2} independent of frequency and the generator impedance a pure resistance R_{I1}.

Solution of the circuit mesh equations shows that the load current is given by

$$I = \frac{jX_3 E}{(R_{I1} + jX_3)[R_{I2} + j(X_2 + X_3)] + X_3^2} \qquad (11\text{-}12)$$

Inasmuch as the variation of $|I|$ with frequency is required, the exact form (inductive or capacitive) of X_2 and X_3 must be known. Since Eqs. (11-8) specify two forms of the network, both will be considered.

Where X_2 is inductive and X_3 capacitive, Eqs. (11-8) may be rewritten as a function of frequency in the form

$$X_2 = \frac{\omega}{\omega_d} \sqrt{R_{I2}(R_{I1} - R_{I2})} \tag{11-13}$$

$$X_3 = - \left(\frac{\omega_d}{\omega}\right) R_{I1} \sqrt{\frac{R_{I2}}{R_{I1} - R_{I2}}} \tag{11-14}$$

where ω_d is 2π times the design frequency. Substitution of these expressions into Eq. (11-12) and considerable algebraic manipulation yield the

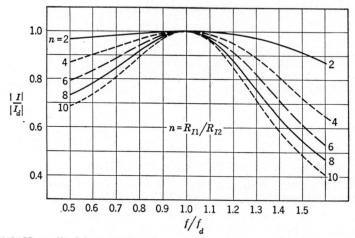

Fig. 11-9. Normalized frequency-response curves for the L matching section with X_2 inductive (see Fig. 11-8). f/f_d is inverted if X_2 is capacitive.

following results for the normalized load-current magnitude:

$$\left.\begin{array}{l} X_2 \text{ inductive} \\ X_3 \text{ capacitive} \end{array}\right\} \quad \frac{|I|}{|I_d|} = \frac{2\sqrt{n}}{\sqrt{(n-1)^2[(f/f_d)^4 - 2(f/f_d)^2] + (n+1)^2}} \tag{11-15}$$

where $n = R_{I1}/R_{I2}$ = impedance transformation ratio
  I_d = load current at design frequency

and

$$|I_d| = \frac{E}{2\sqrt{R_{I1}R_{I2}}} = \frac{\sqrt{n}\,E}{2R_{I1}} \tag{11-15a}$$

Equation (11-15) is plotted in Fig. 11-9 for different values of the impedance-transformation ratio n. It may be observed that, as n increases, the curves become more selective; therefore, if a broad bandwidth is of major consideration, the transformation ratio should be small. This leads to the idea of cascading two or more L sections to achieve a required ratio over a large band and is considered later in Chap. 13.

Equation (11-15a) indicates that, for a fixed generator, $|I_d|$ increases for smaller values of R_{I2}. This result may be verified from physical considerations. For a properly designed L section, a given generator always works into a resistive load of R_{I1} and so delivers constant power of $E^2/4R_{I1}$ watts. Since the L section is lossless, constant power is delivered to R_{I2}, whatever its value. Then, as R_{I2} is decreased, the load-current magnitude must increase by the factor $1/\sqrt{R_{I12}}$.

Similar methods applied to the L section where X_2 capacitive and X_3 inductive show the normalized response to be

$$\left.\begin{matrix} X_2 \text{ capacitive} \\ X_3 \text{ capacitive} \end{matrix}\right\} \frac{|I|}{|I_d|} = \frac{2\sqrt{n}}{\sqrt{(n-1)^2[(f_d/f)^4 - 2(f_d/f)^2] + (n+1)^2}} \quad (11\text{-}16)$$

where again $|I_d| = E/2\sqrt{R_{I1}R_{I2}}$. It should be observed that Eqs. (11-15) and (11-16) are identical except for an inversion of the normalized frequency variable.

11-8. General Requirements of Impedance-matching Networks. While the L section is a minimum-element structure, it is not the only reactive network which may be designed to provide an impedance match at a specified frequency, T or Π sections and tuned transformers being other commonly used networks. Since any four-terminal network may be replaced by an equivalent T section at the design frequency, it is convenient to consider the general requirements of impedance-matching networks in terms of the equivalent T section.

If any asymmetrical T network is terminated in an impedance, the input impedance measured at the input terminals will, in general, be different from the terminating impedance. This property makes the T section suitable as an impedance-transforming device. As explained in Chap. 3, with the asymmetrical T section (see Fig. 3-24), a pair of *image impedances* Z_{I1} and Z_{I2} may be found such that, if end 1 is terminated in Z_{I1}, the input impedance at end 2 is Z_{I2}; and if end 2 is terminated in Z_{I2}, the input impedance at end 1 is Z_{I1}. It was further shown that the image impedances are related to the components of the T section by

$$Z_{I1} = \sqrt{\frac{Z_1 + Z_3}{Z_2 + Z_3}(Z_1Z_2 + Z_2Z_3 + Z_1Z_3)} \quad (3\text{-}100)$$

$$Z_{I2} = \sqrt{\frac{Z_2 + Z_3}{Z_1 + Z_3}(Z_1Z_2 + Z_2Z_3 + Z_1Z_3)} \quad (3\text{-}101)$$

In Chap. 7, Wave Filters, it was shown that a symmetrical network of pure reactances may have a characteristic impedance which is pure resistance. Similarly an asymmetrical network may also have image impedances which are pure resistances. If such a network is connected between a generator whose internal impedance is Z_{I1} and a load whose impedance is Z_{I2}, as in Fig. 11-10, the impedances will match at both junctions, the maximum power will be absorbed from the generator, and since it has been assumed that the arms of the connecting network are pure reactances, no power will be dissipated in the transfer and so this maximum power will be delivered to the load.

Regardless of the generator impedance, any output load can be modified by the network so that the input impedance at the terminals 1, 1' will be anything desired, for if the network is terminated in Z_{I2}, the input impedance will be Z_{I1}.

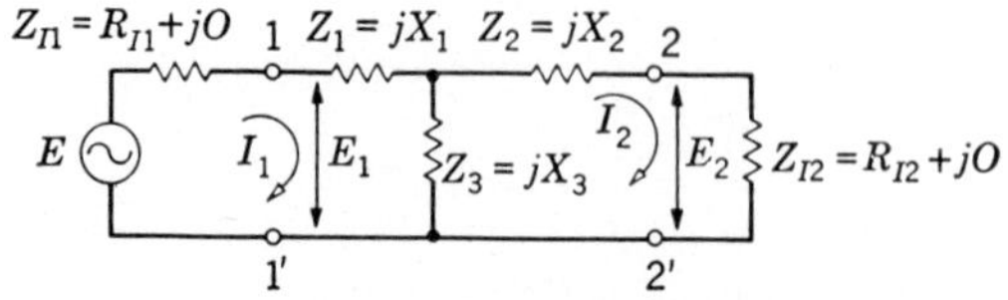

FIG. 11-10. General form of the T impedance-matching network.

If the terminating impedances are not pure resistances, they can be made so at any single frequency by additional reactances in series with them. This has been illustrated in connection with the L section.

11-9. General Requirements for a Matching T Network of Pure Reactances. Consider a T section of pure reactances similar to Fig. 11-10, to match two pure resistances R_{I1} and R_{I2}. Then

$$
\begin{aligned}
Z_1 &= jX_1 \\
Z_2 &= jX_2 \\
Z_3 &= jX_3 \\
Z_{I1} &= R_{I1} \\
Z_{I2} &= R_{I2}
\end{aligned}
\tag{11-17}
$$

X_1, X_2, and X_3 may have either positive or negative values. Then by Eq. (3-100)

$$
R_{I1}^2 = \frac{j(X_1 + X_3)}{j(X_2 + X_3)} j^2(X_1X_2 + X_2X_3 + X_1X_3)
$$

$$
R_{I1}^2 = -\frac{X_1 + X_3}{X_2 + X_3}(X_1X_2 + X_2X_3 + X_1X_3)
\tag{11-18a}
$$

Similarly from Eq. (3-101)

$$
R_{I2}^2 = -\frac{X_2 + X_3}{X_1 + X_3}(X_1X_2 + X_2X_3 + X_1X_3)
\tag{11-18b}
$$

In order to make R_{I1} and R_{I2} pure resistances, the right-hand sides of Eqs. (11-18a) and (11-18b) should be positive numbers, and *therefore one of the reactance arms must be opposite in sign to the other two arms.*

Multiply Eqs. (11-18a) and (11-18b), and extract the square root.

$$
R_{I1}R_{I2} = -(X_1X_2 + X_2X_3 + X_1X_3)
\tag{11-19}
$$

Divide Eq. (11-18a) by Eq. (11-18b), and extract the square root.

$$\frac{R_{I1}}{R_{I2}} = \frac{X_1 + X_3}{X_2 + X_3} \qquad (11\text{-}20)$$

It is frequently desirable, especially in the case of transformers, to consider $X_1 + X_3$ as one term and $X_2 + X_3$ as another. The reactance X_3 is called the "mutual reactance," because it is common to both the input and output circuits. Let

$$X_1 + X_3 = X_p = \text{primary reactance}$$
$$X_2 + X_3 = X_s = \text{secondary reactance}$$
$$X_3 = X_m = \text{mutual reactance}$$

Then Eq. (11-19) becomes

$$R_{I1}R_{I2} = X_m{}^2 - X_p X_s \qquad (11\text{-}19a)$$

while Eq. (11-20) can be written

$$\frac{R_{I1}}{R_{I2}} = \frac{X_p}{X_s} \qquad (11\text{-}20a)$$

In designing a network if only R_{I1} and R_{I2} are specified, one of the three arms may be arbitrarily selected and the other arms then determined from Eqs. (11-19) and (11-20). A set of equations will therefore be obtained for each arm in terms of the others.

Substitute X_s from Eq. (11-20a) in Eq. (11-19a).

$$R_{I1}R_{I2} = X_m{}^2 - \frac{R_{I2}}{R_{I1}} X_p{}^2$$

$$X_p = \pm \sqrt{\frac{R_{I1}}{R_{I2}} (X_m{}^2 - R_{I1}R_{I2})} \qquad (11\text{-}21)$$

Substitute X_p from Eq. (11-20a) in Eq. (11-19a).

$$X_s = \pm \sqrt{\frac{R_{I2}}{R_{I1}} (X_m{}^2 - R_{I1}R_{I2})} \qquad (11\text{-}22)$$

From Eq. (11-19a)

$$X_m{}^2 = X_p X_s + R_{I1}R_{I2} \qquad (11\text{-}23)$$

$$X_m = \pm \sqrt{\frac{R_{I2}}{R_{I1}} X_p{}^2 + R_{I1}R_{I2}} \qquad (11\text{-}23a)$$

$$X_m = \pm \sqrt{\frac{R_{I1}}{R_{I2}} X_s{}^2 + R_{I1}R_{I2}} \qquad (11\text{-}23b)$$

If R_{I1}/R_{I2} is different from unity, then either X_p or X_s will be less than X_m. Now

$$X_1 = X_p - X_3 = X_p - X_m$$

and

$$X_2 = X_s - X_3 = X_s - X_m$$

Therefore, one of the arms X_1 or X_2 of the T section must be the opposite type of reactance to X_m.

11-10. Network Design with One Assumed Element. In the last section design equations were derived for the elements of a reactive asymmetrical T section to match two image resistances. Since only two design conditions are specified, namely, R_{I1} and R_{I2}, but three elements appear in the network; one element is redundant, and it may be chosen arbitrarily, subject to one condition. Equations (11-21) and (11-22) show that $X_m{}^2$ must equal or exceed $R_{I1}R_{I2}$ in order that X_p and X_s remain real and hence physically realizable. Subject to this restriction, the ability to choose one parameter often affords the designer an opportunity of using a component on hand for one of the matching network elements.

The student should observe that $X_m{}^2 = R_{I1}R_{I2}$ represents a critical case, for if $X_m{}^2$ is less than this value, a conjugate impedance match cannot be realized. Furthermore, for this critical case $X_p = X_s = 0$, and $X_1 = X_2$ for the equivalent T. This represents a paradox of sorts, for a *symmetrical* T section may then match two *different* resistances, and the design equations reduce to

$$X_1 = X_2 = -X_3 = \pm \sqrt{R_{I1}R_{I2}} \qquad (11\text{-}24)$$

i.e., the three reactances have equal magnitudes, which are in turn equal to the geometric mean of the two resistances to be matched.

Design a reactive T section to match a load of $250 + j200$ ohms to a 1,000-ohm generator at $\omega = 2 \times 10^6$ radians/sec. Use the critical coupling condition.

To simplify the design procedure, place a reactance of -200 ohms in series with the load impedance so that the effective load is $R_{I2} = 250$ ohms.

$$R_{I1} = 1,000 \text{ ohms.}$$

Then by Eq. (11-24)

$$|X_1| = |X_2| = |X_3| = + \sqrt{R_{I1}R_{I2}} = \sqrt{250 \times 10^3} = 500 \text{ ohms}$$

A single variable capacitor is on hand which will be used as the shunt element, X_3. Then

$$X_3 = -\frac{1}{\omega C_3} = -500 \qquad C_3 = \frac{1}{(2 \times 10^6)(5 \times 10^2)} = 1,000 \ \mu\mu\text{f}$$

$$X_1 = X_2 = 500 \text{ ohms}$$

$$L_1 = L_2 = \frac{500}{2 \times 10^6} = 250 \ \mu\text{h}$$

The resulting network is shown in Fig. 11-11a. Simplification results if X_2 and the compensating reactance of -200 ohms are combined into a single element.

$$X_2' = X_2 - 200 = 500 - 200 = 300 \text{ ohms}$$

$$L_2' = \frac{300}{2 \times 10^6} = 150 \ \mu\text{h}$$

The simplified network is shown at b in the figure.

Equations (11-21) and (11-22) may also be used to design a tuned-transformer-matching network.   An illustrative example follows:

Design a matching network, utilizing a pair of 1 mh coils, to replace the T network of the last example.   The coupling coefficient between the coils may be varied from 0.1 to 0.6 by rotating one coil with respect to the other.   The general configuration of the network is shown in Fig. 11-11c.   Note that the capacitors C_p and C_s are provided so that X_p and X_s may be adjusted even though L_p and L_s are fixed.

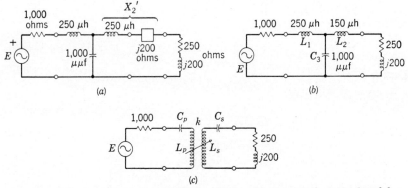

(a)

(b)

(c)

FIG. 11-11. Circuits for the illustrative problem. X_2' of a has been replaced by a single element at b. c shows the equivalent tuned-transformer network.

For critical coupling $X_m = \sqrt{R_{I1}R_{I2}}$.   By definition the coupling coefficient is

$$k = \frac{M}{\sqrt{L_pL_s}} = \frac{\omega M}{\omega \sqrt{L_pL_s}} = \frac{X_m}{\omega \sqrt{L_pL_s}}$$

Since the coils have equal inductances of 1 mh,

$$k = \frac{X_m}{\omega L_p} = \frac{\sqrt{R_{I1}R_{I2}}}{\omega L_p} = \frac{\sqrt{250 \times 10^3}}{(2 \times 10^6) \times 10^{-3}} = \frac{500}{2 \times 10^3} = 0.25$$

This value lies within the specified range of adjustment and hence is satisfactory. By Eqs. (11-21) and (11-22), $X_p = X_s = 0$.

$$X_p = \omega L_p - \frac{1}{\omega C_p} = 0$$

$$C_p = \frac{1}{\omega^2 L_p} = \frac{1}{(4 \times 10^{12}) \times 10^{-3}} = 250 \ \mu\mu f$$

X_s is the *total* reactance of the secondary circuit; thus

$$X_s = \omega L_s - \frac{1}{\omega C_s} + 200 = 0$$

$$C_s = \frac{1}{\omega(\omega L_s + 200)} = \frac{1}{2 \times 10^6[(2 \times 10^6) \times 10^{-3} + 200]}$$

$$= \frac{1}{2 \times 2.2 \times 10^9} = 227 \mu\mu f$$

11-11. Frequency Response of T Section. The response of the T matching section of Fig. 11-10 may be determined by solving for I_2 as a function of frequency. If X_1 and X_2 are chosen to be inductive and X_3 to be capacitive, considerable algebraic manipulation yields the result

$$I_2 = j \frac{E}{R_{I2}} \frac{\omega_d/\omega}{\left\{ \left[\sqrt{\frac{n}{\alpha}} (2\alpha + 1) + \sqrt{\alpha - 1} (n + 1) \right] \right.}$$

$$\frac{}{- \left[\sqrt{\frac{n}{\alpha}} (2\alpha - 1) + \sqrt{\alpha - 1} (n + 1) \right] \left(\frac{\omega}{\omega_d} \right)^2 \right\}}$$

$$+ j \left\{ \left[2 \sqrt{\frac{n}{\alpha}} \sqrt{\alpha - 1} + (n + 1) \right] \frac{\omega}{\omega_d} - (n + 1) \frac{\omega_d}{\omega} \right\} \qquad (11\text{-}25)$$

where $n = R_{I1}/R_{I2}$ = impedance-transformation ratio
$\alpha = X_m{}^2/R_{I1}R_{I2}$

Equation (11-25) is plotted in Fig. 11-12 for several transformation

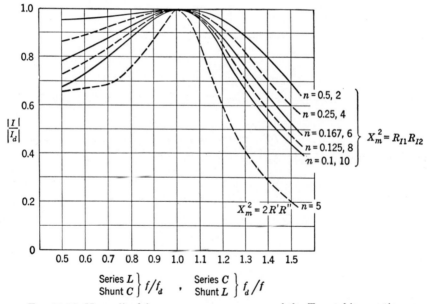

FIG. 11-12. Normalized frequency-response curves of the T matching section.

ratios with critical coupling. It will be observed that the curve becomes more selective as the transformation ratio increases. The effect of increasing the coupling above the critical value is illustrated by the dotted curve in Fig. 11-12, which is plotted for coupling equal to the $\sqrt{2}$ times the critical value ($\alpha = 2$) and $n = 5$. The curve shows that the selectivity of the circuit increases as the coupling increases. The student may show that for this latter case a second maximum of current magnitude occurs at zero frequency. [The student should compare these curves with those for the tuned-transformer circuit (Fig. 11-24), where the two current maxima occur in the same general frequency range.]

11-12. General Relations in Asymmetrical Network. The redundancy of elements in a T section designed on an image-impedance basis alone, as in the previous sections, may be removed by specifying, in addition, the network loss and phase shift. This may be done by means of the "image-transfer constant" Θ of the network. If Θ, Z_{I1}, and Z_{I2} of the asymmetrical T network are all specified, the components of the network are uniquely determined.

In a symmetrical section γ has been defined by the relation that, when the section is terminated by Z_o,

$$e^\gamma = \frac{E_1}{E_2} = \frac{I_1}{I_2} = \sqrt{\frac{E_1 I_1}{E_2 I_2}}$$

In an asymmetrical section, terminated in its image impedance, the ratio of E_1/E_2 is in general different from I_1/I_2, and in the case of matching networks of pure reactance the magnitudes of the two ratios will be reciprocals of each other. The definition adopted for Θ therefore corresponds to the last relation for γ, namely: when the network is terminated in its image impedances,

$$e^\Theta = \sqrt{\frac{E_1 I_1}{E_2 I_2}} \tag{11-26}$$

11-13. Equivalent T Section of Complex Network. It is desirable to obtain a function of Θ in terms of the other constants of the network and, conversely, to find a relation for the values of Z_1, Z_2, and Z_3 in terms of Z_{I1}, Z_{I2}, and Θ, so that a network can be designed to operate between any two impedances and to give any desired loss and/or phase angle. Θ will in general be a complex number. When terminated in the image impedances, the voltage ratio in the network will be

$$\frac{E_1}{E_2} = \frac{I_1 Z_{I1}}{I_2 Z_{I2}}$$

$$e^\Theta = \frac{I_1}{I_2} \sqrt{\frac{Z_{I1}}{Z_{I2}}} \tag{11-26a}$$

In Fig. 11-10

$$\frac{I_1}{I_2} = \frac{Z_2 + Z_3 + Z_{I2}}{Z_3} = \frac{Z_{o2} + Z_{I2}}{Z_3} \tag{11-27}$$

where Z_{o1} and Z_{o2} are, respectively, the open-circuit impedances measured at ends 1 and 2. From Eqs. (3-100) and (3-101)

$$\frac{Z_{I1}}{Z_{I2}} = \frac{Z_1 + Z_3}{Z_2 + Z_3} = \frac{Z_{o1}}{Z_{o2}} \tag{11-28}$$

Substitute Eqs. (11-27) and (11-28) in Eq. (11-26a).

$$e^\theta = \frac{Z_{o2}}{Z_3}\sqrt{\frac{Z_{I1}}{Z_{I2}}} + \frac{Z_{I2}}{Z_3}\sqrt{\frac{Z_{I1}}{Z_{I2}}}$$

$$= \frac{Z_{o2}}{Z_3}\sqrt{\frac{Z_{o1}}{Z_{o2}}} + \frac{Z_{I2}}{Z_3}\sqrt{\frac{Z_{I1}}{Z_{I2}}}$$

$$e^\theta = \frac{\sqrt{Z_{o1}Z_{o2}} + \sqrt{Z_{I1}Z_{I2}}}{Z_3}$$

$$\cosh\theta = \frac{e^\theta + e^{-\theta}}{2}$$

$$= \frac{\sqrt{Z_{o1}Z_{o2}} + \sqrt{Z_{I1}Z_{I2}}}{2Z_3} + \frac{Z_3}{2(\sqrt{Z_{o1}Z_{o2}} + \sqrt{Z_{I1}Z_{I2}})}$$

$$= \frac{Z_{o1}Z_{o2} + 2\sqrt{Z_{o1}Z_{o2}Z_{I1}Z_{I2}} + Z_{I1}Z_{I2} + Z_3{}^2}{2Z_3(\sqrt{Z_{o1}Z_{o2}} + \sqrt{Z_{I1}Z_{I2}})}$$

From Eqs. (3-100) and (3-101)

$$Z_{I1}Z_{I2} = Z_1Z_2 + Z_2Z_3 + Z_1Z_3$$

$$Z_{I1}Z_{I2} + Z_3{}^2 = (Z_1 + Z_3)(Z_2 + Z_3) = Z_{o1}Z_{o2}$$

$$\cosh\theta = \frac{Z_{o1}Z_{o2} + \sqrt{Z_{o1}Z_{o2}Z_{I1}Z_{I2}}}{Z_3(\sqrt{Z_{o1}Z_{o2}} + \sqrt{Z_{I1}Z_{I2}})}$$

$$= \frac{\sqrt{Z_{o1}Z_{o2}}(\sqrt{Z_{o1}Z_{o2}} + \sqrt{Z_{I1}Z_{I2}})}{Z_3(\sqrt{Z_{o1}Z_{o2}} + \sqrt{Z_{I1}Z_{I2}})}$$

$$= \frac{\sqrt{Z_{o1}Z_{o2}}}{Z_3} = \sqrt{\left(1 + \frac{Z_1}{Z_3}\right)\left(1 + \frac{Z_2}{Z_3}\right)} \qquad (11\text{-}29)$$

Similarly

$$\sinh\theta = \frac{e^\theta - e^{-\theta}}{2} = \frac{\sqrt{Z_{I1}Z_{I2}}}{Z_3} \qquad (11\text{-}30)$$

$$Z_3 = \frac{\sqrt{Z_{I1}Z_{I2}}}{\sinh\theta} \qquad (11\text{-}30a)$$

From Eqs. (11-29) and (11-30)

$$\tanh\theta = \sqrt{\frac{Z_{I1}Z_{I2}}{Z_{o1}Z_{o2}}} \qquad (11\text{-}31)$$

Multiply both sides by Z_{o1}, and make use of Eq. (11-28).

$$Z_{o1}\tanh\theta = \sqrt{\frac{Z_{o1}}{Z_{o2}}}\sqrt{Z_{I1}Z_{I2}} = \sqrt{\frac{Z_{I1}}{Z_{I2}}}\sqrt{Z_{I1}Z_{I2}} = Z_{I1} \qquad (11\text{-}32)$$

$$Z_1 + Z_3 = \frac{Z_{I1}}{\tanh\theta}$$

$$Z_1 = \frac{Z_{I1}}{\tanh\theta} - \frac{\sqrt{Z_{I1}Z_{I2}}}{\sinh\theta} \qquad (11\text{-}32a)$$

Similarly

$$Z_{o2} \tanh \Theta = Z_{I2} \tag{11-33}$$

$$Z_2 = \frac{Z_{I2}}{\tanh \Theta} - \frac{\sqrt{Z_{I1}Z_{I2}}}{\sinh \Theta} \tag{11-33a}$$

If a network is to be designed for a given Θ and image impedances, Eqs. (11-30a), (11-32a), and (11-33a) will be used to determine the shunt and series arms of a T section.

Equation (11-32) can also be written

$$\tanh \Theta = \frac{Z_{I1}}{Z_{o1}} = \frac{\sqrt{Z_{o1}Z_{s1}}}{Z_{o1}} = \sqrt{\frac{Z_{s1}}{Z_{o1}}} \tag{11-32b}$$

and, similarly, Eq. (11-33) can be written

$$\tanh \Theta = \frac{Z_{I2}}{Z_{o2}} = \frac{\sqrt{Z_{o2}Z_{s2}}}{Z_{o2}} = \sqrt{\frac{Z_{s2}}{Z_{o2}}} \tag{11-33b}$$

From the symmetry of Eqs. (11-32b) and (11-33b) it is apparent that the constant Θ would be the same if the direction of transmission were reversed.

In the general case Z_{I1}, Z_{I2}, Z_1, Z_2, and Z_3 will all be complex, and the image-transfer constant will be complex; thus

$$\Theta = A + jB \tag{11-34}$$

where A is a loss function analogous to α and B is the phase shift analogous to β. In Chap. 13 the case will be considered where the five impedances and Θ are real.

11-14. Network Design for Specified Phase Shift. Of particular interest in the present chapter is the case where the T network is a lossless structure and the two image impedances are real. Thus, making the substitutions of Eqs. (11-17) into Eq. (11-32b),

$$\tanh \Theta = \frac{R_{I1}}{j(X_1 + X_3)}$$

Since the right-hand member of the equation is imaginary, $\tanh \Theta$ is also imaginary, or $\Theta = 0 + jB$. Furthermore, on substitution of Eqs. (11-17), Eqs. (11-30a), (11-32a), and (11-33a) become

$$X_3 = -\frac{\sqrt{R_{I1}R_{I2}}}{\sin B} \tag{11-35}$$

$$X_1 = -\frac{R_{I1}}{\tan B} + \frac{\sqrt{R_{I1}R_{I2}}}{\sin B} \tag{11-36}$$

$$X_2 = -\frac{R_{I2}}{\tan B} + \frac{\sqrt{R_{I1}R_{I2}}}{\sin B} \tag{11-37}$$

By means of these equations the lossless T section may be designed for a given pair of image impedances and a specified phase shift.

Design a lossless T section to transform a load resistance of 200 ohms into $800 + j0$ ohms at $\omega = 5 \times 10^6$ radians/sec. The load current is to lead the input current by 12°. Let

$$R_{I1} = 800 \text{ ohms} \qquad R_{I2} = 200 \text{ ohms}$$

Since the output current is to *lead* the input current by 12°, $B = -12°$. Then from Eq. (11-35)

$$X_3 = -\frac{\sqrt{800 \times 200}}{\sin(-12°)} = +1,924 \text{ ohms}$$

$$L_3 = \frac{X_3}{\omega} = \frac{1.924 \times 10^3}{5 \times 10^6} = 0.384 \times 10^{-3} = 384 \ \mu\text{h}$$

From Eq. (11-36)

$$X_1 = -\frac{800}{\tan(-12°)} - 1,924 = +3,760 - 1,924 = 1,836 \text{ ohms}$$

$$L_1 = \frac{1.836 \times 10^3}{5 \times 10^6} = 0.367 \times 10^{-3} = 367 \ \mu\text{h}$$

From Eq. (11-37)

$$X_2 = \frac{-200}{\tan(-12°)} - 1,924 = +941 - 1,924 = -983 \text{ ohms}$$

$$C_2 = \frac{1}{X_2\omega} = \frac{1}{(0.983 \times 10^3)(0.5 \times 10^7)} = 2.04 \times 10^{-10} = 204 \ \mu\mu\text{f}$$

The complete network is shown in Fig. 11-13.

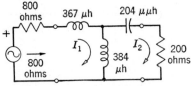

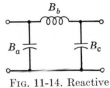

Fig. 11-13. A T network that transforms 200 ohms to 800 ohms with a phase shift of 12°, the output current leading the input current.

Fig. 11-14. Reactive Π impedance transforming network.

11-15. Π Matching Networks. The equations of the previous sections may be readily adapted to the design of reactive Π matching sections by use of the duality principle (see Chap. 3). As a matter of convenience in Fig. 11-14 let $B_p = B_a + B_b$ and $B_s = B_c + B_b$. Then the equations are applicable to the Π network by substituting B_p for X_p, B_s for X_s, B_c for X_2, B_b for X_3, B_a for X_1, G_{I1} for R_{I1}, and G_{I2} for R_{I2}. The condition for an impedance match becomes $B_b{}^2 \geq G_{I1}G_{I2}$.

11-16. Summary of T and Π Networks. It has been shown previously that in T and Π matching networks at least two of the reactive elements must be of opposite sign. For this reason there are only four basic types of such networks possible. These types will now be summarized in terms of three design parameters a, b, and c as an aid for the work of the next section. It will be assumed throughout that $n = R_{I1}/R_{I2} > 1$. This is valid because the networks can transform in either direction and R_{I1} may be chosen as the larger of the image impedances.

Consider first the T sections. From Eqs. (11-35) to (11-37)

$$X_3 = -\frac{\sqrt{R_{I1}R_{I2}}}{\sin B} = R_{I1}\frac{-1}{\sqrt{n}\sin B} = R_{I1}b \tag{11-38}$$

$$b = \frac{-1}{\sqrt{n}\sin B} \tag{11-38a}$$

$$X_1 = -R_{I1}\frac{\cos B}{\sin B} + \frac{\sqrt{R_{I1}R_{I2}}}{\sin B} = R_{I1}\frac{1 - \sqrt{n}\cos B}{\sqrt{n}\sin B} = R_{I1}c \tag{11-39}$$

$$c = \frac{1 - \sqrt{n}\cos B}{\sqrt{n}\sin B} \tag{11-39a}$$

$$X_2 = -R_{I2}\frac{\cos B}{\sin B} + \frac{\sqrt{R_{I1}R_{I2}}}{\sin B} = R_{I1}\frac{\sqrt{n} - \cos B}{n\sin B} = R_{I1}a \tag{11-40}$$

$$a = \frac{\sqrt{n} - \cos B}{n\sin B} \tag{11-40a}$$

Now if the networks introduce a phase *lag*, B is positive as is sin B; hence b is negative, and since $\sqrt{n} > 1$, a is positive. On the other hand, c may be positive, negative, or zero depending upon the magnitude of B. If $0 < B < \arccos(1/\sqrt{n})$, $c < 0$; if $\arccos(1/\sqrt{n}) < B \le 180°$, $c > 0$; and if $B = \arccos(1/\sqrt{n})$, $c = 0$ and the T section degenerates into the L configuration. These conditions define the types 1 and 2 networks of Fig. 11-15.

On the other hand, if the networks introduce a phase *lead*, B is negative as is sin B; hence b is positive, and a is negative. If $0 < |B| < \arccos(1/\sqrt{n})$, $c > 0$; if $\arccos(1/\sqrt{n}) < |B| < 180°$, $c < 0$. The L section results if $|B| = \arccos(1/\sqrt{n})$. These conditions define the types 3 and 4 networks of Fig. 11-15.

The corresponding Π sections may be handled in an analogous manner so that the network elements may be expressed in terms of the same three parameters a, b, and c. Thus, letting $n = R_{I1}/R_{I2} = G_{I2}/G_{I1}$ and manipulating the duals of Eqs. (11-35) to (11-37),

$$B_b = -\frac{\sqrt{G_{I1}G_{I2}}}{\sin B} = -G_{I2}\sqrt{\frac{G_{I1}}{G_{I2}}}\frac{1}{\sin B} = G_{I2}\frac{-1}{\sqrt{n}\sin B}$$

$$= G_{I2}b \tag{11-38b}$$

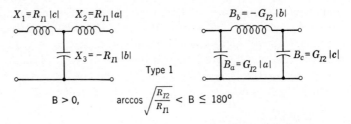

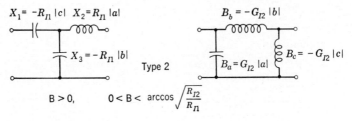

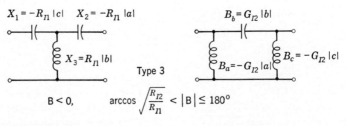

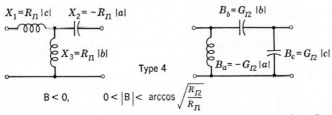

FIG. 11-15. Summary of T and Π impedance-transforming networks. In each case $R_{I1}/R_{I2} = G_{I2}/G_{I1} > 1$. B is the phase shift.

$$B_a = -G_{I1} \frac{\cos B}{\sin B} + \frac{\sqrt{G_{I1}G_{I2}}}{\sin B} = G_{I2} \frac{\sqrt{n} - \cos B}{n \sin B} = G_{I2}a \quad (11\text{-}39b)$$

$$B_c = -G_{I2} \frac{\cos B}{\sin B} + \frac{\sqrt{G_{I1}G_{I2}}}{\sin B} = G_{I2} \frac{1 - \sqrt{n} \cos B}{\sqrt{n} \sin B} = G_{I2}c \quad (11\text{-}39c)$$

Since the Π elements are expressed in terms of the same parameters as the T elements, the same rules of sign apply here as for the T, yielding the four Π networks of Fig. 11-15.

These results may now be used to investigate the effects of losses in the impedance-transforming networks.

11-17. Dissipation in T and Π Networks.[1] In the previous sections the T and Π impedance-transforming sections have been designed on a no-loss basis. As a practical matter, however, the resistance of inductors may not be entirely negligible, and the efficiency of the transforming network will be something less than 100 per cent. The computation of high-efficiency reactance-network losses may be handled by the following approximation (refer to Sec. 10-15): The circuit is initially designed and the currents calculated on a no-loss basis. The Q of the required

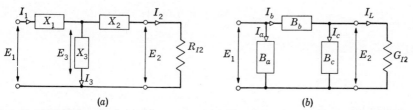

(a)   (b)

FIG. 11-16. Defining the branch currents of (a) T and (b) Π networks for studying the effects of dissipation.

inductors may then be used to calculate the loss and efficiency, the inductor losses being taken into account.

A more general treatment of the losses in T and Π networks is advantageous, however, for, subject to three simplifying approximations, it shows that *the network loss is independent of the number of inductors used* and depends only upon the inductor Q, the impedance-transformation ratio, and the phase-shift angle B. These results in turn may be used as a guide in designing minimum-loss reactive T and Π transforming networks.

In the derivations that follow it will be assumed that all inductor Q's in a given network are identical; that the losses in the capacitors are negligible; and that the *branch currents* are not affected by the presence of the small resistive components, i.e., the *currents* will be computed on the basis of no loss. This latter assumption is warranted when the network efficiency is 90 per cent or greater. The currents and voltages in the following paragraphs are identified in Fig. 11-16.

Consider, first, the type 1 T and Π networks. For the T configuration

$$P_{\text{lost}} = (P_{\text{lost}})_1 + (P_{\text{lost}})_2 = |I_1|^2 R_1 + |I_2|^2 R_2$$

[1] W. L. Everitt, Coupling Networks, *Communications* (*N.Y.*), vol. 18, p. 12, September, 1938, p. 12, October, 1938. See also F. E. Terman, "Radio Engineers' Handbook," p. 210, McGraw-Hill Book Company, Inc., New York, 1943.

where R_1 and R_2 are the resistances of the inductors L_1 and L_2, respectively; thus, utilizing the results of the last section,

$$R_1 = \frac{|X_1|}{Q} = \frac{R_{I1}|c|}{Q} \qquad R_2 = \frac{|X_2|}{Q} = \frac{R_{I1}|a|}{Q}$$

Then

$$P_{\text{lost}} = \frac{|E_1|^2}{R_{I1}^2}\frac{R_{I1}|c|}{Q} + \frac{|E_2|^2}{R_{I2}^2}\frac{R_{I1}|a|}{Q}$$

But since currents are computed on a lossless basis,

$$\frac{|E_1|^2}{R_{I1}} = \frac{|E_2|^2}{R_{I2}} = P_{in}$$

therefore

$$P_{\text{lost}} = \frac{P_{in}}{Q}(|c| + n|a|) \tag{11-41}$$

Let δ be a loss factor defined by

$$\delta = Q\frac{P_{\text{lost}}}{P_{in}} \tag{11-42}$$

and let the loss factor for the type 1 T network be designated δ_1. Then from Eq. (11-41)

$$\delta_1 = |c| + n|a| \tag{11-43}$$

It will now be demonstrated that the type 1 Π network has the same loss factor. For this network

$$P_{\text{lost}} = (P_{\text{lost}})_b = |I_b|^2 R_b$$

where

$$R_b = \frac{1}{Q|B_b|} = \frac{1}{QG_{I2}|b|}$$

and

$$I_b = I_L + I_c = E_2(G_{I2} + jB_c)$$
$$= E_2 G_{I2}(1 + j|c|)$$

Substituting,

$$P_{\text{lost}} = \frac{|E_2|^2 G_{I2}^2(1 + |c|^2)}{QG_{I2}|b|} = \frac{P_{in}}{Q}\left(\frac{1 + |c|^2}{|b|}\right)$$

By Eq. (11-42)

$$\delta = \frac{1 + |c|^2}{|b|} \tag{11-44}$$

This quantity may be shown to be identical to δ_1 by substituting for $|c|$ and $|b|$ from Eqs. (11-38a) and (11-40a). Since for the type 1 networks $|c|$ is positive, $|c| = c$; thus

$$\delta = \left(1 + \frac{1 - 2\sqrt{n}\cos B + n\cos^2 B}{n\sin^2 B}\right)\sqrt{n}\sin B$$
$$= \frac{n + 1 - 2\sqrt{n}\cos B}{\sqrt{n}\sin B}$$

Regrouping the numerator,

$$\delta = \frac{n - \sqrt{n}\cos B}{\sqrt{n}\sin B} + \frac{1 - \sqrt{n}\cos B}{\sqrt{n}\sin B} = na + c$$

Now in the type 1 networks a and c are both positive; hence δ may be written

$$\delta = n|a| + |c| = \delta_1 \tag{11-45}$$

It has, therefore, been proved that the type 1 T and Π networks have the same loss factor δ_1 given by Eqs. (11-43) and (11-45). The student may show in a similar manner that δ_1 is also the loss function for the type 3 T and Π networks, thereby showing that the four networks for which arccos $\sqrt{R_{I1}/R_{I2}} < |B| < 180°$, B being either positive or negative, have the same loss factor δ_1.

By similar methods it may be shown that the four type 2 and type 4 networks have the same loss function δ_2. For example, in the type 4 T structure

$$P_{\text{lost}} = (P_{\text{lost}})_1 + (P_{\text{lost}})_3 \tag{11-46}$$

But
$$I_1 = \frac{E_1}{R_{I1}} \qquad R_1 = \frac{|X_1|}{Q} = \frac{R_{I1}|c|}{Q}$$

Then
$$(P_{\text{lost}})_1 = |I_1|^2 R_1 = \frac{|E_1|^2 R_{I1}|c|}{R_{I1}{}^2 Q} = \frac{P_{in}|c|}{Q} \tag{11-47}$$

Also,
$$I_3 = \frac{E_3}{jX_3} = \frac{E_1 - jX_1 I_1}{jX_3} = \frac{E_1 - j(E_1 X_1/R_{I1})}{jX_3}$$
$$= \frac{E_1}{jR_{I1}} \frac{1 - j|c|}{|b|}$$

and
$$R_3 = \frac{|X_3|}{Q} = \frac{R_{I1}|b|}{Q}$$

Then
$$(P_{\text{lost}})_3 = |I_3|^2 R_3 = \frac{|E_1|^2}{R_{I1}{}^2}\left(\frac{1 + |c|^2}{|b|}\right)\frac{R_{I1}|b|}{Q}$$
$$= \frac{P_{in}}{Q}\left(\frac{1 + |c|^2}{|b|}\right) \tag{11-48}$$

The factor in parentheses may be simplified further, but care must be exercised to preserve the magnitude of c. In the type 4 network $\sqrt{n}\cos B > 1$ and $\sqrt{n} - \cos B < 0$, and $\sin B < 0$; thus

$$|c| = \frac{\sqrt{n}\cos B - 1}{\sqrt{n}\,|\sin B|} \qquad |b| = \frac{1}{\sqrt{n}\,|\sin B|}$$

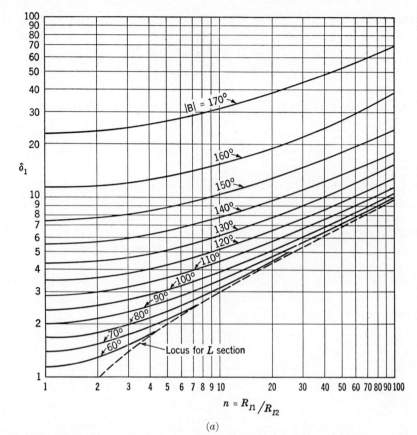

FIG. 11-17. Loss functions for T, Π, and L impedance-matching networks. (a) δ_1 for the types 1 and 3 networks of Fig. 11-15. (b) δ_2 for the types 2 and 4 networks.

Then

$$\frac{1 + |c|^2}{|b|} = \left(1 + \frac{n \cos^2 B - 2\sqrt{n} \cos B + 1}{n|\sin B|^2}\right)\sqrt{n}\ |\sin B|$$

$$= \frac{n - 2\sqrt{n} \cos B + 1}{\sqrt{n}\ |\sin B|}$$

$$= n\frac{\sqrt{n} - \cos B}{n|\sin B|} - \frac{\sqrt{n} \cos B - 1}{\sqrt{n}\ |\sin B|}$$

$$= n|a| - |c|$$

and Eq. (11-48) becomes

$$(P_{\text{lost}})_3 = \frac{P_{in}}{Q}\ (n|a| - |c|) \tag{11-49}$$

Substituting Eqs. (11-47) and (11-49) into Eq. (11-46),

$$P_{\text{lost}} = \frac{P_{in}}{Q}\ n|a| \tag{11-50}$$

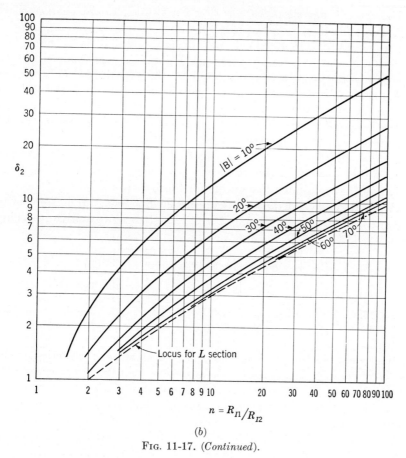

$$n = R_{I1}/R_{I2}$$

(b)

FIG. 11-17. (Continued).

The coefficient of P_{in}/Q may be recognized as the loss factor defined by Eq. (11-42). Let δ_2 designate the loss factor for the type 4 networks; then

$$\delta_2 = n|a| \qquad (11-51)$$

The type 4 II network may also be shown to have the loss function δ_2. In this case

$$P_{\text{lost}} = (P_{\text{lost}})_a = |I_a|^2 R_a$$

But

$$I_a = E_1 j B_a = j E_1 G_{I2} a \qquad R_a = \frac{1}{Q|B_a|} = \frac{1}{Q G_{I2}|a|}$$

or

$$P_{\text{lost}} = \frac{|E_1|^2 G_{I2}{}^2 |a|^2}{Q G_{I2}|a|} = \frac{|E_1|^2 G_{I1}}{Q} \frac{G_{I2}}{G_{I1}} |a|$$

$$= \frac{P_{in}}{Q} n|a|$$

or

$$\delta_2 = n|a|$$

The student may show that the type 2 networks are also characterized by the loss function δ_2 of Eq. (11-51).

The results of the foregoing work may be stated as follows: The efficiency of the transforming network is implicitly determined by the impedance-transformation ratio n and by the magnitude of the phase-shift angle, and not by the choice between T and Π networks and the sign of the phase shift angle. In all cases δ_1 applies to those networks where the phase shift is large ($|B| > \arccos 1/\sqrt{n}$) and δ_2 to networks with smaller phase shifts ($|B| < \arccos 1/\sqrt{n}$).

The loss functions δ_1 and δ_2 are plotted in Fig. 11-17. Inspection of these curves shows that the loss increases with increasing transformation ratio and that minimum loss occurs for the L section.

11-18. Reduction of Loss with Cascaded Sections. It is frequently argued that minimizing the number of inductors in a reactive matching

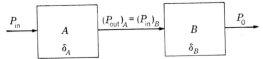

FIG. 11-18. Circuit for calculating the efficiency of two cascaded impedance-matching networks.

section results in the maximum possible efficiency for the section. The results of the last section may be used to show that this is not necessarily true if the network must provide a large specified phase shift as well as a specified impedance-transformation ratio. The loss may sometimes be reduced by cascading two networks.

As an example, consider a network which is to have a transformation ratio $n = 36$ and a phase shift magnitude $|B| = 160°$. Assume inductor Q's of 100. Then, from Fig. 11-17a, $\delta_1 = 23$, and, by Eq. (11-42), the efficiency will be

$$\eta = 1 - \frac{P_{\text{lost}}}{P_{in}} = 1 - \frac{\delta_1}{Q}$$
$$= 1 - 0.23 = 77\%$$

An equivalent network could be designed comprising two sections in cascade, each having $n = 6$ and $|B| = 80°$. Then, from Fig. 11-17a, $\delta_1 = 2.5$ for each section: referring to Fig. 11-18,

$$(P_{\text{out}})_A = P_{in} - (P_{\text{lost}})_A = P_{in}\left(1 - \frac{\delta_A}{Q}\right)$$

$$P_{\text{out}} = (P_{in})_B - (P_{\text{lost}})_B = (P_{in})_B\left(1 - \frac{\delta_B}{Q}\right)$$

But $(P_{out})_A = (P_{in})_B$; thus

$$\eta = \frac{P_{out}}{P_{in}} = \left(1 - \frac{\delta_A}{Q}\right)\left(1 - \frac{\delta_B}{Q}\right)$$

$$= 1 - \frac{\delta_A + \delta_B}{Q} + \frac{\delta_A \delta_B}{Q^2} \tag{11-52}$$

Substituting numerical values for the example

$$\eta = 1 - 0.05 + 0.000625 = 95\%$$

Hence the two sections in cascade give an increase of 18 per cent over the efficiency of the single stage, provided, of course, that $Q = 100$ for all the inductors.

11-19. Frequency Rejection in Matching Networks. Since all the networks of Fig. 11-15 are designed at a single frequency, it will be found

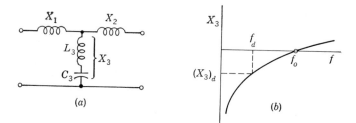

(a)

(b)

Fig. 11-19. Modification of a T matching network to suppress a particular frequency. (a) X_3 is made series resonant at the frequency to be rejected. (b) Reactance curve for X_3. f_d is the design frequency, f_o the frequency to be rejected.

that at frequencies different from the design frequency, they will not provide an impedance match. This filtering action may be useful in many rf applications. It may be made even more effective by utilizing the properties of resonance in the design of one or more of the arms. For example, if any of the shunt branches is modified to be series resonant at some particular frequency, say, f_o, then that branch acts as a short circuit at f_o and energy at that frequency does not appear across the load. Similar action may be obtained by making any of the series branches antiresonant at, say, f_x.

More specifically, let the network of a T section be modified to reject f_o, which is higher than the design frequency f_d. This may be accomplished by changing X_3 to a series combination of L_3 and C_3 as shown in Fig. 11-19a. The reactance curve of X_3 is sketched as a function of frequency at b. The branch elements may then be calculated by application of Foster's reactance theorem, or since only two unknowns are involved, they may be evaluated by setting up two simultaneous equations. At the design frequency f_d X_3 must have the value $(X_3)_d$ determined from Eqs. (11-20) to (11-22) or Eqs. (11-35) to (11-37), that is

$$\omega_d L_3 - \frac{1}{\omega_d C_3} = (X_3)_d$$

and at ω_o the branch must be series resonant, or

$$\omega_o L_3 - \frac{1}{\omega_o C_3} = 0$$

These equations may then be solved simultaneously for L_3 and C_3.

As an example, the T network of Fig. 11-11b is to be modified to reject the second harmonic in the X_3 branch. From a previous problem, on page 416,

$$\omega_d = 2 \times 10^6 \text{ radians/sec.}$$

$(X_3)_d = -500$ ohms. $\omega_o = 4 \times 10^6$ radians/sec.
At ω_d

$$2 \times 10^6 L_3 - \frac{1}{2 \times 10^6 C_3} = -500 \tag{11-53}$$

At ω_o

$$4 \times 10^6 L_3 - \frac{1}{4 \times 10^6 C_3} = 0 \tag{11-54}$$

Solving by determinants,

$$L_3 = \frac{500/(4 \times 10^6)}{-\frac{3}{4} + \frac{1}{2}} = \frac{125 \times 10^{-6}}{1.5} = 83.3 \ \mu h$$

From Eq. (11-54)

$$C_3 = \frac{1}{(16 \times 10^{12})L_3} = \frac{1}{(16 \times 10^{12})(0.833 \times 10^{-4})} = 750 \ \mu\mu f$$

More than one frequency may be rejected in a single branch by using circuits more complicated than a simple series or parallel combination of inductance and capacitance. The design of such branches is greatly simplified by the use of Foster's reactance theorem and the synthesizing techniques of Chap. 4.

11-20. Matching at Several Frequencies. The idea proposed in the last section of using a Foster network rather than a single reactive element in one or more branches of the matching network suggests the possibility of providing an impedance match at more than one frequency. This is quite possible and may provide a distinct operating advantage for short-wave radio transmitters, which often operate on markedly different frequencies during the day and night in order to utilize the best propagation characteristics of the several available bands. The methods for designing the required networks are similar to those of the last section and may best be illustrated by a numerical example.

A single transmitter is to be operated on two different short-wave frequencies: on 11.91 Mc (25-m band) during the daytime, and on 6.1 Mc (49-m band) at night.   It is desired to design a Π network to match 800 ohms to a 50-ohm coaxial line at either frequency without retuning or switching elements.   A 1.336-μh inductor is to be used as the series element if possible.   Only the c branch will be designed for purposes of illustration.

By the specifications

$$\omega_1 = 2\pi(6.1 \times 10^6) = 3.84 \times 10^7 \text{ radians/sec.}$$
$$\omega_2 = 2\pi(11.91 \times 10^6) = 7.56 \times 10^7 \text{ radians/sec.}$$
$$G_{I1} = \tfrac{1}{800} = 0.125 \times 10^{-2} \text{ mho} \qquad G_{I2} = \tfrac{1}{50} = 2 \times 10^{-2} \text{ mho}$$
$$G_{I1}G_{I2} = 0.25 \times 10^{-4} \text{ mho}^2$$

Check to see whether the inductor is small enough so that $B_b{}^2 \geq G_{I1}G_{I2}$
At ω_1

$$B_b = -\frac{1}{\omega_1 L_b} = -\frac{1}{(3.84 \times 10^7)(1.336 \times 10^{-6})} = -1.95 \times 10^{-2} \text{ mho}$$
$$B_b{}^2 = (-1.95 \times 10^{-2})^2 = 3.8 \times 10^{-4} > G_{I1}G_{I2}$$

At ω_2

$$B_b = -\frac{1}{(7.56 \times 10^7)(1.336 \times 10^{-6})} = -0.99 \times 10^{-2} \text{ mho}$$
$$B_b{}^2 = (-0.99 \times 10^{-2})^2 = 0.979 \times 10^{-4} > G_{I1}G_{I2}$$

Therefore, the specified inductor is satisfactory for the series branch B_b.

Next find the values required for B_c at the design frequencies.   By the dual of Eq. (11-22)

$$B_s = \pm \sqrt{\frac{G_{I2}}{G_{I1}} (B_b{}^2 - G_{I1}G_{I2})}$$

At ω_1

$$(B_s)_1 = \pm \sqrt{\frac{2 \times 10^{-2}}{0.125 \times 10^{-2}} (3.8 - 0.25)10^{-4}} = \pm \sqrt{\frac{2}{0.125} \times 3.55 \times 10^{-4}}$$
$$= 7.54 \times 10^{-2}$$

But $B_c = B_s - B_b$

+ root: − root:
$$(B_c)_1 = (7.54 + 1.95) \times 10^{-2} \qquad\qquad (B_c)_1 = (-7.54 + 1.95) \times 10^{-2}$$
$$= 9.49 \times 10^{-2} \text{ mho} \qquad\qquad\qquad = -5.59 \times 10^{-2} \text{ mho}$$

At ω_2

$$(B_s)_2 = \pm \sqrt{\frac{2}{0.125} (0.979 - 0.25) \times 10^{-4}} = \pm \sqrt{\frac{2}{0.125} \times 0.729 \times 10^{-4}}$$
$$= \pm 3.42 \times 10^{-2}$$

+ root: − root:
$$(B_c)_2 = (3.42 + 0.99) \times 10^{-2} \qquad\qquad (B_c)_2 = (-3.42 + 0.99) \times 10^{-2}$$
$$= 4.41 \times 10^{-2} \text{ mho} \qquad\qquad\qquad = -2.43 \times 10^{-2} \text{ mho}$$

The remaining part of the problem is to synthesize the required c branch of the Π section.   The susceptance curves corresponding to the positive and negative roots of B_s are shown at a and b, respectively, in Fig. 11-20. It may be seen that three elements are required to synthesize the curve at a, whereas only two elements are needed for the curve at b. Hence the latter solution will be used, corresponding to L_c and C_c in parallel. (The dashed curve at b shows an alternative two-element possibility, that of L_c and C_c in series.) The parallel-element

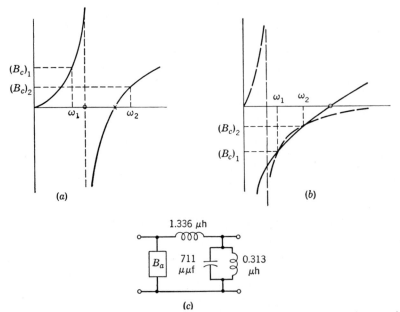

FIG. 11-20. Design of a II section to provide an impedance match at two frequencies. (a) Susceptance curve for positive roots of B_s. (b) Susceptance curve for negative roots of B_s. (c) An antiresonant circuit is used in the c branch.

branch may be designed by setting up two simultaneous equations to evaluate the two unknowns.

$$\omega_1 C_c - \frac{1}{\omega_1 L_c} = (B_c)_1$$

$$\omega_2 C_c - \frac{1}{\omega_2 L_c} = (B_c)_2$$

$$C = \frac{\begin{vmatrix} (B_c)_1 & -\dfrac{1}{\omega_1} \\[2ex] (B_c)_2 & -\dfrac{1}{\omega_2} \end{vmatrix}}{\begin{vmatrix} \omega_1 & -\dfrac{1}{\omega_1} \\[2ex] \omega_2 & -\dfrac{1}{\omega_2} \end{vmatrix}} = \frac{-(B_c)_1/\omega_2 + (B_c)_2/\omega_1}{-\omega_1/\omega_2 + \omega_2/\omega_1}$$

$$= \frac{-\omega_1(B_c)_1 + \omega_2(B_c)_2}{\omega_2{}^2 - \omega_1{}^2} = \frac{[-3.84(-5.59) + 7.56(-2.43)] \times 10^5}{(5.71 - 1.47) \times 10^{14}}$$

$$= \frac{(21.41 - 18.4) \times 10^5}{4.24 \times 10^{14}} = \frac{3.01 \times 10^{-9}}{4.24} = 711 \ \mu\mu f$$

$$L_c = \frac{1}{\omega_1[\omega_1 C_c - (B_c)_1]} = \frac{1}{3.84 \times 10^7[3.84 \times 10^7(0.711 \times 10^{-9}) + 5.59 \times 10^{-2}]}$$

$$= \frac{1}{3.84 \times 10^7(2.73 + 5.59) \times 10^{-2}} = \frac{1}{3.84 \times 8.32 \times 10^5} = 0.313 \ \mu h$$

The resulting network is shown in Fig. 11-20c. The B_a branch may be designed in a similar manner.

11-21. Tuned Radio-frequency Transformers. In an earlier section it was pointed out that a tuned rf transformer as shown in Fig. 11-21

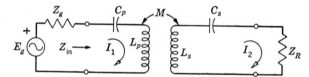

Fig. 11-21. A tuned-transformer impedance-transforming network.

may be designed by the use of Eqs. (11-20) to (11-22). X_p in these equations represents the *total* primary reactance including any in Z_g, while X_s represents the *total* secondary reactance including any in Z_L. X_p can be adjusted by C_p and X_s by C_s. It is usually necessary to add capacitive reactance (C_p and C_s), but occasionally the design equations dictate the addition of inductance in one side or the other. An example showing the design of such a network on a lossless basis *with no phase shift specified* is shown in Fig. 11-11c. Where the transformer network must be designed for a specified phase shift as well as a given impedance-transformation ratio, a T section may first be designed by means of Eqs. (11-35) to (11-37) and then converted to the transformer by the identities preceding Eqs. (11-19a).

It should be observed that more freedom of design is afforded by the transformer than by the T section because it involves five parameters (L_p, L_s, M, C_p, and C_s) rather than three. The coil assembly comprising L_p and L_s, with M often variable, may be chosen from available stock subject only to the restriction that ωM be of sufficient value. C_p and C_s may then be adjusted to give the design values of X_p and X_s. The extra degrees of freedom afforded by the tuned transformer also admit greater variations in the frequency-response curve. This is discussed in a later section.

11-22. Input Impedance of Tuned Transformer. While the last section outlines the method for designing lossless tuned-transformer matching networks, additional insight into the behavior of these circuits may be had by investigating their input impedance in general form.

Since the tuned transformer, generator, and load of Fig. 11-21 comprise a two-mesh circuit, the input impedance of the transformer will be

$$Z_{in} = Z_{11} - \frac{Z_{12}^2}{Z_{22}} \tag{11-55}$$

where Z_{11} = loop primary impedance *not* including Z_g
$\qquad = jX_p$
$\qquad Z_{22}$ = loop secondary impedance
$\qquad = R_s + jX_s$
$\qquad Z_{12}$ = mutual impedance
$\qquad = \pm jX_m = \pm j\omega M$

The sign of Z_{12} depends upon the winding polarities of the transformer and the assumed positive current directions. Substituting and rationalizing,

$$\begin{aligned} Z_{in} &= jX_p - \frac{(\pm jX_m)^2}{R_s + jX_s} \\ &= \frac{X_m^2 R_s}{R_s^2 + X_s^2} + j\left(X_p - \frac{X_m^2 X_s}{R_s^2 + X_s^2}\right) \end{aligned} \tag{11-56}$$

It should be observed that the sign of X_m has no effect on the input impedance since it appears only as the square in Eq. (11-56). Notice also that the secondary reactance is reflected or coupled into the primary with a change of sign.

11-23. Insufficient Coupling. Equations (11-21) and (11-22) specify the values of X_p and X_s for an impedance match where X_m^2 equals or exceeds the critical value $X_m^2 = R_{I1}R_{I2}$. Equation (11-56) allows the determination of X_p and X_s for the case of *insufficient coupling*, i.e., where $X_m^2 < R_{I1}R_{I2}$. In order to make the notation consistent, let $Z_g = R_{I1}$ in Fig. 11-21, and let $Z_R = R_s = R_{I2}$. Then in this case it is desirable to make the input impedance *real* and as large as possible, since it cannot be made sufficient to equal R_{I1}. Thus, to maximize the real term of Eq. (11-56), set

$$X_s = 0 \tag{11-57a}$$

Then
$$Z_{in} = \frac{X_m^2}{R_{I2}} + jX_p \qquad X_s = 0$$

This quantity may be made real by setting

$$X_p = 0 \tag{11-57b}$$

and
$$Z_{in} = \frac{X_m^2}{R_{I2}} \tag{11-58}$$

The student should observe that, if X_m^2 can be increased to

$$X_m^2 = R_{I1}R_{I2}$$

$Z_{in} = R_{I1}$, confirming previous results for critical coupling. He may also verify Eqs. (11-21) and (11-22) for the sufficient coupling case $(X_m{}^2 > R_{I1}R_{I2})$ by suitable manipulation of Eq. (11-56).

11-24. Control of Impedance Match by Circuit Parameters. Equations (11-21) and (11-22) and also Eqs. (11-57a) and (11-57b) are *pairs* of equations which give, for the cases of sufficient and insufficient coupling, respectively, the best adjustments for primary and secondary reactance, *when both adjustments are made.* If X_p cannot be adjusted, then Eqs. (11-22) and (11-57a) do not give the best value of X_s, if the latter is the only value which can be selected at will. Similarly, if X_s must remain fixed, Eqs. (11-21) and (11-57b) will not give the best values of X_p.

In general, in a matching network, if there are two adjustments which can be made, for example, X_p and X_s, or X_p and X_m, or X_s and X_m, both the magnitude and phase of the generator and load impedances may be matched. On the other hand, if only one of the three variables can be adjusted, only one of the complex components of generator and load impedance can be matched.

11-25. Partial Resonance. It is apparent that, when it is possible to adjust only X_p, all other reactances being fixed, the best value of X_p (which has no effect on the real part of Z_{in}) is such as to make the total *reactance* of the equivalent series circuit, as viewed from the generator, equal to zero. This will give the largest value of $|I_1|$ obtainable with this adjustment and hence the largest amount of power delivered to the load which is possible under the conditions laid down. Therefore, when X_p only is adjustable, from Eq. (11-56) it can be seen that the following condition should be met:

$$X_p = \frac{\omega^2 M^2}{R_s{}^2 + X_s{}^2} X_s \qquad (11\text{-}59)$$

Equation (11-59) has been termed by Pierce "partial resonance P."[*]

If, on the other hand, X_s is the only variable, the best adjustment is not readily apparent from Eq. (11-56) because X_s affects both real and imaginary components of Z_{in}. The situation may be handled, however, by Thévenin's theorem. On this basis a coupled circuit supplying a secondary resistance R_s can be considered as a generator with an internal impedance equal to the impedance looking back into the network from the load. If, then, it were possible to adjust only X_s, the best value would be such as to make the total equivalent *reactance* equal to zero and a condition similar to Eq. (11-59) would be obtained, with the exception that primary and secondary values would be interchanged. This

---

[*] G. W. Pierce, "Electric Oscillations and Electric Waves, McGraw-Hill Book Company, Inc., New York, 1920.

has been called by Pierce "partial resonance S" and is obtained when

$$X_s = \frac{\omega^2 M^2 X_p}{R_p{}^2 + X_p{}^2} \tag{11-60}$$

If the conditions for partial resonance P and partial resonance S are satisfied simultaneously the condition is called "optimum resonance." The requirements to satisfy this condition are found by treating Eqs. (11-59) and (11-60) as simultaneous equations, and it will be found that this gives the same relations as Eqs. (11-21) and (11-22).

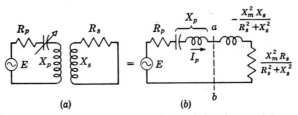

(a)   (b)

Fig. 11-22. Equivalent circuits showing the condition for partial resonance P.

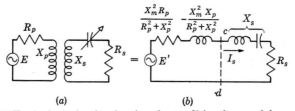

(a)   (b)

Fig. 11-23. Equivalent circuits showing the condition for partial resonance S.

The condition where X_p only is adjustable is illustrated in Fig. 11-22, the equivalent load as viewed from the primary lying to the right of the dotted line ab. The problem is to deliver as much power as possible to the equivalent load, and hence to the actual load. It is apparent that the *resistive* components cannot be matched by any adjustment of X_p, and so the best that can be done is to match the reactive components to resonance as discussed in the derivation of Eq. (11-59).

On the other hand, the circuit may be the one shown in Fig. 11-23a. The equivalent is illustrated in Fig. 11-23b, as far as secondary current is concerned.

In Fig. 11-23b the portion to the left of the line cd is the equivalent circuit obtained from Thévenin's theorem. Again an adjustment of X_s cannot match the resistive components and so can be used only to neutralize the total reactance and thus produces a maximum current in R_s when Eq. (11-60) is satisfied.

If X_m is the only adjustment, a matching of magnitude may be obtained but the phase cannot be changed at will.

In Fig. 11-22, the *magnitude* of the impedance to the right of the line *ab* is

$$|Z_{ab}| = \frac{X_m^2}{\sqrt{R_s^2 + X_s^2}} \tag{11-61}$$

while the magnitude of the impedance to the left of *ab* is

$$|Z_p| = \sqrt{R_p^2 + X_p^2} \tag{11-62}$$

These magnitudes can be made equal by a proper selection of X_m. For this condition,

$$\frac{X_m^2}{\sqrt{R_s^2 + X_s^2}} = \sqrt{R_p^2 + X_p^2}$$

$$X_m^2 = |Z_p|\,|Z_s| \tag{11-63}$$

The principles just discussed can be applied to a more complicated circuit by reducing the latter to an equivalent series circuit.

11-26. Primary and Secondary Currents for Optimum Resonance. When the matching network of pure reactances is adjusted in accordance with Eqs. (11-21) and (11-22) (sufficient coupling), the input impedance of the network will be R_{I1} if the load is equal to R_{I2}. If the generator resistance is also R_{I1}, the input current will be

$$I_1 = \frac{E_g}{2R_{I1}} \tag{11-64}$$

The power delivered to the network will be

$$P = |I_1|^2 R_{I1} = \frac{|E_g|^2}{4R_{I1}}$$

This power will be delivered to the load without loss, since pure reactances have been assumed.

$$P = |I_2|^2 R_{I2} = \frac{|E_g|^2}{4R_{I1}}$$

Therefore
$$I_2 = \frac{E_g}{2\sqrt{R_{I1}R_{I2}}} \tag{11-65}$$

If the coupling is sufficient, Eqs. (11-64) and (11-65) show that the currents are independent of the value of X_m *provided that optimum resonance conditions are satisfied.*

If the transformer has resistance and the resistance of the primary is included in R_{I1} while the resistance of the secondary is included in R_{I2}, Eqs. (11-64) and (11-65) will still hold.

In the case of insufficient coupling it has been shown that the best adjustment is to make $X_p = 0$ and $X_s = 0$. In this case

$$I_1 = \frac{E_g}{Z_{11} - Z_{12}^2/Z_{22}} = \frac{E_g R_{I2}}{R_{I1}R_{I2} + \omega^2 M^2} \qquad (11\text{-}66)$$

$$I_2 = -\frac{Z_{12}E_g}{Z_{11}Z_{22} - Z_{12}^2} = \frac{E_g \omega M}{R_{I1}R_{I2} + \omega^2 M^2} \qquad (11\text{-}67)$$

The currents for the case of insufficient coupling will be less than if the coupling is sufficient and optimum resonance conditions are met.

11-27. Multiple Resonance in Tuned Transformers. Figure 11-21 shows that the tuned-transformer circuit involves two series resonant circuits, and it is apparent that there are two resonant points for such a

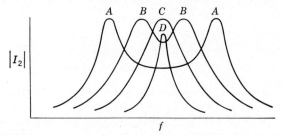

Fig. 11-24. Resonance curves for the tuned-transformer circuit of Fig. 11-21.

combination. Equations (11-21) and (11-22) can be satisfied if X_p and X_s are made either capacitive or inductive, but they must both be of the same type in order to satisfy Eq. (11-20a) at the design frequency.

If a response curve of $|I_2|$ vs. frequency is plotted for the circuit of Fig. 11-21, it will have the general shape of curve A in Fig. 11-24.

If the mutual inductance in the circuit is reduced, the peaks of Fig. 11-24 (curve A) will be moved closer together as shown in curve B. This double resonant characteristic of *tuned* coupled circuits is sometimes used in rf transformers to obtain a so-called BP filter.

In adjusting X_p and X_s to satisfy the conditions expressed by Eqs. (11-21) and (11-22), if the negative values are used, the lower peak of Fig. 11-24 will be set at the frequency of operation, while if the positive or inductive values are used, the upper peak will be set at the frequency of operation.

At critical coupling Eqs. (11-21) and (11-22) call for an adjustment of X_p and X_s equal to zero. There is only one setting which will give best results and the peaks of Fig. 11-24 (curves A and B) will merge into one peak, as shown in curve C.

11-28. Response Curves. The calculation of *general* response curves of the type shown in Fig. 11-24 for the tuned-transformer circuit is extremely difficult because of the large number of variables. It has already been pointed out that Eqs. (11-21) and (11-22) specify X_p and

X_s at only the design frequency f_d. Since both these reactances consist
of inductance and capacitance in series, the design values may be satisfied by an infinite number of combinations of L_p, C_p and L_s, C_s. To
complicate matters further, a general set of curves would necessarily
include still another parameter relating X_m to the critical value, and often
the circuit resistances become frequency-dependent over a wide frequency
range. For these reasons only a special case will be considered, that in
which the primary and secondary circuits resonate at the same frequency
f_r, that is,

$$\omega_r{}^2 = \frac{1}{L_pC_p} = \frac{1}{L_sC_s} \tag{11-68}$$

The specific problem will be to determine the frequencies at which $|I_2|$
becomes maximum or minimum.

The secondary current of a two-mesh circuit is

$$I_2 = -\frac{Z_{12}E_g}{Z_{11}Z_{22} - Z_{12}{}^2}$$

From Fig. 11-21

$$Z_{11} = R_{I1} + j\left(\omega L_p - \frac{1}{\omega C_p}\right) = R_{I1} + j\omega_r L_p\left(\frac{\omega}{\omega_r} - \frac{\omega_r}{\omega}\right)$$

$$Z_{22} = R_{I2} + j\left(\omega L_s - \frac{1}{\omega C_s}\right) = R_{I2} + j\omega_r L_s\left(\frac{\omega}{\omega_r} - \frac{\omega_r}{\omega}\right)$$

$$Z_{12} = \pm j\omega M$$

Substituting and collecting terms,

$$I_2 = \frac{\mp j\omega M E_g}{R_{I1}R_{I2} + (\omega M)^2 - \omega_r{}^2 L_p L_s\left(\dfrac{\omega}{\omega_r} - \dfrac{\omega_r}{\omega}\right)^2 + j\omega_r(R_{I1}L_s + R_{I2}L_p)\left(\dfrac{\omega}{\omega_r} - \dfrac{\omega_r}{\omega}\right)} \tag{11-69}$$

This result may be further simplified by noting that $R_{I1}R_{I2}$ is the square
of the mutual reactance at *critical coupling*. By Eqs. (11-21) and (11-22)
$X_p = X_s = 0$ at the design frequency. For this special case where
$X_p = X_s = 0$ at ω_r,

$$R_{I1}R_{I2} = (\omega_r M_c)^2$$

where M_c is the critical value of mutual inductance. By factoring
$\omega_r{}^2 L_p L_s$ from the denominator, Eq. (11-69) reduces to

$$I_2 = \frac{\mp j\omega M E_g}{\omega_r{}^2 L_p L_s\left[\dfrac{M_c{}^2}{L_p L_s} + \left(\dfrac{\omega}{\omega_r}\right)^2\dfrac{M^2}{L_p L_s} - \left(\dfrac{\omega}{\omega_r} - \dfrac{\omega_r}{\omega}\right)^2 + j\left(\dfrac{R_{I1}}{\omega_r L_p} + \dfrac{R_{I2}}{\omega_r L_s}\right)\left(\dfrac{\omega}{\omega_r} - \dfrac{\omega_r}{\omega}\right)\right]} \tag{11-70}$$

In the interest of further simplification it is noted that at the *design* frequency

$$(X_p)_d = \omega_d L_p - \frac{1}{\omega_d C_p} = L_p\left(\omega_d - \frac{\omega_r{}^2}{\omega_d}\right)$$

$$(X_s)_d = \omega_d L_s - \frac{1}{\omega_d C_s} = L_s\left(\omega_d - \frac{\omega_r{}^2}{\omega_d}\right)$$

Then, dividing and introducing Eq. (11-20a),

$$\frac{(X_p)_d}{(X_s)_d} = \frac{L_p}{L_s} = \frac{R_{I1}}{R_{I2}}$$

Therefore

$$Q = \frac{\omega_r L_p}{R_{I1}} = \frac{\omega_r L_s}{R_{I2}} = \sqrt{\frac{\omega_r{}^2 L_p L_s}{R_{I1} R_{I2}}} = \frac{1}{k_c} \tag{11-71}$$

Introducing the definition of the coupling coefficient and Eq. (11-71), Eq. (11-70) becomes

$$I_2 = \frac{\mp j\omega M E_g}{\omega_r{}^2 L_p L_s \left\{ \left[k_c{}^2 + k^2\left(\frac{\omega}{\omega_r}\right)^2 - \left(\frac{\omega}{\omega_r} - \frac{\omega_r}{\omega}\right)^2 \right] + j2k_c\left(\frac{\omega}{\omega_r} - \frac{\omega_r}{\omega}\right) \right\}} \tag{11-72}$$

Where Q is sufficiently high, the frequency variable $\omega/\omega_r - \omega_r/\omega$ may be replaced by the arithmetic symmetry approximation described in Chap. 4. Thus let $(\omega - \omega_r)/\omega_r = x$. Then

$$\frac{\omega}{\omega_r} - \frac{\omega_r}{\omega} = \frac{x(2 + x)}{1 + x} \approx 2x \qquad \text{for } x \ll 1$$

$$\omega = \omega_r(1 + x) \approx \omega_r \qquad \text{for } x \ll 1 \tag{11-73}$$

Then Eq. (11-72) becomes

$$I_2 = \frac{\pm jk E_g}{\omega_r \sqrt{L_p L_s}(k^2 + k_c{}^2 - 4x^2) + j4k_c x} \tag{11-74a}$$

and

$$|I_2| = \frac{k E_g}{\omega_r \sqrt{L_p L_s} \sqrt{(k^2 + k_c{}^2 - 4x^2)^2 + 16k_c{}^2 x^2}} \tag{11-74b}$$

As stated before, the problem is to find the values of normalized frequency difference, x, at which $|I_2|$ is maximum or minimum. This may be done by differentiating the denominator squared of Eq. (11-74b) with respect to x and equating the derivative to zero. This procedure shows that $|I_2|$ either maximizes or minimizes at the following values:

$$x_b = 0 \qquad \text{or} \qquad f_b = f_r$$

$$x_a = -\tfrac{1}{2}\sqrt{k^2 - k_c{}^2} \qquad f_a = f_r(1 - \tfrac{1}{2}\sqrt{k^2 - k_c{}^2}) \tag{11-75a}$$

$$x_c = +\tfrac{1}{2}\sqrt{k^2 - k_c{}^2} \qquad f_c = f_r(1 + \tfrac{1}{2}\sqrt{k^2 - k_c{}^2}) \tag{11-75b}$$

It is clear, then, that the type of response depends upon the relative magnitudes of k and k_c, i.e. upon the degree of coupling.

Case I. Sufficient Coupling, $k^2 > k_c{}^2$. The values of frequency given by Eqs. (11-75) are all physically realizable when $k^2 > k_c{}^2$. It is easy to show from physical considerations that $|I_2|$ maximizes at f_a and f_c and minimizes at f_b ($= f_r$). Since the coupling is by mutual inductance, $|I_2|$ is zero at zero frequency. It is also zero at infinite frequency because of L_p and L_s. By definition the current *magnitude* is always positive; therefore, as frequency is raised from zero to infinity, the response must maximize first, then minimize, and maximize again. Since $f_a < f_b < f_c$, the maxima occur at f_a and f_c, while $f_b = f_r$ defines a minimum. The bandwidth between the peaks will be

$$(BW)_p = f_c - f_a = f_r \sqrt{k^2 - k_c{}^2} \qquad k^2 > k_c{}^2 \qquad (11\text{-}76)$$

The response at the peaks may be obtained by substituting Eq. (11-75b) into Eq. (11-74b).

$$|I_2|_p = \frac{|E_g|}{\omega_r \sqrt{L_p L_s} 2k_c} = \frac{|E_g|}{2 \sqrt{R_{I1} R_{I2}}} \qquad (11\text{-}77)$$

The response at the minimum occurs at f_r and is

$$|I_2|_r = \frac{k|E_g|}{\omega_r \sqrt{L_p L_s}(k^2 + k_c{}^2)} \qquad (11\text{-}78)$$

The student may show that the bandwidth between the two points on the "skirts" of the response curve at which $|I_2| = |I_2|_r$ is given by

$$(BW)_m = \sqrt{2}\,(BW)_p \qquad (11\text{-}79)$$

These results are summarized in Fig. 11-25a.

It should be noted that the design equations (11-21) and (11-22) specify values for X_p and X_s at either of the two peaks corresponding to f_a and f_c. If the broad-banding properties of the overcoupled circuit are to be realized, the design frequency is chosen to be f_r and maximum power will be delivered to the load at f_a and f_c.

Case II. Critical Coupling, $k^2 = k_c{}^2$. The values of frequency given by Eqs. (11-75) all coalesce into a single value $f_a = f_b = f_c = f_r$ for the critical case; hence the response curve exhibits a single maximum as shown in Fig. 11-25b. From Eq. (11-74b) the response at the peak is

$$|I_2|_r = \frac{|E_g|}{\omega_r \sqrt{L_p L_s}\, 2k_c} = \frac{|E_g|}{2 \sqrt{R_{I1} R_{I2}}} \qquad k^2 = k_c{}^2 \qquad (11\text{-}80)$$

and the normalized response is

$$\frac{|I_2|}{|I_2|_r} = \frac{1}{\sqrt{1 + 4(x/k_c)^4}} \qquad k^2 = k_c{}^2 \qquad (11\text{-}81)$$

The student may show from Eq. (11-81) that the half-power bandwidth for the critical case is

$$BW = \sqrt{2}\, k_c f_r \tag{11-82}$$

It may be observed that the frequency variable appears as the fourth power in Eq. (11-81), while it appears as the square in the universal

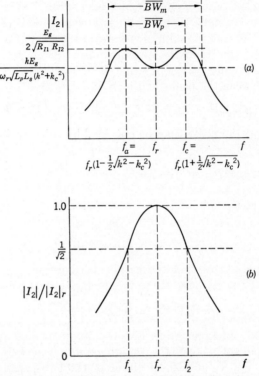

FIG. 11-25. Response of the tuned-transformer circuit when the primary and secondary circuits are both resonant at f_r and the conditions of arithmetic symmetry are assumed. (a) Sufficient coupling. (b) Critical coupling.

resonance curve of a single resonant circuit (Fig. 1-10). Hence for small values of x Eq. (11-81) is flatter than the universal resonance curve.

Case III. *Insufficient Coupling, $k^2 < k_c^2$.* The two values of frequency specified by Eq. (11-75b) become complex when $k^2 < k_c^2$ and so must be ruled out from physical considerations, complex frequency in this sense not being realizable. Thus the undercoupled case gives a response curve exhibiting a single maximum at f_r. The student may demonstrate that, for this case, the normalized response is

$$\frac{|I_2|}{|I_2|_r} = \frac{k^2 + k_c^2}{\sqrt{(k^2 + k_c^2 - 4x^2)^2 + 16k_c^2 x^2}} \qquad k^2 < k_c^2 \tag{11-83}$$

and that the half-power bandwidth is

$$BW = f_r \sqrt{\sqrt{2(k^4 + k_c{}^4)} - (k_c{}^2 - k^2)} \qquad k^2 < k_c{}^2 \qquad (11\text{-}84)$$

11-29. Tuned-transformer Efficiency. Under the assumption of low circuit losses the efficiency of the tuned-transformer circuit may be determined on the same basis which was used in Sec. 11-17, viz., that the *currents* may be computed as if no losses were present. On this basis the power lost in the two inductors in Fig. 11-21 will be

$$P_{\text{lost}} = \frac{|I_1|^2 X_{Lp}}{Q_p} + \frac{|I_2|^2 X_{Ls}}{Q_s} \qquad (11\text{-}85)$$

Under *matched* conditions and for small losses, $|I_1|^2 R_{I1} = |I_2|^2 R_{I2}$; hence

$$P_{\text{lost}} = |I_1|^2 \left(\frac{X_{Lp}}{Q_p} + \frac{R_{I1} X_{Ls}}{R_{I2} Q_s} \right) \qquad (11\text{-}85a)$$

Further investigation of this equation for the general case is difficult because of the large number of circuit parameter combinations which can give the required match. A special case of interest, however, is that in which the coupling is critical so that

$$X_m{}^2 = k_c{}^2 X_{Lp} X_{Ls} = R_{I1} R_{I2} \qquad (11\text{-}86)$$

Then, on eliminating X_{Lp}, Eq. (11-85a) becomes

$$P_{\text{lost}} = P_{in} \left(\frac{R_{I2}}{k_c{}^2 Q_p X_{Ls}} + \frac{X_{Ls}}{R_{I2} Q_s} \right) \qquad (11\text{-}85b)$$

Now by Eq. (11-86) the product $k_c{}^2 X_{Lp} X_{Ls}$ is fixed for a given match. The question then arises: "What ratio X_{Lp}/X_{Ls} will minimize the loss?" In other words, "How shall the two inductances be chosen to minimize the loss?" Assuming constant Q's and fixed input power,

$$\frac{\partial P_{\text{lost}}}{\partial X_{Ls}} = P_{in} \left(\frac{-R_{I2}}{k_c{}^2 Q_p X_{Ls}{}^2} + \frac{1}{R_{I2} Q_s} \right) = 0$$

whence

$$k_c X_{Ls} = \sqrt{\frac{Q_s}{Q_p}} R_{I2} \qquad (11\text{-}87)$$

Substituting into Eq. (11-86),

$$\frac{X_{Lp}}{X_{Ls}} = \frac{R_{I1} Q_p}{R_{I2} Q_s} = n \frac{Q_p}{Q_s} \qquad (11\text{-}88)$$

Equation (11-88), then, gives the inductance ratio for minimum loss at critical coupling.

For comparison with the T and II networks considered earlier, it is interesting to define a loss function δ_{min}. Thus, substituting Eq. (11-87) into Eq. (11-85b),

$$(P_{lost})_{min} = \frac{2P_{in}}{k_c \sqrt{Q_p Q_s}} \tag{11-89}$$

or

$$\delta_{min} = \frac{(P_{lost})_{min}}{P_{in}} \sqrt{Q_p Q_s} = \frac{2}{k_c} \tag{11-90}$$

It is of interest to note that, for the minimum-loss condition, the loss function is independent of the impedance-transformation ratio.

The value of k_c will never be much greater than 0.5 and usually is less. Hence it is apparent than δ_{min} has a magnitude of the order of 4 or greater.

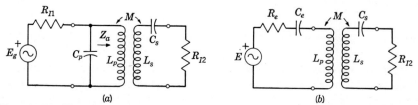

FIG. 11-26. Tuned-transformer impedance-transforming circuit with C_p shunted across L_p. Application of Thévenin's theorem gives the equivalent circuit of b. Compare with Fig. 11-21.

When this is compared with the values for an L section shown in Fig. 11-17, it will be seen that, unless the impedance ratio is quite large, the L section is inherently more efficient than a tuned transformer.

11-30. Tuned Radio-frequency Transformer with Shunt C_p. The tuned rf transformer circuit of Fig. 11-21, which utilizes a capacitor in *series* with L_p, provides an impedance-transformation ratio which is limited by the available value of mutual reactance X_m. Since $X_m^2 \geq R_{I1}R_{I2}$ is necessary for an impedance match,

$$n = \frac{R_{I1}}{R_{I2}} \leq \left(\frac{X_m}{R_{I2}}\right)^2 \tag{11-91}$$

An alternative type of tuned-transformer circuit is provided by *shunting* C_p across L_p as shown in Fig. 11-26a. It will now be shown that this alternative circuit inherently can provide a greater transformation ratio which is limited by X_p rather than by X_m.

One means of analyzing the circuit consists in replacing the circuit to the left of the primary inductor by its Thévenin equivalent circuit as in Fig. 11-26b. The equivalent generator voltage is

$$E = \frac{jX_{Cp}}{R_{I1} + jX_{Cp}} E_g$$

and the equivalent generator impedance is

$$Z_e = R_e + jX_e$$
$$= \frac{jX_{Cp}R_{I1}}{R_{I1} + jX_{Cp}} = \frac{R_{I1}X_{Cp}^2}{R_{I1}^2 + X_{Cp}^2} + \frac{jR_{I1}^2X_{Cp}}{R_{I1}^2 + X_{Cp}^2} \tag{11-92}$$

It can be seen, then, that the shunt C_p circuit of Fig. 11-26a has been reduced to the series capacitor form of Fig. 11-21 except that R_{I1} of the series form has been replaced by R_e. From Eq. (11-92) R_e may be written

$$R_e = \frac{R_{I1}}{1 + (R_{I1}/X_{Cp})^2} \tag{11-93}$$

Since $(R_{I1}/X_{Cp})^2$ is always positive, it follows at once that $R_{I1} > R_e$; hence for the same circuit parameters the shunt C_p circuit is capable of giving a greater transformation ratio than the series capacitor form.

As a specific example of this effect, let the secondary circuit of Fig. 11-26a or its equivalent b be adjusted to resonance such that $X_s = 0$. Then by Eq. (11-20a) X_p, the total series reactance of the primary circuit, must be zero, or

$$X_{Ce} = -X_{Lp} \tag{11-94}$$

Substituting from Eq. (11-92) and solving for $R_{I1}X_{Cp}/(R_{I1}^2 + X_{Cp}^2)$,

$$\frac{R_{I1}X_{Cp}}{R_{I1}^2 + X_{Cp}^2} = -\frac{X_{Lp}}{R_{I1}} \tag{11-95}$$

Then from Eqs. (11-92) and (11-95)

$$R_{I1} = \frac{-X_{Lp}X_{Cp}}{R_e}$$

But, for the condition where $X_p = X_s = 0$, $R_e R_{I2} = X_m^2$, whence

$$n = \frac{R_{I1}}{R_{I2}} = \frac{-X_{Lp}X_{Cp}}{X_m^2} \tag{11-96}$$

In typical circuits it is often true that R_{I1} is much greater than X_{Cp} so that $R_{I1}^2 \gg X_{Cp}^2$. Where this is true, from Eq. (11-92)

$$X_{Ce} \approx X_{Cp} \tag{11-97}$$

and from Eq. (11-94)

$$X_{Cp} \approx -X_{Lp} \tag{11-98}$$

Therefore, if $X_s = 0$ and $X_{Cp} \approx X_{Lp}$,

$$n = \frac{R_{I1}}{R_{I2}} \approx \frac{X_{Lp}^2}{X_m^2} \tag{11-99}$$

These equations may be used to design the network of Fig. 11-26. It is interesting to note that the results here corroborate the results of Chap. 4, where it was shown that parallel resonance is preferred to series resonance when the source impedance is high. The foregoing results will now be used in an illustrative example.

Design the network of Fig. 11-26a to match 10 ohms to 5,000 ohms at

$$\omega = 2 \times 10^6 \text{ radians/sec}$$

The available inductors are $L_p = 100 \ \mu h$, $L_s = 50 \ \mu h$ with a maximum coupling coefficient of 0.7.

$$X_{Lp} = \omega L_p = (2 \times 10^6) \times 10^{-4} = 200 \text{ ohms}$$
$$\frac{R_{I1}}{X_{Lp}} = \frac{5,000}{200} = 25$$

By Eq. (11-99)

$$X_m{}^2 = \frac{R_{I2}}{R_{I1}} X_{Lp}{}^2 = \frac{10}{5 \times 10^3} 4 \times 10^4 = 80$$

Check to see whether k is within the specified limit.

$$k = \sqrt{\frac{X_m{}^2}{X_{Lp}X_{Ls}}} = \sqrt{\frac{80}{2 \times 10^4}} = 0.0633$$

This is satisfactory. By Eq. (11-98)

$$C_p = \frac{1}{\omega X_{Lp}} = \frac{1}{(2 \times 10^6)(2 \times 10^2)} = 2,500 \ \mu\mu f$$
$$C_s = \frac{1}{\omega X_{Ls}} = \frac{1}{(2 \times 10^6)(1 \times 10^2)} = 5,000 \ \mu\mu f$$

The student should notice that the same inductors used with a series C_p would provide a maximum R_{I1} of

$$R_{I1} = \frac{X_m{}^2}{R_{I2}} = \frac{k^2 X_{Lp}X_{Ls}}{R_{I2}} = \frac{0.49 \times 200 \times 10^2}{10} = 980 \text{ ohms}$$

PROBLEMS

11-1. The network of Fig. 11-5b is to provide simultaneously conjugate impedance matches at terminals 1, 1' and 2, 2'. Set up equations stating this fact, and use them to verify Eqs. (11-8).

11-2. (a) Design two L sections to match a 306-ohm resistive load to a generator whose impedance is $81 + j22$ ohms. The frequency is 1 Mc. (b) In what respects will the performance of these two networks differ? (c) Calculate the efficiency of the two L sections. Assume an inductor Q of 100 in each case.

11-3. Calculate and plot a curve of normalized load-current magnitude vs. frequency for the network of Prob. 11-2a which utilizes a series inductor. Cover a frequency range of 10 kc on each side of 1 Mc.

11-4. (a) Starting with Eq. (11-15), derive an expression for the upper and lower half-power frequencies of an L section in which X_2 is inductive. (b) Plot curves of the half-power frequencies vs. n for $n = 2$ to $n = 10$.

11-5. Design an L section by means of Eqs. (11-8) to match two equal resistances. Comment on your result.

11-6. (a) Design a T section to match $100 + j20$ ohms to a 600-ohm generator at 732 kc. Use an 800-$\mu\mu$f capacitance for the shunt arm, and choose X_p to be capacitive. (b) What is the phase shift between the input and output currents?

11-7. (a) Starting with Eq. (11-25), derive an expression for $|I_2|/|I_2|_d$ vs. ω/ω_d for a T section having inductive series arms. Use $X_m{}^2 = R_{I1}R_{I2}$, and let

$$a = \sqrt{n} + \frac{1}{\sqrt{n}}$$

(b) Figure 11-12 shows that the T-section response displays arithmetic symmetry for a limited frequency range near f_d. Simplify your equation to account for this fact (see Chap. 4). (c) How is the resulting equation related to the universal resonance curve? (d) Plot a curve of half-power bandwidth vs. n. Assume arithmetic symmetry.

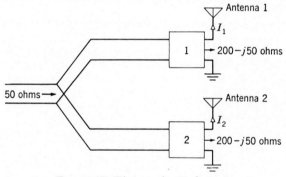

Fig. 11-27. Diagram for Prob. 11-8.

11-8. In Fig. 11-27, the current in antenna 2 is to *lead* the current in antenna 1 by 90° and is to have twice the magnitude of the current in antenna 1, that is, $I_2 = j2I_1$. The combined inputs of networks 1 and 2 are to match a 50-ohm line. All lines are to be flat.

a. What should be the input resistances R_1 and R_2 of the lossless networks 1 and 2?

b. Design a minimum-element lossless network 1 to meet the specifications.

c. Neglecting phase shifts along the transmission lines, design a T section to meet the requirements for network 2.

11-9. Design a reactive II section to match a load of 500 ohms *shunted* by 100 $\mu\mu$f to a 100-ohm line at $\omega = 1 \times 10^6$ radian/sec. The current in the 500-ohm resistor is to lag the input current by 60°.

11-10. Derive the dual of Eq. (11-25) for a II section having shunt capacitances.

11-11. (a) Verify that Eq. (11-45) defines the loss function for the type 3 T and II networks. (b) Verify that Eq. (11-51) defines the loss function for the type 2 T and II networks.

11-12. Investigate the feasibility of cascading L matching sections to improve efficiency. If only two sections are cascaded, should they both be designed for the same value of n?

11-13. Design a network which can be used to couple two transmitters to the same antenna. One transmitter operates at 1,210 kc and is designed to feed into a 600-ohm line balanced to ground. The other transmitter operates at 1,430 kc and is designed to feed into a 70-ohm line with one side grounded. The impedance of the antenna at 1,210 kc is $242 - j70$ ohms, and at 1,430 kc it is $92 - j48$ ohms. Compute the efficiency of the coupling system at each frequency if the Q of the coils is 200.

11-14. A radio amateur plans to operate on 7.15 Mc in the 40-m band. Design a Π section to match a 600-ohm line to a 2,000-ohm source with a shift of $B = +70°$. The second harmonic lies in the 20-m band and must be suppressed. Modify the series branch of the Π network to accomplish this.

11-15. Design a single Π network to match 600 ohms to 2,000 ohms at frequencies of 7.1 and 14.3 Mc. Critical coupling should be used at the higher frequency. The resulting network should be a minimum-element structure.

11-16. In Fig. 11-21 $L_p = 12$ μh, $L_s = 2$ μh, $M = 1.5$ μh, $R_{I2} = 4$ ohms. The resistances of the primary and secondary inductors are $R_1 = 0.5$ ohm, $R_2 = 0.4$ ohm.

  a. What is the maximum purely resistive value of Z_{in} at $\omega = 5 \times 10^6$ radians/sec?

  b. What is the efficiency of the impedance-transforming network with the circuit adjusted to give the condition of part *a*?

11-17. In Fig. 11-21 $L_p = L_s = 100$ μh, $R_{I2} = 10$ ohms, and C_p is shorted out. What values of the coupling coefficient and C_s are required for $Z_{in} = 100 + j0$ ohms at $\omega = 5 \times 10^6$ radians/sec?

11-18. (*a*) Redesign the network of Prob. 11-17 accounting for inductor Q's of 100. (*b*) What is the efficiency of the network?

11-19. An antenna whose impedance is $72 - j5$ ohms is to be matched to a 500-ohm generator at $\omega = 2 \times 10^6$ radians/sec by means of a tuned transformer. The antenna current is to lag the input current by 90°. $L_p = L_s = 500$ μh. Calculate the necessary values of C_p, C_s, and k.

11-20. Calculate the efficiency of the tuned transformer designed in the last illustrative example of the chapter.

CHAPTER 12

IMPEDANCE MATCHING WITH STUBS

It was stated in Chapter 10 that the use of lumped inductors and capacitors is not practical at higher radio frequencies (say, 50 Mc or above) because of the small values of L and C required and that it is common practice in this frequency range to use stubs, i.e., short segments of transmission line, as reactors. This chapter will consider the use of stubs in impedance-transforming networks. The work will be carried out on the assumption that the stubs are lossless, i.e., that αl is so small as to be considered negligible. In many instances it will be found that a stub matching network may be identified with a lumped constant counterpart covered in the last chapter.

12-1. Single-stub Matching. In the sections on the L section it has been shown that, if one is concerned only with the transforming of one resistance R_{I2} into another value R_{I1}, with no regard whatsoever to phase shift, only two adjustable elements are required in the impedance-transforming network. In the L section the adjustable elements were inductors and capacitors. An analogous situation will now be considered where the reactors are replaced by short transmission-line sections. It will be found that a line segment serves in place of the series reactor of the L section and that the shunt reactor is replaced by a shunt short-circuited stub. Because of the latter stub, the problem is handled more easily in terms of admittance than of impedance.

As a starting point, say, a conductance G_R (resistance R_R) is to be transformed to a conductance G_{in} (resistance R_{in}). Let G_R be connected to a lossless line of characteristic impedance $R_o = 1/G_o$ and of adjustable length l as in Fig. 12-1a. Then the normalized input admittance $y_{in} = Y_{in}/G_o$ may be calculated by Eq. (10-28a). The real and imaginary components of y_{in} are plotted in Fig. 12-1b for $g_r = 0.5$. Inspection of the g_{in} curve shows that, by a suitable choice of l, g_r may be transformed to any value lying between 0.5 and 2. By way of illustration let the required value be $g_{in} = 0.674$. Then from the curve, or Eq. (10-28a), $l = 0.1\lambda^*$, or $\beta l = 36°$ and $b_{in} = 0.475$. Therefore, if a suscep-

---

* The student will observe that $g_{in} = 0.674$ at $l = 0.4\lambda$ also. The shorter value is ordinarily used because it is cheaper and has less actual loss.

tance of normalized value -0.475 is shunted across the input terminals, as in Fig. 12-1c, the total susceptance will be zero and the required transformation will be accomplished. From a theoretical standpoint the additional susceptance required across the input terminals may be furnished

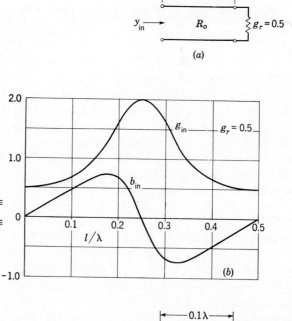

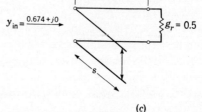

FIG. 12-1. The transmission-line equivalent of the L impedance-transforming section. (a) y_{in} may be changed by varying l. (b) Normalized input admittance for y_{in} as a function of l. (c) A shunt stub of length s is added to make the input admittance real.

by either an open- or a short-circuited stub. Practical considerations rule out the former; the shorted stub is invariably used because it radiates less energy, and its effective length may be varied by means of a sliding, shorting bar. The length s of this shorted stub may be found by Eq. (10-10).

$$Z_{sc} = jR_o \tan \beta s$$

or
$$b_{sc} = -\cot \beta s$$

Then assuming the stub to have the same R_o as the original line segment to which g_r is connected,

$$\beta s = \frac{360s}{\lambda} = \text{arccot } 0.475 = 64.6°$$

$$s = \frac{64.6}{360} \lambda = 0.1798\lambda$$

While the foregoing discussion considered a case where the termination is a pure conductance, the method of single-stub matching is by no

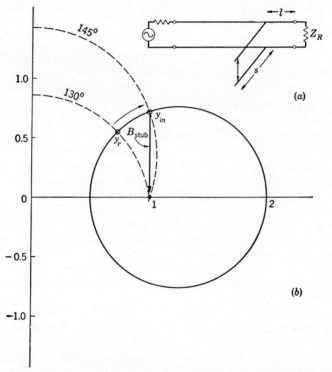

FIG. 12-2. Solution of a single-stub matching problem by means of the bicircular chart.

means restricted in this manner; the basic idea may be extended to yield an *algebraic* solution for l and s where the termination is complex.

By suitable manipulation of Eq. (10-4b), the student may show that for any termination described by ρ

$$y_{in} = \frac{(1 - |\rho|^2) - j2|\rho| \sin (\varphi - 2\beta l)}{1 + 2|\rho| \cos (\varphi - 2\beta l) + |\rho|^2}$$

This equation contains sufficient information for the calculation of l and b_{in} for a required value of g_{in}. $|\rho|$ and φ may be determined from standing wave measurements and Eqs. (10-17), (10-13), and (10-15).

An easier method of solution is afforded by either the bicircular or the Smith chart. Consider the situation shown in Fig. 12-2a. The section of line (characteristic admittance G_o) to the left of the stub is to be terminated in G_o in order that reflections may be eliminated. The problem is to find l and s. Figure 12-2b shows a bicircular chart on which the complex value of normalized Y_R is located. As l is increased from zero, the input admittance (exclusive of the stub) will vary on the constant $-S$ locus; therefore one rotates clockwise (i.e., toward the generator) until the real part of $y_{in} = 1$, corresponding to the condition that the termination for the left-hand portion of the line shall be G_o. From the diagram an electrical length of $\beta l = 145° - 130° = 15°$ is required. Thus $l = 15°/\beta = 15\lambda/360 = 0.0417\lambda$.

The susceptive component of y_{in} is read to be $+0.7$; hence, for the total susceptance to be zero, a shunt short-circuited stub having a susceptance of -0.7 is required. From Fig. 10-10 the required stub length is $\beta s = 55°$, $s = 55\lambda/360 = 0.1528\lambda$. The student should compare Figs. 12-12b and 11-7 in order to see the close similarity between the single-stub and L-matching sections.

The same results can, of course, be obtained from a Smith chart, but the analogy to Fig. 11-7 is less apparent. Furthermore, the actual value of y_r need not be known provided only that the standing wave ratio and the location of a voltage maximum (or minimum) be known.

A parallel-wire line is terminated in an unknown impedance. Standing wave measurements yield the following data: $S = 3$. The first voltage minimum is 54 cm from the termination, and the first voltage maximum is 204 cm away from the termination. Design a single-stub matching section so that the line will be "flat" (that is, $S = 1$) to the left of the stub. The notation of Fig. 12-2a will be used, and l' will designate the distance between the stub and the first voltage minimum.

Draw a circle for $S = 3$ on a Smith chart (Fig. 12-3). Since an admittance maximum and a voltage minimum coincide, locate $E_{\min}$ on the chart at 3 on the real axis. The basic procedure is to rotate on $S = 3$ until the real part of $y_{in} = 1$. Consider, first, rotation toward the *load* (counterclockwise) to point a. From the chart (inner scale)

$$l' = (0.333 - 0.25)\lambda = 0.083\lambda$$

Since a voltage maximum is spaced a quarter wave from an adjacent voltage minimum,

$$\frac{\lambda}{4} = 204 - 54 = 150 \text{ cm}$$

$$\lambda = 600 \text{ cm}$$

or $$l' = 0.083 \times 600 = 49.8 \text{ cm}$$

Note that this solution is possible because the load is 54 cm from the first voltage minimum.

At point a the normalized susceptance is $+j1.16$; hence the stub must have a

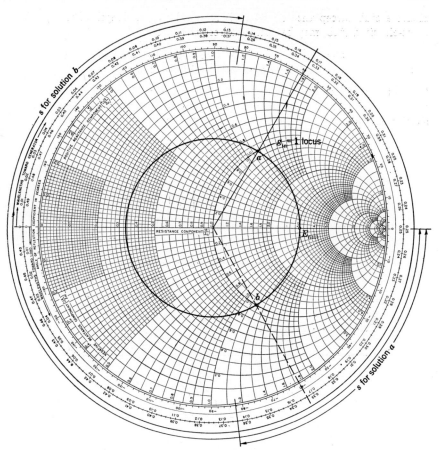

Fig. 12-3. Solution of a single-stub matching problem by means of the Smith chart.

susceptance of $-j1.16$.   Using a shorted stub, the required stub length is read from the chart as

$$s = (0.364 - 0.25)\lambda = 0.114\lambda$$
$$= 0.114 \times 600 = 68.4 \text{ cm}$$

Therefore one solution is to locate a short-circuited stub 68.4 cm long at a point 49.8 cm toward the load from the first voltage minimum (that is

$$l = 54 - 49.8 = 4.2 \text{ cm}$$

from the load).

Another solution is possible by placing the stub on the *generator* side of the voltage minimum, point b in Fig. 12-3.   From the chart

$$l' = (0.333 - 0.25)\lambda = 0.083\lambda = 49.8 \text{ cm}$$
$$b_{in} = -1.16$$

Hence a stub susceptance of $+1.16$ is required. s, the length of the required short-circuited stub, may be obtained from the chart.

$$s = (0.136 + 0.25)\lambda = 0.386 \times 600 = 231.6 \text{ cm}$$

and
$$l = 54 + l' = 54 + 49.8 = 103.8 \text{ cm}$$

Of the two solutions given above, the former is preferred on two accounts: (1) it results in a longer section of the transmission line being flat; (2) it utilizes a stub of shorter length.

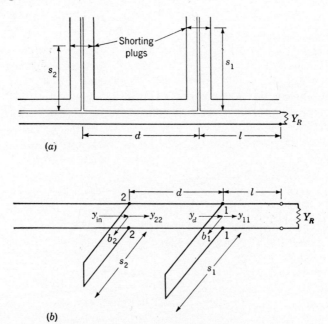

Fɪɢ. 12-4. The double-stub impedance-matching system. (a) Coaxial line. (b) Parallel line.

In practice the methods just described are used for locating the approximate length and position of the stub. Minor final adjustments are made by changing the stub length and moving its position along the line. As a general rule the adjustment is satisfactory when the standing wave ratio on the generator side of the stub is 1.1 or less although the actual acceptable value will vary with the application.

12-2. Double-stub Matching. While the single-stub matching system is quite adequate for open-wire lines, it is not adaptable to coaxial lines because of the difficulty encountered in moving a stub on a coaxial structure. To circumvent this difficulty, two stubs of adjustable length but fixed in position may be used. Since two variables are provided, an impedance match may be obtained in general but no control of the phase shift is provided. The basic structure is illustrated in Fig. 12-4, and the method of solution will be explained by means of the Smith chart, which in this case is much more adaptable than the bicircular chart.

The basic method of adjusting the double-stub section consists in varying the length of stub 1 so that $y_{22} = 1 + jb_{22}$ and setting stub 2 to cancel out b_{22}. With these conditions satisfied, the line to the left of stub 2 will be terminated in G_o and hence will be "flat." Because of the difficulty in adjusting the stubs experimentally, it is desirable to find their approximate lengths by analytical means.

Consider the philosophy behind these adjustments. In Fig. 12-4b $y_{in} = y_{22} + jb_2$ must have the value $1 + j0$ for the line to be flat. Since stub 2 can contribute only susceptance ($g_2 = 0$ under the lossless assumption), y_{22} must be some point on the locus $g = 1$ on a Smith chart. y_d must lie toward the load d wavelengths away from y_{22}, where d is some arbitrarily chosen but fixed value. It will be shown presently that y_d must therefore lie on a particular circular locus on the Smith chart, determined solely by the value of d. This locus will be designated L. Then since $y_d = y_{11} + jb_1$, b_1 must be adjusted to transform y_{11} onto this particular locus.

It will now be shown that the locus $g = 1$ is transformed by a section of line d long into a circular locus, of the same radius and whose center is rotated d wavelengths toward the load (counterclockwise) on the Smith chart. By way of example, let $d = 0.2\lambda$. Then in Fig. 12-5 the arbitrary point a lying on the $g = 1$ locus (whose center is c) is rotated about the origin, on a circle of constant S, 0.2λ toward the load to point a'. Another arbitrary point b on the $g = 1$ locus is rotated in the same manner 0.2λ to b'. The same procedure can be carried out for other points, such as d and e. If, then, the locus L is drawn through all the primed points, it will be found to be the circle shown, whose center c' lies 0.2λ counterclockwise from c. A similar transformation exists for any other value of d; in each case $g = 1$ maps into a circle of the same radius, whose center lies d wavelengths counterclockwise from c.*

With the fact established that a match at points 2-2 requires y_d to lie on the locus specified in the last paragraph, the method of computing the stub lengths for a double-stub section may be illustrated by an example.

* For the student familiar with complex-variable theory the following points may be of interest: For the line section of length d write Eq. (10-28a) in terms of the notation of Fig. 12-4b.

$$y_{22} = \frac{y_d + j \tan \beta d}{1 + jy_d \tan \beta d}$$

Solving for y_d,

$$y_d = \frac{y_{22} + j \tan (-\beta d)}{1 + jy_{22} \tan (-\beta d)}$$

This equation is a linear transformation that maps a given circle of y_{22} into another circle, $y_d - \beta d$ degrees away (toward the load) and having the same radius.

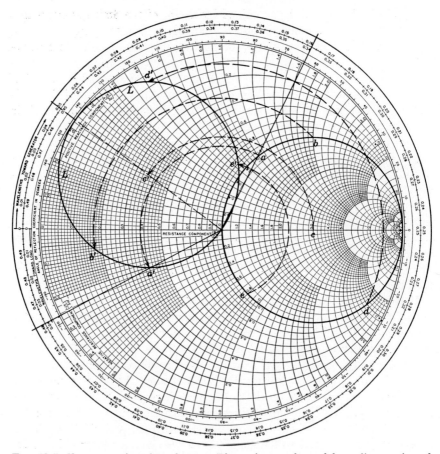

FIG. 12-5. Demonstrating that the $g = 1$ locus is transformed by a line section, d long, into a circle whose center is d wavelengths away from the $g = 1$ locus. Each point is rotated d wavelengths on a circle of constant S to its corresponding primed point.

Calculate the stub lengths required in a double-stub matching system where the normalized load admittance is $y_r = 1.23 - j0.51$. In the notation of Fig. 12-4, $l = 0.1\lambda$, $d = 0.4\lambda$.

In Fig. 12-6 draw the circular locus lying 0.4λ toward the load from the $g = 1$ circle. Locate y_r. Rotate clockwise $l = 0.1\lambda$ on a circle of constant S to find y_{11}. Read $y_{11} = 0.7 - j0.3$. Now, for a match, y_d must lie on the locus at the intersection with the $g = 0.7$ circle. Therefore stub 1 must add a susceptance corresponding to $b_1 = +(0.3 - 0.14) = +0.16$. Since stub 1 is short-circuited, enter the chart independently at $y_r = \infty$, and rotate clockwise around the periphery of the chart to $b_1 = +0.16$, and read

$$s_1 = (0.50 - 0.25 + 0.025)\lambda = 0.275\lambda$$

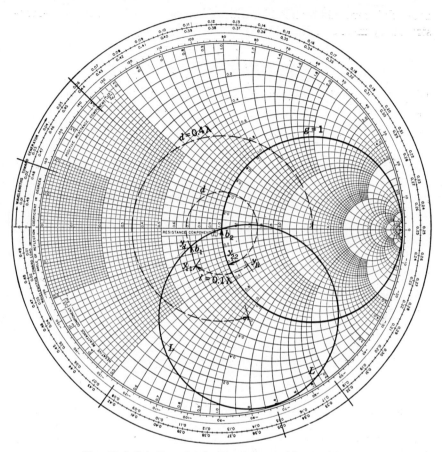

Fig. 12-6. Solution of a double-stub matching problem.

The line length d transforms y_d into $y_{22} = 1 - j0.4$; hence stub 2 must add a susceptance of $+0.4$. To find s_2, enter the chart at $y_r = \infty$ (the stub is short-circuited), and rotate to $b = +0.4$, and read

$$s_2 = (0.50 - 0.25 + 0.06)\lambda = 0.31\lambda$$

Thus y_{22} is transformed to $y_{in} = 1 + j0$, and the match is obtained.

The student is warned that for given values of d and l a match may not be obtained for certain values of y_r. In such cases l or d must be changed. In general, d must not be an integral number of half wavelengths. The proof of this statement is left as an exercise for student.

12-3. The Quarter-wave Transformer. The results of the preceding chapter showed that a lossless symmetrical T or Π section may be used to match two unequal image resistances provided that the network phase shift is $\pm 90°$. A similar situation is present when the lumped-constant network is replaced by a lossless line of length $\lambda/4$. This may be demonstrated by means of Eq. (10-4a).

$$Z_{in} = R_o \frac{Z_R + jR_o \tan \beta l}{R_o + jZ_R \tan \beta l}$$

Dividing numerator and denominator by $\tan \beta l$ and substituting $\beta l = 90°$, Z_{in} becomes

$$Z_{in} = \frac{R_o{}^2}{Z_R} \qquad l = \frac{\lambda}{4} \tag{12-1}$$

Then, if Z_R is a pure resistance R_R, Z_{in} is a pure resistance R_{in}; and the section is designated a *quarter-wave transformer*. Use of Eq. (12-1) may be made in designing an impedance-transforming system.

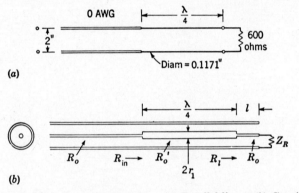

(a)

(b)

FIG. 12-7. Quarter-wave transformers. (a) Parallel line. (b) Coaxial line.

A 600-ohm resistor is to be matched to a parallel-wire line constructed of No. 0 A.W.G. wires (diameter = 0.3249 in.) spaced 2 in. on centers. Design a quarter-wave transformer to make the necessary transformation.

From Prob. 8-2 the characteristic impedance of the main transmission line is

$$R_o = 120 \operatorname{arccosh} \frac{s}{2r} = 120 \operatorname{arccosh} \frac{2}{0.3249}$$
$$= 120 \operatorname{arccosh} 6.15 = 120 \times 2.503 = 300 \text{ ohms}$$

Then the quarter-wave section must have a characteristic impedance R_o' given by

$$R_o' = \sqrt{300 \times 600} = 424 \text{ ohms}$$

As a practical matter, the spacing between the wires of the quarter-wave section should be the same as for the main line. Thus

$$R_o' = 120 \operatorname{arccosh} \frac{2}{2r'}$$

$$2r' = \frac{2}{\cosh (R_o'/120)} = \frac{2}{\cosh (424/120)} = \frac{2}{\cosh 3.53} = \frac{2}{17.08} = 0.1171 \text{ in.}$$

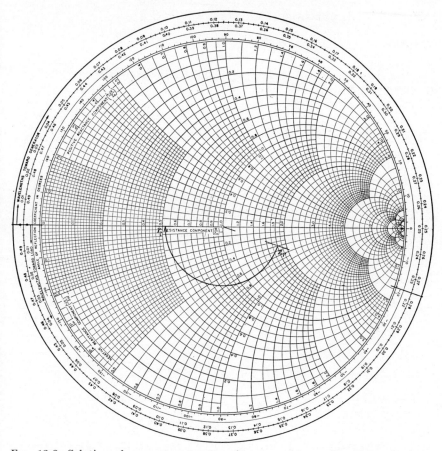

Fig. 12-8. Solution of a quarter-wave-transformer problem. The Smith chart is used to find the location of the quarter-wave transformer with respect to Z_R.

(Number 9 A.W.G. wire has a diameter of 0.1144 in. and might prove satisfactory.) The final configuration of the matching system is shown in Fig. 12-7a.

The use of a quarter-wave transformer is not restricted to applications where Z_R is a pure resistance. For example, in Fig. 12-7b the quarter-wave section may be displaced a distance l from the load so that Z_R is transformed into a pure resistance R_l. The design is then reduced to that of the last problem. Consider an illustrative example.

A 70-ohm coaxial line, having an outer conductor whose inner radius is 1 in., is to be matched to a load of $126 - j28$ ohms. Find the location and inner conductor diameter for the required quarter-wave transformer. The notation of Fig. 12-7b is used.

Normalizing Z_R with respect to R_o of the main line,

$$z_r = \frac{126 - j28}{70} = 1.8 - j0.4$$

Locate z_r on the Smith chart (Fig. 12-8), and rotate toward the generator until the input impedance is real. Read $r_l = 0.51$. The distance rotated is

$$l = (0.500 - 0.276)\lambda = 0.224\lambda$$

Multiply r_l by R_o of the main line to convert to ohms.

$$R_l = r_l R_o = 0.51 \times 70 = 35.7 \text{ ohms}$$

The quarter-wave transformer must therefore match 35.7 ohms to 70 ohms; hence by Eq. (12-1) it must have a characteristic impedance

$$R_o' = \sqrt{70 \times 35.7} = 50 \text{ ohms}$$

From Prob. 8-1

$$R_o' = 138 \log \frac{2r_2}{2r_1}$$

where $2r_2$ = inner diameter of outer conductor
$2r_1$ = diameter of inner conductor

Then

$$\log \frac{2r_2}{2r_1} = \frac{R_0'}{138} = \frac{50}{138} = 0.362$$

$$2r_1 = \frac{2r_2}{2.3} = \frac{2}{2.3} = 0.87 \text{ in.}$$

The student should realize that practical limitations on line dimensions restrict the values of R_o that may be obtained with coaxial lines to 150 ohms or less and with parallel-wire lines to 800 ohms or less. By virtue of Eq. (12-1) these values impose a limitation on the values of R_{in} and R_o that may be transformed by a quarter-wave line section.

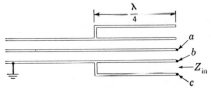

FIG. 12-9. Cross section of a simple form of balun or bazooka used to convert from a grounded coaxial cable to an ungrounded or balanced load. The load is connected between a and b.

12-4. The Balun. Another form of quarter-wave transformer is called the "bazooka," or "balun" because of its ability to transform from a *balanced* (or ungrounded) line or load to an *un*balanced (or grounded) line or load. One form of balun, shown in Fig. 12-9, consists of a short-circuited quarter-wave-long sleeve mounted concentrically about one end of a coaxial cable. The outer surface of the coaxial line is grounded. Since the balun sleeve has a length $\lambda/4$ and is short-circuited, Z_{in}, the input impedance between points b and c on the middle and outer conductors, is infinite; hence b

is isolated from ground, and points a and b are balanced with respect to ground and may be connected to a balanced load or line. The impedance-transformation ratio of the balun shown in Fig. 12-9 is unity. Other forms of baluns may provide a change in impedance level.[1]

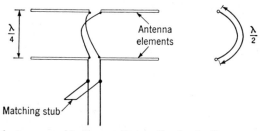

FIG. 12-10. Use of a transposed half-wave line section for feeding two antenna elements in phase.

12-5. The Half-wave Transformer. A line section of length $\lambda/2$ also has useful impedance-transforming properties. In this case the electrical length $\beta l = 180°$, and by Eq. (10-4a) the input impedance is

$$Z_{in} = Z_R \qquad l = \frac{\lambda}{2} \qquad (12\text{-}2)$$

Thus the half-wave transformer behaves like a 1:1 transformer in so far as impedance is concerned. Consider its effect on current and voltage. From Eqs. (10-2) and (10-3)

$$E_x = E_R \cos \beta y + j I_R R_o \sin \beta y$$

$$I_x = I_R \cos \beta y + j \frac{E_R}{R_o} \sin \beta y$$

Substituting $\beta y = \beta l = 180°$, $E_x = E_S$, $I_x = I_S$,

$$E_S = -E_R \qquad I_S = -I_R \qquad l = \frac{\lambda}{2} \qquad (12\text{-}3)$$

Thus the half-wave transformer also transforms current and voltage on a 1:1 *magnitude* basis, but *with a phase shift of* 180°. If the 180° shift is not desired, it may be eliminated by the simple expedient of transposing the two sides of the line. (This corresponds to the reversing of output leads on a lumped-constant transformer.) For these reasons the half-wave section serves admirably as a device for connecting two points in a system with no change in current, voltage, or impedance.

An example of its use is illustrated in Fig. 12-10. The two center-fed antenna elements are spaced a quarter wavelength apart in the vertical

---

[1] See, for example, Staff, MIT Radar School, "Principles of Radar," chap. 7, McGraw-Hill Book Company, Inc., New York, 1946.

plane. They are to be fed *in phase* from a common transmission line. As shown in the diagram, the two elements are connected by a half-wave section which is curved to fit into the required quarter-wave space between the elements. The lines are transposed to satisfy the inphase condition.

12-6. Tapped-line Matching. A case of intermediate interest is one in which power is to be delivered to a length of transmission line. (A case in point is the rf transmission line connected to the "dees" of a

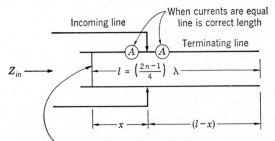

FIG. 12-11. Impedance matching by means of taps to excite a line with low dissipation an odd number of quarter wavelengths long.

cyclotron.) The principle is illustrated in Fig. 12-11. Consider a transmission line which is an odd number of quarter wavelengths long, short-circuited at one end and open-circuited at the other. Two input terminals are secured by tapping either side of the line at the same distance from the ends. Then at this tap there are two branches in parallel, one being the short-circuited line to the left in Fig. 12-11 and the other the open-circuited line to the right. The impedance of these two branches would be given by

$$Z_{sc} = Z_o \tanh \gamma l$$
$$Z_{oc} = Z_o \coth \gamma l$$

In Chap. 10 it was shown that when the attenuation is small the reactive component of the open-circuited impedance could be written

$$X_{oc} = -R_o \cot \beta l = -R_o \cot \frac{2\pi l}{\lambda}$$

Similarly, it may be shown that the reactance of the short-circuited line can be written

$$X_{sc} = +R_o \tan \beta l = +R_o \tan \frac{2\pi l}{\lambda}$$

As applied to Fig. 12-11 the equations would become

$$X_{oc} = -R_o \cot \frac{2\pi(l-x)}{\lambda}$$

$$X_{sc} = +R_o \tan \frac{2\pi x}{\lambda}$$

If l is made an odd number of quarters of a wavelength long, then $2\pi l/\lambda$ would be some odd multiple of $\pi/2$ and

$$\cot \frac{2\pi(l - x)}{\lambda} = \cot \left[\frac{(2n - 1)\pi}{2} - \frac{2\pi x}{\lambda} \right] = \tan \frac{2\pi x}{\lambda}$$

Hence, in this case the reactance of the short-circuited end would be equal and opposite to the reactance of the open-circuited end. This condition is independent of the point at which the tap is connected. The proper length of line may be determined experimentally by connecting an ammeter in the line on either side of a tapped point, applying

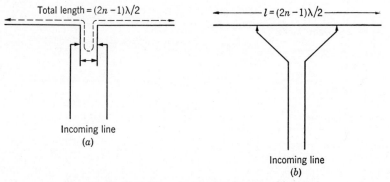

Fig. 12-12. Matching of antennas by movable taps.

voltage to the input terminals, and adjusting the length of line until the currents are equal in the two ammeters. The most convenient adjustment of length is usually made by moving the short-circuiting bar.

Since the reactances of the two branches on either side of the taps are equal, the condition for antiresonance will be set up and a resistive load will be presented to the tap. If the line is subject to dissipation, the magnitude of this load can be adjusted by moving the position of the tap, as this would vary the magnitude of the reactance of each branch while keeping them equal and opposite, just as the moving of a tap on the inductance of an antiresonant circuit was shown in Chap. 4 to vary the magnitude of the effective resistance of the load.

The principle of Fig. 12-11 can be used when the open end of the line is opened out into an antenna as shown in Fig. 12-12a for an antenna of any length or in Fig. 12-12b for an antenna which has a total length which is an odd number of half wavelengths long (end to end). The dissipation is then largely due to the radiation of the antenna portion. The physical length must be slightly less than would be computed, assuming propagation at the velocity of light, but can be found experimentally by the method described. In this case the taps are usually adjusted so as to terminate the incoming line in its characteristic impedance. Such an adjustment may be made by measuring the current along the line with a meter (which may be shunted across a constant portion of the line if it is inconvenient to enter the line) and determining the position of the taps which will eliminate standing waves on the line. If the current rises on the incoming line as one proceeds away from the tap back toward the source, then the termination of the incoming line is less than that of the

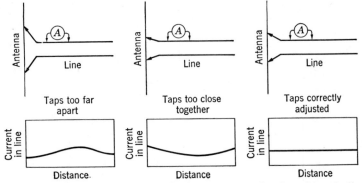

FIG. 12-13. Adjustment of taps to obtain correct termination of supply line.

characteristic impedance and the taps should be moved away from the center. Conversely, if the current in the incoming line drops as one proceeds away from the tap, the terminating impedance is too high and the taps should be moved toward the center. This is illustrated in Fig. 12-13.

PROBLEMS

12-1. (a) Following the method of Fig. 12-1, sketch curves of g_{in} and b_{in} for a general termination y_r. Use $\varphi - 2\beta l$ as the abscissa. (b) Derive equations for the values of l and s in terms of ρ and y_{max}, assuming the input impedance is to be R_o.

12-2. In Fig. 12-2a $Z_R = 2R_o$. Calculate l and s for the longest run of flat line to the left of the stub. Use a minimum stub length.

12-3. Repeat Prob. 12-2 for $y_r = 4 + j0.5$.

12-4. In Fig. 12-4a $y_r = 1.21 + j0$, $l = 0.116\lambda$ and $d = 0.33\lambda$. Stub 1 is to open-circuited and of the shortest possible length. Stub 2 is short-circuited.

a. Find s_1 and s_2 for the main line to be flat.

b. What is the standing wave ratio between stub 1 and the load?

12-5. In Fig. 12-4a if $d = 0.2\lambda$, $l = 0.1\lambda$, and $y_r = g_r + jb_r$, what range of values of g_r cannot be matched by the double-stub system?

12-6. In Fig. 12-4b $R_o = 200$ ohms. The line to the left of stub 2 is flat when $\beta l = 38°$, $\beta d = 120°$, $\beta s_1 = 81.5°$, and $\beta s_2 = 30.5°$. What is Z_R?

12-7. Standing wave measurements on a line indicate that the first minimum of voltage is 30° from the load and $S = 4$. Design a double-stub matching system. If possible, use $l = 0.1\lambda$, if not, use $l = 0.2\lambda$. Use $d = 0.4\lambda$.

12-8. A 70-ohm coaxial cable is terminated in an unknown load. $S = 1.7$, and the first voltage minimum lies at 0.174λ from the load end. The outer pipe of the line has an inner diameter of 1 in. Find the location and inner conductor diameter for a matching quarter-wave transformer.

12-9. In Fig. 12-10 each antenna element has a driving-point impedance of $72 + j0$ ohms. The main feed line has a characteristic impedance of 100 ohms. Find the length and position for the single matching stub.

12-10. Discuss the feasibility of tapping in on the resonant stub of Fig. 12-14 such that $R_{in} = R_o$ of the stub.

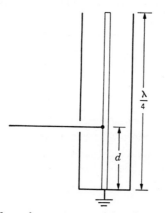

FIG. 12-14. Tapped resonant coaxial stub for Prob. 12-10.

12-11. An oscillator tank circuit is to be made from a coaxial line a quarter wave long. The coaxial elements are copper tubing, for which $r_1 = 0.5$ in., $r_2 = 1$ in. The frequency of operation is to be 10^8 cycles.

a. Locate the tap position for the oscillator tube to work into a load of 30 kilohms. Use $\sigma = 5.75 \times 10^7$ mhos/m, and assume a relative velocity of unity.

b. What is the reactive component of input impedance at the tap?

12-12. A 50-ohm quarter-wave section is used for matching a resonant (that is, $\rho \neq 1$) line to a 12-kilohm load in a radar antenna system. The resonant line is to work into a 5-kilohm load at a wavelength of 1 m. Locate the tap positions if the quarter-wave section has a loop resistance per unit length of 1.38 ohms/m at the operating frequency.

CHAPTER 13

BROAD-BAND IMPEDANCE
TRANSFORMATION

The several impedance-transforming networks described in the last two chapters are inherently narrow-band devices. Relying on the behavior of simple reactive elements, they are sharply frequency-selective and give the required impedance transformation at a single frequency only. (An exception is shown in Fig. 11-20.) The curves of Figs. 11-9 and 11-12 indicate how the response of such circuits varies with frequency.

A number of communication applications, however, require essentially uniform response over a relatively wide bandwidth; for example, a typical television transmitter must work into an essentially constant load over a 4.5-Mc range! This chapter is concerned with these broad-band systems.

Two inherently different types of broad systems are encountered in practice: (1) Audio and video frequency, where the frequency band begins at or near zero frequency. (2) Radio frequency, where the broad band extends on either side of a "center," or "carrier," frequency located far above the limits of the audio range. As a consequence these may be considered as two virtually distinct problems.

AUDIO SYSTEMS

13-1. The Audio Transformer. The basic impedance-transforming device in the audio range is the audio transformer. In contrast to the tuned rf transformer where the primary and secondary inductors are supported in air, at audio frequencies it is common practice to use ferromagnetic materials such as iron or permalloy as a core upon which the primary and secondary windings are placed, this core guiding to a large extent the path of the magnetic flux which links with the two coils. In this type of operation it is usually desirable to make as large a proportion as possible of the flux which links with one coil link also with the other coil. In this case the coefficient of coupling k is nearly unity.

When two coils are wound on a common ferromagnetic core, the reluctance of the paths for the magnetic fluxes which they set up will be

468

practically identical and the ratio of their inductances will be proportional to the ratio of the square of the number of turns on the coils, i.e.,

$$\frac{L_p}{L_s} = \frac{N_1^2}{N_2^2} \tag{13-1}$$

A given flux would induce a voltage in each coil which would be proportional to the number of turns. If this flux were produced by current in coil 1, then the ratio L_p/M would be the ratio of the voltage induced in coil 1 to that induced in coil 2 by the current in coil 1. If *all* the flux set up by one coil linked with the other coil, then the mutual inductance would be related to the self-inductances by the relation

$$\frac{L_p}{M} = \frac{N_1}{N_2} \qquad \frac{L_s}{M} = \frac{N_2}{N_1}$$

Since k represents the proportion of flux set up by one coil which actually links the other, the true equation is

$$M = k \frac{N_2}{N_1} L_p = k \frac{N_1}{N_2} L_s \tag{13-2}$$

From Eq. (13-2) it is apparent that

$$M = k \sqrt{L_p L_s} \tag{13-3}$$

Equation (13-3) also holds for any arrangement of inductances, while Eqs. (13-1) and (13-2) apply only when the reluctances of the flux paths of the two coils are equal and *hence are not applicable to the tuned rf transformer*.

The study of the audio transformer is greatly simplified by means of suitable equivalent circuits. Two basic forms of equivalent circuit will be considered. The mesh equations for the circuit of Fig. 13-1a are

$$
\begin{aligned}
Z_{11}I_1 + Z_{12}I_2 &= E_g & Z_{11} &= R_g + R_{Lp} + j\omega L_p \\
Z_{12}I_1 + Z_{22}I_2 &= 0 & Z_{22} &= Z_R + R_{Ls} + j\omega L_s \\
& & Z_{12} &= -j\omega M
\end{aligned} \tag{13-4}
$$

These equations may be rewritten in the following manner without affecting the currents:

$$
\begin{aligned}
[(Z_{11} - Z_{12}) + Z_{12}]I_1 + Z_{12}I_2 &= E_g \\
Z_{12}I_1 + [(Z_{22} - Z_{12}) + Z_{12}]I_2 &= 0
\end{aligned} \tag{13-5}
$$

Equations (13-5) yield the equivalent T circuit of the transformer which is shown in Fig. 13-1b.

Now if the value of the mutual impedance is multiplied by any factor a and the secondary impedance Z_{22} is multiplied by a^2, then the *primary current will remain the same as before*, while the secondary current will be changed by a factor $1/a$.

This may be shown by inserting aZ_{12} for Z_{12} and a^2Z_{22} for Z_{22} in the expressions for the driving-point and transfer impedances.

$$(z_{11})_{\text{new}} = Z_{11} - \frac{a^2Z_{12}^2}{a^2Z_{22}} = Z_{11} - \frac{Z_{12}^2}{Z_{22}} = (z_{11})_{\text{old}}$$

$$(z_{12})_{\text{new}} = \frac{a^2Z_{11}Z_{22} - a^2Z_{12}^2}{-aZ_{12}} = \frac{a(Z_{11}Z_{22} - Z_{12}^2)}{-Z_{12}} = a(z_{12})_{\text{old}}$$

It may be seen that the value of z_{11}, and hence the value of primary current I_1, has not been altered, but z_{12} has been increased by the factor a,

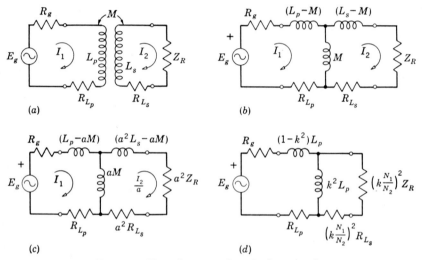

(a)

(b)

(c)

(d)

Fig. 13-1. Transformer and equivalent circuits.

and so the current I_2 has been reduced by a factor equal to the reciprocal of a. The driving-point impedance of Fig. 13-1c is, therefore, the same as that of Fig. 13-1b; hence Fig. 13-1c is often called the equivalent circuit *referred to the primary side.*

It is common practice in the design of audio transformers to make the reactance of the transformer primary large in comparison with the impedance to be presented to its input terminals and to make the reactance of the secondary large in comparison with the load impedance. The reasons for this will be discussed in detail later. Hence in Fig. 13-1c the reactance of the branch aM is usually large in comparison with the impedances a^2R_{Ls} and a^2Z_R. Under these circumstances, if a is so selected that the reactance of $a^2L_s - aM$ is small in comparison with the reactance of aM, then the branch aM could be neglected for a good approximate solution and the equivalent circuit would be a simple series one. One such value of a would be obtained by setting $a^2L_s - aM$ equal to zero, which would give the equation

$$a = \frac{M}{L_s} \tag{13-6}$$

From Eq. (13-2), Eq. (13-6) could also be written

$$a = k\frac{N_1}{N_2} \tag{13-6a}$$

The inductance $L_p - aM$ in Fig. 13-1c would then become, by the use of Eqs. (13-2) and (13-6a), $L_p(1 - k^2)$, and the equivalent circuit would be that shown in Fig. 13-1d. In solving for the currents the branch $k^2 L_p$ can usually be neglected.

Since k is usually nearly equal to unity, a value of a which is more commonly used for equivalent circuits is to make

$$a = \frac{N_1}{N_2} = \sqrt{\frac{L_p}{L_s}} \tag{13-7}$$

For this value of a the arms $L_p - aM$ and $a^2 L_s - aM$ are both equal to $(1 - k)L_p$, and the equivalent circuit is that shown in Fig. 13-2. Notice that, while a value of a equal to the turns ratio is a common and convenient one to choose, it produces only one out of an infinite variety of possible equivalent circuits.

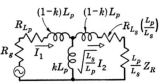

13-2. Ideal Transformers. An ideal transformer is one which will modify the magnitude of the load impedance, as viewed from the sending end, without changing its angle and will not introduce any additional losses. From a consideration of Figs. 13-1c and 13-2, it is apparent that such a transformer would have the following requirements:

FIG. 13-2. Equivalent circuit of Fig. 13-1c when $a = N_1/N_2$ $= \sqrt{L_p/L_s}$.

1. Infinite primary and secondary inductances but a finite ratio L_p/L_s.
2. Coefficient of coupling equal to unity.
3. No resistance in primary and secondary windings.

At audio frequencies one can approximate these conditions. For all practical purposes condition 1 is satisfied if $X_m^2 \gg |Z_g Z_R|$, and this can usually be realized if cores of high permeability are used and are wound with a sufficient number of turns. Condition 2 can be approximated by using cores of high permeability and arranging the windings so that the flux produced by one coil will link with the other coil to as great an extent as possible. Condition 3 can be approximated if the resistance of the primary is small in comparison with the resistance to be presented at the input terminals and if the resistance of the secondary is small in comparison with that of the load.

13-3. Conditions for Impedance Match. Equations (11-21) to (11-23) state the general requirements for a purely reactive T section to give a specified impedance transformation. At af the network must operate over a very wide band measured in octaves. For example, the range of 30 to 15,000 cycles represents about nine octaves. Hence, it is not feasible to build a T section which uses inductances and capacitances and which operates over this range. That is why the matching network is usually built of inductances alone in the form of an iron-core transformer. Under these circumstances a *perfect* impedance match is impossible *at any frequency*. The requirement set by Eq. (11-23) cannot be met, because in a transformer with purely inductive coupling

$$X_m{}^2 = k^2 X_p X_s$$

where $k = M/\sqrt{L_p L_s} < 1$.

However, if the coefficient of coupling can be made nearly equal to unity and if $X_p \gg R_{Lp}$, $X_s \gg R_{Ls}$ (conditions approximating the ideal transformer), then the second terms under the radical of Eqs. (11-23a) and (11-23b), viz.,

$$X_m = \pm \sqrt{\frac{R_{I2}}{R_{I1}} X_p{}^2 - R_{I1} R_{I2}}$$

$$= \pm \sqrt{\frac{R_{I1}}{R_{I2}} X_s{}^2 - R_{I1} R_{I2}}$$

become negligible and the equations become practically

$$X_m = X_s \sqrt{\frac{R_{I1}}{R_{I2}}} = X_p \sqrt{\frac{R_{I2}}{R_{I1}}} = \sqrt{X_p X_s} \qquad (13\text{-}8)$$

If this condition is true, then if X_m, or X_p, or X_s be selected first, the other values are determined only by the magnitude of the impedance-transformation ratio, and not by the individual impedance magnitudes, and it would be possible to alter any terminating resistance by the ratio X_p/X_s with one network.

While such a network does not give a perfect match at any frequency, it does give an *approximate* match over a wide range of frequencies and so is more suitable than the T network containing capacitive elements.

The requirement of a transforming network that one of the *equivalent* arms must have a type of reactance opposite to X_m is met by the transformer, for, with k nearly equal to 1, X_m will be greater than either X_p or X_s but not both (except in the 1:1 transformer, in which case it can be greater than neither), and so either the series arm X_1, which is equal to $X_p - X_m$ in Fig. 13-1b, or the series arm X_2, which is equal to $X_s - X_m$, will have a negative value. The advantage of obtaining the negative reactance in this way is that Eq. (11-20a) may be made to hold over a wide *frequency* range, whereas if a capacitance were used to obtain the negative reactance required for X_1 or X_2, this equation (11-20a) would hold at only one frequency.

13-4. Image Impedances of an Ideal Transformer. The characteristics of the ideal transformer were discussed in a preceding section. In an ideal transformer the input impedance on open circuit is infinite, and the input impedance on short circuit zero, when measured from either pair of terminals. Hence the image impedances would be individually indeterminate as indicated by an application of Eqs. (3-102). However, the *ratio* of the image impedances would have a definite value given by Eq. (11-20a), for in the ideal transformer there is a definite ratio of primary to secondary reactance equal to the ratio of the square of the turns.

13-5. Comparison of Reflected Resistance in Iron-cored and Tuned-transformer Circuits. Another interesting comparison may be made between the reflected resistance in the circuits using iron-cored transformers and those using tuned circuits. The driving-point impedance of a two-mesh circuit is given by

$$z_{11} = Z_{11} - \frac{Z_{12}^2}{Z_{22}}$$

In the tuned rf transformer, if the primary and secondary reactances are made equal to zero, this equation would become

$$z_{11} = R_{11} + \frac{\omega^2 M^2}{R_{22}}$$

The resistance reflected into the primary circuit by the coupling to the secondary circuit would be given by the term $\omega^2 M^2 / R_{22}$ and would be *inversely* proportional to the secondary mesh resistance.

On the other hand, if an iron-cored transformer is used which approximates ideal conditions, then $X_{11} \gg R_{11}$ and $X_{22} \gg R_{22}$ and if the reactance external to the transformer is negligible, $X_{11}X_{22} = X_{12}^2$. Then the equation becomes

$$z_{11} = R_{11} + jX_{11} + \frac{X_{12}^2}{R_{22} + jX_{22}}$$
$$= R_{11} + jX_{11} + \frac{X_{11}X_{22}(R_{22} - jX_{22})}{R_{22}^2 + X_{22}^2} \tag{13-9}$$

R_{22}^2 may be neglected in the denominator in comparison with X_{22}^2, which reduces the equation to

$$z_{11} = R_{11} + jX_{11} + \frac{X_{11}}{X_{22}} R_{22} - jX_{11}$$
$$= R_{11} + \left(\frac{N_1}{N_2}\right)^2 R_{22} \tag{13-10}$$

The resistance reflected into the primary is given by the term $(N_1/N_2)^2 R_{22}$ and so is *directly* proportional to the secondary mesh resistance.

Other circuits may fall between these two extremes, in which case the situation can be examined by the fundamental equations.

13-6. Frequency Response. Figure 13-2 must be regarded as a first-order-approximation equivalent circuit when the frequency response and efficiency of the transformer are to be considered. A more accurate representation of the transformer would show shunt capacitance across the input and output terminals and "mutual" capacitance between the two windings. Furthermore, a conductance G should appear in parallel with the mutual leg kL_p in Fig. 13-2 to account for the eddy-current and hysteresis losses in the core material. As a general rule this equivalent conductance depends upon frequency and varies nonlinearly with primary current and so may introduce frequency, delay, and amplitude (nonlinear) distortion.

As a practical matter, the large majority of iron-core audio transformers (with the exception of interstage vacuum-tube transformers) are used to match impedances in the range from a few ohms to a few thousand ohms. In this type of service the shunt and mutual capacitances are usually so small that their reactances have little measurable effect in the audio band. When the impedance level of one or both windings becomes high, say, above several thousand ohms, the winding capacitance must be taken into account at the higher audio frequencies. In a well-designed transformer the core losses are small enough so that G draws negligible current. Hence the first-order approximation shown in Fig. 13-2 is often adequate for the calculation of frequency response. (This may not be true in inexpensive units, where the behavior of the core may become significant.)

In typical high-quality audio impedance-matching transformers, kL_p will have a value 50 to 500 times as great as the total leakage inductance, $2(1 - k)L_p$. Because of this difference in magnitudes the behavior of the transformer may be considered in three distinct frequency bands, yielding a greatly simplified analysis. At the lower frequencies the voltage drop across the leakage reactance is negligible, and the simplified equivalent circuit of Fig. 13-3a results. At the higher frequencies the drop across the leakage reactance is significant, and ωkL_p is so large that negligible current is diverted through this shunt branch. Then the high-frequency equivalent circuit of Fig. 13-3c is adequate. In the band of frequencies intermediate between these two extremes the series, and shunt reactances may both be neglected, so that the simplified equivalent circuit of Fig. 13-3b may be used. The student may calculate the voltage or current response as a function of frequency quite readily from these equivalent-circuit diagrams (see Prob. 13-1).

Inspection of Fig. 13-3 shows that the low-frequency response is improved by raising kL_p, while the high-frequency response is improved by lowering $(1 - k)L_p$.   If the primary inductance L_p is raised by increasing the number of turns in order to improve the operation at low-frequencies, the transmission at high-frequencies will be affected adversely.   Hence

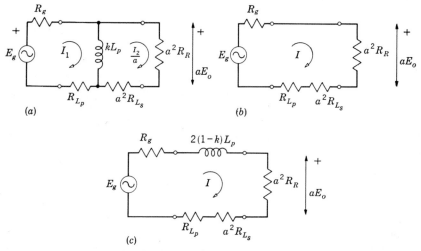

Fig. 13-3. Equivalent circuits for the iron-core impedance-matching transformer. (a) Low-frequency circuit. (b) Mid-frequency circuit. (c) High-frequency circuit.

values of L_p and k should be so selected that the inequalities

$$\omega(1 - k)L_p \ll \frac{L_p}{L_s}|Z_R| \ll \omega k L_p \tag{13-11}$$

will hold over as wide a range of frequencies as is possible.   It is apparent that k must be made as near unity as possible in order to secure this.

In order to ascertain approximate limits for the values of L_p and k, consider the two simplified circuits shown in Figs. 13-3a and c.   Since k nearly equals 1, it may be assumed as such in the arm kL_p but not in the inductance $(1 - k)L_p$.   The resistance of the two windings is neglected, and it is assumed that the transformer is matching two resistances so that the reflected resistance of the load equals the resistance of the generator, that is, $a^2R_R = R_g$.   Then if a perfect, or ideal, transformer were used, the power delivered to the load would equal $E_g^2/4R_g$.

In Fig. 13-3a the output current would be

$$I_1 = \frac{E_g(R_g + j\omega L_p)}{R_g^2 + 2j\omega L_p R_g}$$

$$\frac{I_2}{a} = \frac{E_g j\omega L_p}{R_g^2 + 2j\omega L_p R_g} \tag{13-12}$$

Suppose that at the lowest frequency of interest $R_g = \omega L_p$. Then the current in the load would be

$$\frac{|I_2|}{a} = \frac{E_g}{\sqrt{5}\,R_g}$$

The power delivered to the load would be

$$P = \frac{|I_2|^2}{a^2}\,R_g = \frac{E_g{}^2}{5R_g} \tag{13-13}$$

From Eq. (13-13) it is seen that the ratio of the power delivered to the load of Fig. 13-3a, for the case where $\omega L_p = R_g$, to the power delivered to a load by an ideal transformer would be $\frac{4}{5}$, or 0.8. This would correspond to a loss of about 1 db.

If, at the high-frequency end of the band where $2(1 - k)L_p$ is of importance, $2\omega(1 - k)L_p$ should equal R_g, then the current in Fig. 13-3c would also be given by the relation

$$|I_1| = \frac{E_g}{\sqrt{5}\,R_g}$$

and the power delivered to the load would again be

$$P = \frac{E_g{}^2}{5R_g} \tag{13-14}$$

This would also correspond to a loss of about 1 db as compared with an ideal transformer.

As an example of the use of these relations, suppose that a transformer is to be designed to match a 600-ohm line to a 5,400-ohm load over a range of frequencies from 30 to 15,000 cycles. Neglecting winding resistances determine the primary and secondary inductances and the required coefficient of coupling if the loss of 1 db is allowed at the low- and high-frequency ends of the band.

Then
$$2\pi \times 30 L_p = 600$$
$$L_p = 3.18 \text{ henrys}$$
$$4\pi \times 15,000(1 - k)L_p = 600$$
$$1 - k = 0.001$$
$$k = 0.999$$

It should be observed that this value of k depended only on the frequency range and the tolerance at the extreme frequencies and was independent of the terminating resistances. However, the required value of L_p does depend on the impedance which is to be presented to the source.

Since the ratio of the secondary load impedance to the primary supply network impedance is 9:1, the transformer should have a turns ratio of 1:3. This means that the secondary inductance should be

$$9 \times 3.18 = 28.62 \text{ henrys}$$

It should be realized that these are rough values since the winding resistances and the core losses have been neglected. One important point that must be stressed is the following: When the transformer is used to match a load to the plate circuit of a vacuum tube, the d-c component of plate current flows through the transformer winding. Thus L_p is the *incremental* primary inductance, i.e., the inductance taking into account the saturation of the transformer core caused by the direct current. More about this will be said later.

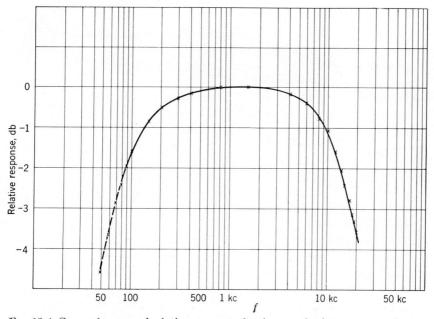

Fig. 13-4. Curve of measured relative response of an inexpensive iron-core transformer.

Push-pull operation of active circuit elements will remove unbalance in the d-c components but may introduce another problem because the leakage reactance between the two sections of a push-pull primary may prove troublesome.

Figure 13-4 shows the measured relative response curve for an inexpensive (manufacture's price, approximately $1) transformer connected between the nominal generator and load resistances and with 1 watt delivered to the load at 1 kc. The d-c primary current is 60 ma. The relative response is

$$N_{db} = -20 \log \frac{(E_o)_{1 \, kc}}{E_o}$$

The transformer is optimistically rated for 5 watts into a 3.5-ohm load when fed from a 2,000-ohm generator. The readings on the dashed portion of the curve below 70 cycles are questionable because of distortion introduced by saturation of the small ($\frac{1}{2}$ by $\frac{1}{2}$ in.) cross-section iron core. A similar curve was run for an output level of 2 watts. It was identical to that in Fig. 13-4 above 130 cycles. Below that frequency the waveform became so poor as to make voltmeter readings meaningless. The measured efficiency of the transformer at 1 kc and 1 watt output was approximately 75 per cent.

The student should note that the output power decreases at the lower frequencies because the shunting susceptance of L_p becomes important. It is apparent that the input impedance of the transformer loaded with a resistance begins to have an appreciable reactive component as the frequency is reduced at about the same frequency as that at which the power delivered starts decreasing. When the transformer is driven by a vacuum tube, this complex impedance causes the path of operation of the vacuum tube to become elliptical rather than linear, which either causes nonlinear distortion or requires a reduction in the maximum output of the tube. This use of the load line in analyzing distortion in combinations of vacuum tubes and loads is discussed in most electronics texts. It may be expected, then, that frequency and nonlinear distortion begin to show up in approximately the same frequency range when the tube is driven to or near its maximum output. Since the power at the higher frequencies is usually small, a similar effect at the upper frequency limit may be neglected.

13-7. Design Considerations for Iron-core Transformers. At low-frequencies the transformer can be represented by the equivalent circuit of Fig. 13-3a. Hence the core volume and number of turns must be large enough to give the desired winding inductance. In addition, the magnetic core should be operated only in the linear portion of the magnetization curve if waveform distortion is to be avoided. The arrangement of the primary and secondary coils is relatively unimportant at low-frequencies.

At high-frequencies the transformer equivalent circuit is that of Fig. 13-3c. As has been pointed out, in some cases it is necessary to include the effects of winding capacitances in addition to the resistances and inductances. There is a fundamental conflict between the requirements for low leakage inductance and low winding capacitances. For low leakage inductance the primary and secondary turns must be wound very near each other. A separation of windings is necessary, however, to reduce interwinding capacitance. A compromise between these considerations is necessary in order to obtain a good design.

In high-impedance windings the capacitance between layers may greatly affect the high-frequency operation. Transformers may include many layers of small wire with very little separation between layers.

The interlayer capacitance may be reduced by using thicker insulation between layers or by winding the coil in a number of sections.   Winding the coil in a number of short segments reduces the voltage gradient between successive layers and thereby reduces the effective capacitance.

The efficiency of impedance-matching transformers is a function of transformer size and core material.   In a small inexpensive transformer the resistances of the windings may be a significant fraction of the impedances being matched.   Winding resistances may be reduced by increasing core size, decreasing turns, and increasing wire sizes.   The efficiency is also improved by using thinner laminations in the core and by the selection of core material with better magnetic characteristics.

In winding coils in a given alloted volume the effect of changing the number of turns on the values of L and R is of interest.   If the number of turns is increased by a ratio m, the cross-sectional area of each turn must be changed by a factor $1/m$ in order to keep the volume constant. If the volume occupied by the insulation is negligible, this would cause the resistance of the winding to be multiplied by a value m^2.   Under these conditions, since the inductance of a coil, whose geometry otherwise is unchanged, is proportional to the square of the number of turns, the value of L would also be multiplied by m^2.   Hence the ratio L/R would remain unchanged.

However, unfortunately, as the size of wire is decreased, the relative amount of space allotted to insulation must be increased.   The thickness of the enamel insulation for fine wire is determined by the value necessary to resist abrasion in the winding process and cannot be reduced below a certain minimum on the finer wires.   Hence, in practice, as the number of turns is increased in a given winding space, the value of the resistance will go up faster than m^2 and so the L/R ratio will drop.

In an audio transformer, particularly when intended to be used with direct current flowing in one of the windings, an air gap is introduced to ensure that the inductance is linear and the reluctance of the magnetic path is determined largely by the length of this air gap, the purpose of the iron being to ensure that as much as possible of the flux linking one coil also links the other (making k as nearly equal to 1 as possible).

For convenience consider the case where all linear dimensions of a transformer are doubled except that the length of the air gap is kept constant.   Then the cross section of the air gap will be multiplied by 4 and the permeance of the magnetic path multiplied by 4.   The cross section of the electrical winding will also be multiplied by 4, and the average length of turn will be doubled.   Therefore, if the number of turns is kept the same, the resistance will be halved.   Since the permeance has been increased by 4, the inductance for the same number of turns will be multiplied by 4.   Therefore, the L/R ratio will be increased by 8, which is also the ratio of the volumes and weights of the two transformers being compared.   This would also be approximately the ratio of the two material costs.

For a given volume the L/R ratio is nearly independent of the number of turns; so advantage of the improved L/R ratio could be taken in terms of higher L or lower R by redesigning the transformer.

The effect of the larger volume with the same air gap would also be to decrease the leakage inductance.   Furthermore, in the larger winding space, it is usually possible to provide more advantageous distribution of windings to reduce capacitances and leakage reactance.

13-8. Resistance Pads.   In all the impedance-transforming networks discussed to this point the design has been based on the use of reactive

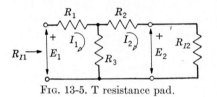

FIG. 13-5. T resistance pad.

elements in order to minimize the losses.   In certain applications, however, fairly high losses may be tolerated and in some instances may even be desirable.   In these applications the matching networks may be built of resistors and hence are inherently broad-band devices, their behavior at high-frequencies limited only by inevitable shunt capacitances, which, like the poor, are with us always. Such resistive matching networks are termed "pads" or "attenuators" and may be designed by application of Eqs. (11-26), (11-30a), (11-32a), and (11-33a).

Consider the T section of pure resistances terminated in its image impedance Z_{I2} as in Fig. 13-5.   By Eqs. (11-26) and (11-34) the image-transfer constant of the network is given by

$$e^\theta = \sqrt{\frac{E_1 I_1}{E_2 I_2}} \qquad (11\text{-}34)$$

$$\theta = A + jB \qquad (11\text{-}26)$$

Since the network contains only resistance, E_1 and E_2 are in phase, as are I_1 and I_2; hence

$$\theta = A \text{ nepers} \qquad B = 0$$

Furthermore, by Eq. (11-28), Z_{I1} and Z_{I2} are real and may be designated R_{I1} and R_{I2}, respectively.   Then by Eqs. (11-30a), (11-32a), and (11-33a) the components of the T pad, to give a specified loss between known image resistances, are given by

$$R_3 = \frac{\sqrt{R_{I1}R_{I2}}}{\sinh A} \qquad (13\text{-}15)$$

$$R_1 = \frac{R_{I1}}{\tanh A} - R_3 \qquad (13\text{-}16)$$

$$R_2 = \frac{R_{I2}}{\tanh A} - R_3 \qquad (13\text{-}17)$$

The student will observe that A is a real number; hence the hyperbolic functions of A are real and may be determined from the tables in the Appendix.

Design a 10-db pad to work between 100 and 200 ohms.
Converting decibels to nepers,

$$A = 10 \text{ db} = 0.115 \times 10 = 1.15 \text{ nepers}$$

From the Appendix tables

$$\sinh 1.15 = 1.421 \qquad \tanh 1.15 = 0.818$$

From Eqs. (13-15) to (13-17)

$$R_3 = \frac{\sqrt{(2 \times 10^2) \times 10^2}}{1.421} = \frac{141.4}{1.421} = 98.4 \text{ ohms}$$

$$R_1 = \frac{200}{0.818} - 98.4 = 244.2 - 98.4 = 145.8 \text{ ohms}$$

$$R_2 = \frac{100}{0.818} - 98.4 = 122.1 - 98.4 = 23.7 \text{ ohms}$$

The II resistance pad of Fig. 13-6 may be designed by applying the duality principle to Eqs. (13-15) to (13-17).

13-9. Minimum-loss Pad. If a resistance pad is to be built for the primary purpose of obtaining a specified impedance transformation, it should be designed such that the loss A is minimum. When designed for

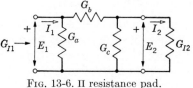

FIG. 13-6. II resistance pad.

this condition, the pad is known as a "minimum-loss pad." Equation (13-17) serves as the basis for finding the minimum-loss condition, namely, that R_2 of the T pad be zero.

For convenience, let R_{I1} be the *larger* of the two image resistances, that is, $R_{I1} > R_{I2}$. Multiplying by R_{I2} and taking the square root,

$$R_{I2} < \sqrt{R_{I1}R_{I2}} \qquad (13\text{-}18)$$

The Appendix shows curves of sinh A and tanh A for positive real values of A. From these curves and inequality (13-18) it may be seen that for A large

$$\frac{R_{I2}}{\tanh A} > \frac{\sqrt{R_{I1}R_{I2}}}{\sinh A} \qquad (13\text{-}19)$$

It may also be seen that, as $A \rightarrow 0$, sinh A $\rightarrow$ tanh A; hence for A small

$$\frac{R_{I2}}{\tanh A} < \frac{\sqrt{R_{I1}R_{I2}}}{\sinh A} \qquad (13\text{-}20)$$

Inequality (13-20) imposes an impossible condition on the resistance pad, for by Eq. (13-17) it requires that R_2 be negative. Thus the minimum possible value of loss must occur at the crossover point between inequalities (13-19) and (13-20), i.e., at

$$\frac{R_{I1}}{\tanh A_{\min}} = \frac{\sqrt{R_{I1}R_{I2}}}{\sinh A_{\min}} \tag{13-21}$$

corresponding to $R_2 = 0$. Equation (13-21) may be solved for $A_{\min}$.

$$\cosh A_{\min} = \sqrt{\frac{R_{I1}}{R_{I2}}} \tag{13-22}$$

It is interesting to note that the minimum loss is a function of the transformation ratio R_{I1}/R_{I2} alone and does not depend on the absolute values

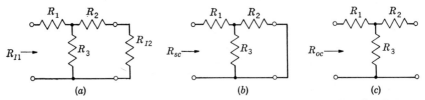

Fig. 13-7. Diagrams for obtaining the input impedance of a T pad under different load conditions.

of R_{I1} and R_{I2}. (It is also of interest to note that the loss increases with the transformation ratio, as was the case in reactive matching sections.) The student may derive simplified expressions for R_1 and R_3 of the minimum-loss pad in terms of R_{I1} and R_{I2} by eliminating A in Eqs. (13-15) and (13-16).

13-10. Isolation from Load Variations. The student might well wonder why a pad other than the minimum-loss type would ever be used as an impedance transforming network. One answer is that the losses of a pad tend to make the input impedance independent of the load. This property may be important when a generator works into a variable load. It will be shown that for a T pad the maximum deviation of R_{in} from R_{I1} is a function of the pad loss, A.

Consider the T pad of Fig. 13-7a. R_1, R_2, and R_3 have been designed to transform the nominal or rated load R_{I2} into the desired input resistance R_{I1}. The load is subject to variation; so the input impedance will be checked for the extreme limits of this variation. If the load becomes a short circuit as in Fig. 13-7b, the input impedance becomes

$$R_{sc} = R_1 + \frac{R_2R_3}{R_2 + R_3} \tag{13-23}$$

Eliminating R_1, R_2, and R_3 by Eqs. (13-15) to (13-17),

$$R_{sc} = R_{I1} \tanh A \tag{13-23a}$$

Then expressing the deviation of R_{sc} from R_{I2} as a fraction of R_{I1},

$$\frac{R_{I1} - R_{sc}}{R_{I1}} = 1 - \tanh A \tag{13-24}$$

The other extreme of load variation is an open circuit. For the open-circuit termination the input resistance of Fig. 13-7c is

$$R_{oc} = R_1 + R_3 \tag{13-25}$$

$$= \frac{R_{I1}}{\tanh A} \tag{13-25a}$$

Expressing the deviation of R_{oc} from R_{I1} as a fraction of R_{I1},

$$\frac{R_{oc} - R_{I1}}{R_{I1}} = \frac{1}{\tanh A} - 1 \tag{13-26}$$

For purposes of comparison, Eq. (13-26) may be rearranged.

$$\frac{R_{oc} - R_{I1}}{R_{I1}} = \frac{1 - \tanh A}{\tanh A} = \frac{1}{\tanh A} \frac{R_{I1} - R_{sc}}{R_{I1}} \tag{13-26a}$$

Since $\tanh A < 1$ for any finite, positive value of A, it follows that the maximum possible deviation of input resistance from R_{I1} is given by an open-circuit termination; hence Eq. (13-26) may be used to design a T pad to keep the input resistance to any specified tolerance regardless of the variations in load.

An oscillator is subject to frequency change with load variations. It is designed to work into a 50-ohm load and is to be coupled to a nominal load of 200 ohms. Design a T pad to make the required nominal impedance transformation and to ensure that the oscillator load remains within 5 per cent of 50 ohms.

Since the largest deviation occurs for an open circuit on the load end of the pad, use Eq. (13-26).

$$\tanh A = \frac{1}{1 + 0.05} = \frac{1}{1.05} = 0.951$$

From the table of hyperbolic functions in the Appendix,

$$A = 1.84 \text{ nepers} \qquad \sinh A = 3.07$$

By Eq. (13-15)

$$R_3 = \frac{\sqrt{R_{I1}R_{I2}}}{\sinh A} = \frac{\sqrt{50 \times 200}}{3.07} = \frac{100}{3.07} = 32.6 \text{ ohms}$$

By Eqs. (13-16) and (13-17)

$$R_1 = \frac{R_{I1}}{\tanh A} - R_3 = \frac{50}{0.951} - 32.6 = 52.5 - 32.6 = 19.9 \text{ ohms}$$

$$R_2 = \frac{R_{I2}}{\tanh A} - R_3 = \frac{100}{0.951} - 32.6 = 105 - 32.6 = 72.4 \text{ ohms}$$

As a check, compute R_{oc} by Eq. (13-25).

$$R_{oc} = R_1 + R_3 = 52.5 \text{ ohms}$$

$$\text{Per cent deviation} = \frac{52.5 - 50}{50} = 5\%$$

It should be noticed that the penalty paid for this isolation from load variation is a loss of 1.84 nepers, or 16 db, representing a ratio of output to input *power* of 0.025!

The student should notice that, in asymmetrical pads where $R_{I1} \neq R_{I2}$, *the decibels loss cannot be calculated as* 20 *log* (E_1/E_2) because of the change in impedance level.

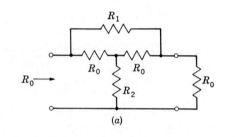

(a)

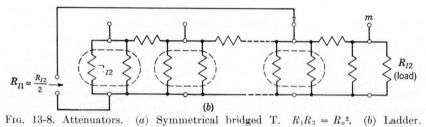

(b)

Fig. 13-8. Attenuators. (a) Symmetrical bridged T. $R_1 R_2 = R_o^2$. (b) Ladder.

13-11. Attenuators. In a number of applications it is necessary to introduce a specified loss between a generator and a *matched* load without upsetting the impedance relationship. Symmetrical T or Π pads may be used for this purpose and are then called "attenuators." If, however, the loss is to be adjustable in fixed steps, the T and Π pads offer an uneconomical solution because of the number of resistors and switch contacts required. An alternate and more economical solution is afforded by the symmetrical bridged T pad of Fig. 13-8a. The loss may be varied by simultaneously switching the values of R_1 and R_2. The student may verify that if $R_1 R_2 = R_o^2$,

$$e^{\alpha} = 1 + \frac{R_1}{R_o} \tag{13-27}$$

for the symmetrical bridged T section.

Still more economical from the viewpoint of switching is the ladder attenuator of Fig. 13-8*b*, which consists of a cascade of symmetrical Π pads terminated at *both ends* in R_{I2}. The ladder attenuator has the principal disadvantage of providing a loss of 3 db in the minimum-loss position (*m* on the diagram). This comes about because the input current divides equally at the tap, only one-half going toward the load, and because of the 1:2 change in resistance level. In constructing the Π ladder attenuator, adjacent shunt elements (circled on the diagram) are combined into a single resistor to reduce cost.

RADIO-FREQUENCY SYSTEMS

In the radio-frequency region there is no direct analog to the audio iron-core transformer to provide a universal broad-band impedance-transforming device. As a result, each radio-frequency problem must be considered on its own merits and a suitable broad-banding means derived. A few general principles may be stated, however, which are of considerable help: (1) As a general rule broad-banding results when a given impedance-transformation ratio is accomplished in several steps rather than a single one. This leads to the concept of cascading impedance-transforming sections. (2) A graphical method of approach is preferable to a purely analytical method. The locus of the terminating impedance is plotted as a function of frequency on either the bicircular or the Smith chart. Since the specified transformation cannot be obtained *exactly* at every point within a broad band, a region lying within a circle of tolerable standing wave ratio may also be plotted. This region defines the limits of allowable input impedance. Then general procedures may be described for mapping the termination locus over the required bandwidth into this region. The remainder of the chapter describes some of these principles and methods.

It should be realized at the outset that the term "broad band" is relative. Bandwidths in radio, as opposed to audio, systems are often only a fraction of a per cent of the "center" frequency, i.e., if f_a and f_b are, respectively, the lower and upper limits of the signal spectrum and f_0 is the arithmetic mean, or center, frequency, the fractional bandwidth is $(f_b - f_a)/f_0 = \Delta f/f_0$. As a general rule the term broad band is reserved for those systems where the fractional bandwidth is 0.05 to 0.1 (5 to 10 per cent) or greater. Typical approximate maximum values for the three broadcasting services are listed below:

Service	$\Delta f/f_0$
Amplitude modulation, AM	0.02
Frequency modulation, FM	0.002
Television, TV	0.1

It may be seen that the amplitude-modulation and frequency-modulation systems are narrow-band, whereas television falls within the broad-band definition.

A frequency-modulation *receiving* antenna and transmission-line system, however, must be capable of working over the entire frequency-modulation band, which extends from 88 to 108 Mc, so that

$$\Delta f/f_0 = {}^{20}\!/_{98} = 0.204$$

This represents a broad band, but fortunately a greater standing wave ratio may be tolerated than at the transmitter. In certain cases, for example, in some aircraft radio systems which must be able to operate in many frequency bands, $\Delta f/f_0$ may be 0.3 or even greater. It is fortunate that, in these "very" broad-band systems, a value of S up to 2 may be satisfactory.

13-12. Frequency Response of Quarter-wave Transformer. The concept of broad-banding by cascading impedance-transforming sections may be demonstrated by means of the quarter-wave transformer which was described in Chap. 12. As a first step, consider how the input impedance varies with frequency when a single quarter-wave section is terminated in a pure resistance. Say $R_R = 4R_o$ is to be matched to a line of characteristic impedance R_o at frequency f_0. Then by Eq. (12-1) the match may be obtained with a quarter-wave section of characteristic impedance R'_o given by

$$R'_o = \sqrt{R_R R_o} = \sqrt{4R_o{}^2} = 2R_o \tag{13-28}$$

It is convenient to find Z_{in} as a function of frequency by using a Smith chart; hence normalize all quantities with respect to R'_o.

$$r'_r = \frac{R_R}{R'_o} = \frac{4R_o}{2R_o} = 2 \tag{13-29a}$$

$$r'_o = \frac{R_o}{R'_o} = \frac{1}{2} \tag{13-29b}$$

A lossless transformer section is assumed; hence the phase velocity is independent of frequency and $f\lambda = f_0\lambda_0$. Then at any frequency f the transformer length as a fraction of the wavelength is given by

$$\frac{l}{\lambda} = \frac{l}{\lambda_0}\frac{f}{f_0} = 0.25\frac{f}{f_0} \tag{13-30}$$

Equation (13-30) is used to compute the electrical length of the transformer in Table 13-1 over the range $0.5 \leq f/f_0 \leq 1.5$.

Since R_R is given as being independent of frequency, enter the impedance chart (Fig. 13-9) at $r'_r = 2$, and rotate l/λ on the $S' = 2$ circle for each frequency to find the corresponding value of normalized input impedance z'_{in}. One such rotation is shown in the figure for $f/f_0 = 0.5$, $l/\lambda = 0.125$. The resulting values are tabulated in Table 13-1. By Eq.

TABLE 13-1. CALCULATION OF z_{in} FOR A QUARTER-WAVE TRANSFORMER

f/f_0	l/λ	z'_{in}	z_{in}
1.5	0.375	$0.80 + j0.60$	$1.60 + j1.20$
1.4	0.350	$0.675 + j0.49$	$1.35 + j0.98$
1.3	0.325	$0.59 + j0.36$	$1.18 + j0.72$
1.2	0.300	$0.54 + j0.24$	$1.08 + j0.48$
1.1	0.275	$0.51 + j0.12$	$1.02 + j0.24$
1.0	0.250	$0.50 + j0.00$	$1.00 + j0.00$
0.9	0.225		
0.8	0.200		
0.7	0.175	Conjugate symmetry	
0.6	0.150		
0.5	0.125		

(13-29b) it may be seen that the match is perfect at f/f_0. The input impedance normalized with respect to R_o is obtained by

$$z_{in} = \frac{Z_{in}}{R_o} = \frac{Z_{in}}{R'_o}\frac{R'_o}{R_o} = 2z'_{in} \qquad (13\text{-}31)$$

Values of z_{in} are shown in Table 13-1 and are plotted along the dashed locus in Fig. 13-9. From the figure it may be seen that, if a standing wave ratio of 2 or less on the line (not the transformer section) may be tolerated, the allowable bandwidth will be approximately

$$\frac{\Delta f}{f_0} = 1.3 - 0.7 = 0.6$$

That is, the frequency could swing roughly 30 per cent on each side of the design value f_0 without S exceeding 2.

13-13. Cascaded Transformers. Figure 13-9 may be used as the basis for showing that the bandwidth for an allowable standing wave ratio decreases with increasing transformation ratio. Let S' be the standing wave ratio on the quarter-wave transformer section. Then, for a given frequency range, the smaller the value of S', the smaller will be the deviation of z'_{in} from the real axis and the desired value of input resistance. Therefore it is desirable to keep S' on the transformer section small.

Now S' is related to the impedance-transformation ratio R_R/R_{in} (or R_{in}/R_R depending upon which is greater than 1). By Eq. (12-1) for the transformer to match R_R to R_{in} at the design frequency f_0 it must have a characteristic impedance

$$R'_o = \sqrt{R_R R_{in}}$$

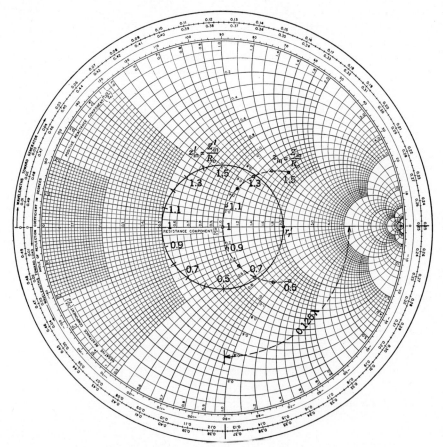

FIG. 13-9. Frequency response of a quarter-wave transformer terminated in a constant resistive load.

Dividing by R_R and inverting,

$$r'_r = \frac{R_R}{R'_o} = \sqrt{\frac{R_R}{R_{in}}} \tag{13-32}$$

Now if $R_R > R_{in}$, $S' = r'_r$, or if $R_R < R_{in}$, $S' = 1/r'_r$; hence

$$S' = \sqrt{\frac{R_R}{R_{in}}} \qquad R_R > R_{in}$$
$$\tag{13-33}$$
$$S' = \sqrt{\frac{R_{in}}{R_R}} \qquad R_R < R_{in}$$

Therefore broad-band considerations dictate that the ratio of impedances transformed by a quarter-wave transformer be kept small.   Any given transformation, then, may be broad-banded by performing the transformation in two or more steps, rather than in one, by means of cascaded quarter-wave transformer sections. (The student should note that this is quite consistent with the results of Chap. 11. Figures 11-9 and 11-12 show that the response of the lumped-constant L and T sections becomes less selective as the transformation ratio is decreased.)

Assuming, then, that two or more quarter-wave sections are to be connected in cascade to transform R_R to R_{in}, the problem is to determine R_o', R_o'', R_o''', the characteristic impedances of these sections. A number of solutions have been proposed. Slater,[1] among others, has suggested that the common logarithms of the impedance ratios at the junctions in the system follow the *coefficients* of the binomial expansion $(a + b)^n$, that is:

No. of $\lambda/4$ sections, n	Logarithm of impedance ratio
2	1 2 1
3	1 3 3 1
4	1 4 6 4 1

As an example, consider the design of a two-quarter-wave-section system. Reading from left to right in the inset of Fig. 13-10, the impedance ratios at the junctions are R_o''/R_o, R_o'/R_o'', and R_R/R_o'. Since the number of sections, n, is 2,

$$\log \frac{R_o'}{R_o''} = 2 \log \frac{R_o''}{R_o} = 2 \log \frac{R_R}{R_o}$$

i.e., from left to right the logarithms of the impedance ratios follow the rule 1 2 1 in accordance with the above table. Then, taking antilogarithms,

$$\frac{R_o'}{R_o''} = \left(\frac{R_o''}{R_o}\right)^2 = \left(\frac{R_R}{R_o'}\right)^2 \qquad (13\text{-}34)$$

Solving for R_o' and R_o'' in terms of R_o and R_R,

$$R_o' = \frac{R_o R_R}{R_o''} \qquad \text{or} \qquad R_o' = \sqrt[4]{R_R^3 R_o} \qquad (13\text{-}35a)$$

$$R_o'' = \frac{R_o R_R}{R_o'} \qquad (13\text{-}35b)$$

[1] J. C. Slater, "Microwave Transmission," pp. 57ff., McGraw-Hill Book Company, Inc., New York, 1942. Slater also explains the theory of broad-banding with cascaded sections by considering the cancellation of the waves reflected at each impedance junction in the system. More recent work has resulted in better solutions for adjusting the impedance levels. See, for example, R. E. Collin, Theory and Design of Wide-band Multisection Quarter-wave Transformers, *Proc. IRE*, vol. 43, no. 2, p. 179, February, 1955.

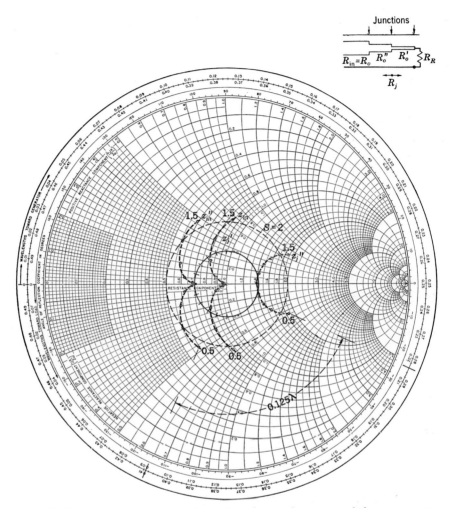

FIG. 13-10. Determination of the input impedance of two cascaded quarter-wave transformers terminated in a constant resistive load.

The student may verify for this case that the impedance at the junction of the two quarter-wave sections is

$$R_j = \sqrt{R_R R_o} \qquad (13\text{-}36)$$

This information will now be used to design a double-section system for an over-all transformation ratio of 4:1. The response will then be computed and compared with the results obtained in the last section.

Thus let $R_R = 4R_o$. Then by Eqs. (13-35)

$$R_o' = \sqrt[4]{4^3 R_o{}^4} = 2.83R_o$$

$$R_o'' = \frac{4R_o{}^2}{2.83R_o} = 1.414R_o$$

As a first step, consider the right-hand section in the diagram, and normalize R_R with respect to R_o'.

$$r_r' = \frac{4R_o}{2.83R_o} = 1.414$$

By Eq. (13-36) the normalized input impedance should be

$$r_j' = \frac{2R_o}{2.83R_o} = 0.707$$

Following the method of the last section, enter the Smith diagram (Fig. 3-10) at r_r', and rotate on a circle of constant S' the appropriate fraction of a wavelength at each frequency. The values of z_j' are tabulated in Table 13-2, and the corresponding locus is shown in the figure.

TABLE 13-2. CALCULATIONS FOR z_{in} OF A DOUBLE QUARTER-WAVE TRANSFORMER

f/f_0	l/λ	z_j'	z_j''	z_{in}''	z_{in}
1.5	0.375	$0.94 + j0.34$	$1.88 + j0.68$	$0.59 + j0.475$	$0.84 + j0.67$
1.4	0.350	$0.85 + j0.30$	$1.70 + j0.60$	$0.56 + j0.29$	$0.79 + j0.41$
1.3	0.325	$0.78 + j0.24$	$1.56 + j0.48$	$0.58 + j0.15$	$0.82 + j0.21$
1.2	0.300	$0.74 + j0.16$	$1.48 + j0.32$	$0.625 + j0.05$	$0.88 + j0.71$
1.1	0.275	$0.71 + j0.08$	$1.42 + j0.16$	$0.68 + j0.01$	$0.96 + j0.01$
1.0	0.250	$0.70 + j0.00$	$1.40 + j0.00$	$0.71 + j0.00$	$1.00 + j0.00$
0.9	0.225				
0.8	0.200				
0.7	0.175		Conjugate symmetry		
0.6	0.150				
0.5	0.125				

Now Z_j is the termination for the left-hand quarter-wave transformer in Fig. 13-10. To handle this section on the Smith diagram, all quantities should be normalized with respect to R_o''. The double prime will indicate these quantities; thus

$$z_j'' = \frac{Z_j}{R_o''} = \frac{Z_j}{R_o'}\frac{R_o'}{R_o''} = z_j'\frac{2.83R_o}{1.414R_o} = 2z_j'$$

These values are computed in Table 13-2 and plotted in Fig. 13-10. Since z_j'' is the termination of the left-hand quarter-wave section, z_{in}'' is obtained by entering the chart at z_j'' at each frequency and rotating toward the generator on a circle of constant S'' the appropriate distance indicated in the table. z_{in} is determined by

$$z_{in} = \frac{Z_{in}}{R_o} = \frac{Z_{in}}{R_o''} \frac{R_o''}{R_o} = z_{in}'' \frac{1.414 R_o}{R_o} = 1.414 z_{in}''$$

Comparison of Figs. 13-9 and 13-10 shows at once the increase in bandwidth afforded by the two cascaded sections. It may be seen that almost the entire locus for $0.5 \leq f/f_0 \leq 1.5$ lies within the $S = 2$ circle, as compared with the range $0.7 \leq f/f_0 \leq 1.3$ for the single section. Stated differently, with a single section a fractional bandwidth of 60 per cent resulted in $S \approx 2$. For the double section a fractional bandwidth of 60 per cent results in $S \approx 1.4$.

The foregoing results apply in general to lumped-constant matching sections as well as to quarter-wave transformers. It is interesting to note, however, that with a 90°-phase-shift T section (the analog of the quarter-wave transformer) the conjugate symmetry of the foregoing example is not present. This point is illustrated later in conjunction with Fig. 13-16.

13-14. Series and Parallel Networks. The second general principle of broad-banding consists in adding series or parallel networks to the actual load or in introducing line transformers between the load and the main transmission line so that the input impedance of the resulting combination lies within a circle of tolerable standing wave ratio on the impedance chart. Bennett, Coleman, and Meier[1] have presented a number of diagrams showing the effect of adding different types of elements. Their results are reproduced here in Smith-chart form in Figs. 13-11 to 13-14. These curves may serve as general guides to the choice of compensating elements to be used for different types of load loci.

An interesting example of the use of a shunt compensating element is afforded by the following example, where a stub is combined with the proper choice of an antenna length to bring about the desired impedance transformation:

[1] F. D. Bennett, P. D. Coleman, and A. S. Meier, The Design of Broadband Aircraft Antenna Systems, *Proc. IRE*, vol. 33, No. 10, p. 671, October, 1945. Their curves are shown on bicircular charts where the impedance and admittance coordinates are rectangular. It is easier to get a physical picture of the effect of adding reactance or susceptance to a Z_R or Y_R locus on these diagrams. The Smith-chart representation is used here because it permits easier location of the standing wave circle (see Chap. 10).

A more analytical approach, which is beyond the scope of this text, has been developed by Nelson and Stavis. See Staff, Radio Research Laboratory, Harvard University, "Very High Frequency Techniques," vol. I, chap. 3, McGraw-Hill Book Company, Inc., New York, 1947. The authors describe a means of setting up boundary curves for a given Z_R locus from which the required transforming elements may be found.

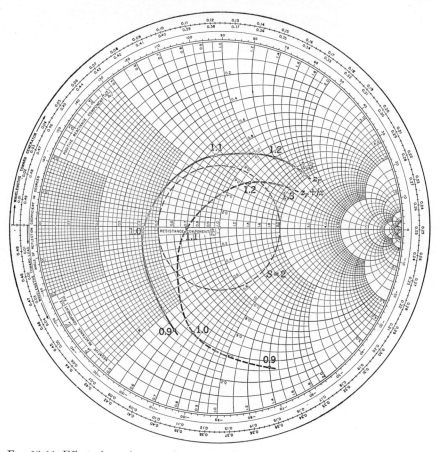

Fig. 13-11. Effect of a series capacitor on a load impedance. (*After Bennett, Coleman, and Meier.*)

A center-fed cylindrical antenna is to be matched to a 100-ohm line. The center frequency f_0 is 42.5 Mc. A shunt stub is to be used, and the standing wave ratio is to be within 1.25 over a fractional bandwidth of 30 per cent.

Now the input impedance (or admittance) of an antenna may be controlled within limits by adjusting the antenna length and radius.[1] Since a shunt stub can modify only the susceptive component of the total admittance terminating the main line, the problem first consists in choosing the antenna dimensions for the correct value of conductance. The stub may then be used to cancel out the susceptance. The dashed locus in Fig. 13-15 shows the input admittance (normalized to $R_o = 100$ ohms) of a center-fed cylindrical antenna as a function of the electrical half length $\beta l/2$ for the case where the ratio of half length to radius is 60. Inspection of the curve shows that the electrical half length

[1] See, for example, E. C. Jordan, "Electromagnetic Waves and Radiating Systems," chap. 13, Prentice-Hall, Inc., New York, 1950.

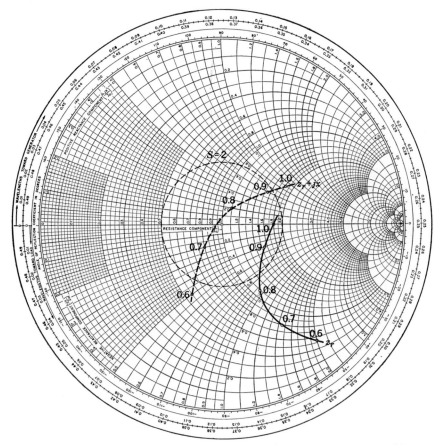

Fig. 13-12. Effect of a series inductor on a load impedance. (*After Bennett, Coleman, and Meier.*)

$\beta l/2 = 1.36$ yields a normalized conductive component of approximately 1 and hence is a satisfactory solution. The physical length of the antenna at

$$f_0 = 42.5 \text{ Mc}$$

must be $\beta l/2 = \omega_0 l/2c = 1.36$, or

$$l = \frac{2c \times 1.36}{\omega_o} = \frac{2(3 \times 10^8) \times 1.36}{2\pi \times 42.5 \times 10^6} = 3.06 \text{ m} = 120 \text{ in.}$$

and the antenna radius will be

$$\frac{l}{2r} = 60 \qquad r = \frac{l}{120} = 1 \text{ in.}$$

The second part of the problem then consists in choosing the proper stub length to cancel out the normalized antenna susceptance of 0.956 at f_0. One method of doing this is to extend the 100-ohm line beyond the antenna as a stub, as shown at inset *a* in Fig. 13-15. The student may easily calculate the length required

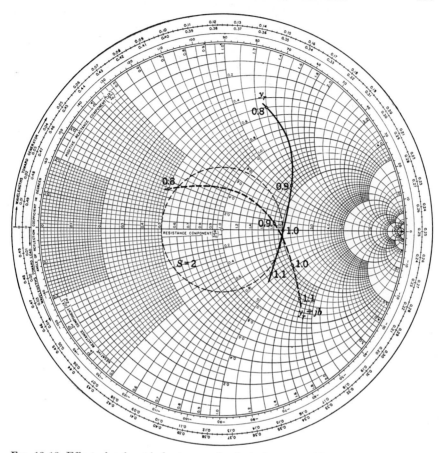

FIG. 13-13. Effect of a shunt inductor on a load admittance. (*After Bennett, Coleman, and Meier.*)

for this stub.   An alternative approach utilizes a coaxial, rather than a parallel-wire, stub which may be fitted *inside* the antenna.   This is quite possible here because the antenna has a 2-in. diameter and hence would be constructed of tubing for economy.   The basic scheme is illustrated at inset *b* in Fig. 13-15. It may be observed that there are two stubs in series in the arrangement; hence each stub should have a susceptance $-2b_r$.

A reasonable value of R'_o for a coaxial line is 70 ohms.   Then, if that value is used, the length of each of the short-circuited stubs at f_0 must be

$$B_s = -2b_r/R_o = -\frac{1}{R'_o}\cot\frac{360s}{\lambda}$$

$$\cot\frac{360s}{\lambda} = \frac{2\times0.956\times70}{100} = 1.34$$

$$s = \frac{36.7}{360}\lambda = 0.102\lambda = 28.3 \text{ in.}$$

The same result may, of course, be obtained from the Smith chart.

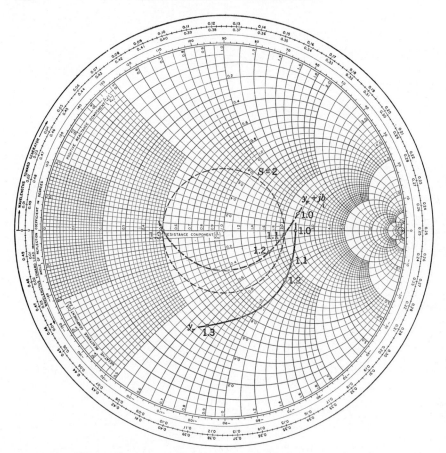

FIG. 13-14. Effect of a shunt capacitor on a load admittance. (*After Bennett, Coleman, and Meier.*)

Assume the antenna tubing to have a $\frac{1}{8}$-in. wall thickness; then the diameter of the outer conductor for the coaxial stubs is $2 - 0.25 = 1.75$ in., and the center conductor must have a diameter

$$R_o' = 138 \log \frac{d_2}{d_1}$$

$$\log \frac{d_2}{d_1} = \frac{70}{138} = 0.507$$

$$d_1 = \frac{d_2}{3.21} = \frac{1.75}{3.21} = 0.545 \text{ in.}$$

The calculations for determining z_{in} are shown in Table 13-3, and the z_{in} locus is shown by the solid line in Fig. 13-15.

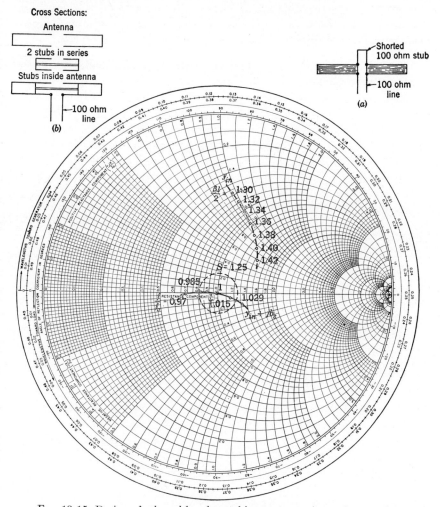

FIG. 13-15. Design of a broad-band matching system using a shunt stub.

TABLE 13-3. CALCULATIONS FOR FIG. 13-15

$\beta l/2$	l/λ	f/f_0	y_{in}	b_s'	b_s	$y_{in} + jb_s$
1.40	0.446	1.029	$1.31 + j0.765$	-2.68	-0.938	$1.31 - j0.173$
1.38	0.439	1.015	$1.15 + j0.890$	-2.70	-0.945	$1.15 - j0.055$
1.36	0.433	1.000	$0.98 + j0.956$	-2.73	-0.956	$0.98 - j0$
1.34	0.427	0.985	$0.82 + j0.980$	-2.77	-0.970	$0.82 + j0.010$
1.32	0.420	0.970	$0.68 + j0.976$	-2.80	-0.980	$0.68 - j0.004$

Note. $b_s = {}^{70}\!/_{100}\,(b_s'/2)$.

Inasmuch as the $f/f_0 = 0.985$ and 1.015 points lie within the $S = 1.25$ circle, the specifications are satisfied. It may be stated, however, that other choices of antenna length and radius permit an even better solution to the problem.

13-15. Quarter-wave Transformers with Varying Load. In earlier sections the response of a quarter-wave transformer was considered where the load was a resistance independent of frequency. The quarter-wave section is also useful as a transforming device when the load varies with *conjugate symmetry* about the center frequency and lies outside the circle of tolerable standing wave ratio on the impedance chart. One type of load which varies in this manner is the resonant antenna. Typical values are shown in the normalized form Z_R/R_o in Table 13-4, where R_o is the

TABLE 13-4. DRIVING-POINT IMPEDANCE OF A RESONANT ANTENNA

f/f_0	z_r
0.8	$3.1 + j1.7$
0.9	$3.8 + j1.0$
1.0	$4.0 + j0$
1.1	$3.8 - j1.0$
1.2	$3.1 - j1.7$

characteristic impedance of the main transmission line. For a perfect match at f_0 the characteristic impedance of the quarter-wave line section will be

$$R_o' = \sqrt{R_R R_o} = \sqrt{4R_o^2} = 2R_o$$

The input impedance locus may be calculated by the methods described earlier and is plotted in Fig. 13-16.

It is interesting to note the behavior of the lumped-constant analog of the quarter-wave line section, viz., the symmetrical T section which has a phase shift of $\pm 90°$. For such a section the design equations at f_0 are

$$|X_1| = |X_2| = |X_3| = \sqrt{R_R R_o} = 2R_o$$

and, choosing X_1 and X_2 to be inductive and X_3 to be capacitive,

$$X_1 = X_2 = 2R_o \frac{f}{f_0} \tag{13-37}$$

$$X_3 = -2R_o \frac{f_0}{f} \tag{13-38}$$

and
$$Z_{in} = jX_1 + j \frac{X_3(Z_R + jX_2)}{Z_R + j(X_2 + X_3)} \tag{13-39}$$

The input impedance locus for the T section may be calculated by direct substitution into Eq. (13-39) or by means of successive transformations on the Smith chart. The resulting locus is shown by the dashed line in Fig. 13-16 and is labeled $z_{in\,(T)}$. It may be observed that the conjugate symmetry obtained with the quarter-wave line is lost with the quarter-wave T section. For this reason in broad-band applications the T is

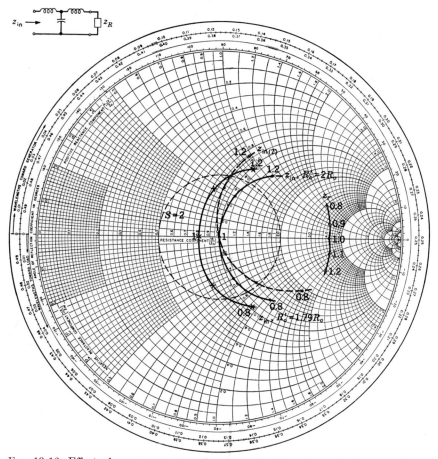

Fig. 13-16. Effect of quarter-wave sections on a load impedance having conjugate symmetry about f_0. The solid line shows z_{in} resulting from a quarter-wave line section, the dashed line from a symmetrical T section.

designed for a perfect match at a frequency lower than f_0. That is, a slight mismatch is tolerated at f_0 in order to force a greater portion of the z_{in} locus into the required standing-wave-ratio circle.

Returning to the quarter-wave line transformer, one notes in Fig. 13-16 that the procedure of designing for a perfect match at f_0 is wasteful of bandwidth: the z_{in} locus lies in only the right-hand portion of the

$S = 2$ circle. A better procedure might be to sacrifice the perfect match at f_0 in order to pull the outer ends of the z_{in} locus into the circle. For example, if the section is designed to transform $r_r = 4$ to $r_{in} = 0.8$ at f_0 by setting $R'_o = \sqrt{0.8 \times 4 \times R_o{}^2} = 1.79R_o$, the z_{in} locus is shifted to the position indicated by the x's in Fig. 13-16. It will be observed that a small, but noticeable, increase in bandwidth results.

13-16. The Line Transformer. In the last section it was shown that the quarter-wave line is useful for transforming loads whose loci display conjugate symmetry about the center frequency f_0. For such loads the section is designed to transform a pure resistance into a pure resistance at f_0. For loads not displaying this property of conjugate symmetry a better solution is afforded by a generalization of the quarter-wave transformer, i.e., a line transformer for which $l \neq \lambda/4$. In the latter case the section may be used to transform a *complex* load into a *complex* input impedance at f_0 or any other frequency.

Let $Z_{in} = R_{in} + jX_{in}$ and $Z_R = R_R + jX_R$; then the design equations for the characteristic impedance R'_o and the length l of the line transformer may be shown to be (see Prob. 12-13)

$$R'_o = \sqrt{(R_{in}R_R - X_{in}X_R) - \frac{(X_R - X_{in})(R_R X_{in} + R_{in} X_R)}{R_{in} - R_R}} \qquad (13\text{-}40)$$

$$\tan \beta l = \frac{R'_o(R_{in} - R_R)}{R_R X_{in} + R_{in} X_R} \qquad (13\text{-}41)$$

These equations may be used as a guide in designing the transformer section; experience is invaluable in making a good guess for the proper values of Z_{in} and Z_R for a particular situation. The general method to be used is illustrated by the following example:

An antenna is to be matched to a 100-ohm parallel-wire transmission line. The normalized antenna impedance is tabulated in Table 13-5 and plotted in Fig. 13-17a. Since the z_r locus does not show conjugate symmetry, it is decided to

TABLE 13-5. CALCULATIONS FOR FIG. 13-17

f/f_0	z_r	z'_r	l/λ	z'_{in}	z_{in}
0.8	$0.40 - j0.80$	$0.989 - j1.975$	0.369	$0.89 + j1.89$	$0.36 + j0.77$
0.9	$0.45 - j0.50$	$1.11\ \ - j1.233$	0.415	$2.96 + j0.50$	$1.20 + j0.20$
1.0	$0.60 + j0.00$	$1.48\ \ + j0$	0.461	$1.38 + j0.28$	$0.56 + j0.11$
1.1	$0.75 + j0.50$	$1.85\ \ + j1.233$	0.507	$2.20 + j1.20$	$0.82 + j0.49$
1.2	$1.10 + j0.85$	$2.72\ \ + j2.1$	0.554	$3.20 - j2.00$	$1.30 - j0.81$

design the transformer to transform $Z_R = 45 - j50$ ohms to $Z_{in} = 120 + j20$ ohms at $f = 0.9 f_0$. (Notice that this is a *guess* based on the general shape of the

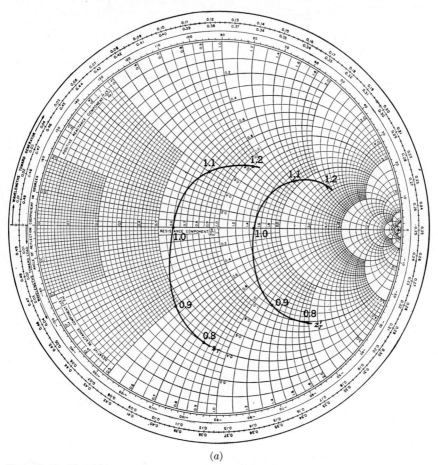

(a)

FIG. 13-17. Matching an antenna to a transmission line by means of a line transformer. (a) Normalized load loci. (b) Normalized input impedance loci.

z_r curve.) The constants of the line transformer are then calculated by Eqs. (13-40) and (13-41).

$$R'_o = \sqrt{120(45) - 20(-50) - \frac{(-50 - 20)[45(20) + 120(-50)]}{120 - 45}}$$
$$= 40.5 \text{ ohms}$$

$z'_r = Z_R/R'_o$ is then calculated and plotted (see Table 13-5 and Fig. 13-17a). The line length at $f = 0.9f_0$ is

$$\tan \beta l = \frac{40.5(120 - 45)}{-5,100} = -0.596 \qquad \beta l = 149.2°$$
$$l = \frac{149.2}{\beta} = \frac{149.2}{360} \lambda = 0.415\lambda$$

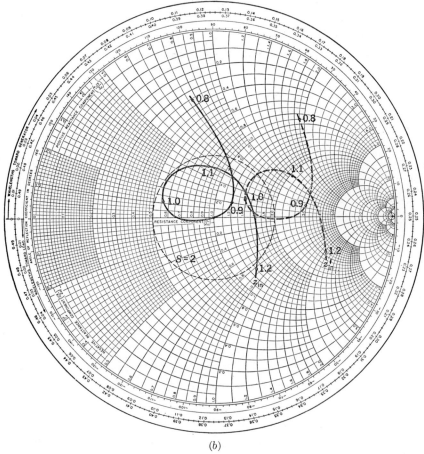

(b)

FIG. 13-17. (Continued).

At any frequency other than $0.9f_0$ the length expressed as a fraction of λ is

$$\frac{l}{\lambda} = \frac{0.415}{0.9} \frac{f}{f_0}$$

These values are given in the table. The input impedance normalized to $R'_o = 40.5$ ohms is then obtained by entering the chart at each point and rotating toward the generator on a circle of constant S the appropriate length. The resulting locus of z'_{in} is shown in Fig. 13-17b as is z_{in}. The latter quantity is obtained by

$$z_{in} = \frac{Z_{in}}{R_o} = \frac{Z_{in}}{R'_o} \frac{R'_o}{R_o} = z_{in} \frac{40.5}{100}$$

The figure shows that a good portion of the input impedance lies within the $S = 2$ circle. Choices of R'_o and l other than 40.5 ohms and 0.415λ may lead to an even better solution. The spiral locus if quite typical of the line transformer whose length exceeds $\lambda/4$.

13-17. Combined Elements. In many instances a combination of two or more of the impedance-transforming devices which have been described result in a better broad-band transformation. The general procedure employed is to use the first element to set up the ideal locus for the second. The interested reader is referred to Coleman's work for details.

PROBLEMS

13-1. Using the equivalent circuits of Fig. 13-3, derive equations in polar form for A_m, A_l/A_m, and A_h/A_m. In each case $A = E_o/E_g$, and the subscripts denote the appropriate frequency band.

13-2. The measured constants of the audio transformer whose response is shown in Fig. 13-4 are:

> D-c primary current = 60 ma
> Primary inductance = 2.2 henry
> Leakage inductance referred to primary = 44.6 mh
> D-c primary resistance = 212 ohms
> D-c secondary resistance = 0.32 ohm
> Primary to secondary turns ratio = 28.5

a. Calculate the response when the transformer is driven from a 2,000-ohm generator and is feeding a 3.5-ohm load. Identify the half-power frequencies. Compare your results with Fig. 13-4, and account for any discrepancies.

b. Neglecting core losses, calculate the *transformer* efficiency.

c. What is the transformer coupling coefficient? State approximations used.

d. Qualitatively, what would be the effect on the low- and high-frequency responses if the d-c primary current were reduced? Explain briefly.

13-3. (*a*) Compute the elements of a T pad to connect a 600-ohm load to a 1,800-ohm line and give a loss of 20 db. (*b*) Design a minimum-loss pad to match the same load and line.

13-4. Equations (13-15) to (13-17) are sometimes difficult to use because they involve differences between two nearly equal numbers. Derive alternative design equations in terms of $p = P_{in}/P_{out}$ in place of the neper loss A.

13-5. Derive the design equations for a Π pad.

13-6. Two identical symmetrical T pads, each having a loss of N db and designed to work between R-ohm resistances, are connected in cascade. Compare the isolation from load variation afforded by this combination with that of a single symmetrical T pad having a loss of $2N$ db and designed to work between R-ohm resistances.

13-7. (*a*) For a Π pad which is greater, $|R_{oc} - R_{I1}|/R_{I1}$ or $|R_{sc} - R_{I1}|R_{I1}$? (*b*) Design a Π pad to match a nominal load of 500 to 500 ohms. The maximum deviation of R_{in} from R_{I1} shall be 10 per cent. (*c*) What is the input admittance if the 500-ohm load resistance is shunted by a 500-ohm capacitive reactance? What conclusions may be drawn from this answer?

13-8. A 600-ohm attenuator ($R_{I1} = R_{I2} = 600$ ohms) is to be designed to provide the attenuation steps of 0, 1, 2, 3, 4, and 5 db.

a. Design a T attenuator to meet the specifications. Sketch the circuit diagram, showing the switching arrangement. Use a multiple-gang rotary switch with as few gangs as possible.

   b. Repeat *a,* but use a bridged T configuration.

   c. Compare the relative costs of the two designs.

   13-9. Verify Eq. (13-27) for the bridged T pad of Fig. 13-8.   Note that $R_1 R_2 = R_o^2$.

   13-10. (*a*) Design a ladder attenuator of Π sections for $R_{12} = 600$ ohms and relative steps of 0, 1, 2, 3, 4, and 5 db.   Sketch the diagram combining adjacent resistors wherever possible.   (*b*) Repeat *a,* but use a ladder of T sections.   (*c*) Compare the two designs from the point of view of economy in construction.

   13-11. (*a*) For the load impedance in Table 13-4 design a series-L shunt-C L section for a perfect match at f_0.   Plot z_{in} on a Smith chart.   (*b*) Repeat *a* for a series-*C* shunt-L network.   (*c*) Modify the design of part *a* to broad-band the transformation.

   13-12. Design two cascaded L sections to meet the specifications of Prob. 13-11*a.* Plot z_{in} on a Smith chart, and compare with the results of Prob. 13-11*a.*

   13-13. Plot a curve similar to $z_{in(T)}$ of Fig. 13-16 for a T section using capacitive series arms and an inductive shunt arm.   Use the load data of Table 13-4.   State your conclusions.

   13-14. Using the y_r data of Fig. 13-15, choose the antenna length, and design a stub to match to an 85-ohm coaxial line.   Sketch a diagram of the system, including a balun (see Chap. 12).   Show the performance (neglecting the effect of the balun) on a Smith chart.   Use $f_o = 42.5$ Mc.

   13-15. Using the z_r data of Table 13-5, design a line transformer to give better performance than that shown in Fig. 13-5.

   13-16. Using the data of Table 13-5, design a quarter-wave line section to give a perfect match at f_0.   Compare the response with Fig. 13-17*b.*

   13-17. A certain load behaves in the following manner

f/f_0	Z ohms
0.8	$310 + j390$
0.9	$340 + j200$
1.0	$360 + j0$

The load displays conjugate symmetry.   A half-wave line transformer with

$$R_o' = 500 \text{ ohms}$$

is used to match the load to a 200-ohm line.   Calculate the input impedance.

CHAPTER 14

EQUALIZATION

14-1. Fundamental Principle of Equalization. It has been shown in Chap. 6 that, for distortionless transmission of a signal consisting of two or more frequency components, all the components should be transmitted with equal attenuation (or amplification) and with equal group velocities (constant delay). Networks which have capacitive or inductive elements do not ordinarily meet these requirements. For example, it was shown in Chap. 8 that the attenuation and group velocity of an unloaded cable pair is approximately proportional to the square root of the frequency.

One method of correcting frequency distortion (α not constant) in telephone cables which is described in Chap. 8 consists in introducing loading to the cable. Loading is becoming less common, however, particularly in intercity telephone facilities, because the filter action resulting from loading precludes use of the system for carrier transmission.

Another method of correcting frequency distortion in a transmission network is to introduce an additional network having an α vs. frequency characteristic such that the total attenuation of the two networks in cascade will be substantially independent of frequency. Where it is desirable to do so, delay distortion may be similarly eliminated, the aim in this case being to obtain a combination in which the total time of transmission is independent of frequency. The problem of delay equalization is considered later in the chapter. In many cases of audio transmission an attenuation equalizer is sufficient, and delay distortion may be neglected.

Figure 14-1 shows graphically how the attenuation equalizer accomplishes its purpose. Curve 1 shows the insertion-loss characteristic of a cable terminated in a 600-ohm resistance. Curve 2 shows the insertion-loss characteristic of an ideal equalizer which would compensate for the frequency distortion of the cable, *together with its termination*. Curve 3 is the total insertion loss of the cable and equalizer, showing a combination in which frequency distortion has been eliminated over the band shown. Actual equalizers do not entirely eliminate frequency distortion since their loss can be made to coincide with the ideal values at only a limited number of frequencies.

In practical cases it is necessary to select a band of frequencies over which it is desirable to make the loss substantially constant. It should be noticed that the total loss of the combination at all frequencies must be greater than the maximum loss of the original network within the band selected. Therefore equalizers are ordinarily used in systems which also include amplifiers that can be used to compensate for the loss introduced by the equalizer.

As applied to telephone cables, a contrast should be drawn between the use of equalizers and loading. The application of loading also reduces the frequency distortion (below the cutoff frequency) and in addition *reduces* the attenuation in this frequency range. However, an equalizer can be designed to give a flatter response and can be applied at the terminals, whereas loading must be introduced at intervals along the line. Hence, loading is feasible only in permanent installations. It is, of course, possible to use equalizers on loaded lines to obtain some of the advantages of both. Equalizers are also of use in transmission systems other than lines, where loading is not applicable.

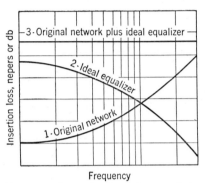

Fig. 14-1. Insertion-loss characteristic of a typical transmission network, and correction by an ideal equalizer.

Basically two different types of four-terminal attenuation equalizers[1] are encountered in practice: (1) Those designed to work between equal resistances of the order of 50 to 600 ohms, i.e., in the range of transmission-line-characteristic impedances. They are ordinarily used to equalize the insertion loss of transmission lines. (2) Those designed to work from low-to-high or high-to-high, but not necessarily equal, resistances. In some instances equalization may be accomplished with a two-terminal corrective network. The constant-resistance network is the most versatile, has the most straightforward method of design, and will be described first, although historically it succeeded the use of two-terminal networks connected in series or shunt. The development of equalizers is largely due to to the work of Hoyt[2] and Zobel,[3] and reference should be made to their publications for a more complete analysis.

[1] "An attenuation equalizer is a corrective network which is designed to make the absolute value (or magnitude) of the transfer impedance, with respect to two chosen pairs of terminals, substantially constant for all frequencies within a desired range." [ASA C42 65.06.546 (1953).]

[2] R. S. Hoyt, U.S. Patent 1,453,980.

[3] O. J. Zobel, Distortion Correction in Electrical Circuits with Constant Resistance Recurrent Networks, *Bell System Tech. J.*, July, 1928.

The simplest termination for a network is a resistor. Furthermore, the impedance of a resistor is independent of frequency except for minor variations due to capacitances and inductances inherent in its physical construction. Consider a network terminated in a resistance whose transmission characteristics, e.g., the insertion loss, have been determined, either experimentally or analytically. These transmission characteristics will, in general, be functions not only of the attenuation of the network but also of any reflections due to impedance mismatches, which

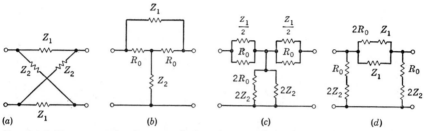

Fig. 14-2. Representative four-terminal constant-resistance networks. In each case $Z_1Z_2 = R_o^2$. (a) Lattice. (b) Bridged T. (c) T. (d) Π.

may occur at either end. An equalizer may be designed which will compensate for variations, with frequency, in these reflections as well as in the attenuation.

From the standpoint of simplicity, if an equalizing network can be designed which can be inserted without modifying the reflection conditions, then it can be designed with attention concentrated on its attenuation characteristic. This can be done by means of constant-resistance networks.

It must be stressed that a constant-resistance equalizer will, in use, be terminated in its iterative impedance. As explained in Chap. 6, when a network is so terminated its attenuation α and its insertion loss become identical. This allows a great simplification in the design problem. For example, the insertion-loss characteristic of a cable terminated in a resistance may be measured. Then the constant-resistance equalizer may be designed to yield a specified α characteristic for which equations are readily available.

14-2. Constant-resistance Networks. Several types of constant-resistance networks are available, four of which are shown in Fig. 14-2. The one with the widest range of application is the lattice network of Fig. 14-2a, although the bridged T section shown at b is often preferable in systems having a common ground lead. The impedances Z_1 and Z_2 in all four of the networks must be chosen so that

$$Z_1Z_2 = R_o^2 \qquad (14-1)$$

where R_o is a resistance which is independent of frequency. Pairs of networks corresponding to Z_1 and Z_2 and which satisfy the relation of Eq. (14-1) are called "inverse networks," and it will be shown later how they may be constructed.

The characteristic impedance and propagation constant of the lattice network of Fig. 14-2a can be determined most readily through an examination of its open- and short-circuited impedances. These can be readily obtained by inspection.

$$Z_{oc} = \frac{Z_1 + Z_2}{2} \tag{14-2}$$

$$Z_{sc} = \frac{2Z_1Z_2}{Z_1 + Z_2} \tag{14-3}$$

Therefore
$$Z_o = \sqrt{Z_{oc}Z_{sc}} = \sqrt{Z_1Z_2} \tag{14-4}$$

If Eq. (14-1) is satisfied, $Z_o = R_o$, that is, the characteristic impedance is a resistance which is independent of frequency, and the input impedance

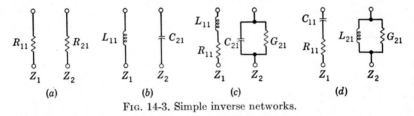

FIG. 14-3. Simple inverse networks.

of the network will be independent of frequency and equal to R_o if the termination of the network is a resistance of magnitude R_o. It is this property which gives the structure the name of "constant-resistance" network.

The complex propagation constant γ may also be found in terms of the open- and short-circuit impedances by means of Eq. (6-22). Thus for the lattice section of Fig. 14-2a

$$\tanh \gamma = \sqrt{\frac{Z_{sc}}{Z_{oc}}} = \frac{Z_o}{Z_{oc}} = \frac{2R_o}{Z_1 + Z_2}$$
$$= \frac{e^\gamma - e^\gamma}{e^\gamma + e^\gamma} = \frac{e^{2\gamma} - 1}{e^{2\gamma} + 1} \tag{14-5}$$

Eliminating Z_2 by Eq. (14-1) and solving for e^γ,

$$e^\gamma = e^\alpha e^{j\beta} = \pm \frac{1 + Z_1/R_o}{1 - Z_1/R_o} \tag{14-6}$$

14-3. Inverse Networks. It is now desirable to determine how two networks can be made inverse. This can be done if the impedance of one network has the general form of the admittance of the other, i.e., if the networks are duals (see Chap. 3), and if definite ratios are kept between corresponding elements in the two networks. Figure 14-3 shows some examples of inverse networks. The simplest pair would be two resistors which satisfy Eq. (14-1). Next in order of simplicity would be an inductance and a capacitance. Since $Z_1 = j\omega L_{11}$ and $Y_2 = j\omega C_{21}$,

$$Z_1 Z_2 = \frac{Z_1}{Y_2} = \frac{L_{11}}{C_{21}} = R_o{}^2 \tag{14-7}$$

Next consider the case where one impedance of the pair is constructed from a resistance in series with an inductance, i.e.,

$$Z_1 = R_{11} + j\omega L_{11} \tag{14-8}$$

The inverse network could be constructed by putting a resistor in parallel

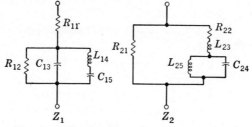

FIG. 14-4. Construction of an inverse network.

with a capacitor and selecting dimensions such that

$$\frac{R_{11}}{G_{21}} = \frac{L_{11}}{C_{21}} = R_o{}^2 \tag{14-9}$$

Now

$$Y_{21} = G_{21} + j\omega C_{21} \tag{14-10}$$

Hence

$$Z_1 Z_2 = \frac{R_{11} + j\omega L_{11}}{G_{21} + j\omega C_{21}} \tag{14-11}$$

Substitute values of G_{21} and C_{21} obtained from Eq. (14-9).

$$Z_1 Z_2 = \frac{R_{11} + j\omega L_{11}}{R_{11}/R_o{}^2 + j\omega L_{11}/R_o{}^2} = R_o{}^2 \tag{14-12}$$

which proves that Z_1 and Z_2 are inverse networks. In a similar way more complicated structures may be constructed. The rule is that for each resistive element in Z_1 there should be a corresponding conductive (resistive) element in Z_2, for each inductive element in Z_1 there should be a corresponding capacitive element in Z_2, and vice versa. Furthermore, when two elements are in series in Z_1, their related elements in Z_2 should be in parallel, while if they are in parallel in Z_1, they should be in series in Z_2. Corresponding elements should satisfy Eq. (14-9), which for general elements may be written

$$R_{1m} R_{2m} = \frac{R_{1m}}{G_{2m}} = \frac{L_{1m}}{C_{2m}} = \frac{L_{2n}}{C_{1n}} = R_o{}^2 \tag{14-13}$$

As an example, consider Fig. 14-4, where a more complicated pair of inverse networks is shown. The corresponding elements, i.e., the ones which are paired, have identical numbers for the second subscript. The equations are then

$$R_{11}R_{21} = R_{12}R_{22} = \frac{L_{23}}{C_{13}} = \frac{L_{14}}{C_{24}} = \frac{L_{25}}{C_{15}} = R_o{}^2 \qquad (14\text{-}13a)$$

14-4. Design of Constant-resistance Lattice Equalizer. As explained earlier, when a constant-resistance equalizer is added to a transmission system, the only modification of the original transmission characteristics will be that due to the propagation constant of the constant-resistance network. If Z_1 is known, Z_2 is immediately derivable from Eq. (14-13). Hence the only problem is the proper selection of Z_1 by means of Eq. (14-6).

If the attenuation constant of the constant-resistance lattice network of Fig. 14-2a is designated by α, then $e^{2\alpha}$ will be given by the square of the absolute value of the right-hand side of Eq. (14-6). If R_1 is the resistance component of Z_1 (usually a function of frequency) and X_1 is the reactive component of Z_1 (also a function of frequency), and if F is an attenuation factor defined by the relation $F = e^{2\alpha}$, then Eq. (14-6) can be written

$$e^{2\alpha} = F = \frac{(1 + R_1/R_o)^2 + (X_1/R_o)^2}{(1 - R_1/R_o)^2 + (X_1/R_o)^2} \qquad (14\text{-}14)$$

It has been explained in the early part of the chapter in connection with Fig. 14-1 how the ideal attenuation characteristic of the equalizing network can be found. As a general proposition, if there are n elements, such as resistance, inductance, or capacitance, in the impedance Z_1, and if the expression for Z_1 is expressed as a function of frequency and these n elements, then Eq. (14-4) will have these n elements as unknowns. If the value of F is selected at n frequencies, then Eq. (14-4) will give a system of n simultaneous equations with n unknowns. From these equations it is theoretically possible to solve for the required elements in Z_1, and this solution constitutes the design of the equalizer. In any given problem it may happen that the solution will not give a physically realizable structure, e.g., one or more of the R, L, or C elements may come out negative.

The solution of a system of simultaneous equations is readily obtainable only in the case where these equations are in a linear form. Equation (14-14) can be reduced to a linear form by the introduction of auxiliary functions of the unknown impedance elements, whose number is often equal to the number of independent elements.

A complicated network is built of simple elements connected successively in series or parallel. The expression for impedance elements in parallel is $Z_{eq} = Z_a Z_b/(Z_a + Z_b)$.

Since the simple elements have impedances which are equal to R_{1m}, $j2\pi fL_{1m}$, or $1/j2\pi fC_{1m}$, the resultant expression for Z_{eq} will have a numerator and a denominator each of which is a polynomial in jf. (A polynomial is a finite series with integral powers of the variable.) Successive combinations in parallel and series will similarly have numerators and denominators which are polynomials in jf, since either the sum or the product of two polynomials is a polynomial. Hence it is possible to write

$$\frac{Z_1}{R_o} = \frac{a_0 + a_1(jf) + a_2(jf)^2 + \cdots}{b_0 + b_1(jf) + b_2(jf)^2 + \cdots} \qquad (14\text{-}15)$$

For a given network, the a's and b's in this expression are constants which are determined by the arrangement and magnitude of the resistances, capacitances, and inductances in the network. The term $a_1(jf)$ means a_1 times jf and not a function of jf as is sometimes the case in such terminology. Both numerator and denominator have a finite number of terms determined by the configuration in any given case.

A similar expression for e^γ, as given by Eq. (14-6), can be written

$$e^\gamma = \frac{g_0 + g_1(jf) + g_2(jf)^2 + \cdots}{h_0 + h_1(jf) + h_2(jf)^2 + \cdots} \qquad (14\text{-}16a)$$

This can also be written

$$e^\gamma = \frac{(g_0 - g_2f^2 + g_4f^4 + \cdots) + j(g_1f - g_3f^3 + g_5f^5 + \cdots)}{(h_0 - h_2f^2 + h_4f^4 + \cdots) + j(h_1f - h_3f^3 + h_5f^5 + \cdots)} \qquad (14\text{-}16b)$$

From Eq. (14-16b) the expression for $F = e^{2\alpha}$ can be obtained. It will be

$$\begin{aligned} F = e^{2\alpha} &= |e^\gamma|^2 \\ &= \frac{(g_0 - g_2f^2 + g_4f^4 + \cdots)^2 + (g_1f - g_3f^3 + g_5f^5 + \cdots)^2}{(h_0 - h_2f^2 + h_4f^4 + \cdots)^2 + (h_1f - h_3f^3 + h_5f^5 + \cdots)^2} \end{aligned} \qquad (14\text{-}17)$$

It is apparent that the squaring of the terms in the numerator and denominator of Eq. (14-17) will result in terms in both numerator and denominator which include only *even* powers of f. Therefore Eq. (14-17) can be written

$$F = e^{2\alpha} = \frac{P_0 + P_2f^2 + P_4f^4 + \cdots}{Q_0 + Q_2f^2 + Q_4f^4 + \cdots} \qquad (14\text{-}18)$$

Furthermore it is always possible to make one of the P's or Q's equal to unity by dividing the numerator and the denominator by a constant. As a rule there will then be as many P's and Q's as there are independent elements in Z_1. Equation (14-18) can be written

$$F(Q_0 + Q_2f^2 + Q_4f^4 + \cdots) = P_0 + P_2f^2 + P_4f^4 + \cdots \qquad (14\text{-}18a)$$

This equation is linear in the P's and Q's. As has been described, if the value of F is selected at as many frequencies as there are independent elements in Z_1, a corresponding number of linear equations may be set up from Eq. (14-18a) and the values of the P's and Q's determined. From these P's and Q's the dimensions of the network elements may be determined.

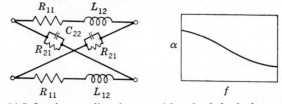

FIG. 14-5. Lattice equalizer for use with unloaded telephone cable.

As an example consider the case of Fig. 14-5. The attenuation constant will vary with frequency in the general manner shown. This network might be used therefore to equalize a cable since the attenuation constant of the latter would increase with frequency. In this network

$$Z_1 = R_{11} + j\omega L_{12}$$
$$\frac{Z_1}{R_o} = \frac{R_{11}}{R_o} + \frac{2\pi L_{12}}{R_o} jf \qquad (14\text{-}19)$$

While it is possible to relate the circuit parameters to the P's and Q's of Eq. (14-18) by going through the intermediate steps of defining the a's and b's of Eq. (14-15), the latter step is unnecessary and the required relationships may be determined directly. Thus by Eq. (14-6)

$$e^\gamma = \frac{(1 + R_{11}/R_o) + 2\pi L_{12}jf/R_o}{(1 - R_{11}/R_o) - 2\pi L_{12}jf/R_o} \qquad (14\text{-}20)$$

and

$$F = |e^\gamma|^2 = \frac{(1 + R_{11}/R_o)^2 + (2\pi L_{12}/R_o)^2 f^2}{(1 - R_{11}/R_o)^2 + (2\pi L_{12}/R_o)^2 f^2} \qquad (14\text{-}20a)$$

which may be identified with the P and Q form of Eq. (14-18). As a practical matter to reduce the number of factors which must be evaluated, it is convenient to divide through by the coefficient of f^2, yielding

$$F = \frac{\left(\dfrac{R_o + R_{11}}{2\pi L_{12}}\right)^2 + f^2}{\left(\dfrac{R_o - R_{11}}{2\pi L_{12}}\right)^2 + f^2} = \frac{P_0 + f^2}{Q_0 + f^2} \qquad (14\text{-}21)$$

and the linear equation will be

$$P_0 - FQ_0 = f^2(F - 1) \qquad (14\text{-}21a)$$

where

$$P_0 = \left(\frac{R_o + R_{11}}{2\pi L_{12}}\right)^2 \qquad Q_0 = \left(\frac{R_o - R_{11}}{2\pi L_{12}}\right)^2 \qquad (14\text{-}22)$$

Since P_0 and Q_0 are the two unknowns in Eq. (14-21a) their values may be obtained by substituting into the equation the numerical values of F and f at two frequencies. It must be stressed that the choice of the two sets of values for F and f is a matter of judicious guessing, guided by experience. If the response resulting from the first guess is not satisfactory, a second or even third guess will be required.

When P_0 and Q_0 have been evaluated, they may be used with Eqs. (14-22) to evaluate the network unknowns, namely, R_{11} and L_{12}. R_{21} and C_{22} may then be evaluated by Eq. (14-13). It should be observed that in solving Eqs. (14-22) for R_{11} and L_{12} four pairs of solutions are mathematically possible, of which only two are physically admissible. This may be demonstrated as follows: From Eqs. (14-22)

$$\frac{R_o + R_{11}}{2\pi L_{12}} = \pm \sqrt{P_0} \qquad \frac{R_o - R_{11}}{2\pi L_{12}} = \pm \sqrt{Q_0} \qquad (14\text{-}23)$$

Adding,

$$\frac{2R_o}{2\pi L_{12}} = \pm \sqrt{P_0} \pm \sqrt{Q_0}$$

Thus the four mathematical solutions are

$$L_{12} = \frac{R_o}{\pi(\sqrt{P_0} + \sqrt{Q_0})} \qquad (14\text{-}24a)$$

$$L_{12} = \frac{R_o}{\pi(\sqrt{P_0} - \sqrt{Q_0})} \qquad (14\text{-}24b)$$

$$L_{12} = \frac{R_o}{\pi(- \sqrt{P_0} - \sqrt{Q_0})} \qquad (14\text{-}24c)$$

$$L_{12} = \frac{R_o}{\pi(- \sqrt{P_0} + \sqrt{Q_0})} \qquad (14\text{-}24d)$$

As will be seen later, $P_0 > Q_0$; hence solutions (14-24c) and (14-24d) are physically impossible because they require either negative R_o or negative L_{12}.

By subtracting Eqs. (14-23) it may be shown that the physical solutions for R_{11} are

$$R_{11} = R_o\pi L_{12}(\sqrt{P_0} - \sqrt{Q_0}) = R_o \frac{\sqrt{P_0} - \sqrt{Q_0}}{\sqrt{P_0} + \sqrt{Q_0}} \qquad (14\text{-}25a)$$

$$R_{11} = R_o\pi L_{12}(\sqrt{P_0} + \sqrt{Q_0}) = R_o \frac{\sqrt{P_0} + \sqrt{Q_0}}{\sqrt{P_0} - \sqrt{Q_0}} \qquad (14\text{-}25b)$$

The pairs of solutions will give identical attenuation characteristics, but they will give different β characteristics.

As an example consider 10 miles of cable terminated at each end in a 600-ohm resistor with an insertion loss given by the curve of Fig. 14-6. The problem is to design an equalizer which, when connected in tandem with the cable, will give substantially constant insertion loss from 100 to 3,000 cycles.

First, select a total insertion loss which is somewhat greater than the maximum attenuation of the cable in the frequency range to be equalized. As a guess, let this insertion loss be 2.6 nepers. Since the equalizer has two independent elements in Z_1, the total loss can be chosen at two frequencies. These frequencies will be selected slightly inside the limits of the frequency band to be equalized. Let them be 200 and 2,400 cycles. The insertion loss of the cable at these two frequencies is as follows:

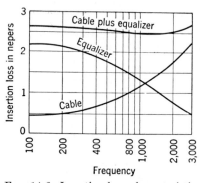

Fig. 14-6. Insertion-loss characteristic of 10 miles of telephone cable terminated in a 600-ohm resistance and fed from a 600-ohm generator.

$$f = 200 \text{ cycles} \qquad \text{Cable loss} = 0.494 \text{ neper}$$
$$f = 2,400 \text{ cycles} \qquad \text{Cable loss} = 1.949 \text{ nepers}$$

The required value of attenuation for the equalizer will be

$$f = 200 \text{ cycles} \qquad \text{Equalizer loss} = 2.6 - 0.494 = 2.106 \text{ nepers}$$
$$f = 2,400 \text{ cycles} \qquad \text{Equalizer loss} = 2.6 - 1.949 = 0.651 \text{ neper}$$

The values of F will be

$$F_{200} = e^{2 \times 2.106} = 67$$
$$F_{2,400} = e^{2 \times 0.651} = 3.68$$

Substitute these values in Eq. (14-21a) to obtain a pair of simultaneous equations.

$$P_0 - 67Q_0 = 66 \times (200)^2 = 264 \times 10^4$$
$$P_0 = 3.68Q_0 = 2.68 \times (2,400)^2 = 1,512 \times 10^4$$

Solve for P_0 and Q_0.

$$Q_0 = 20.2 \times 10^4$$
$$P_0 = 1,616.4 \times 10^4$$

Then by Eqs. (14-24), (14-25), and (14-13) we have the following:

Solution a

$$R_{11} = 478 \text{ ohms} \qquad L_{12} = 42.8 \text{ mh}$$
$$R_{21} = \frac{(600)^2}{478} = 754 \text{ ohms}$$
$$C_{22} = \frac{42.8 \times 10^{-3}}{(600)^2} = 0.119 \ \mu\text{f}$$

Solution b

$$R_{11} = 751 \text{ ohms} \qquad L_{12} = 53.3 \text{ mh}$$

$$R_{21} = \frac{(600)^2}{751} = 480 \text{ ohms}$$

$$C_{22} = \frac{53.3 \times 10^{-3}}{(600)^2} = 0.148 \ \mu\text{f}$$

The choice between the two solutions might be made on the basis of the phase shift. It would be found that Solution *b* has a tendency to equalize the delay distortion of a cable at low-frequencies.

The attenuation of the equalizer can be computed at frequencies other than 200 cycles and 2.4 kc by means of Eq. (14-21). For the equalizer just designed the resultant curve is shown in Fig. 14-6, together with the total insertion loss of the combination. If this is not flat enough, another choice of over-all insertion loss and correction frequencies may be made or, failing this, a more complicated structure should be used so that the attenuation can be specified at more than two frequencies. Similarly, if the equalizer is to be used over a wider band of frequencies, it will ordinarily be necessary to use a structure with three or more independent elements.

It is apparent from the symmetry of the lattice structure that Z_1 and Z_2 can be interchanged in position without affecting the characteristics of the constant-resistance network. Therefore, if an analysis is made for any configuration of Z_1, an identical result will be obtained if the inverse configuration is used in the Z_1 position, except for a phase change of π radians.

Figure 14-7 shows some configurations of Z_1 together with sketches of the manner in which the attenuation constant will vary with frequency. The linear equation for attenuation is also given. The equations for the network elements, in terms of the P's and Q's, can be derived in the manner which has been described. For more details reference should be made to Zobel,[1] from whose paper these were obtained.

The student should realize that, while the foregoing equations have been developed for the lattice equalizer, the same general methods of approach also apply to the bridged T, T, and II equalizers of Fig. 14-2*b* to *d*.

14-5. Corner Plots. The results of the foregoing sections present an analysis of the lattice attenuation equalizer which is based on the solution of an equation linear in P_0 and Q_0, namely, Eq. (14-21). By calculating the response at several frequencies for a typical structure the student may readily appreciate the amount of tedious, though not difficult, algebraic work required. Another method of calculating the attenuation response curve which is graphical, rather than algebraic, will now

[1] Zobel, *op. cit.*

be considered. The method is based on the concept of "corner plots" and is applicable to any network whose complex response characteristic T is of the general form[1]

$$T = Ka \frac{(1 \pm jf/f_{o1})(1 \pm jf/f_{o2}) \cdots}{(1 \pm jf/f_{x1})(1 \pm jf/f_{x2}) \cdots}$$

where $\qquad a = jf, \dfrac{1}{jf}, \text{ or } 1 \hspace{3cm} (14\text{-}26)$

$\qquad\qquad K = \text{scalar constant}$

It will be found that many, though not all, common equalizers are amenable to the corner-plot method of response calculation, as are a number of other types of circuits.[2]

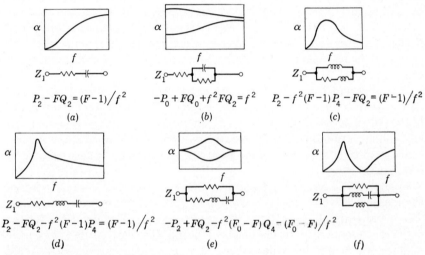

$$P_2 - FQ_2 = (F-1)/f^2$$
(a)

$$-P_0 + FQ_0 + f^2 FQ_2 = f^2$$
(b)

$$P_2 - f^2(F-1)P_4 - FQ_2 = (F-1)/f^2$$
(c)

$$P_2 - FQ_2 - f^2(F-1)P_4 = (F-1)/f^2$$
(d)

$$-P_2 + FQ_2 - f^2(F_0 - F)Q_4 = (F_0 - F)/f^2$$
(e)

(f)

FIG. 14-7. Attenuation characteristics of constant-resistance lattice structures with different Z_1 configurations.

The corner-plot method determines how each of the factors a, $1 \pm jf/f_{on}$, and $1 \pm jf/f_{xn}$ affects the response and then graphically sums up the individual contributions to give the over-all response. Attention will be directed primarily to the amplitude response. As a matter of convenience $f_{o1}, f_{o2}, \ldots$ will be designated "positive corner frequencies,"

[1] G. E. Anner, Corner Plots, *Radio Television News, Radio-Electronic Engineering Edition*, March, 1954, p. 14.

[2] For an extension of the corner-plot method which applies to equations involving more complicated factors than Eq. (14-26) see Research Council of the Academy of Motion Picture Arts and Sciences, "Motion Picture Sound Engineering," chap. XVI, D. Van Nostrand Company, Inc., New York, 1938.

or simply "positive corners," while $f_{x1}, f_{x2}, \ldots$ will be designated "negative corner frequencies," or "negative corners."[1]

Consider the magnitude of Eq. (14-26).

$$|T| = K|a| \frac{\sqrt{1 + (f/f_{o1})^2} \sqrt{1 + (f/f_{o2})^2} \cdots}{\sqrt{1 + (f/f_{x1})^2} \sqrt{1 + (f/f_{x2})^2} \cdots} \tag{14-27}$$

Since amplitude response functions are frequently expressed in logarithmic units such as decibels or nepers, convert Eq. (14-27) to decibels.

$$|T|_{db} = 20 \log K + 20 \log |a| + 10 \log \left[1 + \left(\frac{f}{f_{o1}}\right)^2\right]$$
$$+ 10 \log \left[1 + \left(\frac{f}{f_{o2}}\right)^2\right] + \cdots - 10 \log \left[1 + \left(\frac{f}{f_{x1}}\right)^2\right]$$
$$- 10 \log \left[1 + \left(\frac{f}{f_{x2}}\right)^2\right] - \cdots \tag{14-28}$$

Consider, now, how each type of term in Eq. (14-28) affects the over-all response.

TABLE 14-1. DATA FOR CORNER RESPONSES

f/f_o or f/f_x	Frequency ratio	$|T|$, db*	Approx response difference, db	$|T|$, nepers*	Approx response difference, nepers	$\theta°$†
0.10	Decade	0.043	0	0.005	0	5.7
0.125	. . . . . .	0.067	. . .	0.008	. . . .	7.1
0.25	. . . . . .	0.26	. . .	0.030	. . . .	14.0
0.50	Octave	0.97	1	0.112	0.1	27.0
1.0	Corner	3.01	3	0.345	0.35	45.0
2.0	Octave	7.00	1	0.805	0.1	63.5
4.0	. . . . . .	12.30	. . .	1.415	. . . .	76.0
8.0	. . . . . .	18.10	. . .	2.808	. . . .	82.9
10.0	Decade	20.00	0	2.303	0	84.3

* Values are positive for a positive corner, negative for a negative corner.

† Same sign as contained in the factor $1 \pm jf/f_o$ in Eq. (14-26), opposite sign as contained in the factor $1 \pm jf/f_x$ in Eq. (14-26).

14-6. Positive Corner Response. Each of the positive corner frequencies f_{on} appears in Eq. (14-28) in a term of the form

$$|T_{on}|_{db} = 10 \log \left[1 + \left(\frac{f}{f_{on}}\right)^2\right] \tag{14-29}$$

[1] The student will observe that the positive corner frequencies are *real* zeros and that the negative corner frequencies are *real* poles (see Chap. 2). The corner notation is used here as a matter of convenience.

Direct substitution of numerical values for f/f_{on} yields the values of $|T_{on}|_{db}$ shown in Table 14-1. These values are plotted (dashed line) against a *logarithmic* frequency scale in Fig. 14-8.

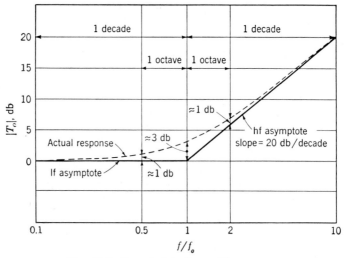

FIG. 14-8. Corner plot of a positive corner.

Now the heart of the method being developed lies in comparing the actual response, just considered, and the asymptotic responses at frequencies much lower—and much higher—than the corner frequency. Thus the asymptote at very low frequencies is given by

$$\frac{f}{f_{on}} \ll 1 \qquad |T_{on}|_{db} \approx 10 \log 1 = 0 \qquad (14\text{-}30)$$

and the high-frequency asymptote by

$$\frac{f}{f_{on}} \gg 1 \qquad |T_{on}|_{db} \approx 10 \log \left(\frac{f}{f_{on}}\right)^2 = 20 \log \frac{f}{f_{on}} \qquad (14\text{-}31)$$

The low-frequency asymptote [Eq. (14-30)] is a horizontal line at 0 db; the high-frequency asymptote [Eq. (14-31)] *when plotted against a logarithmic frequency scale* is a straight line with a positive slope of 20 db/decade (or 6.02 db/octave) of frequency and a frequency axis intercept of f_{on} (or of $f/f_{on} = 1$ when normalized frequency is used). These two asymptotes are shown by the solid lines in Fig. 14-8. The reason for the designation "positive corner" is at once apparent: the asymptotes meet to form a corner at f_{on} with a positive high-frequency asymptote slope.

In comparing the actual and asymptotic responses in the figure, one notes that *they differ by approximately 3 db at the corner, by approximately 1 db at an octave above and below the corner, and by essentially 0 db at a decade above and below the corner.* This, then, is the basis for the corner-plot method of sketching responses: given the positive corner frequency, one may draw its asymptotes and then sketch the actual response from the known differences at five particular frequencies, the corner and the octaves and decades on either side of the corner.

The same basic method may be applied where the response is desired in nepers rather than decibels. Taking the natural logarithm of Eq. (14-27),

$$|T|_{\text{nep}} = \ln K + \ln |a| + \frac{1}{2} \ln \left[1 + \left(\frac{f}{f_{o1}} \right)^2 \right] + \frac{1}{2} \ln \left[1 + \left(\frac{f}{f_{o2}} \right)^2 \right]$$

$$+ \cdots - \frac{1}{2} \ln \left[1 + \left(\frac{f}{f_{x1}} \right)^2 \right] - \frac{1}{2} \ln \left[1 + \left(\frac{f}{f_{x2}} \right)^2 \right] - \cdots \quad (14\text{-}28a)$$

The student may show that the slope of the high-frequency asymptote is 2.3 nepers/decade (or 0.694 neper/octave) and that the differences between the actual response and the asymptotes at the five critical frequencies have the values listed in Table 14-1.

It is apparent from Eq. (14-26) that the angle contributed by a positive corner factor, $1 \pm jf/f_{on}$, is

$$\theta_{on} = \pm \arctan \frac{f}{f_{on}} \quad (14\text{-}32)$$

Values of θ_{on} are tabulated in Table 14-1.

14-7. Negative Corner Response. Each of the negative corner frequencies f_{xm} appears in Eq. (14-28) in a term of the form

$$|T_{xm}|_{\text{db}} = -10 \log \left[1 + \left(\frac{f}{f_{xm}} \right)^2 \right] \quad (14\text{-}33)$$

Since Eqs. (14-33) and (14-39) are identical except for a change in subscript and *sign*, it follows that amplitude response data of Table 14-1 also apply to a negative corner, provided that a negative sign is inserted before each value. The actual response and the asymptotes for a negative corner are plotted in Fig. 14-9, and it is evident that the previously stated rules for sketching the response may be carried over to a negative corner with a shift in sign.

It may be seen from Eq. (14-26) that the angle contributed by a negative corner factor $1 \pm jf/f_{xm}$ is

$$\theta_{xm} = \mp \arctan \frac{f}{f_{xm}} \quad (14\text{-}34)$$

Hence the angular data of Table 14-1 also apply to the negative corner provided that the proper sign is associated with each value.

14-8. External-factor Response. The external factor a in Eqs. (14-26) and (14-28) may have any one of the three forms jf, $1/jf$, and 1. The effect of these three forms on the over-all response will now be considered.

1. $a = jf$.   From Eq. (14-28)

$$|T_a|_{db} = 20 \log f \qquad (14\text{-}35)$$

Thus the *actual* response is a straight line of $+20$ db/decade, crossing the logarithmic frequency axis at unit frequency.   On a neper plot the corresponding slope is $+2.303$ nepers/decade.   From Eq. (14-26) the angular response will be $\theta_a = +90°$.

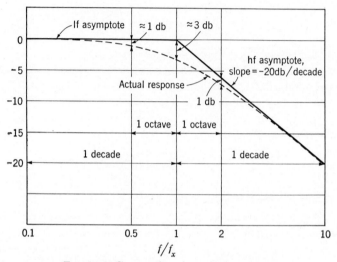

Fig. 14-9. Corner plot of a negative corner.

In many instances it is convenient to combine the external factor jf with the first negative corner factor to give a modified corner factor. For example, considering these two factors in Eq. (14-26) and rearranging by multiplying through by $-jf_{x1}/f$,

$$\frac{jf}{1 + jf/f_{x1}} = f_{x1} \frac{1}{1 - jf_{x1}/f} \qquad (14\text{-}36)$$

The modified factor on the right-hand side of Eq. (14-36) involves an inverted frequency variable and may be termed a "lower negative corner."   The amplitude response may be obtained from the left-hand member of the equation and is obtained as shown in Fig. 14-10a.   As a first step, the asymptotes are combined as shown and then the final response drawn by using the amplitude data of Table 14-1.   It will be of advantage to the student to be able to recognize the lower negative corner factor and to plot its response directly.   It will be of use in the

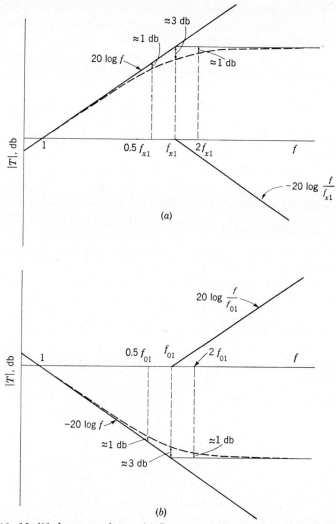

Fig. 14-10. Modified corner plots. (a) Lower negative corner resulting from combining an external factor jf and a negative corner. The total asymptote follows $20 \log f$ up to f_{x1}. At higher frequencies the two asymptotes cancel. The actual response is drawn from the differences listed in Table 14-1. (b) Lower positive corner resulting from combining an external factor $1/jf$ and a positive corner.

next chapter. The angular response of the lower negative corner is
$$\tan (f_{x1}/f) = \cot (f/f_{x1})$$
2. $a = 1/jf$. From Eq. (14-28)

$$|T_a|_{\mathrm{db}} = 20 \log \frac{1}{f} = -20 \log f \qquad (14\text{-}37)$$

Hence the response is identical to that for case 1 except for a change in the sign of the slope. From Eq. (14-26) the angular response will be $\theta_a = -90°$. The external factor $1/jf$ may be combined with the first positive corner factor to give a "lower positive corner." Considering these two factors in Eq. (14-26) and multiplying through by $-jf_{o1}/f$,

$$\frac{1 + jf/f_{o1}}{jf} = \frac{1}{f_{o1}}\left(1 - j\frac{f_{o1}}{f}\right) \tag{14-38}$$

The resulting amplitude response is shown in Fig. 14-10b, and the angular response is $- \arctan (f_{o1}/f) = - \operatorname{arccot} (f/f_{o1})$.

3. $a = 1$. In this case, a has no effect on either the amplitude or the angular responses.

14-9. Over-all Response. Equation (14-28) indicates that the over-all amplitude response $|T|$ is a linear combination of the individual responses contributed by the several corners and the external factors a and K; hence $|T|$ may be found by graphically adding the individual responses.

From Eq. (14-26) the over-all angular response may be shown to be

$$\theta = \theta_a + \theta_{o1} + \theta_{o2} + \cdots + \theta_{x1} + \theta_{x2} + \cdots$$

and hence may be plotted by graphically by summing up the individual angular responses.

To illustrate the method of summing up responses, consider the following problem:

The response function T of a network is given by

$$T = K\frac{1 + jf/f_o}{1 - jf_x/f}$$

where
$$K = 0.5$$
$$f_x = 0.2 \text{ kc}$$
$$f_o = 1 \text{ kc}$$

Plot $|T|$ in decibels. The work of sketching the response is shown in Fig. 14-11. The asymptotes for the lower negative corner are drawn in, the corner being at $f_x = 0.2$ kc. Then the actual response for this factor is plotted by joining the points at 0.2 kc, 0.1 and 0.4 kc, and 2 kc, which lie, respectively, *below* the asymptote by 3, 1, and 0 db.

The asymptotes for the upper corner are also shown, the corner lying at

$$f_o = 1 \text{ kc.}$$

The actual response is sketched in a similar manner. The relative over-all response $|T|/K$ is obtained by graphically adding the two dotted curves.

As a last step, the scalar constant K is taken into account. Since

$$20 \log K = 20 \log 0.5 = -20 \log 2 = -6 \text{ db,}$$

K has the effect of lowering the over-all response by 6 db.   This is shown by the corrected ordinate scale on the right-hand margin of the figure.

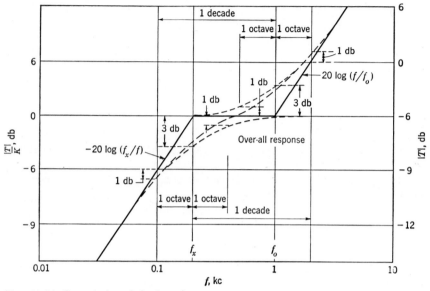

FIG. 14-11. Corner plot of the function

$$T = K \frac{1 + jf/f_o}{1 - jf_x/f}$$

where $K = 0.5$, $f_x = 0.2$ kc, $f_o = 1$ kc.

14-10. Response of Lattice Equalizer.   Another example which may be used to illustrate the corner-plot method is the lattice equalizer in Sec. 14-4.   The numerical values of Solution b will be used.   The basic equation for the response is Eq. (14-20).   Rearranging to get e^γ in the corner-plot form of Eq. (14-26),

$$\left.\begin{aligned} e^\gamma &= \left(\frac{R_o + R_{11}}{R_o - R_{11}}\right) \frac{\left(1 + j \dfrac{2\pi L_{12}}{R_o + R_{11}} f\right)}{\left(1 - j \dfrac{2\pi L_{12}}{R_o - R_{11}} f\right)} \\ &= \frac{f_o}{f_x}\left(\frac{1 + jf/f_o}{1 + jf/f_x}\right) \end{aligned}\right\} \quad (14\text{-}39)$$

where

$$f_o = \frac{R_o + R_{11}}{2\pi L_{12}} = \frac{600 + 751}{2\pi(53.3 \times 10^{-3})} = 4.04 \text{ kc}$$

$$f_x = \frac{R_{11} - R_o}{2\pi L_{12}} = \frac{751 - 600}{2\pi(53.3 \times 10^{-3})} = 0.45 \text{ kc}$$

The student may notice that $f_o = \sqrt{P_0}$ and $f_x = \sqrt{Q_0}$ where P_0 and Q_0

are the design parameters used in Eqs. (14-22). Solving Eq. (14-39) for α in nepers,

$$\alpha = \ln |e^\gamma| = \ln \frac{f_o}{f_x} + \frac{1}{2} \ln \left[1 + \left(\frac{f}{f_o} \right)^2 \right] - \frac{1}{2} \ln \left[1 + \left(\frac{f}{f_x} \right)^2 \right] \quad (14\text{-}40)$$

The determination of α by corner plots is illustrated in Fig. 14-12a. The individual response for each corner factor is determined from the asymptotes and the values of differences shown in Table 14-1. The over-all response is obtained by adding the two corner responses with a pair of dividers.

The student should notice that the neper ordinate scale on the left-hand margin is for $\alpha - \ln (f_o/f_x)$, that is, for the corners alone, exclusive of the scalar factor $K = f_o/f_x$. The scale on the right-hand margin is obtained by adding $\ln (f/f_o)$ to give α.

Observe that at high-frequencies the over-all response approaches 0 nepers asymptotically. This fact may be verified from Eq. (14-39) as a check on the graphical method. Dividing numerator and denominator by f and taking the limit as $f \to \infty$,

$$\lim_{f \to \infty} e^\gamma = \lim_{f \to \infty} \frac{f_o}{f_x} \left(\frac{1/f + j/f_o}{1/f + j/f_x} \right) \to 1$$

Then $\lim_{f \to \infty} \alpha \to \ln 1 \to 0$ nepers.

From Eq. (14-39) the phase response of the lattice equalizer may be seen to be

$$\beta = \arctan \frac{f}{f_o} - \arctan \frac{f}{f_x} = \theta_o + \theta_x$$

The values of θ_o and θ_x may be obtained from Table 14-1 and are plotted in Fig. 14-12b, as is β, which is obtained by adding the two θ curves with dividers.

14-11. Lattice Design by Corner Plots.[1]   Contrary to first appearance, the lattice-equalizer design procedure of Sec. 14-4 is not a "cut-and-dried" one; an element of intelligent guessing is involved in the choice of the over-all insertion loss of the line and equalizer and in the choice of the frequencies at which the equalization is to be exact. An alternative design procedure consists in guessing the values of the corner frequencies f_o and f_x (tantamount to guessing the values of P_0 and Q_0). The choice is guided by a knowledge of the α-curve shape (Fig. 14-12a) and the fact that at low-frequencies $\alpha \approx 2.3 \ln (f_o/f_x)$ nepers above 0 as indicated in the figure. This fact, in essence, sets the *ratio* of f_o to

[1] For an extension of the method outlined here, see A. D. Bresler, On the Approximation Problem in Network Synthesis, *Proc. IRE*, vol. 40, no. 12, p. 1724, December, 1952. Bresler presents means for matching slopes so that a large degree of guessing is removed from the design problem.

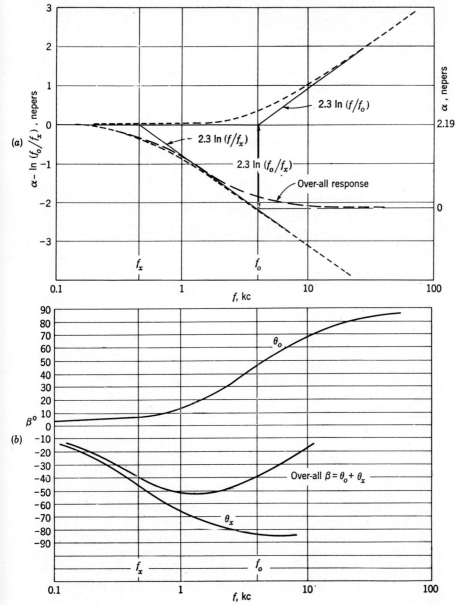

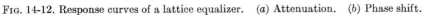

FIG. 14-12. Response curves of a lattice equalizer. (a) Attenuation. (b) Phase shift.

f_x. f_0 may then be chosen to place the α curve properly along the frequency axis.

It must be stressed that this "corner" method of equalizer design is no more arbitrary, and, in fact, may be faster to use, than the algebraic method, at least when $Z_1 = R_{11} + j\omega L_{12}$. The graphical design procedure is greatly facilitated by the sacrifice of a sheet of semilogarithmic paper to the construction of a template based on the data of Table 14-1. Such a template simplifies the drawing of the response curves.

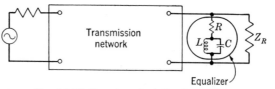

Fig. 14-13. Two-terminal shunt equalizer.

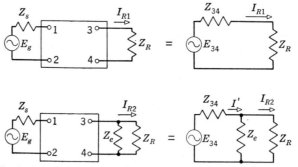

Fig. 14-14. Equivalent networks for determining the insertion loss of two-terminal shunt equalizers.

14-12. Two-terminal Equalizer. Another type of equalizer is the two-terminal type in which a network is connected in series or shunt with the sending or receiving end of the network to be corrected. One of the configurations most widely used is shown in Fig. 14-13. By inspection it is apparent that the loss it will introduce would be negligible at the antiresonant frequency of the LC combination, and the loss would increase as the frequency is varied away from antiresonance. If this structure is to be used to equalize a cable, the antiresonant frequency would be set at or above the highest frequency which it is desirable to transmit.

If the system is originally terminated in an impedance Z_R, the equalizer will modify this termination and this modification must be taken into account in determining the characteristics. Consider the case where the structure is connected in shunt at the receiving end. By Thévenin's theorem the original network can be considered as a generator in series with an impedance, as shown in Fig. 14-14, where the equivalent systems are shown with and without the equalizer Z_e in shunt. Z_{34} is the impedance looking to the left of terminals 3, 4, while E_{34} is the open-circuit voltage at the terminals 3, 4. The insertion loss introduced by the equalizer can be determined by computing the ratio I_{R1}/I_{R2}. By inspection it will be seen

$$I_{R1} = \frac{E_{34}}{Z_{34} + Z_R}$$

$$I' = \frac{E_{34}}{Z_{34} + \dfrac{Z_e Z_R}{Z_e + Z_R}} = \frac{E_{34}(Z_e + Z_R)}{Z_{34}Z_e + Z_{34}Z_R + Z_e Z_R}$$

$$I_{R2} = \frac{Z_e I'}{Z_e + Z_R} = \frac{E_{34}Z_e}{Z_{34}Z_e + Z_{34}Z_R + Z_e Z_R}$$

Therefore
$$\frac{I_{R1}}{I_{R2}} = \frac{Z_{34}Z_e + Z_{34}Z_R + Z_e Z_R}{Z_{34}Z_e + Z_e Z_R}$$

$$= 1 + \frac{Z_{34}Z_R}{Z_e(Z_{34} + Z_R)}$$

Let Z'_R be the impedance of Z_{34} and Z_R in parallel. Then

$$Z'_R = \frac{Z_{34}Z_R}{Z_{34} + Z_R} \tag{14-41}$$

and to correspond to the notation in the case of the constant-resistance equalizer, let

$$\frac{I_{R1}}{I_{R2}} = e^\gamma$$

where, of course, this γ is not a true propagation constant. Then

$$e^\gamma = 1 + \frac{Z'_R}{Z_e} \tag{14-42}$$

This is the general equation for the two-terminal shunt equalizer which corresponds to Eq. (14-6) for the constant-resistance equalizer. Both Z'_R and Z_e will be functions of frequency. The problem is to select dimensions for Z_e so that the real part of γ will equalize the variation in insertion loss which takes place in the original structure.

In the configuration shown in Fig. 14-13 the value of Z_e will be

$$Z_e = R_e + \frac{j\omega L_e}{1 - \omega^2 L_e C_e} \tag{14-43}$$

There are three independent elements, and hence the loss can be set at three frequencies. The first step is to make a selection of the antiresonant frequency at which no loss will occur. Let this frequency be f_3.

Then

$$L_e C_e = \frac{1}{(2\pi f_3)^2}$$

and Eq. (14-43) can be written

$$Z_e = R_e + \frac{j\omega L_e}{1 - f^2/f_3{}^2}$$
$$Z_e = R_e + j\omega' L_e \qquad (14\text{-}44)$$

where ω' is a function of frequency given by the relation

$$\omega' = \frac{2\pi f}{1 - f^2/f_3{}^2} \qquad (14\text{-}45)$$

Let

$$Z'_R = R' + jX'$$
$$\gamma = \alpha + j\beta$$

Then Eq. (14-42) becomes

$$e^\gamma = \frac{R' + R_e + j(X' + \omega' L_e)}{R_e + j\omega' L_e}$$
$$F = |e^\gamma|^2 = e^{2\alpha} = \frac{(R' + R_e)^2 + (X' + \omega' L_e)^2}{R_e{}^2 + (\omega' L_e)^2} \qquad (14\text{-}46)$$

Two frequencies may now be selected at which equalization is to take place. The values of R' and X' will be known at these two frequencies from the data on the original network. Therefore, two simultaneous equations can be set up from Eq. (14-46) in which R_e and L_e are the only unknowns. Unfortunately, in the general case, Eq. (14-46) cannot be reduced to a *linear* equation in two unknowns. If X' is negligible in comparison with R' (e.g., a loaded line properly terminated), Eq. (14-46) can be written

$$F = \frac{\left(\dfrac{R' + R_e}{L_e}\right)^2 + (\omega')^2}{(R_e/L_e)^2 + (\omega')^2}$$
$$= \frac{P_0 + (\omega')^2}{Q_0 + (\omega')^2} \qquad (14\text{-}47)$$

which is linear in P_0 and Q_0, and can be readily solved for P_0 and Q_0. R_e and L_e can be obtained from P_0 and Q_0 by the expressions

$$L_e = \frac{R'}{\sqrt{P_0} - \sqrt{Q_0}} \qquad (14\text{-}48a)$$

$$R_e = \frac{R' \sqrt{Q_0}}{\sqrt{P_0} - \sqrt{Q_0}} \qquad (14\text{-}48b)$$

If the attenuation can be specified at zero frequency, then Eq. (14-46) becomes

$$F_0 = \frac{(R_0' + R_e)^2}{R_e{}^2} \tag{14-49a}$$

The subscript zero in this case indicates the value at zero frequency that is to be substituted. Equation (14-49a) can be solved directly for R_e.

$$R_e = \frac{R_0'}{\sqrt{F_0} - 1} \tag{14-49b}$$

The equalizer network under discussion will have a low value of $\omega'L$ at low-frequencies, and an approximate equation can neglect $\omega'L$. Let the subscript 1 indicate an evaluation at a low-frequency. Equation (14-46) then becomes

$$F_1 = \frac{(R_1' + R_e)^2 + (X_1')^2}{R_e{}^2} \tag{14-50a}$$

This can also be solved for R_e with the following result:

$$R_e = \frac{R_1' + \sqrt{F_1(R_1')^2 + (F_1 - 1)(X_1')^2}}{F_1 - 1} \tag{14-50b}$$

After R_e has been determined by Eq. (14-50b) at a low-frequency, Eq. (14-46) can be used at another frequency f_2 to solve for L_e. Since everything is now known in Eq. (14-46) except L_e, this equation is a quadratic in L_e and can be solved directly. The solution will be

$$L_e = \frac{X_2' + \sqrt{F_2(X_2')^2 + (F_2 - 1)[(R_e + R_2')^2 - F_2 R_e{}^2]}}{\omega_2'(F_2 - 1)} \tag{14-51}$$

Equations (14-50b) and (14-51) give first approximations for R_e and L_e. Where a more accurate solution is necessary, a second approximation could be obtained for R_e by substituting in Eq. (14-46) the first approximation for L_e and a second approximation for L_e could be obtained by substituting in Eq. (14-51) the second approximation for R_e.

As an example of the design of a shunt equalizer, consider the cable for which the constant-resistance equalizer was originally designed. The data for this cable, terminated in a 600-ohm resistor, are approximately

$f = 100$	$Z_o = 1{,}034 - j1{,}034$	Insertion loss $= 0.47$ neper
$f = 1{,}600$	$Z_o = 258 - j258$	Insertion loss $= 1.53$ nepers
$f = 3{,}200$	$Z_o = 183 - j183$	Insertion loss $= 2.37$ nepers

Assume $f_3 = 3{,}200$, $f_2 = 1{,}600$, and $f_1 = 100$. If the equalizer is adjusted so as to have zero loss at 3,200 cycles, it should have $2.37 - 1.53 = 0.84$ neper loss at 1,600 cycles and $2.37 - 0.47 = 1.90$ nepers loss at 100 cycles. Assume the cable is long enough so that Z_{34} of Fig. 14-14 is approximately equal to Z_o. Then by Eq. (14-41) at $f = 100$.

$$Z'_{R1} = \frac{(1{,}034 - j1{,}034) \times 600}{1{,}634 - j1{,}034} = 442 - j99 = R'_1 + jX'_1$$

at $f = 1{,}600$

$$Z_{R2} = \frac{(258 - j258) \times 600}{858 - j258} = 215 - j116 = R'_2 + jX'_2$$

$$F_1 = e^{2 \times 1.90} = 44.8$$
$$F_2 = e^{2 \times 0.84} = 5.37$$

Substitute these values in Eq. (14-50b). Then

$$R_e = \frac{442 + \sqrt{44.8 \times (442)^2 + 43.8 \times (99)^2}}{43.8}$$

$$= 79 \text{ ohms}$$

From Eq. (14-45)

$$\omega'_2 = \frac{2\pi \times 1{,}600}{1 - (1{,}600/3{,}200)^2} = 13{,}380$$

Next make substitutions in Eq. (14-51) for a frequency at 1,600 cycles.

$$L_e = \frac{-116 + \sqrt{5.37 \times (116)^2 + 4.37[(215 + 79)^2 - 5.37 \times (79)^2]}}{13{,}380 \times 4.37}$$

$$= 7.45 \times 10^{-3} \text{ henry}$$

$$C = \frac{1}{\omega_3^2 L_e} = \frac{1}{(2\pi \times 3{,}200)^2 \times 7.45 \times 10^{-3}} = 0.332 \times 10^{-6} \text{ farad}$$

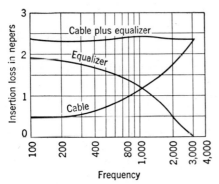

FIG. 14-15. Insertion-loss characteristic of a 10-mile cable terminated in 600 ohms, and correction by a two-terminal equalizer.

The effect of adding this shunt equalizer to the cable is shown in Fig. 14-15.

14-13. Experimental Line-up of Equalizers. It is sometimes desirable to line up an equalizer experimentally. The two-terminal type is much easier than the constant-resistance equalizer to adjust in this manner, for four arms would have to be adjusted in the latter type. With the two-terminal type of Fig. 14-13 it is quite common to make L and C fixed and R adjustable. In this case the insertion loss of equalizer and line is measured at a frequency near the antiresonant frequency of LC and at a low-frequency, and R is adjusted until the losses at the two frequencies are equal. A transmission-frequency run may then be made and the resistance of the equalizer slightly readjusted to obtain the best compromise results.

14-14. Non-constant-resistance Equalizers. A third type of equalizer to be considered works between unequal impedances and hence need not be designed on a constant-resistance basis, i.e., the input impedance may vary with frequency. Such equalizers are generally incorporated as part of the interstage coupling between two vacuum tubes so that the equalizer works into the grid circuit of a tube which, to all intents and purposes, may be considered as an open circuit. A typical application is the equalization of the recording characteristic of a phonograph record as used in a good-quality audio amplifier system. A brief discussion of the basic problem may be desirable.

The mechanical parts of a recording system comprise a motor-driven turntable which rotates a recording disk at a constant angular velocity. A recording, or cutting, head is made to traverse the record by a feed-screw mechanism perpendicular to the record motion so that the head follows a spiral path over the record surface.

The electrical system consists of a microphone, correcting network, amplifier, and the cutting head itself. (These are the elements of a basic system. In practice a magnetic tape system is used between the microphone and cutting head.) The microphone converts the original sound into a corresponding electrical signal which, in turn, is amplified and used to drive the cutting head. In this head an electromechanical system utilizes the amplified electrical signal to produce a lateral vibration of the recording, or cutting, stylus which contacts the disk surface. Then, under the influence of the sound signal, the stylus cuts a groove in the disk surface. For pickups which generate voltage proportional to the magnitude of the needle deviation, the wiggles in the groove should have the exact waveform of the sound intensity, i.e., the period of the wiggles should be proportional to the period of the sound signal, and the amplitude of the wiggles should be proportional to the amplitude (or intensity) of the sound.

Mechanical problems in the cutter head, however, prevent the latter 1:1 amplitude relationship. To illustrate, say that the stylus is to cut a sinusoidal wiggle, perpendicular to the direction of record rotation, and that the stylus motion is given by $s = \hat{s} \sin \omega t$, s being the instantaneous displacement of the stylus from its "no-signal" position. The velocity of the stylus will be $v = ds/dt = \omega \hat{s} \cos \omega t$. Or, at any frequency $\omega/2\pi$, the maximum stylus velocity will be $\hat{v} = \omega \hat{s}$. Then, for a constant-amplitude sound signal, $\hat{v}$ increases linearly with frequency. At high audio-frequencies a typical cutting head would be unable to move the stylus fast enough to meet this requirement. To overcome this difficulty, the amplitude of the electrical signal is modified by a correcting network to decrease linearly with frequency so that $\hat{v}$ of the stylus is independent of frequency. This works satisfactorily for the higher audio-frequencies and results in "constant-velocity recording."

At low audio-frequencies constant-velocity recording would result in large values of $\hat{s}$, so large, in fact, that wiggles of adjacent grooves cut into the disk might overlap. To prevent this from happening, a transition is made in the corrective network at the so-called "turnover" frequency so that at lower frequencies the 1:1 amplitude relationship is maintained. Below the turnover frequency, then, the recording characteristic is "constant-amplitude." The two regions, constant-amplitude and constant-velocity, are illustrated by the dashed lines in Fig. 14-16.

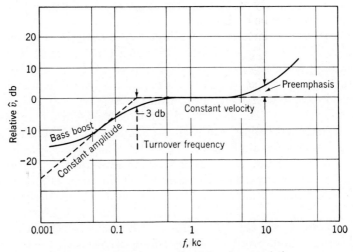

Fig. 14-16. Basic record-cutting characteristic.

This, then, is the basic recording characteristic which the correcting network must derive from a constant-amplitude electrical signal.

Further modifications of this basic characteristic are introduced to mask noise which arises in the playback system. Phonograph turntables are subject to low-frequency vibrations of about 30 cycles. These are transmitted to the playback, or reproducing, head and are reproduced in the audio system as a "rumble." Furthermore, nonuniformities in the disk material and dirt particles in the grooves bring about spurious motion of the stylus during playback. These are reproduced by the audio system as sounds in the vicinity of 3 to 5 kc and are known as "surface noise." To keep the signal above the rumble and surface noise, "preemphasis" is also introduced by the corrective network, i.e., the very low and very high signal characteristics are raised above the basic characteristic of Fig. 14-16. This "bass boost" and "treble preemphasis" are shown by the solid line in the figure.[1] It should be noticed that the treble preemphasis is given in decibels of boost at 10 kc above the basic

[1] See, for example, F. H. Slaymaker, Equalization and Tone Controls on Phonograph Amplifiers, *Trans. IRE*, Professional Group on Audio, AU-3, no. 1, p. 5, January–February, 1955.

constant-velocity characteristic. While many recording characteristics have been used in the past, some standardization resulted in 1954 when the bulk of the industry agreed to adopt the RIAA (Record Industry Association of America) characteristic, which is plotted in Fig. 14-17.

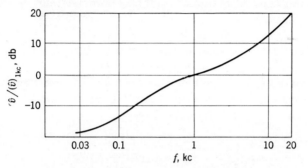

FIG. 14-17. RIAA recording characteristic.

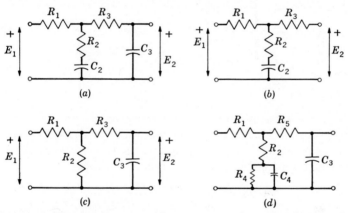

FIG. 14-18. Double-L equalizers. (a) RCA Victor. $R_1 = 330$ kilohms, $R_2 = 7.5$ kilohms, $R_3 = 27$ kilohms, $C_2 = 0.03$ μf, $C_3 = 0.002$ μf. (b) Low-frequency equivalent circuit. (c) High-frequency equivalent circuit. (d) RIAA. $R_4 = 82$ kilohms, $R_5 = 30$ kilohms, $C_4 = 0.04$ μf. R_1, R_2, and C_3 same as in a.

The function, then, of the phonograph equalizer is to provide the complement of the recording characteristic so that the over-all system, from microphone to loudspeaker, is flat. This equalization may be accomplished for any of the recording characteristics that have been used by a double-L section containing only resistance and capacitance. The response of these equalizers is usually easy to obtain by the corner-plot method.

14-15. Double-L Equalizer. A typical phonograph equalizer is shown in Fig. 14-18.[1] Since the network works into essentially an open circuit,

[1] C. P. Boegli, New Developments in Phono Equalizers, *Radio Television News*, vol. 49, no. 4, p. 54, April, 1953.

the transfer function $|T| = |E_2/E_1|$ is generally considered, rather than e^{α} as in the lattice equalizer. If the student sets up the nodal equations for the network and solves for T, he will find that the expression is not in the general form of Eq. (14-26) and hence is not amenable to the corner-plot method of solution. Suitable approximations, however, overcome this difficulty.

The parameter values specified in Fig. 14-18 show that $C_2 = 15C_3$. As a result of this difference in capacitance values, C_2 and C_3 control T in different parts of the audio spectrum. At very low-frequencies the branch containing C_3 approaches an open circuit, and the approximate equivalent circuit is that of Fig. 14-18b. By inspection the approximate low-frequency transfer function will be

$$T_l = \frac{R_2 + 1/j\omega C_2}{R_1 + R_2 + 1/j\omega C_2} = \frac{1 + j\omega C_2 R_2}{1 + j\omega C_2(R_1 + R_2)}$$

$$T_l = \frac{1 + jf/f_{o1}}{1 + jf/f_{x1}}$$

where   (14-52)

$$f_{o1} = \frac{1}{2\pi C_2 R_2} = \frac{1}{2\pi(3 \times 10^{-8})(7.5 \times 10^3)} = 709 \text{ cycles}$$

$$f_{x1} = \frac{1}{2\pi C_2(R_1 + R_2)} = \frac{1}{2\pi(3 \times 10^{-8})(330 + 7.5) \times 10^3} = 15.7 \text{ cycles}$$

At high audio-frequencies, on the other hand, the reactance of C_2 approaches a short circuit, and the approximate equivalent circuit of Fig. 14-18c may be used. Using this diagram, the student may show that the approximate high-frequency transfer function will be

$$T_h = \frac{R_2}{R_1 + R_2} \frac{1}{1 + jf/f_{x2}}$$

where $$f_{x2} = \frac{1}{2\pi C_3\left(R_3 + \dfrac{R_1 R_2}{R_1 + R_2}\right)}$$ (14-53)

Since R_1 is much larger than R_2, their parallel combination is approximately equal to R_2, the smaller of the two values; hence

$$f_{x2} \approx \frac{1}{2\pi C_3(R_3 + R_2)} = \frac{1}{2\pi(2 \times 10^{-9})(27 + 7.5) \times 10^3} = 2.34 \text{ kc}$$

(14-53a)

The corner-plot responses are shown in Fig. 14-19. It should be noted that the f_{x2} corner is plotted at a level of -33 db corresponding to the effect of the scalar factor $R_2/(R_1 + R_2)$ in Eq. (14-53). It may be observed that there is a break between $|T_l|$ and $|T_h|$ in the region between

200 cycles and 5 kc. This is the result of using the approximate low- and high-frequency equivalent circuits of Fig. 14-18b and c. Since the network will give a continuous response, the $|T_l|$ and $|T_h|$ curves should be averaged out in this region. The response is usually plotted on a relative basis with the value at 1 kc as the zero-decibel reference level.

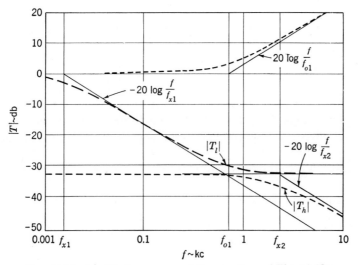

Fig. 14-19. Amplitude response of the equalizer of Fig. 14-18a.

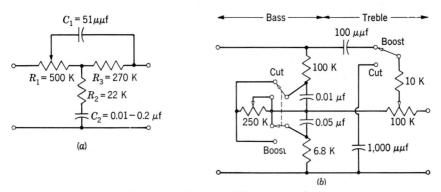

Fig. 14-20. Typical RC tone controls.

14-16. Tone Controls. In audio reproducing systems it is often desirable to provide, by tone-control circuits, additional means of shaping the playback characteristic to allow for variations in the playback system, in the recorded material, and in the listening environment. Two typical RC tone-control circuits are shown in Fig. 14-20.

Circuit $a*$ has the general form of a bridged T network but is not designed on a constant-resistance basis. C_2 controls the turnover frequency, while the potentiometer R_1 provides a variable treble boost.

Circuit $b\dagger$ in Fig. 14-20 provides a greater degree of control in that bass and treble may be cut or boosted. The behavior of the circuit is easy to predict, given a set of switch positions, and the transfer function may be computed by means of corner plots.

In some instances the RC tone-control network is incorporated into the feedback network of the audio amplifier.$\ddagger$ In that event RC networks are also used and the basic method of determining the response is the same as that which has been demonstrated.

In audio work the phase characteristic has little if any effect which may be discerned by the ear. As a consequence, no attention is paid to the phase angles introduced by the equalizer and tone controls.

14-17. Delay Equalizers. Transmission lines exhibit frequency-dependent phase-shift — as well as insertion-loss — characteristics. In applications where the preservation of the *waveform* of the input signal is important, e.g., in facsimile and television signal transmission over lines, a delay equalizer§ may be inserted in the system to equalize the group velocities in order that delay distortion shall be minimized. As is the case with attenuation equalizers, the delay equalizer should be a constant-resistance network so that its insertion in the system does not upset any of the impedance relationships. The lattice and the bridged T configurations are ordinarily used. In order to keep the equalization of the attenuation characteristic independent of the delay equalization, the delay equalizer should be an all-pass structure, that is, $\alpha = 0$ for all frequencies in the desired band.

It has been shown in Chap. 7 that a lattice structure in which Z_1 and Z_2 are pure reactances and inverse with respect to R_o is such an "all-pass" structure and so may be used as a delay equalizer. The student may easily show that the phase shift of the network (Fig. 14-21a) is given by

$$\beta = \pm 2 \arctan \frac{X_1}{R_o} \tag{14-54}$$

The general method of designing a lattice phase equalizer may be

---

* Allan M. Ferres, A Bass-boost Control, *Radio Television News*, vol. 52, no. 1, p. 52, July, 1954.

† Philip Cheilik, Audio Amplifier—Preamp for Home Use, *Radio Television News*, vol. 52, no. 5, p. 68, November, 1954.

‡ See, for example, Arthur J. Rose, Simplified Design of Feedback Equalizers, *Radio Television News*, vol. 52, no. 3, p. 54, September, 1954.

§ A delay equalizer is a corrective network which is designed to make the phase delay or envelope delay of a circuit or system substantially constant over a desired frequency range." [ASA C42, 65.06.548 (1953).]

described as follows: X_1 will generally be some combination, more or less complicated, of inductance and capacitance, and its behavior may, by Foster's reactance theorem, be uniquely expressed in terms of its poles and zeros and a scale factor H. Then, given a desired β characteristic, the poles, zeros, and H may be determined. A Foster network to give the required X_1 may then be designed by the procedures described in Chap. 4. X_2 may be determined from $X_2 = -R_o{}^2/X_1$, since X_1 and

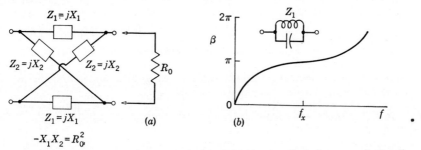

Fig. 14-21. Lattice delay equalizer. b shows the β characteristic for a particular Z_1 configuration.

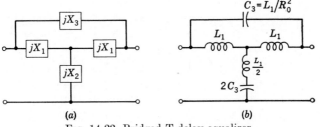

Fig. 14-22. Bridged T delay equalizer.

X_2 are inverse networks. The phase response for a simple example is illustrated in Fig. 14-21b.

A suitably designed bridged T reactive structure may also serve as an all-pass equalizer. Consider the requirements on Fig. 14-22a for it to be a constant-resistance network: by evaluating Z_{oc} and Y_{sc} the student may show that

$$Z_o{}^2 = \frac{Z_{oc}}{Y_{sc}} = \frac{-X_1X_3(2X_2 + X_1)}{2X_1 + X_3} = R_o{}^2 \tag{14-55}$$

One possible solution is to make X_1 and X_3 inverse so that

$$-X_1X_3 = R_o{}^2 \tag{14-56a}$$

Then from Eq. (14-55)

$$\frac{2X_2 + X_1}{2X_1 + X_3} = 1$$

or

$$X_2 = \frac{X_1 + X_3}{2} \tag{14-56b}$$

If, for example, X_1 is chosen as ωL_1, the structure will have the form illustrated in Fig. 14-22b. It is left as an exercise for the student to show that $\alpha = 0$ and to derive an expression for β for the bridged T equalizer of Fig. 14-22a.

PROBLEMS

14-1. Prove that, in a constant-resistance lattice equalizer, α is unaffected if the positions of Z_1 and Z_2 in the lattice are interchanged. What is the effect on β?

14-2. Prove that the circuits of Fig. 14-2b to d exhibit the constant-resistance property if $Z_1 Z_2 = R_o^2$.

14-3. Draw a network containing eight or more elements including R, L, and C, and then draw the inverse network.

14-4. Design a constant-resistance equalizer to equalize, up to 3,000 cycles, the insertion loss of 40 miles of 16-gage cable, unloaded.

Note. It is sometimes more convenient to use more than one equalizing section.

14-5. (*a*) Derive the design equations for the bridged T equalizer where

$$Z_1 = R_{11} + j\omega L_{12}.$$

(*b*) Sketch the shape of the α vs. frequency curve, using corner plots. (*c*) Comment on the simplicity of the bridged T design equations as compared with those of the lattice.

14-6. A length of telephone cable is driven from a 600-ohm generator and is terminated in a 600-ohm resistance load. The measured insertion loss in decibels is:

f...............	30	100	200	500	1,000	2,000	2,400	4,000	6,000
Loss............	3.8	3.8	3.9	4.6	6.6	10.5	11.9	16.4	20.7

Design a lattice network to equalize the cable within 2 db from 30 to 3,000 cycles. The over-all insertion loss of the cable and equalizer must not exceed 20 db.

14-7. Using the insertion-loss data of Prob. 14-6, design a suitable bridged T equalizer by means of the corner-plot method. As a starting point, assume f_o is 2 octaves above f_x.

14-8. A length of 75-ohm coaxial cable is to be used in a community television distribution system. The cable is terminated in $R_o = 75$ ohms. The attenuation of the cable is given by:

f, Mc.............	40	100	150	200	400
α, db.............	5.50	9.50	12.00	14.25	21.75

Design an equalizer to work over the vhf television channels, 54 to 220 Mc. Should a lattice or bridged T equalizer be used? Why?

14-9. A constant-resistance lattice equalizer has $Z_1 = R_{11} - j/\omega C_{12}$.

a. If $R_{11} = 1$ kilohm, $R_{21} = 250$ ohm, $C_{12} = 0.0212$ μf, and $L_{22} = 5.3$ mh, what is the characteristic impedance?

b. Plot a curve of insertion loss in decibels vs. frequency.

14-10. A bridged T equalizer is to be used to attenuate 60-cycle hum picked up on a long audio line which is terminated in a 600-ohm resistance. Z_2 consists of an inductor L_{21} and capacitor C_{22} in series. $C_{22} = 4.426$ μf, and $L = 1.591$ henrys, with a Q of 100 at 60 cycles.

a. Find the elements of Z_1 so that the equalizer is a constant-resistance network.

b. Find the equalizer insertion loss at 60 cycles as compared with 600 cycles in decibels.

14-11. (a) Derive the design equations [similar to (14-20a) to (14-22)] for the Z_1 configuration of Fig. 14-7a. (b) For which of the Z_1 configurations of Fig. 14-7 may the corner-plot method be used?

14-12. Plot the β curve for Solution a of the lattice equalizer designed in the text (Sec. 14-4).

14-13. Repeat Prob. 14-4, using a shunt two-terminal equalizer.

14-14. Derive the design equations for a series equalizer to be placed in series with the load Z_R in Fig. 14-13 but otherwise to have the same characteristics as the shunt equalizer shown in that figure.

14-15. Apply the equations derived in Prob. 14-14 to the design of an equalizer for the cable used in the examples in the text.

14-16. Plot the response $|T|$ of the RIAA equalizer of Fig. 14-18d. Compare the curve with Fig. 14-17. Are they complementary?

14-17. Design an equalizer to give the complement of the curve of Prob. 14-16. What use could be made of this circuit in a recording system?

14-18. (a) Plot the transfer-function magnitude vs. frequency curve for the circuit of Fig. 14-20a. Use $C_2 = 0.01$ μf and the tap at the left-hand end of R_1. (b) Repeat with $C_2 = 0.2$ μf and with the tap at the right-hand end of R_1.

14-19. Plot $|T|$ vs. frequency for the circuit of Fig. 14-20b in both cut and boost positions. Assume the taps of both potentiometers are at the mid-position.

CHAPTER 15

LINEAR AMPLIFIERS

An amplifier is a device which, by enabling a received wave to control a local source of power, is capable of delivering an enlarged reproduction of the essential characteristics of the wave. [ASA C42 65.06.105 (1953).] Two basic types of linear vacuum-tube amplifiers which differ in their amplitude vs. frequency-response characteristics, will be treated here, the quasi-LP and the BP types.[1] In the former the amplifying property is exhibited from a low to some finite upper-frequency limit. In the BP type the amplifying property is exhibited over a more or less limited frequency band, centered on a frequency far removed from zero. (Compare with the LP and BP filters of Chap. 7.) Attention will be directed to the *voltage amplification*, or *gain*, which is defined as the ratio of output to input voltage,[2] i.e.,

$$A = E_{\text{out}}/E_{in} \tag{15-1}$$

15-1. Linear Equivalent Circuit of Vacuum Pentode. In contrast to the circuits which have been discussed earlier, the vacuum-tube amplifier is an active unilateral, rather than a passive bilateral, circuit. Although the vacuum tube is not linear, in that the alternating component of plate current is not an exact linear function of the input-voltage signal, still if the amplitude of the signal is limited and if certain design precautions are adopted, the nonlinearity may be neglected. With these assumptions an actual pentode as shown in Fig. 15-1a may be replaced by the Norton equivalent circuit of Fig. 15-1b, in so far as the alternating components of the signals are concerned. g_m is the "mutual conductance," or "grid-plate transconductance," and r_p the a-c "plate resistance," of the tube.

The *unilateral* property of the vacuum tube under the assumed condi-

---

[1] So-called d-c amplifiers can also be built which are true LP amplifiers, but they introduce considerable difficulties and so are used only where absolutely necessary to amplify very slowly changing unidirectional signals.

[2] The student may observe that the definition of voltage amplification given here is identical to that for the transfer function in Chap. 14 and is also one form of the immittance function described in Chap. 2. It is common practice to use A for active networks in which $|E_{\text{out}}|/|E_{in}| > 1$ and T for passive networks where, in general, $|E_{\text{out}}|/|E_{in}| < 1$.

tions is apparent from the equivalent circuit (Fig. 15-1b). A signal E_g applied between the grid and ground affects the plate circuit through the *dependent* current generator $g_m E_g$, but the plate circuit has no corresponding effect on the input or grid circuit. The importance of this unilateral property in isolating the load circuits of adjacent amplifier stages in a cascade will be discussed later in the chapter.

It is a physically demonstrable fact that g_m and r_p are independent of frequency below the uhf or vhf ranges; hence it is evident from Fig. 15-1b that the frequency response of the vacuum-tube amplifier is dependent

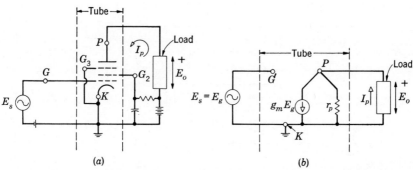

FIG. 15-1. Basic pentode amplifier. (*a*) Actual circuit. It is assumed that G_2 is at a-c cathode potential. (*b*) Equivalent a-c circuit. Linear operation is assumed.

solely upon the linear passive circuit elements comprising the load and the plate-to-cathode and grid-to-cathode interelectrode capacitances (C_{pk} and C_{gk}). For this reason, even though a vacuum tube is part of the circuit, the frequency-response ($|A|$ vs. f) problem is one involving linear passive elements, and the methods of analysis used in the previous chapters may be applied.

15-2. Basic RC Amplifier. The basic amplifier circuit is the familiar resistance-capacitance-coupled amplifier of Fig. 15-2a and also discussed in Chap. 2. C_c is the coupling, or blocking, capacitor which serves to isolate the output terminals from the d-c plate voltage. C_o is the output capacitance of the vacuum tube plus the ever-present stray capacitances of the tube socket and plate lead to ground. C_i is the input capacitance of whatever circuit is connected across the output terminals plus the stray capacitances between the output lead and C_c to ground. It is convenient to define the total shunt capacitance as

$$C_s = C_o + C_i \tag{15-2}$$

The equivalent circuit which results from replacing the tube by its Norton equivalent is shown at b in Fig. 15-2.

In typical broad-band applications the circuit values are such that

$R_L \ll R_g < r_p$ and $C_s \ll C_c$. As was shown in Chap. 2, these differences in order of magnitude permit the circuit behavior to be analyzed in terms of three different frequency bands which are determined by the relative significance of the capacitive reactances. The mid-band region will be considered first because it serves as a basis of normalizing the response.

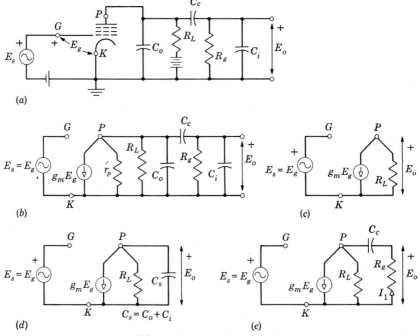

(a)

(b)

(c)

(d)

(e)

FIG. 15-2. Basic RC amplifier. (a) Complete circuit. (b) Complete equivalent circuit. Approximate circuits: (c) Mid-band. (d) High-band. (e) Low-band.

Mid-band. In the mid-band of frequencies the reactance magnitude of C_c is negligibly small, and that of C_s very large compared with R_L. Hence C_c may be considered as a short circuit and C_s as an open circuit. Then since $R_L \ll R_g < r_p$, the approximate mid-band equivalent circuit has the form shown in Fig. 15-2c, and by Eq. (15-1) the mid-band voltage amplification or gain will be

$$A_m = \left(\frac{E_o}{E_s}\right)_{\text{mid-band}} = -g_m R_L \qquad (15\text{-}3)$$

High-band. At frequencies above the mid-band the reactance of C_c remains negligibly small, but the reactance of C_s approaches R_L in magnitude; hence the approximate equivalent high-band circuit has the form of Fig. 15-2d. The high-band gain will be

$$A_h = \left(\frac{E_o}{E_s}\right)_{\text{high-band}} = -\frac{g_m R_L}{1 + j\omega C_s R_L} \qquad (15\text{-}4)$$

and, normalizing with respect to the mid-band gain of Eq. (15-3),

$$\frac{A_h}{A_m} = \frac{1}{1 + j\omega C_s R_L} = \frac{1}{1 + jf/f_2} \qquad (15\text{-}4a)$$

where $$f_2 = \frac{1}{2\pi C_s R_L}$$

Comparison of Eqs. (15-4a) and (14-26) shows that the former can be handled by the corner-plot method and that f_2 is a negative corner fre-

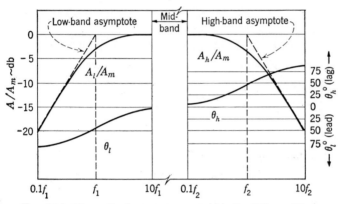

FIG. 15-3. Normalized response curves for the RC amplifier.

quency. In the study of amplifiers f_2 is often called the "upper half-power frequency" because it lies near the upper end of the response curve and because at f_2 the output voltage is 3 db below the mid-band value, corresponding to a voltage ratio of $1/\sqrt{2}$. Since power is proportional to the square of voltage for a constant R_L, the power delivered to R_L at f_2 is one-half the value delivered in the mid-band.

From Eq. (15-4a) the angle between A_h and A_m is

$$\theta_h = -\arctan\frac{f}{f_2} \qquad (15\text{-}4b)$$

that is, the high-band output voltage *lags* the mid-band output voltage. The high-band normalized amplitude and phase responses are plotted in Fig. 15-3.

Low-band. At frequencies below the mid-band the reactances of C_o and C_i become very large, while the reactance of C_c is of the same order of magnitude as R_g; hence the approximate low-band circuit has the form shown in Fig. 15-2e. By the current-division theorem

$$E_o = -I_1 R_g = -\frac{g_m E_g R_L R_g}{(R_g + R_L) - j/\omega C_c}$$

But $R_L \ll R_g$; hence the low-band gain is

$$A_l = \left(\frac{E_o}{E_s}\right)_{\text{low-band}} = -\frac{g_m R_L}{1 - j/\omega C_c R_g} \tag{15-5}$$

Normalizing with respect to A_m of Eq. (15-3),

$$\frac{A_l}{A_m} = \frac{1}{1 - jf_1/f} \tag{15-5a}$$

where

$$f_1 = \frac{1}{2\pi C_c R_g}$$

Comparison with Eq. (14-36) shows that f_1 is a lower negative corner frequency; hence Eq. (15-5a) may be handled by the corner-plot method. In usual amplifier parlance f_1 is called the "lower half-power frequency."

From Eq. (15-5a) the angle between A_l and A_m is

$$\theta_l = \arctan\frac{f_1}{f} \tag{15-5b}$$

i.e., the low-band output voltage *leads* the mid-band output voltage. The normalized low-band responses are shown in Fig. 15-3.

15-3. Figure of Merit. The foregoing results show that the upper half-power frequency f_2 and the mid-band gain magnitude $|A_m|$ are interrelated through the plate-load resistance R_L and that, for typical circuit-parameter values, f_1, the lower half-power frequency, is independent of R_L. As a consequence a figure of merit for the RC stage may be defined as the product of $|A_m|$ and f_2. Thus from Eqs. (15-3) and (15-4a)

$$|A_m|f_2 = \frac{g_m}{2\pi C_s} \tag{15-6}$$

As a practical matter for typical circuit values, $f_1 \ll f_2$; hence, to a good approximation, the half-power bandwidth is

$$BW = f_2 - f_1 \approx f_2 \tag{15-7}$$

and Eq. (15-6) may be written as

$$|A_m|(BW) \approx \frac{g_m}{2\pi C_s} \tag{15-6a}$$

The practical consequence of this equation is that, by lowering R_L, one may sacrifice mid-band gain for increased bandwidth, but the product

$|A_m|(BW)$ remains constant. Equation (15-6a) shows that for broadband amplifiers a tube should be chosen that has a high mutual conductance g_m and a low value of C_s. C_i and whatever stray capacitances are present should be held to a minimum by careful wiring techniques. Some typical orders of magnitude may be obtained from the following example:

A 6AC7 is to be used as a broad-band amplifier. $g_m = 9{,}000$ μmhos, and $C_s = 20$ $\mu\mu$f. What R_L is required for $f_2 = 4.5$ Mc? What is $|A_m|$?

By Eq. (15-4a)

$$R_L = \frac{1}{2\pi f_2 C_s} = \frac{1}{2\pi(4.5 \times 10^6)(2 \times 10^{-11})} = 1.77 \text{ kilohms}$$

By Eq. (15-3)

$$|A_m| = g_m R_L = (9 \times 10^{-3}) \times 1.77 \times 10^3 = 15.9 \text{ numeric}$$

It should be noted that, if f_2 is doubled, $|A_m|$ is halved, or vice versa, by virtue of Eq. (15-6).

Typical values for C_c and R_g might be 0.1 μf and 100 kilohms, respectively. For these values the lower half-power frequency is by Eq. (15-5a)

$$f_1 = \frac{1}{2\pi C_c R_g} = \frac{1}{2\pi \times 10^{-7} \times 10^5} = 15.9 \text{ cycles}$$

15-4. Effect of Self-bias Circuit. It is usual practice to use self-bias for the RC stage, the common circuit being the parallel combination of R_K and C_K in the cathode return as shown in Fig. 15-4a. The bias voltage is provided by the d-c plate and screen currents of the pentode flowing through R_K, which will generally have a value between 100 and 200 ohms. C_K is generally made very large so that the a-c impedance between cathode and ground is small. Thus in typical circuits $C_K \gg C_c$ and $R_K < R_L$. The presence of C_K introduces another frequency effect on the gain characteristic, confined to the low end of the band, because C_K is so large that, in the mid- and high-frequency-bands, the a-c impedance between the cathode and ground is essentially zero. The effect of the $C_K R_K$ combination on the low-band response may be determined by setting up and solving the nodal equations for the equivalent low-band circuit (Fig. 15-4b). The nodal equations for Fig. 15-4b are

$$(G_K + j\omega C_K)E_K = g_m E_g = g_m(E_s - E_K)$$
$$(G_L + j\omega C_c)E_p - j\omega C_c E_o = -g_m E_g = -g_m(E_s - E_K) \qquad (15\text{-}8)$$
$$-j\omega C_c E_p + (G_g + j\omega C_c)E_o = 0$$

Solution of these equations, simplified by the fact that $R_g \gg R_L$, yields the result

$$\frac{A_l}{A_m} = \frac{1 + j\omega C_K R_K}{(1 + g_m R_K) + j\omega C_K R_K}\left(\frac{1}{1 - j/\omega C_c R_g}\right) \qquad (15\text{-}9)$$

Comparison of Eqs. (15-9) and (15-5a) shows that the effect of the self-bias combination is to multiply the normalized low-band response by the

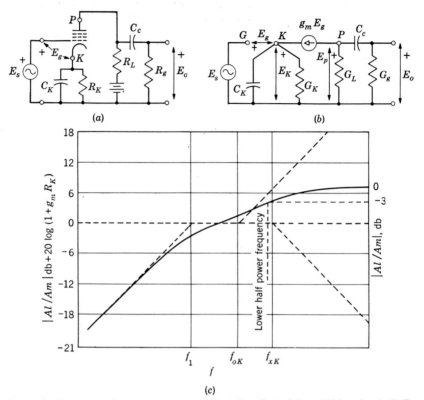

Fɪɢ. 15-4. Circuits and response curve showing the effect of the self-bias circuit $C_K R_K$.

factor $(1 + j\omega C_K R_K)/[(1 + g_m R_K) + j\omega C_K R_K]$. This effect may be shown graphically by means of corner plots. Rearranging Eq. (15-9),

$$\frac{A_l}{A_m} = \frac{1}{1 + g_m R_K}\left(\frac{1 + jf/f_{oK}}{1 + jf/f_{xK}}\right)\left(\frac{1}{1 - jf_1/f}\right)$$

where
$$f_{oK} = \frac{1}{2\pi C_K R_K}$$

$$f_{xK} = \frac{1 + g_m R_K}{2\pi C_K R_K}$$

$$f_1 = \frac{1}{2\pi C_c R_g}$$

(15-10)

The resulting amplitude response is shown by the solid line in Fig. 15-4c for a case where $f_1 < f_{oK} < f_{xK}$. The asymptotes for the three corners are shown by the dashed lines. It should be observed for the case illustrated that the lower half-power frequency is determined predominantly by the self-bias combination rather than by R_g and C_c.*

15-5. Cascaded Stages. Because of the isolation afforded by a vacuum-tube the over-all response of two or more amplifiers connected in cascade is the product of the individual responses. This may be shown from Fig. 15-5. By definition the over-all, or total, gain is $A_T = E_{o2}/E_{s1}$. From the diagram

$$A_T = \frac{E_{o2}}{E_{s1}} = \frac{E_{o1}}{E_{s1}} \frac{E_{o2}}{E_{s2}} = A_1 A_2 \tag{15-11}$$

Furthermore the isolation property allows adjustments to be made on one stage without affecting the individual responses of any of the other

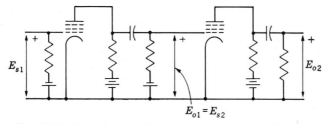

E_{s1}

E_{o2}

$E_{o1} = E_{s2}$

Fig. 15-5. Circuit for calculating the gain of cascaded stages.

stages in the cascade, even though the over-all response reflects a corresponding change. It is of interest to observe what happens to the bandwidth and mid-band gain when n *identical* stages are cascaded. By Eq. (15-11) the over-all mid-band gain will be

$$|A_m|_T = |A_m|^n \tag{15-12}$$

The effect on the over-all upper half-power frequency F_2 of cascading identical stages may be observed by the student if he will sketch the asymptotic high-band responses for, say, one, two, and three identical RC stages. The problem may be approached analytically in the following manner: From Eq. (15-4a) the magnitude of the normalized high-band gain for each stage is

$$\left|\frac{A_h}{A_m}\right| = \frac{1}{\sqrt{1 + (f/f_2)^2}} \tag{15-13}$$

where f_2 is the half-power frequency of each individual stage. By Eqs. (15-11) and (15-13) the normalized gain of n identical stages will be

$$\left|\frac{A_h}{A_m}\right|^n = \frac{1}{[1 + (f/f_2)^2]^{n/2}} \tag{15-13a}$$

* The effect of an inadequately bypassed screen grid is similar to that of the self-bias circuit. See, for example, F. E. Terman, "*Radio Engineer's Handbook*," p. 358, McGraw-Hill Book Company, Inc., New York, 1943.

Now by definition, at the over-all upper half-power frequency, say, F_2, the normalized response is down 3 db or is equal to $1/\sqrt{2}$; hence, substituting $f = F_2$ in Eq. (15-13a) and inverting,

$$[1 + (F_2/f_2)^2]^{n/2} = 2^{\frac{1}{2}}$$

or
$$F_2 = f_2 \sqrt{2^{1/n} - 1} \qquad (15\text{-}14)$$

The quantity $F_2/f_2 = \sqrt{2^{1/n} - 1}$ is often designated the "bandwidth shrinkage factor" and is tabulated in Table 15-1. The student may

TABLE 15-1. BANDWIDTH SHRINKAGE FACTOR $\mathfrak{F}$
For RC amplifier $\mathfrak{F} = F_2/f_2 \approx (BW)_T/BW$
For single-tuned amplifier $\mathfrak{F} = (BW)_T/BW$

n........	1	2	3	4	5	6	7	8	9	10
$\mathfrak{F}$........	1.000	0.644	0.510	0.434	0.385	0.350	0.323	0.308	0.284	0.268

derive a similar factor for F_1/f_1, F_1 being the over-all lower half-power frequency and f_1 the lower half-power frequency of each stage in the cascade. In typical cascades of wide-band RC stages $F_1 \ll F_2$; hence to a good approximation the over-all bandwidth $(BW)_T$ is given by

$$(BW)_T = F_2 - F_1 \approx F_2$$

Then the gain-bandwidth product of n identical, cascaded stages is

$$|A_m|_T (BW)_T = |A_m|^n (BW) \sqrt{2^{1/n} - 1} \qquad (15\text{-}15)$$

It may be observed that, as n increases, the gain increases faster than the bandwidth shrinks.

An amplifier is to be designed to have an over-all upper half-power frequency of 5 Mc and an over-all voltage gain of at least 50 db. Determine the number of identical stages required in cascade if 6AC7's are used ($g_m = 9,000$ μmhos). The shunt capacitance per stage is estimated to be 20 $\mu\mu$f.

Converting the decibels gain to a numeric,

$$|A_m|_T = 10^{50/20} = 10^{2.5} = 316$$

A trial-and-error process is used. By Eq. (15-6a) for $n = 1$

$$|A_m| f_2 = \frac{g_m}{2\pi C_s} = \frac{9 \times 10^{-3}}{2\pi(2 \times 10^{-11})} = 71.5 \text{ Mc}$$

$$f_2 = 5 \text{ Mc} \qquad |A_m| = \frac{71.5}{5} = 14.3 \text{ numeric}$$

For $n = 2$ by Table 15-1 f_2 must be

$$f_2 = \frac{5}{0.644} \qquad |A_m| = \frac{71.5 \times 0.644}{5} = 9.2 \qquad |A_m|^2 = 84.4$$

For $n = 3$

$$f_2 = \frac{5}{0.51} \qquad |A_m| = \frac{71.5 \times 0.51}{5} = 7.3 \qquad |A_m|^3 = 390$$

Since 390 exceeds the minimum required over-all gain, three identical stages each having an $f_2 = 9.8$ Mc and a mid-band gain of 7.3 will be satisfactory. By Eq. (15–3) the required plate-load resistance for each stage must be

$$R_L = \frac{|A_m|}{g_m} = \frac{7.3}{9 \times 10} = 811 \text{ ohms}$$

The method of corner plots affords a good means of determining over-all gain-bandwidth products when cascades of stages not identical are encountered.

15-6. Compensation. Equation (15-6) shows that the mid-band gain of the basic RC stage may be reduced in exchange for a higher upper half-power frequency, and vice versa, their product remaining constant. Such a trading by changing the value of R_L, however, has no effect whatsoever on the *shape* of the gain vs. frequency curve, as shown by Eqs. (15-4a) and (15-5a). In both the low and high bands the magnitude of the gain decreases toward a 6 db/octave asymptote.

A change in this characteristic shape may be brought about by modifying the basic RC stage with additional components, a process known as "compensation." Compensation of the low- and high-frequency ends of the response curves is handled independently. The general methods which may be used are discussed in the following sections.

15-7. High-frequency Compensation. The decrease in high-frequency gain of the RC amplifier is due to the presence of C_s, the total shunt capacitance across the coupling network. A method of modifying the high-frequency response is to add inductance in the network to cancel out partially the effects of this capacitance. Some typical high-band compensating circuits are shown in Fig. 15-6, the "shunt-compensated" network a being the most commonly used. Attention, for the most part, will be devoted to this circuit.

By writing the circuit equations for the shunt-compensated network of Fig. 15-6a the student may readily verify that

$$\frac{A_h}{A_m} = \frac{1 + j(\omega_2 L/R_L)(\omega/\omega_2)}{[1 - (\omega_2 L/R_L)(\omega/\omega_2)^2] + j\omega/\omega_2} \tag{15-16}$$

where $\omega_2 = 2\pi f_2$

f_2 = upper half-power frequency *without* compensation
  $= 1/2\pi C_s R_L$

In the work which follows it is convenient to replace $\omega_2 L/R_L$ by a design parameter Q, which is the effective figure of merit of the inductive branch

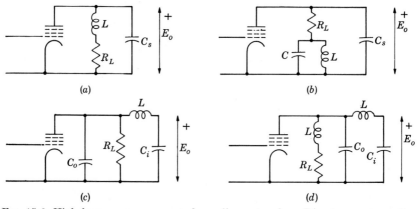

FIG. 15-6. High-frequency-compensated coupling networks. Direct-current supplies, C_c, and R_g are omitted for simplicity. (a) Shunt-compensated. (b) m-derived network. (c) Series-compensated. (d) Series-shunt-compensated. Networks a and b are of the two-terminal type, c and d of the four-terminal type.

at f_2, and f/f_2 by y, the normalized frequency variable. Thus

$$\frac{A_h}{A_m} = \frac{1 + jQy}{(1 - Qy^2) + jy}$$

$$Q = \frac{\omega_2 L}{R_L} \qquad y = \frac{f}{f_2} \tag{15-16a}$$

Reducing to polar form,

$$\left|\frac{A_h}{A_m}\right|^2 = \frac{1 + Q^2 y^2}{1 + (1 - 2Q)y^2 + Q^2 y^4} \tag{15-17a}$$

$$\theta_h = \arctan Qy - \arctan \frac{y}{1 - Qy^2} \tag{15-17b}$$

The expression for θ_h may be simplified by means of the familiar trigonometric identity.

$$\tan(\varphi_1 \pm \varphi_2) = \frac{\tan \varphi_1 \pm \tan \varphi_2}{1 \mp \tan \varphi_1 \tan \varphi_2} \tag{15-18}$$

Let

$$\tan \varphi_1 = x_1 \qquad \varphi_1 = \arctan x_1$$
$$\tan \varphi_2 = x_2 \qquad \varphi_2 = \arctan x_2 \tag{15-19}$$

Substituting,

$$\arctan x_1 \pm \arctan x_2 = \arctan \frac{x_1 \pm x_2}{1 \mp x_1 x_2} \tag{15-20}$$

Thus, by Eq. (15-20), Eq. (15-17b) may be simplified to

$$\theta_h = -\arctan[y(1 - Q + Q^2 y^2)] \tag{15-17c}$$

A more satisfactory parameter than θ_h is the group delay τ_g defined by Eq. (6-49) because τ_g should be constant for no delay distortion. Since

θ_h is a lagging angle, τ_g for the shunt-compensated amplifier is

$$\tau_g = \frac{d|\theta_h|}{d\omega} = \frac{1}{\omega_2}\frac{d|\theta_h|}{dy}$$

Then, substituting from Eq. (15-17c),

$$\tau_g = \frac{1}{\omega_2}\frac{(1-Q)+3Q^2y^2}{1+y^2[(1-Q)+Q^2y^2]^2} \tag{15-17d}$$

Curves of $\omega_2\tau_g$ are plotted for several values of Q in Fig. 15-7b.

It may be shown from Eq. (15-17a) that the high-frequency asymptote of the shunt-compensated amplifier gain is -20 db/decade (-6 db/octave) regardless of the value of Q. At very high frequencies $y^4 \gg y^2 \gg 1$, and the equation reduces to

$$\left|\frac{A_h}{A_m}\right| \approx \sqrt{\frac{Q^2y^2}{Q^2y^4}} = \frac{1}{y} \tag{15-21}$$

Hence the hf asymptote will be

$$\left|\frac{A_h}{A_m}\right|_{db} = -20\log y \tag{15-21a}$$

which corresponds to a -20 db/decade slope. While this result may seem odd at first glance because inductance is present, it is easy to reconcile with the physical situation. It may be seen from Fig. 15-6a that C_s *shunts* the R_LL branch. Thus, as frequency is raised, the reactance of C_s, and the total load impedance as well, approaches zero; so C_s becomes the important element in determining the response.

While the hf asymptote is independent of the value of Q, the shape of the actual response curve below and in the vicinity of f_2 may be controlled by a suitable choice of Q. This is illustrated in Fig. 15-7a. It may be noted that the addition of inductance causes the actual response to approach the asymptote in an entirely different manner from what it does for the basic RC stage ($Q = 0$ in the figure). Figure 15-7b illustrates how Q may also be used to control the time-delay characteristic.

15-8. Maximally Flat Amplitude Response. It has been shown in connection with Eq. (14-17) in the last chapter that the square of the amplitude response of a network may be written as the ratio of two polynomials involving only *even* powers of the frequency variable. Equation (15-17a) further verifies this statement, and one may write in general

$$|T|^2 = \frac{a_0 + a_2y^2 + a_4y^4 + a_6y^6 + \cdots}{b_0 + b_2y^2 + b_4y^4 + b_6y^6 + \cdots} \tag{15-22}$$

T being a generalized response function and y a normalized frequency variable. The amplitude response $|T|$ is said to be "maximally flat"

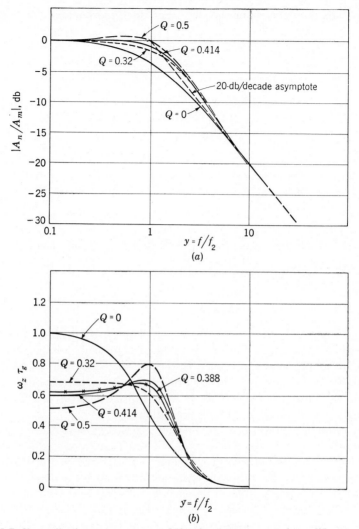

Fig. 15-7. Normalized response curves of the shunt-compensated amplifier as a function of $Q = \omega_2 L/R_L$. (a) Amplitude. (b) Group delay.

when $|T| \approx K$, K being a scalar constant, over the widest possible range of the frequency variable. If the a's and b's are subject to adjustment, they are chosen to bring about the maximally flat condition in the following manner: Factor out a_0 and b_0 from Eq. (15-22).

$$|T|^2 = \frac{a_0}{b_0} \frac{1 + (a_2/a_0)y^2 + (a_4/a_0)y^4 + (a_6/a_0)y^6 + \cdots}{1 + (b_2/b_0)y^2 + (b_4/b_0)y^4 + (b_6/b_0)y^6 + (b_8/b_0)y^8} \quad (15\text{-}22a)$$

Then, for maximal flatness, the coefficients of corresponding powers of y

in the numerator and denominator must be equated for as many of the terms as possible, i.e., one sets

$$\frac{a_n}{a_0} = \frac{b_n}{b_0} \tag{15-23}$$

starting with the lowest powers of y.* This concept may be applied to the shunt-compensated circuit of Fig. 15-6a and described by Eq. (15-17a) to find the value of Q which yields a maximally flat response. It is apparent from Eq. (15-17a) that only one pair of coefficients may be matched in this case, those of the y^2 terms; hence by Eq. (15-23)

$$Q^2 = 1 - 2Q$$

or
$$Q = -1 \pm \sqrt{2} \qquad \text{maximally flat response}$$

It may be noted that the negative sign preceding the radical gives a result that cannot be realized: since $Q = \omega_2 L/R_L$, if $Q = -2.414$, either negative inductance or resistance is required; hence the positive sign is chosen. Then $Q = 0.414$ gives a maximally flat response. The response shape is shown in Fig. 15-7a.

It may also be demonstrated that the maximally flat condition gives an increase in half-power frequency above the value of the uncompensated stage. Let f_2' be the upper half-power frequency *with compensation*. By definition, at f_2', $|A_h/A_m| = 1/\sqrt{2}$. Then substituting $Q = 0.414$ in Eq. (15-17a),

$$\left|\frac{A_h}{A_m}\right|^2_{f_2'} = \frac{1 + (0.414)^2(y_2')^2}{1 + [1 - 2(0.414)](y_2')^2 + (0.414)^2(y_2')^4} = \frac{1}{2}$$

Solving for y_2',

$$y_2' = \frac{f_2'}{f_2} = 1.72$$

$$f_2' = 1.72 f_2 \tag{15-24}$$

It may be seen, then, that the maximally flat condition gives a 72 per cent increase in upper half-power frequency over the basic stage.

Redesign the 6AC7 amplifier of Sec. 15-3, using shunt compensation adjusted for the maximally flat condition. Note the increase in mid-band gain that results.

To simplify comparison, let primes be used to designate modified values of load resistance and mid-band gain. By the specifications $f_2' = 4.5$ Mc. By Eqs. (15-4a) and (15-24)

$$R_L' = \frac{1}{2\pi f_2 C_s} = \frac{1.72}{2\pi f_2' C_s} = 1.72 R_L = 3.04 \text{ kilohms}$$

---

* It may be demonstrated that the maximally flat condition also results by setting equal to zero as many as possible of the successive derivatives of $|T|^2$ with respect to y, evaluated at $y = 0$ (see Prob. 15-5).

By Eqs. (15-16a) and (15-24)

$$L = \frac{QR'_L}{\omega_2} = \frac{1.72QR'_L}{\omega'_2} = \frac{(1.72 \times 0.414)(3.04 \times 10^3)}{2\pi(4.5 \times 10^6)} = 76.4 \ \mu\text{h}$$

$$|A'_m| = g_m R'_L = 1.72 g_m R_L = 1.72|A_m| = 27.4 \text{ numeric}$$

It may be observed that the addition of compensation has given a 72 per cent increase in mid-band gain over the original design.

15-9. Maximally Flat Delay Characteristic. The technique outlined in the last section may also be used to find the value of Q which gives the most linear phase response, or maximally flat group delay characteristic, with the shunt-compensated circuit. It is left as an exercise for the student to show from Eq. (15-17d) that the value of Q required for this condition is 0.32. The resulting response curves are shown in Fig. 15-7.

15-10. Transient Response of a Shunt-compensated Amplifier. The results thus far in the chapter have been concerned with the steady-state response of a quasi-LP amplifier. In communication systems where the waveform of the transmitted signal must be maintained to a reasonable accuracy, e.g., in television, it is the transient response which becomes of importance. As pointed out in Chap. 2 the steady-state and transient responses are interrelated through the poles and zeros of the network response function. It was also shown that the "leading edge" of the transient response to a step voltage is related to the high-band steady-state characteristics. Thus the edge response may be predicted for the shunt-compensated stage by examining the zeros and poles of the equivalent circuit of Fig. 15-6a. Reading from the diagram,

$$E_o = -g_m E_g \frac{R_L + j\omega L}{1 + j\omega C_s R_L + (j\omega)^2 LC_s} \tag{15-25}$$

Factoring out L/LC_s and replacing $j\omega$ by the complex frequency variable p,

$$E_o(p) = -\frac{g_m}{C_s} E_g(p) \frac{p + (R_L/L)}{p^2 + R_L p/L + 1/LC_s} \tag{15-26}$$

Let the grid voltage be a negative step function $-EU(t)$. Then from Table 2-1

$$E_g(p) = -\frac{E_g}{p} \tag{15-27}$$

Then

$$E_o(p) = \frac{g_m}{C_s} E_g \frac{p + p_o}{p(p - \alpha)(p - \beta)} \tag{15-28}$$

where $p_o = -R_L/L$, a zero, and

$$\begin{matrix} \alpha \\ \beta \end{matrix} = -\frac{R_L}{2L} \pm \sqrt{\left(\frac{R_L}{2L}\right)^2 - \frac{1}{LC_s}}, \text{ poles} \tag{15-29}$$

It is convenient to restate Eq. (15-29) in terms of Q and ω_2 to provide a better correlation with the steady-state curves. From Eq. (15-16a)

$$\frac{R_L}{2L} = \frac{\omega_2}{2Q} \tag{15-30a}$$

and from Eq. (15-16)

$$C_s = \frac{1}{\omega_2 R_L} \tag{15-30b}$$

Then

$$LC_s = \frac{Q}{\omega_2{}^2} \tag{15-30c}$$

By means of these identities the poles of Eqs. (15-29) may be rewritten as

$$\frac{\alpha}{\beta} = \frac{\omega_2}{2Q}(-1 \pm \sqrt{1 - 4Q}) \tag{15-29a}$$

It may be seen, then, that the location of the poles in the complex plane, and hence the transient response, depends upon the value of Q.

For example, consider the case where $4Q < 1$ or $Q < 0.25$. Then the two poles are real, negative, and of different values as shown in Fig. 15-8a. Expanding Eq. (15-28) by partial fractions

$$E_o(p) = \frac{g_m E_g}{C_s}\frac{p + p_o}{p(p - \alpha)(p - \beta)} \tag{15-26a}$$

$$= \frac{g_m E_g}{C_s}\left(\frac{A}{p} + \frac{B}{p - \alpha} + \frac{C}{p - \beta}\right) \tag{15-26b}$$

and by the mates listed in Table 2-1

$$e_o(t) = \frac{g_m E_g}{C_s}(A + Be^{\alpha t} + Ce^{\beta t}) \tag{15-31}$$

indicating an overdamped transient response as shown in Fig. 15-8a.

On the other hand, if $4Q = 1$ or $Q = 0.25$, the two poles of Eq. (15-29a) coalesce into a single second-order pole which gives the critically damped response of Fig. 15-8b.

A third possibility is afforded if $4Q > 1$ or $Q > 0.25$, in which case the poles [Eq. (15-29a)] become

$$\frac{\alpha}{\beta} = \frac{\omega_2}{2Q}(-1 \pm j\sqrt{4Q - 1}) \tag{15-32}$$

that is, the poles are complex conjugates leading to an overshoot type of response as shown in Fig. 15-8c.

The degenerate case for $Q = 0$, which corresponds to the uncompensated RC stage, has been covered in Chap. 2 but is shown again in Fig. 15-8d for comparison.

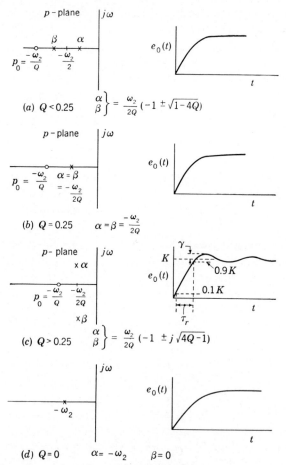

$$(a) \quad Q < 0.25 \qquad \left.\begin{array}{c}\alpha\\\beta\end{array}\right\} = \frac{\omega_2}{2Q}(-1 \pm \sqrt{1-4Q})$$

$$(b) \quad Q = 0.25 \qquad \alpha = \beta = \frac{-\omega_2}{2Q}$$

$$(c) \quad Q > 0.25 \qquad \left.\begin{array}{c}\alpha\\\beta\end{array}\right\} = \frac{\omega_2}{2Q}(-1 \pm j\sqrt{4Q-1})$$

$$(d) \quad Q = 0 \qquad \alpha = -\omega_2 \qquad \beta = 0$$

Fig. 15-8. Pole and zero locations and the transient response to step function of a shunt-compensated amplifier for different ranges of Q.

Transient-response curves for the shunt-compensated amplifier are plotted to scale for different values of Q in Fig. 15-9. These curves illustrate the effect of Q on the "rise time," "overshoot," and "ring." These and related quantities are defined as follows:

Pulse amplitude is the maximum instantaneous value of a pulse. *Note.* Spikes and ripples superimposed on the pulse are commonly considered to be separate transients and are ignored in considering the dimensions of the pulse itself. [ASA C42 65.02.078 (1953).]

A *spike* is a transient of short duration, comprising part of a pulse, during which the amplitude considerably exceeds the average amplitude of the pulse. [ASA C42 65.02.087 (1953).]

Overshoot is the initial transient response to a unidirectional change in input which exceeds the steady-state response. [ASA C42 65.02.085 (1953).] See γ in Fig. 15-8c.

Pulse rise time is the interval of time required for the leading edge of a pulse to rise from 10 per cent to 90 per cent of the pulse amplitude. [ASA C42 65.02.081 (1953).] See τ_r in Fig. 15-8c.

The term *ring*, while not defined by the ASA in this sense, is often used to describe the presence of oscillatory variations in the pulse about the steady-state amplitude.

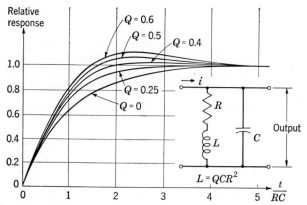

Fig. 15-9. Transient response to a step function of the shunt-compensated amplifier as a function of Q. (*Proc. IRE.*)

It may be seen from Fig. 15-9 that τ_r may be shortened either by raising Q or by raising f_2, the uncompensated upper half-power frequency. Both these methods, however, produce disadvantages. If Q is raised above 0.25, the response "rings" and exhibits overshoot, γ. [From Eq. (15-32) it may be seen that the approximate angular frequency of the oscillation is $(\omega_2/2Q)\sqrt{4Q-1}$.] If f_2 is raised, the mid-band gain of the amplifier is lowered. In designing a shunt-compensated stage, then, a compromise must be made between short rise time, on the one hand, and small overshoot and reasonable mid-band gain, on the other.

Palmer and Mautner[1] have calculated curves of rise time and overshoot as a function of Q for a single shunt-compensated stage and recommend a value of $Q = 0.388$ as an optimum value. The corresponding approximate overshoot and rise time are $\gamma = 2$ per cent, $\tau_r = 1.27/\omega_2$. As a practical matter Q's between 0.32 and 0.4 are often used, indicating a compromise between the steady-state maximally flat amplitude and maximally flat delay conditions (see Fig. 15-7).

[1] R. C. Palmer and L. Mautner, A New Figure of Merit for the Transient Response of Video Amplifiers, *Proc. IRE*, vol. 37, p. 9, September, 1949.

Where n identical stages are connected in cascade, the design of each stage becomes more severe because overshoots and rise times accumulate, though not in a linear fashion, with n.   As a general guide,[1] if γ per stage is 2 per cent or less, the rise time for n stages is approximately $\sqrt{n}$ times τ_r for a single stage and γ will increase slowly.   Where γ per stage is 5 to 10 per cent, γ increases approximately by the factor $\sqrt{n}$.

Comparison of the steady-state $|A_h/A_m|$ and transient responses of Figs. 15-7a and 15-9 shows an interesting correlation between the two responses.   The higher values of Q give sharper "roll-offs," i.e., steeper cutoff characteristics above f_2 on the $|A_h/A_m|$ curve and a greater tendency to ring and overshoot in the transient curve, a tendency which was noted in connection with the so-called "ideal" filters discussed in Chap. 2. This serves as an excellent guide in predicting the transient response from a knowledge of the steady-state high-band characteristics; the sharper the cutoff, the shorter the rise time and the greater the tendency to ring. Also, high upper half-power frequency is related to short rise time.

The following example will give the reader some idea of the magnitudes involved in an actual stage:

Design a shunt-compensated stage using a 6AU6. $g_m = 5,000$ μmhos, and C_s is estimated at 20 $\mu\mu$f.   The rise time shall be 0.025 μsec and the overshoot 2 per cent.

From previous data use $Q = 0.388$; then $\tau_r = 1.27/\omega_2$.

$$\omega_2 = \frac{1.27}{\tau_r} = \frac{1.27}{0.25 \times 10^{-7}} = 5.08 \times 10^7 \text{ radians/sec}$$

By Eq. (15-4a)

$$R_L = \frac{1}{\omega_2 C_s} = \frac{1}{(5.08 \times 10^7)(2 \times 10^{-11})} = 983 \text{ ohms}$$

By Eq. (15-16a)

$$L = \frac{QR_L}{\omega_2} = \frac{0.388 \times 983}{5.08 \times 10^7} = 7.5 \ \mu\text{h}$$

The corresponding mid-band gain will be

$$|A_m| = g_m R_L = (5 \times 10^{-3})(0.983 \times 10^3) = 4.9 \text{ numeric}$$

As a practical matter the rise time specified in the example is rather severe.   It is impossible to realize in practice any input pulse of zero rise time such as is assumed when the step function is used in calculating the transient response.   As a general rule, τ_r for the amplifier need only be less than T_p, the rise time of the applied pulse, for a satisfactory response.   Of course, the shorter the value of τ_r, the better will be the

[1] G. E. Valley, Jr., and H. Wallman (eds.), "Vacuum Tube Amplifiers," MIT Radiation Laboratory Series, vol. 18, McGraw-Hill Book Company, Inc., New York, 1948.

response. Moskowitz and Racker[1] have suggested as a rule of thumb that f_2 of the amplifier should exceed or equal $1/2T_p$.

15-11. m-derived Network. In the preceding section it has been tacitly assumed that the inductor placed in series with R_L contributes only inductance. As a practical matter any inductor has shunt capacitance associated with it, and this capacitance may introduce effects not included in the preceding section. When this shunt capacitance (or additional capacitance intentionally introduced across L) is taken into account, the circuit has the form shown in Fig. 15-6b and is known as an m-derived shunt peaking network. It may be demonstrated without much difficulty that a proper choice of m gives a mid-band gain roughly 50 per cent greater than does the shunt-compensated stage for a given value of $\omega_2 = 1/C_s R_L$. As may be expected from the last section, the increase in gain is bought at the expense of good transient response.

The student may show that the normalized steady-state response of the m-derived network is given by

$$\frac{A_h}{A_m} = \frac{(1 - mQy^2) + jQy}{[1 - (m + 1)Qy^2] + jy(1 - mQy^2)} \tag{15-33}$$

where
$$m = \frac{C}{C_s} \qquad Q = \frac{\omega_2 L}{R_L} \qquad \omega_2 = \frac{1}{C_s R_L} \qquad y = \frac{f}{f_2} \tag{15-34}$$

The corresponding magnitude squared will be

$$\left|\frac{A_h}{A_m}\right|^2 = \frac{1 + (Q^2 - 2mQ)y^2 + m^2 Q^2 y^4}{1 + [1 - 2(m + 1)Q]y^2 + [(m + 1)^2 Q^2 - 2mQ]y^4 + m^2 Q^2 y^6} \tag{15-33a}$$

It is apparent that the presence of the y^6 term in the denominator means that the roll-off above f_2 will be steeper than it was for the shunt-compensated stage. The potential consequences are a shorter rise time and greater overshoot. It may also be seen that the high-frequency asymptote is still -20 db/decade. This may also be verified from physical considerations. At high frequencies the shunt capacitance C_s becomes the response-determining element, just as it was in the shunt-compensated circuit.

It may also be deduced that the maximal-flatness design condition in the m-derived network gives a flat response over a wider frequency range than does the shunt-compensated stage. This comes about because two, rather than one, design parameters are available; hence two pairs of terms in the numerator and denominator of Eq. (15-33a) may have their coefficients matched.

[1] S. Moskowitz and J. Racker, Pulse Amplifier Design, *Radio Television News*, Radio-Electronic Engineering Edition, vol. 10, p. 2, February, 1948.

The p-plane equation for the output-voltage response of the m-derived network to a *negative* step function $-E_g U(t)$ is

$$E_o(p) = \frac{g_m E_g}{C_s p} \frac{p^2 + (\omega_2/m)p + (\omega_2{}^2/mQ)}{p^3 + \dfrac{1+m}{m}\omega_2 p^2 + \dfrac{\omega_2{}^2}{mQ} p + \dfrac{\omega_2{}^3}{mQ}} \qquad (15\text{-}35)$$

where m, ω_2, and Q are defined as in Eqs. (15-34).

The character of the transient response will be determined by the poles of Eq. (15-35), i.e., by the factors of the third-degree polynominal in the denominator. It is immediately apparent that the determination of these

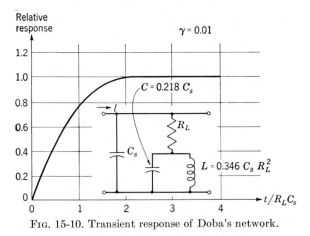

FIG. 15-10. Transient response of Doba's network.

poles (or the roots of the polynomial equated to zero), and hence the transient response, cannot be immediately deduced unless numerical values are known. A few general observations may be made, however.

The third-degree polynomial must have at least one *real* root, i.e., Eq. (15-35) has at least one real pole. The two other poles may be real and equal, real and unequal, or complex conjugates. The first two possibilities lead to a damped type of transient response with no ring. If two of the poles are complex conjugates, the transient response will overshoot and ring. The restrictions on m and Q corresponding to these conditions may be deduced by means of Tartaglia's solution of the general cubic equation;[1] however, the resulting expressions are so complicated as to be of little value. When numerical values of m and Q are specified, Tartaglia's solution may be used to find the poles of Eq. (15-35) and the equation expanded by partial fractions to obtain the transient response. (Alternatively, the real root of the polynomial may be found by plotting the value of the polynomial vs. assumed real negative values of p. The

[1] See, for example, W. L. Hart, "College Algebra," D. C. Heath and Company, Boston, 1926.

root is then the value of p for which the polynomial is zero. Division of the polynomial by this factor reduces the degree to 2 so that the two remaining roots may be found by the quadratic formula.)

S. Doba of the Bell Telephone Laboratories has recommended the values $m = 0.218$ and $Q = 0.346$ as giving a good transient response. The m-derived network with these values is frequently called "Doba's network." Its transient response is shown in Fig. 15-10.

15-12. Four-terminal Compensating Networks. The two high-band compensating circuits of Fig. 15-6c and d are four-terminal networks since a compensating inductance maintains the input and output terminals at different potentials. It is important to notice that C_o and C_i no longer combine as a single element C_s shunting R_L. As a consequence it may be expected that a higher mid-band gain may be realized for a given value of $f_2 = 1/2\pi C_s R_L$.

Consider the series-compensated circuit of Fig. 15-6c. Analysis of the circuit shows that the normalized high-band gain is given by

$$\frac{A_h}{A_m} = \frac{1}{1 - mQy^2/(1 + m) + j[y - mQy^3/(1 + m)^2]} \qquad (15\text{-}36)$$

where

$$m = \frac{C_i}{C_o} \qquad C_s = C_i + C_o \qquad \omega_2 = \frac{1}{C_s R_L}$$
$$Q = \frac{\omega_2 L}{R_L} \qquad y = \frac{f}{f_2} \qquad\qquad (15\text{-}37)$$

The corresponding magnitude squared and angle will be

$$\left|\frac{A_h}{A_m}\right|^2 = \frac{1}{1 + \left(1 - \dfrac{2mQ}{1 + m}\right)y^2 + \dfrac{mQ}{(1 + m)^2}(mQ - 2)y^4 + \dfrac{(mQ)^2}{(1 + m)^4}y^6}$$
$$(15\text{-}36a)$$

and

$$\theta_h = \arctan y\, \frac{1 - mQy^2/(1 + m)^2}{1 - mQy^2/(1 + m)} \qquad (15\text{-}36b)$$

It may be noted that the roll off above f_2 is quite steep because of the y^6 term. The high-frequency asymptote may be shown to be

$$\left|\frac{A_h}{A_m}\right|_{db} = 20 \log \frac{(1 + m)^2}{mQ} - 60 \log y \qquad (15\text{-}38)$$

Thus the asymptote has a negative slope of 60 db/decade, and its starting point on the ordinate scale at f_2 is a function of both m and Q. Hence the whole character of the high-band response differs from that for the previously considered circuits.

The edge response to a negative step function of amplitude $-E_g$ may be determined from the p-plane equation.

$$E_o(p) = \frac{g_m R_L E_g}{p} \frac{(1 + m)^2 \omega_2^3/mQ}{p^3 + (1 + m)\omega_2 p^2 + (1 + m)^2 \omega_2^2 p/mQ + (1 + m)^2 \omega_2^3/mQ} \quad (15\text{-}39)$$

The problem here is similar to that of the m-derived stage because the factors of the third-degree polynomial must be evaluated. A satisfactory transient response is provided by $Q = 0.467$ and $m = 2$. This latter value for the ratio C_i/C_o is typical for usual circuits.

Another four-terminal network, the series-shunt-compensated type, is shown in Fig. 15-6d. Still another is Dietzhold's network, which is a combination of Fig. 15-6b and a series-compensating inductance L_2. The network is named for R. L. Dietzhold of the Bell Telephone Laboratories, who specified the optimum values for the circuit parameters. The design parameters and transient performance for these and the previously discussed networks are summarized in Table 15-2.

TABLE 15-2. SUMMARY, HIGH-FREQUENCY COMPENSATION*

Network	Parameter values	$\tau_r \omega_2$	γ, %
Shunt	$L = \dfrac{0.388 R_L}{\omega_2}$	1.27	2
Doba's	$\dfrac{C}{C_s} = 0.218, L = \dfrac{0.346 R_L}{\omega_2}$	1.24	1
Series	$\dfrac{C_i}{C_o} = 2, L = \dfrac{0.467 R_L}{\omega_2}$	0.99	6.4†
Series-shunt	$\dfrac{C_i}{C_o} = 2, L_1 = \dfrac{0.133 R_L}{\omega_2}, L_2 = \dfrac{0.467 R_L}{\omega_2}$	0.907	1.8
Dietzhold	$\dfrac{C_i}{C_o} = 2, \dfrac{C}{C_s} = 0.145$ $L_1 = \dfrac{0.133 R_L}{\omega_2}, L_2 = \dfrac{0.467 R_L}{\omega_2}$	0.888	0.34

* R. C. Palmer and L. Mautner, A New Figure of Merit for the Transient Response of Video Amplifiers, *Proc. IRE*, vol. 37, p. 9, September, 1949.

† 6.4 is the magnitude of the first undershoot. The overshoot is significantly smaller.

15-13. Low-band Compensation. It has been shown in the early sections of the chapter that the loss in gain in the low band of the basic RC amplifier stage is due to the effects of the RC coupling network and to the degeneration caused by inadequate bypassing by C_K in the self-bias circuit. Either of these effects may be reduced by the lf compensating elements, C_1 and R_1, of Fig. 15-11. In the following work it will be assumed that $R_L \ll R_g$, the typical situation in broad-band applications.

Neglecting the self-bias circuit for the moment, it is easy to see from physical considerations how the compensating elements function. In the high and mid-bands C_1 effectively shorts out R_1 so that the plate load is

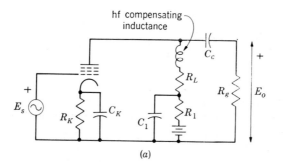

(a)

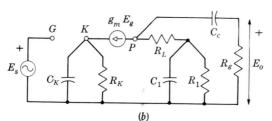

(b)

Fig. 15-11. Circuits for studying low-frequency compensation. R_1 and C_1 are the compensating elements.

R_L alone. At lf, however, the current generator $g_m E_g$ works into a higher load, $R_L + R_1/(1 + j\omega C_1 R_1)$, causing E_p, the plate voltage, to increase with lowered frequency. Stated mathematically,

$$E_p = -g_m E_g \left(R_L + \frac{R_1}{1 + j\omega C_1 R_1} \right) = -g_m E_g R_L \frac{(1 + R_1/R_L) + j\omega C_1 R_1}{1 + j\omega C_1 R_1}$$

$$= -g_m E_g (R_L + R_1) \frac{1 + j\omega C_1 R_L R_1/(R_L + R_1)}{1 + j\omega C_1 R_1} \qquad (15\text{-}40)$$

Thus, as the frequency is lowered from the mid-band toward zero, $|E_p|$ rises from $g_m E_g R_L$ toward $g_m E_g (R_L + R_1)$, giving the desired compensating action. The student may show that the low-band output voltage including the effects of the compensating, self-bias, and coupling networks is

$$E_o = -g_m E_g R_L \frac{(1 + R_1/R_L) + j\omega C_1 R_1}{1 + j\omega C_1 R_1} \frac{1 + j\omega C_K R_K}{(1 + g_m R_K) + j\omega C_K R_K}$$

$$\frac{1}{1 - j/\omega C_c R_g} \qquad (15\text{-}41)$$

and that

$$\frac{A_l}{A_m} = \underbrace{\frac{(1 + R_1/R_L) + j\omega C_1 R_1}{1 + j\omega C_1 R_1}}_{a} \underbrace{\frac{1 + j\omega C_K R_K}{(1 + g_m R_K) + j\omega C_K R_K}}_{b} \underbrace{\frac{1}{1 - j/\omega C_c R_g}}_{c}$$

$$(15\text{-}41a)$$

15-14. Bias-circuit Compensation. Since the factors a and b in Eq. (15-41a) are reciprocal in form, the first and most obvious use of the compensating circuit is to cancel out the degenerative effect of the self-bias circuit. Thus, to make $ab = 1$,

$$R_1 = g_m R_K R_L$$
$$C_1 = \frac{C_K R_K}{R_1} \qquad \text{bias-circuit compensation} \qquad (15\text{-}42)$$

When Eqs. (15-42) are satisfied, the normalized low-band response is determined solely by the $C_c R_g$ coupling network as described by Eq. (15-5a).

Actually this condition gives reasonably good results in practice. For example, if $C_c = 0.1$ μf and $R_g = 100$ kilohms, by Eq. (15-5a) the lower half-power frequency will be

$$f_1 = \frac{1}{2\pi \times 10^{-7} \times 10^5} = 15.9 \text{ cycles}$$

It should be noted, however, that this value tends to be a lower limit on f_1 for the following reasons: Tube manufacturers specify 100 to 500 kilohms as a maximum limit on R_g for most vacuum tubes. Also, increasing C_c above 0.1 μf generally will increase the physical size of the capacitor to the point where its contribution to the total shunt capacitance to ground, C_s, has an adverse effect on the *high-band* response.

It has been the usual practice to use an electrolytic-type capacitor for C_K, the value being 10 μf or more, shunted by a paper or mica dielectric unit of capacitance ranging around 0.01 to 0.1 μf. The need for this smaller unit is that the structure of the electrolytic units is such that in the high band they become inductive. The small shunt capacitor ensures adequate bypassing at the high-frequencies. Of course, in low-band calculations the small shunt unit may be neglected. Some idea of typical circuit values may be obtained from the following example:

A 6AC7 is used in a wide-band amplifier. $R_K = 160$ ohms, and

$$g_m = 9,000 \text{ μmhos}$$

R_L is chosen to be 3 kilohms from high-band considerations (maximally flat response with $f_2' = 4.5$ Mc, $f_2 = 2.62$ Mc). Assume $C_K = 10$ μf.

The compensating-network elements are determined from Eqs. (15-42).

$$R_1 = g_m R_K R_L = (9 \times 10^{-3}) \times 160 \times (3 \times 10^3) = 4.32 \text{ kilohms}$$
$$C_1 = \frac{C_K R_K}{R_1} = \frac{10^{-5} \times 160}{4.32 \times 10^3} = 0.37 \ \mu\text{f}$$

It may be noted, in passing, that at $0.1f_2$, which effectively defines the upper limit of the mid-band, the reactance of C_1 has a magnitude

$$\frac{1}{\omega C_1} = \frac{1}{2\mu(0.262 \times 10^6)(0.37 \times 10^{-6})} = 1.64 \text{ ohms}$$

This indicates adequate bypassing of R_1 in the high band so that the plate load is effectively R_L alone.

Professor M. H. Crothers of the University of Illinois has suggested that with bias-circuit compensation C_K need not be of so large a value that an electrolytic capacitor must be used. Since the compensating circuit cancels the effect of self-bias circuit degeneration, C_1 and C_K may be chosen so that R_1 is adequately bypassed in the high band. This is essential because C_s shunts the plate load and R_L is made small to satisfy the high-band design conditions.

By way of illustration, a 5 per cent increase in plate-load impedance may be tolerated at $0.1f_2$. Then, using the figures of the last example, it is desired that $1/2\pi(0.1f_2)C_1 \leq 0.05R_L$. Substituting,

$$C_1 \geq \frac{1}{2\pi(0.292 \times 10^6)(5 \times 10^{-2})(3 \times 10^3)} = 0.00363 \ \mu\text{f}$$

Let the next larger standard value be chosen so that

$$C_1 = 0.0039 \ \mu\text{f}. \quad \text{Then by Eq. (15-42)}$$
$$C_K = \frac{C_1 R_1}{R_K} = \frac{0.0039 \times 4.32}{0.16} = 0.117 \ \mu\text{f}$$

The saving in capacitor size (and hence cost) is quite apparent from these figures. Crothers has also suggested that, for bias-circuit compensation, tolerances should be specified for the *ratios* C_K/C_1 and R_1/R_L rather than on the values of the four components separately.

15-15. Coupling-circuit Compensation. In amplifiers using fixed bias or very large values of C_K (say, of the order of 100 μf) so that no degeneration occurs in the frequency band of interest, the compensating network R_1C_1 of Fig. 15-11 may be used to *partially* cancel out the low-band response of the coupling network R_gC_c. Since cathode degeneration is out of the picture, the factor b in Eq. (15-41a) is unity and the low-band response becomes

$$\frac{A_l}{A_m} = \frac{(1 + R_1/R_L) + j\omega C_1 R_1}{1 + j\omega C_1 R_1} \frac{1}{1 + 1/j\omega C_c R_g} \tag{15-43}$$

It may be observed that the two remaining factors are not inverse in form; hence complete or perfect compensation cannot be effected. For this reason a better idea of the compensating process may be had by use of corner plots.

Rearranging Eq. (15-43) into suitable form,

$$\frac{A_l}{A_m} = \frac{f_{o1}}{f_{x1}}\left(\frac{1 + jf/f_{o1}}{1 + jf/f_{x1}}\right)\left(\frac{1}{1 - jf_1/f}\right) \tag{15-44}$$

where

$$f_{o1} = \frac{R_1 + R_L}{2\pi C_1 R_1 R_L}$$

$$f_{x1} = \frac{1}{2\pi C_1 R_1} \tag{15-44a}$$

$$f_1 = \frac{1}{2\pi C_c R_g}$$

The response, then, is characterized by three corners, two of which, f_{o1} and f_{x1}, are subject to control by choice of C_1 and R_1, the compensating elements.

Say the design condition chosen is that $f_{o1} = f_1$. Then from Eqs. (15-44a)

$$\frac{C_1}{C_c} = \frac{R_g}{R_L}\left(1 + \frac{R_L}{R_1}\right) \qquad \text{coupling-network compensation} \tag{15-45}$$

The response for this design condition is shown in Fig. 15-12a. It may be observed that f_{x1} becomes the response-determining corner, so that f_1', the lower half-power frequency with compensation, is identical to f_{x1}. A low value of f_1' may be obtained by using a large value of C_1. It should be noted that C_1 does not contribute to C_s as does C_c; hence compensation allows a better low-band response without adversely affecting the high band.

Alternatively, C_1 and R_1 may be chosen such that $f_{x1} < f_1 < f_{o1}$ as illustrated in Fig. 15-12b. It may be seen that, for this case, a hump appears in the response curve, and the network is often said to be "over-compensated." Considerable freedom is available in choosing values of f_{o1} and f_{x1} relative to each other and to f_1. As may be seen from the diagram, the height of the "hump" depends upon the ratio f_{o1}/f_1. A study of the transient response will shed more light on this design condition.

15-16. Low-band-compensation Transient Response. The transient response of the low-band-compensated amplifier may be obtained by replacing $j\omega$ by the complex frequency variable p and E_g by a suitable step function in Eq. (15-41). A negative step function $-E_g U(t)$ will be assumed.

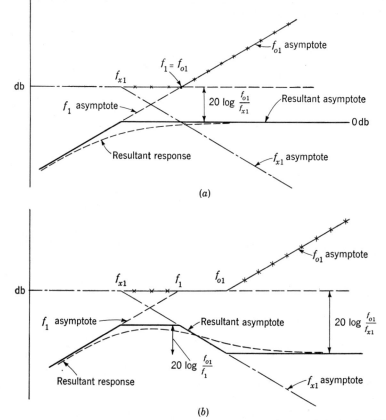

Fig. 15-12. Corner plots showing the effect of lf compensation. (a) $f_{o1} = f_1$. The lf response is determined by the f_{x1} corner. (b) $f_{o1} > f_1 > f_{x1}$. The response curve exhibits a hump and is said to be overcompensated.

With bias-circuit compensation [Eqs. (15-42)] two of the factors in Eq. (15-41) cancel, and the equation in p becomes

$$E_o(p) = g_m E_g R_L \frac{p}{p(p + \omega_1)} \qquad \omega_1 = \frac{1}{C_c R_g} \qquad (15\text{-}46)$$

It is apparent, then, that the transient response consists of a single exponential decay,

$$e_o(t) = g_m E_g R_L e^{-\omega_1 t} \qquad (15\text{-}46a)$$

which is characteristic of the basic RC amplifier (see Fig. 2-18c).

Furthermore, if cathode degenerative effects are unimportant and coupling-network compensation, in accordance with Eq. (15-45), is used, the p-plane equation reduces to

$$E_o(p) = g_m E_g R_L \frac{p}{p(p + \omega_{x1})} \qquad \omega_{x1} = \frac{1}{C_1 R_1} \qquad (15\text{-}47)$$

and the response is again a single decaying exponential. Since $\omega_{x1} < \omega_1$, the sag will be less than for the basic, uncompensated amplifier, indicating that compensation results in a better transient response.

Much more interesting are the possibilities afforded by the "over-compensated" conditions described in the last section. Assuming no cathode-degeneration effects, the p-plane equivalent of Eq. (15-41) with an applied negative step function $-E_g U(t)$ is

$$E_o(p) = g_m E_g R_L \frac{[p + (R_1 + R_L)/C_1 R_1 R_L]p}{p(p + 1/C_1 R_1)(p + 1/C_c R_g)} \qquad (15\text{-}48)$$

As a matter of convenience, to relate the transient and steady-state responses, introduce Eqs. (15-44a).

$$E_o(p) = g_m E_g R_L \frac{p + \omega_{o1}}{(p + \omega_{x1})(p + \omega_1)} \qquad (15\text{-}48a)$$

Expanding by partial fractions,

$$E_o(p) = g_m E_g R_L \left(\frac{A}{p + \omega_{x1}} + \frac{B}{p + \omega_1} \right) \qquad (15\text{-}48b)$$

where
$$A = \frac{(\omega_{o1} - \omega_{x1})}{(\omega_1 - \omega_{x1})}$$
$$B = -\frac{(\omega_{o1} - \omega_1)}{(\omega_1 - \omega_{x1})} \qquad (15\text{-}49)$$

Then
$$e_o(t) = g_m E_g R_L (A e^{-\omega_{x1} t} + B e^{-\omega_1 t}) \qquad (15\text{-}50)$$

Thus the response is characterized by the sum of two decaying exponentials. Now the problem in compensation here is to minimize the sag or the decay due to the exponentials. This may be done by making the *initial* slope of Eq. (15-50) zero at $t = 0$. To find the values of $R_1 C_1$ to satisfy this condition, set the time derivative of Eq. (15-50) equal to zero.

$$\frac{de_o(t)}{dt}\bigg|_{t=0} = g_m E_g R_L(-\omega_{x1} A - \omega_1 B) = 0$$

Substituting for A and B from Eqs. (15-49),

$$\frac{-\omega_{x1}(\omega_{o1} - \omega_{x1}) + \omega_1(\omega_{o1} - \omega_1)}{(\omega_1 - \omega_{x1})} = 0$$

$$\frac{(\omega_1 - \omega_{x1})\omega_{o1} - (\omega_1 - \omega_{x1})(\omega_1 + \omega_{x1})}{(\omega_1 - \omega_{x1})} = 0$$

or
$$\omega_{o1} - \omega_1 - \omega_{x1} = 0$$

Substituting from Eqs. (15-44a),

$$C_1 R_L = C_c R_g \tag{15-51}$$

Equation (15-51) places no design condition on R_1 of the compensating network, i.e., the condition for making $de_o(t)/dt = 0$ at $t = 0$ is independent of R_1. R_1 is chosen to minimize the sag at $t > 0$. The student may readily show that the sag decreases if R_1/R_L increases. The practical upper limit on R_1 is determined by the rated d-c plate voltage for the pentode and the available plate-supply voltage.

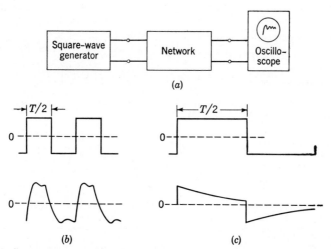

(a)

(b)   (c)

FIG. 15-13. Square-wave testing of transient response. (a) A square wave generator feeds the network whose output is viewed on an oscilloscope. (b) For edge response, $T/2$ of the square wave is chosen to be long enough for the ring to die out. (c) For tilt or sag, $T/2$ is so long that the edge response is not visible.

15-17. Square-wave Testing. In this chapter frequent reference has been made to the transient response of the quasi-LP amplifier to an applied step voltage. The question arises: "How is this transient response determined experimentally?" Since the transient response consists of an output voltage as a function of *time*, the input being a step function, the cathode-ray oscilloscope suggests itself as an ideal device for displaying the output signal. One basic difficulty arises, however: the oscilloscope should be driven by a repetitive function rather than a single, nonrecurrent signal.

In testing, a compromise is made by replacing the step function (used in calculations) by a "repetitive step function" or square wave as shown in Fig. 15-13a. The principal problem in making this substitution consists in choosing the proper half period, $T/2$, of the square wave to permit display of that portion, i.e., the edge, or sag, of the transient response which is of interest during a particular test. This problem may readily be resolved.

The results of this chapter and of Chap. 2 have shown that the edge response is governed by the same components of the circuit that determine the high-band steady-state response and that the sag is governed by those circuit components which determine the low-band steady-state response. To observe the edge response, one chooses a high-frequency square wave, the restriction being that $T/2$ be sufficiently long so that

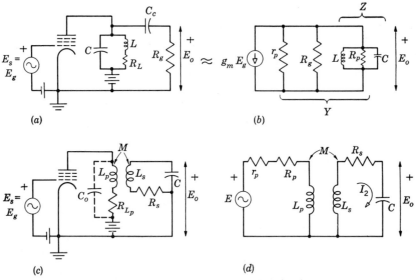

FIG. 15-14. Single-tuned amplifier circuits.

any ring dies out before the square wave changes amplitude (see Fig. 15-13b). The sag, or tilt, is dependent on the low-frequency response-determining components; hence the square wave is chosen to have a frequency so low that the edge response occupies an insignificant portion of the trace time and the sag becomes visible.

15-18. Bandpass-amplifier Types. The remainder of the chapter will be devoted to three common types of BP, or tuned, amplifiers, i.e., those having a steady-state amplitude response which is approximately symmetrical about some center frequency far removed from zero. The amplifiers will be grouped in accordance with their number of tuned circuits.

15-19. Single-tuned Amplifiers. Two basic amplifiers which employ a single-tuned circuit and which are equivalent in behavior are shown in Fig. 15-14. The circuit shown at a is commonly called a "single-tuned" amplifier. At b the tube is replaced by its linear equivalent circuit, viz., the current generator $g_m E_g$ shunted by its a-c plate resistance r_p. C_c, whose reactance is made negligible at the operating frequencies, is omitted. The inductance L, its equivalent *shunt* resistance $R_p = Q_r \omega_r L$, and the capacitance C are lumped into an antiresonant circuit labeled Z. From Chap. 4 Z may be written in the universal-resonance-curve form,

$$Z = \frac{R_p}{1 + jQ_r(f/f_r - f_r/f)} \qquad (15\text{-}52)$$

where $Q_r = R_p/\omega_r L$
$\qquad \omega_r{}^2 = 1/LC$

Then the output voltage will be

$$E_o = -\frac{g_m E_g}{Y} = \frac{-g_m E_g}{\dfrac{1}{r_p} + \dfrac{1}{R_g} + \dfrac{1 + jQ_r(f/f_r - f_r/f)}{\omega_r L Q_r}} \qquad (15\text{-}53)$$

Dividing by E_g and clearing to find the amplification,

$$A = \frac{E_o}{E_g} = \frac{-g_m \omega_r L Q_r}{1 + \omega_r L Q_r(1/r_p + 1/R_g) + jQ_r(f/f_r - f_r/f)} \qquad (15\text{-}54)$$

At $f = f_r$, the resonant gain, or amplification, will be

$$A_r = \frac{-g_m \omega_r L Q_r}{1 + \omega_r L Q_r(1/r_p + 1/R_g)} = -g_m \omega_r L Q_e$$

$$= -\frac{g_m}{\omega_r C} Q_e \qquad (15\text{-}55)$$

where
$$Q_e = \frac{Q_r}{1 + \omega_r L Q_r(1/r_p + 1/R_g)} \qquad (15\text{-}56)$$

By Eq. (4-29) the bandwidth of a resonant circuit is given by the expression $BW = f_r/Q_r$, where Q_r is the value at resonance. Hence for this case

$$A_r = \frac{-g_m}{2\pi C(BW)} \qquad (15\text{-}55a)$$

The effective Q, Q_e of the entire circuit is defined as a matter of convenience.

In a number of broad-band applications, $R_g \ll r_p$, and $Q_r \gg R_g/\omega_r L$, in which case Q_e reduces to

$$Q_e = \frac{R_g}{\omega_r L} = \omega_r C R_g \qquad r_p \gg R_g \qquad Q_r \gg \frac{R_g}{\omega_r L} \qquad (15\text{-}56a)$$

and
$$A_r = -g_m R_g \qquad (15\text{-}55b)$$

The normalized gain of the single-tuned stage is obtained by dividing Eq. (15-54) by Eq. (15-55); thus

$$\frac{A}{A_r} = \frac{1}{1 + jQ_e(f/f_r - f_r/f)} \tag{15-57}$$

It may be seen at once from Eq. (15-57) that the normalized response follows the universal resonance curve (see Fig. 4-10) and that the half-power bandwidth is

$$BW = \frac{f_r}{Q_e} \tag{15-58}$$

In this chapter it will be assumed that the conditions for arithmetic symmetry prevail (see Chap. 4) so that Eq. (15-57) may be written

$$\frac{A}{A_r} = \frac{1}{1 + j2Q_e\delta} \tag{15-57a}$$

where
$$\delta = \frac{f - f_r}{f_r} \tag{15-57b}$$

For the single-tuned amplifier the gain bandwidth product is, by Eqs. (15-55) and (15-58),

$$|A_r|(BW) = \frac{g_m}{2\pi C} \tag{15-59}$$

It may be noted that this is identical to the corresponding quantity for the quasi-LP amplifier [Eq. (15-6a)]; hence gain may be traded for bandwidth, and vice versa, their product remaining constant, if Q_e is changed.

The student may see here another example of the LP-BP analog which was used in Chap. 7. From Eqs. (15-57b) and (15-58)

$$2Q_e\delta = 2Q_e\frac{f - f_r}{f_r} = \frac{f - f_r}{BW/2} \tag{15-60}$$

Hence Eq. (15-57a) may be written

$$\frac{A}{A_r} = \frac{1}{1 + j(f - f_r)/BW/2} \qquad \text{BP} \tag{15-61}$$

The analogous LP amplifier would have the form shown in Fig. 15-15a, and its normalized gain would be

$$\frac{A}{A_r} = \frac{1}{1 + jf/f_2}$$

But for this LP case $f_2 = BW = 1/2\pi C_s R_L$, therefore,

$$\frac{A}{A_r} = \frac{1}{1 + jf/BW} \qquad \text{LP} \tag{15-61a}$$

The amplitude responses of Eqs. (15-61) and (15-61a) are plotted in Fig. 15-15b and c. It will be observed that, if the resonant frequency f_r in Eq. (15-61) is "transferred to zero," the two responses become identical except for a 2:1 ratio in half-power bandwidths. For analogous behavior, C_s should be chosen so that

$$2(BW)_{\text{LP}} = (BW)_{\text{BP}}$$

whence
$$C_s R_L = 2CR_g \qquad (15\text{-}61b)$$

This LP-BP analog will be of use in a later section.

As a general rule, the method of tuning used in the single-tuned stage of Fig. 15-14a varies with the frequency range. Up to a few megacycles,

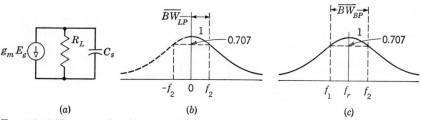

(a)   (b)   (c)

FIG. 15-15. Low-pass bandpass analog. (a) Low-pass amplifier which is the analog of Fig. 15-14a. (b) Amplitude response of the LP amplifier. Negative frequencies are included for symmetry. (c) Amplitude response of the BP amplifier.

C is made variable. At higher frequencies where L gets quite small, the tube and stray capacitances make up C, no external capacitance being added. Where this condition prevails, tuning is accomplished by varying L, often by means of a movable high-permeability slug.

Another circuit having a response identical to that of the single-tuned stage is shown in Fig. 15-14c and is often designated the untuned-primary, tuned-secondary (UPTS) amplifier. In the physical circuit, L_p will be shunted by C_o, the output capacitance of the vacuum tube, as shown in the figure. In typical applications, however, L_p is chosen to be small compared with L_s and C large relative to C_o, such that

$$\omega_r{}^2 = \frac{1}{L_s C} \ll \frac{1}{L_p C_o} \qquad (15\text{-}62)$$

It has been shown in Chap. 4 that under this condition the parallel combination $L_p C_o$ will behave like an inductance L_p at frequencies near f_r; hence in the equivalent circuit of Fig. 15-14d, C_o may be omitted. It may be seen, then, that the UPTS amplifier effectively involves only one tuned circuit and for typical circuit values may be shown to have the same type of response as the single-tuned amplifier of Fig. 15-14a. The circuit may be analyzed by means of the equivalent two-mesh circuit of Fig. 15-14d.

$$E_o = \frac{I_2}{j\omega C} = \frac{-Z_{12}E}{j\omega C Z_{11}(Z_{22} - Z_{12}{}^2/Z_{11})} \qquad (15\text{-}63)$$

where
$$E = g_m r_p E_g$$

$$Z_{22} = R_s + j\left(\omega L_s - \frac{1}{\omega C}\right)$$

$$= R_s + j\omega_r L_s\left(\frac{f}{f_r} - \frac{f_r}{f}\right) \tag{15-64}$$

$$\omega_r{}^2 = \frac{1}{L_s C}$$

$$Z_{12} = \pm j\omega M$$

$$Z_{11} = r_p + R_p + j\omega L_p$$

As a practical matter, in typical circuits r_p will be of the order of 1 megohm, R_p of a few ohms, and ωL_p of a few hundred ohms; hence to an excellent approximation

$$Z_{11} = r_p \tag{15-64a}$$

Substituting Eqs. (15-64) and (15-64a) into Eq. (15-63),

$$E_o = \mp \frac{g_m E_g M}{C} \cdot \frac{1}{R_s + j\omega_r L_s\left(\dfrac{f}{f_r} - \dfrac{f_r}{f}\right) + \dfrac{(\omega M)^2}{r_p}} \tag{15-65}$$

Now $1/C = \omega_r{}^2 L_s$; thus, substituting and factoring $R_s + (\omega M)^2/r_p$ from the denominator,

$$E_o = \mp \frac{g_m E_g \omega_r M \omega_r L_s}{\left[R_s + \dfrac{(\omega M)^2}{r_p}\right]\left[1 + j\,\dfrac{\omega_r L_s}{R_s + (\omega M)^2/r_p}\left(\dfrac{f}{f_r} - \dfrac{f_r}{f}\right)\right]} \tag{15-66}$$

That this equation may be reduced to the universal-resonance form by defining a suitable effective figure of merit will now be shown. Let

$$Q_e = \frac{\omega_r L_s}{R_s + (\omega M)^2/r_p} \tag{15-67}$$

Substituting Q_e into Eq. (15-66) and dividing by E_g to find the gain,

$$A - \mp \frac{g_m \omega_r M Q_e}{1 + j Q_e(f/f_r - f_r/f)} \tag{15-68}$$

At $f = f_r$ the resonant gain will be

$$A_r = \mp g_m \omega_r M Q_e \tag{15-69}$$

and the normalized gain will be

$$\frac{A}{A_r} = \frac{1}{1 + j Q_e(f/f_r - f_r/f)} \tag{15-70}$$

It may be observed, then, that, subject to the assumption that C_o is negligible and that $Z_{11} \approx r_p$, the UPTS and single-tuned amplifiers have identical responses of the universal-resonance type. As stated before, it will be assumed in the remainder of the chapter that Q_e is sufficiently

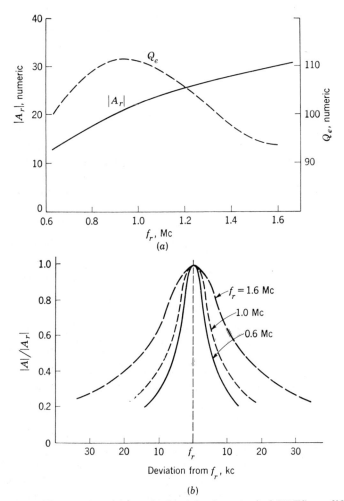

FIG. 15-16. Curves of Q_e, $|A_r|$, and selectivity for a typical UPTS amplifier.

high that the approximations of arithmetic symmetry may be used, so that Eqs. (15-57) and (15-70) may be written as

$$\frac{A}{A_r} = \frac{1}{1 + j2Q_e\delta}$$

$$\delta = \frac{f - f_r}{f_r}$$

normalized response of UPTS and single-tuned amplifiers, arithmetic symmetry assumed   (15-71)

The UPTS amplifier of Fig. 15-14c is often incorporated as part of a broadcast-band radio receiver. In this application its *resonance-response curve* is important as well as its selectivity curve. In the broadcast band each transmitting station is allocated a total bandwidth of 10 kc, centered on a "carrier" frequency. Consider three stations:

Station	Carrier f, Mc	Band limits, Mc
A	0.600	0.595–0.605
B	1.000	0.955–1.005
C	1.600	1.595–1.605

For the receiver to operate properly, it must be able to "tune" to any one of these stations, that is, f_r must be made to coincide with any one of the carrier frequencies, usually by varying C. Furthermore, it would be desirable that $|A_r|$ and the selectivity be constant over the entire broadcast band (0.535 to 1.605 Mc) so that all stations are amplified in the same amount and manner. It may be seen from Eq. (15-69) that $|A_r|$ is frequency-dependent, being proportional to f_r and Q_e. A typical manner in which Q_e varies with frequency is shown by the dashed curve of Fig. 15-16a. (Notice that an expanded ordinate scale is used in the figure.) A typical resonance-response curve, $|A_r|$ vs. f_r, is shown by the solid line.

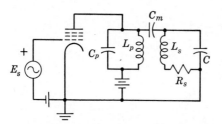

FIG. 15-17. Tuned amplifier employing capacitive coupling to flatten the resonance response characteristic, $|A_r|$ vs. f_r.

Since Q_e varies nonlinearly with frequency, the half-power bandwidth varies from station to station. Typical selectivity curves, $|A|/|A_r|$ vs. f, are shown at Fig. 15-16b. Since each station occupies only a small fraction of the entire broadcast band, Q_e may be assumed constant in calculating any one of these curves. The curves of Fig. 15-16 show that the UPTS amplifier is more selective for low-frequency stations and less selective for high-frequency stations. These effects may be minimized by using circuits employing two tuned circuits having *different* resonant frequencies and coupled by capacitance as shown in Fig. 15-17.[1]

15-20. Envelope Response. The BP amplifiers which have been the subject of the foregoing sections are ordinarily used to amplify *modulated* signals which are centered on a carrier frequency f_c which is equal to f_r of the amplifier. Under these conditions one is concerned with the

---

[1] See, for example, F. E. Terman, "Radio Engineering," p. 343, 3d ed., McGraw-Hill Book Company, Inc., New York, 1947.

envelope response rather than the transient response. In the process of amplitude modulation the intelligence is superimposed on the carrier by making the carrier amplitude A vary about a mean value E_c in accordance with the intelligence as shown in Fig. 1-14 such that, if a single modulating frequency $\omega_i/2\pi$ is used,

$$e(t) = (\hat{E}_c + \hat{E}_i \sin \omega_i t) \sin \omega_c t \tag{15-72}$$

(the equation of the amplitude-modulated signal developed in Chap. 1). It is apparent from the Fig. 1-14 that the intelligence is contained in the *envelope* of the modulated wave. By the methods of Chap. 2 an intelligence signal more complicated than a single sine wave could be analyzed in a series, or band, of sinusoidal terms so that the same argument would apply.

Now with LP amplifiers the transient response to a step-function signal has been calculated. By analog, then, one is concerned with the envelope response of a BP structure to a test signal consisting of a carrier modulated by a step function. Such a signal would be

$$e(t) = U(t)E_g \sin \omega_r t \tag{15-73}$$

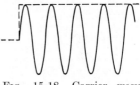

as shown in Fig. 15-18. The envelope here is, of course, simply $\hat{E}_c U(t)$.

Fig. 15-18. Carrier wave modulated by a step function used for determining envelope response.

The LP-BP analog suggests itself as the basis for a simplified method of determining the envelope response of a single-tuned amplifier to an applied signal of the form of Eq. (15-73). One easy way of transferring f_r to zero is by defining a new complex frequency variable $p' = j(\omega - \omega_r)$ so that by Eqs. (15-71)

$$E_o(p') = \frac{-g_m R_g E_g(p')}{1 + 2Q_e p'/\omega_r}$$

But $Q_e/\omega_r = R_g C$. Hence

$$E_o(p') = -\frac{g_m E_g(p')}{2C} \frac{1}{p' + 1/2R_g C} \tag{15-74}$$

Transferring the carrier frequency to zero in Eq. (15-73), $E_g(p')$ becomes

$$E_g(p') = -\frac{E_g}{p'} \tag{15-75}$$

the negative sign being chosen to give a positive-going envelope response. Then

$$E_o(p') = \frac{g_m E_g}{2C} \frac{1}{p'(p' + 1/2R_g C)} \tag{15-74a}$$

Since this is identical to the response of the analogous LP amplifier to an applied step signal, the response will have the shape of Fig. 15-19a. On transferring the carrier frequency from zero to f_r, the response will have the form shown in Fig. 15-19b. It is apparent that good envelope response is related to low Q_e and is obtained at the sacrifice of selectivity against other signals.

The student should observe that the factor 2 appearing in Eqs. (15-74) and (15-74a) indicates the adjustment required in C by the LP-BP analog as discussed in the last section.

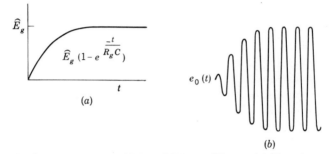

FIG. 15-19. Analogous responses of LP and BP amplifiers.   (a) Transient response of LP amplifier to a step function.   (b) Envelope response of BP amplifier to the signal of Fig. 15-18.

15-21. Cascade of n Identical Stages.   It has been demonstrated that the gain-bandwidth product $|A_r|(BW)$ is equal to $g_m/2\pi C$ for the single-tuned stage.   If one such stage does not provide a high enough value of this product, two or more stages may be connected in cascade.   One possibility is to have all n stages tuned to the same center frequency f_r, in which case the stages are said to be "synchronously tuned" or "synchronous."   Furthermore, if the stages are all identical, i.e., same f_r, bandwidth, and A_r, the over-all gain will be

$$A_T = A^n = \left(\frac{A_r}{1 + j2Q_e\delta}\right)^n \tag{15-76}$$

The student may show that the over-all bandwidth in this case is

$$(BW)_T = (BW)\sqrt{2^{1/n} - 1}$$

The bandwidth shrinkage factor, $\sqrt{2^{1/n} - 1}$, is tabulated in Table 15-1. As in the RC amplifier case, as n increases, the center gain increases faster than the bandwidth decreases, indicating an over-all improvement in $|A_r|_T(BW)_T$.

A much more interesting possibility is afforded by having the individual stages nonsynchronous, or *stagger-tuned*.

15-22. Stagger-tuned Amplifier.[1] Where the n stages of the cascade are nonsynchronous, a change in notation is helpful. For the kth stage in the cascade let

$$g_m = g_k \qquad R_g = R_k$$
$$Q_e = Q_k \qquad f_r = f_k$$
$$BW = (BW)_k \qquad \delta = \delta_k = \frac{f - f_k}{f_k} \qquad (15\text{-}77)$$

Then for the kth stage

$$A_k = - \left[\frac{g_k}{2\pi C_k (BW)_k} \right] \frac{1}{1 + j2Q_k\delta_k} \qquad (15\text{-}78)$$

The over-all gain will be the product of the n-stage gains, which may be represented by

$$A_T = A_1 A_2 \cdots A_k \cdots A_n$$

$$= \prod_{k=1}^{n} - \left[\frac{g_k}{2\pi C_k (BW)_k} \right] \frac{1}{1 + j2Q_k\delta_k} \qquad (15\text{-}79)$$

where the symbol $\displaystyle\prod_{k=1}^{n}$ means the *product* of the n factors just as the sym-

bol $\displaystyle\sum_{k=1}^{n}$ means the *sum* of the n terms.

The student should observe that Eq. (15-79) comes about because of the isolation property of the vacuum tubes in the cascade, which property allows *independent* adjustment of the poles by individual physical parameters such as the L and C of an individual stage without effect on other poles controlled in turn by their stages. In contrast, in a multi-mesh bilateral network each pole is a function of the physical parameters of all meshes, and independent control is very difficult if not impossible. Hence, in network synthesis, the use of vacuum tubes introduces an important advantage, entirely independent of their amplifying property.

This might be a good time to introduce a general principle in engineering synthesis. In general there are certain physical constants which may be controlled, such as inductors, capacitors, etc. These in general determine, through transformations of variables, certain constants of the system, such as the frequencies of the poles, which are not in themselves of primary interest to the designer or user. These secondary dependent

---

[1] The method of setting up the gain function which is employed here follows R. F. Baum, Design of Broad Band I. F. Amplifiers, *J. Appl. Phys.*, vol. 17, no. 6, p. 519, June, 1946. Baum also considers the case of the Tschebyscheff-type response. The method of factoring the denominator of Eq. (15-88a) follows Henry Wallman, Stagger-tuned I. F. Amplifiers, *MIT Radiation Lab. Rept.* 524, 1944. See also Valley and Wallman, *op. cit.*, chap. 4.

variables determine in turn certain tertiary dependent variables which are of interest to the designer, such as the response at certain frequencies which determine the shape of some characteristic curve desired. Expressed mathematically, if x_1, x_2, x_3, x_4, . . . , x_i are the physically independent variables, y_1, y_2, . . . , y_i the secondary design parameters, and z_1, z_2, . . . , z_i the tertiary dependent variables, then in general

$$y_1 = f_1(x_1,x_2,x_3,. . .,x_i)$$
$$y_2 = f_2(x_1,x_2,x_3,. . .,x_i)$$
$$. . . . .$$
$$y_i = f_i(x_1,x_2,x_3,. . .,x_i) \qquad (15\text{-}80a)$$

and
$$z_1 = g_1(y_1,y_2,y_3,. . .,y_i)$$
$$z_2 = g_2(y_1,y_2,y_3,. . .,y_i)$$
$$. . . . .$$
$$z_i = g_i(y_1,y_2,y_3,. . .,y_i)$$

However, the designer should seek and secure some way, if he possibly can, to control the system so that $y_1 = F_1(x_1)$, $y_2 = F_2(x_2)$, $y_i = F_i(x_i)$ and if possible so that

$$z_1 = G_1(y_1) \cdot \cdot \cdot z_i = G_i(y_i) \qquad (15\text{-}80b)$$

If he can do this, then either analytically or experimentally it will be much easier to determine the values of x's he should choose in order to fit the conditions on the z's he has imposed.

For instance, in the case under discussion the x's may be the physical value of the inductors, the y's the frequencies of the poles, and the z's the responses at certain frequencies. In ordinary multimesh networks the first set of equations (15-80a) apply, while with resonant-tuned circuits connected in cascade between vacuum tubes the second set (15-80b) apply. It will be shown in Sec. 15-28 that a double-tuned amplifier does not afford this desirable isolation.

Since n different values of f_r or δ_k are involved in Eq. (15-79), it is convenient to introduce a new frequency variable normalized with respect to f_0, the center frequency of the over-all response curve. This may be introduced as follows:

$$\delta_k = \frac{f - f_k}{f_k} = \frac{f - f_0}{f_k} + \frac{f_0 - f_k}{f_k}$$

Let the new frequency variable be

$$x = \frac{2(f - f_0)}{(BW)_T} \qquad (15\text{-}81)$$

where $(BW)_T$ = system half-power bandwidth. Since $(BW)_k = f_k/Q_k$,

$$2Q_k\delta_k = 2Q_k\left[\frac{(BW)_Tx}{2f_k} + \frac{f_0 - f_k}{f_k}\right]$$
$$= \frac{(BW)_T}{(BW)_k}x + \frac{2(f_0 - f_k)}{(BW)_k} \tag{15-82a}$$

For convenience let

$$a_k = \frac{(BW)_T}{(BW)_k} \qquad b_k = \frac{2(f_0 - f_k)}{(BW)_k} \tag{15-82b}$$

The gain of the kth stage may therefore be written

$$A_k = \frac{-g_k}{2\pi C_k(BW)_k}\frac{1}{1 + j(a_kx + b_k)}$$

and the over-all response as

$$A_T = \prod_{k=1}^{n}\frac{-g_k}{2\pi C_k(BW)_k}\frac{1}{1 + j(a_kx + b_k)} \tag{15-83}$$

15-23. Maximally Flat Amplitude Stagger. One basic method of broad-banding an amplifier is to adjust its parameters to give a maximally flat amplitude response. To get this condition for the stagger-tuned amplifier, consider the magnitude squared of Eq. (15-83).

$$|A_T|^2 = \prod_{k=1}^{n}\left[\frac{g_k}{2\pi C_k(BW)_k}\right]^2\frac{1}{1 + (a_kx + b_k)^2} \tag{15-84}$$

At the center frequency f_0, $x = 0$, and

$$|A_T|_0{}^2 = \prod_{k=1}^{n}\left[\frac{g_k}{2\pi C_k(BW)_k}\right]^2\frac{1}{1 + b_k{}^2} \tag{15-84a}$$

So the normalized gain squared becomes

$$\frac{|A_T|^2}{|A_T|_0{}^2} = \prod_{k=1}^{n}\frac{1 + b_k{}^2}{1 + (a_kx + b_k)^2} = \frac{\displaystyle\prod_{k=1}^{n}(1 + b_k{}^2)}{D} \tag{15-84b}$$

where $D = \displaystyle\prod_{k=1}^{n}[1 + (a_kx + b_k)^2]$. The problem of designing for a maximally flat reponse, then, consists in selecting the proper values of the a's and b's. This is implemented by expanding the denominator, D, of Eq. (15-84b) into a polynomial in x.

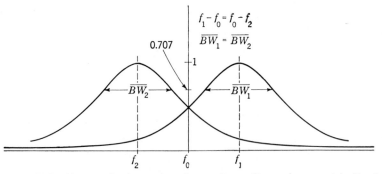

FIG. 15-20. Pairs of stages in the staggered cascade are disposed symmetrically about the center frequency f_0.

Some intelligent guessing may simplify the work. The response will be symmetrical about f_0; hence assume that pairs of stages will be displaced symmetrically on each side of f_0 as in Fig. 15-20. Then, if n is *even*,

$$a_{n+1-k} = a_k$$
$$b_{n+1-k} = -b_k \tag{15-85}$$

and D would become

$$D = \prod_{k=1}^{n/2} [1 + (a_k x + b_k)^2][1 + (a_k x - b_k)^2] \qquad n \text{ even} \quad (15\text{-}86)$$

It may readily be shown that D is therefore a polynomial involving only even powers of x, the highest power being x^{2n} and having the coefficient $\prod_{k=1}^{n/2} a_k^4$. The zero-power term will be $\prod_{k=1}^{n/2} (1 + b_k^2)^2$. Therefore, for n even, Eq. (15-84b) becomes

$$\frac{|A_T|^2}{|A_T|_0^2} = \frac{\displaystyle\prod_{k=1}^{n/2} (1 + b_k^2)^2}{\displaystyle\prod_{k=1}^{n/2} (1 + b_k^2)^2 + p x^2 + q x^4 + \cdots + \prod_{k=1}^{n/2} a_k^4 x^{2n}} \tag{15-87}$$

On the other hand, if n is *odd*, one guesses that the odd stage will be centered on f_0 such that

$$b_{(n+1)/2} = 0 \tag{15-85a}$$

the other stages being symmetrically disposed pairs in accordance with Eqs. (15-85). Under this condition D becomes

$$D = (1 + a_{(n+1)/2}{}^2 x^2) \prod_{k=1}^{(n-1)/2} [1 + (a_k x + b_k)^2][1 + (a_k x - b_k)^2] \qquad n \text{ odd}$$

$$(15\text{-}86a)$$

which is still a polynomial in x^2 and the normalized response is the same as Eq. (15-87) except for a change in the upper limits of the products from $n/2$ to $(n-1)/2$. Therefore the same argument applies whether n is odd or even.

Now the maximally flat response is obtained by setting $p, q, \ldots,$ that is, all the coefficients but the first and last, equal to zero. If this is done, the maximally flat amplitude response squared becomes

$$\left. \begin{aligned} \frac{|A_T|^2}{|A_T|_0{}^2} &= \frac{\displaystyle\prod_{k=1}^{n/2} (1 + b_k{}^2)^2}{\displaystyle\prod_{k=1}^{n/2} (1 + b_k{}^2)^2 + \prod_{k=1}^{n/2} a_k{}^4 x^{2n}} \\ &= \frac{1}{1 + K^{2n} x^{2n}} \end{aligned} \right\} \qquad (15\text{-}88)$$

where $K^{2n} = \displaystyle\prod_{1}^{n/2} a_k{}^4 / (1 + b_k{}^2)^2$.

The numerical value of K may be evaluated easily. Let F_2 be the upper half-power frequency of the over-all response. Then, at $f = F_2$, $x = x_2$, and $|A_T|^2 / |A_T|_0{}^2 = \frac{1}{2}$. Substituting in Eq. (15-88),

$$1 + K^{2n} x_2{}^{2n} = 2$$

$$x_2 = \frac{1}{K}$$

But from Eq. (15-81)

$$x_2 = \frac{2(F_2 - f_0)}{(BW)_T} = 1$$

Therefore, $K = 1$, and the normalized response squared becomes

$$\frac{|A_T|^2}{|A_T|_0{}^2} = \frac{1}{1 + x^{2n}} \qquad (15\text{-}88a)$$

Now the values of the a's and b's which reduce the coefficients $p, q, \ldots$ of the denominator polynomial to zero must be found. This may be done by factoring $1 + x^{2n}$, that is, by finding the roots of $1 + x^{2n} = 0$.

Let α_k be the roots of this equation, i.e., the $2n$ roots of -1. Then

$$\alpha_k{}^{2n} = -1 = e^{j(2k-1)\pi}$$

$$\alpha_k = e^{j\left(\frac{2k-1}{2n}\pi\right)} = \cos\frac{2k-1}{2n}\pi \pm j\sin\frac{2k-1}{2n}\pi \qquad (15\text{-}89)$$

But, from Eq. (15-84b), D is also zero if $\displaystyle\prod_{k=1}^{n}[1 + (a_k\alpha_k + b_k)^2] = 0$; or if $(a_k\alpha_k + b_k)^2 = -1$,

$$\alpha_k = -\frac{b_k}{a_k} \pm \frac{j}{a_k} \qquad (15\text{-}89a)$$

Then, comparing corresponding terms in Eqs. (15-89) and (15-89a),

$$\frac{-b_k}{a_k} = \cos\frac{2k-1}{2n}\pi$$

$$\frac{1}{a_k} = \sin\frac{2k-1}{2n}\pi$$

Substituting from Eqs. (15-82b) and (15-85),

$$\frac{(BW)_k}{(BW)_{n+1-k}} = \pm(BW)_T \sin\frac{2k-1}{2n}\pi \qquad (15\text{-}90a)$$

$$\frac{f_k}{f_{n+1-k}} = f_0 \pm \frac{(BW)_T}{2}\cos\frac{2k-1}{2n}\pi \qquad (15\text{-}90b)$$

Since for each stage

$$\omega_k{}^2 = \frac{1}{L_kC_k} \qquad (BW)_k = \frac{f_k}{Q_k}$$

sufficient equations are available to design a maximally flat stagger-tuned amplifier.

One additional relationship is of considerable help in calculating $|A_T|_0$. From Eq. (15-84a)

$$|A_T|_0 = \prod_{k=1}^{n}\frac{g_k}{2\pi C_k(BW)_k\sqrt{1 + b_k{}^2}} \qquad (15\text{-}91)$$

But from Eqs. (15-88) and the fact that $K^{2n} = 1$

$$\prod_{k=1}^{n}\sqrt{1 + b_k{}^2} = \prod_{k=1}^{n}a_k$$

Substituting for a_k from Eq. (15-82b),

$$\prod_{k=1}^{n}\sqrt{1 + b_k{}^2} = \prod_{k=1}^{n}\frac{(BW)_T}{(BW)_k} = (BW)^n{}_T\prod_{k=1}^{n}\frac{1}{(BW)_k}$$

Substituting into Eq. (15-91),

$$|A_T|_0 = \frac{1}{[2\pi(BW)_T]^n} \prod_{k=1}^{n} \frac{g_k}{C_k} \qquad (15\text{-}92)$$

The use of these equations will now be illustrated by a numerical example.

Design a staggered triple ($n = 3$) using 6AK5's. $g_m = 4{,}300$ μmhos,

$$r_p = 420 \text{ kilohms}$$

$C = 120$ $\mu\mu$f, for all stages. The center frequency is to be 500 kc, and the over-all half-power bandwidth 20 kc.

By Eq. (15-90b)

$$\begin{aligned}
\frac{f_1}{f_3} &= f_0 \pm \frac{(BW)_T}{2} \cos \frac{180°}{6} = f_0 \pm \frac{2 \times 10^4}{2} \cos 30° \\
&= f_0 \pm 8.66 \times 10^3 \\
f_1 &= 508.66 \text{ kc} \\
f_3 &= 491.34 \text{ kc}
\end{aligned}$$

By Eq. (15-90b)

$$f_2 = f_0 + \frac{(BW)_T}{2} \cos \frac{3 \times 180°}{6} = f_0 = 500 \text{ kc}$$

Also by Eq. (15-90a)

$$(BW)_1 = (BW)_3 = (BW)_T \sin 30° = \frac{2 \times 10^4}{2} = 10 \text{ kc}$$
$$(BW)_2 = (BW)_T \sin 90° = 20 \text{ kc}$$

Consider the parameters for stage 1.

$$L_1 = \frac{1}{\omega_1{}^2 C_1} = \frac{1}{4\pi^2(5.0866 \times 10^5)^2(1.2 \times 10^{-10})} = 816 \text{ }\mu\text{h}$$
$$Q_1 = \frac{f_1}{(BW)_1} = \frac{508.66}{10} = 50.9$$

The student should remember that this value represents the *effective Q* of the entire coupling network. Since it is highly improbable that the inductor Q will be very much greater than this value, the approximations of Eqs. (15-55b) and (15-56a) are not valid and the more exact forms must be used. By way of illustration, say the inductor Q_r is 80. Then by Eq. (15-56)

$$\begin{aligned}
\frac{1}{R_1} &= \frac{1}{\omega_1 L_1 Q_r} \left(\frac{Q_r}{Q_1} - 1 \right) - \frac{1}{r_p} \\
&= \frac{0.573}{2\pi(5.09 \times 10^5)(0.816 \times 10^{-3})(8 \times 10^1)} - \frac{1}{0.42 \times 10^6} \\
&= (0.274 - 0.238) \times 10^{-5} \\
R_1 &= 2.78 \text{ megohms}
\end{aligned}$$

The components of the other stages may be computed in a manner similar to this.

The over-all gain at f_0 will be by Eq. (15-92)

$$|A_T|_0 = \left[\frac{g_m}{2\pi C(BW)_T}\right]^3$$

$$= \left[\frac{4.3 \times 10^{-3}}{2\pi(1.2 \times 10^{-11})(2 \times 10^4)}\right]^3 = 23 \times 10^9 = 207.2 \text{ db}$$

The over-all normalized response of the staggered triple is shown in Fig. 15-21. The dashed line shows the normalized response for the second

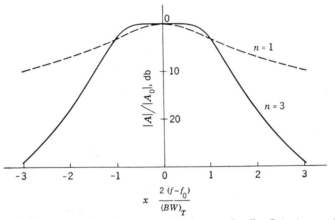

Fig. 15-21. Normalized amplitude response of a maximally flat staggered triple. The dashed curve shows the normalized response of the center stage of the triple for comparison. Note the improvement in selectivity afforded by staggering.

stage of the cascade which has the same bandwidth, $(BW)_T$. The great improvement in selectivity afforded by the stagger-tuned stages 1 and 3 is immediately apparent.

15-24. Limitation of Arithmetic Symmetry. In deriving the conditions for the maximally flat staggered "n-uple" it has been assumed that the conditions of arithmetic symmetry prevail. This assumption, in turn, imposes a limit on the maximum value of $(BW)_T/f_0$ for which the design equations are valid. This limit will now be considered.

Wallman[1] has derived design equations for the maximally flat amplitude case based on the exact forms involving geometric symmetry. For values of $(BW)_T/f_0$ less than 0.3 his design equations reduce to the so-called "asymptotic forms":

$$(BW)_k = (BW)_{n+1-k} = \pm(BW)_T \sin\frac{2k-1}{2n}\pi \qquad (15\text{-}93a)$$

[1] *Op. cit.* See also Valley and Wallman, *op. cit.*

$$f_k = f_0 \left(1 + \frac{(BW)_T}{2f_0} \cos \frac{2k-1}{2n} \pi \right) \qquad (15\text{-}93b)$$

$$f_{n+1-k} = \frac{f_0}{1 + \dfrac{(BW)_T}{2f_0} \cos \dfrac{2k-1}{2n} \pi} \qquad (15\text{-}93c)$$

Comparison of these equations with Eqs. (15-90) shows that they are identical except for f_{n+1-k}. Then the upper limit of $(BW)_T/f_0$ for which Eq. (15-90b) is satisfactory is that value for which Eq. (15-93c) reduces to Eq. (15-90b). This limit may be found by means of the binomial expansion. For example,

$$(1 + a)^{-1} = 1 - a + a^2 + \cdots \qquad (15\text{-}94)$$

and the error introduced by replacing $(1 + a)^{-1}$ by $1 - a$ is less than a^2. By applying this principle the student may find the limit on $(BW)_T/f_0$ as a function of n for which Eq. (15-90b) may be used correct, say, to better than 1 per cent.

15-25. Pole Locations for Maximally Flat Amplitude Response.[1] The values of α_k specified by Eq. (15-89) are the roots of $D = 0$ in Eq. (15-86) and hence are the poles of the maximally flat staggered n-uple. It is of interest to observe the location of these poles in the complex x plane.

From Eq. (15-89) $\alpha_k = e^{j\left(\frac{2k-1}{2n}\pi\right)}$. Clearly, for any k, $|\alpha_k| = 1$; hence all k poles lie on a circle of unit radius. Furthermore the angular spacing between poles of successive values of k is $2\pi/2n$ radians or $360/2n$ degrees. There are n poles, and they will be in the left-hand half plane. These statements are illustrated for a maximally flat quintuple in Fig. 15-22a. The image poles are shown as an aid in locating the correct positions. It may be observed from earlier work that the over-all half-power frequencies occur at $x = \pm1$; hence the circle diameter in Fig. 15-22a is equal to the normalized system bandwidth. These results may be carried over into the complex frequency plane as in Fig. 15-22b.

15-26. Envelope Response of Staggered n-uple. The envelope response of a stagger-tuned amplifier may be calculated by use of the LP-BP analog as described earlier in the chapter. The student should note that Eq. (15-79) is in a good form for this calculation because the poles are clearly identified for easy expansion by partial fractions.

When pairs of stages are symmetrically displaced about f_0, the corresponding poles occur as complex conjugates and the response will be

---

[1] Pole positions have been described for a number of responses other than the maximally flat type. See, for example, W. H. Huggins, The Natural Behavior of Broadband Circuits, *Electronics Research Lab.* (*Air Materiel Command*) *Rept.* E 5013A; W. E. Bradley, A Theory of Wide Band Amplifier Design, *Philco Research Division Rept.* 98M; Baum, *op. cit.*

oscillatory in nature.   In the maximally flat amplitude case both over-shoot and rise time increase with increasing n.*

15-27. Double-tuned Amplifier.   Another basic type of BP amplifier employs two tuned circuits as shown in Fig. 15-23a and is often desig-nated an intermediate frequency (if) or tuned-primary, tuned-secondary

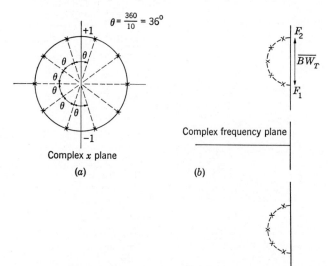

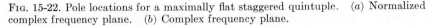

Fɪɢ. 15-22. Pole locations for a maximally flat staggered quintuple.   (a) Normalized complex frequency plane.   (b) Complex frequency plane.

(TPTS) amplifier.   This circuit will now be considered under the assump-tions that both tuned circuits have the same resonant frequency and that the primary and secondary inductors have the same value of Q which is sufficiently high that arithmetic symmetry may be assumed; thus

$$\omega_r{}^2 = \frac{1}{L_p C_p} = \frac{1}{L_s C_s} \tag{15-95a}$$

$$Q = \frac{\omega_r L_p}{R_{L_p}} = \frac{\omega_r L_s}{R_{L_s}} \tag{15-95b}$$

The circuit is redrawn in Fig. 15-23b with the vacuum pentode replaced by the current generator $g_m E_g$ shunted by r_p.   In typical applications, however, $r_p \gg 1/\omega C_p$; hence r_p may usually be omitted from the diagram.

By Thévenin's theorem the portion of the circuit to the left of the pri-mary inductor can be reduced to the equivalent circuit of Fig. 15-23c. This circuit is identical in form to the tuned-transformer impedance-transforming network of Fig. 11-21; hence the analysis of Sec. 11-28 may be adapted to the TPTS amplifier, provided R_{I1} is replaced by R_{L_p}, R_{I2}

*See Valley and Wallman, *op. cit.*, sec. 7-5.

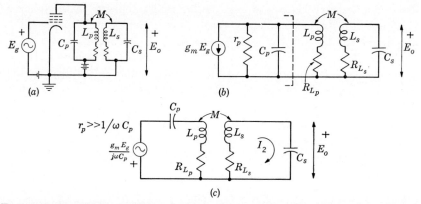

FIG. 15-23. The TPTS amplifier. (a) Basic circuit. (b) The vacuum tube is replaced by its equivalent linear circuit. (c) Equivalent circuit with $g_m E_g$, r_p, and C_p simplified by Thévenin's theorem.

by R_{Ls}, and E_g by $g_m E_g / j\omega C_p$. Then under the assumed conditions the secondary-current magnitude will be by Eq. (11-74b)

$$|I_2| = \frac{g_m E_g k}{\omega C_p \omega_r \sqrt{L_p L_s} \sqrt{(k^2 + k_c^2 - 4x^2)^2 + 16k_c^2 x^2}} \qquad (15\text{-}96)$$

where $x = (f - f_r)/f_r$
$k = M/\sqrt{L_p L_s}$
$k_c = 1/Q$

The output-voltage magnitude will be

$$|E_o| = \frac{|I_2|}{\omega C_s} \qquad (15\text{-}97)$$

Then, substituting Eq. (15-96) into Eq. (15-97) and noting that for arithmetic symmetry $\omega \approx \omega_r$ and that $\omega_r^4 C_p C_s \sqrt{L_p L_s} = 1/\sqrt{L_p L_s}$,

$$|E_o| = \frac{g_m E_g \omega_r k \sqrt{L_p L_s}}{\sqrt{(k^2 + k_c^2 - 4x^2)^2 + 16k_c^2 x^2}} \qquad (15\text{-}98)$$

The student may verify that the normalized gain of the TPTS stage is

$$\left| \frac{A}{A_r} \right| = \frac{k^2 + k_c^2}{\sqrt{(k^2 + k_c^2 - 4x^2)^2 + 16k_c^2 x^2}} \qquad (15\text{-}99)$$

where $$|A_r| = \frac{g_m \omega_r k \sqrt{L_p L_s}}{k^2 + k_c^2} \qquad (15\text{-}99a)$$

Comparison of Eqs. (15-99), (15-98), and (11-74b) shows that the denominators are identical except for a constant factor; therefore the discussion in Sec. 11-28 and Fig. 11-25, which concern the response of the impedance-transforming network, apply equally well to the TPTS amplifier.

15-28. Poles of Tuned-primary, Tuned-secondary Amplifier. It may be shown that the denominator of Eq. (15-98) before rationalization may be written in terms of a complex frequency variable p whose imaginary part is $(\omega - \omega_r)/\omega$ as

$$D = 4p^2 + 4k_cp + k^2 + k_c^2$$

The poles of Eq. (15-98) are the roots of $D^2 = 0$ and have the values

$$p = \tfrac{1}{2}(-k_c \pm jk) \tag{15-100}$$

Consider, then, the conditions for a maximally flat amplitude response. From Sec. 15-25 the angular spacing between the poles must be $^{360}\!/_4 = 90°$, yielding the pole pattern shown in Fig. 15-24. To satisfy this configuration, $k = k_c$ in Eq. (15-100); thus, when the primary and secondary circuits are tuned to the same frequency, the maximally flat condition occurs when the coupling is critical.

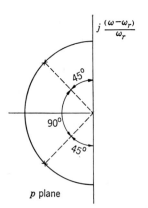

The contrast between a staggered pair and a TPTS amplifier is apparent. In the former a vacuum tube prevents any coupling or interaction between the two resonant circuits which are tuned to different frequencies, i.e., the poles may be adjusted independently. In the TPTS circuit, on the other hand, the poles depend upon the coupling between two resonant circuits tuned to the same frequency and so may not be adjusted independently.

Fig. 15-24. Pole locations for maximally flat amplitude response in TPTS amplifier.

In general any response curve obtainable with a high-Q TPTS amplifier may be synthesized with a properly adjusted staggered pair. This comes about because both circuits are characterized by a single pair of poles. In the staggered pair there are no zeros, while in the high-Q approximation the effect of the zero of the two-mesh resonant circuit is assumed to be negligible.

15-29. Feedback. No discussion of linear amplifiers would be complete without mention of the use of *inverse*, or *negative*, feedback in controlling their response characteristics. One of the principal applications of inverse feedback will be demonstrated by a specific example.

Consider the high-band response of two identical RC stages having mid-band gains of A_{m1} and upper half-power frequency f_2. Then letting $A_m = A_{m1}^2$ and $A_h = A_{h1}^2$, one has from earlier results

$$A_h = \frac{A_m}{(1 + j\omega/\omega_2)^2} = \frac{E_o}{E_s} \tag{15-101}$$

or

$$E_o = \frac{\omega_2{}^2 A_m E_s}{(\omega_2 + j\omega)^2} \tag{15-101a}$$

It is clear from this equation that the over-all response of these two stages will be characterized by a second-order real pole at $p = -\omega_2$.

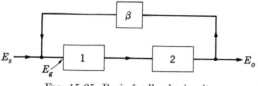

Fig. 15-25. Basic feedback circuit.

Now let a feedback loop be introduced around the two stages as shown in Fig. 15-25 such that a fraction βE_o of the output voltage is added to E_s. Then the grid voltage on stage 1 will be $E_{g1} = E_s + \beta E_o$. Since the amplifier proper has a gain $A_h = E_o/E_{g1}$, one obtains from the figure

$$E_o = A_h(E_s + \beta E_o) \tag{15-102}$$

or

$$E_o = \frac{A_h E_s}{1 - A_h \beta}$$

Substituting from Eq. (15-101),

$$E_o = \frac{A_m E_s}{(1 + j\omega/\omega_2)^2 - A_m \beta}$$

Multiplying by $\omega_2{}^2$, replacing $j\omega$ by p, and clearing,

$$E(p) = \frac{\omega_2{}^2 A_m E_s(p)}{p^2 + 2\omega_2 p + (1 - A_m \beta)\omega_2{}^2} \tag{15-103}$$

With feedback, then, the network response will be characterized by two poles

$$\genfrac{}{}{0pt}{}{\alpha}{\beta} = \omega_2(-1 \pm \sqrt{A_m \beta}) \tag{15-104}$$

Now, if the feedback is *negative*, $A_m \beta = -|A_m \beta|$ and the poles become

$$\genfrac{}{}{0pt}{}{\alpha}{\beta} = \omega_2(-1 \pm j \sqrt{|A_m \beta|}) \tag{15-105}$$

Thus, if $|A_m \beta|$ differs from zero, the two poles are complex conjugates, with $|A_m \beta|$ controlling their imaginary parts. Reference to Sec. 15-10 will show, then, that the effect of negative feedback in this case is similar to that of shunt compensation in a video amplifier except that $|A_m \beta|$ has no effect on the real part of the poles. For example, a maximally flat amplitude response results if $|A_m\beta| = 1$ so that $\dfrac{\alpha}{\beta} = \omega_2(1 \pm j)$.

Negative feedback has other important applications; for example, it can be used to reduce distortion arising within the feedback loop. It further introduces a problem of stability in that the amplifier and feedback loop tend to oscillate unless certain criteria are satisfied. It is beyond the scope of this volume to consider these and other important aspects of feedback. The interested reader is referred to any modern text on electronics.

PROBLEMS

15-1. A 6AG7 is to be operated under conditions such that

$$g_m = 11,000 \ \mu\text{mhos} \qquad r_p = 0.13 \text{ megohm}$$
$$\text{D-c plate voltage} = 300 \text{ volts} \qquad \text{bias voltage} = -3.24 \text{ volts}$$
$$\text{D-c plate current} = 32 \text{ ma} \qquad \text{d-c screen current} = 8 \text{ ma}$$

The total shunt capacitance is estimated to be 25 $\mu\mu$f. With $C_c = 0.05 \ \mu$f, $C_K = 25 \ \mu$f, $R_L = 1$ kilohm, and $R_g = 100$ kilohms:

a. Determine the cathode resistor R_K.

b. Calculate and plot $|A/A_m|$ and the phase shift.

c. Determine the upper and lower half-power frequencies and the mid-band gain.

15-2. The amplifier for Prob. 15-1 is preceded by another stage using fixed bias and for which $f_1 = 200$ cycles, $f_2 = 3$ Mc, $|A_m| = 10$. Plot the over-all gain characteristic, and determine the over-all half-power frequencies.

15-3. Derive an expression for F_1/f_1 for n identical cascaded RC stages.

15-4. Redesign the stage of Prob. 15-1, using shunt compensation to give a maximally flat high-band amplitude response. Specify the new values of R_L and $|A_m|$.

15-5. Verify the value of Q for the maximally flat high-band amplitude response by setting

$$\left(\frac{d^2|A_h/A_m|}{d^2y}\right)_{y=0} = \left(\frac{d|A_h/A_m|}{dy}\right)_{y=0} = 0$$

15-6. Derive the value of Q required to give a maximally flat delay characteristic with shunt compensation.

15-7. (a) Calculate and plot the transient response for the shunt-compensated amplifier for $Q = 0.32$ and 0.414. (b) Tabulate τ_r and γ (in per cent) for the two cases.

15-8. Design a shunt-compensated stage using a 6AK5 with $Q = 0.388$ to give a rise time of 0.05 μsec. Use $g_m = 4,300 \ \mu$mhos, $r_p = 420$ kilohms, $C_s = 12 \ \mu\mu$f. What is the mid-band gain?

15-9. Verify Eq. (15-33) for the m-derived compensating network.

15-10. (a) Evaluate m and Q to give a maximally flat amplitude response, using an m-derived network. (b) Plot $|A_h/A_m|$ for this case. (c) Determine f_2'/f_2 analytically. (d) Calculate and plot the edge response. (e.) Compare the edge response with Fig. 15-10.

15-11. Repeat Prob. 15-10 for a maximally flat delay characteristic.

15-12. Verify Eq. (15-36) for the series-compensated amplifier.

15-13. Plot the transient response of a series-compensated stage for $m = 2$,

$$Q = 0.467$$

Tabulate $\tau_r f_2$ and γ (in per cent).

15-14. A 6AG7 is to operate under the conditions specified in Prob. 15-1, except that C_K is raised to 100 μf. The power supply limits the value R_1 to 3 kilohms.

a. Determine the value of C_1 for the best low-band transient response.

b. Plot the low-band transient response to an applied step function.

c. Plot $|A_l/A_m|$ vs frequency for the low-band range.

15-15. (a) Design a single-tuned amplifier capable of being tuned over the standard broadcast band. Use a 20- to 365-$\mu\mu$f variable capacitor. Bandwidth is to equal 10 kc at $f_r = 1$ Mc. Assume $g_m = 2,000$ μmhos, $r_p > 1$ megohm. (b) Qualitatively discuss the variation of resonance response and selectivity over the broadcast band.

15-16. The amplifier of Prob. 15-15 is tuned to 1 Mc. A 1-Mc sine wave of amplitude $\hat{E}$ is applied for an interval of 1 msec. Calculate and sketch the envelope response. Use reasonable approximations in your calculations.

15-17. Two identical UPTS stages are connected in cascade. For each stage, at 560 kc, $L_p = 90$ μh, $Q_p = 90$, $L_s = 220$ μh, $Q_s = 85$, $M = 20$ μh, $r_p = 660$ kilohms, $g_m = 1,600$ μmhos. Calculate the over-all gain and half-power bandwidth.

15-18. (a) Plot the frequency spectrum of $E_i \sin \omega_i t$, including both positive and negative values of frequency. (b) Expand Eq. (15-72) by means of trigonometric identities, and plot the resulting frequency spectrum. (c) From your results, propose a LP-BP analog relating the spectra of a modulated wave and its modulation envelope.

15-19. Design a minimum-stage synchronously tuned amplifier to meet the following specifications: center frequency = 30 Mc; minimum gain at 30 Mc = 50 db; over-all half-power bandwidth = 4 Mc. 6AC7's are to be used: $g_m = 9,000$ μmhos, $r_p > 1$ megohm. The total shunt capacitance per stage is 25 $\mu\mu$f.

15-20. In this problem you are to study a stagger-tuned pair, independent of the method discussed in the text. Assume arithmetic symmetry throughout. Both stages have the same half-power bandwidth BW and have center frequencies of

$$f_{\frac{1}{2}} = f_0 \pm \frac{BW}{2} b$$

Use a normalized frequency variable defined by

$$x = \frac{2(f - f_0)}{BW}$$

a. Write the equation for the normalized over-all gain.

b. At what values of x does the gain maximize or minimize? Sketch the shape of normalized gain vs. frequency for the three cases $b < 1$, $b = 1$, $b > 1$. Which value of b gives the maximally flat response?

c. Under the maximally flat conditions how is the over-all bandwidth $(BW)_T$ related to BW?

15-21. Design a maximally flat stagger-tuned pair to meet the specifications of the sample problem in Sec. 15-23. Calculate and plot the normalized amplitude response. How does it compare with Fig. 15-21 for the staggered triple?

15-22. Design a maximally flat stagger-tuned quadruple ($n = 4$) to meet the specifications of the sample problem in Sec. 15-23. Compare the response with Fig. 15-21.

15-23. For the two single-tuned stages described in Prob. 15-20 let $b > 1$.

a. What is the normalized gain at a peak?

b. What value of *b* (in equation form) will give a specified ratio of gain at a peak to center gain?

c. What is $(BW)_T$?

15-24. A voltage $U(t)\hat{E}_g \sin(2\pi \times 5 \times 10^5 t)$ is applied to the maximally flat staggered triple of Sec. 15-23. Calculate the envelope response.

15-25. Three stages identical to stage 2 of the sample problem in Sec. 15-23 are connected in cascade. If $U(t)\hat{E}_g \sin(2\pi \times 5 \times 10t)$ is applied, calculate the envelope response. Compare with Prob. 15-24.

15-26. By comparing Eqs. (15-90*b*) and (15-93*c*) determine the maximum values of $(BW)_T/f_0$ for which Eq. (15-90*b*) is correct to within 1 per cent. Calculate for $n = 2$ to $n = 5$. Tabulate your results.

15-27. The circuit parameters of a TPTS amplifier are $g_m = 2{,}000$ μmhos, $r_p > 1$ megohm, $L_p = L_s = 1$ mh, $Q = 100$, $C_p = C_s = 117.2$ $\mu\mu$f, $M = 24.14$ μh.

a. What is the center frequency of the response?

b. What is the "dip" in decibels?

c. What is bandwidth?

d. What is the gain at the peaks and center frequencies?

e. At what frequencies do the peaks occur?

CHAPTER 16

ELECTROMECHANICAL
COUPLING

In the introductory chapter, reference was made to the fact that electrical systems for both power and communication purposes often receive their energy in a mechanical form and must deliver their energy in a similar mechanical form. One may consider the system as a complete network and the electromechanical coupling between electrical and mechanical meshes as similar to the electrical coupling between two adjacent meshes of a network of electrical impedances.

Both unilateral and bilateral electromechanical coupling units are available. The carbon-grain microphone is an example of a unilateral type as the mechanical movement of the diaphragm can control the flow of electrical current, but this current does not react on the mechanical system. An ordinary telephone receiver, on the other hand, is a bilateral device, for it may be used either as a motor or a generator, i.e., it can transfer energy either from the electrical to the mechanical system, or vice versa. In Bell's original telephone the same device was used as both transmitter and receiver.

16-1. Analogs. In communication work the mechanical movements of most interest are alternating in character. The principles which have been developed for the analysis of alternating currents can be applied directly to the study of mechanical and acoustical vibrations.

In extending one's knowledge into new fields, use may be made of analogs which relate one's past experience to the new situation. A distinction should be made between qualitative and quantitative analogs. A quantitative analog occurs when equations relating new quantities are of exactly the same form as those relating old quantities. New and old quantities occupying the same positions in the equations are then said to be analogous. A common analog is the one comparing the flow of water in pipes to the flow of electrical current in wires. However, the relation between pressure and velocity in the water system does not have the linear character of Ohm's law, and so the analog is qualitative and not quantitative. It is, however, possible to build a nonlinear electrical analog which is quantitative, and this has been done to construct pipe-line analyzers for the prediction of complicated situations.

On the other hand, many of the differential equations of the linear electrical circuit are similar to those of mechanical motion. Some of these will now be discussed.

Newton's second law may be written

$$f = \frac{d(mv)}{dt} \tag{16-1}$$

$$= m\frac{dv}{dt} + v\frac{dm}{dt}$$

$$= m\frac{d^2x}{dt^2} + v\frac{dm}{dt} \tag{16-1a}$$

where f is the *applied* force.

Similarly the law of induced emf is

$$e = \frac{d(n\Phi)}{dt} \tag{16-2}$$

where e is the *applied* voltage.

One might therefore draw these comparisons: *Force is analogous to emf. Momentum is analogous to flux linkages.*

Another concept which is frequently introduced is that of inductance, or flux linkages per ampere. For the case where L is not a function of current but may be a function of time (there is no mechanical analog to saturation),

$$L = \frac{n\Phi}{i} \tag{16-3}$$

Introducing Eq. (16-3) into (16-2),

$$e = \frac{d(Li)}{dt}$$

$$= L\frac{di}{dt} + i\frac{dL}{dt}$$

$$= L\frac{d^2q}{dt^2} + i\frac{dL}{dt} \tag{16-4}$$

Compare Eqs. (16-4) and (16-1a) to find the following analogs: *Mass is analogous to inductance. Velocity is analogous to current. Displacement is analogous to charge.*

A further substantiation of these comparisons is contained in the expressions for kinetic energy and the energy stored in a magnetic field. Let W represent this energy:

$$W = \frac{Li^2}{2} \text{ in an electrical system where } L \text{ is independent of } i \tag{16-5}$$

$$W = \frac{mv^2}{2} \text{ in a mechanical system} \tag{16-6}$$

Consider the case of a spring disturbed by a force. Then the force *exerted* on the spring to produce the displacement will be

$$f = kx \qquad (16\text{-}7a)$$

where k is the coefficient of stiffness and it is assumed that the stretching is below the elastic limit.

In an electrical circuit it is common to write

$$e = \frac{q}{C} \qquad (16\text{-}7b)$$

where the voltage e is the external applied voltage which produces the charge q in the capacitor.

The reciprocal of capacitance is sometimes termed "elastance." Therefore *stiffness is analogous to electrical elastance.*

The reciprocal of mechanical stiffness is called the "compliance," and so *compliance is analogous to capacitance.*

The analog for the case of resistance is not so generally perfect. In the case of low velocities the mechanical force due to viscous friction is nearly proportional to the velocity. This is also true of internal mechanical forces due to the velocity of bending, etc. The equation of the force which must be applied to a body in a viscous medium would then become

$$\mathbf{f} = r_{\text{mech}}v \qquad (16\text{-}8a)$$

where r_{mech} is a proportionality factor called the "mechanical resistance." Compare this equation with Ohm's law

$$e = Ri \qquad (16\text{-}8b)$$

where e is the voltage applied to the resistance.

Therefore *mechanical resistance is analogous to electrical resistance.*

The dimensions of a mechanical ohm can be obtained from Eq. (16-8a).

$$r_{\text{mech}} = \frac{\mathbf{f}}{v} \text{ newton-sec/m.}$$

When the frictional force is not directly proportional to the velocity, the same principles which are applied to nonlinear electrical resistances may be used.

A simple mechanical system vibrating in a viscous medium is shown in Fig. 16-1. The positive direction of force and displacement is assumed to be downward. The equation would be

$$\mathbf{f} = m\frac{d^2x}{dt^2} + r\frac{dx}{dt} + kx \qquad (16\text{-}9)$$

It will be seen that this is similar to the equation that would be obtained for the circuit consisting of a resistance, inductance, and capacitance in series, viz.,

$$e = L\frac{di}{dt} + Ri + \frac{1}{C}\int i\,dt$$

$$e = L\frac{d^2q}{dt^2} + R\frac{dq}{dt} + \frac{q}{C} \tag{16-10}$$

These equations, together with the boundary conditions, will describe the transient oscillations of the mechanical and electrical systems. When the mechanical system is subjected to steady alternating impressed forces, the resultant velocities will be related to these forces in both magnitude and phase, in the same manner as the corresponding relations between voltage and current. Therefore, steady-state impedance operators will be introduced which are quantitative analogs of electrical impedances and may be treated in the same way, for example, by the use of complex quantities. A mechanical impedance of Z ohms would indicate that the ratio of the maximum alternating force measured in newtons to the maximum alternating velocity measured in meters per second would have the numerical value Z. There would also be a shift in phase which would be computed in the same way as for the analogous a-c circuit.

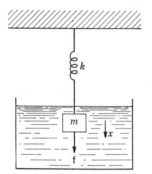

FIG. 16-1. Simple mechanical vibrating system.

It should be observed that the summing up of the voltages *around a mesh* in an electrical circuit gives the same type of equation as the summing up of the forces *on a mass* in a mechanical system. In a complicated mechanical system the displacements, velocities, and accelerations will require more than one space variable to describe their configuration as a function of time. In this case more space variables must be introduced. There will then be as many independent equations as there are space variables. If there are n such variables, the system is said to have n degrees of freedom. The n equations would be analogous to the n independent equations obtained in an electrical circuit containing n independent meshes. If the equations of motion are set up for the mechanical system, the analogous electrical system can be recognized. The equations for an n-mesh electrical system were given in Chap. 3 as Eqs. (3-6). This group of equations can be made to apply to instantaneous currents and voltages by replacing the impedance operator Z_{mn} by an integro-differential operator of the form

$$-\left(L_{mn}\frac{d}{dt} + R_{mn} + S_{mn}\int dt\right)$$

The general mutual term $Z_{mn}I_n$ would then become

$$Z_{mn}I_n = -\left(L_{mn}\frac{di_n}{dt} + R_{mn}i_n + S_{mn}\int i_n \, dt\right)$$

where L_{mn}, R_{mn}, and $S_{mn} = 1/C_{mn}$ are the circuit elements common to

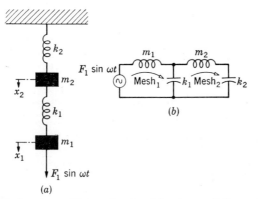

(a)

(b)

FIG. 16-2. Mechanical system with two degrees of freedom and the analogous electrical circuit.

two meshes. The mechanical equations are usually given in terms of displacements instead of velocities, and the general electrical term could also be written

$$Z_{mn}I_n = -\left(L_{mn}\frac{d^2q_n}{dt^2} + R_{mn}\frac{dq_n}{dt} + S_{mn}q_n\right) \tag{16-11}$$

As was explained in Chap. 3, the negative sign would be used for mutual terms but the positive sign would be used for self-impedances ($m = n$). This gives

$$Z_{nn}I_n = L_{nn}\frac{d^2q_n}{dt^2} + R_{nn}\frac{dq_n}{d_t} + S_{nn}q_n \tag{16-12}$$

As an example consider the mechanical system shown in Fig. 16-2a with the masses m_1 and m_2 hung by the two springs with stiffness coefficients k_1 and k_2. Let the weights take their initial extension due to gravity, which can then be neglected, and study the motion due to an alternating force $\hat{F}_1 \sin \omega t$. Assume that frictional or dissipative forces are negligible.

Let

x_1 be the displacement of m_1 from its initial position downward
x_2 be the displacement of m_2 from its initial position downward
Forces be positive when exerted downward

Then spring 2 would be stretched an amount x_2 from its initial position and would exert a restoring force $-k_2x_2$ on mass 2. Spring 1 would be stretched an amount $x_1 - x_2$ and would exert a force $+k_1(x_1 - x_2)$ on mass m_2 and a force

$-k_1(x_1 - x_2)$ on mass m_1. The equations of motion would then be obtained by summing up the forces acting on *each* mass and equating it to ma for that mass. This would give two equations as follows:

$$\hat{F}_1 \sin \omega t = m_1 \frac{d^2x_1}{dt^2} + k_1x_1 - k_1x_2 \qquad (16\text{-}13)$$

$$0 = m_2 \frac{d^2x_2}{dt^2} + (k_1 + k_2)x_2 - k_1x_1 \qquad (16\text{-}14)$$

An examination of Eqs. (16-13) and (16-14) shows that two variables and two equations are necessary to describe the mechanical system, and so the equivalent electrical system would be a two-mesh circuit. The most general equations for a two-mesh electrical circuit would be

$$E_1 = Z_{11}I_1 + Z_{12}I_2$$
$$E_2 = Z_{21}I_1 + Z_{22}I_2$$

which can be given in more detail in the differential form as

$$e_1 = \left(L_{11}\frac{d^2q_1}{dt^2} + R_{11}\frac{dq_1}{dt} + S_{11}q_1\right) - \left(L_{12}\frac{d^2q_2}{dt^2} + R_{12}\frac{dq_2}{dt} + S_{12}q_2\right) \qquad (16\text{-}15)$$

$$e_2 = -\left(L_{21}\frac{d^2q_1}{dt^2} + R_{21}\frac{dq_1}{dt} + S_{21}q_1\right) + \left(L_{22}\frac{d^2q_2}{dt^2} + R_{22}\frac{dq_2}{dt} + S_{22}q_2\right) \qquad (16\text{-}16)$$

A comparison of Eqs. (16-13) and (16-14) with Eqs. (16-15) and (16-16) shows the following quantitative analogies:

$$x_1 \rightarrow q_1 \qquad \hat{F}_1 \sin \omega t \rightarrow e_1 \qquad m_1 \rightarrow L_{11}$$
$$x_2 \rightarrow q_2 \qquad 0 \rightarrow e_2 \qquad m_2 \rightarrow L_{22}$$
$$k_1 \rightarrow S_{11} \qquad k_1 \rightarrow S_{12} \qquad \text{All } R\text{'s} = 0$$
$$k_1 + k_2 \rightarrow S_{22} \qquad k_1 \rightarrow S_{21} \qquad L_{12} = L_{21} = 0$$

Since L_{nn} and S_{nn} are the total values around the nth mesh, the equivalent circuit would be that shown in Fig. 16-2b.

Since the differential equations correspond and have the same solutions, the two systems are analogous in both the transient and the steady state. In the mks system the force in newtons can replace the voltage in volts, the mass in kilograms can replace the inductance in henrys, the stiffness in newtons per meter can replace the reciprocal of the capacitance in farads, and the effective or maximum velocity in meters per second can replace the effective or maximum current in amperes. This means that the notions of impedance and effective values which are used in a-c electrical circuits will also be useful in vibrating mechanical systems and Eqs. (3-6) of Chap. 3 can be used directly. The "mechanical impedance" will be defined as the phasor ratio of the applied alternating force to the alternating velocity.

It is not necessary to make force analogous to emf and displacement analogous to charge in setting up mechanical equations. Other coordinates could be used provided that the quantity analogous to emf times the quantity analogous to charge had the dimensions of work. For example, it is quite common to write equations in terms of torque and angular displacement, and these would occupy the same positions in the differential equations and hence be analogous, respectively, to voltage and charge. Furthermore, torque times angular displacement equals work.

It was shown in Chap. 3 that duals in electrical circuits are themselves analogs. Therefore it would be possible to make force the analog of current, velocity the analog of voltage, mass the analog of capacitance, etc. In this case the equivalent circuit would be the equivalent of the dual of the circuit obtained with the analogs developed earlier in the chapter. This is particularly useful when the driving function is a known velocity rather than a known force as in a phonograph pickup.

It is possible to set up simultaneous equations in electromechanical systems in which both current and velocity will appear, and these will correspond to a multimesh system with a certain difference in the character of the mutual impedance, to be explained later. An example will be given in connection with the discussion of motional impedance. It is also possible to use more than one type of space and force coordinate in a mechanical system provided that dimensional homogeneity is maintained. For example, the motion of a body which has both translation and rotation might be described in terms of both linear and angular displacements. These coordinates in turn may be made analogous to electrical charge in an equivalent electrical circuit obtained by examination of the simultaneous differential equations.

16-2. Acoustical Analogs. Since acoustical vibrations involve the mechanical movement of gases, similar analogs to those which have been applied to mechanical systems can be applied to acoustical networks. Rayleigh, in his "Theory of Sound," laid down the fundamentals of acoustics in a masterful manner, and after many years his work is still the authority on the subject. Webster, in his analysis of horns, first introduced the idea of acoustical impedance, and this application of an electrical analog has proved one of the most powerful tools which has been introduced since the work of Rayleigh.

16-3. Effect of Low Velocity of Propagation on Acoustical and Mechanical Analogs. It has been pointed out that, when the dimensions are of the order of a wavelength in electrical circuits, analyses must be made on the basis of distributed constants and wave propagation. This occurs on long telephone lines at af and with much smaller dimensions at high rf. Since the wavelength is equal to the velocity of propagation divided by the frequency, a low velocity of propagation will reduce the dimensions at which the effect of distributed constants must be taken into account. In mechanical and acoustical vibrations the velocity is very low, e.g., the velocity of sound in air at normal temperatures and pressures is 1,120 ft/sec, which means that the wavelength of a 1,000-cycle wave is only 1.12 ft. Therefore, many of the same phenomena which appear in electrical circuits with frequencies of the order of 10^9 cycles appear in acoustical systems of the same approximate dimensions in meters at af. A short length of pipe can be considered acoustically on the same basis as an electrical line, but analyses made on the basis of lumped constants must be examined carefully to determine the order of error which is there introduced. A vibrating diaphragm will have multiple-resonant frequencies due to its distributed mass and compliance.

In general, operation below and in the neighborhood of the first resonant frequency can be treated on the basis of lumped constants, while operation above that frequency must be treated on the basis of distributed constants except in special cases.

16-4. Stiffness, Mass, and Resistance Control of Mechanical Systems. One of the ideals in the construction of most communication equipment is the elimination of frequency distortion. In the electromechanical devices such as microphones, receivers, and loudspeakers it will be found that the desirable relations between *mechanical force* and *motion* can be obtained by controls which will fall into three principal classifications. These are called stiffness, resistance, and mass control. They correspond, respectively, to electrical circuits in which capacitance, resistance, and inductance predominate. As in the electrical systems it is not possible to have capacitance without inductance, so in the mechanical systems it is impossible to produce stiffness without the presence of some mass, and vice versa. By reference to Chap. 4, Resonance, it will be seen that, if the resistance is small in a series electrical circuit containing both capacitance and inductance, the capacitive reactance will predominate below the resonant frequency, in which range the inductance may be practically neglected. On the other hand, at frequencies above resonance the inductive reactance will predominate, and the capacitance may be neglected. In the same way, the stiffness will be the controlling factor below the resonant frequency in the case of a diaphragm, while the mass will be the controlling factor at frequencies higher than resonance until the distributed character of the constants begins to be of importance as still higher resonant frequencies appear. Some additional characteristics are discussed below and are summarized in Fig. 16-3.

16-5. Stiffness Control (Resonant Frequency above Operating Range of Frequencies). In this case the mechanical impedance will be reactive and nearly *inversely proportional to the frequency*. In the following equations the inductance is neglected.

See note*	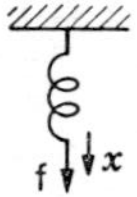 $f = kx$	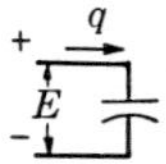 $e = Sq = \dfrac{q}{C}$	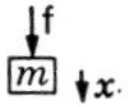 $f = m\dfrac{d^2x}{dt^2}$	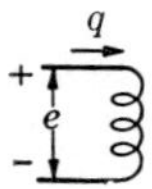 $e = L\dfrac{d^2q}{dt^2}$	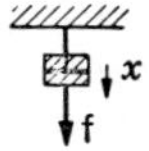 $f = r\dfrac{dx}{dt}$	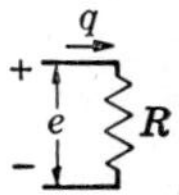 $e = R\dfrac{dq}{dt}$
$f = \hat{F}\sin\omega t$ and $e = \hat{E}\sin\omega t$	$x = \dfrac{\hat{F}}{k}\sin\omega t$	$q = C\hat{E}\sin\omega t$	$\dfrac{d^2x}{dt^2} = \dfrac{\hat{F}\sin\omega t}{m}$	$\dfrac{d^2q}{dt^2} = \dfrac{E\sin\omega t}{L}$	$\dfrac{dx}{dt} = \dfrac{\hat{F}\sin\omega t}{r}$	$\dfrac{dq}{dt} = \dfrac{\hat{E}\sin\omega t}{R}$
Velocity and current..	$v = \dfrac{dx}{dt} = \dfrac{\omega\hat{F}\cos\omega t}{k}$	$i = \dfrac{dq}{dt} = \omega C\hat{E}\cos\omega t$	$v = \int \dfrac{d^2x}{dt^2}\,dt = -\dfrac{\hat{F}\cos\omega t}{\omega m}$	$i = \int \dfrac{d^2q}{dt^2}\,dt = -\dfrac{\hat{E}\cos\omega t}{\omega L}$	$v = \dfrac{\hat{F}\sin\omega t}{r}$	$i = \dfrac{\hat{E}\sin\omega t}{R}$
Maximum value......	$V_m = \dfrac{\omega\hat{F}}{k}$	$\hat{I} = \omega C\hat{E}$	$\hat{V} = \dfrac{\hat{F}}{\omega m}$	$\hat{I} = \dfrac{\hat{E}}{\omega L}$	$\hat{V} = \dfrac{\hat{F}}{r}$	$\hat{I} = \dfrac{\hat{E}}{R}$
Effective value......	$V = \dfrac{\omega F}{k}$	$I = \omega C E$	$V = \dfrac{F}{\omega m}$	$I = \dfrac{E}{\omega L}$	$V = \dfrac{F}{r}$	$I = \dfrac{E}{R}$
Absolute value of the impedances ($= F/V$ and E/I)..........	$Z = \dfrac{k}{\omega}$	$Z = \dfrac{1}{\omega C}$	$Z = \omega m$	$Z = \omega L$	$Z = r$	$Z = R$
Phasor impedances...	$Z = -j\dfrac{k}{\omega}$	$Z = -\dfrac{j}{\omega C}$	$Z = j\omega m$	$Z = j\omega L$	$Z = r$	$Z = R$

* In these cases, f and e are the forces and voltages exerted *on* the elements. The forces exerted *by* the elements are equal and opposite.

Fig. 16-3. Chart showing common analogs between electrical and mechanical impedances.

603

Electrical equation: $\qquad\qquad I = jE2\pi fC$ $\qquad\qquad$ (16-17a)

Mechanical equation: $\qquad\qquad V = jF\,\dfrac{2\pi f}{k}$ $\qquad\qquad$ (16-17b)

$$Z_{\text{mech}} = -\frac{jk}{2\pi f} \qquad\qquad (16\text{-}17c)$$

where V = rms velocity, cm/sec
$\qquad F$ = rms force, in newtons
$\qquad f$ = frequency
$\qquad k$ = mechanical stiffness, newtons/m

These are effective values. In instantaneous values the equations may be written as below.

Electrical equation: $\qquad\quad i = \hat{E}2\pi fC \cos 2\pi ft$ $\qquad\qquad$ (16-18a)

Mechanical equation: $\qquad v = \hat{F}\,\dfrac{2\pi f}{k}\cos 2\pi ft$ $\qquad\qquad$ (16-18b)

The charge or displacement can be found by integrating with respect to time.

Electrical equation: $\qquad q = \displaystyle\int_0^t i\,dt_1 = \hat{E}C \sin 2\pi ft$ $\qquad$ (16-19a)

Mechanical equation: $x = \displaystyle\int_0^t v\,dt_1 = \dfrac{\hat{F}}{k}\sin 2\pi ft$ $\qquad$ (16-19b)

Hence, with stiffness control the maximum displacement is directly proportional to the maximum force and independent of frequency just as the maximum charge on a capacitor is proportional to the maximum voltage applied and independent of the frequency.

16-6. Mass Control (Resonant Frequency below Operating Range of Frequencies). In this case the mechanical impedance will be reactive and *directly proportional to the frequency.*

Electrical equation: $\qquad\qquad I = \dfrac{-jE}{2\pi fL}$ $\qquad\qquad$ (16-20a)

Mechanical equation: $\qquad\qquad V = \dfrac{-jF}{2\pi fm}$ $\qquad\qquad$ (16-20b)

$$Z_{\text{mech}} = j2\pi fm \qquad\qquad (16\text{-}20c)$$

where m = mass in kilograms.

16-7. Resistance Control. In certain cases it is possible to provide a mechanical load in which the velocity will be in phase with a sinusoidal applied force and their ratio will be independent of frequency. Hence no resonant effects are of importance.

As in the electrical case this is called resistance control.

Electrical equation: $\qquad\qquad I = \dfrac{E}{R}$ $\qquad\qquad$ (16-21a)

Mechanical equation: $\qquad\qquad V = \dfrac{F}{r_{\text{mech}}}$ $\qquad\qquad$ (16-21b)

16-8. Coupling Units. Electromechanical systems used in communication may be classed in several ways. On the basis of use, the classification might be in terms of the following:

1. Electrical to mechanical couplers.
    a. Receivers which operate pressed against the ear.
    b. Loudspeakers which operate into free air.
2. Mechanical to electrical couplers.
    a. Microphones.
    b. Devices for reflecting mechanical elements as electrical constants in a circuit.

As far as their use is concerned, these elements, with the exception of those falling under 2*b* above, may be either unilateral or bilateral. As a matter of fact, most of the useful elements, with the exception of the carbon-grain transmitter, are bilateral and hence may be applied to any of the uses described above.

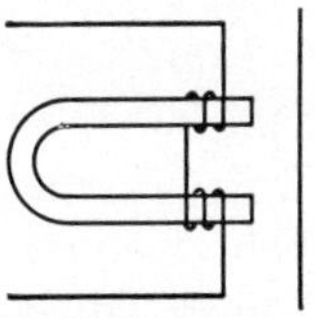

16-9. Telephone Receivers. The essential parts of a telephone receiver are shown in Fig. 16-4. They consist of a permanent magnet, a coil to modify the flux in accordance with the fluctuations in current, and an iron diaphragm.

Fig. 16-4. Elements of a simple telephone receiver.

The pull of a magnet is proportional to the *square* of the flux. Since the flux is proportional to current, if no permanent magnet were used the force on the diaphragm would be proportional to the square of the current. If a pure sine wave of voltage were impressed on the coil in such a case, the motion of the diaphragm would occur at twice the frequency of the voltage. This is illustrated in Fig. 16-5. Mathematically such a condition is illustrated by the equation

$$f = k_1\Phi^2 \qquad (16\text{-}22)$$

Let

$$i = \hat{I}_1 \sin \omega_1 t \qquad (16\text{-}23)$$

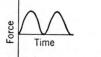

Fig. 16-5. Current and force on the diaphragm of a telephone receiver with no permanent magnet.

If there is neither a d-c component of current nor a permanent flux, then

$$\Phi = k_2 i = k_2\hat{I}_1 \sin \omega_1 t \qquad (16\text{-}24)$$

$$f = k_1 k_2{}^2 \hat{I}_1{}^2 \sin^2 \omega_1 t = \frac{k_1 k_2{}^2 \hat{I}_1{}^2}{2} - \frac{k_1 k_2{}^2 \hat{I}_1{}^2}{2} \cos 2\omega t$$

$$(16\text{-}25)$$

The second term of Eq. (16-25) shows the existence of the second harmonic in the force on the diaphragm.

Similarly, if a complex wave with several sinusoidal components were impressed on the coil, the force, and hence the motion, would have components equal to the sum and difference of each frequency and every other frequency in the input, as well as second harmonics.

If a direct component is added to the flux, by means of either a permanent magnet or a d-c component in the electrical circuit, the situation will be greatly improved. In this case let

$$\Phi = \Phi_1 + k_2 i \qquad (16\text{-}24a)$$

where Φ_1 is a constant unidirectional flux

Substitute Eq. (16-24a) in Eq. (16-22).

$$\begin{aligned} f &= k_1(\Phi_1 + k_2 i)^2 \\ &= k_1(\Phi_1{}^2 + 2k_2\Phi_1 i + k_2{}^2 i^2) \end{aligned} \qquad (16\text{-}26)$$

Equation (16-26) contains three terms. The first is the permanent pull $k_1\Phi_1{}^2$, which is independent of the signal. The second is the term $2k_1k_2\Phi_1 i$, which will be proportional to i and will contain all the component frequencies of the input current. The third is the term $k_1k_2{}^2 i^2$, which will contain all the distortion terms which are present when no permanent flux is provided. The ratio of the desired to the undesired term is then

$$\frac{\text{Amplitude of desired frequencies}}{\text{Amplitude of undesired frequencies}} = \frac{2k_2\Phi_1 i}{k_2{}^2 i^2} = \frac{2\Phi_1}{k_2 i} \qquad (16\text{-}27)$$

By making the permanent flux large in proportion to that produced by the current, the ratio given by Eq. (16-27) can be made large.

The effect of the permanent flux can be seen qualitatively by considering the motion of the diaphragm of Fig. 16-4 in two cases. If no magnet or d-c component is provided, the diaphragm will have no tension upon it when the current is zero. If a sine wave of current is sent through the coil, the diaphragm will be attracted during the positive alternation, restored to normal when the current reaches zero, and again be attracted when the current becomes negative. It will therefore execute two cycles of motion during one electrical cycle. When the permanent flux is added, the diaphragm will be flexed even when no current is flowing. When the mmf, due to the current, aids the permanent flux, the attraction will increase and the diaphragm will move inward, while during the opposite alternation of current the attraction will be decreased and the motion will be outward. Therefore, one cycle of current will produce one cycle of mechanical motion.

In addition to the reduction of distortion, it is apparent that the permanent magnet increases the sensitivity of the receiver. The amplitude of the desired output, as represented by the middle term of Eq. (16-26), is proportional to the permanent flux Φ_1.

A form of electromechanical coupling commonly used to drive loudspeakers and some of the better telephone receivers is shown in Fig. 16-6. The electrical element, or voice coil, is a solenoid which is attached to the diaphragm. The permanent magnet is cylindrical with one pole in the center and the other pole concentric around it so that the voice coil is in a magnetic field of constant flux density. The force on the magnetic field will be

$$f = Bli \qquad (16\text{-}28)$$

where f = force, newtons
B = flux density, webers/ sq m
l = length of wire wound in voice coil, m
i = current in voice coil, amp

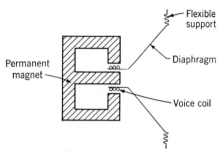

FIG. 16-6. Elements of an electrodynamic coupler commonly used for loudspeakers and microphones.

Since the force is directly proportional to the current, no distortion is introduced of the type present in the receiver of Fig. 16-4. However, at low frequencies, the motion of the coil may be so large that the coil is carried out of the region of constant flux density, and in this case nonlinear distortion may be severe.

16-10. Motional Impedance. The coupler of Fig. 16-6 may also be used as a generator for converting mechanical to electrical energy. The voltage generated will be

$$e = Blv \qquad (16\text{-}29)$$

where v is the velocity in meters per second. Hence this coupler may also be used as a microphone.

A device which can act as either a generator or a motor will act as both simultaneously. When a current is sent through the coil and mechanical motion takes place, this motion induces a voltage in the coil which modifies the impedance. This change in impedance due to the mechanical motion is called "motional impedance."

In a d-c motor the equation of voltages in the armature is

$$E_t = I_a R_a + E_b \qquad (16\text{-}30)$$

where E_t = terminal voltage applied to armature
I_a = armature current
R_a = armature resistance
E_b = counter emf due to motion of armature

Equation (16-30) can be rewritten

$$\frac{E_t}{I_a} = R_a + \frac{E_b}{I_a} \qquad (16\text{-}31)$$

E_t/I_a is the apparent resistance of the armature. It is made up of two parts, the normal resistance R_a and the term E_b/I_a, which is due to the motion of the armature and so might be called the "motional resistance."

As the load on the motor increases, it should be noted that the armature current increases and the motional resistance decreases. Therefore, this motional resistance in the electrical circuit is *inversely proportional* to the mechanical resistance of the load.

The electrodynamic coupler differs from the d-c motor in that an alternating voltage is impressed on the winding and the motion of the diaphragm is also alternating. The diaphragm has the mechanical properties of mass, stiffness, and resistance. The resistance is due to internal friction and to the acoustical load which is presented by the air. Below and in the neighborhood of the first resonant frequency the mechanical system can be represented by simple lumped elements. The mechanical and electrical systems are coupled by bilateral action, and the system may be solved by a pair of simultaneous equations.

The analysis of the mechanism of Fig. 16-6 as a coupler between a mechanical and electrical system may be developed as follows: Assume the receiver diaphragm has mass and stiffness and is loaded with a mechanical resistance. These mechanical values can be lumped in a complex impedance Z_{mech}. Let the coil be connected in an electrical circuit whose impedance, including that of the coil, is Z_{elec}. Let the circuit have a voltage E impressed on it.

Then the complex current I in the coil will produce a complex force on the diaphragm

$$F = BlI \qquad (16\text{-}32)$$

The resultant complex velocity of the diaphragm will be given by

$$V = \frac{F}{Z_{mech}} = \frac{BlI}{Z_{mech}} \qquad (16\text{-}33)$$

This will induce a voltage in the coil

$$E_{ind} = BlV = \frac{(Bl)^2 I}{Z_{mech}} \qquad (16\text{-}34)$$

Hence the electrical-circuit equation will be

$$E_{app} = Z_{elec}I + \frac{(Bl)^2 I}{Z_{mech}} \qquad (16\text{-}35)$$

$$\frac{E_{app}}{I} = Z_{elec} + \frac{(Bl)^2}{Z_{mech}} \qquad (16\text{-}36)$$

The term $(Bl)^2/Z_{mech}$ is called the *motional impedance*. It is seen that the motional impedance is inversely proportional to the mechanical impedance, and hence inversion takes place in a similar way to that for two electrical circuits [see Eq. (11-56)].

An alternate way of writing the two meshes is as two simultaneous equations as follows:

$$E = Z_{\text{elec}}I + BlV \tag{16-37}$$

$$BlI = Z_{\text{mech}}V$$

or
$$0 = -BlI + Z_{\text{mech}}V \tag{16-38}$$

It will be observed that Eqs. (16-37) and (16-38) are similar to the equations for two coupled electrical circuits except for the important difference that the signs on the mutual-impedance terms are opposite. Therefore care must be taken in any attempt to represent an electromechanical system in terms of an equivalent circuit, since the mutual impedance between a mechanical and an electrical system is not quite the same as the mutual impedance between two electrical meshes or, for that matter, two mechanical meshes.

In this derivation the effects of hysteresis and eddy currents have been neglected. In practice such effects would cause the flux to lag behind the mmf which produces it. This causes the motional impedance of the actual receiver to lag the impedance which would be obtained if the magnetic circuit were ideal.

16-11. Motional-impedance Circles. In Chap. 4, Resonance, it was shown that the locus of admittances of a series resonant circuit is a circle. Therefore, the locus of the motional impedance of a telephone receiver is also a circle, since it is proportional to the mechanical *admittance* of the diaphragm. When the motional impedance has been obtained over a range of frequencies, the resonant frequency, effective resistance, and sharpness of resonance of the receiver diaphragm may be obtained.

In order to determine the motional impedance, the impedance of the receiver is first measured with the diaphragm blocked, so that no motion can occur. Then the receiver impedance is measured with the diaphragm operating normally. The *phasor* difference between the two impedances is the motional impedance.

Figure 16-7 shows how this phasor may be measured at different frequencies. This figure was obtained by measuring the impedance of a Western Electric 555W loud-speaking receiver through an efficient 600/15-ohm transformer. This receiver is of the type shown in Fig. 16-6 and is intended to be loaded with an exponential horn. The dotted curve is the one obtained with the diaphragm blocked. This curve gives the phasor locus of impedances, in which any point represents the terminal point of a phasor starting at the origin. The solid-line curve is obtained when the diaphragm is allowed to move. In this case no horn was attached, so that the resonant effect of the diaphragm alone was emphasized. Small increments of frequency must be taken when passing around the loop, as the changes are rapid near the resonant frequency. A line, connecting points on the two curves which correspond to the same frequency, will give the phasor of motional impedance at that frequency. If these phasors are obtained over a range of frequencies extending around the loop of the solid line of Fig. 16-7 and are replotted from a common center, their terminal points will lie on a circle as shown in Fig. 16-8. The diameter of this circle OA will be depressed below the horizontal axis by the angle due to hysteresis and eddy currents.

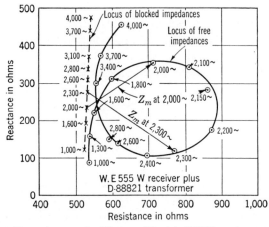

Fig. 16-7. Locus of impedances of a Western Electric 555W receiver measured through a 600/15-ohm transformer with the diaphragm free and with it blocked.

The maximum mechanical admittance will occur at the resonant frequency of the diaphragm, and so the maximum motional impedance will occur at this same frequency. This is the frequency at which the phasor OA is obtained in Fig. 16-8. If no measurement was made at this particular frequency, it can be determined by interpolation between the frequency of phasors lying on either side.

The sharpness of resonance of an electrical circuit has been defined in Chap. 4 in terms of the difference between the two frequencies at which the admittance drops to $1/\sqrt{2}$ of the maximum value. Similarly, the sharpness of resonance of the telephone diaphragm can be defined in terms of the difference in frequencies between these two half-power points. The frequencies at which the mechanical admittance drops to 0.707 of the maximum value are those where the phasors OB and OC are obtained in Fig. 16-8. The line BC passes through the center at right angles to the line OA. If f_1 is the frequency for the phasor OB and f_2 is the frequency for the phasor OC, then the effective Q of the diaphragm can be obtained from Eq. (4-29).

$$\frac{f_2 - f_1}{f_r} = \frac{1}{Q} = \frac{R_{\text{mech}}}{2\pi f_r L_{\text{mech}}} \tag{16-39}$$

A diaphragm does not have lumped constants, but rather distributed ones, and so may be resonant at several frequencies. At each of these resonant frequencies loops will appear in the impedance curve, and they

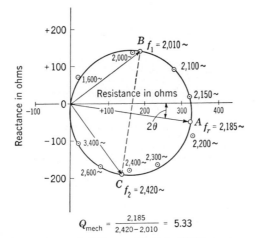

$$Q_{\text{mech}} = \frac{2{,}185}{2{,}420 - 2{,}010} = 5.33$$

FIG. 16-8. Motional impedance of a Western Electric 555W receiver measured through a 600/15-ohm transformer.

can readily be measured. In the neighborhood of each resonant frequency an equivalent series circuit of lumped constants can be assumed.

16-12. Mechanical-control Requirements for Receiver of Low Distortion. An ordinary telephone receiver is used clamped fairly tightly against the ear. This causes the ear to present an acoustical load to the diaphragm which is largely capacitive in character. The alternating motion of the diaphragm will cause a varying pressure on the eardrum which is superimposed on the atmospheric pressure. The instantaneous value of this varying pressure will, by Boyle's law, be proportional to the *displacement* of the diaphragm provided that the ear-cavity dimensions are a small proportion of a wavelength. The telephone receiver is a very inefficient device except near the resonant frequency, and so the motional impedance is not an important factor in determining the current which flows in its coil. Hence, the desirable relation for minimum distortion is that the *displacement* of the diaphragm should be proportional to the *current* in the coil and independent of frequency. The force on the diaphragm is directly proportional to the current. It was shown in an earlier paragraph that under conditions of stiffness control the displacement would be proportional to the force and so this type of control would be desirable in a telephone receiver.

It has been shown that stiffness control exists in a resonant mechanical system below the first resonant frequency, and so the resonant frequency should be located at the upper end of the frequency band which the receiver is designed to reproduce. This is not always done in receivers for ordinary substations, as efficiency is desired even at the expense of good quality. Figure 16-9 shows the measured characteristics of a telephone receiver as obtained by Inglis, Gray, and Jenkins[1] and indicates that its response is relatively free from distortion below the first resonant frequency. This curve also shows the effect of the multiple resonance of the diaphragm, which causes corresponding peaks to appear in the response curve. This measurement was made with air leakage around the ears, which accounts for the falling off at the lower frequencies.

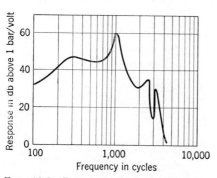

FIG. 16-9. Response characteristic of a desk-stand receiver on ears. (*American Telephone and Telegraph Company.*)

16-13. Other Electromagnetic Couplers. In addition to the simple types of telephone receivers shown in Figs. 16-4 and 16-6 several other types of couplers are available. These types are used for receivers, loudspeakers, and microphones.

Another type of receiver used is that shown in Fig. 16-10. The current in the coil will make the armature a north pole at one end and a south pole at the other, tending to rock it about its center and so operate the diaphragm. The force on the armature will be reversed when the current is reversed. This arrangement is magnetically similar to a push-pull circuit, and so second-order distortion terms which are not present in the electrical input are balanced out and do not appear in the motion of the diaphragm.

This type of unit is sometimes used in phonograph pickups to convert mechanical to electrical energy. High efficiency is not important for this application, as pickups are always used in connection with vacuum-tube amplifiers.

---

[1] A. H. Inglis, C. H. G. Gray, and R. T. Jenkins, A Voice and Ear for Telephone Measurements, *Bell System Tech. J.*, vol. 11, p. 293, 1932.

The ribbon type of coupling unit is extensively used for certain purposes. It is illustrated in Fig. 16-11. The ribbon is hung in a transverse magnetic field, and the current is conducted through it. The ribbon acts as both the conductor of current and the diaphragm. The ribbon is usually bent in a zigzag manner so as to reduce its stiffness and hence its resonant frequency. The low mass of the mechanically moving parts also contributes to this same result.

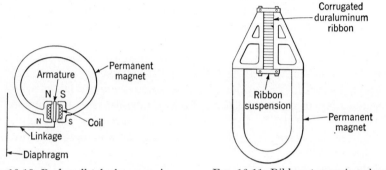

Fig. 16-10. Push-pull telephone receiver.   Fig. 16-11. Ribbon-type microphone.

16-14. Piezoelectric Couplers. Another type of coupling between electrical and mechanical networks is important and makes use of the piezoelectric effect of certain crystals. This effect was discovered by the Curies.

When a crystal possessing piezoelectric properties is mechanically strained, a dielectric polarization or electric stress will result, the magnitude of which is proportional to the strain. Conversely, if an electric field is impressed on the crystal to polarize it, a mechanical stress will be set up.

Since these crystals can transfer energy from a mechanical to an electrical network or back again, they may be used as telephone receivers or transmitters by mechanically linking them to a diaphragm. This was demonstrated by Nicolson prior to 1919. Crystals have also been found to be applicable in the generation, in air or water, of ultrasonic waves of the order of 20,000 to several million cycles.

Previous to 1940, two piezoelectric-crystal materials were in common use. Natural quartz was used exclusively for electric-wave filters and frequency control of oscillators. Rochelle-salt crystals were used in phonograph pickups and underwater transducers.

Since 1940, a variety of new piezoelectric crystals have been put to use. Because of its desirable mechanical characteristics, quartz, although less active, still remains as the only piezoelectric crystal used for oscillator frequency control. However, two new synthetic crystals have been developed for use in electric-wave filters. These are ethylenediamine tartrate and dipotassium tartrate. These two crystals have zero temperature coefficient cuts, high Q's, and a high electromechanical coefficient, are relatively unaffected by atmospheric humidity conditions, and have stability against aging changes.

In the field of underwater transducers ammonium dihydrogen phosphate has largely displaced Rochelle salt. This crystal, commonly referred to as ADP, is also used for phonograph pickups. It has no water of crystallization and will withstand temperatures up to 100°C. It also has a high electromechanical coupling coefficient and can be used to radiate considerable acoustic power, per unit area, without suffering breakdown. Its stability with respect to water vapor is a considerable advantage when contrasted with that of Rochelle salt.

In addition to the first-order effect, piezoelectric materials also exhibit a second-order, or electrostrictive, effect (strain or stress proportional to the square of the electric displacement). This effect is extremely small in all materials except the ferroelectric type. It was discovered in 1947 that the ferroelectric crystal barium titanate exhibits a large electrostrictive effect when made up in multicrystalline form. This ceramic material is now receiving wide application in underwater sound transducers. By applying a d-c polarizing field and exciting the material with an a-c field which has an amplitude small compared with the d-c polarization one obtains a ceramic material which acts as a linear piezoelectric crystal. This ceramic material has considerable advantage over other piezoelectric crystals in that practically any desired shape of element and direction of polarization can be achieved. This advantage, combined with the fact that the material has a large coupling coefficient, is relatively rugged, and is insoluble in water, makes this material especially desirable for use in underwater transducers and processing machines for industrial uses, which require large amounts of ultrasonic energy. Barium titanate is also used for phonograph pickups.

16-15. Electrostatic Couplers. Another electromechanical coupling device of interest is the ordinary capacitor. If one of the plates is permitted to vibrate, it can be used as either a microphone or a receiver.

If a charge is placed on a capacitor, its potential is given by the equation

$$E = \frac{Q}{C} \tag{16-40}$$

If the charge is maintained constant and the capacitance changed, the potential E will vary and so a capacitor with movable plates could be used as a microphone. A typical circuit is shown in Fig. 16-12.

There is a force tending to attract the two plates, and work must be done on the capacitor in decreasing its capacitance, while work is done by the field when the capacitance is increased. If a varying potential were impressed upon the two plates, it would cause a varying force between them, and if one of the latter were free to move, this motion would absorb energy from the electrical circuit in accordance with the work done.   Therefore a capacitor could be used as a receiver.

In a capacitor receiver it is necessary to apply a polarizing, or steady, electric field for the same reason that a polarizing, or permanent, magnetic field is used in the magnetic receiver.   This is because the force

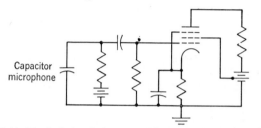

Fig. 16-12. Typical circuit for use with a capacitor microphone.

between the plates is proportional to the square of the potential and the polarization reduces the relative importance of distortion terms.

16-16. Loudspeakers.   While the same type of couplers may be used in the operation of telephone receivers, loudspeakers, and microphones, the design of the mechanical systems associated with the driving units must be quite different for the different applications.   One of the important applications is the loudspeaker, which differs from the receiver in that it must operate into free air instead of the confined space of the ear. Two principal types of loudspeaker are in use: (1) cone loudspeakers, which use a large diaphragm in order to obtain a large acoustic load; (2) horn loudspeakers, which use a horn as an impedance-matching device to connect a small diaphragm to the air.

In the loudspeaker the energy must be imparted as wave motion to the air.   Its problem is therefore quite similar to that of the radio antenna.

In order to deliver acoustical power directly and efficiently to the air, a relatively large diaphragm should be used.   The power in watts delivered *at any frequency* is equal to a constant times the square of the rms velocity of the diaphragm in meters per second.   This constant, or coefficient of proportionality, is termed the "radiation resistance." Space limitations prevent the derivation of the expression for the radiation resistance of a diaphragm.   It was first given by Rayleigh, but it may also be found in other references.   The equation for radiation resistance for a diaphragm in which all parts of the surface are moving together in phase is given by

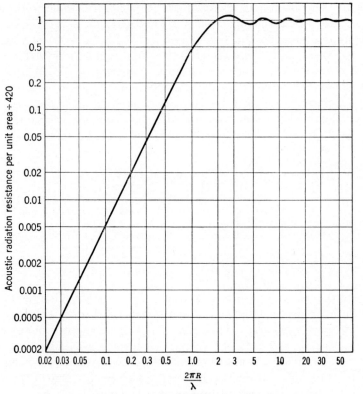

FIG. 16-13. Radiation characteristic of a vibrating piston.

$$r_{\text{rad}} = \rho c \pi R^2 \left[1 - \frac{J_1(2kR)}{kR} \right] \qquad (16\text{-}41)$$

$$= 420 \pi R^2 \left(\frac{k^2 R^2}{2} - \frac{k^4 R^4}{2^2 3} + \frac{k^6 R^6}{2^2 3^2 4} - \cdots \right) \qquad (16\text{-}42)$$

where ρ = density of air, kg/cu m.

= 1.205 for air.

c = velocity of sound, m/sec

= 344 for air.

R = radius of diaphragm, m

J_1 = Bessel function, whose series is given in Eq. (16-42)

$k = 2\pi f/c = 2\pi/\lambda$

A plot of Eq. (16-41) is given in Fig. 16-13. The abscissa is proportional to frequency for a given size of diaphragm. For the lower frequencies the radiation resistance is given by the first term in the series, or

$$r_{\text{rad}} = \frac{420 \times 2\pi^3 R^4 f^2}{c^2}$$

$$r_{\text{rad}} = 0.22 R^4 f^2 \qquad (16\text{-}43)$$

From an inspection of Fig. 16-13 it is apparent that this expression could be used as an approximation up to the point where $2\pi R/\lambda \approx 1.5$ or about $R = \lambda/4$. For frequencies above this the radiation resistance is approximately constant and given by

$$r_{\text{rad}} = 420\pi R^2 \tag{16-44}$$

For an 8-in. cone, which is a common size for broadcast receivers,

$$R = 0.0254 \times 4 \approx 0.10 \text{ m}$$

The radiation resistance will be proportional to the square of the frequency up to

$$\lambda \approx 4 \times 0.10 \approx 0.40 \text{ m}$$
$$f \approx \frac{c}{\lambda} = \frac{344}{0.40} \approx 860 \text{ cycles}$$

The first problem to be considered is the character of the mechanical control which would be desirable in order to reproduce the lower frequencies without distortion. For a given current in the driving coils the acoustic power output should be independent of frequency, in order that there shall be no frequency distortion. By the definition of radiation resistance the output power P in watts is given by

$$P = |V^2|r_{\text{rad}} \tag{16-45}$$

where V is the effective or rms velocity, i.e., $V = \hat{V}/\sqrt{2}$.

The relation between force and velocity in a mechanical system is given by

$$|V| = \frac{|F|}{|Z_{\text{mech}}|} \tag{16-46}$$

Therefore

$$P = F^2 \frac{r_{\text{rad}}}{|Z_{\text{mech}}^2|} \tag{16-47}$$

Since the force on the diaphragm is directly proportional to the driving current, if $r_{\text{rad}}/Z_{\text{mech}}^2$ can be made independent of frequency, the output will be independent of frequency. Since it has been shown by Eq. (16-41) that the radiation resistance is proportional to the square of the frequency up to about 1,000 cycles, the mechanical impedance in this frequency range should be *directly proportional to the frequency*. By reference to Eq. (16-20c) it will be seen that this calls for mass control, i.e., the resonant frequency should be placed at the lower end of the frequency range to be reproduced. Hence, the suspension of the cone should have a large degree of compliance, i.e., it should have very little stiffness. Below the resonant frequency the mechanical impedance will be inversely proportional to the frequency, and so the radiated power P as given by Eq. (16-47) will be proportional to the fourth power of the frequency. Hence the radiation drops off very rapidly, and it is a good approximation to say that there is no appreciable acoustic output below the resonant frequency of the diaphragm. Contrast the operation of the diaphragm in free space as a loudspeaker with the operation of the receiver held against the ear, where it was shown that the distortion was least below the resonant frequency of the diaphragm. This difference is very noticeable in the change in quality when a receiver is removed from the ear and laid on the table. It then becomes a cone loudspeaker, and the reproduction of the frequencies below resonance disappears, with the result that the reproduction is high-pitched and distorted.

It has been shown that at the higher frequencies the radiation resistance of the cone does not continue to increase but flattens off, if all cone parts continue to move in phase. At lower frequencies the cone tends to move as a whole, i.e., all parts are in phase; at higher frequencies the distributed nature of the mass and stiffness of the cone comes into play. At such frequencies the cone would have an analogous electrical circuit which would be similar to that of a line with distributed characteristics, and with dissipation due to the radiation resistance of the elemental parts. The difficulty of developing one speaker which can cover a large number of octaves has given rise to the custom in high-fidelity systems of using two to four speakers each covering a limited range and fed from dividing networks such as were discussed in Chap. 7.

The coupling device in a horn loudspeaker may have a small diaphragm which would have a very small radiation resistance if it were exposed directly to the air. By the use of a horn, the radiation resistance represented by the large area at the outer end of the horn can be matched to the driving device.

The horn is not an amplifying device. It is an impedance-matching device to connect the diaphragm of high impedance to the atmosphere of low impedance. This must be done by a gradually changing unsymmetrical network of distributed constants.

Webster has shown that an exponential horn is best suited for this purpose. Such a horn acts as an HP filter, transmitting no sound below a certain frequency. The theory is, in many respects, similar to that of a transmission line, except for the changing of the circuit constants with increasing length. Two factors enter into the design of the horn, the propagation constant along the horn and reflection at the ends. The less the rate of taper, the lower will be the limit of the frequencies transmitted.

The equation of the cross section of an exponential horn is

$$S = S_1 e^{mx} \tag{16-48}$$

where S_1 = initial area at throat
x = distance from throat

m is determined by the lowest frequency to be transmitted. Such a horn is shown in Fig. 16-14.

Crandall has given the equation for the cutoff frequency of the horn as

$$f_c = \frac{mc}{4\pi} \tag{16-49}$$

where c = velocity of sound in air

m = coefficient in exponent of Eq. (16-48)

If c is given in meters per second, then the x of Eq. (16-48) will be measured in meters. Below f_c there will be no appreciable transmission of sound along the horn; above f_c the transmission increases rapidly to a maximum.

Below the cutoff frequency, the pressure and velocity become almost 90° out of phase, as do the voltage and current in an electrical filter, and so cannot transfer energy effectively between the two ends.

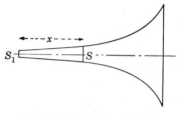

FIG. 16-14. Exponential horn.

The rate of taper determines the transmission along the horn, while the area at the large end determines the termination and hence the reflection at this point. The reflection does not change as suddenly with frequency as the transmission characteristics. An exact theory without approximations has not been developed, but an assumption may be made that the end of the horn represents a weightless diaphragm radiating into the free air. It is desirable that this radiation resistance representing the termination of the horn should be constant at all frequencies which it is desirable to radiate. Referring to Fig. 16-13 and to the discussion which followed, it was pointed out that the radiation resistance is approximately constant when the radius of the diaphragm is greater than one-quarter wavelength. Hence, the diameter of the large end of the horn should be about half the wavelength of the lowest frequency which is to be reproduced.

The requirement of small taper and large area at the end calls for long horns in order to give good reproduction of the lower frequencies, the long length often being obtained by folding. Such horns can provide a large load for the diaphragm of the receiver, and the power factor will be close to 100 per cent. In such cases the motional-impedance circle will have a small diameter and the damping will be high.

The load of the horn on the diaphragm of the coupling unit will provide resistance control. The mass of the diaphragm and the stiffness of the suspension should be made small so that this resistance control will predominate, and the velocity of the diaphragm will be directly proportional to the force on it and hence to the current through the windings. The diaphragm should be stiffened across its face, so that all parts will move in phase, but the stiffness at the edge should be kept small.

16-17. Microphones. In a microphone, the acoustical vibrations strike the diaphragm, causing it to vibrate, and this in turn sets up a voltage which is to be introduced into the electrical circuit. The alternating force on the diaphragm is directly proportional to the alternating pressure in the acoustic wave. An ideal microphone would generate a voltage which is independent of frequency but directly proportional to the acoustic pressure, and hence to the mechanical force on the diaphragm. Microphones with diaphragms may be divided into two groups:

Group 1. The generated voltage is proportional to the *displacement* of the diaphragm.

Group 2. The generated voltage is proportional to the *velocity* of the diaphragm.

In a carbon-type transmitter the generated voltage is proportional to the resistance variation. This resistance variation is produced by the packing and release of the carbon granules and hence is proportional to the displacement of the diaphragm. Therefore, the carbon-grain microphone falls in Group 1. In connection with the discussion of the electrostatic coupler or capacitor microphone it was shown in Eq. (16-40) that the generated voltage for this type is inversely proportional to the capacitance. Since the capacitance is inversely proportional to the separation between plates, the generated voltage will be proportional at any instant to the displacement of the diaphragm and this type also falls in Group 1. In the piezoelectric crystal the generated voltage is also proportional to the displacement.

In the electrodynamic type of microphone the generated voltage is produced by the motion of a conductor in a magnetic field. In such a microphone the generated voltage is proportional to the velocity of the conductor, which in turn is proportional to the velocity of the diaphragm. Similarly, if the generated voltage is produced by a change in magnetic field due to a variation in the air gap, the induced voltage will be proportional to the velocity of the microphone. Therefore these types will fall in Group 2.

The type of mechanical control for a distortionless microphone will be different in the case of the two groups. In Group 1 the maximum displacement of the diaphragm for a given force should be made independent of frequency. On referring to Eq. (16-19b) it is seen that this occurs when the mechanical system is stiffness-controlled. This stiffness control is obtained by making the resonant frequency of the diaphragm fall at a frequency above the frequencies to be reproduced.

In Group 2 the *velocity* of the diaphragm should be directly proportional to the impressed force. This calls for resistance control. Such resistance control is usually obtained by air damping of the diaphragm through narrow tubes or slits between the air enclosure in the back of the diaphragm and the outside air.

A third type of microphone is available in which the voltage is generated as in Group 2, but with a diaphragm consisting of a ribbon exposed on both sides to the passing acoustic wave. This is the ribbon microphone shown in Fig. 16-11. A plane acoustic wave can be represented as a function of time and space by the following equation (compare with the equation of a traveling wave in Chap. 6):

$$p = A \sin 2\pi f \left(t - \frac{x}{c} \right) \tag{16-50}$$

where p = instantaneous *difference* in pressure between a point in the wave and the average atmospheric pressure

x = distance measured in the direction in which wave is traveling

c = velocity of sound

The force on the microphone ribbon at any instant will be proportional to the difference between the pressures on the two sides.

Let p_1 be the pressure on one side. Then the pressure on the other side will be

$$p_1 + \frac{\partial p}{\partial x} \Delta x \tag{16-51}$$

where Δx is the distance between the two exposed sides and is small in comparison with a wavelength.

Hence the force will be

$$f = k \left[p_1 - \left(p_1 + \frac{\partial p}{\partial x} \Delta x \right) \right]$$

$$= -k \frac{\partial p}{\partial x} \Delta x \tag{16-52}$$

Insert Eq. (16-50) in Eq. (16-52).

$$f = \frac{2\pi k A f \Delta x}{c} \cos 2\pi f \left(t - \frac{x}{c} \right) \tag{16-53}$$

It is seen that the force on the ribbon of the microphone is directly proportional to frequency. At the same time the mechanical impedance should be selected so that the velocity is independent of frequency. This means that the mechanical impedance should be directly proportional to frequency. On referring to Eq. (16-20c) it is seen that this dictates mass control. Therefore, the resonant frequency of the ribbon should be set at a frequency below the lowest frequency to be reproduced.

TABLE 16-1. ANALYSIS OF TYPES OF MECHANICAL CONTROL FOR MINIMUM DISTORTION

Type of instrument	Force on diaphragm proportional to—	Required relation for minimum distortion	Additional information	Mechanical control required	Location of resonant frequency of diaphragm
Telephone receiver	Current	Pressure in enclosed volume independent of frequency	Pressure proportional to diaphragm displacement	Stiffness	Above transmission band
Cone-type loudspeaker	Current	Radiated power independent of frequency	Radiation resistance proportional to square of frequency	Mass	Below transmission band
Horn-type loudspeaker	Current	Radiated power independent of frequency	Radiation resistance independent of frequency	Resistance	Absent
Carbongrain, capacitor, crystal microphones	Pressure of sound wave	Induced voltage independent of frequency	Induced voltage proportional to displacement of diaphragm	Stiffness	Above transmission band
Dynamic microphone	Pressure of sound wave	Induced voltage independent of frequency	Induced voltage proportional to velocity of diaphragm	Resistance	Absent
Ribbon microphone	Pressure of sound wave times frequency	Induced voltage independent of frequency	Induced voltage proportional to velocity of ribbon	Mass	Below transmission band

The determination of the type of control for the various types of telephone receivers, loudspeakers, and microphones is summarized in Table 16-1.

16-18. Mechanically Controlled Resonance. The piezoelectric crystal finds its greatest usefulness in the reflection of its mechanical constants back into the electrical circuit. The ratio of effective reactance to effective resistance in most mechanical systems is much higher than is attainable in any electrical network. The use of mechanical meshes will give greatly improved results where sharply resonant systems are desired. It is essential that the coupling between the electrical network and mechanical mesh operate in both directions, in order that the electrical system may react in the same manner as though an electrical mesh of very high Q were introduced.

It has been shown how the mechanical characteristics of the diaphragm of a telephone receiver appear in the electrical circuit in the form of motional impedance. In the receiver, however, this motional impedance is added by phasors to the impedance of the winding. Since the latter is rather large and does not have a high value of Q, the effective reactance of the diaphragm is not sufficient to make the Q of the receiver as a whole so very high.

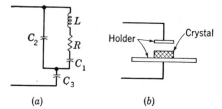

(a)   (b)

FIG. 16-15. Equivalent circuit and mounting of a piezoelectric quartz crystal.

The advantage of the piezoelectric crystal is that it is actuated by an electric field instead of a magnetic field. Electric fields can be set up with less loss than magnetic fields. This is illustrated by the fact that a well-constructed capacitor of a given reactance will have a much smaller resistance than is attainable in an inductance of the same reactance. The mechanical constants of the crystal can therefore be reflected back into the circuit with practically no superimposed resistance due to the driving circuit.

16-19. Equivalent Circuit of Piezoelectric Crystal. Van Dyke and Dye have given the equivalent network of the crystal as that of Fig. 16-15a. The crystal is mounted in the general fashion of Fig. 16-15b. The upper plate may or may not be in contact with the crystal.

In the equivalent network of Fig. 16-15a L is the effective mechanical inductance due to the mass of the crystal, R is the effective resistance due to its internal losses, and C_1 is the effective mechanical capacitance due to the stiffness of the crystal. C_2 is the capacitance which the crystal introduces between its faces due, largely, to its straight capacitive action and may be computed from a knowledge of the dielectric constant. C_2 is of the order of $100C_1$. C_3 is the effective series capacitance introduced by the air gap when the upper plate of Fig. 16-15b does not touch the crystal.

The reactance curve of the circuit of Fig. 16-15a can be obtained by sketching in the standard manner described in Chap. 4. It is illustrated in Fig. 16-16, where the effect of C_3 is neglected. Since C_2 is so much larger than C_1, the slope of the susceptance curve of C_2 will be much greater at the origin than that of the curve for the branch LC_1.

This circuit will have one zero and one pole. Owing to the high value of C_2/C_1 these two frequencies will be very close together.

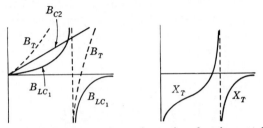

Fig. 16-16. Reactance curves for a piezoelectric crystal.

A measurement of the crystal in the neighborhood of its antiresonant frequency will give a circle for the locus of the impedance phasors, of much the same type as the telephone receiver. The damping will be found to be very small. If an emf is impressed across the crystal, the current vs. frequency curve will be similar to the one shown in Fig. 16-17·

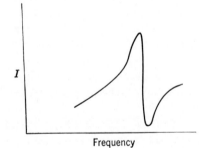

Frequency

Fig. 16-17. Resonance curve for a piezoelectric crystal.

The curve of Fig. 16-17 shows very clearly the presence of the resonant frequency, and slightly above it the antiresonant frequency.

As explained in Chap. 7, one important use of the piezoelectric crystal is as a high-Q filter element. The most common use of a crystal is to serve as the "tank" circuit of an oscillator. As such, because of its high Q, it gives an extremely stable operation, the frequency depending only slightly on the other constants of the circuit.

PROBLEMS

16-1. Determine the equations of motion and the equivalent electrical circuit for a horizontal rod suspended by a spring at each end, with a force $F_1 \sin \omega t$ applied at the center. Assume the springs have different stiffness coefficients k_1 and k_2.

16-2. Draw the analogy between sound waves in a pipe and electrical waves on a long line. Show the equivalent electrical circuit for a closed organ pipe. Repeat for an open organ pipe. From these equivalents determine the configuration which would give an acoustical inductive reactance. Determine the configuration which would give an acoustical capacitive reactance.

16-3. A mass of 1 kg is suspended by a spring with a stiffness coefficient

$$k = 10^3 \text{ newton/m.}$$

What is the natural frequency of the system? A force $f = \hat{F} \sin \omega t$ is applied to the mass. If $\hat{F} = 10^{-1}$ newton, plot a curve of *amplitude* of oscillation vs. frequency from 0 to 10 cycles. $r = 1$ newton-sec/m.

16-4. A 10-in. cone vibrates as a piston. What must be the amplitude of vibration in order to deliver an acoustical power to the air equal to 100 mw when the frequency is 100 cycles? Repeat for a frequency of 1,000 cycles.

16-5. The cone of Prob. 16-4 has a mass of 0.1 kg, and the stiffness of the suspension is such that the mechanical resonant frequency is 50 cycles. Determine the force at the apex of the cone which must be applied to secure the radiation specified in Prob. 16-4. Neglect mechanical resistance.

16-6. The driving mechanism for the cone of Prob. 16-4 is similar to that of Fig. 16-6. The flux density is 1.5 webers/sq m. The voice coil has a diameter of 3 cm and is wound with 150 turns. What must be the effective current at 100, 500, and 1,000 cycles in order to radiate an acoustic power of 100 mw? If the resistance of the voice coil is 10 ohms, what is the efficiency of the loudspeaker?

HYPERBOLIC FUNCTIONS

Complex Hyperbolic Functions. The three primary hyperbolic functions are defined in terms of exponentials.

$$\sinh \theta = \frac{e^\theta - e^{-\theta}}{2} \tag{A-1}$$

$$\cosh \theta = \frac{e^\theta + e^{-\theta}}{2} \tag{A-2}$$

$$\tanh \theta = \frac{\sinh \theta}{\cosh \theta} = \frac{e^\theta - e^{-0}}{e^\theta + e^{-\theta}} = \frac{e^{2\theta} - 1}{e^{2\theta} + 1} \tag{A-3}$$

Note that, for real values of θ, $0 < \sinh \theta < \infty$, $1 < \cosh \theta < \infty$, $0 < \tanh \theta < 1$. Curves to show the general range are shown in Fig. A-1. The functions are tabulated in Table A-1 for real values of θ

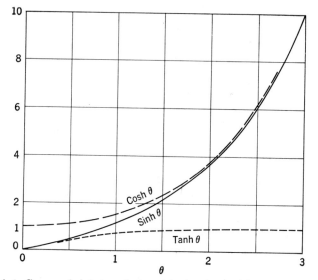

FIG. A-1. Curves of sinh θ, cosh θ, and tanh θ for positive real values of θ.

Algebraic manipulation of the definitions can be used to prove the sum and difference formulas.

$$\sinh (A \pm B) = \sinh A \cosh B \pm \cosh A \sinh B \qquad \text{(A-4)}$$
$$\cosh (A \pm B) = \cosh A \cosh B \pm \sinh A \sinh B \qquad \text{(A-5)}$$

It may be shown that the hyperbolic and circular (trigonometric) functions are related to each other, for by definition

$$\sin x = \frac{e^{jx} - e^{-jx}}{2j}$$

Let
$$x = j\theta$$
$$\sin j\theta = (e^{-\theta} - e^{\theta})/2j = j(e^{\theta} - e^{-\theta})/2$$

or
$$\sin j\theta = j \sinh \theta \qquad \text{(A-6)}$$

Similarly
$$\cos j\theta = \cosh \theta \qquad \text{(A-7)}$$
$$\tan j\theta = j \tanh \theta \qquad \text{(A-8)}$$

The last three identities may be used to convert any of the trigonometric identities into the corresponding hyperbolic identities. For example, given $\cos^2 x + \sin^2 x = 1$, let

$$x = j\theta$$
$$\cos^2 j\theta + \sin^2 j\theta = 1$$

Substituting from Eqs. (A-6) and (A-7),

$$\cosh^2 \theta - \sinh^2 \theta = 1 \qquad \text{(A-9)}$$

As another example, consider the familiar trigonometric identity

$$\sin 2x = 2 \sin x \cos x$$

Let
$$x = j\theta$$
$$\sin j2\theta = 2 \sin j\theta \cos j\theta$$

Therefore
$$j \sinh 2\theta = j2 \sinh \theta \cosh \theta$$

or
$$\sinh 2\theta = 2 \sinh \theta \cosh \theta \qquad \text{(A-10)}$$

As another example, one has the alternative half-angle identity

$$\sin^2 x = \frac{1 - \cos 2x}{2}$$

Let
$$x = j\theta$$
$$(\sin j\theta)^2 = \frac{1 - \cos j2\theta}{2}$$
$$- \sinh^2 \theta = \frac{1 - \cosh 2\theta}{2}$$

or
$$\sinh^2 \theta = \frac{\cosh 2\theta - 1}{2} \qquad \text{(A-11)}$$

The inverse of Eqs. (A-6) to (A-8) may be derived to relate the hyperbolic functions of an imaginary variable to the circular functions of a real variable.

Replacing θ by $j\theta$ in Eq. (A-1),

$$\sinh j\theta = \frac{e^{j\theta} - e^{-j\theta}}{2} = j \sin \theta \qquad \text{(A-12)}$$

Similarly

$$\cosh j\theta = \cos \theta \qquad \text{(A-13)}$$
$$\tanh j\theta = j \tan \theta \qquad \text{(A-14)}$$

The foregoing identities may be used to evaluate the hyperbolic function of a complex variable. For example, let it be required to evaluate $\sinh (A \pm jB)$. By Eq. (A-4)

$$\sinh (A \pm jB) = \sinh A \cosh jB \pm \cosh A \sinh jB$$

By Eqs. (A-13) and (A-14)

$$\sinh (A \pm jB) = \sinh A \cos B \pm j \cosh A \sin B \qquad \text{(A-15)}$$

Similarly

$$\cosh (A \pm jB) = \cosh A \cos B \pm j \sinh A \sin B \qquad \text{(A-16)}$$

In polar coordinates

$$\sinh (A + jB) = \sqrt{\sinh^2 A \cos^2 B + \cosh^2 A \sin^2 B} \Big/\arctan \frac{\tan B}{\tanh A}$$
$$= \sqrt{\sinh^2 A(1 - \sin^2 B) + (1 + \sinh^2 A) \sin^2 B}$$
$$\Big/\arctan (\tan B \coth A)$$
$$= \sqrt{\sinh^2 A + \sin^2 B} \Big/\arctan (\tan B \coth A) \quad \text{(A-15a)}$$

Similarly,

$$\cosh (A + jB) = \sqrt{\cosh^2 A \cos^2 B + \sinh^2 A \sin^2 B}$$
$$\Big/\arctan (\tan B \tanh A)$$
$$= \sqrt{\sinh^2 A + \cos^2 B} \Big/\arctan (\tan B \tanh A)$$

Proof of Eqs. (6-20) and (6-23). Frequently the hyperbolic function of a complex number is known, and it is required to find the complex number itself. To do this, it is necessary to manipulate the equations so that the real and imaginary parts of the number may be solved for independently. As an illustration say that $\cosh (\alpha + j\beta) = A + jB$, A and B being known quantities. It is required to evaluate α and β. Then by Eq. (A-16)

$$A + jB = \cosh (\alpha + j\beta) = \cosh \alpha \cos \beta + j \sinh \alpha \sin \beta$$

Equating reals,

$$A = \cosh \alpha \cos \beta$$

Equating imaginaries,

$$B = \sinh \alpha \sin \beta$$

Squaring and adding,

$$A^2 + B^2 = \cosh^2 \alpha \cos^2 \beta + \sinh^2 \alpha \sin^2 \beta$$

Eliminating $\cos^2 \beta = 1 - \sin^2 \beta$,

$$A^2 + B^2 = \cosh^2 \alpha(1 - \sin^2 \beta) + \sinh^2 \alpha \sin^2 \beta$$
$$= \cosh^2 \alpha - \sin^2 \beta$$

Adding 1,

$$1 + A^2 + B^2 = \cosh^2 \alpha + \cos^2 \beta \qquad \text{(A-17)}$$

Completing the square by adding $2A = 2 \cosh \alpha \cos \beta$,

$$1 + 2A + A^2 + B^2 = \cosh^2 \alpha + 2 \cosh \alpha \cos \beta + \cos^2 \beta$$

Taking the square root,

$$\sqrt{(1 + A)^2 + B^2} = \cosh \alpha + \cos \beta \qquad \text{(A-18)}$$

Completing the square by subtracting $2A = 2 \cosh \alpha \cos \beta$ in Eq. (A-17),

$$\sqrt{(1 - A)^2 + B^2} = \cosh \alpha - \cos \beta \qquad \text{(A-19)}$$

Then from Eqs. (A-18) and (A-19)

$$\cosh \alpha = \frac{\sqrt{(1 + A)^2 + B^2} + \sqrt{(1 - A)^2 + B^2}}{2}$$
$$\cos \beta = \frac{\sqrt{(1 + A)^2 + B^2} - \sqrt{(1 - A)^2 + B^2}}{2} \qquad \text{(6-20)}$$

Inasmuch as only real quantities are involved in the last two equations, α may be found by reference to Table A-1, and β from a table of circular functions.

Frequently the hyperbolic tangent of a complex number is known and the number itself must be found. Let

$$C + jD = \tanh (\alpha + j\beta) = \frac{\sinh (\alpha + j\beta)}{\cosh (\alpha + j\beta)}$$

$$C + jD = \frac{\sinh \alpha \cos \beta + j \cosh \alpha \sin \beta}{\cosh \alpha \cos \beta + j \sinh \alpha \sin \beta}$$

$$C + jD = $$
$$\frac{(\sinh \alpha \cosh \alpha)(\cos^2 \beta + \sin^2 \beta) + j(\sin \beta \cos \beta)(\cosh^2 \alpha - \sinh^2 \alpha)}{\cosh^2 \alpha \cos^2 \beta + \sinh^2 \alpha \sin^2 \beta}$$

$$C + jD = \frac{\sinh \alpha \cosh \alpha + j \sin \beta \cos \beta}{\sinh^2 \alpha + \cos^2 \beta}$$

By equating the real and imaginary parts of this equation,

$$C = \frac{\sinh \alpha \cosh \alpha}{\sinh^2 \alpha + \cos^2 \beta} = \frac{\sinh 2\alpha}{2(\sinh^2 \alpha + \cos^2 \beta)}$$

$$D = \frac{\sin \beta \cos \beta}{\sinh^2 \alpha + \cos^2 \beta} = \frac{\sin 2\beta}{2(\sinh^2 \alpha + \cos^2 \beta)}$$

$$C^2 + D^2 = \left| \frac{\sinh^2 \gamma}{\cosh^2 \gamma} \right| = \frac{\sinh^2 \alpha + \sin^2 \beta}{\sinh^2 \alpha + \cos^2 \beta}$$

$$1 + C^2 + D^2 = \frac{2 \sinh^2 \alpha + 1}{\sinh^2 \alpha + \cos^2 \beta} = \frac{\cosh 2\alpha}{\sinh^2 \alpha + \cos^2 \beta}$$

$$1 - (C^2 + D^2) = \frac{\cos^2 \beta - \sin^2 \beta}{\sinh^2 \alpha + \cos^2 \beta} = \frac{\cos 2\beta}{\sinh^2 \alpha + \cos^2 \beta}$$

Therefore

$$\tanh 2\alpha = \frac{2C}{1 + C^2 + D^2}$$

$$\tan 2\beta = \frac{2D}{1 - (C^2 + D^2)}$$

(6-23)

From these equations real functions of the components of γ can be computed, and α and β can then be determined from tables of these real functions.

COMMUNICATION ENGINEERING

TABLE A-1. REAL HYPERBOLIC FUNCTIONS*

x, radians	sinh x	cosh x	tanh x	x, radians	sinh x	cosh x	tanh x
0.00	0.00000	1.00000	0.00000	0.45	0.46534	1.10297	0.42190
0.01	0.01000	1.00005	0.01000	0.46	0.47640	1.10768	0.43008
0.02	0.02000	1.00020	0.02000	0.47	0.48750	1.11250	0.43820
0.03	0.03000	1.00045	0.02999	0.48	0.49865	1.11743	0.44624
0.04	0.04001	1.00080	0.03998	0.49	0.50984	1.12247	0.45422
0.05	0.05002	1.00125	0.04996	0.50	0.52110	1.12763	0.46212
0.06	0.06004	1.00180	0.05993	0.51	0.53240	1.13289	0.46995
0.07	0.07006	1.00245	0.06989	0.52	0.54375	1.13827	0.47770
0.08	0.08009	1.00320	0.07983	0.53	0.55516	1.14377	0.48538
0.09	0.09012	1.00405	0.08976	0.54	0.56663	1.14938	0.49299
0.10	0.10017	1.00500	0.09967	0.55	0.57815	1.15510	0.50052
0.11	0.11022	1.00606	0.10956	0.56	0.58973	1.16094	0.50798
0.12	0.12029	1.00721	0.11943	0.57	0.60137	1.16690	0.51536
0.13	0.13037	1.00846	0.12927	0.58	0.61307	1.17297	0.52267
0.14	0.14046	1.00982	0.13909	0.59	0.62483	1.17916	0.52990
0.15	0.15056	1.01127	0.14889	0.60	0.63665	1.18547	0.53705
0.16	0.16068	1.01283	0.15865	0.61	0.64854	1.19189	0.54413
0.17	0.17082	1.01448	0.16838	0.62	0.66049	1.19844	0.55113
0.18	0.18097	1.01624	0.17808	0.63	0.67251	1.20510	0.55805
0.19	0.19115	1.01810	0.18775	0.64	0.68459	1.21189	0.56490
0.20	0.20134	1.02007	0.19738	0.65	0.69675	1.21879	0.57167
0.21	0.21155	1.02213	0.20697	0.66	0.70897	1.22582	0.57836
0.22	0.22178	1.02430	0.21652	0.67	0.72126	1.23297	0.58498
0.23	0.23203	1.02657	0.22603	0.68	0.73363	1.24025	0.59152
0.24	0.24231	1.02894	0.23550	0.69	0.74607	1.24765	0.59798
0.25	0.25261	1.03141	0.24492	0.70	0.75858	1.25517	0.60437
0.26	0.26294	1.03399	0.25430	0.71	0.77117	1.26282	0.61068
0.27	0.27329	1.03667	0.26362	0.72	0.78384	1.27059	0.61691
0.28	0.28367	1.03946	0.27291	0.73	0.79659	1.27849	0.62307
0.29	0.29408	1.04235	0.28213	0.74	0.80941	1.28652	0.62915
0.30	0.30452	1.04534	0.29131	0.75	0.82232	1.29468	0.63515
0.31	0.31499	1.04844	0.30044	0.76	0.83530	1.30297	0.64108
0.32	0.32549	1.05164	0.30951	0.77	0.84838	1.31139	0.64693
0.33	0.33602	1.05495	0.31852	0.78	0.86153	1.31994	0.65271
0.34	0.34659	1.05836	0.32748	0.79	0.87478	1.32862	0.65841
0.35	0.35719	1.06188	0.33638	0.80	0.88811	1.33743	0.66404
0.36	0.36783	1.06550	0.34521	0.81	0.90152	1.34638	0.66959
0.37	0.37850	1.06923	0.35399	0.82	0.91503	1.35547	0.67507
0.38	0.38921	1.07307	0.36271	0.83	0.92863	1.36468	0.68048
0.39	0.39996	1.07702	0.37136	0.84	0.94233	1.37404	0.68581
0.40	0.41075	1.08107	0.37995	0.85	0.95612	1.38353	0.69107
0.41	0.42158	1.08523	0.38847	0.86	0.97000	1.39316	0.69626
0.42	0.43246	1.08950	0.39693	0.87	0.98398	1.40293	0.70137
0.43	0.44337	1.09388	0.40532	0.88	0.99806	1.41284	0.70642
0.44	0.45434	1.09837	0.41364	0.89	1.01224	1.42289	0.71139

* Reprinted by permission from "Smithsonian Physical Tables."

TABLE A-1. REAL HYPERBOLIC FUNCTIONS (*Continued*)

x, radians	sinh x	cosh x	tanh x	x, radians	sinh x	cosh x	tanh x
0.90	1.02652	1.43309	0.71630	1.35	1.79909	2.05833	0.87405
0.91	1.04090	1.44342	0.72113	1.36	1.81977	2.07643	0.87639
0.92	1.05539	1.45390	0.72590	1.37	1.84062	2.09473	0.87869
0.93	1.06998	1.46453	0.73059	1.38	1.86166	2.11324	0.88095
0.94	1.08468	1.47530	0.73522	1.39	1.88289	2.13196	0.88317
0.95	1.09948	1.48623	0.73978	1.40	1.90430	2.15090	0.88535
0.96	1.11440	1.49729	0.74428	1.41	1.92591	2.17005	0.88749
0.97	1.12943	1.50851	0.74870	1.42	1.94770	2.18942	0.88960
0.98	1.14457	1.51988	0.75307	1.43	1.96970	2.20900	0.89167
0.99	1.15983	1.53141	0.75736	1.44	1.99188	2.22881	0.89370
1.00	1.17520	1.54308	0.76159	1.45	2.01427	2.24884	0.89569
1.01	1.19069	1.55491	0.76576	1.46	2.03686	2.26910	0.89765
1.02	1.20630	1.56689	0.76987	1.47	2.05965	2.28958	0.89958
1.03	1.22203	1.57904	0.77391	1.48	2.08265	2.31029	0.90147
1.04	1.23788	1.59134	0.77789	1.49	2.10586	2.33123	0.90332
1.05	1.25386	1.60379	0.78181	1.50	2.12928	2.35241	0.90515
1.06	1.26996	1.61641	0.78566	1.51	2.15291	2.37382	0.90694
1.07	1.28619	1.62919	0.78946	1.52	2.17676	2.39547	0.90870
1.08	1.30254	1.64214	0.79320	1.53	2.20082	2.41736	0.91042
1.09	1.31903	1.65525	0.79688	1.54	2.22510	2.43949	0.91212
1.10	1.33565	1.66852	0.80050	1.55	2.24961	2.46186	0.91379
1.11	1.35240	1.68196	0.80406	1.56	2.27434	2.48448	0.91542
1.12	1.36929	1.69557	0.80757	1.57	2.29930	2.50735	0.91703
1.13	1.38631	1.70934	0.81102	1.58	2.32449	2.53047	0.91860
1.14	1.40347	1.72329	0.81441	1.59	2.34991	2.55384	0.92015
1.15	1.42078	1.73741	0.81775	1.60	2.37557	2.57746	0.92167
1.16	1.43822	1.75171	0.82104	1.61	2.40146	2.60135	0.92316
1.17	1.45581	1.76618	0.82427	1.62	2.42760	2.62549	0.92462
1.18	1.47355	1.78083	0.82745	1.63	2.45397	2.64990	0.92606
1.19	1.49143	1.79565	0.83058	1.64	2.48059	2.67457	0.92747
1.20	1.50946	1.81066	0.83365	1.65	2.50746	2.69951	0.92886
1.21	1.52764	1.82584	0.83668	1.66	2.53459	2.72472	0.93022
1.22	1.54598	1.84121	0.83965	1.67	2.56196	2.75021	0.93155
1.23	1.56447	1.85676	0.84258	1.68	2.58959	2.77596	0.93286
1.24	1.58311	1.87250	0.84546	1.69	2.61748	2.80200	0.93415
1.25	1.60192	1.88842	0.84828	1.70	2.64563	2.82832	0.93541
1.26	1.62088	1.90454	0.85106	1.71	2.67405	2.85491	0.93665
1.27	1.64001	1.92084	0.85380	1.72	2.70273	2.88180	0.93786
1.28	1.65930	1.93734	0.85648	1.73	2.73168	2.90897	0.93906
1.29	1.67876	1.95403	0.85913	1.74	2.76091	2.93643	0.94023
1.30	1.69838	1.97091	0.86172	1.75	2.79041	2.96419	0.94138
1.31	1.71818	1.98800	0.86428	1.76	2.82020	2.99224	0.94250
1.32	1.73814	2.00528	0.86678	1.77	2.85026	3.02059	0.94361
1.33	1.75828	2.02276	0.86925	1.78	2.88061	3.04925	0.94470
1.34	1.77860	2.04044	0.87167	1.79	2.91125	3.07821	0.94576

TABLE A-1. REAL HYPERBOLIC FUNCTIONS (*Continued*)

x, radians	sinh x	cosh x	tanh x	x, radians	sinh x	cosh x	tanh x
1.80	2.94217	3.10747	0.94681	2.25	4.69117	4.79657	0.97803
1.81	2.97340	3.13705	0.94783	2.26	4.73937	4.84372	0.97846
1.82	3.00492	3.16694	0.94884	2.27	4.78804	4.89136	0.97888
1.83	3.03674	3.19715	0.94983	2.28	4.83720	4.93948	0.97929
1.84	3.06886	3.22768	0.95080	2.29	4.88684	4.98810	0.97970
1.85	3.10129	3.25853	0.95175	2.30	4.93696	5.03722	0.98010
1.86	3.13403	3.28970	0.95268	2.31	4.98758	5.08684	0.98049
1.87	3.16709	3.32121	0.95359	2.32	5.03870	5.13697	0.98087
1.88	3.20046	3.35305	0.95449	2.33	5.09032	5.18762	0.98124
1.89	3.23415	3.38522	0.95537	2.34	5.14245	5.23878	0.98161
1.90	3.26816	3.41773	0.95624	2.35	5.19510	5.29047	0.98197
1.91	3.30250	3.45058	0.95709	2.36	5.24827	5.34269	0.98233
1.92	3.33718	3.48378	0.95792	2.37	5.30196	5.39544	0.98267
1.93	3.37218	3.51733	0.95873	2.38	5.35618	5.44873	0.98301
1.94	3.40752	3.55123	0.95953	2.39	5.41093	5.50256	0.98335
1.95	3.44321	3.58548	0.96032	2.40	5.46623	5.55695	0.98367
1.96	3.47923	3.62009	0.96109	2.41	5.52207	5.61189	0.98400
1.97	3.51561	3.65507	0.96185	2.42	5.57847	5.66739	0.98431
1.98	3.55234	3.69041	0.96259	2.43	5.63542	5.72346	0.98462
1.99	3.58942	3.72611	0.96331	2.44	5.69294	5.78010	0.98492
2.00	3.62686	3.76220	0.96403	2.45	5.75103	5.83732	0.98522
2.01	3.66466	3.79865	0.96473	2.46	5.80969	5.89512	0.98551
2.02	3.70283	3.83549	0.96541	2.47	5.86893	5.95352	0.98579
2.03	3.74138	3.87271	0.96609	2.48	5.92876	6.01250	0.98607
2.04	3.78029	3.91032	0.96675	2.49	5.98918	6.07209	0.98635
2.05	3.81958	3.94832	0.96740	2.50	6.05020	6.13229	0.98661
2.06	3.85926	3.98671	0.96803	2.51	6.11183	6.19310	0.98688
2.07	3.89932	4.02550	0.96865	2.52	6.17407	6.25453	0.98714
2.08	3.93977	4.06470	0.96926	2.53	6.23692	6.31658	0.98739
2.09	3.98061	4.10430	0.96986	2.54	6.30040	6.37927	0.98764
2.10	4.02186	4.14431	0.97045	2.55	6.36451	6.44259	0.98788
2.11	4.06350	4.18474	0.97103	2.56	6.42926	6.50656	0.98812
2.12	4.10555	4.22558	0.97159	2.57	6.49464	6.57118	0.98835
2.13	4.14801	4.26685	0.97215	2.58	6.56068	6.63646	0.98858
2.14	4.19089	4.30855	0.97269	2.59	6.62738	6.70240	0.98881
2.15	4.23419	4.35067	0.97323	2.60	6.69473	6.76901	0.98903
2.16	4.27791	4.39323	0.97375	2.61	6.76276	6.83629	0.98924
2.17	4.32205	4.43623	0.97426	2.62	6.83146	6.90426	0.98946
2.18	4.36663	4.47967	0.97477	2.63	6.90085	6.97292	0.98966
2.19	4.41165	4.52356	0.97526	2.64	6.97092	7.04228	0.98987
2.20	4.45711	4.56791	0.97574	2.65	7.04169	7.11234	0.99007
2.21	4.50301	4.61271	0.97622	2.66	7.11317	7.18312	0.99026
2.22	4.54936	4.65797	0.97668	2.67	7.18536	7.25461	0.99045
2.23	4.59617	4.70370	0.97714	2.68	7.25827	7.32683	0.99064
2.24	4.64344	4.74989	0.97759	2.69	7.33190	7.39978	0.99083

TABLE A-1. REAL HYPERBOLIC FUNCTIONS (*Continued*)

x, radians	sinh x	cosh x	tanh x	x, radians	sinh x	cosh x	tanh x
2.70	7.40626	7.47347	0.99101	3.0	10.0179	10.0677	0.99505
2.71	7.48137	7.54791	0.99118	3.1	11.0765	11.1215	0.99595
2.72	7.55722	7.62310	0.99136	3.2	12.2459	12.2866	0.99668
2.73	7.63383	7.69905	0.99153	3.3	13.5379	13.5748	0.99728
2.74	7.71121	7.77578	0.99170	3.4	14.9654	14.9987	0.99777
2.75	7.78935	7.85328	0.99186	3.5	16.5426	16.5728	0.99818
2.76	7.86828	7.93157	0.99202	3.6	18.2855	18.3128	0.99851
2.77	7.94799	8.01065	0.99218	3.7	20.2113	20.2360	0.99878
2.78	8.02849	8.09053	0.99233	3.8	22.3394	22.3618	0.99900
2.79	8.10980	8.17122	0.99248	3.9	24.6911	24.7113	0.99918
2.80	8.19192	8.25273	0.99263	4.0	27.2899	27.3082	0.99933
2.81	8.27486	8.33506	0.99278	4.1	30.1619	30.1784	0.99945
2.82	8.35862	8.41823	0.99292	4.2	33.3357	33.3507	0.99955
2.83	8.44322	8.50224	0.99306	4.3	36.8431	36.8567	0.99963
2.84	8.52867	8.58710	0.99320	4.4	40.7193	40.7316	0.99970
2.85	8.61497	8.67281	0.99333	4.5	45.0030	45.0141	0.99975
2.86	8.70213	8.75940	0.99346	4.6	49.7371	49.7472	0.99980
2.87	8.79016	8.84686	0.99359	4.7	54.9690	54.9781	0.99983
2.88	8.87907	8.93520	0.99372	4.8	60.7511	60.7593	0.99986
2.89	8.96887	9.02444	0.99384	4.9	67.1412	67.1486	0.99989
2.90	9.05956	9.11458	0.99396	5.0	74.2032	74.2099	0.99991
2.91	9.15116	9.20564	0.99408	5.1	82.0079	82.0140	0.99993
2.92	9.24368	9.29761	0.99420	5.2	90.6334	90.6389	0.99994
2.93	9.33712	9.39051	0.99431	5.3	100.1659	100.1709	0.99995
2.94	9.43149	9.48436	0.99443	5.4	110.7010	110.7055	0.99996
2.95	9.52681	9.57915	0.99454	5.5	122.3439	122.3480	0.99997
2.96	9.62308	9.67490	0.99464	5.6	135.2114	135.2151	0.99997
2.97	9.72031	9.77161	0.99475	5.7	149.4320	149.4354	0.99998
2.98	9.81851	9.86930	0.99485	5.8	165.1483	165.1513	0.99998
2.99	9.91770	9.96798	0.99496	5.9	182.5174	182.5201	0.99999
				6.0	201.7132	201.7156	0.99999

If x is larger than the values given in this table, e^{-x} is negligible and

$$\sinh x = \cosh x = \frac{e^x}{2}$$

$$\tanh x = 1$$

INDEX